During the tumultuous period of world history from 1660 to 1815, three complex movements combined to bring a fundamental cultural reorientation to Europe and North America, and ultimately to the wider world. The Enlightenment transformed views of nature and of the human capacity to master nature. The religious reawakenings brought a revival of heart-felt, experiential Christianity. Finally revolution, the political and social upheavals of the late eighteenth and early nineteenth centuries, challenged established ideas of divine-right monarchies and divinely ordained social hierarchies, and promoted more democratic government, notions of human rights, and religious toleration. A new religious climate emerged, in which people were more likely to look to their own feelings and experiences for the basis of their faith. During this same period, Christianity spread widely around the world as a result of colonialism and missions, and responded in diverse ways to its encounters with other cultures and religious traditions.

STEWART J. BROWN is Professor of Ecclesiastical History at the University of Edinburgh. His publications include *William Robertson and the Expansion of Empire* (1997) and *The National Churches of England, Ireland and Scotland 1801–1846* (2001).

TIMOTHY TACKETT is Professor of History at the University of California, Irvine. His publications include *Priest and Parish in Eighteenth-century France* (1977); and *Religion, Revolution, and Regional Culture* (1986).

CHRISTIANITY

The *Cambridge History of Christianity* offers a comprehensive chronological account of the development of Christianity in all its aspects – theological, intellectual, social, political, regional, global – from its beginnings to the present day. Each volume makes a substantial contribution in its own right to the scholarship of its period and the complete *History* constitutes a major work of academic reference. Far from being merely a history of Western European Christianity and its offshoots, the *History* aims to provide a global perspective. Eastern and Coptic Christianity are given full consideration from the early period onwards, and later, African, Far Eastern, New World, South Asian and other non-European developments in Christianity receive proper coverage. The volumes cover popular piety and non-formal expressions of Christian faith and treat the sociology of Christian formation, worship and devotion in a broad cultural context. The question of relations between Christianity and other major faiths is also kept in sight throughout. The *History* will provide an invaluable resource for scholars and students alike.

List of volumes:

Origins to Constantine
EDITED BY MARGARET M. MITCHELL AND FRANCES
M. YOUNG

Constantine to c. 600
EDITED BY AUGUSTINE CASIDAY AND FREDERICK
W. NORRIS

Early Medieval Christianity c. 600–c. 1100
EDITED BY THOMAS NOBLE AND JULIA SMITH

Christianity in Western Europe c. 1100–c. 1500
EDITED BY MIRI RUBIN AND WALTER SIMON

Eastern Christianity
EDITED BY MICHAEL ANGOLD

Reform and Expansion 1500–1660
EDITED BY RONNIE PO-CHIA HSIA

Enlightenment, Reawakening and Revolution 1660–1815
EDITED BY STEWART J. BROWN AND TIMOTHY TACKETT

World Christianities c. 1815–1914
EDITED BY BRIAN STANLEY AND SHERIDAN GILLEY

World Christianities c. 1914 to c. 2000
EDITED BY HUGH McLEOD

THE CAMBRIDGE
HISTORY OF
CHRISTIANITY

★

VOLUME VII
Enlightenment, Reawakening and Revolution 1660–1815

★

Editors

STEWART J. BROWN

and

TIMOTHY TACKETT

CAMBRIDGE
UNIVERSITY PRESS

CAMBRIDGE UNIVERSITY PRESS
Cambridge, New York, Melbourne, Madrid, Cape Town, Singapore, São Paulo

Cambridge University Press
The Edinburgh Building, Cambridge CB2 2RU, UK

Published in the United States of America by Cambridge University Press, New York

www.cambridge.org
Information on this title: www.cambridge.org/9780521816052

First published 2006

Printed in the United Kingdom at the University Press, Cambridge

A catalogue record for this publication is available from the British Library

ISBN-13 978-0-521-81605-2 hardback
ISBN-10 0-521-81605-X hardback

Contents

PART II

CHRISTIAN LIFE IN THE EUROPEAN WORLD, 1660–1780

PART III

MOVEMENTS AND CHALLENGES

Contents

PART IV
CHRISTIAN DEVELOPMENTS IN THE
NON-EUROPEAN WORLD

Contents

PART V
REVOLUTION AND THE CHRISTIAN WORLD

Illustrations

Maps

Contributors

NIGEL ASTON is Reader in Early Modern European History at the University of Leicester. His books include *Religion and revolution in France* and *Christianity and revolutionary Europe c.1750–1830*.

FR CHARLES J. BORGES S. J. was a member of the Xavier Centre of Historical Research in Goa between 1981 and 2000, and served as director of the Centre for six years. He is currently Assistant Professor of History at Loyola College in Maryland. His books include *The economics of the Goa Jesuits 1542–1759: An explanation of their rise and fall* and eight edited volumes on Indo-Portuguese history.

JAMES E. BRADLEY is the Geoffrey W. Bromiley Professor of Church History at Fuller Seminary in Pasadena California. His books include *Religion, revolution, and English radicalism: Non-conformity in eighteenth-century politics and society* and *Religion and politics in Enlightenment Europe* (with Dale K. Van Kley).

CHRISTOPHER LESLIE BROWN is Associate Professor of History at Rutgers University. His books include *Moral capital: Foundations of British abolitionism*, and *Arming slaves: Classical times to the modern age* (with Philip Morgan).

STEWART J. BROWN is Professor of Ecclesiastical History at the University of Edinburgh. His books include *Thomas Chalmers and the godly commonwealth in Scotland* and *The national churches of England, Ireland and Scotland 1801–1846*.

LOUIS CHÂTELLIER is Directeur d'étude at the Ecole pratique des hautes études (Paris), Section des sciences religieuses. Among his books are *Les espaces infinis et le silence de Dieu: science et religion, XVIe–XIXe siècle; The Europe of the devout: The Catholic reformation and the formation of a new society;* and *The religion of the poor: Rural missions in Europe and the formation of modern Catholicism, c.1500-c.1800*.

J. C. D. CLARK is Hall Distinguished Professor of British History at the University of Kansas. His books include *English society 1660–1832: Revolution and Rebellion* and *The language of liberty 1660–1832*.

List of contributors

SUZANNE DESAN, Professor of History at the University of Wisconsin-Madison, has published books on *Reclaiming the sacred: Lay religion and popular politics in revolutionary France*; and *The family on trial in revolutionary France.*

JORIS VAN EIJNATTEN is a member of the Department of History at the Free University of Amsterdam. His books include *'God, Nederland en Oranje': Dutch Calvinism and the search for the social centre* and *Liberty and concord in the United Provinces: Religious toleration and the public in the eighteenth-century Netherlands.*

WILLEM FRIJHOFF is Professor of History at the Free University of Amsterdam. He has published numerous books on Dutch, French, and European history, including *Embodied belief: Ten essays on religious culture in Dutch history*; *Dutch culture in a European perspective*; and *Prophètes et sorciers dans les Pays-Bas, XVIe–XVIIIe siècle* (with Robert Muchembled and Marie-Sylvie Dupont-Bouchat).

PHILIP T. HOFFMAN holds the Richard and Barbara Rosenberg chair in History and Social Science at the California Institute of Technology. His books include *Church and community in the diocese of Lyon, 1500–1789*; and *Growth in a traditional society: The French countryside, 1450–1815*.

ANDREW R. HOLMES is a Research Fellow at the Institute of Irish Studies, Queen's University, Belfast. He is the author of *The shaping of Ulster Presbyterianism belief and practice 1770–1840: Tradition, reform and revival* and of several articles on Irish Protestant history.

MARGARET C. JACOB is Professor of History at the University of California, Los Angeles. Among her books are *The Newtonians and the English Revolution, 1689–1720*; *The Radical Enlightenment: Pantheists, freemasons and republicans*; *The cultural meaning of the scientific revolution*; and *Living the Enlightenment: Freemasonry and politics in eighteenth-century Europe.*

DOMINIQUE JULIA is Director of the Centre d'anthropologie religieuse européenne at the Ecole des hautes études en sciences sociales (Paris) and Directeur de recherche with the Centre national de recherches scientifiques. Among his publications are *Les trois couleurs du tableau noir: la Révolution*; *L'éducation en France du XVIe au XVIIIe siècle* (with Roger Chartier and Marie-Madeleine Compère); and *Pèlerins et pèlerinages dans l'Europe moderne* (with Philippe Boutry).

HARTMUT LEHMANN is Director of the Max-Planck Institute for History at Göttingen and Honorary Professor at the Universities of Göttingen and Kiel. His books include *Jansenismus,Quietismus, Pietismus* and *Pietismus und weltliche Ordnung in Württemberg. Vom 17. bis zum 20. Jahrhundert* (with Heinz Schilling and Hans-Jürgen Schrader).

JEAN-MICHEL LENIAUD is Directeur d'étude at the Ecole pratique des hautes études (Paris), Section des sciences historiques et philologiques. His books include *L'administration des cultes pendant la période concordataire*; *Viollet-le-Duc, ou, Les délires du système*; and *Jean-Baptiste Lassus, 1807–1857, ou, Le temps retrouvé des cathédrales.*

FRANCES MALINO is Sophia Moses Robison Professor of Jewish Studies and History at Wellesley College. Among her books are *The Sephardic Jews of Bordeaux: Assimilation and emancipation in revolutionary and Napoleonic France*; and *A Jew in the French Revolution: The life of Zalkind Hourwitz*.

MARTIN E. MARTY is the Fairfax M. Cone Distinguished Service Professor Emeritus of the History of Modern Christianity at the University of Chicago. He is the author of over fifty books, including *Religion, awakening and revolution* and the three-volume *Modern American religion*.

MARK A. NOLL is the McAnaney Professor of History at the University of Notre Dame. He is the author or editor of over thirty books, including *A history of Christianity in the United States and Canada* and *America's God: From Jonathan Edwards to Abraham Lincoln*.

JAMES D. RILEY is Associate Professor of History at the Catholic University of America. His works include *Hacendados Jesuitas en Mexico: La Administracion de los Bines Inmuebles del Colegio Maximo de San Pedro y San Pablo de la Ciudad de Mexico, 1687–1767*; and *Landholding and provincial society: The Labradores of Tlaxcala, 1640–1730*.

MARIO ROSA is Professor of Modern History at the Scuola Normale Superiore in Pisa. Among his books are *Settecento religioso: politica della ragione e religione del cuore*; *Politica e religione nel '700 europeo*; and *Religione e società nel Mezzogiorno tra Cinque e Seicento*.

HELENA ROSENBLATT is Associate Professor at Hunter College in New York City. She has published *Rousseau and Geneva: From the First Discourse to the social contract, 1749–1762*.

ANDREW C. ROSS, a former Senior Lecturer in the History and Theology of Missions, is currently an Honorary Fellow in the School of Divinity at the University of Edinburgh. His books include *A vision betrayed: The Jesuits in Japan and China 1542–1742* and *David Livingstone: Mission and empire*.

LAMIN SANNEH is the D. Willis James Professor of Missions and World Christianity at Yale University. His books include *Encountering the West: Christianity and the global cultural process: The African dimension*, and *Abolitionists abroad: American blacks and the making of modern West Africa*

TIMOTHY TACKETT is Professor of History at the University of California, Irvine. Among his books in religious history are *Priest and parish in eighteenth-century France*; *Religion, revolution, and regional culture in eighteenth-century France*; and *Atlas de la Révolution française*, vol. 9: *Religion* (with Claude Langlois and Michel Vovelle).

R. G. TIEDEMANN is currently a Lecturer in History at the School of Oriental and African Studies at the University of London, and is soon to take up a research position at the Ricci Institute for Chinese-Western Cultural History at the University of San Francisco. He is the editor of and principal contributor to *The handbook of Christianity in China*, vol. 2: *1800 to the present* and the author of a number of scholarly articles on Christianity in East Asia.

DALE K. VAN KLEY is Professor of History at Ohio State University. He has published three major monographs on *The Jansenists and the expulsion of the Jesuits from France* (1975), *The Damiens affair and the unraveling of the ancien régime, 1750–1770*, and *The religious origins of the French Revolution*; as well as numerous articles on church–state relations in *ancien régime* France and the impact of Jansenism on French culture and politics.

W. R. WARD is Professor Emeritus of Modern History at the University of Durham. Among his books are *The Protestant Evangelical awakening* and *Christianity under the ancien régime 1648–1789*.

MERRY WIESNER-HANKS is Professor of History at the University of Wisconsin-Milwaukee. She is author, editor, or co-editor of over a dozen books, including *Christianity and sexuality in the early modern world: Regulating desire, reforming practice* and *Gender, church, and state in early modern Germany*.

Acknowledgements

The editors wish to express their appreciation to Dr Katharina Brett, Ms Gillian Dadd, Mr Kevin Taylor and other members of the staff at Cambridge University Press for their valued support in the preparation of this volume. Professors Ulrike Strasser, Daniel Schroeter, and Stephen Topik, all of the University of California, Irvine, provided valuable advice in the early stages of the project. Micah Alpaugh, from the same University, assisted us with the chronology. The editors also wish to note a special debt of gratitude to Dr Andrew C. Ross of the School of Divinity at the University of Edinburgh for his advice and assistance on sections relating to Christianity in the non-western world, and to Miss Margaret Acton of the Centre for the Study of Christianity in the Non-Western World at the University of Edinburgh. Finally, we record our thanks to our many authors, for their efforts in preparing their chapters and their co-operation and good humour through the editorial process.

Introduction

STEWART J. BROWN AND TIMOTHY TACKETT

Every historical age is an age of transition. But it is clear that from the mid-seventeenth century to the early nineteenth century – the period covered in the present volume – the Christian world would confront a series of exceptionally difficult transformations and challenges. By the end of this period, forces of intellectual and political opposition had arisen that put into question not only the nature of Christian doctrine and the authority of the church – as in the age of the Protestant Reformation – but also the authenticity of the Christian religion itself. Yet the same period also gave birth to a number of movements for religious revitalization and renewal, remarkable for their energy and impact, movements that would arouse major controversies within the established churches. The great wave of revolutions that marked the end of the period would serve to intensify the currents of both religious confrontation and religious renewal.

Here the editors will briefly underline some of the major motifs which emerge from this collective study. After a rapid survey of the geography of Christendom during the early modern period, we will touch on each of the three central themes that serve as the conceptual troika for this volume – Enlightenment, Reawakening, and Revolution. We will argue that those themes did not exist as independent and separate historical strands, but were inextricably interwoven, reacting and interacting with one another throughout the age.

The geography of early modern Christendom

Towards the middle of the seventeenth century, Europe was just emerging from a long series of brutal inter-Christian wars of religion. The basic confessional geography that crystallized by the end of the Thirty Years' War and the civil wars fought in the British Isles persisted with only minor modifications into the twentieth century. The Roman Catholic faith was now

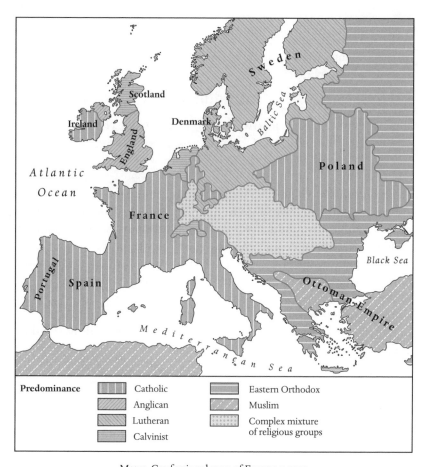

Map 1 Confessional map of Europe *c.* 1700

overwhelmingly dominant across much of southern Europe and the western Mediterranean – including Portugal, Spain, France, and the Italian peninsula – but also in most of Ireland, the Austrian Lowlands, Bavaria, Poland, and Lithuania. The various Protestant denominations, for their part, were deeply entrenched throughout north and north-central Europe, from Great Britain and Northern Ireland to the 'Lutheran sea' of the Baltic – including most of the north German states, Prussia, Scandinavia, Finland, Estonia, and Latvia. Somewhat further south, strong Protestant bridgeheads were also to be found in Silesia, south-west Germany and across the Swiss plateau.

Almost everywhere, of course, there were dissident minorities, clinging to existence within seas of state-supported orthodoxies. But the confessional jumble was particularly complex in a central band of territories extending from the United Provinces in the west, across south-central Germany, Austria, Bohemia, Hungary, and Transylvania. Here intricate juxtapositions and inter-mixtures of Catholics, Lutherans, Calvinists, various Protestant minorities, and Jews, jostled each other in a kind of continuing religious cold war. Further east and south the Catholic and Protestant populations blended into the sphere of the Eastern Orthodox churches, largely dominant in the Russian Empire and the Balkans. But the latter also contained a sizable Muslim minority of Europeans converted during the long occupation by the Ottoman Turks. This was in fact the one area of major religious warfare in Europe after 1648, with Christians and Turks locked in a struggle that continued intermittently to the end of the eighteenth century.

Although Europe remained the heartland of Christendom, home to by far the largest concentration of Christians, the previous period had also seen an unprecedented expansion of Europeans across much of the planet. By the mid-dle of the seventeenth century, Christian missionaries and settlers – sometimes following in the train of warriors and explorers, sometimes advancing on their own – had made contact with all of the major world civilizations.

Throughout large areas of Mexico, the Caribbean, and Central and South America, Spanish and Portuguese mendicants and Jesuits had permanently converted the indigenous populations to the faith. Christianity had also touched wide areas of North America above the Gulf of Mexico. But here in the mid-seventeenth century, European settlements were still relatively sparse, tenaciously clinging to coastlines and river valleys. Compared to the efforts of the Spanish and Portuguese, the Europeans in these areas had been far less successful in converting native peoples.

Much the same could be said for the great expanses of Sub-Saharan Africa. For the most part the European presence consisted of coastal trading stations and a small Dutch colony only just established at the Cape of Good Hope. Yet in two zones – the coasts of Congo and Angola and the lower Zambezi and coastal Mozambique – regulars from Portugal and other nations had succeeded in establishing tenuous Christian communities that survived into the nineteenth century.

In Asia, the small Portuguese province of Goa on the west coast of the Indian subcontinent served as a bridgehead for significant missionary activities throughout south India and Ceylon (Sri Lanka), with a few intrepid Jesuits and Capuchins pushing north to the heart of the Mughal Empire and beyond into Nepal and Tibet. Further east, the situation appeared even more hopeful for the Christian mission. The Spanish had won spectacular success in the

Philippines, permanently converting much of the population within three generations. The Portuguese and the regulars of several other nations had also achieved substantial numbers of baptisms in China, Indochina, Indonesia, and Japan – although much of the progress achieved in the latter region was beginning to crumble by 1650 as the Tokugawa Shogunate launched a broad movement of Christian persecution.

The late seventeenth and eighteenth centuries were to witness a continuing expansion of Christianity in certain areas of the world. Spain and Portugal pursued their conversions in the Americas, moving into the Californias and parts of Amazonia and Patagonia. In British and French North America, conversions remained relatively limited, although the period saw a huge influx of permanent European settlers, professing a wide variety of Christian denominations and sects. The eighteenth century also marked the advent of the first systematic Protestant missions activity, especially under the influence of the Pietists, who sponsored missionary efforts in North America, Africa, and India. But perhaps the most spectacular new conversions occurred among black African slaves on plantations across the Americas and the Caribbean. Free blacks from the nascent United States would themselves play an important role in proselytizing certain regions of West Africa.

Elsewhere, however, Christian missions experienced major disappointments and setbacks. In the eighteenth century, state-sponsored attacks on the Christian clergy and laity spread from Japan to China, Indochina, Siam, and Korea. Moreover, by the second half of the eighteenth century almost all areas of the world saw a sharp decline in the numbers of missionaries and a general flagging of energy. In part, it was a question of non-western nations coming increasingly to identify Christianity with European political and cultural imperialism. But in part the decline was also related to developments occurring within Europe itself: to the increasing rivalries for empire between European nations; to the pope's rejection of Jesuit efforts to adapt Christian rites to non-European cultures; to the broad attacks on the regular clergy by several European regimes, culminating in the suppression of the Society of Jesus; and to a sharp decrease in recruitment among both regular and secular clergies.

Enlightenment

Many of these developments occurring within Europe can be linked to an array of intellectual trends emerging near the end of the seventeenth century and commonly described as 'the Enlightenment'. This sweeping intellectual movement had varied roots. It was in one sense a reaction to the religious warfare that had so devastated Europe up through the mid-seventeenth century and to the politics of intolerance by both Protestant and Catholic states that threatened to revive such warfare: for example, the Revocation of the Edict of Nantes in France in 1685, or the expulsion of the Protestants from Salzburg in 1730, or the anti-Catholic penal laws in eighteenth-century Britain and Ireland. Surely, some began arguing, it was time to envisage forms of social organization that did not require efforts to impose religious uniformity. The new intellectual trends were also influenced by the growing European exposure to other world religions and cultures through the developing networks of global trade and communication. This exposure promoted among some European thinkers an intense interest in studying other religions – thus, for instance, the so-called British 'Orientalists' in India, who helped to gather and publish the ancient texts of Hinduism. Such studies would lead some European thinkers to a new sense of cultural relativism and a belief that religious systems, even Christianity, were largely human constructs. Perhaps most important, however, was the rise of science, which promoted an alternative means, apart from religious authority, for understanding nature and humanity. Careful observation, mathematical analysis, and logical calculation – the power of reason – would, it was believed, reveal the laws which governed the natural and the social worlds. The experimental method, with experiments that could be repeated by people everywhere, demonstrated sound truths which all rational men and women could accept. Science would show the way to practical improvements in material life, and also to new forms of social organization, based on the natural laws of society and the natural rights of man.

The early proponents of the 'Scientific Revolution' were convinced that its teachings provided more potent proofs of the existence of the Christian God and might even help restore the unity of Christendom. The revelations of science, they believed, confirmed the revelations of Scripture, while at the same time ensuring a more rational grounding for the Christian religion, based on the universal laws of nature. This in turn would diminish confessional divisions and strife. The laws of nature and the ethical precepts of Scripture, they insisted, came from the same source – that is, a benevolent God, the creator of a harmonious universe, who intended humankind to live together in charity and mutual respect. Most of those who embraced the ideals of the Enlightenment remained within the Christian tradition, viewing human reason and natural laws as aspects of God's created order, and seeking to bring a more moderate and ethical spirit to Christianity. An example of this Christian moderatism was William Robertson, Presbyterian clergyman, celebrated historian, Principal of the University of Edinburgh from 1762 to 1793, and acknowledged leader of the Church of Scotland, who endeavoured to move that church away from the fierce Calvinism of the seventeenth century towards a rational Christianity emphasizing practical morality and toleration. Such tendencies also had a powerful influence on a generation of European monarchs, who used Enlightened precepts as justifications for exercising an increased control over the churches within their domains. 'Enlightened despots', among them Frederick II of Prussia, Charles III of Spain, and above all Joseph II of Austria, issued sweeping edicts ranging from the imposition of toleration to the reorganization of churches and even the seizure of some ecclesiastical lands and the suppression of certain clerical orders.

While most proponents of the Enlightenment remained within a broadly defined Christian orthodoxy, many were drawn away from a strict dependence upon scriptural revelation to embrace a natural religion, which viewed reason as a sufficient guide to truth. What was the need for scriptural revelation, they asked, if reason and the natural laws revealed the mind of the Creator? Such a path led some to deism, or the belief in a first cause, a divine Creator, who had instilled in humans an innate knowledge of his attributes and the fundamentals of the ethical life. For deists, like John Toland or Voltaire, this innate human knowledge of the godhead lay at the foundation of all the great world religions, and Enlightened men and women could now strip away the accretions and corruptions of the centuries, and embrace the essential truths of God's existence and his moral imperatives. Other Enlightened thinkers, however, went beyond deism to a radical scepticism about the existence of God or of any divinely ordained morality. Such thinkers, to be sure, were a minority, but they included such influential figures as Denis Diderot, the baron d'Holbach and possibly David Hume. In its more extreme expressions the later Enlightenment could be conceived as fundamentally opposed to Christianity and as a precursor of a purely secular world-order.

Reawakening

The late seventeenth century also witnessed the emergence of movements of Christian renewal and reawakening within both the Protestant and Catholic churches. The Protestant reawakening first emerged among certain displaced and dispossessed Protestant communities in central Europe following the devastation of the Thirty Years' War. Some Protestant groups had felt alienated from the religious settlement imposed within their state by the Peace of Westphalia; they found no spiritual home within the church as it was established under the civil law and they felt vulnerable to persecution. In response, they developed their own forms of religious expression outside the established order in church and state, emphasizing personal conversion, regular Bible study, the formation of conventicles for prayer and devotion, a strict methodical manner of living, and the practice of charity. Some believed that the millennium was imminent, and they lived in the fervent expectation of Christ's return. These Protestant groups became known as Pietists, and their movement spread, assisted by the printing press, networks of correspondence, the migration of Europeans to the New World, and the missionary zeal of one of their groups, the small colony of Protestant Bohemian refugees that had settled on the Saxon estate of Count Zinzendorf and whose members became known as the Moravian brethren. The Protestant awakening reached Britain, initially Wales, in the 1730s, finding support among labouring men and women who were largely outside the established churches. The emotional itinerant preaching of John Wesley and George Whitefield attracted vast crowds, often in great outdoor meetings, while Wesley organized his converts on the model of continental Pietists into Methodist class meetings. At about the same time, a series of revivals swept through the British colonies in North America, transforming and renewing the religious life in what became known as the Great Awakening.

It was not only the Protestant churches that were affected by a heart-felt and experiential faith. Beginning in the mid-seventeenth century, the Roman Catholic Church in France also experienced a movement of spiritual renewal known as Jansenism that had some similarities to the Protestant awakenings. Jansenism emerged largely as a reaction against the triumphalist 'Baroque' orthodoxy of the Catholic Reformation – especially as promoted by the Society of Jesus. Profoundly influenced by the writings of St. Augustine, Jansenists sought to revive an emphasis on predestination and individual conversion through the grace of God, and to cultivate an emotional devotional life. They formed communities of the faithful, practised a rigorous morality, elevated the role of the laity, and engaged in acts of charity. Some strands of Jansenism, especially the more popular 'Convulsionaries' of the early eighteenth century, believed in miraculous healings and felt moved by the Holy Spirit to prophesize. When the Catholic establishment and the Bourbon kings sought to repress the movement, Jansenists became increasingly politicized, intensifying both their anticlerical rhetoric and their opposition to the absolute monarchy. In the course of the eighteenth century, despite the condemnation of some aspects of Jansenism by the papacy, the movement spread among Catholics in the Netherlands, Germany, Spain, and the north of Italy.

The Christian awakenings were not initially opposed to the contemporary movements of scientific investigation and the Enlightenment, and indeed many of those embracing the new religious zeal also shared in the fervent hopes of social improvement raised by science and reason. The Pietists were strong advocates of both popular and higher education, and the Pietist-dominated University of Halle promoted the study of science, especially the practical applications of scientific learning, and of world cultures. In Britain, John Wesley was a keen student of science and philosophy, and wrote learned treatises on epistemology. The Jansenists included among their number Blaise Pascal, a leading French scientist, who grounded both his scientific and his religious knowledge upon his personal experience. Those influenced by the Enlightenment and those influenced by the Awakening could unite in criticizing the established order in church and state, and in promoting programmes aimed at the extension of education. Protestant Dissenters and philosophers joined forces, moreover, in the first concerted attacks upon the slave trade and the slavery of black Africans. Nonetheless, evangelical Christians strenuously opposed the deism and scepticism that became prevalent in the later Enlightenment, and they grew to abhor the tendency of Enlightened philosophers to promote a moderate, rational, and ethical Christianity, which downplayed the doctrines of human sinfulness, eternal damnation, and Christ's atonement on the cross. By the beginning of the nineteenth century, this distrust had evolved into fundamental opposition.

Revolution

The wave of revolutions that swept across the Atlantic world in the later eighteenth century originated in developments that are largely outside the concern of this volume. In their long-term development, the revolutions can be linked to geopolitical competition for empire and the profits of maritime trade, especially the struggle between Great Britain and France. In the aftermath of Britain's victory in the Seven Years' War, the English-speaking colonies in North America violently resisted efforts by the British parliament to impose greater fiscal and political control over its expanded land empire, and this resistance led between 1775 and 1783 to a declaration of independence, a prolonged war, and the formation of a new republic. The French Revolution began in 1789 as a direct result of the monarchy's efforts to stave off fiscal collapse resulting from a century of imperial conflict, including France's military intervention in the American war. This is not to say, however, that the Enlightenment and Christian Awakenings did not play significant roles in the revolutions. Many

Enlightened philosophers directed a relentless assault on political institutions that were seen as not reflecting the natural laws and 'inalienable rights' of man, as endowed by the Creator and revealed through reason. Such 'corrupt' political institutions included a distant British monarchy and an imperial parliament imposing taxation on its colonies without due representation, or a divine-right French monarchy granting fiscal privileges to certain social orders or corporate bodies. Moreover, the Great Awakening of the 1730s and 1740s had played an important role in shaping an American identity and a sense of shared destiny under Providence. In France, the Jansenist criticisms of church and state throughout the eighteenth century contributed to the formation of a revolutionary discourse.

Once the revolutions began, they divided Christians. For some Christians, revolution was a rebellion against the divinely ordained order, a revolt, born of sin, against the 'powers that be', the worldly authority provided by God. For others, however, revolution was part of the providential plan for humankind, a movement that promised to strip away corruption and restore both church and state to purer forms; it would end clerical privilege, extend religious toleration, and elevate human aspirations. Many of these Christian supporters welcomed the way in which both the American and French revolutions aroused powerful support to the anti-slavery movement.

While the American Revolution did inspire, in the name of freedom, attacks upon the principle of established churches, it did not bring a break with Christianity. In France, however, the revolution ultimately went much further. After an initial period of support for a reformed Catholic Church within a regime of religious toleration – reforms that led, however, to a schism with Rome – the most radical French revolutionaries turned in 1793 against Christianity itself, portraying it as the ideological prop of the old order and a rallying centre for reaction, which would have to be swept away. To be sure, even the most radical de-Christianizers commonly maintained an attachment to the ethical teachings of Jesus, sometimes portrayed as a 'sans-culottes revolutionary'. Yet at the height of the 'Reign of Terror' they pursued their attacks on all clergy – Catholic and Protestant – and on the physical infrastructure of the church with brutal determination. While the de-Christianization campaign eased in the late 1790s, the churches remained subject to varying degrees of harassment and persecution by revolutionary officials. As the revolutionary and Napoleonic armies advanced beyond the borders of France, moreover, they spread the revolution's anticlerical and even anti-Christian policies to many other parts of Europe. The religious policies of the French Revolution thus stand as a landmark in the history of Christianity.

The onslaught on Christianity also led to further movements of Christian reawakening in both Protestant and Catholic Europe. These included millenarian movements, as many grew convinced that the political convulsions presaged profound spiritual events, perhaps even the Second Coming of Christ. They also included popular Christian movements of resistance – in Italy, Spain, Russia, and Germany – to what was viewed as a 'godless' French Revolutionary and Napoleonic domination. Among many artists and intellectuals, moreover, there was a celebration of a religion of feeling and a yearning for a restored Christendom. In North America there was a related revival activity known as the Second Great Awakening. The Awakenings contributed to a renewed onslaught on the iniquities of slavery, and to an agreement among the great powers in 1815 to end the slave trade. They also inspired a major increase in Protestant overseas missions activity and a renewal in Catholic overseas missions, laying the foundations for the 'great missionary century' and the renewed spread of Christianity to the wider world.

The plan of the volume

As the reader will discover, the essays in this volume have been divided into five parts. Four chapters in the first part examine the problems of church, state, and society in seventeenth- and eighteenth-century Europe. They are conceived to provide a broad overview of the political and social context of the Christian experience during the period. Part II then examines a variety of issues related to Christian life, primarily in Europe, prior to the French Revolution: from the nature and origins of the Catholic and Protestant clergies, to Christian education, sermons and oratory, religious architecture, Christianity and gender, and Christianity and the Jews. In Part III, particular emphasis is placed on the sources of change affecting the Christian world, including both the Scientific Revolution and the Enlightenment and the various movements of Protestant evangelicalism and Catholic Jansenism. A final chapter in this section explores the currents of toleration and Christian reunion that arose in the eighteenth century before the French Revolution. Part IV takes up the story of Christianity in the non-European world, exploring the advance of Christian settlers and missionaries in five major areas of the planet as well as the general problem of the relations of Christianity with the other major world religions. The final section of the book then picks up three central topics in the 'Age of Revolution': Christianity as it was involved in the American Revolution, the French Revolution, and the movement of opposition to slavery. The ultimate chapter, on Christian reawakenings between 1790 and 1815, provides an overview of

Christianity in Europe at the end of the period under consideration in this volume.

No collective work of this kind can hope to be entirely inclusive. The reader will find very little here on the immense areas of Australia, New Zealand, and Oceania, where the first Christian settlers and missionaries were only just arriving at the end of our period. Our volume has also not included the various groups within the sphere of the Eastern Orthodox churches which were in communion with the pope in Rome – the so-called 'Uniates' of eastern Europe, and the Maronites and certain elements of the Armenian and Coptic churches in the Middle East. Nor is there a treatment of the role of religion and the clergy in the early nineteenth-century movements of national independence in Iberian America. However, some of these topics will be taken up in the volume on Christianity in the nineteenth century.

PART I

⋆

CHURCH, STATE, AND SOCIETY IN THE EUROPEAN WORLD, 1660–1780

Continental Catholic Europe

NIGEL ASTON

General trends

The equilibrium sought in church–state relations during the later early modern era was a prize seldom attained. That failure was not a new development. This fundamental relationship in European public life had been contested as long as it had existed: which institution should be supreme in matters of law, appointments, and policy-making? By the mid-seventeenth century, it was obvious that the power of the state was becoming predominant. It was not that the princely houses of Europe were uninterested in promoting the values of Tridentine Catholicism, but they would do it on their terms, at their pace, and rarely unconditionally. The final destruction of Christendom at the Reformation and the persistent Ottoman threat had awarded them a leverage they were never slow to exploit at the expense of the papacy and the episcopate. The defence of the faith was no meaningless task and both sides appreciated well enough that the church militant on earth was dependent on how monarchs chose to understand that phrase. Lutherans had been open about this point since the Reformation and accepted that princely protection compromised institutional independence. Catholic clergy were reluctant to admit that their church was in its way no less reliant on the temporal powers and therefore no less vulnerable to Erastian incursions and policy decisions contrary to their own preferences.

In this period, the church could never assume that rulers would put the interests of Catholicism before the good of their states or the prestige of their dynasty. The Thirty Years' War graphically drove home that lesson. What may have looked like a Catholic *reconquista* in the 1620s was little more than a struggle for European dominance between France and Spain two decades later, with successive cardinal ministers, Richelieu and Mazarin, unashamedly enlisting heretical help (first the Dutch, then the English) in order to ensure the triumph of 'His Most Christian Majesty' of France. In the negotiation of the general European settlement at Westphalia in 1648, the Austrian Habsburgs were also willing to put confessional allegiance aside in the interests of making the empire work, of finally coming to terms with the persistence of Protestantism.

Like it or not, from as early as the mid-seventeenth century, the Catholic Church was obliged by international law to recognize Protestant rights across Germany. Thus, after 1648, non-Catholics at Strasbourg shared the official status of members of the cathedral chapter and Catholics and non-Catholics rotated in the see of Osnabrück. The church honoured the treaty to the letter on the basis of historic concessions capable of legal demonstration, of rights and liberties resting on regional and local differences. The Westphalia provisions also encouraged a form of co-existence with Protestant polities that would later act as a model for tolerating them *within* Catholic states. Only four years before the revocation of the Edict of Nantes in 1685, French troops occupied Strasbourg, and the great temple 'so long defiled by Lutheran rites' was reconsecrated. Even Louis XIV was careful, however, to permit Protestant congregations in the city to go on worshipping as before. Nevertheless, in the century after Westphalia, the Catholic hierarchy in Germany was tempted to encroach where it could, so that, as one scholar has put it, 'the bitter Protestant experience was that, as at more exalted levels, the tide went pretty consistently against them'.[1]

The Catholic hierarchy preferred to think in terms of religious reunion rather than toleration, of absorbing Protestants rather than accommodating them. In the 1680s, Bishop Rojas y Spinola pursued a vision of religious reunion within the empire that was given additional urgency by the need to contain the Turkish challenge. That vision commended itself long after the Ottomans had retreated from the plains of eastern Europe, and was reiterated by Benedict XIV in 1749. Despite (or perhaps because of) the Seven Years' War, inter-confessional relationships flourished in eighteenth-century Germany, with educated Catholics displaying an openness towards Protestants in line with Febronian precepts. Secular rulers were encouraging for a harmonious society made for loyalty and stability, and the Catholic Church went along with the trend in the interests of minimizing any reduction in its confessional privileges.

Outside Germany, the church was slow to make legal allowances for its religious rivals in the absence of any equivalent to the Westphalia stipulations. Intolerance was readily condoned in societies accustomed to considering confessional diversity as tending to political instability. The semblance of religious uniformity also suited rulers keen to show their rivals that their subjects knew that loyalty did not end with secular obligations. Louis XIV's long-premeditated revocation of the Edict of Nantes confirmed that the Bourbon monarchy's toleration of the *religion prétendue réformée* was a tactical gambit rather than a principled commitment.

France reverted to a pattern of official denominational exclusiveness that was very much the European norm in 1700. It took another well-publicized measure of anti-Protestant repression, the expulsion of Pietists from the archbishopric of Salzburg in the early 1730s, to bring about a gradual European reaction in favour of toleration. After the Salzburg affair, European advocates of limited toleration were constantly alert to the sort of *cause célèbre* that would call for passionate prose, and they found Enlightened absolutists like Frederick II of Prussia ready to listen on the grounds of state construction. However, less-enlightened rulers long continued to use coercion as a means of obtaining religious uniformity. In Portugal, John V was still persecuting heretics through the Inquisition with fifty-one individuals burnt between 1734 and 1743.

Catholic kings were commonly the combined *de facto* and *de iure* heads of their state churches. Indeed, the theology and traditions of the Roman faith were at least as respectful of the deference required for rulers as were any of the Protestant communions. In the post-Tridentine era, absolutist tendencies, the powers vested in bishops for instance, were as fashionable within the church as in the state. Rulers were easily convinced that Catholicism was the natural prop of authority; that Protestantism was born in disobedience with a propensity to republicanism. There was nothing more likely to sanction and uphold royal powers than the Catholic Church, for kingship itself was inconceivable without the blessing of the church. Little wonder that as many as fifty-one German princes converted to Catholicism during the seventeenth and eighteenth centuries. Even when the Catholic Stuarts lost their throne in England and Scotland in 1688–89 and in Ireland in 1690–91, the church could continue to recognize their family right to appoint to sees in the Irish Catholic bishoprics. This recognition dignified decades of exile, and its withdrawal in 1766 by Clement XIII was a reminder of the supreme legitimating power reposing in the hands of the hierarchy. Though the throne–altar 'alliance' was increasingly weighted in favour of the former, the advantage was not wholly one-way. Churches were highly privileged corporations with rights guaranteed by sovereigns at their coronation, and their leaders took precedence over their counterparts within the nobility.

Of course, though state and church had a clear idea of each other's distinctive roles and of where they could be mutually supportive, there were still frequent conflicts in most decades and in most states about the prerogatives properly belonging to both. By the 1760s, monarchies were adamant that the church must accept limits more strictly defined than previously, particularly in matters of taxation. In Milan, where the *Giunta Economale* (1765) disposed of state powers over the clergy, instructions of 1768 stated: 'There is no prerogative, no interference of ecclesiastics in the temporal sphere which can be proclaimed as legitimate if it does not originate in the consent and voluntary grant of the sovereign . . .'.[2] The anti-Jesuit campaign and the rash of mid-century concordats between princes and the papacy showed that tendency, while later Jansenism encouraged state power as a form of protection for itself, in effect, a variant within the Erastian tradition. In the Austrian Netherlands, the goal was to insert the church into 'the natural order of the state' as Zeger-Bernard van Espen (1646–1728), Professor of Canon Law at Louvain, said. Priests should not forget that they were both subjects and citizens.

The administrative services of the clergy remained at a premium in the running of Catholic states. Monarchs and ministers put a lot of thought into nominating bishops whose political skills were at least as conspicuous as their pastoral ones. At the same time, the fact that promotion was conditional on winning royal favour made bishops and higher clergy as skilled as ever in courtly arts and naturally sympathetic to entrenching regal powers at the expense of papal ones. Any minister expected the co-operation of the episcopate and used the patronage system to make it more likely than not. Thus when Pombal made his first moves against the Jesuits in 1757, he had his brother appointed Inquisitor-General and relied throughout on the compliancy of prelates. In France as elsewhere, bishops were prominent in managing Provincial Estates while cardinals Fleury and Brienne followed the precedent of Richelieu and Mazarin and served in practice as Principal Minister of the realm. Legislative roles were commonplace. In Poland, the seventeen bishops sat in the Senate; the Archbishop-primate of Gniezno was the second dignitary of the commonwealth after the king. In most French *parlements* a number of magisterial posts (six in Bordeaux, twelve in Paris) were reserved for the clergy. In Spain, Cardinal Portocarrero of Toledo intrigued with some effect in the late 1690s for the accession of the Bourbon dynasty, and as many as nine of the twelve presidents of the Council of Castile in 1700–51 were clerics. Spanish prelates were always caught up in activities that ranged far beyond the pastoral and the charitable. Lorenzana of Toledo tried to revive the decaying silk industry of his seat; Fabían y Fuero of Valencia and Llanes y Argüelles of Seville opened public libraries in their palaces; Bertran of Salamanca founded a vocational school for the training of goldsmiths. The parish clergy, too, were vital spokesmen for, and upholders of, royal authority in their parishes that were, after all, the primary agencies of administration across Europe. It was from the pulpits that villagers were likely to learn of royal edicts. Imaginative sovereigns grasped well enough that no agents in their realm possessed a greater reach into the lives and hearts of subjects than the parish clergy. In the church–state disputes of the middle decades of the century, persuading the lower clergy to view public affairs from the crown's perspective became crucial. Hence the interests of Charles III of Spain and Joseph II in securing the 'correct' education of parish priests through seminary consolidation and reform. Where that policy failed to produce results, as it had in the Austrian Netherlands by the late 1780s, the obduracy of the clergy in stirring up the people against imperial plans could be a prime explanation for their failure.

The papacy

Roman Catholicism was, at one level, embodied in an international church with a set of canon laws and observances having ubiquitous application; at another, the irrational structures and working practices of all early modern institutions applied at national, provincial, and local levels. Historical precedents were never lightly set aside and the scope for national churches to nourish and protect their independence from Rome was well rehearsed by the end of the seventeenth century. There had seldom been a point in the history of the papacy when secular rulers had not been assertive in the defence of their own leadership rights in their own states against papal pretensions. If encroachment was possible, then monarchs would attempt it, much as they always had: the process merely accelerated during the eighteenth century.

The Treaty of Westphalia is commonly supposed to have ushered in a period of progressive papal decay culminating in Clement XIV's humiliating consent to dissolve the Society of Jesus in 1773 and Pius VI's ignominious exile from the Holy City twenty-five years later. For Hanns Gross, the Roman see was suffering from 'post-Tridentine syndrome', one denoted by the largely successful completion of the programme laid down nearly two centuries earlier without articulating anything to replace it. This view is not uncontroversial.[3] It tends to underestimate the extent to which Tridentine policy initiatives in doctrinal and pastoral matters persisted throughout the eighteenth century. The evolution of the pontifical office during that period drew on a proven capacity for adaptation, suggesting that it was less diminished than different.

Within Italy, a long-standing leadership role in the city of Rome and the papal states was expanded through the assumption of primatial authority through-out the peninsula. Papal determination to assert metropolitan jurisdiction in the Roman province was underlined by the summoning of a Provincial coun-cil to Rome in 1725. In Catholic Europe as a whole, the Holy Father was still honoured as the patriarch of the west, the 'bishop of the universal Church'. He enjoyed continuing rights of ecclesiastical patronage on a scale unknown to any secular ruler even though the exercising of those rights occasionally gen-erated controversy. Thus the refusal to make Alberoni Archbishop of Seville in 1720 blew up a diplomatic crisis with Philip V that resulted in the expulsion of the nuncio. The unwillingness of a pope to recognize a ruler could have lasting repercussions. Neither Innocent X nor Alexander VII would counte-nance the Braganza claimant, John IV of Portugal (1640–56), nor fill sees with his nominees. John's response was to leave them unfilled, appropriate their incomes, and even contemplate setting up a national church. It was not until Portuguese independence was conceded by Spain in 1668 that the situation was stabilized. Issues such as preferment, regalian rights, clerical immunities and suzerainty over papal fiefs could also provoke conflicts.

In addition, the pope had unique responsibilities in securing the boundaries of Catholic Europe against Muslim encroachment and encouraging Christian monarchs, principally the emperor, to recover lands lost to the infidel. Alexan-der VII in the 1660s tried to organize a league of European powers against the Ottomans but was thwarted by the minimal help extended by France. Clement X (1670–76) gave financial aid to John Sobieski who defeated the Turks at the Dniester and later led the army that broke the siege of Vienna in 1683. A Holy League was put together by Innocent XI in 1684, consisting of the empire, Venice and Poland, and the pope deployed a military contingent until the close of campaigning in 1687. The results were spectacular: Hungary was liberated in 1686 and Belgrade recovered two years later. Clement XI's preoccupations brought the crusading ideal down into the *siècle des lumières*, and the Peace of Passowitz (1718) would be a landmark in the expansion of Christendom. By the 1740s, however, Catholic–Ottoman relations had stabi-lized much as Catholic–Protestant ones had a century earlier. Benedict XIV enjoyed such amicable diplomatic relations with Othman II that he dubbed him, 'The *Good* Turk'. Another aspect of papal pastoral concern was for the Uniate churches of eastern Europe which acknowledged Petrine primacy in general terms. Their vulnerability to Orthodox pressures rose sharply after the first Partition of Poland in 1773 when Catherine II of Russia promised to patronize those in White Russia without reference to Rome. Under the circumstances, Clement XIII and Pius VI had no choice but to rely on the good offices of Maria Theresa to support the independence of the Uniates.

A vacancy in St Peter's chair always precipitated a furious level of diplomatic activity as the Catholic powers lobbied to secure their candidate's election, a sign that having the right man in the post could facilitate policy-making appreciably and confer a slight advantage in international relations that was worth a good deal. Failure to obtain the right result could have long-term consequences. Thus Alexander VII (1655–67) could not develop a close working relationship with Mazarin, who had initially worked against his election. It was therefore vital for every Catholic ruler to have cardinals nominated on whose loyalties he could draw at election time. The explicit claims of France and Spain to name 'crown' cardinals had been rejected in 1667, and Benedict XIII met French plans to limit his freedom in creating cardinals by threatening to resign the papacy and retire to his other see of Benevento.

Despite the opportunities it presented, the papal office was a heavy burden, even for the outstandingly able Benedict XIV. Like other supreme pontiffs, Benedict relied heavily on the professional assistance of his secretary of state and those other officers (usually cardinals) holding the post of nuncio in the various Catholic capitals of Europe. The long eighteenth century witnessed the rapid maturation of papal administration. In the half century from Westphalia to the accession of Clement XI in 1700, the traditional role of the cardinal nephew became marginal as part of a steady drive against nepotism. Thus, in 1692 Innocent XII decreed in *Romanum decet pontificem* that popes could nominate only one kinsman to the cardinalate. There was a corresponding growth in significance of the secretary of state's office. Postings for lengthy periods to a nunciature became normative for senior members of the Curia, and the reports they filed rank as some of the most professional and insightful of their age. Some were outstandingly talented, such as Cardinal Garampi, nuncio to Poland in the aftermath of the first partition, who disarmingly made himself 'the pivot of an international network which set about refuting the policies favouring national churches and their legal rights'.[4] Considerable prestige came to be attached to this office, with rulers of the revived and elected monarchies of Portugal and Poland insistent that nuncios to their courts be created cardinals so as to place them on a basis of equality with larger states. It was a sure sign of diplomatic pressures when a nuncio was either expelled or had his office reduced to an ordinary embassy, as occurred in Florence in the 1780s.

Church and state in France

The Concordat of Bologna (1516) was an established and efficient protocol for the conduct of church–papal relations throughout the period with the Holy Father generally content to confirm royal nominations to dioceses. Failure to do so commonly led to temporary French military occupation of the Avignon and Venaissin enclaves. The Gallican church was, to all intents and purposes, a royal church, the model of a church–state polity to which every lesser Catholic monarch aspired. Despite possessing formidable structures of self-government (the quinquennial General Assembly of the Clergy was the most prestigious) and being exempted from direct taxation (it offered its own 'free gift', set at a rate and incidence of its choosing), the church was a dependent institution that looked to the monarchy for protection. It was not always forthcoming, but the majority of bishops and priests rarely faltered in their loyalty, even when the Gallican Articles of 1682 were discarded in favour of using the pope as an instrument to obtain the royal policy objective of crushing Jansenism. They well knew that the crown controlled senior appointments, and those higher clergy who sought a mitre had to exercise the arts of the courtier. Throughout the fifty-four years of his personal rule, Louis XIV had no regard for any version of Gallicanism that complicated the regalian authority of the sovereign. That stance enabled the King of France to pursue such classically non-Gallican policies as securing and then imposing the papal bull *Unigenitus* of 1713. After the king's death two years later, the content of Gallicanism would be interminably contested between the canonists and clergy on one side, and the lawyers and magistrates on the other.

Louis XIV's determination to act as the model of a Catholic king was inconsistent and less persuasive than he cared to admit. He was under pressure from the General Assembly of the Clergy to eliminate the legal existence of the Huguenot faith in his realm and the king was sympathetic to this broad objective. Protestants could be conveniently presented as republicans as well as heretics. On the other hand, as recently as 1662 Louis had rewarded Protestant loyalty during the Fronde with a royal declaration confirming the toleration granted at Nantes in 1598. After the Peace of Nijmegen in 1679, Louis backtracked and made it a domestic priority to cancel the Edict of Nantes, and in 1685 the deed was done. The king was acclaimed by a chorus of Gallican bishops with Bossuet of Meaux in the vanguard, but Catholic opinion outside France was either unimpressed or hostile. The vicious campaign of 'persuasion' visited on the Huguenots in the early 1680s was anathema to progressive opinion and reawakened interest in the possibility of toleration as an act of state. Leopold I of Austria, the main defender of Christendom against the Turkish threat, was still furious that Louis had sent a derisory French force to join in the relief of Vienna in 1683. Pope Innocent XI remained at logger-heads with Louis over the king's insistence on extending crown rights to draw income from certain vacant bishoprics (the *régale*) as well as his aggressive pol-icy in the Rhineland and elsewhere on the German frontier. Papal opposition to Louis' candidate for the vacant electoral diocese of Cologne had prompted the occupation of Avignon, the detention of the French nuncio and the king's raising the conciliarist threat. The wrangling got worse before it got better when Innocent in 1687 refused to accept the new French ambassador and, in December 1688, secretly excommunicated Louis and his ministers.

After Innocent's death in 1689, relations between Versailles and Rome slowly improved. Louis was ageing, and he wanted to enlist papal support of his grand-son Anjou to the Spanish succession and, above all, to eliminate Jansenism. There was no necessary reason for Jansenists to constitute a threat to royal power in the 1690s, but the king's insensitive conduct quickly pushed them to adopt the conciliarism that was classically Gallican and at odds with the pro-pontifical policy of convenience that Louis pursued in the quarter cen-tury before his death. He was convinced that unless Jansenism was authorita-tively and comprehensively condemned before his death it could threaten the continuation of the dynasty that was to be bequeathed to his three-year-old great-grandson. In fact, the king's reckless policy of extracting *Unigenitus* from a very reluctant Clement XI in 1713 would greatly destabilize French politics after his death.

Cardinal Fleury's long ministry (1726–42) saw a firm, resourceful handling of the Jansenist question by one who in his own person embodied the institutional overlap between church and state in eighteenth-century France. Fleury in the 1730s, having declared *Unigenitus* a law of the French state, relied primarily on patronage to install moderates of his own cast into key vacancies in the church. The policy restored a degree of harmony to church–state relations that lasted beyond his death. But in the 1750s the Archbishop of Paris, Christophe de Beaumont, provoked a constitutional clash with the Paris *parlement* over Jansenism that had profound implications for the entire polity and damaged the public standing of the First Estate (the clergy). The crown turned out to be an unreliable ally for the majority party in the church. Louis XV was not ready to defend its claims unconditionally and its vulnerability to pressure from anticlericalists in the sovereign courts was apparent to all. Only on the issue of direct taxation had the church been able to preserve its immunities, seeing off the attempt of the Controller-General, Orry, to impose the *vingtième* tax on the clergy in 1749. On that occasion, royal tergiverzation had, for once, worked to the advantage of the clergy.

The expulsion of the Jesuits in 1764 was undeniably a blow to the church, yet it put a term to the First Estate's disputes with the *parlementaires* and restored a degree of stability to church–state relations, a stability further confirmed by the accession of the pious Louis XVI in 1774. However, the new king was no more inclined to view public affairs from the hierarchy's perspective than his grandfather Louis XV had been. At each General Assembly of the Clergy, the king was abjured to issue an authoritative decree against the flood of impious *philosophe* or *philosophe*-inspired literature that was said to be corrupting the morals of France. Louis expressed his sympathy but remained inactive. In 1787, to the vexation of the clergy, his government granted very restricted civic rights to Calvinists in France. The edict was disingenuously presented as the working-out of the 1685 Edict of Fontainbleu rather than what it really was, the state sanctioning of a measure of toleration with kingdom-wide validity. With some justification, the clergy as a whole saw it as signalling the start of the dismantling of the French confessional state. They were particularly aghast that it was made law during the ministry of one of their own number: Loménie de Brienne, Archbishop of Toulouse, who had led 'the opposition' in the first Assembly of Notables (February–June 1787). But if the summons of Brienne to office suggested the continuing importance of the First Estate in affairs of state, the edict of 1787 indicated that a relegation in status of the clergy might not be far off.

Regalist trends in Spain and Portugal

On several occasions in the first half of the seventeenth century, Philip IV and his ministers had been at loggerheads with Rome, but the pressures of war and rebellion had made it impossible to press their points. However, the conferring of the throne of Spain on the Bourbon dynasty in 1700 (confirmed by the Treaty of Utrecht, 1713) signalled the turn towards a more Gallican style of royal control over the church. The post-1700 monarchy negotiated concordats with the papacy in 1737 and 1753, both emphatically confirming royal authority, a tendency known as 'regalism' within a Spanish context. The 1753 concordat was particularly significant: the papacy handed over to the crown the rights of presentation to most benefices, 12,000 in all, leaving only fifty-two in his Holiness's hands. It was also made clear that the crown did not recognize the papal grant of jurisdiction as the necessary foundation of its overseas *patronato*. It became the norm for clerics to exalt the Bourbon monarchy (especially after 1750), often by comparing Charles III's rule to the kingship of David and Solomon. The extraction of powers comparable to those belonging to their cousin, Louis XV, did nothing to encourage anti-Catholic or anticlerical tendencies in either Ferdinand VI or his half-brother, Charles III. The latter had no interest in either toleration or freedom of expression and in 1761 he triumphantly named Mary of the Immaculate Conception the official patroness of Spain. The Inquisition remained in existence and though a 'sleeping dog', it 'often woke and growled and occasionally bit'.[5]

After 1753, the crown nominated to the eight archbishoprics and fifty-two bishoprics of the kingdoms through a chamber of the Council of Castile, and involved procedures were put in place to ensure the exclusive selection of men of honour and reputation for episcopal office. These arrangements did not prevent wide suspicion that some ecclesiastical appointments were simonical, though such accusations were always hard to prove. The involvement and cooperation of the episcopate was considered essential to the implementation of the regalist programme and to the introduction of good government and sound religious practices into the bishops' jurisdictions. Thus, in 1767, the Council of Castile sent a circular to the bishops ordering them to curb abuses and superstition in their dioceses. Central administration could be ruthless when episcopal policies seemed at odds with what was sought: as when José Climent, Bishop of Barcelona, fell under unjustified suspicion of encouraging separatism in Catalonia and was obliged to resign his see.

The Bourbon crown energized those aspects of the Tridentine agenda neglected by the previous dynasty, particularly the production of an educated parochial clergy. Only eight seminaries were created between 1600 and 1747; but the suppression of the Jesuits added opportunity and urgency to the enterprise and eighteen were established between 1747 and 1797. Their curriculum and organization gave them the semblance of quasi-universities, though many were poorly staffed and too small as viable units. Beyond the crown's complicity in the anti-Jesuit policies of most European Catholic monarchies in the 1760s, there was also a serious effort at introducing state control (at the expense of Rome) over the other religious orders, numerically superior to the parish clergy and not known for their pastoral relevance. In 1776, a national vicar was forced on the Franciscans by the crown, which then extended this innovation to the Trinitarians, Carthusians, and Augustinians in the 1780s. There was, however, an unexpected twist to this imposition of royal authority. Monks and nuns developed the habit of appealing to the Council of Castile for resolution of internal conflicts, so that factionalism actually increased, and the crown's hope of reviving the religious motivations of the regulars was pushed aside.

In Portugal, the Braganca monarchy was determined that its status *vis-à-vis* the Holy See should not be less than that of any other Catholic monarchy, and the award of the title 'Most Faithful Majesty' to John V (1706–50) in 1748 gratified him immensely. Relations between John and the papacy had been constantly fraught over his demand that the office of patriarch of Lisbon (attached to his court chapel at Mafra) should be confirmed. He was ready to break with Rome over this stipulation, and indeed diplomatic relations were severed completely between 1728 and 1732. A concordat finally secured in 1737 brought the office into existence and, by a secret clause, laid down that the holder of the patriarchate would carry assured elevation to the college of cardinals (a point confirmed in 1766). State–church links were consistently tight in Portugal, and under John V the monarchy was happy to spend its wealth for ecclesiastical purposes. Thus Brazilian bullion paid for the great church-monastery of Mafra between 1717 and 1730 as well as church repairs and new buildings in Lisbon after the devastation caused by the earthquake of 1755. With the church a vital part of the national economy, and led by a wealthy, cultivated higher clergy (of 156 bishops in office in 1668–1820 four-fifths belonged to the nobility), the Braganca monarchy could usually rely on the episcopacy for support in any disagreement with the Vatican. Such relations were most valuable to the minister Pombal, who led the way in the Europe-wide campaign to secure the abolition of the Jesuits. The minister's uncompromising stance resulted in the progressive breakdown of diplomatic links with Rome in the 1760s. Pombal also limited clerical privileges generally and transformed the Inquisition into a royal tribunal, though he became in time a figure tending to compromise Portugal's international standing. He was arrested after 1775 and a new concordat was signed with Pius VI. The accession of Maria I in 1777 inaugurated a period of stability in relations between Lisbon and Rome previously unknown in the century.

Italy

Relations between secular rulers and the papacy were nowhere more acute and sensitive than in the Italian peninsula. The papal states were invaded three times in the course of the century before the French Revolution by foreign armies in the Wars of the Spanish, Polish and Austrian Successions. Even in peace, the Holy See might have to cede ground. In 1731, papal suzerainty over Parma and Piacenza was renounced. A concordat of 1727 with the House of Savoy gave the new Kingdom of Sardinia only a share of the rights it asked for, but a second of 1741 obliged Benedict XIV to permit church appointments in that state to be regulated exclusively according to royal preferences. Rights of sanctuary were also virtually abolished, and it was further agreed that the church's property acquired since 1620 should be subject to normal civil taxation. In the Kingdom of Naples, there was a long-standing regalist tradition suspicious of both the Jesuits and the Holy Office, and resentful of the annual tribute of the *chinea*, the traditional symbol of papal suzererainty over Naples itself. Anti-curial sentiment intensified over papal hesitation at sufficiently recognizing the Bourbon succession in 1734. It ended with a 1741 concordat (there was a second in 1745) and the final abolition of the Holy Office's authority in questions of state. The Bourbon dynasty showed itself unhesitatingly determined to police the church–state boundary lines in its own favour and, over the course of the next half century, diminished rights of sanctuary were established, clergy became liable for taxation, and the principle that only Neapolitans should hold benefices in the kingdom was put beyond dispute. The last symbolic act in this very Catholic form of Erastianism came in 1788 when Ferdinand refused the *chinea*. A four-year standoff between himself and Pius VI ensued. Eventually, with almost half the sees in southern Italy vacant and the French Revolution demanding his undivided attention, the pope gave way. But the *locus classicus* of state-sponsored reform Catholicism in the late eighteenth century was the Grand Duchy of Tuscany, a small state of about one million people, run by Maria Theresa's son, Peter Leopold. Catholic reform was not a new current in the duchy but Peter Leopold came to see himself as an 'external bishop' interfering in clerical education and prescribing reading lists almost on the scale of his elder brother, the emperor Joseph II. It was the century's ultimate expression of Caesaropapism, one in which the church seemed programmed for absorption by the state. This was the position in 1780 when the Grand Duke recruited the new Bishop of Pistoia and Prato, Scipione de' Ricci, to be his principal collaborator, the prelate who became known as 'the pope of Tuscany'.

Church and state in Germany and the Habsburg Empire

The pronounced state loyalties of Catholic clergy in most German princi-palities is well attested, a feature of the political landscape even before the Treaty of Westphalia, and it was nowhere stronger than in the three elec-toral principalities of Mainz, Trier, and Cologne where state and church alike were governed by their prince-archbishop. The Elector of Mainz, the senior archiepiscopal elector, was also the arch-chancellor of the empire, giving him a diplomatic status that far outweighed his territorial importance. His colleagues at Cologne and Trier were scarcely less significant as an international presence, a point that helps to explain Louis XIV's determination to intrude his candidate at Cologne in the mid-1680s, at the height of his own imperial ambitions. As Simon Schama once observed, 'the endurance of Mainz was a witness to the viability of anachronism'[6] and successive archbishops behaved confidently as Enlightened absolutists in miniature, ready to take on and overcome the strength of popular, noble, and clerical hostility to change. The greatest of them was Friedrich Karl (1774–1802), who used the demonstratively anti-Austrian and Protestant-dominated *Fürstenbund* in 1785 as a springboard for achieving a 'German national church', much to the amusement of Frederick the Great.

Friedrich Karl's success marked the culmination of the development of an essentially *German* church within Catholicism. Academics at universities like Trier, Mainz, and Würzburg had been at the fore in this trend, and by the 1730s the scholarship of outstanding historians such as Muratori and the concepts of natural law were used to validate long-standing attacks on targets like annates paid to Rome and papal nuncios. This strand of reasoning was also influenced by Jansenism and by a warmer regard for German Protestantism, as Catholics became accustomed to the confessional co-existence laid down in the 1648 settlements. This pronounced anti-ultramontanism was at its strongest in those principalities where princes looked to academics for theoretical support against the popes and in transforming their territories into sovereign states. Febronianism was the end-product and part of a distinctive Catholic reform movement. Taken together, the ascendancy of such views by the 1760s famously led Heribert Raab to talk of an 'intellectual revolution' in Catholic Germany.

The coming of Febronianism and the apparent confidence of German Protestantism were an imperial policy concern for the Empress Maria Theresa (1740–80). She, no more than her father (Charles VI) or her grandfather (Leopold I), could be viewed as unconditionally responsive to the Curia or to the bishops within the Habsburg territories. She wanted to govern her church while respecting the papacy's spiritual primacy, and guard Catholicism (of which she was, in theory, the leading defender on earth) from further, aggressive Protestant incursions. With her family, she attended Mass daily, as did Joseph II in his ten-year sole reign. The institutional strength of the Austrian church at the turn of the eighteenth century was impressive, though diocesan and provincial boundaries were often awkwardly aligned. The creation of new dioceses in the eighteenth century in the Hereditary Lands was well behind demographic growth: only three episcopal seats were added, although the population increased by 50 per cent. Habsburg powers of patronage over a relatively small episcopate were limited. Bishops were elected by cathedral canons in the first instance, according to German custom. Prelates were also well represented in the diets and the clergy furnished up to a quarter of the administrators chosen by these assemblies. The imperial monarchy was determined to reduce the tax immunities of the clergy and achieved this objective at mid-century: after 1749, the regular orders had to pay taxes for a ten-year period and could no longer discuss the amount to be paid annually.

The detachment of the monarchy after mid-century from Jesuit influences was a historic rupture, because Austrian Catholicism had been deeply marked by them. However, the empress was bent on a programme of educational reforms that would increase the role of the secular clergy and the laity. The Habsburg tradition of anti-curialism was reactivated again by Paul Joseph Ritter von Riegger, Professor of Canon Law at Vienna University, drawing on Jansenist-inspired canonists like van Espen, whose own pupil was Febronius himself. The latter's ideas were condemned in 1764 by Clement XIII, who feared that the Habsburg monarchy and the German principalities had a common agenda that would end in greatly reducing papal power in central Europe. Maria Theresa was no Febronian, but she pressed on with the policy of secularizing intellectual life in the interests of the monarchy. In 1767, a new administrative department was created to initiate and implement ecclesiastical legislation in the empire. The major participants were her son and co-sovereign, Joseph II, Chancellor Kaunitz, and (from 1769) Franz Joseph Heinke, senior official of ecclesiastical affairs. All were persuaded that state power was fundamental to the task of Catholic reform. Maria Theresa still worried about betraying her family's historic role as the defenders of Catholic culture. In fact, her empire contained a number of non-Catholic minorities, including, in Vienna, an estimated 2,000 Protestants – 1 per cent of the population – and a substantial number of Jews. In the Kingdom of Hungary, the Magyar elite was divided between Catholics, Lutherans, and Calvinists. Jews also resided in Trieste, Goricia, and Mantua, though community and public worship remained unauthorized there and in both Bohemia and Moravia. In Bohemia, adherence to Protestantism was punishable by death in Charles VI's reign (1711–40), although covert Protestants were tolerated after the annexation of neighbouring Silesia by Prussia in 1745. In 1777, whole Moravian villages declared themselves Protestant, and Kaunitz argued that persecution was inimical both to the interests of true Christianity and to the true interests of the state. But continued disagreement on how to treat religious minorities soured relations between the empress and Joseph II in the 1770s.

After his mother's death in 1780, Joseph was at last in an unfettered position to introduce a general patent of toleration into the empire and to embark on an unprecedented policy of reforming the church: banning the entry of papal bulls, closing monasteries, rationalizing the organization and number of seminaries to form six general seminaries, with the state assuming the task of educating its parish clergy. The latter would be turned into servants of the state, whatever their personal preferences and irrespective of the provincial privileges which apparently invalidated such centralizing plans. Religion would be the cement of empire, and Jansenist works would be permitted as well as textbooks minimizing papal authority. For Joseph, conversion to Catholicism was in principle desirable but coercion was inadmissible. It was to be a matter of charity and persuasion and he reserved special clerical preferment for those priests who acted according to these guidelines.[7]

The emperor's controversial agenda had plenty of defenders, especially when Pius VI made his visit to Vienna in 1782 to plead unsuccessfully with the emperor to modify his policies. Was there a danger of a second German Reformation? Pius's anxiety was acute that Joseph's extreme Erastianism was converging with Febronian tendencies in Germany and that his own power-base outside Italy looked close to collapse. Joseph visited Rome in 1783 in a bid to force his claim to appoint all bishops in Milanese territory, a breach of traditional papal prerogatives. Pius tried to save face by making concessions, and a concordat followed in 1784 without fully resolving the jurisdictional dispute. Another bone of contention was Joseph's intent on making his ally Johann Karl von Herberstein Archbishop of Ljubljana, an archdiocese Joseph had created himself. Only the candidate's death in 1787 forestalled outright schism between the emperor and Pius. It was at this middle point of Joseph's reign that opposition began rising over the emperor's ecclesiastical policies. Numerous pamphlets drew attention to the hesitancy and inconsistency in his idiosyncratic approach, such as his refusal to discard clerical celibacy. Confronted with this avalanche of criticism, Joseph brought back censorship and tried to silence the opposition. His heavy-handedness only increased his problems and gave the clergy increased confidence to urge their flocks to resist him. It was a salutary reminder that no eighteenth-century monarch could ever take the good offices of either lower or higher clergy for granted.

The point is well made by Jeremy Black that, 'it is important not to ignore the relationship between "reforming" governments and clerics, and the attempt to adjust the ideologies and practices of Church–State co-operation to new aspirations and circumstances'.[8] What is striking in the long eighteenth century is less the mutual competition than the capacity of both parties to build on the experience of mutual co-existence over the centuries and the fundamental awareness that each side needed the other. Nowhere was there much sympathy for ultramontane ideals as they would be articulated after 1815. The outreach of papal power may have contracted between 1648 and 1780; yet most of the popes adopted a *realpolitik* that served the institution well, and they benefitted from the increased professionalization of the advice available to them. The institutional foundations would thus be strong enough to survive the double blow of the dissolution of the Jesuits in 1773 and the French occupation of Rome in 1798. Rome was still capable of acting as the focus of the Christian world, as at the Jubilee of 1750 when St Leonard of Port-Maurice preached the penitential mission before the pope and cardinals and an audience of 100,000 people.

It would be quite misleading to say that it was all downhill for the Catholic Church from the mid-eighteenth century. If Tridentine initiatives were coming to a close, it was because the need for them scarcely existed. They had been completed successfully. Although symptoms of de-Christianization have been detected, Europe was really at its most Christianized, its populations ready to be mobilized against 'Enlightened' opposition to Christianity. One should not forget that, in a moderate form, Catholic opinion had its own Enlightenment imperatives. The increased importance of natural rights and Enlightenment debate shifted consciousness away from the denominational group to the individual believer. Joseph's Edict of Toleration extended newly defined rights from previous areas of denominational co-existence into the areas of Catholic uniformity. But what may be called 'civil rights' still fell short of those awarded Catholic subjects, as the 1787 edict in France indicated. Toleration may have indicated revised limits to confessional churches, it was never intended to cancel their powers and privileges. These still had their uses for any reforming monarch. The real problem for the church between 1750 and 1780 was producing a post-Tridentine agenda and here its imaginative and pastoral failure is evident. Monarchs were not interested in responding to clergy-led initiatives when their own concerns centred primarily on making the church into an efficient unit of state agency. Prelates largely complied because their own ambitions could be gratified by enhanced leadership roles within the polity. For its part, the papacy after Benedict XIV was too preoccupied with dealing with the international crisis caused by demands for the abolition of the Jesuits and its aftermath to have much time for constructing a new strategy for changed times. Church–state relations had become so fraught in the 1760s, so central to the domestic and foreign strategies of most Catholic powers, that all sides lost sight of the harm to their credibility that such a war of attrition was likely to cause.

Notes

1. W. R. Ward, *Christianity under the ancien régime, 1648–1789* (Cambridge: Cambridge University Press, 1999), p. 5.
2. Quoted in Norbert Jonard, *Milan au siècle des Lumières* (Dijon: University of Dijon, 1974), p. 50.
3. Hanns Gross, *Rome in the age of the Enlightenment: The post-Tridentine syndrome and the ancien régime* (Cambridge: Cambridge University Press, 1990). Cf. the emphasis in Anthony David Wright, *The early modern papacy: From the Council of Trent to the French Revolution, 1564–1789* (Harlow: Longman, 2000), especially pp. 7–8. See also Owen Chadwick, *The popes and European revolution* (Oxford: Clarendon Press, 1990).
4. Dries Vanysacker, *Cardinal Giuseppe Garampi (1725–92), an Enlightened Ultramontane* (Brussels: Brepols, 1995), p. 11.
5. Charles C. Noel, 'Clerics and crown in Bourbon Spain, 1700–1808: Jesuits, Jansenists, and Enlightened reformers', in James E. Bradley and Dale K. Van Kley (eds.), *Religion and politics in Enlightened Europe* (Notre Dame, Ind.: University of Notre Dame Press, 2001), p. 144.
6. See S. Schama's review of T. C. W. Blanning, *Reform and revolution in Mainz* (Cambridge: Cambridge University Press, 1974) in the *Times Literary Supplement* (28 March 1975), p. 333.
7. Joseph himself was 'certainly not a Jansenist, but a sort of Christian Stoic': W. R. Ward, 'Late Jansenism and the Habsburgs', in Bradley and Van Kley (eds.), *Religion and politics in Enlightened Europe*, p. 180. See Derek Beales, *Joseph II*, vol. 1: *In the shadow of Maria Theresa* (Cambridge: Cambridge University Press, 1987), p. 192, for the emperor's sense of the divine voice speaking within him.
8. Jeremy Black, *Eighteenth-century Europe*, 2nd edn (Basingstoke: Palgrave, 1999), p. 241.

2

Continental Protestant Europe

HARTMUT LEHMANN

The rise and decline of Pietism

In the period between the end of the Thirty Year's War and the era of the French Revolution, no religious movement changed the face of continental Protestantism more than Pietism. The followers of Pietism, as this religious revival soon came to be called, developed new centres of social, cultural, and political activity for all Protestants. But more importantly, perhaps, those Protestants who were inspired by the ideas of Pietism exhibited a new kind of self-esteem. They believed, it seems, that they were completing whatever had remained unfinished in Luther's Reformation. In short, they saw themselves as a better kind of Protestant.

Philipp Jakob Spener was the undisputed leader of the first generation of Pietists. Born in 1635, Spener received theological training at Strasbourg and rose to the leading position of pastor to the Protestant Church in Frankfurt by the 1660s. Deeply concerned about the sincerity of the members of the flock who were entrusted to him in this thriving centre of international trade, he decided in 1670 to assemble some of the most devout members of his congregation in special meetings. In Spener's view, this first Frankfurt conventicle (or 'ecclesiola in ecclesia') was an attempt to form a kind of Christian elite that in turn would, he hoped, help to better the condition of his congregation and even contribute to reforming the church as a whole. A few years later, in 1675, Spener explained his ideas in some detail in a preface to the new publication of one of the works of Johann Arndt. This preface, soon to be published as a separate tract under the title *Pia Desideria*, that is, 'pious wishes', can be considered the founding document of Pietism. It served as the most influential guide for future generations of Pietists. Spener stressed three points in particular in the *Pia Desideria*. First, he argued, sincere Christians should assemble regularly and support one another spiritually. Second, he insisted that it was the obligation of all devout Christians to help reform the church.

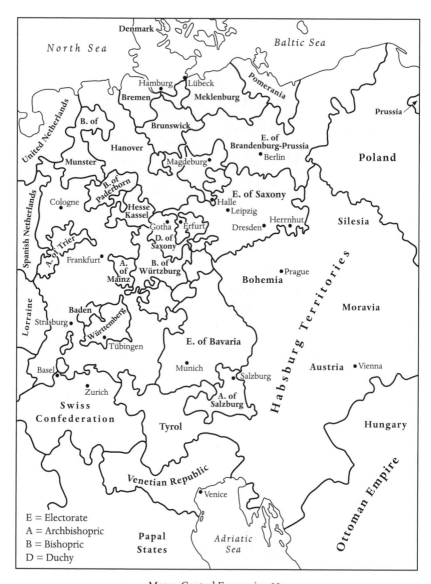

Map 2 Central Europe in 1660

They should not separate themselves from the church, but try to build a better church. Third, Spener argued, although salvation history had progressed, as all the signs of his time indicated, God had promised to His children before Christ's return a prolonged period in which they could and should build God's kingdom. This hope for better times, as it was called, was a most startling and innovative interpretation of Protestant eschatology. This theological notion meant that all of those who followed the example of Spener were expected to labour most actively in the affairs of this world so that they would, with God's blessing, successfully lay the foundations for His kingdom. Rather than prepare themselves for the Day of the Last Judgement in the fear that this day was imminent, Christians should recognize that God demanded social responsibility and a high standard in the conduct of one's affairs. Through this, Spener redirected the activity particularly of those Protestants who were afraid that they would not gain eternal life. Instead of fearfully observing the signs of the times, he argued, they should initiate and shoulder reform projects that served the good of the church, and indeed the community of all Christians hoping for salvation.

Spener's various initiatives at Frankfurt soon attracted attention. While some of his fellow-pastors applauded what he had done and attempted to proceed in the same manner, others criticized him severely. They argued that by assembling a part of his congregation in a special meeting, Spener was about to divide the church effectively into two camps, those who were brought to believe that they were reborn, and the rest, the so-called children of the world ('*Weltkinder*'), who were supposedly doomed. Not surprisingly, there were soon also tensions right in the midst of the Frankfurt conventicle. While Spener tried to ensure that the energy of his conventicles would help reform the church, his most important collaborator, the Frankfurt lawyer Johann Jakob Schütz, believed that the church could not be saved and that any efforts in that direction were futile. For Schütz, as salvation history had progressed rapidly, the assembly of those who now met in conventicles was the true church of the end-time.

After long discussions and what was certainly a most painful process, the Frankfurt conventicle split in two. The followers of Schütz met separately, and after some years they decided to migrate to Pennsylvania where they hoped to find a place of refuge as the apocalypse approached. Spener, meanwhile, continued his work for some time in Frankfurt, but in 1686 he decided to accept the position of court preacher in Dresden. Although the Dresden post was considered to be the most prestigious position in Protestant Germany and within Lutheranism, Spener soon found out that he was unable to implement any of his proposed reforms in surroundings defined by the luxury of a Baroque court and a prince more interested in operas, fireworks, and hunting than in social reform. Thus in 1692, after only a few years, Spener left Dresden and moved to Berlin, to a somewhat inferior position, but to a court that was open to his ideas. Spener stayed in Berlin until his death in 1705.

In Berlin, Spener became what can be called the patriarch of the Pietist movement. He took an active part in reforming the social system of this socially very diverse city by supporting plans that helped beggars and the very poor, and he used his influence at court and among the high Prussian military officer class to protect Pietists who were persecuted in other territories. Most importantly, however, he counselled literally hundreds of persons who turned to him for help in practical matters and for spiritual advice. Spener answered all of the requests in long and detailed letters that were published even before his death as 'Theologische Bedenken', which means theological considerations or reflections. For historians of Pietism, these 'Theologische Bedenken' form a most informative source. Through his answers, Spener was keen to build a network that reached far beyond Berlin and even beyond the Holy Roman Empire. By the end of his life, Spener had developed the two most important means through which Pietists were able to communicate and gain influence: conventicles and letters. Other means of religious socialization, which were soon being exercised effectively, were regular visits of those who considered one another as brothers and sisters in the community of the reborn, meetings of the like-minded, and the establishment of Pietist educational and social institutions. Furthermore, Pietists soon made substantial contributions to the body of edifying tracts and hymns through which they expressed Pietist spirituality. By the beginning of the eighteenth century, the new movement had gained many followers all over central Europe and, what was perhaps even more important, an unmistakable profile. In other words, a new tradition had begun. To be considered a Pietist, one had to place the influence of Spener and Johann Arndt next to that of Martin Luther.

Already in the 1680s, pious Protestants met regularly in conventicles in cities like Erfurt, Magdeburg, Lübeck, and Quedlinburg as well as in many other places. Very early on, women participated actively in many of these meetings, while pastors often played only a marginal role. This indicates that these early disciples of Spener were suspicious of the teachings of Lutheran orthodoxy as taught in theological faculties at German universities. At the same time, they were prepared to listen to what they considered direct inspiration and revelation, and such direct revelation could be given, as they believed, to women as well as to men. Rather than defer to the authority of the corps of male pastors, they relied on spiritual bonding, on improvised prayers, and on the hope that they would receive direct instruction from God on how to understand certain passages in the Scripture. As might be expected, the ecclesiastical authorities did not take long before they intervened. Wherever conventicles led by lay persons were detected, they were forbidden and dissolved. In many of the Lutheran territories within the Holy Roman Empire, edicts banning Pietist conventicles were passed and executed, sometimes with unnecessary force, by local authorities. But such measures could not stop those who were convinced of Spener's ideas and who felt that they were part of an international religious revival directly guided and inspired by God. That they were persecuted by the official church was, they believed, a sure sign that they were God's elected children. To them, out of repentance for their sins followed rebirth, and out of rebirth the task of sanctification, and out of sanctification the certainty of salvation.

One of Spener's early followers and an active participant in the religious revival of the 1680s was August Hermann Francke, who was a generation younger than Spener. When the church authorities disbanded the conventicles in which he had taken part at Quedlinburg, Francke moved to the city of Halle where he soon made a spectacular career. In his capacity as a talented scholar who was well versed in all of the classical languages, Francke was appointed to a professorship at the newly founded University of Halle. In addition, he became very active in the social field. He founded an orphanage which he expanded into a primary school, to which he added a secondary school, and then a training centre for teachers. But this did not exhaust Francke's remarkable capacities as an organizer. Within only a few years, he founded, in addition to his schools, a pharmacy and also a print-shop in which he printed edifying tracts and bibles which he distributed to the poor. Soon many members of the Prussian aristocracy sent their children to Halle. Alumni of Francke's educational empire found posts as teachers across Europe. As early as 1706, some went as missionaries to India, and this was just the beginning of a wide network of international contacts and connections.

Francke's success would not have been possible without the guiding hand of Spener in Berlin, and certainly not without the special privileges and the protection that he received from the Hohenzollern court. The Hohenzollern dynasty had converted to Calvinism in the early seventeenth century, and they were now ruling a state with a strong Lutheran majority that had close ties to the local estates. In the last decades of the seventeenth century the Hohenzollerns, like the princes of many other territories, attempted to curb the influence of the estates in their realm. As the Lutherans supported the estates, the Pietists' wish to establish themselves in the Hohenzollern lands came just at the right time. By helping Spener in his social activities in Berlin, but above all by granting special privileges to Francke at Halle, the Prussian sovereign was able to curtail the influence of the Lutheran establishment and this, as he knew, in turn served to weaken the political role of the estates. It was not love for Pietism that led the Hohenzollerns in their decision to support Halle Pietism; rather, they used the Pietists at Halle for their own political ends.

Francke proved to be more than an equal in dealing with Prussian sovereigns. Francke was committed to building a kingdom of his own, or, rather, one should say, he was convinced that he was the instrument chosen by God to build His kingdom. When Frederick William I became King of Prussia in 1713, he sent an ultimatum to Francke, demanding that he stop his involvement in worldwide projects. Instead, he should concentrate his efforts on helping to improve society and educational provision within Prussia. Francke knew that he had to give in, or at least to give the king the impression that he agreed. In truth, Francke pursued what can be called a double strategy. On the one hand, he sent some of his alumni to teach at the military orphanage in Berlin and he also supplied the Prussian army with military chaplains. Through this and other means he attempted to demonstrate to the king that Halle served the king's policies and nothing else. On the other hand, Francke not only continued to keep contact with Pietists in many other countries, but he actively expanded Halle's sphere of influence. As recent research has clearly shown, Francke corresponded with like-minded Christians in east-central Europe, especially Hungary and Bohemia, and in northern Europe, most notably in Latvia, Lithuania, and Russia. He even sent an expedition to Siberia. Francke also developed close ties to the court in Copenhagen, to the Society for the Propagation of the Gospel in England and to many of the German communities which had migrated to the British colonies in North America. He also supplied them with bibles and with pharmaceutical products, most notably the *essentia dulcis*. As a result, between the time of Spener's death in 1705 and Francke's death in 1727, Halle not only was the most important centre of Pietism within Prussia – such that some historians argue that the rise of Prussia and the very special Prussian values can only be understood if one takes into account the influence of Pietism – but also the most active centre of Pietism worldwide. Two centuries after the Reformation, and after a long period of German Lutheran self-centeredness, the Halle Pietists were the first German-speaking Christians to become active outside of Germany and contribute significantly to the development of Christianity as a world religion.

The most active and perhaps even the most influential representative of a third generation of Pietists was Ludwig Nikolaus Graf Zinzendorf, born in 1700 and an alumnus of Francke's foundations at Halle. Since the 1720s, Zinzendorf had assembled pious Protestants on his estate at Herrnhut, among them many refugees from Moravia and Bohemia who traced their religious faith back to Johann Hus. In 1727, to the surprise and joy of all who were involved, something that can be called a collective revival occurred at Herrnhut. This event convinced Zinzendorf that God had entrusted to him a very special mission. In the 1730s, the number of Zinzendorf's followers grew rapidly. Pietists from various German regions joined his cause. Soon Herrnhut became too small. Zinzendorf did not hesitate to act. Within the following years, he established new communities in other places, even in other countries, as for example Zeist in the Netherlands, and Neuwied in the Rhineland. Zinzendorf also travelled a great deal. Historians have called him the count who crossed all borders, a characterization that has multiple meanings. Not only did Zinzendorf travel, more than once, to North America where the Herrnhuter, or Moravians as they were called in the English-speaking world, had founded the community of Bethlehem; Zinzendorf also had a close spiritual relationship with common people who counted as his most loyal supporters. For his second marriage he chose a partner from a non-noble family.

As early as the 1730s, Zinzendorf sent missionaries to faraway places. Best known are the missionary endeavours of the Moravians among African slaves on sugar plantations in the West Indies and among the Eskimos in Greenland. As a rule, Zinzendorf's missionaries were skilled artisans, preferably carpenters (although this turned out to be quite useless in Greenland where no trees for building houses could be found). Most certainly, the secret of the success of the missionaries sent from Herrnhut was that they always combined biblical teaching with practical help. Zinzendorf's theology can best be described as an early form of ecumenism. He thought little of confessional differences. Rather, what he attempted to create was an international army of committed reborn Christians of which he would be the undisputed leader. Within Herrnhut, Zinzendorf divided people according to gender, family status and age by forming so-called choirs. In the late 1740s, another wave of spiritual excitement swept through Herrnhut and other Moravian communities. This widely publicized event convinced traditional Protestants and also the Pietists at Halle that Zinzendorf could not be trusted. When Zinzendorf died in 1760, his heritage was as rich as it was problematic. By the time of his death he had compiled a huge financial debt. But his legacy was inspiring because he had managed to found the first truly international missionary movement, with outposts on all continents.

The Pietists of Württemberg were among those who had been most reserved, if not unfriendly and at times even hostile, towards Zinzendorf. They had always been closely associated with the estates in their territory, and they remained so throughout the eighteenth century. In fact, one can say that the strict asceticism that Württemberg Pietists espoused formed the basis of the political opposition of the Württemberg estates in their struggle with the prince who strove, like most other German princes of the time, to rule in an absolutist manner and to imitate the life of the court at Versailles. At the same time, Württemberg Pietists were not very active in the social field. While they concentrated on spiritual edification and personal sanctification, and while they strengthened family ties and local networks, their primary aim was not to create new institutions or to send out missionaries. Those young men from Württemberg who wanted to become missionaries went to Herrnhut.

What made Württemberg Pietists special was their strong interest in eschatology and in the apocalypse, and the person who gained most influence and scholarly authority in this respect was Johann Albrecht Bengel. By carefully assembling all numbers that he could find in the Old and New Testaments and in particular in the Revelation of St John, and by combining these numbers in what he believed to be a meaningful way so that they would disclose the hidden chronology of salvation history, Bengel concluded that the exact date of the Second Coming would be June 1836, and the place, of course, Jerusalem. Bengel was convinced that God had revealed this insight to him so that he could admonish His most loyal children to prepare themselves for this most crucial event. Bengel died in 1752. Even after they had lost their spiritual leader, the Pietists of Württemberg never forgot that the world-order in which they lived and which presented them with so many hardships would be totally transformed in the not too distant future. In the 1790s, as the sequence of upheavals caused by the French Revolution unfolded, Württemberg Pietists were convinced that this was the beginning of the final raging of the devil that preceded Christ's return. As we will see in the final chapter of this volume, some of them decided to migrate to Palestine where they hoped to find a safe place of refuge until 1836 and the Second Coming.

In assessing the impact of Pietism on continental Protestantism, the year 1740 formed a watershed. Before 1740, the movement was growing, especially due to the favours that Halle received from the Prussian king and also because of the attraction of Zinzendorf's initiatives. When Frederick the Great assumed power in Berlin in 1740, things changed drastically. The new King of Prussia was a fervent believer in the ideas of the Enlightenment. He despised the kind of piety that Halle propagated and did not hesitate to make his thoughts on the matter clear. In 1723, due to pressure from Francke, Frederick William I had decided to ban the Enlightened philosopher Christian Wolff from Halle University. In 1740, one of the first actions of his son, Frederick the Great, was to reinstall Wolff in his chair at Halle. To Halle Pietists and beyond, this was an unmistakable signal that the time in which they had enjoyed the protection of the Berlin court was over.

Zinzendorf's movement was also affected by the beginning of the first of the Silesian Wars. Perhaps it is not sheer speculation to assume that Zinzendorf's strong interest in Pennsylvania in the 1740s was due to his impression that with Frederick the Great's assumption of the throne, central Europe was lost to the followers of true faith and that God's remaining children needed an alternative place to live and labour until Christ returned. Perhaps, at least in part, the same conviction can also be found among Halle Pietists. This would explain why the followers of Halle and Herrnhut bitterly confronted each other in Pennsylvania in the 1740s and in the 1750s, as each group attempted to gain influence and control.

Eighteenth-century continental Protestantism between orthodoxy and nonconformity

Important as Pietism was within continental Protestantism in the first half of the eighteenth century, it would be misleading to create the impression that Pietists completely dominated Protestant church life during this period. Resistance to Pietism has been mentioned, and most of this resistance was formulated and pursued by other Protestants, orthodox Lutherans and traditional Calvinists alike. Protestant orthodoxy possessed and maintained three main spheres of influence well into the eighteenth century: first, theological faculties at leading universities; second, the large body of clergy including most church leaders; third, most members of territorial governments and local administrations. In other words, in most Protestant territories well into the eighteenth century the rule of territorial princes over the church (the 'Landes-herrliche Kirchenregiment') was intact and functioning effectively. Just as they were expected to provide loyal legal experts for the government, universities had the obligation to educate pastors who would be loyal to the government. In all universities an impressive body of orthodox theological literature was available that could be put to use in the academic training of future pastors.

Protestant clergymen, in turn, were expected to represent church and state on the local level. Pastors were responsible for the proper administration of marriages, baptisms, funerals, and, of course, Sunday services. But above and beyond this they had to see that the local order was not interrupted and that those who disturbed others, on workdays as well as Sundays, were brought to justice. In many places pastors served also as teachers; some gave medical advice and, when needed, also medical help. Everywhere, the duties of pastors were far more extensive than preaching the pure faith. In fact, one can say that Sunday services were the least important of their duties and functions. When lay people formed conventicles without the consent and approval of the pastor, he had the duty to interfere. When groups of radical dissenters appeared in villages or cities, the pastors were expected to act. In short, pastors were the extended arm of territorial governments, and just as most members of territorial governments clung to traditional orthodox belief, so did many pastors. There were, of course, many pastors who were not content to hold to traditional orthodoxy or to act as government functionaries. Some of these pastors, as we have seen, were drawn to Pietism. Others, however, were attracted by the ideas of the early Enlightenment. Indeed, by the 1730s and certainly by the 1740s, the number of pastors who embraced Enlightenment thought was larger than the number of those who favoured Pietism or the number of those who still clung to orthodox doctrine.

Further, in certain regions Protestant radicalism in the tradition of the radical reformation played a much greater role than either Pietism or orthodoxy. Typically, these were regions in which some of the lesser princes reigned in a patriarchal manner, that is, in parts of the Palatinate, of Hesse, of Thuringia, and in some areas on the lower Rhine. In most instances, these radicals were inspired by eschatology. As the apocalypse was near, their leaders proclaimed, the remaining true children of God had to separate from the official and established churches that had fallen, as they thought, into the hands of the devil. These radicals held, wherever possible, separate services and practised communion without the assistance of the local pastor. In the tradition of sixteenth-century Anabaptists they often insisted upon adult baptism. Lay preaching was the rule as was the belief that God's word in the Bible could best be understood by those who were not corrupted by learned theology. From the late seventeenth century and well into the eighteenth century, self-appointed itinerant preachers travelled over the German countryside. Often they were persecuted and driven out of the villages and towns that they visited. But to the degree they suffered humiliation, they gained authority in the eyes of people in search of the divine truth. For many decades, for example, the former tanner Johann Friedrich Rock travelled through southern Germany. Protestant dissenters venerated him as a prophet and saint.

Almost all local governments considered Protestant separatists a serious political danger. Leaders of such groups were put into prison, and all means available were used to break up regional networks of separatists and to discourage these nonconformist faithful. From the 1680s onwards, and especially between 1700 and 1730, but again also in the 1750s, as they were confronted with mistrust and repression, many groups of Protestant dissenters decided to leave Germany. While some migrated to Transylvania, most went to the British colonies in North America, and especially to Pennsylvania. Whether Germany's loss was America's gain in this matter depends on one's view of the role of the church and on how religious life should develop. If one believes that church ordinances should be obeyed under all circumstances and that any kind of dissent only serves to disrupt the spiritual growth of congregations, one can approve the actions of those pastors who did not tolerate dissent. However, if one acknowledges the importance of every person's individual conscience and concludes that religious liberty is an essential ingredient for the building of God's kingdom, then he or she must believe that the Protestant state officials and Protestant pastors failed in their Christian vocation when they suppressed nonconformists and expelled dissenters. In any event, by getting rid of separatists and dissenters, German Protestantism, both Lutheran and Calvinist, lost a vital religious element that might have led to a situation in which religion could prosper exactly because it was no longer expected first and foremost to serve political ends.

The consolidation of Protestant states in post-1648 central Europe

The Peace of Westphalia in 1648 confirmed the Treaty of Augsburg of 1555, with some important modifications. In addition to territories ruled by Catholic princes or prince-bishops, and territories ruled by Lutheran princes, Calvinist princes were now also accepted as equals within the legal framework of the Holy Roman Empire. The Lutheran and Calvinist princes were also the official heads of the churches in their states. In most Lutheran and Calvinist territories within the empire, church government was entrusted to consistories. Superintendents were in charge of supervising deans who in turn were obliged to control church life down to the parish level in villages and towns. The consistories were also in charge of organizing the education of future pastors; they had to control the way active pastors fulfilled their duties; they were responsible for administering church finances and church property. In short, they were not only representatives of the prince in his position as the head of the church, but they were also empowered to enforce the edicts concerning church doctrine and church life that the prince wanted to put into effect. In some Lutheran states church affairs were run by bishops, as for example in Sweden, where the church was headed by the Archbishop of Uppsala. In regard to practical matters of church life as well as the preservation and defence of Lutheran or Calvinist doctrine, only small differences existed between Protestant churches under the leadership of bishops and those run by consistories. In both cases, the princes attempted to incorporate the churches into the emerging bureaucracy of their absolutist rule and, to varying degrees, were successful in doing so. Only in a small number of Protestant states in central Europe did estates continue to exert some power in church matters. Within the empire, the Mecklenburg duchies and the Duchy of Württemberg were such cases. Outside the empire, this was true of some Calvinist provinces of Hungary that were, as we shall see, under continued Catholic pressure, as well as the Protestant cantons of the Swiss federation.

Within the Protestant states of central Europe, the backbone of the established churches was the support first by the ruling princes and then, especially in towns, by the families that belonged to the well-educated middle classes. By contrast, noble families very often took pride in their legal autonomy as well as in their social distinction and cherished their own confessional tradition, which might be different from the established tradition within the state. In the decades after 1648, moreover, it took a long time before confessional indoctrination made any significant impact among members of the lower classes. As servants of artisans or farmers the lower classes adhered, as a rule, to the faith practised by their masters. When they had the opportunity to migrate to other regions in search of a better life, or when they were forced to migrate, they often showed little confessional loyalty. Even among artisans there are examples of people who changed their confessional affiliation several times.

But there were also spectacular examples of confessional loyalty. The Huguenots who decided to leave France in 1685 rather than convert to Catholicism formed close confessional communities and congregations in the states that offered them places of refuge. They were led by Reformed pastors who in turn were supported by a large number of well-educated merchants and artisans. In their host societies they managed to create communities adhering to the Reformed faith which remained loyal to the religious tradition of their heroic forefathers well into the nineteenth century. The Waldensians who were forced to emigrate only a few years after the Huguenots also showed a remarkable degree of religious loyalty to their special tradition. They, too, continued to preserve their Waldensian faith in the places that were offered to them as new settlements. Even the Salzburgers who were expelled by an intransigent Catholic archbishop in the early 1730s and had to leave their native Alpine valleys retained their confessional identity for several generations. As they migrated to faraway places, some to East Prussia, others as far as the new British colony of Georgia, they were praised by their fellow Protestants as heroes of true Protestant faith. In the territories in which they were able to settle they received, in most cases, special privileges, including the right to practise their faith. As a result, they were able to celebrate the memory of their special religious destiny.

The privileges granted to Huguenots, Waldensians, and Salzburgers should not be considered an expression of religious tolerance on the part of the host princes, however. The Huguenots, for example, were famous as extremely talented and productive artisans, and the Lutheran princes were pursuing their own economic interests when they permitted the Huguenots to settle in their territories and retain their own Reformed traditions. The princes' position was marked by economic pragmatism, as dictated by the theories of mercantilism, not by a deliberate policy of toleration. Nor were those princes who granted refuge to the Salzburgers inspired by Enlightened ideas of religious toleration. As they paid tribute to the fame the Salzburgers had gained on their journey through the empire, they attempted to stylize themselves as champions of true Protestant faith. Even in Prussia, a policy of religious toleration came later.

The principle of 'cuius regio ejus religio', first proclaimed in 1555 and confirmed in 1648, was put to a severe test in the late seventeenth and early eighteenth centuries when several Protestant princes decided to convert to Catholicism. The most spectacular case occurred in 1697 when the Elector of Saxony had the opportunity to become King of Poland on condition that he convert to Catholicism, which he did. And there were also other, similar cases. In 1733, for example, a Catholic prince inherited the Lutheran Duchy of Württemberg. Since the early Reformation of the sixteenth century, both Saxony and Württemberg had been first among the defenders of Lutheran faith. What could be done in Saxony and Württemberg to honour this tradition if their prince was a Catholic? How could the confessional balance of power in the Holy Roman Empire be preserved if leading princes changed confessional sides? In both cases the estates successfully claimed the right to protect Lutheranism and to be responsible for the course of church government. Through this compromise, the delicate relationship between Protestant and Catholic powers within the empire could be maintained.

But there were also political events that threatened the confessional balance within the European concert of powers. In the decades after 1648, the revocation of the Edict of Nantes in 1685 had severely hurt the position of Protestantism in western Europe. In a similar manner, the Habsburgs set out to strengthen Catholicism in east-central Europe. After they had consolidated the rule of the Catholic Church in Bohemia, they reclaimed, step by step, the Alpine provinces for the Catholic religion. By 1700, after the Turks had been defeated and large parts of the Balkans were opened to Habsburg influence, the Habsburgs' main aim was to support the Counter-Reformation in the Kingdom of Hungary. Once again, the leaders of Hungarian Calvinism were determined to resist. In the early seventeenth century, Count Gabor Bethlen and Duke George Rákóczi had led, though unsuccessfully, many of their Calvinist countrymen in an uprising against the Habsburg policy of Counter-Reformation, and now, in 1703, so did Duke Francis Rákóczi. By 1711, Vienna had succeeded in suppressing the opposition, bringing continued misery to the Protestants in Hungary. Their situation improved somewhat three decades later as Empress Maria Theresa showed a certain degree of respect for Hungarian Protestants. But it was not until 1782, that is two years after she had passed away, that her son, Emperor Joseph II pronounced his famous Toleration Edict that provided for confessional autonomy within the Habsburg Empire, including confessional autonomy for Hungarian Protestants.

The Habsburg Counter-Reformation was no less aggressive in Silesia. After 1648, with the exception of two small duchies and the city of Breslau, freedom of religion was no longer granted to Silesian Lutherans. While three so-called peace churches (*Friedenskirchen*) were entrusted to them, a total of over 1,200 Protestant churches were reclaimed for Catholic worship and incorporated into Catholic congregations. In the following decades, some 200,000 Silesian Lutherans decided to emigrate. Many others remained and attended secret Lutheran services in the woods (*Buschkirchen*), and some Lutherans regularly travelled long distances to attend services across the border in a neighbouring Lutheran territory. Help came late, and unexpectedly, from a power that had rescued Protestantism in central Europe before. In 1707, the Swedish king Charles XII, backed by a strong army, forced Emperor Joseph I to sign the convention of Altranstädt. This treaty guaranteed the return to Lutherans of 130 formerly Protestant churches that had been expropriated in Silesia and the establishment of an additional six new churches (so-called *Gnadenkirchen*). Also, schools for Protestants were reopened. Through these measures, Protestantism in Silesia was saved several decades before Frederick the Great annexed Silesia in 1740. It is also important to note that the Habsburg

Counter-Reformation not only produced mass emigration and widespread despair in Silesia but, in opposition to Catholic Vienna, also an impressively rich Silesian literary culture. Of the many Silesian poets of the pre-1740 era, perhaps Andreas Gryphius was the most talented.

As these examples demonstrate, the consolidation of Protestantism in central Europe was challenged by a series of attempts to continue the Counter-Reformation even after the peace treaty of Westphalia. At the same time, however, we should note that Protestantism blossomed in some states of Europe that had, each in a different manner, a strong influence on confessional matters in the region. With the support of absolutism, Lutheranism in both Sweden and Denmark developed a strong tradition that was not weakened as Pietism replaced Lutheran orthodoxy. But there were also other ways of influencing Protestantism in central Europe. In close relation, not to absolutist princes, but to the estates, Protestantism became a strong force in the Netherlands. On the other hand, the Protestant cantons of Switzerland had to fight several battles before they were able to defend their confessional autonomy. Perhaps nothing inspired Protestants on the European continent more than the success of Puritanism in England. English Puritanism provided a rich source of edifying literature. In most cases, these books were brought to central Europe via the Netherlands. Puritanism also served as an example that Protestantism could be successfully defended in the arena of power-politics.

The consolidation of Protestant states in post-1648 Europe should be seen, therefore, as a process that occurred on two levels – the level of European politics and the level of popular religion. First, at the level of European politics, the rise of the Protestant powers helped to stabilize Protestantism as a whole. In direct and indirect ways, both Sweden and Denmark continued after 1648 to provide protection to Protestantism in central Europe, and so did the Netherlands, though mainly as an economic power and as a centre of culture. After 1689, Great Britain became the premier Protestant power in Europe, joined, a few decades later, by the new Kingdom of Prussia. By 1700, and certainly by 1740, we can therefore observe a kind of double confessional balance of power in Europe: first, and most notably, within the Holy Roman Empire; but also among the leading powers of Europe, whose influence helped to reinforce the first. Second, under the protection of the Protestant powers and when no longer threatened by the forces of the Counter-Reformation, Protestantism was consolidated at the level of popular religion. During the first half of the eighteenth century, Protestantism became an undisputed way of life for people in many parts of central Europe. So much so, that when the

Archbishop of Salzburg decided to expel the Protestants from his territory in the early 1730s, most Europeans considered such behaviour to be anachronistic.

The aims and the attraction of the Enlightenment

The new ideas of the Enlightenment first captured the minds of Protestants in the north west of Europe, in Great Britain and the Netherlands. While British and Dutch thinkers made bold moves towards a new world-view, their counterparts in German Protestantism were, as a rule, more cautious, if not timid when it came to expressing new ideas. This was true, for example, of the political writings of the German Protestant, Samuel Pufendorf, as well as of the philosophical treatises of his fellow German, Christian Thomasius. Both lacked the vision and the determination of such Scottish or English authors as David Hume, Thomas Hobbes, or John Locke. And the same was equally true of the writings of such early eighteenth-century German Protestant theologians as Johann Franz Buddeus, Johann Lorenz von Mosheim, Johann Georg Walch, Christoph Matthaeus Pfaff, and Johann August Ernesti. Their writings appear like cautious adjustments to new ideas when compared to the works on Deism by British and Irish authors like Anthony Collins, John Toland, William Whiston, Thomas Woolston, or Matthew Tindal. During his lifetime, Baruch Spinoza, writing in the Netherlands, had no influence in Germany. Not until almost a hundred years after his death in 1677 were his ideas discussed or greatly appreciated. The books of Pierre Bayle and of Christian Wolff had an impact on German intellectual life somewhat earlier, but not before the middle of the eighteenth century. Even the celebrated German philosopher Gottfried Wilhelm Leibniz received little attention from his contemporaries. Only in retrospect have the quality of his philosophical reflections and his contribution to paving the way towards an Enlightened theological discourse found the necessary attention and received their due praise.

What has to be stressed once again is the importance of the caesura of 1740. The Enlightenment had little impact in Protestant Germany before Frederick the Great became king. The Enlightenment then gained momentum between 1740 and the end of the Seven Years' War in 1763. In the years between 1763 and the beginning of the French Revolution, the public sphere, including the theological faculties of the German universities, became dominated by the themes that were central to the Enlightenment. It was in this period that Lessing published some of the texts on biblical criticism written by Hermann Samuel Reimarus, that Johannes Joachim Spalding explained the principles of Enlightened thought in his writings, that August Friedrich Wilhelm Sack and

Johann Friedrich Wilhelm Jerusalem began to discuss central topics of Christian theology in a critical manner, and that Christoph Friedrich Nicolai applied literary criticism to biblical texts. It was in the two decades before the fall of the Bastille that Johann Salomo Semler, Gotthold Ephraim Lessing, and Immanuel Kant in their writings discussed and fully developed the programme of the Enlightenment. Religious and theological tradition, these writers insisted, had to stand the test of reason ('*Vernunft*'); further, Christianity had to adhere to the principle of tolerance. For Lessing, the ideas of Moses Mendelssohn were more important and inspiring than Protestant tradition. For Kant, criticism based on reason outweighed dogma.

To be sure, the programme of Enlightenment had two faces. One face was characterized by the application of the principles of rationalism and criticism. The other face was determined by the implementation of practical reforms in many spheres of life. One can even say that while the impact of biblical criticism within German Protestantism always remained limited to a relatively small circle of university theologians, it was these practical reforms which changed German Protestantism fundamentally and which helped to create and shape a new generation of Protestant clergy who understood their task in a new way. At least in the beginning, Pietists supported many of the Enlightened reforms wholeheartedly. In Halle, for example, Christian Thomasius stood behind the educational initiatives of August Hermann Francke. But while Pietists and Enlightened circles could co-operate in carrying through practical reforms, they parted ways when it came to matters of eschatology and Christology, and most certainly when Enlightened thinkers addressed questions of biblical criticism. Very often, and in many places, however, this was not the case before the middle of the eighteenth century. What we can observe, at least for some decades, are local coalitions between single members of both reform movements that were designed to carry through specific projects.

Enlightenment reforms mainly addressed six different spheres of German life. First, for the early Enlightenment as well as for the Enlightenment in the second half of the eighteenth century, the improvement of education was a central goal. Education meant that children should attend school regularly and learn how to write and read. Education also meant that people should learn the fundamentals of personal hygiene, that if illness occurred, they should consult a doctor and apply the right kind of medicine. In short, people were themselves responsible for their lives and should use the intellectual capabilities entrusted to them by God in order to improve their personal condition as well as the condition of their families and the communities in which they lived. It went without saying that curricula in secondary schools as well as academic teaching should be improved. New universities were established which were completely devoted to the programme of the Enlightenment, such as the University of Göttingen.

Second, for the Enlightenment, useful knowledge was no longer found only in traditional religious texts or in edifying literature. Rather, supporters of the Enlightenment produced and propagated an impressive amount of new and highly specialized literature. Many of these texts possessed a practical dimension. Such literature could address medical problems, matters of agriculture, legal reform and the like. Besides, Enlightened thinkers thought that educated people should take an interest in poetry, novels, and the theatre. While up until the early eighteenth century most texts published in Protestant Germany had been devoted to religious and theological themes, by 1750 such matters were discussed in less than 20 per cent of all publications.

Third, for many people, the legal reforms that were demanded by Enlightened writers were of more importance than anything else. In addition to the application of due legal procedures these legal reforms addressed major questions such as capital punishment or how one should deal with infanticide. Following the great Italian reformer Cesare Beccaria, German legal experts also demanded the abolition of torture as well as the abolition of capital punishment. While up until then women who had been found guilty of infanticide could not expect any mercy, the discussion now turned to the question of the guilt of those men who had seduced young women, while these women were given advice, counselling, and practical help. Furthermore, in its extreme form, the Enlightenment did not tolerate any kind of superstition. The witchcraft trials of the seventeenth century were looked upon with contempt and horror. Hence, even before 1789 many popular myths and legends were demystified. What we find particularly in Protestant Germany towards the end of the eighteenth century, therefore, is a fascinating vision of a just and tolerant society based on the rational application of law.

Fourth, Enlightened writers insisted that the reform programme should also include agriculture, manufacturing, and commerce. In these areas the Enlightenment introduced an interest in inventions and the practical application of new techniques. A telling example in this respect was the severe hunger crisis of 1770–72 caused by harvest failure in two consecutive years. In previous years of severe shortage, for example in the 1570s and in the 1690s, all commentators had implored their fellow-citizens to stop sinning, to repent and live once again the lives of good Christians so that God would cease punishing them and show mercy. In 1770–72, by contrast, the majority of those who wrote about the crisis demanded that their contemporaries use the power of reason given to them by God more effectively than in the past. They should introduce crop rotations, build better storage facilities for food, use fertilizer and better seeds. In short, the crisis, they believed, could have been avoided if the Enlightened programme for improvements in the field of agriculture had been implemented.

Fifth, those inspired by the Enlightenment took a new interest in the cultures outside of Europe. While the Pietists sent missionaries to foreign lands, Enlightened scientists attempted to explore and describe societies in Asia and Africa, particularly in non-Christian countries like Iran, India, China, and Japan. They looked at these cultures not as the missionaries did, that is as heathens who needed nothing more than the light of the gospel, but with the eyes of ethnologists. In the belief that all cultures and all peoples were equal, as explained by Johann Gottfried Herder, they tried to learn. European imperialism and colonialism came later.

Sixth and finally, a special concern of committed members of the Enlightened elite was the toleration of Jews. Well into the eighteenth century Jews in Germany were barely tolerated. In order to secure residence, they had to pay extra fees, without ever reaching a state of civil acceptance. This was so when the Enlightened elite began to demand the complete equality of all members of all religions, including the Jews. Major steps in this direction were first made by Emperor Joseph II of Austria. Other sovereigns, including Frederick the Great, followed his example. At the time of the outbreak of the French Revolution, Jewish citizens of many towns had been given a more secure status, but popular hostility, both in the Catholic as well as in the Protestant parts of Germany, persisted. Many Protestants, and especially those who felt attached to the cause of mission, propagated the idea that the conversion of all Jews to Christianity (the 'Judenmission') would be the solution to the problem. It was still a long way before the vision of a multi-faith Germany that would include all the various forms of Protestants, Catholics, and Jews would be realized. By 1789, the programme of religious tolerance so eloquently and impressively spelled out by Lessing in his *Nathan der Weise* was far from being accepted as a way of life.

As can be imagined, it took an enormous effort before such a comprehensive and challenging agenda as the one proposed by the representatives of the Enlightenment could be implemented, even if only in part. When the French Revolution totally changed European affairs, much had not been completed. As many observers of the events in France came to believe that the radical Enlightenment was to blame for the sudden upheaval of the old order, it became much harder to carry through reforms based on Enlightened ideas after 1789. The backlash began even before the Enlightened offensive had been successful.

Enlightened despotism as a form of secularization

At best, Enlightened despots ruling in the various Protestant states of central Europe in the second half of the eighteenth century advocated religious tolerance; very often, however, they had no interest in religion other than as a matter of traditional decorum on certain holidays and on special occasions. For example, Enlightened despots ordered that burial grounds which up until then had often been placed in churchyards located in town centres should be closed for hygienic reasons, and that new cemeteries should be opened outside of towns and villages. Sacred ground mattered little to them. Sacred objects they valued as art forms. Just as many Catholic rulers of the time dissolved the monasteries of those orders that did not provide useful services to society, for many Protestant rulers pastors were only helpful and necessary as long as they told people to live an orderly life, to work hard, and to obey the authorities. More often than not the Enlightened despots lacked respect for religion, or any substantial emotional tie to religion. It is not wrong, therefore, to view the rule of the Protestant Enlightened despots as a major step towards secularization. Had these rulers opened the door for a gradual separation of state and church, and had they extended effective political support to religious minorities, absolute rule combined with Enlightened insight might have served, at least temporarily, a useful function. But as these rulers insisted both on absolute obedience in political matters and on imposing their authority over church life, their regimes challenged the sanctity of individual conscience in a manner that contradicted their Enlightened precepts, and that resulted in regimes that could not be upheld for very long.

Before new forms of political rule had been established, opposition, particularly in Protestant regions of Germany, against the church policy of Enlightened despots began to grow. As early as 1780 a Society of Defenders of True Christianity (the '*Christentumsgesellschaft*') was founded. Within a decade, branch societies had sprung up in many parts of central Europe. At first, the members of these societies published tracts in which they disputed Enlightened views on theology. After a few years, however, and especially from the early 1790s, they actively opposed Enlightened church policies. For example, when Protestant consistories introduced new hymnals or new liturgies that followed Enlightenment principles, the societies organized local resistance. Furthermore, they provided support when a missionary society was founded in Basel and when, a few years later, Bible societies were created in a number of German cities. In both of these cases, important outside support had come from anti-revolutionary Protestant circles in Great Britain. The members of the *'Christentumsgesellschaft'* saw themselves as fighting for a common cause, and also to be within the tradition of Pietism. Most certainly, these groups opposing Enlightened despotism represented the beginning of a religious revival within continental Protestantism that lasted well into the nineteenth century and which embodied the *'Erweckungsbewegung'*, that is, the German Protestant equivalent to the Second Great Awakening in North America or the *Reveil* in Protestant French-speaking Switzerland. After the Napoleonic Wars were over, in most Protestant territories of Germany a compromise had to be found between the remaining representatives of the Enlightenment, the new followers of Pietism, and some circles for whom, in the turmoil of the times, Protestant orthodoxy had assumed an unexpected attraction. In the course of the nineteenth century, this compromise was challenged by liberalism and socialism and, above all, by German nationalism which had erupted in unexpected ways for the first time in the fight against Napoleon in 1813.

3

Great Britain and Ireland

J. C. D. CLARK

The state church ideal

The civil wars fought within the British Isles from the Scottish 'Bishops' Wars' of 1638–39 into the 1650s were essentially wars of religion, often initiated as bids for control of national churches. Almost all parties to these conflicts had initially held the rightness of a homogeneous, authoritative church congruent with the polity; what distinguished the participants were their goals for that united body. Yet the realities of conflict splintered this ideal: in the 1640s the 'plural society' triumphed as each man did what was right in his own eyes. This teeming, passionate sectarianism meant that at the Restoration of the monarchy in 1660 a revived state church was the least likely of political possibilities. Yet the ideal of a national church was first reinstituted, and then enjoyed a hegemonic position into the 1820s.

This was especially so in England. The idea of an 'Ecclesia Anglicana' had a millennium of varied development behind it by 1660; the Thirty-Nine Articles of 1563 had drawn upon older assumptions in referring without explication to 'Every particular or National Church' (Article 34). The sense in which the church in England was regarded as the Church of England was strengthened but not invented in the 1530s and 1550s. The mutually supporting relation between the secular and the sacred was a high ideal as well as a set of administrative procedures, and a legitimate role for the Christian prince in governing the church was conventionally traced back to Constantine. In 1660, each of the component territories of a restored composite monarchy sought to apply a still-powerful ideal. England, Scotland, and Ireland all had their national churches, and each shared a vision of a homogeneous Christian society that the status of these churches expressed.

William Warburton echoed a truism of his age when he argued that 'wherever there are diversities of religion, each sect, believing its own the true, strives to advance itself on the ruins of the rest . . . What persecutions, rebellions, revolutions, loss of civil and religious liberty, these intestine struggles between sects have occasioned, is well known even to such as are least acquainted with the history of mankind . . . the obvious remedy was to *establish* one church, and give a *free toleration* to the rest.'[1] This ideal would continue to dominate the relations of church and state; in 1780, a state church was still the norm, powerfully entrenched and defended with much sophistication.

In 1785, even the latitudinarian William Paley could advance an analysis of establishment as if it were uncontroversial:

> The notion of a religious establishment comprehends three things; – a clergy, or an order of men secluded from other professions to attend upon the offices of religion; – a legal provision for the maintenance of the clergy; – and the confining of that provision to the teachers of a particular sect of Christianity.[2]

Yet this was a minimalist doctrine. More was involved when, in 1660, one alternative – episcopal Anglicanism – emerged as dominant. William Sancroft, later Archbishop of Canterbury, implored God that He would 'digest that *Chaos*, and *Confusion*, and Strife of *Opinions* into one beautifull, and Harmonious *Composure*'.[3] This was not to be: the triumph of episcopacy henceforth defined the separated alternatives as 'denominations'. Each denomination possessed a set of teachings on ecclesiology or ecclesiastical polity that justified its claims on the basis of scriptural history, revelation, or natural law. These teachings continued to compete, especially during the period *c.* 1660–1725: this was the era in which the challenge of Protestant and Roman Catholic Dissent generated the most powerful Anglican responses.

The 'established church' was a term whose meaning nevertheless differed across the monarchy's possessions. In Wales, it might appear as the church associated with the union of 1536, like the system of shires and JPs. In Scotland, a Presbyterian polity was enforced after the Revolution of 1688. The Church of Ireland could be seen as the church of the English ascendancy, imposed in different ways by Henry VIII, Elizabeth, Cromwell, and William III. In England the church had never been established in this politically proactive sense, never chosen from among competing alternatives. An established church, in this English perspective, was strengthened, not founded, by its relations with the state. In this English sense, Samuel Johnson defined 'establishment' in his *Dictionary* of 1755 as 'Confirmation of something already done; ratification'. The church was also 'an establishment' in the sense that it was served by an elaborately endowed hierarchy of archbishops, bishops, deans, and archdeacons, and vouched for by the endowed universities and grammar schools; it performed acts of charity through endowed hospitals, orphanages, and asylums, was supported by tithes which it claimed by divine right, and collected them with the assistance of the civil power. For Low Churchmen like Gilbert Burnet, by contrast, it was not the church as such but 'the Protestant religion' that had been 'established'.[4] Yet neither Luther nor Calvin was to provide the rationale for England's state church; this became the achievement of English divines and lawyers.

The nature of the English church

The Restoration in 1660 did not follow a Laudian blueprint, but it was primarily High Churchmen who exploited Laud's legacy in order to shape a reinstituted regime: royal supremacy, episcopacy, the threefold ministry of bishops, priests and deacons, church courts, and liturgical uniformity. They coupled this ecclesiastical polity with a High Church ecclesiology: their keynote was the church's hierocratic nature. Sancroft, preaching at the great restocking of episcopal ranks in 1660, did not defend the relation of the church to the state, but rather promoted the church itself as an ecclesiastical polity whose form and authority derived from the Apostles. Besides that momentous theme, the exact nature of the church's connection with the state was not his priority, as long as the state accorded it protection.[5]

An episcopal regime in which the church claimed an independent source of authority was potentially a challenge to the monarchy as well as a support to it. It was therefore necessary to argue that episcopacy might be by divine right in the weaker sense of copying Christ's or the Apostles' example or institution, rather than in the sense of obeying an express divine command. Coercive jurisdiction derived from the crown alone. Papists, Presbyterians, and Independents challenged the king's supremacy, but not episcopalians.[6] This explanatory formula did not prevent their collision, and the resistance of the church helped to bring down a Catholic sovereign in 1688. The general claim of this church to the support of the civil magistrate was not that it was merely the church chosen for pragmatic reasons by the state but that it embodied religious truth. William Lloyd, later a bishop, argued in this sense of the term 'established', defending first the church's Apostolic status and its doctrine; then condemning the errors of Rome; and only then offering as a motive for supporting it 'the *Safety of the King's Person*, and the Prerogative of the Crown . . . according to the powers invested in the *Jewish* Kings under the Law, and exercised by the first Christian Emperours'.[7]

In England, the nature of the church and its link to the state was continually debated. In the absence of statutory definitions, individual churchmen offered views that sometimes came to carry semi-official status; the most famous was Richard Hooker (c. 1554–1600). When the eight books of his *Laws of Ecclesiastical Polity* were first printed together in 1662, edited for anti-Laudian ends by the new Bishop of Exeter, John Gauden, Book VII's endorsement of episcopacy in other than divine right terms and Book VIII's constitutional restrictions on monarchy were embarrassments. Hooker's work was therefore republished in 1666 on the instructions of Archbishop Gilbert Sheldon, this version re-edited by Isaak Walton, prefaced by a new life of Hooker and containing prominent editorial doubts as to the authenticity of the last three books. Hooker himself had looked charitably on non-episcopal churches and had not denied the validity of their orders, but his work could now be read as that of a Caroline High Churchman, insisting that civil and ecclesiastical authority were linked because they were equally communicated by divine appointment. After the Restoration Hooker enjoyed his greatest vogue, hailed by churchmen as an antidote to the new phenomenon of separated denominations of Protestant Dissenters on the strength of his demolition of the old Puritan claim to a right of private judgement.

To justify the role of the prince in non-Roman churches, Hooker had implicitly ignored the Apostolic succession and argued instead that 'Truth of Religion is the proper difference whereby a Church is distinguished from other Politique societies of men'. If the church was not separately grounded on its Apostolicity, it could follow that church and state were the same: 'We hold that seeing there is not any man of the Church of *England* but the same man is also a member of the Common-wealth; not any, member of the Common-wealth, which is not also of the Church of *England*', whether one called the body a church or a commonwealth was determined by 'chance'.[8] Having made that anti-papal point, Hooker had then said little about the rest of the issues that were later to be subsumed under the question of 'establishment'. Others now did so for him.

A High Church ecclesiology was clearly defined between about 1660 and 1725 by the need to respond to two powerful threats: Protestant and Roman Catholic Dissent. The first of these was the major challenge in the 1660s and 1670s, in the aftermath of the sectarianism of the interregnum. Simon Patrick, later Bishop of Ely, provided one among many critiques of schism that identified the key points at issue: private conscience, unlicensed ministry, extempory prayer and pretences to personal revelation. Against them he advanced a defence of Apostolical ordinations and the lawfulness of the official regulation of things indifferent.[9] Archbishop Sheldon's chaplain, Samuel Parker, later Bishop of Oxford, provided an influential restatement, commissioned by Sheldon, of the 'Unanswerable' Hooker, but without Hooker's constitutional limitations on the crown. The point was now to use Hooker to resist the new phenomenon of separated Dissent and to insist on the Christian duty of obedience in place of Dissent's appeal to private judgement. For Parker, it was enough that the Church of England's 'Forms *and* Institutions *are not only countenanced by the best and purest times of Christianity, but establisht by the Fundamental Laws of the Land*', since 'the Supreme Magistrate of every Common-wealth should be vested with a Power to govern and conduct the Consciences of Subjects in Affairs of Religion'.[10]

The second challenge, that of Roman Catholic Dissent, came to prominence from the 1670s with the conversion to Catholicism of the heir presumptive, James, Duke of York. The response to this challenge produced not only the definition of a new secular political ideology, Whiggism, but also a remarkable outpouring of Anglican ecclesiological and theological writing dedicated to rebutting the claims of Rome. In the Exclusion Crisis of 1679–81, produced by a Whig attempt to bar James from the succession, churchmen defended the monarchy without giving prominence to the idea of establishment. Rather, they claimed that the Church of England 'doth hold, teach, and practice Loyalty above all others in the World; the Divines thereof generally holding *Monarchy* to be of Divine Right', by contrast with the Roman Church, which held that kings derived their authority from the people and were open to being censured or deposed by the pope. This political stance followed from the fact that 'The present Religion of the *Church of England* is no new device of ours, but the very same that our Lord Jesus and his Apostles have left upon Record'. Religious truth was the yardstick: 'As for the penalties inflicted on Dissenters by our Laws, they are rather for disturbing the Peace of the Civil Government, than for differing from us in Judgment'.[11]

In 1707 the Whig High Churchman John Potter provided the classic summation of this ecclesiology. Still aimed equally against Rome and Geneva, it professed to vindicate both the '*inherent Rights*' of the Church of England since the Reformation and the '*just Prerogative*' of the civil magistrate on the basis of the '*Constitution, Government and Rights of the Christian Church*' as established by the Scriptures and the Fathers. It was a work intended '*towards the putting a Stop to those Erastian and other licentious Principles, which are too rife, and have been too much countenanc'd by some among us*'. Potter argued that the church possessed only spiritual powers; nevertheless, the church was 'not a mere *voluntary* Society, but one whereof Men are oblig'd to be Members' since 'this Society is appointed with an inforcement of Rewards and Punishments'. It was governed after Christ's death by 'a Succession of the same *Officers* in the following Ages' to the world's end, the orders of ministers like their powers being by divine commission. '*To continue this Account after the Church was taken into the Protection of the Civil Powers, to vindicate the Supremacy of Christian Princes, and to adjust it with the Rights of the Church*', Potter recognized, 'will require another Book'. This he never completed, becoming instead Bishop of Oxford in 1715 and Archbishop of Canterbury in 1737.[12]

It remained for another Whig High Churchman, Edmund Gibson, Bishop of London from 1723 to 1748, to give the lasting legal interpretation of the relation of the church, as conceived by Potter, to the state. Gibson's *Codex*, published in two folio volumes in 1713 and reprinted in 1761, was recognized as the definitive compendium on canon law. Gibson insisted both on the union of church and state, and also on the church's separate authority. From a detailed historical survey, he argued that the documents defining the church's relation to the state acknowledged the church's spiritual independence. Statutes were generally only 'Enforcements of the ancient Ecclesiastical Laws' designed to strengthen them '*in the same Chanel*', not to be replacements of them. Bishops therefore exercised 'Government and Disciplin' upon 'the foot of Divine, as well as Human, Authority'. The church was not, therefore, 'a *meer Creature* of the State'. But this was not a preliminary to an alliance, since the Christian prince's supremacy in the state and the church gave the two an inseparable unity.[13] The jurist Sir Edward Coke, argued Gibson, had been wrong to claim that only the clergy, and not the laity, would be bound by legislation passed by Convocation (the provincial assembly of the clergy) but not by parliament. It was this High Church vision that was made problematic, but not necessarily refuted, by the suspension of Convocation in 1717.

A similar but importantly modified position was expressed by the lawyer Thomas Wood in a standard compendium of 1720. '*Law* in General' was built most notably on 'the *Law of Nature*' (commonly called 'the Law of *Reason*'), and 'the *Revealed* Law of God: Hence it is that our Law punishes Blasphemies, Perjuries &c. and receives the *Canons* of the Church duly made, and supposeth a Spiritual *Jurisdiction* and *Authority* in the Church'. Wood gave a careful account of the mutual roles of ecclesiastical and civil courts: both were subject to the royal supremacy, and there was in Wood's account no evident clash of jurisdictions. For Wood, however, 'the Legislative Power in the Church, and the Canons that are made concerning the Church with the Royal Assent bind the Clergy, but not the Laity'.[14] So it was for a churchman and lawyer like Richard Burn, who by 1763 explicitly accepted the doctrine of the common lawyers in *Cox's case* (1700) and *Middleton v. Croft* (1736) that 'The canons of a convocation do not bind the laity without an act of parliament'.[15]

If lawyers almost always reiterated Wood's position, clergymen were prominent in questioning Gibson's. Benjamin Hoadly and his allies sought to guard against the threat of a Catholic Stuart restoration by countering a High Church ecclesiology with Low Church minimalism. Hoadly was only the most notorious among the Whig clergy who seized the common ground of the legitimate role of the state in regulating the church, but he used it to vilify both the Nonjurors and High Church theology: the political acceptability of the first critique shielded him from the consequences of attacking the second.

Hoadly insisted that the Nonjurors' target was nothing less than the principle of established religion: 'The *Establishment* is now openly and directly charged with the Want of all Right'. But it was a valid establishment, replied Hoadly, despite the Revolution of 1688, since God had not instituted 'a *Regular Uninterrupted Succession*' either of bishops or of monarchs. Instead, every man's 'Title to God's favour cannot depend upon his actual being, or continuing, in any particular Method; but upon his *Real sincerity* in the conduct of his Conscience, and of His own Actions, under it . . . The Favour of God, therefore, follows *Sincerity*, consider'd as such'.[16] Hoadly's Erastianism in ecclesiology was reflected in his theology: unfettered private judgement was the essence of Christianity; no church could claim to exercise a direct divine mandate. Christ

> hath, in those Points, left behind Him, no visible, humane *Authority*; no *Vicegerents*, who can be said properly to supply his Place; no *Interpreters*, upon whom his Subjects are absolutely to depend; no *Judges* over the Consciences or Religion of His people . . . All his Subjects are *equally* his Subjects; and, as such, *equally* without Authority to alter, to add to, or to *interpret*, his *Laws* so, as to claim the absolute Submission of *Others* to such *Interpretation*.[17]

The majority of churchmen who agreed with Hoadly's arguments on the legitimacy of the Revolution nonetheless reviled these theological arguments. Whig politicians, however, were more often in sympathy with Hoadly's theology, since they rightly interpreted the church's claims to civil authority, claims which they emphatically rejected, as rooted in the belief that the church carried a direct divine commission. The early years of the Whig ascendancy saw a series of parliamentary attempts to repeal legislation that churchmen held to be integral to 'the establishment'. Part was repealed, but part survived. Walpole finally backed away from extending 'the Toleration' at the expense of 'the Establishment' in the face of an unprecedented storm. The 'Bangorian Controversy' was an outcry against the minimalist interpretation of Christianity held by Hoadly, then bishop of Bangor. Although triggered by the political aspect of Hoadly's teaching, the controversy came to centre on the spiritual authority of the church. Hoadly's most effective opponent was a Nonjuror, William Law.[18] He appealed to an understanding of the English church as it had been defined by the sixteenth-century reformers, with its claim to spiritual authority resting on the evidences of Christ, the Apostles, the Fathers, and the Councils. This was to be a generally prevalent argument in the latter part of the century.

In the 1660s, the church had seen itself as being assailed from both Geneva and Rome. By the 1730s, it was becoming evident that both challenges had been beaten off: the church would retain the position which had been defined for it by law. The High Church party, meanwhile, suffered a major defeat. In emphasizing the divine mandate for the church, High Churchmen had some-times ascribed separate authority to the church's legislature. Hooker had not defined the relation between Convocation and parliament, and this relation-ship remained uncertain after 1660. Convocation surrendered the right to set clerical taxation in 1664, and was rewarded by not being summoned between 1664 and 1688. It met again in 1689, but there was increasing controversy over its role. The 'Convocation Controversy' was fought on political grounds after William III once more prorogued that body in 1689.[19] Convocation's chief champion became Francis Atterbury, from 1713 Bishop of Rochester, a juror but also a Jacobite; the leading champions on the other side were Edmund Gibson, bishop of Lincoln from 1716, and William Wake, from 1716 Archbishop of Canterbury. Hoadly now became the last straw. His theological heterodoxy was a challenge that Convocation could not avoid, and Convocation's evi-dent intention to discipline him raised the stakes. The Whig regime took pre-emptive action. After several turbulent annual sessions Convocation was suspended in 1717. With Convocation's suspension it became necessary to treat parliament, however implausibly, as the lay synod of the Church of England.

A principled defence of establishment, in deliberately Whiggish language, was now provided by William Warburton. Yet Warburton was in his own day not widely credited with having provided the church's official rationale. This is because Hooker's model of the essential unity of church and state, as rein-terpreted from the 1660s, precluded Warburton's model of a contract between two essentially separate bodies, church and state. Anglican doctrine asserting the essential unity of the secular and the sacred had been fully formed by 1713. Warburton's tract of 1736 was one of few in the later period centrally to address the question of church–state relations, because the issue could be regarded as having been settled in the era of Potter and Gibson. In this light, people tended to see Warburton's theory as a route to a shared conclusion. The underpinnings of Warburton's position were also revealed in his reply to Bolingbroke in 1766. Only Christian doctrine was God given, he argued. 'Church-government', on the other hand, 'may be administered by an Episcopacy, a Presbytery, or an Independency', since its 'specific form' was 'not prescribed'. On the contrary, Jesus had left it 'to particular churches to follow such as were most agreeable to the forms of those civil societies, in which they were to be established'.[20] Warburton's view, however, was not shared by most mid- and late eighteenth-century churchmen.

If Warburton in the 1730s expressed the idea of establishment in the language of natural law and contract, Paley in the 1780s equally captured the idiom of his day when he expressed a similar idea in the language of utility. On the surface, both Warburton and Paley denied that the civil magistrate had any concern with the truth status of religion. Warburton presented his key defence of the establishment as not truth, but utility.[21] Read more closely, however, even Warburton and Paley ultimately grounded the claims of the church on the truth of its doctrine. Warburton argued that the state would ally with the larger church in the realm as that best 'enabled . . . to answer the ends of an *alliance*', but only 'where there is an equality in other points'. In the first edition of 1736, the key qualification was '(where the difference [between churches] is not in Essentials)': clearly the Church of England claimed its foundation on natural law. Warburton also included in a footnote a strongly positive commendation of the church: 'I would recommend that excellent Treatise intit[uled] *A Vindication of the Corporation and Test Acts*'.[22] But Thomas Sherlock's tract of 1718 had, as a premise, truth as the basis of the church's authority.[23] Although Warburton later omitted this argument, he continued to include his closing claim that the alliance 'secures . . . *the advancement of truth*'.[24]

In his bestselling work of 1785, William Paley, at least on the surface, adopted a similar argument: 'The authority . . . of a church establishment is founded in its utility'. This position was not an anticipation of the utilitarian Jeremy Bentham, but rather a latitudinarian belief (like Warburton's) that no form of church government was prescribed in Scripture. Paley did not, however, claim that no theology whatever was there authoritatively set out. His other latitudinarian premise was that 'In religion, as in other subjects, truth, if left to itself, will almost always gain the ascendancy'. It followed that 'of different systems of faith, that is the best, which is the truest . . . we are justified in pronouncing the *true* religion, by its very *truth*, and independently of all considerations of tendencies, aptness, or any other internal qualities whatever, to be universally the *best*'. Consequently, even 'The justice and expediency of toleration we found *principally* in its conduciveness to truth'.[25]

Hoadly and Warburton failed to destroy a High Church rationale for establishment. This was also shown by the rapidly acclaimed *Commentaries* of William Blackstone, who treated Christianity as integral to civil society.[26] For Blackstone, the value of the Church of England was grounded in the truth of its doctrines, combined with its resistance to the threat posed to the state by Dissenters.[27] Consequently, the civil magistrate 'is bound indeed to protect the established church, by admitting none but it's genuine members to offices of trust and emolument: for, if every sect was to be indulged in a free communion of civil employments, the idea of a national establishment would be at once destroyed, and the episcopal church would no longer be the church of England'.

Blackstone pointed to 'two bulwarks', the Corporation and Test Acts, 'which secure both our civil and religious liberties', but he offered no deeper reflection on the sense in which the church was 'established'.[28] The old common law doctrine that 'christianity is part of the laws of England', repeated by Blackstone,[29] was still relied on by judges into the early nineteenth century in cases of blasphemous libel. Not only did Blackstone pour scorn on the Whig contractarian account of the origin of the state,[30] but his account of the history of the church left no room for a contract either: the origins of its established status were implicitly revealed in his chapter on the clergy, for Blackstone there traced their 'large privileges' back before Charlemagne, beyond any demonstrable moment of alliance between church and state.[31]

The argument for practical advantages of an established church was strong into the early nineteenth century. But from the 1760s a rival strand was reasserted in Anglican ecclesiology that criticized the Hoadly–Warburton–Paley tradition and identified it as a falling away from High Church ecclesiology. Represented by George Horne, William Jones of Nayland, Samuel Horsley, and Charles Daubeny, this tradition offered various readings of divine-right monarchy and episcopacy: it portrayed the church as part of the origins of the state, by divine institution. For them, Scripture provided the texts for an account of a Providential, not a contractual, social order.

This reassertion of a Catholic ecclesiology led by 1815 to a defence of the establishment, despite the fact that the church's 'high and transcendent claims' were 'not of a temporal nature', and that the church's position as 'a National Establishment' meant only state provision for its worship and state protection against other denominations, not a right to coerce the laity. Thus a reasserted claim of the church's Apostolical authority (a 'far higher character than that of an establishment') could be a route to a pragmatic defence of its established status, in which the civil magistrate supported the establishment only 'to keep alive a sense of religion, with a view to the well-being of society'. The magistrate's choice of which church to support was not, however, exactly unconstrained, since in this account only one church could claim Apostolical authority: 'Every other association, assuming the name of a Church, must . . . be a mere human institution'. Only a difference on an essential matter of faith could justify separation: 'when an Established Church is, in its constitution, an Apostolical Church, such a difference alone can justify separation from that Church'.[32] It was this rationale, at once utilitarian and Catholic, that underpinned the last flowering of the state church ideal in the years 1808–28. Disestablishment as an ideal waited for the formation of the 'Liberation Society' in 1844.

Ireland

The Church of Ireland, too, was a 'national' church – albeit one which paradoxically antedated its 'nation' and which was continually debating issues of continuity. The Church of Ireland had, like the Church of England, been subjected to reorganization by sixteenth-century legislation. Its members had a similar monopoly of political office after the test law of 1704; its archbishops and bishops sat in the Irish House of Lords, participating in state ceremonial and offering an endorsement of the political order. Its clergy, too, unavailingly sought to voice their views in a Convocation which enjoyed meetings only between 1703 and 1714 and which was resisted by Irish Protestant MPs; despite Convocation's general abeyance, the network of church courts continued to function. The Irish church, like the English, was bitterly divided on political lines after 1688, the Whigs denouncing their Tory and High Church opponents as standing for the independence of the church from the civil power, the Tories denigrating Whig landowners for being irreligious as well as anticlerical, and Low Church clergy for being Erastian or latitudinarian. From this system no fundamental reform of church finances, pluralism, or patronage was to emerge. The preoccupations of the Church of Ireland were too often with political threats to its very survival.

The political events of the seventeenth century served to place emphasis on the premise that Catholics, if given power, would seek the total expropriation, and perhaps the deaths, of Protestants. By 1700, about a quarter of the population was polarized into the identity of 'Protestant', half of them members of the episcopal Church of Ireland, half Presbyterians located mainly in Ulster. This latter group posed a second challenge to the episcopal state church. According to Swift, 'the zealous *presbyterians* of the *north* are more alienated from the established clergy, than the *romish* priests; taxing the former with idolatrous worship, as disguised *papists, ceremony-mongers,* and many other terms of art; and this for a very powerful reason; because the clergy stand in their way, which the *popish* priests do not'.[33] Yet the Presbyterians themselves suffered schism in 1725 between the 'Old Lights', supporters of the Westminster Confession of Faith, and a 'New Light' party rejecting the imposition of creeds, often for anti-Trinitarian reasons.

Defeat in 1691 was a disaster for the Catholics. William III did little to shield them from a Protestant Dublin parliament. By a series of acts, from the 1690s to the 1720s, Catholics were subjected to a catalogue of civil disabilities. Such legislation, passed piecemeal, soon earned the systematizing title 'the penal laws'. This code was, arguably, effective: there were no Jacobite Irish risings like those of 1715 and 1745 in Scotland, and the position of the Irish Catholic interest steadily weakened. The anti-Catholic legislation on the statute book was therefore less and less enforced after *c.* 1720 and Catholic worship won a *de facto* toleration. Yet although coercing people into religious belief later acquired a bad name, the provision of material reasons for adherence to religious truth posed no problem for the clergy of the Church of Ireland: they adopted a strategy which would have been pursued by their Catholic co-religionists had the result of the war of 1689–91 been different.

Moreover, this strategy proved largely successful: before the emergence of Daniel O'Connell's populist Irish nationalism in the 1820s, Roman Catholics in Ireland as well as in England were increasingly seen as potential supporters of a monarchical state, a reversal that the American and French revolutions served to confirm. So evident was this shift that the Irish parliament felt able to pass Catholic Relief Acts in 1778 and 1782, which dismantled the penal code with respect to religious worship, education, and landownership; further relaxations followed in 1792–93. In 1780, the rural plebeian violence with its revolutionary and republican undertones that was to characterize the last two decades of the century could hardly be foreseen: as in England, the state church in Ireland appeared to be the route to increasing harmony and prosperity.

Legal discrimination against Protestant Dissenters was less effective. Presbyterians flourished in Ulster; their sense of grievance, combined with their ancient resistance theory, found expression in colonial America, which witnessed mass emigration from Ulster in the early 1770s, and in a domestic political campaign that almost saw Ireland break free from English domination during the American war. As in England, it was Protestant rather than Roman Catholic Dissent that posed the major challenge.

Irish High Churchmen identified their church as a true branch of the Universal Church, its ancient Catholic but non-Roman identity established by the Briton, Saint Patrick. Apostolicity and purity of primitive doctrine rather than majority status had to be the backbone of its rationale, and into the 1780s Irish clergy continued to deploy this ecclesiology against challenges from Catholicism or Presbyterianism. Some churchmen emphasized one threat, some the other; all agreed that there was a lasting danger to the church's position. Where in England this pattern of controversy had faded, in Ireland it remained the essence of debate.

If Apostolicity and primitive doctrine were the Irish church's foundations, one other component of the English church's rationale was lacking. The relatively small numbers of adherents had made a Warburtonian vision of the identity of church and state implausible in Ireland from the outset. Where England had a debate on 'church and state', Ireland had a debate on the 'penal code'. An Irish Toleration Act in 1719 provided for freedom of worship for Protestant Dissenters, but attempts to repeal the Irish Test of 1704 failed in 1719 and 1733. The Irish church generated little debate on ecclesiology, drawing rather on English rationales. The Irish church was insufficiently endowed fully to support a native intelligentsia. For that reason, it held even more firmly to teachings of the Caroline divines.

State churches were also exactly that: churchmen might confine their rationales to their own country without feeling any pressing need to test their formulae against a neighbouring one. Warburton failed to mention Ireland, or any other polity in which many denominations enjoyed an approximate equality. On the surface, his position was that numbers, not truth, justified the Reformation: after a change of numbers, 'the *alliance* between the POPISH CHURCH and the kingdom of England was broken; and another made with the PROTESTANT, in its stead'.[34] Yet Warburton's argument was ultimately an appeal to truth, not to utility. In the 1736 edition, he had used an Irish analogy that he later deleted. It would, he argued, produce 'Confusion . . . had every Sect free Entry into the Administration'; 'He who would see a lively Image of the intolerable Mischiefs, that arise from thence to Civil Society may read two Tracts wrote by a great Wit in defence of the *Irish Test*; and particularly that fine Discourse above referred to, intitled a *Vindication of the Corporation and Test Acts*'.[35] He thereby fell back both on Thomas Sherlock and, by clear allusion, Jonathan Swift.[36] Yet Swift, as an Irish High Churchman, had argued on quite different grounds.[37] Nor was Warburton alone in avoiding writing on the religious settlements of neighbouring countries: in 1798, the English High Churchman Charles Daubeny, who more openly based the title of the English church on truth, equally ignored Scotland and Ireland.[38]

The 'established' church in Ireland thus lacked a powerful rationale for its public role; an alternative model, the idea of a 'Protestant Ascendancy', was not formulated until late in the century. Rural terrorist disturbances from the 1780s encouraged Richard Woodward, Bishop of Cloyne, to identify the Church of Ireland and its established status with the Protestant landowning interest. This formulation proved attractive to that social constituency but unappealing to a ministry in London which was seeking a broader base for Anglo-Irish co-existence: from 1791–92, the British government began to pursue the opposite policy of granting political rights to Irish Catholics.[39] Woodward's new formulation was functional; yet even he recognized that the utilitarian aspect of Paley's rationale for established churches was 'subversive of the Protestant government of Ireland', and so, arguably, it proved to be.[40]

Scotland

The Church of Scotland inherited the established status of the medieval church, but was fundamentally reformed into a Presbyterian polity in the late sixteenth century and again after 1688. It was more plausible to contend that the Reformation in Scotland had broken the link between church and crown, whereas in England that conclusion was harder to draw. Yet this key issue was not clear, since Episcopalians and Presbyterians remained locked in conflict for possession of a single Scots church. The episcopal system restored in 1660 was more of an attempt at compromise than its English parallel; it did not, for example, challenge existing presbyterial ordinations. Nonetheless, this solution failed, first in the face of armed resistance by the Presbyterian Covenanters, and again when the Scots bishops made clear the limits of their allegiance to William III. In 1690, the Presbyterian system was instituted by an act of the Scots parliament in an embittered setting,[41] and the Presbyterian settlement was continually threatened by a possible Stuart Restoration for which the Episcopalians longed.

The Scots church had been subject to a much larger dose of Calvinism in the later sixteenth century than the English. Consequently it found it difficult to present itself as the church of all the Scots; its Genevan zeal cast it increasingly as a gathered church of the elect. It subscribed to what looked like a foundation document, the Westminster Confession of Faith, ratified by the Edinburgh parliament in 1647. The Confession was based on the Scottish Solemn League and Covenant of 1643, a document that had led to a Scots attempt to impose Calvinism and Presbyterianism on England. Ironically, this attempt to separate church and state meant that the Church of Scotland became more like a parliamentary church.

In Scotland the union of church and state after 1688 was effected implicitly, from the bottom up. Presbyterianism militantly rejected the idea of the civil magistrate as simultaneously the head both of church and state, and rejected an episcopacy chosen by the king. Instead it developed, as English Presbyterianism did not, an elaborate formal structure of church governance to regulate itself without state intervention, rising in a pyramid from the parish kirk-session through the presbyteries and synods to the General Assembly, meeting annually in Edinburgh. It entailed the separation of the church from the state: following the union of 1707, Scots ministers could not vote in parliamentary elections, as clergy did in England; Scots ministers could not sit in the Westminster House of Commons; the Scots church had no direct representation in the House of Lords. No Scots equivalents of England's Corporation or Test Acts restricted civil office to Presbyterians; but, in so heavily and coercively Presbyterian a society, such provisions were unnecessary. So effective was the link between church government and local government that few ministers became magistrates, in strong contrast to English practice.

This formal separation of church and state generated little Scottish reflection on the nature of the establishment. Instead it gave rise to conflict within the ranks of Presbyterians, and to limited but bitter controversy in the one area where the church might claim wholly to regulate its own affairs: its claim to appoint ministers, a claim set against landowners' and the crown's pre-Reformation rights of patronage. Patronage was property and therefore inheritable; so were rights to the teind (tithe), for, as with the tithe in England, the teinds in Scotland had often been appropriated by landowners at the Reformation, and (despite repeated and unavailing petitions to parliament from the General Assembly after 1740) only a proportion of it now found its way to the local minister. Both practices were offensive to zealous Presbyterians, who in their campaigns against them drew on popular egalitarianism and resentment at local wealth.

Patronage had been revived along with the restored episcopacy in 1660. Triumphant Presbyterianism abolished private patronage in 1690, and in 1707 the Act of Union had embodied guarantees to maintain the existing Scottish church settlement. In 1712, however, the Tory-dominated Westminster parliament restored lay patronage in Scotland, and Whig ministries after 1714 declined to remedy what many Scots perceived as a major grievance. Many patrons initially responded to the popular anti-patronage feeling by declining to impose their own candidates. However, from the reign of George II they increasingly did so, thus gradually changing the character of the ministry, moving it in a more moderate direction. This tendency was clearly understood by the so-called Popular party in the Scots church, which resisted private patronage as emblematic of worldliness and spiritual lukewarmness, characteristics that they claimed to detect in the softened Calvinism of the Moderate party from the 1750s.

Presbyterianism tended to fragment; but the fragments generally agreed on the principle of a state church, and divided on which of them was worthy of that role. Only during the eighteenth century did these divisions slowly lead to new denominations and a *de facto* voluntarism. In 1733, the Secession Church broke from the established Presbyterian Church over adherence to the Covenants, patronage and unhappiness with the growing moderatism among the clergy. They began to absorb numbers of surviving Covenanters in the south west. Rancorous in tone, and sometimes millenarian, its members preserved the resistance theories of the Covenanters but without renouncing the principle of a state church. This sect split again in 1747 over the legitimacy of its members taking an oath of allegiance to the crown on accepting local office. The state church ideal was however soon explicitly rejected by another body of Presbyterian seceders, the so-called Relief Church, founded in 1761 by Thomas Gillespie, a minister who had been deposed from his charge in the national church in 1752 for his opposition to patronage. This sect lacked the stark Calvinism of the Secession Church; with latitudinarian attitudes to membership, its numbers expanded substantially by 1800.

Among the other seceders were the Glassites; they took their name from John Glas (1695–1773), ejected from his living in 1730 for challenging the Presbyterian tenet of a national church. Such a challenge attracted few Scots supporters, although the position was inherited by Robert Sandeman (1718–71), who gave his name to what was in effect a Congregational challenge to Presbyterianism. These growing (and, in some areas, substantial) secessions from the established church predated the revival of Dissent in England after about 1780, and more seriously weakened the state church ideal north of the border.

It has been argued that, after 1707, the Kirk's General Assembly became a substitute for the Scots parliament. If so, it was a substitute that acted in general accord with the Whig authorities in London, not as a catalyst of anti-unionist feeling, let alone of a proto-nationalism. In the seventeenth century, Scots Presbyterianism had been closely correlated with resistance theory and its application; in the eighteenth, this correlation was eroded, just as the tendency of Presbyterianism to fragment prevented any nationalist flowering like that promoted by the Roman Catholic Church in Ireland: there was to be no Scots version of Daniel O'Connell.

In the first quarter of the nineteenth century, the government of the United Kingdom deliberately used its established churches to forward its social policy, acknowledging clergy as agents of the state in the work of social improvement and political stabilization. This had already worked in England, Wales, and Scotland; after 1801, it was applied to Ireland. By 1829 it had failed there, and a candid acceptance of its failure by the London government meant fundamental redefinition in England also. None the less, in 1780, even in the middle of a momentous war of religion in the North American colonies, the extent of the later challenge to the establishment ideal was seldom foreseen.

Notes

1. [William Warburton], *The alliance between church and state* (London, 1736); here cited from the 1766 edn, in Richard Hurd (ed.), *The works of the Right Reverend William Warburton D.D.*, 12 vols. (London, 1811), vol. 7, pp. 241–2, 250.
2. William Paley, *The principles of moral and political philosophy* (London, 1785), p. 556.
3. W[illiam] S[ancroft], *A sermon preached in S. Peter's Westminster, on the first Sunday in Advent* (London, 1660), p. 39.
4. [Gilbert Burnet], *An impartial survey and comparison of the Protestant religion, as by law established* (London, 1684).
5. [Sancroft], *Sermon*, pp. 9–11.
6. Robert Sanderson, *Episcopacy (as established by law in England) not prejudicial to regal power* (London, 1661), pp. 13–15, 21, 32, 40.
7. [William Lloyd], *A seasonable discourse shewing the necessity of maintaining the established religion, in opposition to popery* (London, 1673), pp. 10–17.
8. *The Works of Mr. Richard Hooker*, ed. Isaak Walton (London, 1666), pp. 447–8.
9. [Simon Patrick], *A friendly debate between a Conformist and a Non-Conformist* (London, 1669).
10. [Samuel Parker], *A discourse of ecclesiastical politie* (London, 1670), pp. ii, 10, 112–13, 174, 199–200.
11. [Thomas Comber], *Religion and loyalty supporting each other* (London, 1681), pp. 37, 39–40, 59.
12. John Potter, *A discourse of church-government* (London, 1707), sigs. A2r–A3v, pp. 2, 11–12, 53, 124, 139–40, 213.
13. Edmund Gibson, *Codex Juris Ecclesiastici Anglicani*, 2 vols. (London, 1713), vol. 1, pp. i, iv, xvii–xix.
14. Thomas Wood, *An institute of the laws of England* (London, 1720; 2nd edn, 1722), pp. 2, 4, 396, 498–500.
15. Richard Burn, *Ecclesiastical law*, 2 vols. (London, 1763), vol. 1, p. 406.

16. Benjamin Hoadly, *A preservative against the principles and practices of the nonjurors both in church and state* (London, 1716), pp. 2, 72, 78, 90–1.

17. Benjamin Hoadly, *The nature of the kingdom, or church, of Christ. A sermon . . . March 31, 1717* (London, 1717), pp. 11–12, 30.

18. William Law, *Three letters to the Bishop of Bangor* (London, 1721).

19. Thomas Lathbury, *A history of the convocation of the Church of England*, 2nd edn (London, 1853).

20. Warburton, *Works*, vol. 7, p. 368 (postscript to the fourth edition).

21. Warburton, *Works*, vol. 7, pp. 281–2.

22. Warburton, *Works*, vol. 7, pp. 242–3; [Warburton], *Alliance* (1736), pp. 110–11.

23. Thomas Sherlock, *A vindication of the Corporation and Test Acts. In answer to the Bishop of Bangor's reasons for the repeal of them* (London, 1718), p. 31.

24. Warburton, *Works*, vol. 7, p. 287.

25. 'Of religious establishments and of toleration', in Paley, *Principles of moral and political philosophy*, pp. 554–7, 579.

26. William Blackstone, *Commentaries on the laws of England*, 4 vols. (Oxford, 1765–9), vol. 4, pp. 41–65; for Blackstone's indebtedness to Wood, see Thomas A. Green's introduction to the Chicago edition (1979), vol. 4, p. iii.

27. Blackstone, *Commentaries*, vol. 4, pp. 52–3.

28. Blackstone, *Commentaries*, vol. 4, pp. 53, 57–8, 432.

29. Quoting 1 Ventris p. 293: Blackstone, *Commentaries*, vol. 4, p. 59.

30. Blackstone, *Commentaries*, vol. 1, pp. 47–9.

31. Blackstone, *Commentaries*, vol. 1, pp. 364–83, at 367.

32. [John Bowles], *The claims of the established church; considered as an apostolical institution, and as an authorised interpreter of Holy Scripture. By a layman* (1815; London, 1817), pp. 2–5, 15, 75, 78.

33. *The advantages proposed by repealing the sacramental test, impartially considered* (1732), in *The works of Jonathan Swift*, 6 vols. (London, 1755), vol. 5, p. 222.

34. Warburton, *Works*, vol. 7, pp. 242–4.

35. [Warburton], *Alliance* (1736), p. 117.

36. [Swift], *The advantages propos'd by repealing the sacramental test; idem, The Presbyterians plea of merit; In order to take off the test, impartially examined* (Dublin, 1733).

37. Swift consistently adopted a pose of moderation, but did so in a way that virtually endorsed one of the positions between which he professed to steer: *The sentiments of a Church of England man with respect to religion and government* (London, 1708), in Swift, *Works*, vol. 2, pp. 53–80, at 57.

38. Charles Daubeny, *A guide to the church, in several discourses* (London, 1798).

39. Jacqueline Hill, 'The meaning and significance of "Protestant Ascendancy", 1787–1840', in Lord Blake (ed.), *Ireland after the Union* (Oxford, 1989), pp. 1–22.

40. Woodward, *Present state of the Church of Ireland*, p. vii; Peter Nockles, 'Church or Protestant sect? The Church of Ireland, high churchmanship and the Oxford Movement, 1822–1869', *Historical journal*, 41 (1998), pp. 457–93, at 467.

41. John Sage, *An account of the late establishment of Presbyterian government by the Parliament of Scotland in Anno 1690. Together with the methods by which it was settled, and the consequences of it* (London, 1693).

4

The church in economy and society

PHILIP T. HOFFMAN

In early modern Europe, Christianity touched most people's lives, from their baptism shortly after birth to the funeral services after death. Christianity affected even mundane details of daily existence. Tolling church bells marked the time of day, and at least in Catholic regions, saints' feast days were used to designate when a market was held or a debt was due. The Sabbath and feast days dictated when Christians rested, and the vast majority of Europeans who toiled in the fields turned a significant portion of what they produced (often on the order of 7 per cent or so of the major crops) over to churches that had rights to the tithe.

Christian churches owned large amounts of property too, particularly in Catholic countries, and throughout Europe they ran or supervised charities, schools, and universities. They were also what we would today call major employers, for they provided both men and women with a religious calling. And of course they exhorted the faithful to lead Christian lives. Precisely what that meant might be different in Rome and Geneva, but it would certainly influence a believer's dealings in early modern society.

Since Christianity extended its reach into nearly every corner of life, one can naturally ask what effect it had on economy and society, especially in a period (1660–1815) that witnessed not just the dislocations of the French Revolution but the beginnings of the Industrial Revolution in England. One can turn the question around too, and ask how the economy affected the Christian churches. These questions have long interested historians and social scientists – notably the sociologist Max Weber (1864–1920). But the connection he detected nearly a century ago between a 'Protestant ethic' and a 'spirit of capitalism' is far from the last word on the links between Christianity and the economy. There is much more that can be said today about the ties between Christianity and the economy, especially about the central question of economic history – explaining economic growth.

Church property and rights to the tithe

In Protestant Europe, the Reformation had stripped away a considerable amount of church property, much of it coming from monasteries that were dissolved. The land, real estate, and other assets that had once belonged to the church fell into the hands of secular authorities or served to fund schools, universities, and charities. Protestant churches did possess some property and still retained most rights to the tithe, but they owned far less than religious institutions in Catholic territories.

Precisely how much property the Catholic Church had is not easily determined. One reason is that contemporary accounts of the church's assets and early historical analyses of what it owned were often biased. Eighteenth-century reformers who wanted their governments to confiscate church land often exaggerated the church's holdings. Nineteenth-century historians of suppressed religious houses, who lamented what the church had gone through, would do the same, while their anticlerical opponents might be tempted to minimize the damage. Further complicating the task of estimating the church's wealth is the way it varied from country to country, from region to region, and over time as well. If we limit ourselves to real estate, then in France, for instance, the clergy held some 6 per cent of the land on the eve of the French Revolution, but their holdings dropped to below 2 per cent in parts of the south and rose to nearly 40 per cent in parts of the north. In Bavaria, the percentage is even higher: over half the forest and farm land was in church hands. For Catholic Europe as a whole, it has been asserted that the regular clergy alone possessed perhaps 10 and even as much as 30 per cent of the real estate in Catholic countries, but the true figure, which we will never know, may well be different. And real estate was not the Catholic Church's only asset. It also had pensions, the tithe, cash gifts from the faithful, and rights to a variety of seigniorial dues, and the income from its land and other assets made it a major employer not just of artists, musicians, craftsmen and servants, but of lawyers and estate managers as well.

The wealth the Catholic Church had was not evenly distributed – some (though not all) parish priests might have very little, while the abbot of an ancient monastery might have a great deal – but it turned the richer Catholic institutions into political plums for rulers and the aristocracy. In France and Spain, monarchs exercised control over a number of the major benefices and used them as a form of patronage to reward supporters and officials and their families. The practice was pushed to extremes in France, where the king could give supporters (or a member of their families) control over wealthy religious houses by making them absentee priors or abbots. The abbots and priors did not have to be members of the religious orders, and they could hold several of these benefices at the same time. The reward was the large income benefices generated once the expenses of the priory or abbey had been paid. Richelieu, for instance, earned roughly a third of his immense revenue from such benefices in the early seventeenth century, and in the eighteenth century, the King of France had rights to nominate nearly a thousand absentee abbots, plus over one hundred bishops and numerous pension holders as well.

Monarchs were not the only ones in Catholic lands with control over benefices – far from it. In the Holy Roman Empire, families from the upper Catholic aristocracy had power over many cathedral chapters. They used the canonries (and other benefices too) to support their kin and to advance their interests and those of princely families to whom they were allied. Nobles in many parts of Italy could also appropriate the income from benefices, even though the Counter-Reformation papacy managed to impose a bit of meritocracy in appointments to the church livings it controlled. Not that the income from the Catholic Church's assets was all squandered on political spoils. It supported nuns who worked in hospitals and regular clergymen who taught in schools and colleges, and it provided charity for the poor and a refuge for unmarried women in societies that offered little place for ladies without husbands – all this even when absentee benefice holders were skimming much of the revenue off from the top. Nor was the Catholic Church alone in having such problems, for there were in fact parallels within the Lutheran and Anglican Churches. In Scandinavia and Germany, a young Lutheran cleric usually needed a patron, such as a local lord or a city councillor, to get a better paying post, for otherwise he risked being out in the countryside, where he was likely to subsist on a modest stipend. Similarly, in England, patronage in the Anglican Church was often used for political purposes, and the income from the tithe and glebe lands did not all end up in the pockets of the parson it was meant to support. Instead, much of it went to bishops, cathedral chapters, or the local gentry who often controlled clerical appointments.

Beyond using church assets as political plums, Catholic rulers also sought to tax the church's wealth, even though in theory its property was tax exempt. Needless to say, the pope and clergy struggled to resist, but they were far from completely successful. The kings of Spain taxed church property, as did the Habsburgs, notably when they had to defend their Austrian lands from the Turks. In France, the clergy developed a representative body that offered the king what was called a 'free gift' but in reality it was little different from taxation. If Catholic rulers were limited in the taxes they could impose on the church's wealth, they could at least try to keep donors from giving the church additional property, for once it was in church hands, it would escape the full force of the state's levies. Their worry was that each new donation would erode the tax base, leaving Catholic rulers at a disadvantage relative to their Protestant counterparts – a fear that seemed particularly pronounced in the divided confessional map of Germany.

Concerns of this sort furnished one of the motives (though certainly not the only one) for the religious reforms that Maria Theresa initiated in the Habsburg lands in the eighteenth century and that her son, Joseph II, pushed even further. Maria Theresa and Joseph II wanted both to strengthen the state and to help reform the Catholic Church. In particular, they sought to redistribute the church's holdings in a more useful way. As Maria Theresa's 'Political Testament' explained, bequeathing more property to the church was not 'laudable' but 'culpable', for the clergy did 'not need it' and made bad use of what it already had. Maria Theresa and her son therefore suppressed a number of monasteries, confiscated their property, and limited further donations to the church. Many of the assets they seized from monasteries (and from the Jesuits when they were suppressed in 1773) were then redeployed to support parishes, schools, and charities.[1]

In France, the unequal distribution of the Catholic Church's wealth fed into the grievances voiced by parish priests, grievances directed at the upper clergy on the eve of the French Revolution. The parish priests believed that they were the most useful members of the clergy and felt that they should therefore be exercising greater authority within the Catholic Church. In instances where they were relatively poor – which, once again, was not always the case – their complaints against the regular clergy or the bishops could be quite vociferous, particularly over the issue of the minimum income (the so called *portion congrue*) that rich absentee tithe owners had to provide for parish priests. The parish priests were of course not the only ones to criticize the Catholic Church's wealth, for a number of the philosophers mounted their own attack. They might argue, as Turgot did for instance, that money left to the church would eventually be diverted from the pious goals that the donors intended and that even money earmarked for support of the poor would only encourage paupers to cease working and to take up begging.

It was hardly startling then that the revolutionary regime confiscated the Catholic Church's property in France and abolished the tithe. Nor was it surprising that the confiscations spread once the French armies had conquered other Catholic territories, where church's wealth had provoked similar criticisms. Beyond its appeal to critics of the Catholic Church, the nationalization of church land had a number of political advantages. In France, it was a means of staving off government bankruptcy. Elsewhere – in Italy, for instance – it could give the French invaders revenue that they needed to fight their wars. The French, though, were not the only ones who profited from confiscating church property. In Germany, both the Protestant rulers of Prussia and the Catholic rulers of Bavaria were eager to lay their hands on the church's assets; the French invasion and the collapse of the Holy Roman Empire facilitated their task.

The secularization had a devastating effect on education and charity in some Catholic regions, particularly in Germany, where it wiped out eighteen Catholic universities as well as schools that had been supported by monasteries. The effect was a lasting one, for little of the secularized property was returned the church during the Restoration. Secularization also affected what we might call the market for 'careers' in the Catholic Church, at least at the highest levels, for there were no longer large numbers of high income benefices that could be reserved for nobles and political insiders. Most patronage was now gone, and bishops had more say about where priests were to be assigned. Lucrative benefices that had once attracted a disproportionate number of Catholic clergymen to cities were now suppressed, making the priesthood less attractive, at least to some candidates. That may be one of the causes (though certainly not the only one) for a decline in ordinations observed in some parts of Catholic Europe in the late eighteenth century. The loss of wealth harmed other professions as well. In Germany, prince-bishops and their courts disappeared, meaning fewer jobs for 'musicians, librarians, painters, [and] architects'.[2]

One thing that loss of the church's property did not affect, however, was agriculture, even though much of the property the church lost was farm land. Although one might imagine this land would be farmed more effectively by its new lay owners, nothing of the sort happened, and for a good reason: the monasteries, churches, and other ecclesiastical institutions that had owned the property before nationalization had already been working it efficiently. Most of the church property was rented out, and churches and monasteries administered their property just as adeptly as secular landlords. They developed the expertise needed to manage property well and with their wealth they could make investments and also take on some risks. Around Paris, for example, the Cathedral of Notre Dame leased its farms to the highest bidder, but it was careful not to squeeze so much from its tenants that they would be ruined. Like a good landlord, the cathedral knew that it should reward good tenants and cut them some slack if weather destroyed crops. Its practices here followed the advice given by early modern experts and fit what a modern economist would advise as well. The same held for the cathedral's investments. It did put money into its agricultural properties – by paying for the construction of new barns, for example, or by helping tenants to undertake improvements – but it apparently only did so if the return on its investments exceeded what it could earn elsewhere. It was behaving, in short, just the way an economist would want. And Notre Dame was not unusual. Evidence from many other parts of Catholic Europe suggests that monasteries administered their farmland in the same way that secular landlords did, and in some instances – in Bavaria, for example – farms fell into ruin when they left the church's hands.

Christianity's effect on labour markets and other economic transactions

Most early modern Europeans were peasants, and historians have long imagined that they produced nearly all that they needed for themselves. They were by and large self-sufficient, this historical tradition maintains, and they did not participate in markets. Theirs was a moral economy, isolated from market forces.

Recent research suggests, however, that this historical tradition is wrong, at least for much of western Europe. By the eighteenth century, if not long before, many peasants in western Europe sold what they produced, rented land, and worked for wages or hired help in local labour markets. There were also markets – and labour markets in particular – in cities and towns, markets for skilled artisans, unskilled lawyers, and also professionals, such as lawyers or even clergymen, who were deeply interested in what their benefice or living happened to pay.

Christianity, one might assume, must have influenced these economic transactions, and especially labour markets. After all, Christianity drew members of the educated elite into the clergy and thus diverted them from occupations that a modern secular observer (and perhaps some of the most radical eighteenth-century reformers too) might consider more 'productive'. It also admonished the faithful to observe the Sabbath, and at least in some churches, not to work on holy days. But what real impact did its teachings and its employment of clergy ultimately have on labour markets?

One can quickly set aside the idea that the clergy were somehow an immense drag on the economy. To begin with, their numbers were simply too small to have had much of an effect on the economy, no matter how productive one might imagine that they would have been had they been working at other tasks. In southern Italy, for instance, the regular and secular clergy amounted to perhaps 1 or 2 per cent of the population. The figures might be a bit higher in cities such as Rome, which had attractive benefices, but overall the male clergy and female religious too were never close to being a sizeable fraction of the population. In late eighteenth-century France, the numbers were even tinier: some 0.6 per cent of the population, including female religious. The figures were smaller still in Protestant regions – perhaps 0.1 or 0.2 per cent of the population, for instance, in parts of Lutheran Germany.

Moving 1 per cent, or at most 2 per cent, of the population to other work would simply not have had much of an effect on the overall economy. And even imagining such a redeployment of the clergy ignores the fact that the clerics were, in many cases, doing precisely what many Europeans wanted. They were preaching or saying Masses or providing solace for the bereaved, and putting an end to their ministry would upset people, as the popular opposition to radical de-Christianization during the French Revolution demonstrates. Having the clergy do something else, even if it had been possible, would have left these faithful Christians worse off, and in that sense would have actually set the economy back. In addition, many of the clerics and female religious were already doing work that even the most anti-religious modern observer would have to concede was useful. In Catholic territories, nuns worked in hospitals, and male religious staffed schools. Lutheran ordinands in Scandinavia and Germany served as tutors or teachers. Shifting them to other work would disrupt schools and charity, as it did during the secularization of church property in Catholic lands.

Christianity affected labour markets in other ways besides hiring members of the clergy, however. It taught the faithful to honour the Sabbath and not to work on Sundays, and the ban on working extended, at least in the mind of much of the population, not just to the liturgical calendar's major feast days, but to numerous saints' days as well, most of which were usually the occasion for festivals and celebrations. In Bamberg in Germany, for example, there were forty-four feast days on which work was completely forbidden in 1642, and another ten on which work was outlawed for half the day – all in addition, of course, to the fifty-two Sundays of the year. The Protestant Reformation suppressed a number of these feast days; so did many Catholic Reformers, who, although they took longer to act than the Protestants, shared their concern with the drunkenness, lechery, violence, and 'superstition' that the festivals and celebrations seemed to cause. For similar reasons, civil authorities also cracked down on the feast days. In 1669, for instance, Louis XIV's finance minister, Jean-Baptiste Colbert exhorted the kingdom's bishops to cut back the number of feast days in their dioceses.

As a result, the number of feast days fell. In Bamberg, for example, it dropped by 1789 to a total of only eighteen feast days on which work was completely forbidden and none on which it was partially outlawed. Cutting back on the feast days did provoke popular opposition, but it also meant that men and women worked more each year. The longer working year, it has been argued, may in turn explain much of the increase in output observed during the early years of Industrial Revolution. If so, then the Industrial Revolution did not really boost productivity much before 1800, despite all the new technology of steam engines and cotton textile production. Nor did it really increase per capita consumption. People did have more money to spend on new consumer goods, but they were simply working longer, and their higher incomes had been purchased at the expense of their free time, a valuable 'commodity' that they now did without. All in all, then, they were not that much better off, at least by 1800, but they were working harder, thanks to a broad campaign that made people more 'industrious' than they had been in the past.[3]

It is conceivable that Christian charity also had an impact on early modern labour markets. Philosophers such as Turgot feared that pious bequests would encourage paupers to give up work for a life of begging, and critics could always point to cases in which beggars took money they had collected at a church door and immediately drank it up at the nearest tavern or cabaret.[4] Religious zeal induced both Protestants and Catholics to leave money to the poor and to create institutions to help them, and this sort of charity was particularly pronounced under the resurgent Catholicism of the Counter-Reformation, at least if we judge from work by French historians, who have paid particularly close attention to religious charity in the early modern period. Do they find that religious charity actually drew a significant number of people away from the labour market?

The answer, in all likelihood, is no. That at least is the conclusion that emerges from what happened in Grenoble in south-eastern France. To judge from bequests made in wills, Catholic religious charity in Grenoble peaked in the 1690s and then was forced down by an economic downturn. Many of the paupers who received this charity, however, were not employed in the first place and so could not have been drawn away from the labour market, no matter what critics such as Turgot might have thought. They were aged, sick, orphans, or women with young children, who could not be expected to work. Furthermore, religious charity in early modern Europe was simply too small to have much of an impact on the labour market. Philosophers such as Turgot were not the only ones to fret about the incentives that assistance might create, whether it was religious or public, but despite all the worrying over the centuries, sizeable help for the poor from any source was a twentieth-century creation.

The greatest effect Christianity had on labour markets, however, came from the role it played in the abolition of slavery and the slave trade. Although abolition was a nineteenth-century achievement, its roots go back to this period, to Enlightenment attacks on slavery and even more so to the campaign against slavery mounted by English evangelicals such as William Wilberforce (1759–1833). Wilberforce and his fellow evangelicals fought for a wide variety of social reforms, but their greatest achievement was the abolition of the slave trade in the British Empire in 1807. Their campaign helped end slavery itself within the Empire by 1840, and it led the British government to press other European powers to withdraw from the slave trade in the years after the end of the Napoleonic Wars. This was the first major step against slavery, for it had a far greater impact than the anti-slavery measures adopted during the French Revolution, which were reversed by Napoleon. It was no doubt one of Christianity's finest moments, for as recent research has shown, slavery was in fact profitable and would not have disappeared on its own. Thanks in large part to the evangelicals, the traffic that had hauled some eleven million human beings out of Africa in chains finally came to an end, and by 1888 slavery itself would disappear from the western world.

Christianity's economic influence certainly extended beyond the labour market. Usury legislation immediately comes to mind, and so too do church teachings on marriage and the family, for in early modern Europe the decision to wed and have children was in large part an economic one. Marriages were often arranged by parents eager to secure their children's fortunes or their own. As a result, a young man and woman, even if they were peasants, did not usually wed until they possessed enough (either through their own savings or gifts and inheritances from their families) to support one another. There were still a number of bans on marrying relatives in Catholicism (some survived in Protestantism too), and these barriers limited the number of eligible marriage partners available for a prospective bride or groom.

There is also a possible connection between Christianity and the early use of birth control, at least in France, where the practice of *coitus interruptus* began to spread in the late eighteenth and early nineteenth centuries, particularly in areas where the clergy supported the Revolution. The likely reason, according to Donald Sutherland, is that the Revolutionary regime eventually drove away most of these priests, even though they had supported the Revolution, at least in its early stages. Many regions ended up with no one who could denounce birth control from the pulpit, and their anticlerical parishioners were in any case not likely to heed sermons against birth control.[5]

Nonetheless, Christianity's greatest impact was no doubt on labour markets, not on financial transactions or the 'marriage' market. Theological arguments against lending at interest had come under attack by the end of the Middle Ages, and by the seventeenth century there were enough loopholes in both Protestant and Catholic lands to allow all sorts of innovative financial transactions, from stock markets in Amsterdam to short-term money markets in Lyon. And the eighteenth century, with its stock market bubbles in London and Paris, witnessed even more financial innovation. It is doubtful whether the legislation restricting marriages was very effective either, for even in Catholic lands a young couple could often get an exemption, and from an economic perspective marriages between individuals who were not related might actually have been beneficial because it would help couples diversify their assets. And whether they were Protestant or Catholic, the other European countries were much slower to adopt birth control than was France.

Where Christianity made its most definitive mark was thus in the abolition of the slave trade and in the contribution Protestant and Catholic Reformers made to the campaign to reduce the number of feast days. There are of course still other ways that Christianity affected the economy: the religious intolerance of the period, for example, divided Protestant from Catholic and Christian from Jew, thereby making it impossible for many individuals to trade with one another. The economic damage this lamentable intolerance did, however, has yet to be determined.

The Protestant ethic, the spirit of capitalism, and the Industrial Revolution

The Industrial Revolution changed the world forever. From its beginnings in eighteenth-century Britain, it set capitalist economies on the path of sustained economic growth, something unknown in the pre-modern world. That meant unending technical change and repeated increases in per capita income, first in Britain and then, after 1800, in other parts of western Europe and countries of European settlement. Initially, growth was slow (up until 1800, as we have seen, most of the increased income in Britain came at the expense of longer working hours and so was not growth at all), and it came at the expense of dislocating social change, as people left the countryside to toil in urban mills. Nor were its benefits evenly spread throughout society, particularly at the outset. Yet by 1870 the average citizen of Britain (and the same is true for much of the rest of western Europe and of the United States, Australia, and New Zealand) lived longer and was better off than his ancestors had been. He was also far richer than the average African, Asian, or Latin American.

Explaining why the Industrial Revolution started in England and why it was western Europe (and not some other part of the world such as China) that jumped ahead is the great enigma of economic history, one that has interested historians and social scientists alike. What was it that gave western Europe – and Britain in particular – a head start on the path of capitalist economic growth?

Given the central role that Christianity has played in European history, one might look to religion for the answer. The best-known attempt to connect Christianity and capitalist growth is no doubt Max Weber's *The Protestant Ethic and the Spirit of Capitalism*. In this famous work, Weber did not say Calvinism caused the Industrial Revolution; rather, he posited a more subtle link between Calvinism and capitalist growth. At bottom, his argument was that the teachings of Calvin and of Puritan divines unintentionally helped legitimate capitalist behaviour. In particular, they encouraged savings, investment, and the relentless pursuit of profit, all of which Weber considered hallmarks of capitalism. The Calvinist doctrine of predestination left anxious believers looking for some sign that they had been saved. That sign would come from success as a capitalist, and capitalist behaviour would be reinforced by Protestant injunctions against idleness and extravagant consumption.

Much ink has been spilled over the Weber thesis, which has had a particularly strong appeal in sociology and among historians who work on Great Britain and New England. But it has encountered less success among historians of early modern religion, particularly those who work on continental Europe. They actually find an ethos similar to Weber's Protestant ethic in Counter-Reformation Catholicism and argue that both Calvinism and post-Tridentine Catholicism shared a common commitment (despite all their other differences) to the sort of disciplined behaviour associated with capitalism. If they are correct, then Weber's argument may reflect not a perceptive reading of the evidence, but his own psychology and the political attitudes of his milieu. From contemporary theology and Bismarck's battle against Catholicism, Weber had imbibed the belief that Protestantism was the better religion for modern society. But he also admired English and American Puritanism as a bulwark against the debilitating authoritarianism he despised in Germany. From there, the step to inventing the Protestant ethic was a short one indeed.

Weber's proponents would of course disagree. They would contend that Weber's critics have mangled his argument, which did not connect

Protestantism and capitalism, but a Protestant 'ethic' and a 'spirit' of capitalism. Such subtlety, however, may in fact be a weakness, and it is not the only one that critics can point to. Weber's method of ideal types – in other words, his practice of constructing an idealized image from the blurred historical reality – may in fact do an injustice to the historical record, since it means shutting one's eyes to the messiness of reality. It may also have meant taking a situation that was specific to Germany, where Catholic education had suffered greatly from the confiscations of the revolutionary era, and mistakenly assuming that it was a generality true throughout the western world.

Is there then any hard evidence that bears Weber out? There is really none in Weber's original essay, for what little statistical evidence it contains does not stand up well to scrutiny. And much of the evidence that Weber's supporters point to – that Protestants were over represented among merchants, inventors, and entrepreneurs – is in fact inconclusive, for it could easily result from factors unrelated to Weber's Protestant ethic. If many of the early inventors and entrepreneurs in England happened to be Nonconformists, it could simply be that they were barred from pursuing careers in the government or the military. Similarly, the fact that Britain was the birth place of the Industrial Revolution might stem not from the influence of Puritanism, but from the country's secure property rights, low transportation costs, and abundant supply of skilled metal workers.

A real test of Weber's thesis has to take into consideration all these other factors that influence economic growth and try to distinguish their effect from that of Protestantism. One way to do that is to use statistics. When statistical techniques are applied to historical evidence from the countries of Europe over a long period stretching from 1300 to 1850, however, they suggest that there was no firm relationship between Protestantism and economic growth. Similar studies, which have been done using modern data, are also relevant here, for if the Weber thesis held in the past, it should hold today as well. But the most careful of these recent studies finds no clear evidence that Protestantism is more favourable for economic growth than Catholicism.

Another way to test the Weber thesis in an unambiguous way is to study Protestants and Catholics who live in the same community. Because they are both part of the same economy and polity, the non-religious factors affecting their economic success would therefore be nearly the same. The only major difference would be their religion, and by examining their fortunes, one could see, for instance, whether the Protestants saved more and were thus more likely to increase their wealth.

Philip Benedict actually carried out such a study for the years 1605–59 in the French city of Montpellier, which was roughly equally divided between Calvinists and Catholics. He found no evidence that the Calvinists accumulated more wealth than their Catholic neighbours. The Calvinists did eventually lose political power in the city, but the loss did not seem to harm their fortunes. Indeed, their wealth grew as the city prospered. Yet Catholic wealth kept pace and in some instances forged ahead.[6]

What then is one to do with the Weber thesis? One option is to rework what he says, taking into account what we have learned about the history of early modern Europe since his day. That effort, which seeks to retain what is valuable in Weber, is currently underway. Alternatively, it may be time to remove Weber's thesis from the box of tools that historians use and consign it instead to the realm of quaint claims that make interesting subjects for historical study. The argument here would be that years of research in history and the social sciences have disproved both Weber's thesis about the Protestant ethic and a number of his key assumptions. Weber believed, for instance, that rational calculation was simply inconceivable without competitive markets.[7] Yet much recent work in economics has been devoted to exploring rational behaviour outside of markets, behaviour that both economists and other social scientists have found quite prevalent, even in developing countries. Historical evidence also points to rational behaviour long ago in the past, even when markets were absent. The evidence thus seems to suggest that Weber was mistaken, and if so, we should perhaps look elsewhere for a connection between Christianity and the origins of the Industrial Revolution.

Where might one seek this connection? Perhaps in education and the transmission of skills, for it has been argued that established religion – and Catholicism in particular – worked against acquiring the sort of practical mechanical knowledge that was widespread in Britain and seemed to play such an important role in the Industrial Revolution.[8] If this argument is correct, religious control of education was one of the barriers keeping students in continental Europe from learning the practical Newtonian mechanics that they needed to catch up with the British. The issue, though, is still controversial, not least because many historians do not accept the connection between this sort of knowledge and the Industrial Revolution. And others would point to very different paths to acquiring knowledge about mechanics and new technology – paths that may have had little at all to do with Christianity.[9]

In Catholic Europe, church property generated enough income to turn major benefices into attractive political plums for kings and noble families. The property – chiefly land, but also buildings, pensions, and tithe rights – made the Catholic Church an inviting target for reform in the eighteenth century and for confiscation during the French Revolution. The loss of the church's property affected recruitment of the clergy and it damaged charitable and educational establishments in Germany. It did not help agriculture, though, because ecclesiastical institutions were already expert and efficient landlords.

Christianity did influence labour markets. British evangelicals began a great battle to end the slave trade, and a quieter campaign – this one waged by Protestants and Catholics alike – helped reduce the number of feast days and increase the amount of time people spent at work. The additional labour helped purchase new consumer goods and it may even account for much of the growth in per capita income in the early stages of the Industrial Revolution in Britain. There are of course other links between Christianity and the economy, but at least one of the connections that scholars thought they perceived – Weber's Protestant ethic – now seems mistaken.

Notes

1. Ernst Wangermann, *The Austrian achievement: 1700–1800* (London: Thames and Hudson, 1973), pp. 73–105; Karl Otmar Freiherr von Aretin, *Vom Deutschen Reich zum Deutschen Bund, Deutsche Geschichte*, ed. Joachim Leuschner (Göttingen: Vandenhoeck und Ruprecht, 1980), pp. 54–5; Derek Beales, *Prosperity and plunder: European Catholic monasteries in the age of revolution, 1650–1815* (Cambridge: Cambridge University Press, 2003), pp. 179–230; Owen Chadwick, *The popes and European revolution* (Oxford: Clarendon Press, 1981), pp. 250–2, 412–17.

2. Chadwick, *Popes and European revolution*, pp. 96–101, 503. For an example of declining vocations in Italy and their link to Joseph II's reforms, see Xenio Toscani, *Il clero lombardo dall'ancien regime alla restaurazione* (Bologna: Il Mulino, 1979), pp. 341–7, 359–60.

3. Hans-Joachim Voth, 'The longest years: New estimates of labor input in England, 1760–1830', *Journal of economic history*, 61 (2001), pp. 1065–82, and 'Time and work in eighteenth-century London', *Journal of economic history*, 58 (1998), pp. 29–58; Jan De Vries, 'Between purchasing power and the world of goods: Understanding the household economy in early modern Europe', in Roy Porter and John Brewer (eds.), *Consumption and the world of goods* (London: Routledge, 1993), pp. 85–132, and 'The Industrial Revolution and the industrious revolution', *Journal of economic history*, 54 (1994), pp. 249–70. See also Gregory Clark and Ysbrand Van Der Werf, 'Work in progress? The industrious revolution', *Journal of economic history*, 58 (1998), pp. 840–3.

4. Anne-Robert-Jacques Turgot, 'Fondation', in *Encyclopédie ou dictionnaire raisonné des sciences, des arts et des métiers, par une société de gens de lettres*, ed. Denis Diderot, 28 vols. (Paris, 1751–72), vol. 7, pp. 72–5; Kathryn Norberg, *Rich and poor in Grenoble, 1600–1814* (Berkeley: University of California Press, 1985), p. 169.

5. D. M. G. Sutherland, *The French Revolution and Empire: The quest for a civic order* (Malden: Blackwell, 2003), pp. 194, 344–5; and personal communication with the author.

6. Philip Benedict, 'Faith, fortune and social structure in seventeenth-century Montpellier', *Past and present*, 152 (1996), pp. 46–78.

7. Max Weber, *Gesamtausgabe, Die Wirtschaftsethik der Weltreligionen*, ed. Helwig Schmidt-Glintzer and Petra Kolonko (Tübingen: J. C. B. Mohr, 1989), pp. 488–9.

8. Margaret C. Jacob, *Scientific culture and the making of the industrial west* (Oxford: Oxford University Press, 1997), pp. 106–11, 135–6, 145, 157–62.

9. See, for example, Joel Mokyr, *The gifts of Athena: Historical origins of the knowledge economy* (Princeton: Princeton University Press, 2002).

PART II

*

CHRISTIAN LIFE IN THE EUROPEAN WORLD, 1660–1780

5

The Catholic clergy in Europe

MARIO ROSA

This survey of the Catholic clergy in Europe, from 1650 to the eve of the French Revolution, will present a comparative outline of the various ecclesiastical groupings, divided into two main branches. The first of these, the secular clergy, consisted of the episcopal hierarchy and the lower clergy of parish priests, clerics belonging to the major orders, and the floating population of those who were in minor orders or merely tonsured. The regular clergy consisted of the male and female members of the monastic orders, the mendicant orders, and the regular congregations. If any conclusion may be drawn from these pages, it is that the different models and forms of Catholicism which developed in Europe between the Counter-Reformation and the Enlightenment, were all affected by the general trend towards uniformity and universalism directed by the Roman Church. But these new models were also influenced by both the ancient religious and political traditions which had permeated religious institutions and religious life for centuries, and by the specific political and social conditions which existed in different parts of Europe.

The Spanish and Portuguese bishops

Although they no longer possessed the religious and political status of the sixteenth-century episcopate, the Spanish bishops of the early seventeenth century continued to provide the principal model for the episcopal hierarchies of the whole of Europe. In the fifty-four Spanish dioceses, expanded to sixty in the eighteenth century, the bishops were all chosen by royal appointment. The majority had previously been canons of the cathedral chapters, and possessed university qualifications, most commonly degrees in canon and civil law. However, there were also bishops who had emerged from the regular orders, generally from the ranks of the Franciscans and Dominicans, who were for the most part graduates in theology. In every case, the candidates were asked to provide evidence of *limpieza de sangre*, i.e., proof that they were not descendants of recently Christianized families (*cristianos nuevos*). Although the royal appointment system meant that there was the possibility of openings for candidates from economically modest backgrounds, nonetheless, candidates with aristocratic origins, whether from the upper or lower nobility, were very considerable in number.

Even if the Inquisition attempted to encroach in those areas which it believed to be within its competence, and sometimes attacked the bishops' authority and jurisdiction, the bishops remained very active in pastoral care. The residence requirement was generally respected, excepting the large dioceses of Toledo and Seville, whose incumbents were often assigned to political and diplomatic missions on behalf of the monarchy.

No prominent personalities stand out among the Spanish bishops of the seventeenth and eighteenth centuries. They were stately individuals who had a heightened awareness of the responsibilities of their office. In the seventeenth century, they dedicated themselves to extensive charitable activities on behalf of the poor. During the eighteenth-century Enlightenment, this interest was extended to some extent into civil, cultural, and social concerns. In the later eighteenth century the Spanish episcopacy generally supported Charles III's reform initiatives, in particular, the battle which would lead first to the expulsion of the Society of Jesus from Spain, and then to the Jesuits' suppression by the papacy in 1773. But the bishops also maintained a strong sense of tradition in relation to 'modernity', and a belief in the harmful consequences of ideas deriving from the French Enlightenment, the French Revolution, and the Napoleonic invasion.

The Portuguese episcopate was similar to the Spanish, in terms of its appointment by the king, its pastoral activity, and its relations with the Inquisition, although it differed in its eighteenth-century evolution towards a more aristocratic recruitment. The patriarchal office of the see of Lisbon, obtained from John V at the beginning of the century, was reserved for the nobility, and the bishops of the other twelve Portuguese dioceses all originated in the court aristocracy or the minor nobility. As a consequence the ecclesiastical and episcopal structures were more closely linked to the state in Portugal than they were in Spain. Such links helped produce the long *Rotura* between Portugal and Rome from 1759 to 1769, and facilitated the minister Pombal's policies against the religious orders, especially the Jesuits.

The French bishops

The French episcopate seemed to develop rather differently, as an alternative model to that of its Spanish counterparts, especially in the early decades of the seventeenth century. France was a country with a strong and active Calvinist minority, recognized by the Edict of Nantes in 1598. With the end of the wars of religion, a reconstruction of Catholic religious and ecclesiastical life became necessary. This was pursued within the framework of the approximately 130 French dioceses, dioceses which differed dramatically in size from the very large in the north of the country, to the very much smaller in the south. Here, as in the Iberian peninsula, the nomination of bishops was the monarch's privilege, and in the seventeenth century these appointments were generally successful. There was an increasing preference for candidates from the upper nobility, so that the aristocracy controlled all the French dioceses by the late eighteenth century.

Though in all Catholic European countries, the episcopate formed a prestigious ecclesiastical elite, in France the bishops were at the head of the first order of the state, with its own unique representative system (the Assembly of the Clergy). This Assembly was first convened in 1561 to contribute an agreed amount of money for the financial needs of the monarchy. Rapidly developing into a permanent body meeting every five years, the Assembly of the Clergy sought to overcome various financial and administrative problems within its areas of competence and to support the Gallican policies of the monarchy. Thus, it generally approved the four Gallican articles of 1682 and the king's repressive policies against the Calvinists, especially those in the dioceses of the Midi. Initially somewhat divided on the problem of Jansenism, a large anti-Jansenist majority developed among the bishops, as the effects of this opposition movement began to be felt in the religious, political, and cultural life of eighteenth-century France.

There was certainly no lack of abuses and scandal within the ranks of the seventeenth-century French episcopate, abuses which were reinforced by the sumptuous lifestyle and the irregular residence of the bishops. But a new model for the bishops was also emerging, based on a new theological and pastoral concept of the episcopacy, influenced by Saint Francis de Sales, by the Jansenist Duguet, and by the Borromaic and Vincentian movements. In the late seventeenth and early eighteenth centuries the bishops increased their efforts to train the diocesan clergy, creating many new seminaries and improving the pedagogy in those already established. Above all, the eighteenth-century

French episcopate aimed to assert itself in both the 'national' and the European contexts: confronting, on the one hand, the Calvinists, who had remained in France after the revocation of the Edict of Nantes; and on the other, the non-believers and proponents of the Enlightenment. These efforts would become decisive after 1770, as the bishops attempted to consolidate traditional Catholic forces in defence of the Christian faith and the political order, both of which were thought to be under threat. However, the bishops continued to have little regard during the century for the economic conditions of the lower clergy, a situation that would lead to an accumulation of hostility which exploded at the time of the Revolution.

The Italian bishops

As Claudio Donati has suggested, it is better to speak of the bishops of the different Italian states, than of 'the Italian bishops', even if the latter expression can legitimately be used to underline the exceptional relationship between the Italian 'church' and Rome.

There was a larger number of dioceses in Italy than in any other European region: eighteen, for example, in Tuscany; thirty-two under Venetian jurisdiction, and about 130 distributed throughout the Kingdom of Naples. The state's intervention in episcopal appointments in the Italian peninsula was similar to that in other European regions, although the array of specific practices was greater. These ranged from direct appointments by the sovereign in Sicily and the Kingdom of Naples, to the practice which prevailed elsewhere, where the pope was given the final choice from up to three candidates proposed by the local political authority.

The majority of the Italian bishops were drawn from the ranks of the secular clergy, from cathedral canons or vicars-general, most of whom held doctoral degrees. Only 15 to 30 per cent – especially those appointed by the papacy – came from the monastic and mendicant orders or from congregations of regular clerics such as the Theatines and the Barnabites, and most of these were destined for undistinguished sees. The growing aristocratic character of the episcopacy was most marked in the Duchy of Savoy, in Sardinia, in the Venetian Republic, and in Sicily. By contrast, only 30 per cent of prelates could claim noble birth in the Kingdom of Naples during the eighteenth century, and a similar trend towards 'bourgeois' bishops was to be found in Tuscany and Lombardy.

Despite the contradictory positions of Rome, which did not always favour the implementation of Tridentine discipline in the dioceses, the papacy's control over the Italian bishops was generally more direct than over the other European episcopacies. This authority had been achieved through the Congregation of the Council in 1564, and through the Congregation of bishops in 1571–72, later (in 1601) the Congregation of bishops and regular clergy. Papal authority was further strengthened through the ruling of Sixtus V in 1585, requiring Italian bishops to make regular *ad limina* visits to Rome every three years (every four years for bishops of other European countries) and deliver reports in person or via an intermediary on the state of their dioceses.

Despite these efforts, however, the early decades of the seventeenth century revealed substantial weaknesses on the part of both Rome and the Italian bishops, due in large measure to the growing expansion of the regular orders and difficult relations with the Inquisition. This situation would be resolved only slowly during the more secular period of the papacy, beginning with Innocent XI in 1676. The bishops' functions would be particularly extolled during the long pontificate of Benedict XIV (1740–58) who, inspired by the writings of Ludovico Antonio Muratori, sought to spread the model of a prelate who was not only a good diocesan administrator, but also a pastor capable of wise 'moderation' in civil and religious matters.

An anti-papal offensive led by various 'Enlightened' rulers of the peninsula began in the 1760s in Venice, Tuscany, Lombardy, and Naples, an offensive which created a large degree of uncertainty among the bishops, especially after the expulsion of the Jesuits. The most advanced anti-Roman and pro-statist episcopalism occurred in Tuscany, with the ecclesiastical reforms of Peter Leopold and of Bishop Scipione de' Ricci of Pistoia and Prato, and with the unsuccessful attempt to create a 'national' church at the Pistoia synod of 1786. At the same time, however, a substantial pro-papal movement was emerging elsewhere within the Italian episcopate. A position in favour of pontifical primacy could be seen, in particular, among the bishops of the Papal States, the Kingdom of Sardinia, the Venetian Republic and the small states of the Po Valley, such as Parma and Modena. After the period of reform, the French Revolution, and the Napoleonic period, this moderate 'Roman' majority would ensure a non-traumatic transformation from the 'Italian churches' of the *ancien régime* to the Italian church of the nineteenth century.

The bishops of the empire, the Habsburg domains, and Poland

In the territories of the empire, the Catholic Church was divided into an 'episcopal' Germany and a 'monastic' Germany, depending on the relative regional power of the bishops or the great abbots. 'Episcopal' Germany – which included some fifty of the sixty-seven dioceses where 'prince-bishops' reigned – was characterized by a large degree of autonomy from Rome and by a unity between political and religious structures which had endured for centuries. It covered a wide area in a mosaic of jurisdictions and ecclesiastical divisions, extending from the north-west to the south of Germany, and from the Rhine to Salzburg. Bishops, abbots, and priors all sat in the Imperial Diet, together with the princes and nobles from the minor dynasties and imperial cities. The great power of the bishops – all of noble birth and elected by the cathedral chapters – was increasingly marked by a sense of autonomy from Rome, especially after the Peace of Westphalia in 1648. The result was an ever stronger episcopalism, a position supported in the eighteenth century by the *De statu ecclesiae* (1763) of Justinus Febronius. At the same time, the region experienced a consolidation of certain secularization programmes, programmes that would be pursued during the Napoleonic occupation through to the dissolution of the ecclesiastic principalities.

While they remained active in both the religious life and the administration of their dioceses, the German bishops were also engaged in sponsoring the great architectural projects of Baroque Catholicism, ranging from churches and sanctuaries to secular buildings such as the palatial residence at Würzburg. Neither should one disregard the bishops' contributions to the figurative and musical arts of the age, of which prince-bishop Girolamo Colloredo's patronage of Mozart is only one example.

In east-central Europe, in the hereditary Habsburg domains and in the territories of the Bohemian and Hungarian thrones, the episcopacy strongly supported both the secular struggles against the Turks and the Protestants, and the creation of strong links between ecclesiastical institutions and the political power of the monarchy. Among the seventeenth-century bishops of the twelve dioceses in the hereditary domains, few made a mark in the spiritual and religious sphere. The typical 'Baroque' Austrian bishop could hardly be described as 'Tridentine', given his aristocratic origins and his involvement in diplomatic and administrative tasks in the service of the Habsburgs. A new type of bishop began to emerge, however, during the period of reforms in the early to mid-eighteenth century. They revealed a curious mixture of influences, both from Trent (as seen in the bishops' frequent appeals to the Council), and from the Enlightenment (as seen in their opposition to traditional expressions of popular religion, in the name of a 'rational' Christianity). In general agreement with state policies, as embodied in the *Concessus in Publico-Ecclesiasticis* of 1769, the bishops opposed devotional practices judged to be superstitious, such as indulgences, processions, confraternities, and pilgrimages. The policies of Joseph II between 1780 and 1790 accentuated the statist characteristics of these reforms, but the bishops were not always united behind the decisions of this monarch. Even if they approved the suppression of monasteries, convents, and confraternities and the strengthening of parish life, they were opposed to any drastic interventions by the emperor in liturgical, religious or devotional practices, areas in which the state generally retreated after the death of Joseph II in 1790.

In a territory which contained such a patchwork of religions, comprising not only royal Hungary but also Transylvania and the so-called Triple Kingdom of Croatia, Slavonia, and Dalmatia, the bishops assumed great cultural influence, especially after the Habsburg reconquest following the siege of Vienna in 1683. This was true partly because of their training which often took place at the German-Hungarian College in Rome; and partly because of the considerable political weight accrued from sitting *ex officio* in the upper House, where their allegiance to the reigning dynasty was conjoined with a solid feeling of Hungarian 'nationality'. In 1776 Maria Theresa responded to the growth of the population and pressure from Catholics by creating several new dioceses out of the primate's archdiocese of Esztergom. Other dioceses were established in the following years, reaching a total of twenty-one by the end of the century, a number largely in line with the standards of western Europe. Through its suppression of the institutions of the regular clergy, Josephism undoubtedly strengthened the dioceses and the parishes, especially in Hungary, but this trend was the result of the directives of the state, not of the bishops. Indeed, the reaction of the Hungarian nobles and peasants against the Josephist reforms was reinforced by a strong reaction of both the bishops and the church in general.

In the mid-seventeenth century the Polish-Lithuanian episcopate consisted of nineteen dioceses and the two archbishoprics of Gniezno (the primate's see) and Lwow. All Catholic bishops were nominated by the king, as were those of both the Eastern Orthodox Church (with one metropolitan and six bishops) and the Greek Catholic 'Uniates' (with one metropolitan and seven bishops). The Roman bishops were chosen from the ranks of the lower nobility (*szlachta*), which also had a monopoly on the high offices and canonries of the cathedral chapters. But in other respects, their social and political positions were scarcely replicated in any other European country. Not only were they senators of the 'royal republic' (unlike the Uniate bishops), but their control of large estates assimilated them into the great land-owning classes. Their studies in Rome exposed them to western culture, while their links with the court, their familial relations, and their seats in the Senate all made them exponents of a 'national' church, a church which was very different from the other European churches, and which contrasted markedly with both German Protestantism and Russian Orthodoxy.

After the strong impact of the Tridentine reforms, inspired by Cardinal Hosius, the Archbishop of Warmia, the Polish bishops of the mid-seventeenth century had become profoundly different from their predecessors. Under the reign of Jan Sobieski (1674–96), the liberator of Vienna from the Turkish siege, the earlier crisis of revolts and wars seemed to come to an end. There followed a long constructive period, which facilitated a second phase of Tridentine reforms within the Polish episcopate, especially under the monarchs of the House of Saxony, Augustus II (1697–1733), and Augustus III (1733–63). In this climate, ecclesiastical culture appeared more sensitive to a particular kind of 'Catholic Enlightenment', supported by the bishops and by some religious orders such as the Jesuits and the Piarists. Renewed difficulties arose, however, in the later eighteenth century, with the suppression of the Society of Jesus, and with the political and constitutional crisis which led to the three successive territorial partitions of Poland in 1772, 1793, and 1795.

The secular clergy in Spain and Portugal

By the end of the eighteenth century, the secular clergy of Spain totalled some 70,000 individuals out of a clerical population of 148,000 and a general population of 10.5 million. The majority of the seculars were concentrated in the cities, living largely from benefices or from bequests for Masses. To those clerics who had received sacerdotal ordination, must be added a 'clerical proletariat' who had only taken minor orders and who enjoyed privileges such as exemptions from taxes and from lay jurisdiction. Distributed irregularly through the vast peninsula, these clergymen originated predominantly from rural backgrounds and were of modest means. They were strongly integrated into Spanish society in terms of their standard of living, their family ties, and their highly localized sense of identity.

The ecclesiastical reforms initiated in the eighteenth century during the reign of Charles III did not substantially change the position of the secular clergy, especially those in the parishes – unlike the reforms in Habsburg Austria and Italy during roughly the same period. At the turn of the nineteenth century the defensive and theocratic vision which affected the episcopacy also had a strong impact on the lower clergy. This perspective would long influence the political, social, and religious characteristics of Spanish history.

The make-up of the Portuguese secular clergy was similar to that of the Spanish, though the data available give conflicting results as to their numerical presence. Foreign travellers, generalizing from the situation observed in the cities, speak of a superabundance of clerics. But just as in Spain, the lower clergy was unevenly distributed. Not only were they concentrated in the urban centres of medium-to-large towns, but they were also more widespread in the north of the country than in areas of large estates in the south. It seems likely that the number of clergy in Portugal was reduced in the 1780s, as a result of the reformist activities of the minister Pombal. But these reforms did not directly affect the organization of the seculars. Their principal aim was the transformation of the religious orders, rather than the ecclesiastical society of the parishes. Thus, the Pombaline policies were more closely allied with those of the Spanish than with the reforms pursued by the Habsburgs.

The secular clergy in France

In the seventeenth century, the French secular clergy numbered approximately 100,000 out of a total of 18 million inhabitants, a number which would rise in the eighteenth century to approximately 130,000 out of 25 million. Despite the fact that the French parish priest was commonly appointed by an ecclesiastical or lay patron (and more rarely, by the bishop), and despite the considerable presence of chaplains and other priests without cure of souls who occasionally celebrated Mass, there was nonetheless a much enhanced awareness in France of the rights of the parish priests. Such rights had been strongly supported in 1611 by the Gallican author Richer. In addition, the dignity of the priesthood had been greatly exalted during the seventeenth century by Cardinal Bérulle, Saint Francis de Sales, and Saint Vincent de Paul. Another characteristic of the French secular clergy was the strong presence of companies or congregations of priests, some of whom took simple vows. Examples of such congregations include the Fathers of Christian Doctrine (or the Doctrinaires) who appeared in Italy in 1560 and were established in France by César de Bus; the French Oratory, created by Bérulle in 1611 following the Italian model of Saint Philip Neri; the mission priests, or Lazarists, founded by Saint Vincent de Paul in 1625; the Congregations of Jesus and Mary, or Eudists, established in 1643 by Saint John Eudes; and the Sulpicians, founded in 1645 by Jean-Jacques Olier, the vicar of the large Parisian parish of Saint-Sulpice. The Sulpicians, the Oratorians and the Lazarists were all committed to teaching in the seminaries.

The French secular clergy of the seventeenth century clearly had its share of moral and disciplinary irregularities, as can be seen in the numerous *abbés* without cure of souls living mostly in the towns, or in the numbers of rural priests whose lifestyle was largely indistinguishable from that of the laity. However, notwithstanding such difficulties and compromises, the image and the reality of the 'good priest' had endured, reinforced by the newly developing theology of the priesthood, and by a Jansenist religious and moral vision. Such movements and traditions not only provided exemplary models of doctrine and personal piety for French ecclesiastics, but also fortified the bond between the priest and his parish community. At the same time, the lower clergy helped guarantee religious and civil commitment to both church and state via the regular readings from the pulpit of episcopal instructions and royal decrees.

By the beginning of the eighteenth century, under the firm control of the bishops, the French secular clergy had been substantially reformed. But the century would also bring a series of ecclesiastical crises: first from the effects of the renewed condemnation of Jansenism in the bull *Unigenitus* (1713), and second from the decline in the number of sacerdotal ordinations in many areas of the country after 1760 – a decline due in part to the increasing secularization of society and the diffusion of Enlightenment ideas. At the same time, tensions were growing throughout the century between the lower clergy on the one hand (particularly the parish priests), and the bishops, canons, and religious orders, on the other. The existence of such tensions would help explain the position taken by the lower clergy in 1789.

The secular clergy in Italy

On the Italian peninsula the post-Tridentine bishops were particularly concerned with the excessive numbers of the secular clergy. Seminaries, created to train and improve clerical behaviour, operated only irregularly and for short periods. The attention of both ecclesiastical and lay authorities was focused primarily on the necessity of controlling the great numbers of clergymen, particularly in southern Italy. The principal causes of this plethora of clerics were economic and social. But the particular institution of the *'ricettizio'* system, present in up to 70 per cent of parishes in the southern provinces, also contributed. In these parishes, the care of souls was collective, delegated by the capitular body to a vicar-curate, who was chosen from within the local chapter. The chapter would then give its *'ricetto'* ('reception' or 'shelter') to all clerics originating from the parish, priests and tonsured clerics alike, according to well-defined rules. Strong local and family interests, and the lay patronage of oligarchal groups, meant that this system was both autonomous and well-integrated within southern Italian society. Not only did this institution lead to the creation of an overly large secular clergy, who were mostly uninvolved in the parish ministry, but it also obstructed the pastoral work of the post-Tridentine prelates. The bishops of the different Italian states in the second half of the seventeenth century sought less to reduce the number of ordinations, than to reorder the clergy and guide clerics towards the major orders. This process was facilitated by pastoral policies under the pontificates of Innocent XI and Innocent XII, which broke new ground for the Catholic Church in Italy, by defining the public face of secular ecclesiastical institutions and religious life in the peninsula for at least the first fifty years of the eighteenth century.

Throughout these years, the age of Muratori and Benedict XIV, a spirit of reform continued to permeate ecclesiastical structures from top to bottom. But in the second half of the century this process was interrupted, or at least greatly slowed by the church's hardening position in the face of Enlightenment culture and the beginnings of Enlightened reforms. Political authorities took increasingly radical initiatives against the institutions of the church, in particular with the Habsburg reformism of Joseph II and his brother Peter Leopold (the future emperor Leopold II). Within the framework of these reforms, the number of secular clergymen was dramatically reduced. In Austrian Lombardy, which was one of the territories where Josephism was put to the test, the clergy as a whole experienced a massive reduction of 57 per cent between 1772 and 1792. Although less drastic than Josephism, the policies of Peter Leopold also made considerable modifications to the regular and secular ecclesiastical institutions in Tuscany, leading to an 8 per cent reduction in the ecclesiastical population between 1765 and 1782.

At the other end of the peninsula in the Kingdom of Naples, the Bourbon ecclesiastical reforms, like those of the Habsburgs, did not set the problem of clerical training and the definition of a new clerical profile as the first priority. Nonetheless, the Bourbons did institute policies to control the numbers of the secular clergy, which underwent a gradual but notable reduction from about 56,000 to 36,000 between 1765–66 and 1801, a 35 per cent reduction in a little less than forty years.

The secular clergy in central and eastern Europe

The Catholic re-conquest of the Habsburg territories was directed essentially by the religious orders, in particular by the Jesuits and Capuchins, who were favoured not only by the Habsburg authorities in Austria and Bohemia, but also by the bishops themselves. These two orders were supported because of their pastoral work and their preaching, deemed particularly valuable in the face of an extremely poor parochial organization. In Bohemia, the religious orders were also important as a consequence of particular historical conditions linked to the seventeenth-century re-conquest. It was within this framework that Joseph II began his reforms of the secular parish clergy, providing the parish priests with an annual stipend paid for from the assets of the Jesuits and other religious orders which had been suppressed. In Hungary, as well, Josephism had a decisive effect, leading to the suppression of 134 monasteries of the contemplative orders. Under state control, the income gained from these suppressions was used to create a thousand new parishes, while clergymen from the suppressed religious orders were secularized and used for parish service.

The secular clergy in the Polish-Lithuanian region was touched by less dramatic transformations than in the Habsburg lands. Here the accumulation of benefices and the non-residence of priests in their parishes would continue to characterize the secular clergy in a parochial framework, where the patronage and appointment of priests belonged to the nobility in 80 to 90 per cent of the 5,000 existing parishes. However, one element which distinguished the secular Roman Catholic clergy of Poland from that in other western and east-central European countries was the stability of the ecclesiastical population, which remained close to 10,000 or 11,000 throughout the two centuries from the Council of Trent to the partition of Poland. In this sense, the Catholic seculars closely resembled the 10,000 married priests of the Uniate Church, apart from the different rites used and the greater poverty and lower educational level of the Uniate clergy.

The regular clergy in Spain and Portugal

The question of the numbers of the regular clergy remained a controversial problem in Spain throughout the modern age. The most notable increase in the regulars had occurred between the end of the sixteenth century and the first half of the seventeenth, especially with the establishment of the Capuchins, the Jesuits, the Hospitallers, and later the Piarists. At the same time there was an increase in the number of mendicant convents, while the Benedictine orders remained largely constant. The new religious impulse of the age, the generosity of certain members of the nobility, rivalries between different communities known for their large memberships, and the piety of the rulers: all contributed to this increase in numbers. Even in 1787, after the expulsion of the Jesuits, there were still over 52,000 religious in 2,067 convents throughout the kingdom.

The members of the mendicant orders generally came from the middle to lower classes of Spanish society, since entry into these orders did not require proof of nobility, but only evidence of *limpieza de sangre*. Individuals of aristocratic origins tended to gravitate towards the monastic orders and, in particular, towards the Hieronymites. The regular Spanish clergy was perhaps best typified by the lively body of Franciscan friars, who were thriving according to the 1787 census, with a total of 15,000 members inhabiting 700 of the 2,000 convents of male religious still in existence at that time. Another important group, especially in Castile, were the discalced or 'barefoot' religious, who followed a severe rule within the various orders. These included, in addition to the discalced Franciscans, the Carmelites, the Augustinians, the Trinitarians, and the Mercedarians. Such movements often provoked strong tensions within the original orders, as can be seen in certain Carmelite monasteries linked to the figures of Saint Teresa of Avila and Saint John of the Cross.

The Society of Jesus deserves a separate discussion. Its expansion in Spain was impressive and by the reigns of Philip III and Philip IV its numerous religious houses held some 2,000 members. However, relations between the Jesuits and the other religious orders – and in particular with the influential Dominicans – were not always cordial. But whether Jesuits or Dominicans, Augustinians or Carmelites, the regulars succeeded in creating a 'Spanish model' of religious and spiritual culture which by the early seventeenth century had established itself throughout the whole of Europe and beyond – before being overtaken and eventually giving way to a 'French model'.

The central crisis for the regular clergy in eighteenth-century Spain would come with the expulsion of the Jesuits in 1767. The members of this order were subjected to a highly secular polemic regarding their moral doctrines, the presumed or real extent of their wealth, and their missionary methods in the colonial territories. Their expulsion accentuated a widespread hostility against the monastic orders in general. Only the mendicant orders seemed not to have experienced such traumatic effects, thanks to their wide popularity in Iberian society.

The female convents, which numbered approximately 1,000 in the 1787 census and contained some 25,000 religious, were mostly 'open' institutions, in which post-Tridentine cloistered life was either not practised at all, or only practised with difficulty. The majority of these convents were controlled by their respective male orders. But in addition to the women religious, a phenomenon particular to Spain was the presence of the *beaterios*, groups of unmarried women and widows living as a community within the parish, and governed by the Augustinian rule. The concept of a 'less regular' religious life would often provoke suspicion on the part of the ecclesiastical authorities. Yet intense manifestations of piety and devotion flourished in both the observant and discalced monasteries and in the *beaterios*, a piety that would profoundly mark female religiosity (and general religious practice) in Spain during the modern age.

The regular clergy in Portugal, like the seculars, was very similar to that in Spain, notwithstanding some important differences. Detailed enumerations reveal that the number of Portuguese religious houses rose from 477 in 1739 to 493 in 1765. By the latter period there was a total of 42,200 regulars (30,772 male religious and 11,428 female). In any case it is certain that the reforms introduced by Pombal's government in the mid-eighteenth century had a strong positive impact on the organization of the Portuguese regular clergy – especially by comparison with the more tentative contemporary efforts carried out in Spain. The reforming efforts in Portugal culminated with two royal decrees issued in 1782 and 1788, one forbidding the establishment of new orders, and the other requiring the authority of the sovereign for admission to a religious order.

The regular clergy in France

With the end of the wars of religion in France, there was a strong revival of the regular orders. In the early 1600s, even before the bishops' reforms of the secular ecclesiastical structures, a vast movement of French 'reforms' swept through the older religious orders and monastic congregations, with profound repercussions not only for religious life in France, but in all of Europe. A general tendency towards the centralization of existing institutions through a system of federal connections was initiated among the Benedictines. The first community to undergo such transformations was the congregation of Saint-Vanne and Saint-Hydulphe in 1604. This occurred in Lorraine, in an area of strong friction between Catholics and Protestants, and thereafter it spread through France. These regulars went on to found the Congregation of Saint-Maur. By the end of the seventeenth century the reforming process had advanced so far that very few French Benedictine monasteries were still linked to the ancient and formerly glorious abbey of Cluny.

Outside the Benedictine world, in the first three decades of the 1600s waves of reform also permeated those institutions which lived according to the Augustinian rule, through a revival of the congregations of regular canons. These included the Union, or the congregation of regular canons of Our Saviour in Lorraine (*Le Sauveur*), established by Saint Pierre Faurier and approved by Rome in 1628; and the congregation of Prémontrés or Norbertines, reorganized in Lorraine, in 1630, and rapidly spreading not only in France, but in Bohemia and Poland as well, where they gave assistance to the parish clergy.

The mendicant orders appear somewhat more removed from these reforming impulses, with the notable exception of the Carmelites. The decalced reforms of Saint Teresa of Avila and Saint John of the Cross were welcomed in France with the establishment in 1611 of a male branch of the Carmelites, a group which would have a profound effect on religious life in France in the seventeenth century.

Already 'reformed', so to speak, were those new congregations of regular and secular clerics, such as the Jesuits and the Oratorians, who arrived and spread through France between the second half of the sixteenth century and the first decades of the seventeenth. The Jesuits were long opposed by the universities, the *parlements*, and the bishops who defended the Gallican traditions. The Oratorians, by contrast, were more readily integrated into French society.

However, despite their active presence, the religious orders in France would never assume the role they acquired in Spain, Italy, and those areas which experienced a Catholic re-conquest in the Habsburg monarchy and Poland. The French church was never dominated by religious orders – notwithstanding the major contributions of certain eminent individuals and reformed congregations. It was rather a church dominated by bishops and the secular clergy, and by those previously mentioned companies or congregations of priests who were dedicated to parish and missionary work. If anything, the impact of the French religious orders would be felt primarily outside Europe, where the work of the Capuchins, Dominicans, and Carmelites in the Levant; of the Jesuits in Canada and China; and of the priests of the *Missions étrangères* from 1664 onwards, would contribute to furthering the diffusion of Catholic Christianity and promoting a French presence in the Near and Far East and the New World.

A particularity of religiosity in France can be seen in the new engagement of women in religious life and society, in a context which was more dynamic than that of either Spain or Italy. In the course of the seventeenth century, women were able to choose an active religious and social mission within the framework of open congregations with simple vows which sprang up during the century. Such congregations included the Daughters of Charity, founded in 1634 by Saint Vincent de Paul and Louise de Marillac, and the congregation of Notre Dame, under the Augustinian rule. The latter was launched in Lorraine by Saint Pierre Faurier and Mother Alix Le Clerc in 1597, and quickly spread throughout France, serving primarily in the education of middle-class girls.

Active in preaching, popular missions, social welfare, and teaching, the male religious orders had about 25,000 members in 1768, living in 2,966 houses, monasteries, and convents. In that year a royal commission on the regular clergy began a series of investigations which would continue through to 1780, leading to a renewed dynamism for the regulars in the fields of education and teaching. The schools of the Christian Brothers, which had been founded by Jean-Baptiste de La Salle between 1694 and 1705 and were formally approved in 1725–26, flourished under this new impulse. Even if no systematic reforms took place in France in the later eighteenth century, there was nonetheless a consistent reduction in the numbers belonging to the male religious orders: from the some 25,000 in 1768 to slightly more than 16,000 in 1789, with a particularly large drop of 40 per cent among the Franciscans, and a more moderate decline of 27 per cent among the female orders. The structural weaknesses of the regulars, combined with an ever more pervasive hostility towards them in public opinion, would lead to their suppression by the French National Assembly in the early years of the Revolution.

The regular clergy in Italy

In the face of the relative weakness of the secular ecclesiastical structure in Italy, it was the religious orders that ensured the success of the Counter-Reformation in the sixteenth and seventeenth centuries. The development of the regulars was overseen by the Roman Curia through a congregation of the regular clergy in 1596, a congregation of bishops and regular clergy in 1601, and a congregation on regular discipline in 1598. It was also expedited by a series of privileges granted by two popes who had come from the ranks of the regular clergy: the Dominican Pius V (1566–72) and the Franciscan Sixtus V (1585–90). From the early 1600s onwards, the enormous expansion of the regular clergy in Italy brought negative consequences for their discipline. As a result, Rome began an investigation of the numbers and wealth of the religious orders in 1649 and initiated a series of reforms which would also benefit the secular ecclesiastical structure.

The data gathered at this time by the investigating commission reveal the extraordinary extent of the network of regulars in Italy. Not including monasteries and friars in Sardinia and Corsica and the congregations of the Oratorians and Lazarists, there were almost 70,000 religious distributed in 6,238 convents and colleges. Sixty-three per cent of the religious and 65 per cent of the institutions were situated in the Papal States, the vice-royalty of Naples, and Sicily. Some 1,513 monasteries and convents were suppressed in the first wave of reforms, but by 1654, when the commission completed its work, the Franciscans had already regained 200 convents out of the 442 which had been suppressed, while the Hermits of Saint Augustine had regained 123 out of 342. A total of 323 institutions had thus reopened. This rapid rebound of the regulars came both from pressure exerted by the orders themselves and from requests made by local authorities, arguing the usefulness of the 'conventini' (little convents) for pastoral service in inaccessible and isolated places, as small hospices for pilgrims and travellers, and as therapeutic centres where exorcist friars operated.

Developing in parallel to these reforms were initiatives which applied the recommendations of the Council of Trent to the female convents. The cornerstone of these reforms was the financial reorganization of the convents and the imposition of the cloister for all nuns who had made solemn vows. The latter transformation was particularly difficult, due to the resistance of the nuns themselves and their families, especially in the noble convents. But economic improvements were also difficult to achieve. The administration of the convents was reorganized, and many were changed into schools for girls, a process which was explicitly ratified in the eighteenth century by Leopold's reforms in Tuscany.

Rome would return to the reform of the male orders after 1694 during the pontificate of Innocent XII through the establishment of another commission for regular discipline. But once again the different orders succeeded in blocking the reforms, and in 1695 they even achieved a *de facto* suppression of the maximum number of entries, which had been in force for forty years. As a consequence there would be a continuing rise in the number of regulars throughout the first half of the eighteenth century.

The ecclesiastical reforms of Habsburg Enlightened despotism were particularly successful with regard to the regular clergy. In Josephist Lombardy, the 291 male monasteries and convents which existed in 1767–72 would be reduced to 200 by 1790–92, while the total number of regulars was reduced by 74 per cent. A similar trend may be found for the female convents, which were reduced from 164 in 1771 to only sixty-seven by 1790. In the Tuscany of Peter Leopold, 130 monasteries and convents out of 345 disappeared between 1765 and 1789, with a total reduction in the religious population of 43 per cent. Here too the female religious orders underwent an even more dramatic reduction, with the 237 convents existing in 1765 declining to 128 by 1768. In the meantime the number of 'veiled' nuns was almost cut in half: from 5,141 in 1767 to 2,670 in 1782.

In the absence of an overall plan, the Bourbon reforms in the Kingdom of Naples primarily affected the widespread Franciscan community, which made up more than 28 per cent of the entire male regular clergy in the realm. Various other suppressive measures were adopted after 1783 as part of the reconstruction of those areas following the terrible earthquake which had devastated Calabria and as a result of other more general political and socio-economic trends in southern Italy. In the end, the population of regular male clergy in the Mezzogiorno declined from about 30,000 individuals in 1765–66 to about 17,000 in 1801, a 44 per cent drop in thirty-five years. But Bourbon reformism was more hesitant with regard to the female orders. Between 1766 and 1787 the monastic population of this sector fell by only 16 per cent – from 22,828 to 18,777. The numbers of women religious would remain at approximately this level until the French occupation of the kingdom in 1801.

The regular clergy in the Habsburg domains and in Poland

In the hereditary Habsburg domains the contemplative orders, the mendicant orders, and the congregations of regular clergy had all played a role in the Catholic re-conquest of territories which had been lost to the Turks or to the Protestant Reformations. Perhaps more than any other groups, it was the Jesuits and the Capuchins who effectively embodied Austrian Catholicism: the Jesuits, with their schools and colleges at Vienna, Graz, Klagenfurt, and Innsbruck, but also with cultural and religious outposts in Wittelsbach Bavaria and the Catholic areas of the Holy Roman Empire; the Capuchins, with their aggressive missions active in the most difficult moments of the fight against Protestantism and, above all, against the Ottoman Empire. The situation in Bohemia was similar, where the Jesuits were solidly entrenched after the re-conquest, with eight colleges and eight residences, and where the Capuchins could claim thirty convents by 1782.

In Hungary and the Triple Kingdom the religious orders were more varied. Here at the time of the Josephist suppressions, there were some 152 male monasteries and convents with a total of 3,234 religious, to which could be added an additional twenty-five convents and monasteries in Transylvania. The majority of the male regulars belonged to the eighty-four Franciscan institutions, but twenty-five were in Jesuit houses, and another twenty-four belonged to the Piarists. In Hungary, in particular, Josephism would take a heavy toll on this clergy, with the suppression in 1781 of 134 male and female houses, with the expulsion of 1,484 male religious and 190 female religious, and with the transfer of the buildings and revenues of these orders to the secular clergy.

However, it was in the Habsburg hereditary domains that the Josephist suppressions of the regular clergy took on paradigmatic significance. A relatively short span of time saw the disappearance of some 700 male and female institutions, so that the population of the regular clergy was reduced from 65,000 to 27,000. The buildings and revenues of the suppressed religious orders were used not only for the secular clergy, but also for the needs of the general public. In addition, those regular clergy who had escaped suppression were redeployed into 'public service' positions. In sum then, in the space of only a few years, Josephism produced a veritable 'revolutionary' upheaval over a vast area where the Counter-Reformation and the religious and social forces which embodied it had once been so strong.

In Poland in the mid-sixteenth century, there had been fourteen monastic and mendicant male orders, and eight female orders. Over time other orders and congregations originating in Spain and Italy were also established, as well as the Lazarists who had come from France. A substantial increase occurred in the 1620s and 1630s, when another 250 houses were added to the 277 already in existence. Two-thirds of these belonged to mendicant orders, such as the Dominicans and the reformed observant Franciscans. The Jesuits were also particularly successful, their initial twenty-five colleges and residences expanding to forty-two by 1626, while the Jesuit corps of 512 members grew to nearly a thousand.

In the second half of the seventeenth century, despite the general political and social crisis that beset the country, another seven male religious orders were added to those already in existence, bringing the total number to twenty-seven – or twenty-eight if the Basilian Order, the only religious order of the Uniate Church, is included (whose male branch numbered in the eighteenth century over a thousand, distributed in 191 monasteries). Older religious orders like the Capuchins, and new congregations such as the Lazarists and the Bartholomists, found a prominent role as educators in the seminaries. The increase in the male religious orders would continue uninterrupted into the second half of the eighteenth century, through the first partition of Poland in 1772, when there were 14,600 religious in 860 institutions – a number which was equivalent, or perhaps even superior, to the numbers of the secular clergy. Unlike other areas of Catholic Europe, over 60 per cent of Polish religious were ordained priests, a factor which facilitated the pastoral work and ministry of the regulars and which probably explains the relatively few instances of indiscipline among the regular clergy, especially by comparison with other parts of Europe.

The female religious orders in Poland followed a similar upward trajectory, though the increases were not so dramatic. To the ninety-five houses in existence by the mid-seventeenth century, sixteen were added during the second half of the century, and a further thirty-two in the first half of the eighteenth century. These orders were eminently practical in their orientation. They included the Ursulines, known for their teaching, the Sisters of Mercy, who cared for the sick, and the Sisters of the Life of Mary, who originated in Lithuania and were established in 1737–39 with the aim of converting Jewish women and neophytes.

The first serious blow to the organization of the regular clergy was the suppression of the Society of Jesus in 1773, an event which had an especially grave impact on teaching institutions in Poland – even though the Jesuits survived without papal sanction in the then Polish territories of Byelorussia. Further damage was inflicted in the 1780s by the Josephist suppressions in Galicia, which had been awarded to Austria in the first partition. As a result, the population of the regular male clergy was reduced by a quarter and the female religious by a third from the mid-eighteenth to the early nineteenth centuries. But, although much reduced, the regular orders continued to play a prominent role during the century and a half when Poland disappeared from the map. Both regulars and seculars would profoundly stamp the religious life of the country, creating a model of Catholicism which was both similar to and distinct from the models found in the other nations of Europe. (Translation by Guyda Armstrong and Timothy Tackett)

6

The Protestant clergies in the European world

ANDREW R. HOLMES

The Reformation had radically altered the religious role and social standing of the clergy. The Protestant Reformers insisted on a general priesthood of believers, though it was rarely realized, and they rejected the view that ordination was a sacrament. Despite the apparent reduction in status this implied, the Protestant clergies remained a privileged body through the symbolism of their ordination, their university education, and their links by marriage with the ever-emerging middle classes. Their domestic arrangements helped to define religious and social respectability within the community, as they performed their role as the godly head of their household. In Zurich they modelled appropriate behaviour and piety as a reflection of the authoritarian state, while Toby Barnard notes that the Anglican parsonages of eighteenth-century Ireland were to be 'miniature godly commonwealths'. The reformers' ideal for an educated parish ministry was eventually achieved, but the process was a long drawn-out and complex affair. As with cultural change more generally in early modern Europe, the influence of tradition and the constant interplay between ideals and reality were often more important than revolutionary changes.

Between 1660 and 1780, the confessional rancour of the previous century gradually subsided and the Enlightenment exerted a moderating influence upon European religious life. The churches of Europe began to consolidate their position within society and in Protestant countries the general understanding of the status and function of the clergy outlined above was widely understood. Yet it is clear that the Protestant clergies of Europe between 1660 and 1780 must be described in the plural. Economic, geographical, and cultural differences shaped the type of minister called to a particular parish or church and how he was likely to approach his pastoral role. Different types of church organization, or ecclesiology, also influenced how a clergyman related to his congregation and what he felt able or unable to do. The nature of the state and the power relationships therein determined the precise association between the secular authorities and the clergy in matters such as appointment, promotion, education, and income. Matters were further complicated by the remnants of a ramshackle medieval system that bequeathed to established churches perennial problems regarding property rights and ownership of parish income. In countries such as Sweden, England, the Netherlands and numerous German states, the parish structure formed the basis of political and social organization and the prime means of Christianizing the people, thus providing the formal context in which a minister did his job. The position of voluntary and persecuted Protestant churches was more complex and led to a considerable degree of uncertainty as to the function and status of their clerical leaders. In areas where Protestants faced determined persecution, such as in France and Hungary, the authority of the clergy was seriously weakened and their power within the church was increasingly delegated to the laity.

Theological developments also shaped the Protestant clergies both in terms of how they saw their calling and the content and style of their preaching. Amongst more advanced sections of the clergy in this period, there was a drift from lengthy doctrinal sermons to lighter homilies that stressed morality and the common good. On the other hand, traditionalists and evangelicals sought to counter the influence of moral preaching either by focusing upon confessional orthodoxy or preaching personal salvation through Christ alone. The latter was a prominent feature of the Protestant revival in its Pietist and evangelical forms. The revival emerged in the face of Habsburg persecution and was shaped by social changes associated with the movement of populations, problems caused by urban growth and the early Industrial Revolution. As far as the spiritual life of the Protestant churches was concerned, the revival inculcated a more zealous and active commitment to the Christian faith that exercised a profound influence upon how many ministers understood and practised their vocation. The leading Lutheran Pietist, Philipp Jakob Spener, was concerned that the ministry was seen as merely an arm of the state and irrelevant to the everyday lives of the laity. Spener was a committed Lutheran pastor who wanted to reform the Church by reminding ministers of their pastoral responsibilities and realizing the priesthood of all believers through small fellowship groups. Though religious revival began as a means of self-preservation amongst persecuted Protestant minorities in eastern and central Europe, it became an indispensable pastoral strategy in the west. As social and economic change challenged how the church would minister to the surrounding population, evangelism and pastoral care became more important than the maintenance of confessional structures. At the same time as they intensified the sense of divine calling amongst the clergy they influenced, Pietism and evangelicalism also challenged the established status of the clergy by increasing the self-confidence of the laity and producing new denominations such as Methodism and Moravianism with their own distinctive, and protean, understandings of the ministry. The period between 1660 and 1780 therefore saw the emergence of a significant challenge to the religious and social status of the established Protestant clergies.

With this broader context in mind, this chapter examines the structures and experiences of the Protestant clergies of Europe in the decades between 1660 and 1780 and considers how their position in church and society developed over time. The five sections of this chapter examine key aspects of clerical life: social background, education, methods of appointment and subsequent career patterns, income levels, and status within the state and local community. A recurring theme will be whether or not the Protestant clergies can be described as a professional group during this period. It will become obvious that the early modern Protestant clergy were in an ambiguous position, poised between a traditional understanding of their calling and place within parish communal life, and an emerging sense of being members of a separate occupational group.

Social background

Compiling a collective prosopographical profile of the early modern Protestant clergy is almost an impossibility given the wide geographical and cultural variations between states and territories. This problem is further compounded by the conflicting conclusions that historians have drawn from the available evidence. Nevertheless, clerical recruitment did reflect the social and cultural characteristics of the society from which recruits came and it is possible to point to some general features. The Protestant clergies were predominately drawn from the middling or lower-middling ranks of society (sizeable farmers and the urban middle classes) with few noblemen or peasants amongst their number. As Nigel Aston points out, men decided to become clergymen for a variety of reasons, including personal religious commitment, hopes among younger sons for status and decent incomes, desire to continue a family tradition, and the prospects for social advancement. Over time, there was an increase in the proportion of clerics who were themselves sons of clergymen, which led to a process of self-recruitment amongst the Protestant clergies. In both the sixteenth and eighteenth centuries, the sons of clergymen provided the largest contingent of pastors in Württemberg, supplying respectively 63 per cent and 44 per cent of the manpower. By the late seventeenth and early eighteenth centuries, over a third of all Lutheran clergymen in German territories were the sons of pastors; in the years between 1680 and 1740 the proportion in Sweden was between 40 and 45 per cent. The social origins of the lower clergy of the Diocese of London during the eighteenth century conformed to this pattern: clergy 35.4 per cent; professions 30.6 per cent; plebeians 19.4 per cent; landed gentry 12.4 per cent; lesser nobility 1.2 per cent; schoolmasters 1 per cent. More generally in the Church of England the social status of recruits began to rise from the 1720s, owing to the increasing cost of university education and the pattern of self-recruitment. Though self-recruitment was important, studies that draw their examples from urban areas in Germany show that the clergy were just one part of the broader educated middle classes in urban areas, associated with legally trained office-holders in the state. Their position in this social group was consolidated through intermarriage that provided a ready-made structure for social and financial advancement.

It would be misleading to assume that the urban middle classes monopolized recruitment to the ranks of the Protestant clergy. Nicholas Hope has observed that after 1700 the majority of the Lutheran clergy of the German states and Scandinavia came from 'clergy families, better-off peasant farmers, the crafts, and a few civil servant families'. Both the lower and higher clergy were of 'extremely modest social background'. This accounts for the patterns of preferment and the provisions made for old age, as, for example, when a new incumbent would marry the widow or daughter of his predecessor in order to secure his financial future through the continuous occupation of the rectory and glebe. In Brandenburg-Prussia, 98 per cent of the clergy of the Lutheran state church were of 'rural commoner origin', while the remaining 2 per cent were from the lesser gentry. More significantly, the social backgrounds of nearly half the clergy in this region were not recorded, which suggests that their fathers may have been either artisans or peasants. The continued centrality of agriculture to the early modern economy was also reflected in patterns of recruitment in other areas. Given the minority status of the Anglican population in Ireland, the established church clung tightly to the Protestant state and local landed society. This link was reinforced by the lay appropriation of tithes and marriage patterns that resulted in, for instance, sixty-eight of the 118 beneficed clergymen in County Down either originating from landed society or marrying into it. In the Presbyterian-dominated north-east, of the 619 ministers who served the Synod of Ulster in the eighteenth century, 71 per cent were sons of farmers, 20 per cent sons of clergy, 4 per cent sons of merchants, 1 per cent of others, while 4 per cent were of unknown origin. It is clear from this summary that the clergy did not come from either the highest or lowest social groups within society but from the middling ranks broadly conceived. Yet, the social complexion of the clergy depended to a large degree upon the local economic and cultural circumstances from which it was derived.

Education

An educated ministry was an indispensable requirement for the Protestant churches of Europe. The clergy were not there simply to perform rituals but to teach God's word, and to teach it well they must be educated. The Reformers had achieved much by the early seventeenth century. By 1600 only a quarter of the pastors in Mecklenburg had no academic training while in England three-quarters of the clergy in most areas were graduates by the 1640s. The figures were higher in more solidly Calvinist areas. By 1619, 94 per cent of ministers in the Palatinate had a formal education in theology, while in the Netherlands a mere 1 per cent were not suitably qualified by 1630. The ideal was, however, prone to lapse in periods of civil strife, no more so than in England during the 1640s and 1650s. In the Canterbury diocese, 87 per cent of the clergy were graduates in 1637, but the proportion fell to only 66 per cent by 1662. Thereafter, the educational attainments of the Church of England clergy improved, and most English and Welsh dioceses required evidence of a university education prior to ordination. This did not mean that all ordinands had to be graduates and in more remote areas a graduate ministry could be rare; for example, only 5.9 per cent of the clergy resident in the diocese of St David's in Wales between 1750 and 1800 held degrees. Amongst non-established Protestant denominations, the ideal of an educated ministry was maintained with arguably more enthusiasm though possibly with less effect in some cases. One of the most successful examples was the Synod of Ulster, founded in 1690. Following the practice in Presbyterian Scotland, the Synod from the last decade of the seventeenth century demanded that their candidates for the ministry be graduates and in 1702 it was resolved that no man be entered for trials unless he had studied divinity for four years after he had graduated.

Unsurprisingly, the clergy of the state churches studied in the universities of their homeland. In central Europe, fifteen of the twenty-nine territorial universities were Lutheran, and this was repeated in Scandinavia and the Baltic region with such foundations as Copenhagen, Uppsala and Dorpat. Theology students also comprised the largest grouping within the student body and the church continued to exercise a significant influence upon the lives of ministerial students. Tübingen in south-west Germany had twice as many theology students as any other faculty and no less than a third of these had to take jobs outside of the church due to an oversupply of candidates. Even after university training replaced the education received in diocesan secondary schools in Sweden in the 1650s, the local diocese continued to supervise the education received at university. The clergy of the established churches of England and Ireland were educated respectively at Oxford and Cambridge and at Trinity College, Dublin. While at university, these students for the Anglican ministry had the opportunity to mingle with gentry and to establish contacts that would become indispensable when they eventually sought a parish.

Though the geographical mobility of students had decreased since the early seventeenth century, many students for the ministry continued to receive their education outside of their country of birth. According to W. R. Ward, Slovaks travelled to Jena, Germans to England and the Netherlands, the Swiss to Saumur, Heidelberg, Herbon, Leiden and Franeker, Hungarian Lutherans to Wittenberg and their Reformed countrymen to the Netherlands, Switzerland, and Oxford. Exclusion from territorial universities and active harassment meant tolerated Dissenters and persecuted Protestants had to seek their education elsewhere. In their quest to maintain the ideal of an educated ministry, English Old Dissent established their own academies. Over time these foundations encouraged the dilution of doctrinal conservatism that in turn was countered by the establishment of a number of evangelical academies from the 1730s. Despite their importance to the emergence of Dissent, these academies varied greatly in size and in the standard of education they offered. Other Dissenters and persecuted groups were forced to receive their training in other countries. Owing to their exclusion from Trinity College, Dublin, Presbyterians of Ulster were forced to travel to Scotland, particularly Glasgow, to receive a university education. In the Habsburg lands, the need to travel abroad was imperative, though it did have the advantage of establishing international links. For the Hungarian Reformed Church in particular, these links were forged early and maintained throughout the period. Special bursaries were formed for Hungarian students and the colleges at Sarospatak, Nargyenyed, and Debrecen received foreign endowment. Prospective French Protestant ministers were also forced by persecution to find opportunities for education abroad, establishing, with the surreptitious help of Bénédict Picet of Geneva, a seminary at Lausanne that functioned from 1727 to 1809.

The education and training of ministers did not end with their attendance at university, as church authorities continued to supervise them to ordination. The supervision of candidates for the ministry provided by hierarchical church structures was less intensive than that provided by Presbyterianism. In the churches of England and Ireland ordination examinations were usually less than demanding, and in some German states examination by the consistory was a mere formality once a patron had appointed the candidate to a church living, though this did not necessarily mean that he was unfit to do the job. In Presbyterian churches, presbyteries and ministerial conferences known as privy censures were better suited to ensure standards were maintained and to foster a sense of group identity. The imposition of bishops in Scotland by the Stuart monarchs between 1660 and 1690 did not entirely dismantle the Presbyterian system. After Presbyterianism was fully re-established in 1690, the examination by presbytery of students for the ministry (known as 'trials') was established by an act of the Scottish General Assembly in 1698. The Scottish model was predictably adopted in Ulster where, despite harassment by the Anglican authorities between 1660 and 1690, Presbyterians maintained a careful system of oversight by the presbytery, though in order to escape the notice of the state, the time and place of ordinations were kept from the congregation. In 1672, the general committee drafted an extensive list of regulations for trials and ordinations. The trials could extend over a period of seven months and encompassed the following elements: popular sermons; set exercises, known as 'common heads', on various themes such as Protestant tenets, Presbyterian principles, polemics and pastoral issues; disputations; an explanation of contradictions in Scripture; and examinations in foreign languages, history, and theology. With some modifications, the system would remain substantially the same in the following century. In 1770, a series of five regulations concerning the licensing and training of ministers was passed by the Synod of Ulster to ensure that candidates remained in university for at least four years. The regulations stipulated that candidates should attend natural and moral philosophy classes and were to be examined by the presbytery in science, Hebrew, Greek, Latin, logic, metaphysics, natural and moral philosophy, theology and church history. These examinations were spread over three meetings of presbytery, though if the candidate had attended university for four years only one meeting was necessary.

The subjects chosen for study demonstrate the extent to which Protestant clergies across Europe were shaped by the values and priorities of the times. The desired education for ministers reflected both the concerns of the Enlightenment and the desirability of a classical education. These regulations also hint at the disparity, sometimes great, between the theory and practice of ministerial education and preparation. For whatever reason, by the early eighteenth century in Scotland there was little insistence by church authorities upon attendance at divinity classes. An act of the General Assembly in 1711 further complicated matters by stipulating that ministers ought to study divinity for six years upon graduation. However, this did not mean full-time attendance at university but private study under the control of the presbytery, during which time probationers taught in parish schools to secure an income. The need of students to do so highlights the financial burden of a university education. Students from modest backgrounds could simply not afford to attend university for long periods of time. As Hope demonstrates, there was a considerable difference in Lutheran Germany between a gifted and well-connected elite who received an education of between five and ten years, and a poor ordinand who could expect at most two years of theological education on a course that was itself dependent on the whim of the lecturer.

With the exception of the Presbyterian churches in Scotland and Ireland, most European Protestant churches did not insist on demonstrated theological competence as a necessary qualification for new clergy. As noted, the Church of England only required evidence of a university education in the arts as a qualification for the ministry. The number of theology degrees held by Lutheran pastors remained small until well into the seventeenth century. In addition, there was a definite hierarchy in the type of qualification one could expect. Masters degrees were given to urban ministers (or graduates of Tübingen) and doctorates to superintendents or court preachers. When theological education was offered, it reflected the values of the church authorities and the often-outdated confessional politics that arose after the Council of Trent. Yet the so-called Lutheran scholasticism this produced had been weakened during the seventeenth century by the influence of Reformed theology and the development of a more spiritual and devotional approach, which laid the basis for the triumph of Pietist pastoral theology. These developments have led Nicholas Hope rightly to caution against overstating the 'coercive power' of theology. Most ordinands in the late seventeenth and early eighteenth centuries preferred 'customary and pastoral' rather than controversial doctrines. Beyond the inadequacy of theological education, practical training for the realities of parish life was in the words of Aston 'either minimal or nonexistent'. The picture that emerges is of clergymen generally ill-equipped to grapple with theological matters and thrust into parish ministry without any semblance of formal training in practical or pastoral matters.

There were exceptions to this pattern and attempts were made by church authorities to improve the oversight, education, and practical training of potential ministers. A number of instances may be cited. First, the tradition in Scandinavia was to train the Lutheran clergy in pastoral theology, and, given the attachment of the people to the state churches, this seems to have paid dividends. Second, during his tenure as Professor of Divinity at Oxford between 1763 and 1776, Edward Bentham gave annual lectures to Anglican ordinands, providing them with an overview of the Bible and the rudiments of Greek. The most significant attempt to make ministerial education more relevant emerged with the growth of Pietism and evangelicalism. Pietists were wary about old-fashioned scholastic Lutheranism and demanded a return to the simplicity of the New Testament church. They argued that ministerial training should not concentrate upon dry theology or homiletics, but upon the Bible, prayer, preaching, visitation and the organization of prayer meetings. These concerns were reflected in the curriculum of the university at Halle, founded in 1694. Until 1727 between 800 and 1,200 students passed each year through Halle, where they were exposed to the ethos and practices of Pietism. Evangelicalism in Britain also pioneered new approaches to ministerial education. One of the most remarkable institutions was Trevecca College, founded in 1768 in Wales to educate itinerant preachers for the Countess of Huntingdon's Connexion. Trevecca had no direct precedent though it did maintain the conviction of Protestants more generally that an educated ministry would be more socially respectable and better able to commend the gospel. The novelty of Trevecca was that it aimed to prepare men for the ministry rather than training the intellect. Classical learning and doctrine were not ignored, but lecturers concentrated upon personal religion and apologetics. Between 1768 and its demise in 1791, 212 students received an education at the college, the great majority of whom went into the ministry. Although there was no set duration of time for study and many attended for only a short period, Trevecca indicated the changing mood brought about by evangelicalism and provided the model for the better organized and regulated evangelical academies formed between 1780 and 1830 in England. An educated ministry remained indispensable, but the challenges accompanying the emergence of a modern society called for new methods of preparing individuals to minister to it.

Appointment and career patterns

The ways in which ministers were appointed to congregations reflected the ecclesiology of the denomination and the nature of the church–state relationship. Owing to their strong autonomous position, the church authorities in Württemberg appointed ministers directly to vacancies. In more absolutist states, the central government made great attempts to control all church patronage. The Swedish Church Law of 1688 had taken patronage from the hands of the nobles and given it to the crown. By 1693 the patronage of no fewer than 178 of Finland's 199 parishes was in the hands of the monarch. In a similar vein, a royal declaration in 1701 by Frederick, King of Prussia, determined that all pastoral appointments made by lay patrons must be ratified by his consistory. In other established churches the religious settlements of the sixteenth century produced a more complex situation and led to the alienation from church hands of parish appointments. Reflecting the situation as it had been for the previous century, in 1830 the proportion of patronage rights for parishes in the Church of England was in the following hands: 48 per cent laity, 24 per cent capitulary and parochial clergy, 12 per cent bishops, 9 per cent crown, with the remaining 7 per cent spread amongst a variety of groups. These bald national figures, however, mask regional variations. In the diocese of Canterbury, 60 per cent of the patronage of the 279 parishes was in ecclesiastical hands, including 105 parishes in the archbishop's alone.

The existence of lay patronage gave rise to a variety of problems. It could have a damaging effect upon the pastoral effectiveness of the parish clergy and the independence of the church. In Mecklenburg, lay patrons deliberately chose non-graduate ministers to ensure they remained in control of the parish. In the Netherlands, the rather weak position of the Reformed Church led to a conflict between regents and the church over the appointment of ministers and the content of sermons.[1] The position was just as complicated and fractious in Scotland where the ideal of a congregational call clashed with the reality of landlord and crown patronage. The right of the people of the congregation to call their own minister had been claimed by church leaders since the Reformation and a form of congregational call had been adopted with the establishment of Presbyterianism in 1690. Despite assurances given in the articles of union in 1707 that there would be no parliamentary interference in the Scottish religious settlement, parliament passed the Scottish Patronage Act in 1711, which put the right of presentment to a vacant parish in the hands of the legal patron, who in most cases was a local landowner. This reimposition of patronage fomented congregational strife that was in turn compounded by the occasional appointment of 'riding committees' by the General Assembly. These were special bodies of ministers charged with installing in parishes unpopular candidates who had been presented by the landlord against the wishes of the local congregation and presbytery. The problem was that the various parties in the patronage controversy were not united about the key issues, particularly amongst opponents of patronage who could not agree as to which groups of people should be eligible to call a minister. These disputes also had strong social and political dimensions, as patronage was controlled by the large landowners, including the crown, to the detriment of small and middle-sized landowners who comprised the majority of the board of heritors, the Scottish equivalent of the parish council.

The system of congregational calls tended to work more smoothly in non-established denominations, yet even here there were important differences as to who exactly had the right to choose a minister. English Presbyterians had a variety of methods and, depending on the congregation, 'the people' could mean the trustees of the congregation, regular contributors, or the majority of hearers. In some cases the incumbent simply appointed his successor. Compared with congregational and Baptist churches, English Presbyterians had a much higher view of appointment to the clerical office. The former saw an appointment to a vacant charge as a transaction between the individual pastor and the congregation whereas Presbyterians emphasized the importance of the presbytery in ordination, a rite which could sometimes be extended over a couple of days. In a similar vein, Ulster Presbyterians in the late seventeenth century issued a call to a minister through the presbytery, which often proved problematical as a shortage of ministers meant that presbyteries had to adjudicate between the respective needs of several congregations when deciding which call to approve. Procedures for calling a minister were tightened over the course of the eighteenth century, as presbyteries further consolidated control over the process and as the Synod of Ulster introduced a form of social segregation by which a minister could only be appointed to a congregation if he had received the support of two-thirds of the membership and those who contributed two-thirds of the minister's stipend. Although Presbyterian and independent churches were in theory more egalitarian than Episcopalians, which groups actually comprised 'the people' was determined by the hierarchical assumptions of the period.

The means of appointing a minister had an obvious impact upon clerical career patterns and promotion opportunities. Even in Presbyterian and Congregational churches there developed definite hierarchies of remuneration, and certain congregations, especially in urban areas, were much sought after by candidates. In Episcopalian churches across seventeenth-century Europe, there emerged an identifiable career structure for clergymen. A prospective clergyman often began as a schoolteacher and could potentially work his way towards a bishopric and once there towards a better endowed see or even the primacy. In the Church of England, the league table of episcopal incomes was headed by Canterbury, which had an annual income of £7,000, and extended downwards through sees such as Lincoln, valued at £1,500, to poor sees such as Bristol at £450 per annum. Although the English episcopate became an increasingly aristocratic body over the course of the eighteenth century, this did not mean that those who were appointed to bishoprics lacked the necessary pastoral and administrative talents. The archbishops of Canterbury generally displayed intellectual ability and had developed good administrative skills in a clearly defined career structure that extended from parish ministry, through appointment to a cathedral prebendary and then to the see. The same was true of the Church of Ireland where there existed both a well-defined hierarchy of sees and a definite career path to them; English appointees came through the vice-regal chaplaincy and Irishmen were usually deans. On average, an individual bishop in Ireland served a total of ten years each in two sees, with the greatest turnover occurring in the first round of appointments. Compared with appointments to the French episcopate, promotion within the English and Irish system was much more gradual and based upon obvious ability rather than noble birth, hence English bishops tended to be older than their French contemporaries.[2] Though such a defined career ladder suggests a degree of professionalization, initial appointment and promotion depended upon patronage networks, recommendations and family connections in addition to the candidate's ability. Appointments were therefore based on a mixture of influence and proven ability.

Though hierarchical structures provided a well-defined career ladder and curacies could, as in England, spell the first step in advancement, life was hard for the majority of the clergy. Graduates lacking family influence or the support of a patron were often consigned to poorly endowed, obscure rural livings that sometimes led to problems of clerical poverty, isolation, and loneliness. Many became curates, paid by the incumbent clergyman to perform his parish duties, and frequently forced to survive and maintain a degree of respectability on a mere pittance. Peter Virgin has concluded that no less than a fifth of curates in late Georgian England would remain as curates for the rest of their careers. An equally lonely existence awaited many Lutheran clergy in the German states and Scandinavia, especially in east Brandenburg with its poor livings and serious language problems, and in the Baltic regions where the clergy simply did not have the agricultural skills to live comfortably. Surrounded by an overwhelmingly Catholic population, Anglican clergymen in Ireland sought to alleviate the sense of isolation through correspondence, reading and some travel, though any companionship sprang from personal friendships rather than official arrangements. Churches did provide opportunities for those with ability to ascend to the dizzying heights of a bishopric or a wealthy urban congregation, yet for the majority of ministers, obtaining an adequate living was as much as could be hoped for, while many found themselves in isolated and dispiriting situations.

Income

Clerical income derived from two main sources: legal exactions or voluntary contribution. Established churches used the former, though as with appointments, the precise relationship between church and state determined the manner and method of payment. The pastors of the Reformed Church of Geneva were appointed directly by the Venerable Company of Pastors and paid a fixed public salary of £30 per annum. The Lutheran pastors of Württemberg were also paid a regular wage directly by the state, as were ministers of the state church in the Netherlands. In states with a more complicated church–state relationship, however, the clergy were forced to negotiate the complex and disheartening tithe system. The tithe was simply a notional tenth of the annual productive value of the parish, though it became more complicated when it was subdivided into various types and was levied and paid for in different ways. Over the course of this period, payment in cash became the norm, though in more rural areas payment in kind, whether through crops, labour or other payments, remained. To make matters more complicated, in Prussia, Scotland and England, tithes were often alienated to a lay proprietor. In Scotland, each parish was overseen by the board of heritors, a body comprising the main landowners in the parish and members of the Kirk session. They were responsible for the collection of the Scottish equivalent of the tithe, the teind, which covered the bulk of the minister's stipend. They were also responsible for the upkeep of the meetinghouse, manse, school, and glebe. Teinds were paid in kind or cash and were traditionally collected at harvest. The teind holder in a parish, usually a large landowner, was legally bound to pass on to the heritors a proportion of the teind, from which the heritors were to pay the minister. Ministers however were in a vulnerable position as teinds were heritable property and many teind holders resisted paying the full amount due to the minister.

The Scottish example illustrates the complexity of the tithe system and the clash between religious and secular priorities. The value of the tithe depended on a host of factors including climate, soil type, population density, the legal framework, the willingness or otherwise of the parishioners to contribute, the legacy of medieval endowments, and the broader political context. For example, the power of lay tithe owners in East and West Prussia, Mecklenburg and the Pomeranias, reduced the local Lutheran clergy to poverty with no hope of redress. The plight of Prussian pastors forced them into becoming in effect employees of their patrons, a situation that could easily alienate them from their parishioners. Tithe contributions nose-dived and clerical stipends drastically fell in value in Sweden and Finland as a consequence of the Great Northern War and seven major harvest failures between 1700 and 1721. These various factors produced an enormous diversity in clerical incomes across regions and forced clergymen to rely upon other sources of income. Given the difficulty of collecting the tithe from hard-pressed tenant farmers, Irish clergymen appointed tithe proctors who were empowered to collect parish dues in return for which they were allowed to keep everything above the sum agreed with the clergyman.

Extravagance and luxury did not characterize the bulk of the Protestant clergy of Europe. Indeed of the Lutheran clergy in Württemberg, who enjoyed a much more comfortable position within the state than the rest of the Protestant clergies of Europe, 30 per cent had incomes below the recognized living wage. Many Church of England incumbents were obliged to teach, farm or engage in other tasks, while in Ireland clergymen supplemented their income by preaching funeral sermons, collecting small dues for performing rites of passage, marrying into money, or sometimes conducting illegal marriages. The paucity of income and lack of parsonages contributed to the much discussed and potentially vexing issues of pluralism and non-residence. In England between 1705 and 1776 the incidence of clergymen who were incumbents of more than one parish increased from 16 per cent to 36 per cent, and though poverty was a reason it may also be related to a decline in the number of ordinands. Yet neither non-residence nor pluralism necessarily entailed pastoral neglect as many clergymen simply lived in a neighbouring parish or employed a curate. The case for pluralism in Ireland was more compelling given the extreme poverty of some dioceses. Of the parishes in the diocese of Ferns in 1712, for example, only thirty-two out of ninety-nine provided any income for the clergy.[3] The inequality of the legal means of payment did in some cases produce a two-tiered system. The traditional losers were the curates who, as noted for England, could often remain in their impoverished and vulnerable position for their entire careers. Yet, measures were taken to improve clerical incomes. Despite its drawbacks, Queen Anne's Bounty formed in 1704 to raise the incomes of small livings, paid out £3,401,600 between 1713 and 1844. Owing to the impact of the Bounty and, more importantly, increased land values and commutation windfalls resulting from land enclosure acts, the average income for the Church of England clergy increased significantly over the course of the eighteenth century. It has been calculated that in 1736 that 5,638 benefices out of an approximate total of 10,500 were valued below £50 a year and that 20 per cent of that number were below £10; by the early nineteenth century, only a third of the entire clergy earned below £150 a year. The greatest increases occurred amongst the lower clergy; the income of perpetual curacies (a type of endowed curacy, which provided the curate with a degree of security of tenure), for instance, increased by a staggering 686 per cent over the same period.

Compared with established churches, non-established churches across Europe were on the whole less wealthy, the payment and collection of stipend more haphazard, and the variation in levels of income greater. This was especially true of persecuted French Protestant pastors who could often expect nothing more than a bed for the night provided by a member of the congregation. In more settled areas such as Ulster, stipend arrears were a serious problem for many Presbyterian ministers in the late seventeenth century, though the existence of a strong system of church courts made it possible to force at least some of the recalcitrants to pay. In 1674, the Antrim Meeting decided to set a minimum stipend of £30 per annum, while congregations were instructed to provide their minister with housing, fuel, land, and grain. Often a minister's stipend was paid in kind, congregations providing peat, land, bolls of oats, labour and other commodities as well as money. Though arrears remained common, the regulations had made a salutary impact upon income levels by the 1690s when the average stipend rose to £33 9s 6d. The minimum stipend was increased to £40 in 1753 and to £50 in 1770. Nevertheless inequalities remained. By the 1790s, the ministers of only two congregations had incomes over £150 and 131 ministers received less than £60 per annum. As in established churches, overall economic, political and social developments determined the actual payment of the agreed stipend. For example, owing to poor harvests, only one minister in Ireland's Route Presbytery was paid his stipend in 1717. Old Dissent in England also experienced enormous variations in the level of stipend. An enquiry in 1690 found that actual incomes of Dissenting ministers could vary anything from 40s to £100 per annum, with the average stipend being between £20 and £40. These income levels left little margin in the event of poor harvests or other economic difficulties, and many ministers had to find alternative sources of income. By the turn of the eighteenth century, various funds were established to ease the financial pressures upon Dissenting ministers, yet local congregations remained primarily responsible for a minister's stipend and this proved a considerable burden for many. Perhaps ironically, both Presbyterians in Ireland and Old Dissenters in England received an annual grant from the crown known as the *regium donum*, or Royal Bounty, which was intended in part to ensure their political quiescence. This was symbolically important in Ireland and was augmented on a number of occasions over the course of the eighteenth century, though the actual share per minister would always remain small: £600 between eighty congregations in 1689 worked out at £15 each and an increase in the number of congregations reduced the share to only £8 of a competent stipend of £40 in 1702. The piecemeal augmentations of the Royal Bounty were dwarfed by a massive endowment after the Act of Union of Great Britain and Ireland, enacted in 1800, partly out of a desire to secure the loyalty of Presbyterians in the wake of the 1798 rebellion.

If the French Huguenots, English Dissenters and Irish Presbyterians often found it difficult to provide for their ministers, the problem for newly formed Dissenting groups was even more formidable. A Methodist itinerant preacher relied upon free board and penny-a-week subscriptions from class and quarterly meetings. Reflecting Wesley's own convictions, this system was predicated upon the interplay of voluntarism and connexionalism – the collection of money was a means to an evangelistic end rather than an end in itself. As with their better-established contemporaries, Methodist preachers attempted to supplement their income in other ways, including the sale of homemade medicines, though a ban on receiving an additional income was enacted in 1770. Such was the financial plight of local preachers that many did not become itinerants; indeed, half of the 200 preachers accepted between 1741 and 1765 failed to become career preachers. As their expectations began to increase in the late eighteenth century, the lack of financial resources became acute and the system showed increasing signs of vulnerability. After all, as David Hempton points out, the entire system depended upon 'frugality, goodwill, and bonds of affection' that could so easily be strained over financial issues.

Status in the state and local community

Depending upon the precise balance of power within confessional lands, the clergy were often part of the apparatus of the state which was reinforced by their educational attainments and family links with the secular elite. In central Europe, scholars have argued that there was a 'bureaucratization' of the Lutheran office from the seventeenth century, a process that produced a type of clergyman who became 'in effect yet another middle-ranking official'.[4] By his Church Law of 1688, Charles XI of Sweden stripped the clergy of their independence, reducing them in the exercise of church discipline to, in the judgement of Michael Roberts, 'the mere agents of the state in a matter of public policy' and paving the way for the dominance of lay control over the church in the eighteenth century. There can be no question that the clergy adopted various administrative and judicial functions on behalf of the state and in some cases became indistinguishable from secular authority. Yet there is a danger of overestimating the politicization of the established clergy. The clergy were not solely or, in many cases, even partly, servants of the state. They had their own sense of calling and responsibilities that often conflicted with the aims and intentions of secular state policy. The majority were more concerned with the practicalities of running a parish, collecting stipends, and caring for the souls of their parishioners. The state in this period may have been extending its influence and structures but it was not so powerful as to be able to interfere systematically with the complexity of traditional parish life and day-to-day ministry.

The status of the clergy within voluntary or persecuted Protestantism was different again from that of their legally established counterparts. Owing to their geographical concentration and well-established church structures, the Presbyterian minister in Ulster occupied a prominent place in local communities. More significantly in political terms, Dissenting ministers in both Britain and Ireland were often found at the vanguard of republican politics as a result of their exclusion from the power structures of the state. An estimated sixty-three Presbyterian ministers in Ulster were implicated in the 1798 rebellion that aimed to overthrow British rule and establish an independent Irish republic. For less fortunate clergymen in Hungary and France the possibility of political activism was severely curtailed and the laity assumed their role as the political leaders of their communities.

How did the social origins, education, methods of appointment, career patterns, and income levels of the clergy affect their status in their local communities? On the whole, their status was ambiguous. On the one hand, on account of his education, ordination and income, the local clergyman was a person set apart, the representative of official religion and of the state if he was a minister of the established church. The absence of an extensive nobility in Württemberg and Sweden allowed the clergy to act as equals with the gentry and thus assume a conspicuous place in local society. In England the social and financial improvement of the clergy led to what has been termed their 'gentrification' over the course of the eighteenth century as they self-consciously became part of 'a propertied hierarchy' by the late Georgian period. More generally, the clergy were aware that they were part of the educated middle class that set them above the parochialism and ignorance of their rural parishes. Such an elevated status and an increasing identification with the social elite ran the risk of alienating the laity whose souls had been charged to their care. This was precisely the concern that animated Spener to seek ways of making the Lutheran pastoral office more responsive to the spiritual and practical needs of parishioners. Yet the danger of irrelevancy was tempered by the fact that the majority of the Protestant clergy were immersed in rural life, ministering to the people of the locality, sharing their joys and sorrows, working the same land and dealing with the same climate. According to Nicholas Hope, Lutheran pastors in the German lands and Scandinavia derived their status from being part of a local clerical family rather than from their social background. They were the guardians of the local Reformation tradition that was reinforced by their family's continuous occupation of the vicarage farm. In many areas such as central Europe, England and north-east Ireland, parochialism was strengthened by the tendency to appoint local men to vacancies. Such a close relationship with the local community undoubtedly had its advantages, but ministers could be hampered in their efforts to reform unofficial practices and beliefs by tradition, etiquette, patron interference, and the insularity of pre-modern parish life.

In general terms, the relationship between the clergy and the laity was symbiotic. In return for a salary and attentiveness during public worship, the laity expected ministers to conduct the weekly services, to preach adequately, to visit the sick and to be aware of significant developments in the life of the parish. The equilibrium of clerical–lay relations was upset when the traditional pattern of doing things was disrupted by the ignorance or calculation of the minister, the narrow-mindedness of the laity, or changes within society more generally. For example, compared to the systemic character of anticlericalism in France, incidents of anticlericalism in Britain were usually the result of local conflicts rather than a criticism of the system. Disputes only became common from the 1760s as a consequence of the rising financial status of the clergy and their appointment as magistrates. Yet in Scotland, Callum Brown has noted that hostility towards the clergy was 'hardly present at all' owing to their shared experience of hardship produced by the modernization of the Scottish economy.

Whether the developments outlined above promoted the professionalization of the Protestant clergies depends to a considerable degree upon what is taken as the measure. In addition to their monopoly of preaching, they took on other marks of an early modern profession, including a specialized education and training, a sense of belonging to a defined occupational group with its own language and symbols, and a clear sense of their role within the broader community. It is clear that despite changes in the intellectual, economic and political climate, they retained a commitment to a number of standard duties such as preaching, catechizing, pastoral visitation, and the performance of the rites of passage (baptism, confirmation or first communion, marriage, and burial). Pietism and evangelicalism certainly ensured that the performance of these duties was more thorough and focused, but it would be unwise to denigrate the sincere efforts of clergymen who did not share these views and who did the best they could in often trying and demoralizing situations. Arguably, the Protestant clergy could never become simply a professional group. As with the relationship between Christianity and culture more generally, the precise relationship between the spiritual vocation of a minister and the secular understanding of that calling would always be ambiguous. Yet it was within this context that individuals decided to become clergymen and it is the struggle they experienced between their spiritual calling and the demands of the world that should be of perennial interest to scholars of the Christian tradition.

Notes

1. J. L. Price, *Holland and the Dutch Republic in the seventeenth century: The politics of particularism* (Oxford: Oxford University Press, 1994), pp. 74–80.
2. D. J. Roorda, 'Contrasting and converging patterns: Relations between church and state in western Europe, 1660–1715', in A. C. Duke and C. A. Tamse (eds.), *Church and state since the Reformation: Britain and The Netherlands vol. VII – papers delivered at the seventh Anglo-Dutch historical conference* (The Hague: Martinus Nijhoff, 1981), p. 139.
3. S. J. Connolly, *Religion, law and power: The making of Protestant Ireland 1660–1760* (Oxford: Clarendon Press, 1992), p. 183.
4. R. Po-Chia Hsia, *Social discipline in the Reformation: Central Europe 1550–1750* (London: Routledge, 1989), pp. 17–18.

7

Reaching audiences: Sermons and oratory in Europe

JORIS VAN EIJNATTEN

During the 'long' eighteenth century, the social and intellectual pressures brought to bear on the sermon as a medium of communication were stronger than ever before. Other channels – the newspaper, the journal, the novel, the public lecture, the coffee house, the debating club, the learned society – were rapidly appropriating its educational and moralizing functions, while audiences were beginning to shift their attention elsewhere. Nevertheless, the sermon remained a chief conduit of public instruction throughout the period, its presence prominent, its appearance varied. The following account is divided into four sections. 'Manifestation' describes the general appearance of the sermon between 1660 and 1800; 'Aspiration' examines its aims; 'Tradition' discusses the confessional type of sermon; and 'Transformation' outlines the successful response of the eighteenth-century sermon to the challenges it faced.

Manifestation

Sermons still catered mostly to organized groups of hearers gathered in a church, but throughout the period there were notorious instances of informal assembly, including the Pietist conventicle and the revivalist gathering. Pietist lay preachers such as the Norwegian Hans Nielsen Hauge (1771–1824) travelled considerable distances on foot to preach, in violation of the law, and he was frequently imprisoned for doing so. Female preachers too could be found outside the dominant institutions, among Quakers and nonconforming Pietists, and in private enclaves within churches, especially among evangelicals. Whilst the place of venue was usually a church – public or clandestine – it might just as well have been a field, a park, a public hall, or a marketplace. Wesley turned to the open air when he found the Anglican pulpit closed to him, and he persisted in doing so, three or four times a day, for half a century until he was eighty-eight years of age. Methodist preachers bypassed official channels through their itinerancy, as did Moravians or Herrnhutters. But most sermons were held at prescribed times in fixed locations by established clergymen.

Year in, year out, the message of the gospel was broadcast to urban or rural congregations of varying size, gender, profession, and social standing. Social distinctions were significant, perhaps even more so in this period than before. The French priest who addressed one audience as *mes sœurs* but felt compelled to address another as *mesdames* is not atypical. In the commercial, bourgeois society of western Europe it was also not unusual to find an audience of highly educated lawyers, magistrates, politicians and academics, such as the Rolls Chapel in London where Joseph Butler (1692–1752) preached as a young man, or the Walloon church at Utrecht where eloquent speakers addressed Francophone high society. The court sermon was an exclusive event, the forum of the most articulate and the best paid sermonizers, where dignitaries, despite the protocol, might send their servants to occupy the best pews in advance. At Versailles seats were kept warm from six in the morning when it was known that the Jesuit Bourdaloue would preach in the afternoon. A charismatic individual and boundlessly popular sermonizer like George Whitefield (1714–70) attracted larger crowds, stemming mainly from the lower middle class, and reached an even greater audience through advertisements and press coverage in newspapers.[1] The role of listeners before, during, and after the sermon ranged from active participation to passive consumption. There were those who cried out, quaked and fell prostrate, those who read newspapers and those who slept throughout. Inner compulsion and social obligation were obvious reasons for attending a sermon. In this age of perfumes and periwigs, sermon attendance might just as well be an excuse to flirt with an eligible marriage partner, or show off a new dress in the latest fashion, or simply hear the recent news. Good sermons were 'info-tainment', early modern style; an excellent preacher was as worthwhile a visit as a celebrated actor at the theatre. It was said in England in the 1740s that 'those who had not heard Farinelli sing and Foster preach, were not qualified to appear in genteel society'.[2]

Sermons were held in the mornings, in the afternoons and sometimes in the evenings, usually every Sunday, and on the festive days as well. Extraordinary sermons held during Advent and Lent and missionary sermons were specific to the Catholic world; occasional sermons, on the other hand, were an ecumenical enterprise. Occasions for holding sermons included official celebrations, the jubilees of princely rulers, days of lamentation, the commencement of a war or the signing of a peace treaty. Epidemics, scarcities, natural disasters, fires and omens in the heavens (the latter less frequently as time went on) were all interpreted in sermons. A major catastrophe such as the Lisbon earthquake of November 1755 induced a variety of theological readings from the pulpit. There were sermons for every rite of passage, including baptism, confession, and marriage. Death and entry into a convent offered yet other occasions. There were sermons, provoked by the ups and downs of daily parish life and the information in press reports, on drinking, dancing, luxury, frivolity, and a host of other bad habits. Sermons recording or celebrating important political or ecclesiastical events (the birth of a prince or the opening of a synod) now and again developed into voluminous histories, chronologies, and genealogies. Bibliographers are sometimes hard put to distinguish between this kind of sermon and a reference book.

Following the recommendations of Trent, most Catholic homiletic guidelines suggested that fifteen to thirty minutes for a sermon preached (in the vernacular) during Sunday Mass was quite satisfactory. Extraordinary sermons, as distinct urban events taking place independently of the celebration of the Eucharist, were substantially longer. In any case, homiletic rules were regularly trespassed upon, especially in Protestant pulpits where sermons of up to two hours were hardly uncommon. For Catholics the sermon was not usually the main event during public worship, a view shared by some Protestants, if for different reasons. The Moravian leader Nikolaus Ludwig, Graf von Zinzendorf (1700–60), rated the efficacy of liturgy at least as high as that of sermons. He believed that to sing of salvation and to read the Bible was no less pertinent to gatherings of the faithful – which did not prevent this gifted, imaginative if somewhat disorderly spiritual leader from delivering a great many extemporaneous *Reden* and *Ansprachen* (talks and addresses). They were copied earnestly by listeners in Berlin, London, the Dutch Republic, and Pennsylvania, and subsequently published.

Between 1660 and 1800 published sermons appeared in enormous numbers. Such publications are not necessarily representative of what preachers actually offered their audiences and they tend to reflect an urban rather than a rural setting. Sermons intended for the press were generally expanded and polished after delivery. The Pietist August Hermann Francke (1663–1727) was one exception. Students wrote down his sermons and Francke habitually committed them to the printing press after a usually cursory examination. Occasional sermons were among the most commonly printed. They were delivered from the pulpit only several times a year, so that we know less than we should like about the regular run-of-the-mill Sunday sermon. For publishers, sermons were an interesting investment, a commodity saleable to an anonymous public. The commercial context, however, was usually more complicated than the simple laws of supply and demand might indicate. Especially Catholic festive sermons were regularly paid for by the organizers and spread or presented as gifts, just as funeral sermons were usually funded by relatives of the deceased. There was in any case a large demand for instructional literature, including sermons. For the illiterate, published sermons read aloud may have been instrumental in achieving literacy. Sermons for the 'common man' and sermons for children appeared with increasing frequency, often in cheap duodecimo editions. As ideals of social and educational reform gained momentum, the market began to be supplied with sermons for the peasantry (a group that figured particularly large), sailors, soldiers, spouses, youths, young ladies, and the elderly.

Preachers-in-print ranged from village pastors to university professors, bishops, and superintendents. If prefaces and forewords are to be believed, sermons were published with a view to instructing flocks and assisting less talented or less experienced colleagues. Publications served also to augment meagre incomes, to further ecclesiastical or academic careers and generally to affirm the reputation of sermonizers; preachers who aimed to advance from the provinces to Paris, and from Paris to the court, realized that achieving a certain standing as a sermonizer was mandatory. Posthumous publications were quite common. Bought and kept as mementos, such collections were issued by relatives, friends, or colleagues. Review writers in the new periodicals faulted the practice because few such compilations lived up to their standards of literary taste, and because defunct authors were regrettably not amenable to correction. Some renowned experts on oral delivery set examples of modesty by stipulating in their wills the destruction of their manuscripts. The Dutch Calvinist minister Bernard Smytegelt (1665–1739) left such an instruction, and the only reason why his 145 discourses on the single text of Isaiah 42:3 ('a bruised reed shall he not break') are still extent in seventeen quarto volumes is because pious disciples took the trouble of transcribing them in church. From Berlin to London, transcription was a chief means of obtaining copy for the many profitable pirate editions of sermons by famous preachers.

Published sermons could, and spoken sermons often did, borrow extensively from the oratorical work of others. Such plagiarism was not necessarily frowned upon. The Anglican episcopate made a point of recommending the practice to young preachers, and few priests denied the utility of quoting passages from Bossuet. Busy, inexperienced, unimaginative, maladroit or merely indolent clergymen put sermon collections to good use, employing them to find relevant themes, suitable passages, apposite quotes, and even complete texts. The culture of consumption thus extended to sermons; in England there apparently existed a market for sermon texts supplied by hack writers and frequented by needy clergymen.[3] The proliferation of printed media even turned sermons into a collector's item. Out of appreciation for their consolatory character, the *Reichsgräfin* Eleonore zu Stolberg-Stolberg (1669–1745) amassed some 25,000 different funeral sermons.[4] A prolific and bestselling writer was the Capuchin Prokop von Templin (1608–80), whose more than 2,600 sermons were published in thirty volumes characteristically titled Eucharistiale, Poenitentiale, Orationale, Mariale, and Decalogale. The sermons of Franz Volkmar Reinhard (1753–1812), Lutheran court preacher in Dresden, filled no less than forty-two volumes (published 1815–21); he is said to have addressed three or four thousand people every Sunday. But there were many prolific sermon writers, some of whom reached audiences far beyond their native lands: they included the English Nonconformist Philip Doddridge (1702–51), the Scots Presbyterian brothers Ralph (1685–1752) and Ebenezer (1680–1756) Erskine and the German Lutheran Johann Jakob Rambach (1693–1735), to name but a few. Series of collected sermons became more popular towards the end of the eighteenth century, such as the (much-translated) sermons of Georg Joachim Zollikofer (1730–88) or Hugh Blair (1718–1800). Each nation produced its own steady sellers, but in this period in western Europe, John Tillotson (1630–94) was certainly one of the most revered sermon writers. His sermons were published and republished in English, French, Dutch, and German, and his influence was pervasive.

Aspiration

Some Catholic preachers – including Jacques Bénigne Bossuet (1627–1704) in a sermon held in 1661 on Matt. 17:5 ('This is my beloved Son, with whom I am well pleased; listen to him') – conceived the sermon in analogy to the Eucharist. Where the altar symbolized the physical reality of Christ, the pulpit represented his verbal reality; whilst hearers experienced 'inner preaching' through the Eucharist, they witnessed 'outer preaching' through the sermon.[5] The impact of the early modern sermon might be enhanced by combining oratory with other, audio-visual methods of communication. Jesuit, Oratorian, or Capuchin missionary sermons were sometimes integrated into elaborate shows replete with banners, processions, choruses and dramatic action performed in front of imposing stage designs. Evangelicals set spiritual texts to spirited melodies. If a lengthy Calvinist exposition and application of a passage from the Bible seems far removed from such exuberance, the aim and form of most if not all sermons was quite similar. For the purpose of this outline, we may regard the early modern sermon as an oral discourse on the Christian faith intended to instruct and motivate a congregation, and frequently but not invariably centred on the exegesis, interpretation, and application of a biblical text. Such a discourse might take on the form of a thorough exposition of doctrine, a prolonged biblical commentary, or a brief, edifying address or 'homily'.

In both the Protestant and Catholic Reformations, sermons were regarded as requisite to internalizing the faith. Tridentine reforms had been implemented by the newly established orders of the sixteenth century, among which the Jesuits in particular remained significant as preachers, at least until the dissolution of the order in 1773. The seventeenth century also produced a number of highly active preaching congregations, such as the Capuchins and the French Lazarists or Vincentians, founded specifically for the purpose of preaching missions to the poor in the countryside. Missionary priests specialized in sermonizing, and were capable of adapting their sermons to wholly different types of public. One of the great French evangelizers of the period, Jacques Bridaine (1701–67), held 256 missions in towns and villages throughout France, gathering the slothful townspeople by walking ostentatiously through the streets, loudly ringing a bell.[6] Despite this prominent role of the religious orders, the period as a whole witnessed a relative shift in overall sermon production from the regular to the secular clergy.

The self-image of the preaching clergy remained largely undented, despite the anticlericalism of Pietist and Enlightenment critics. Post-Tridentine homiletic guidelines, usually written by Jesuits, had enlarged on the preacher's sense of self. They tended to emphasize the disconcerting void between the elevated deity and the lowly preacher. The latter acted as an emissary of the Lord – as an angel, according to some – bringing the message of salvation to earthly vales of lamentation. To be able to mediate between God and the audience, the high office of preacher required, above all, humility, obedience, and a sense of unworthiness.[7] Much emphasis was put on the preacher's vocation, piety, and humility: homiletic reforms in the confessional period thus involved the sermonizers more than they did the hearers. Metaphorical self-representations of the preacher abounded among both Protestants and Catholics; the more colourful included the hawker of comestibles (serving milk to beginners and strong meat to the advanced), the innkeeper supervising a Christian banquet and the physician who ministers spiritual cures to ailing patients.

Sermons frequently had a highly structured format, with complex divisions and subdivisions. In the course of the period, however, less artificial arrangements became more common. Sermons were increasingly informed by literary standards and the conviction that simple ideas simply expressed were more effective in moving the human heart. The structure of the sermon could be based on the discursive development of a biblical or moral theme, as in the Reformed sermon, which usually took the exegesis of a biblical verse as its point of departure. Catholic preachers were more inclined to organize their sermons according to an external theme. Thus, in Germany, the popular 'class' sermon (*Ständepredigt*) mirrored the social order, successively reviewing each social level, age group, and profession. Another well-liked genre was the 'letter sermon'. The name JESUS, for instance, offered the more imaginative sermonizer an opportunity to enlarge on the typological meanings implicit in the letter 'I'; he might consider Jacob, Joseph, Joshua, and Isaiah, as well as *iustus, iudex*, and illuminator.[8] Reformed preachers, less constrained than their colleagues in the choice of subject matter, liked to employ the *lectio continua*, that is, producing series on a particular biblical book or a catechism. Among the Lutherans, the Württemberger preacher Georg Conrad Rieger (1687–1743) sermonized no less than one thousand times on Matthew, and even then only got to chapter 19. There were other methods of 'invention'; John Newton (1722–1807), the Anglican evangelical, published fifty sermons on the biblical verse used in Handel's *Messiah*. In the Lutheran world the use of pericopes and a fixed preaching scheme that reflected the liturgical year was obligatory, putting the less resourceful at a disadvantage. Preachers therefore utilized rhetorical schemes which allowed the sermon to take on different forms, or ensured variety by taking recourse to collections of anecdotes, parables, examples, and quotes from pagan and patristic antiquity.

Calvinist preachers followed older theorists such as Johannes Hoornbeek (1617–66), who regarded the sermon as 'a holy act in which Scripture is explained and applied with the aim of edifying the church'.[9] Most preachers of the confessional period would have agreed that the sermon ought to convey instruction, intellectual and moral, to an audience. The Pietist Philipp Jakob Spener (1635–1705) censured excesses in his *Pia Desideria* (1675), an influential call for urgent reform combining theological reflection with a practical attitude. He insisted on *Erbauung*, or edification, as the sermon's central aim and contended that a sermon should, above all, be intelligible and clear. Followers of the German philosopher Christian Wolff set great store by rational argument, concise terminology and transparent arrangement, precisely to counter what they regarded as amorphous Pietist oratory. The Prussian king Frederick William I even attempted to introduce the Wolffian sermon model by officially prescribing the homiletics of Johann Gustav Reinbeck to his clergy in

1739. Clarity, in effect, was stressed by all writers on homiletics before and after Spener; and most affirmed that a sermon's objective was cognitive (knowledge of the faith) as well as active (the godly life).

What changed in the course of the period was, firstly, the relative emphasis put on moral edification rather than doctrinal instruction, and, secondly, the appropriation of methods considered most suitable to transmitting a timeless message to a tangible audience. The growing stress on effective transmission and on the perennial hermeneutic problem of communicating the Bible's good tidings to the modern world suggested that the sermon's language and content had to be accommodated to the listeners. One of the outstanding sermon reformers of that age, Johann Lorenz von Mosheim (1639–1755) – who like Spener insisted on *Erbauung* – argued that only clarity of argument enlightened the intellect, and that only an Enlightened intellect edified the will. A sermon had to convince, which in Mosheim's influential view meant that Scripture and reason must not and could not contradict one another, that pulpit oratory reflected the same rhetorical principles as secular oratory, and, above all, that preachers must address themselves to specific audiences in specific contexts. For the Scots Presbyterian, Hugh Blair, a no less authoritative writer on the subject, pulpit oratory was the 'art of placing truth in the most advantageous light for conviction and persuasion'.[10]

Apart from the publications of Mosheim and Blair, the major homiletic writings of the period include Charles Rollin's *De la manière d'enseigner et d'étudier les belles-lettres* (1726–28) and Fénelon's *Dialogues sur l'éloquence en general et sur celle de la chaire en particulier* (written in 1681, first published in 1718). Both were read and quoted throughout Europe. For Fénelon, the aim of pulpit oratory was to instruct minds and improve morals, and the way to achieve this was to *prouver, peindre et toucher* respectively the intellect, the fancy, and the emotions. What Mosheim was to Protestantism, Jean-Siffrein Maury (1746–1817) was to Catholicism; his *Discours sur l'éloquence de la chaire* ran to thirteen French editions between 1777 and 1851. Such books were prescribed at academies and seminaries or utilized by preachers in the field. Other aids included sermon collections (*Postillen*) in all shapes and sizes. Some provided continuous commentaries on a book of the Bible; some offered encyclopaedic overviews of *praedicabilia*, ordered thematically or alphabetically; some appeared as theological tracts to which the author appended an index *concionatorius*. Reference works and auxiliaries included emblematic lexicons, encyclopaedias, thesauruses, anthologies of metaphors, parables, antitheses, and histories, many of which were given exotic titles such as *aurifodinae, promptuaria,* or *deliciae*. Growing interest in education eventually resulted in expositions of simple homiletic rules and in magazines and journals devoted to the sermon.

A sermon failing to appeal to the emotions was considered barren. That conviction was shared by the evangelicals of the age, who used every homiletic device at their disposal (rhetorical question, antithesis, sheer repetition) to achieve their one great aim: saving men and women from hell by confronting them with their own iniquity, awakening their consciences and bringing them to conversion. Such preaching, couched in simple language, was all the more effective for being delivered extemporaneously; success in spontaneous delivery might indicate divine inspiration. George Whitefield was one master preacher who delivered some 18,000 sermons off-hand with the skill of a great actor, keeping a goodly stock of anecdotes at hand. He possessed a voice of such amplification that (according to Benjamin Franklin's computations) it was theoretically capable of reaching an audience of several tens of thousands in the open field. Some groups, Dutch Arminians and Scottish Calvinists for example, were unanimously and adamantly opposed to sermons being read verbatim from the pulpit. By contrast, many reformers (Hugh Blair was a notable exception) increasingly favoured the memorized or even the read sermon, since preaching extempore hardly vouchsafed eloquence. Most Catholic theorists apparently preferred sermons to be memorized, but it is questionable whether more than a minority of French *curés* or Austrian *Pfarrer* ever did so. Bossuet, after all, had not learnt his sermons by heart, and Fénelon objected to the practice. All writers on the topic, however, agreed that even when a speaker planned to improvise, he should assiduously prepare himself beforehand in his study.

The prayer-day sermon was probably the most common occasional Protestant sermon, held at the behest of the secular authorities in times of war and disaster, in order to implore divine help, confess communal sins and ward off divine punishment. The popularity of these 'jeremiads' declined only towards the end of the period; rather than reflect on the sins of the people and prophesy immediate divine intervention, the later sermons discussed society's moral deficiencies and the providential threat of imminent, immanent national decline. Prayer sermons fulfilled a similar 'nationalizing' role in Protestant Europe as did the festive sermons of the Catholic Baroque. In Austria after 1663, the so-called Leopold sermons held in honour of the Austrian patron saint spread among the populace a consciousness of Austria as a cohesive national unit subordinate to one reigning house.[11] Specific kinds of sermons had specific aims. The purpose of the Catholic *Heiligenpredigt* or festive sermon was twofold. It encouraged adoration of the saints by evoking admiration for their deeds and it inspired imitation of their virtues. This species of sermon was closely related to the funeral sermon, the aim of which was to praise the dead, console the bereaved and instruct the audience. Funeral sermons were idiosyncratic in the sense that they contained a biographical sketch of the deceased. Especially common among, but by no means restricted to, Lutherans in the central part of the empire, funeral sermons increasingly developed into unadulterated panegyric in the decades around 1700. Only nobles and wealthy burghers could afford the splendid printed sermons which preachers vied among each other to produce. Adorned with sumptuous portraits, Hebrew and Greek types, and even funeral music, sermons in folio or quarto format served as epitaphs to the dead, as extravagant portable gravestones commissioned in limited editions by the family. Critics, such as the Rostock theologian Heinrich Müller (1631–75) who discarded *Leichpredigten* as *Leichtepredigten* (funeral preaching as slight or trifling preaching) censured a genre increasingly given to eulogizing the deceased rather than encouraging the living.[12] Yet the fashion of printing sumptuous funeral sermons declined only after about 1750, partially in response to changing attitudes to death; among Catholics these sermons flowered, albeit less profusely, until well into the 1780s.

Towards the end of the eighteenth century, sermons focused on improving the moral condition of the congregation. They consequently took into account the various spheres of life, civilian, social and private; clergymen could now sermonize on philosophy, nature or the realms of politics, and economics. A 'nature sermon' on a tree, for example, might give thought to the selfless person who had planted it for the benefit of posterity.[13] Pulpit oratory devoted to economics might treat subjects such as commercial fraud, parsimony, the utility of hygiene and the harmfulness of superstition to agriculture. Others addressed such topics as Frederik II, the Society of Jesus, political revolutions, the corruption of court life, shipping and press freedom. Sermons had, of course, long been utilized for political ends. Before the Revolution, the French clergy had been obliged to inform Sunday congregations about administrative and legal directives; since 1695, government notices were read from the pulpit towards the end of Mass. Neither Enlightened regimes nor revolutions changed the political function of the pulpit. In the Austrian Netherlands, Joseph II typically used the pulpit as a medium for disseminating the contents of imperial edicts and ordinances. It may be argued that sermons were (and are) political in yet another sense. As public statements, sermons are inherently political, in that they reflect presuppositions concerning the relations between religion, the public sphere, and political power. It is to this latter, 'political' meaning that we shall now turn.

Tradition

The history of the sermon in the century and a half between 1660 and 1800 has been described in terms of a turn from 'Baroque' to 'neo-Classical'. This is one plausible perspective. To a literary historian focusing on rhetorical theory, the contrast between Baroque and neo-Classical may seem more relevant than to a theologian interested in the doctrinal differences between post-Tridentine Catholicism and Lutheran orthodoxy. No method of organizing the variegated oratorical landscape of the period will be entirely satisfactory. The labels 'confessional' and 'polite' used here may be helpful to the extent that they shed some light on the engagement of early modern pulpit oratory with political change, communication processes and the development of public opinion. From this point of view, the 'confessional sermon' may be seen as an extension of a public sphere premised on authority and subordination, and the 'polite sermon' as reflecting a public sphere based on such Enlightened virtues as liberty, moderation and articulateness.

Contemporary research tends to evaluate the sermon within the historical context in which it originated, as a means of communication, as a rhetorical instrument implicitly sustaining (and sometimes subverting) the social and political order, and as a mode of discourse reflecting religious mentalities.[14] Nineteenth-century historians, who were particularly harsh in their judgement of the later seventeenth-century and the eighteenth-century sermon, set a trend that has begun to fade away only quite recently. The more traditional sermon has long been either associated with old-fashioned devotion or condemned as obscure and unpalatable. Eighteenth-century innovations to the sermon have been denounced as practical, utilitarian, moralistic and superficial, or, alternatively, as reflecting the poised rationality and supposed secularism of the Enlightened mind. Pedantry, pomposity, polemics, and prolixity were qualities already attributed to the confessional sermon in the eighteenth century, when the impulse to reform also led to the first historical surveys of pulpit oratory.[15] Partisans of new methods of preaching regretted the slow pace of change. The sermon certainly underwent substantial modifications, but very gradually, and only to a certain extent. A significant number of preachers stuck to traditional ways and methods until well into the period, and among traditionalists, looking wistfully back towards the era of the 'Fathers', demand for the old familiar sermons remained high.

Thus, for much of the period, elaborate and heavily structured sermons, modelled after seventeenth-century examples, were by far the more common. Calvinist sermons were generally analytic, devoting much space to the explanation of individual words and to controversy. Texts were carefully divided into divisions and subdivisions, generals and particulars, and numerous heads, points, doctrines, uses and improvements, with due attention paid to the *quid*, the *quale* and the *quantum*. These sermons appear arbitrary in the sense that virtually any biblical verse was liable to be employed in substantiating any line of reasoning or embellishing any theme. In early eighteenth-century Lutheran circles, preachers commonly used concordances to plunder the Scriptures, making reference to or discussing any biblical passage even remotely related to a particular topic, or drawing attention to similar words in different places in the Bible. Catholic sermons could be no less byzantine.

The point is that to the confessional preachers as well as, presumably, a large part of their audiences the contents of the Bible were as self-evident as their confessional interpretations were authoritative. If, as critics point out, the fear of hell evoked from (especially Catholic) pulpits braced existing clericalism, it responded also to common beliefs and assumptions.[16] In pillaging the Bible as a storehouse of divine utterances and in appealing to traditions of scholarship, preachers were believed to show due respect and add lustre to the Christian tradition. This is not to say that they were fastidious in their display of learning. The type pages of confessional sermons are peppered indiscriminately with words and phrases in Hebrew, Greek, and Latin; renowned authorities ranging from Maimonides to Grotius were commonly cited in the margins and the footnotes, but so were writers of trifling distinction. Catholic sermons of the 'Baroque' variety similarly took truths of faith for granted. They made use of biblical texts, not necessarily to explain them, but to develop moral points. A biblical text or a Sunday or feast-day pericope was often merely used as an opportunity to elaborate on or embellish a particular theme. The festive sermon functioned as ritual, as part of a liturgy, as one ornament among others; the popular play with words was principally intended to contribute to the glory of the saint whose feast-day was celebrated. There is much to say, then, for underscoring the similarity between the Catholic Baroque sermon and the Protestant analytic sermon, despite the Tridentine predilection for a theology of the Sacrament and the Reformation emphasis on a theology of the Word. Both shared a love for metaphor. Where a Bavarian Jesuit preached, in the Passion Week, on a winepress yielding blood, a Lutheran elaborated on the *Geistliche Ölkammer*. A Catholic preacher might strike at the walls of Jericho with bugles *analogica, tragica, rustica,* and *clementina;* a Protestant sounded trumpets of national penance with equal zeal.

Prolonging a deeply rooted medieval habit, confessional preachers of any provenance – Catholic, Lutheran, Calvinist – relished allegories, deeper meanings, symbols, types, and emblems. Hence the 'emblematic sermon', so popular in the German-speaking world, which made graphic use of numerous images and similes to internalize the emblem's meaning in the hearer. One of the best-known representatives in this tradition was the Viennese court preacher and Augustinian Abraham a Sancta Clara (Johann Ulrich Megerle, 1644–1709), whose sermons, couched in popular language, were notably rich in imagery, wit, word play, anagrams, anecdotes, and emblems. Lutheran preachers, too, employed the emblematic form. In a sermon comparing the Lord's Prayer to a well-built edifice, Valentin Ernst Löscher (1674–1749) led his audience through the court, the chapel, the chancery, the loft and the armory, as so many metaphors of the various supplications contained in this exposition.[17] Doctrinal, liturgical, and scholarly traditions informed the confessional sermon to a large extent – so much so that in Catholic sermons until the end of the eighteenth century, biblical texts often fulfilled the same purpose as stories, fables and examples, or folk tales about sinners chastised, prayers answered and miracles performed, or accounts of witches and devils and giants and water spirits, or the histories of mottos and proverbs, or farces in which various social ranks or domestic relationships were ridiculed with a view to moral instruction.[18] Only with the reforms of the Bavarian bishop Johann Michael Sailer (1751–1832) did Catholic sermons become more unequivocally oriented towards the Bible.

In Spain, the species of confessional sermon is represented by the 'concetto' sermon. Divided into numerous paragraphs or articles, the *concetto* sermon exploited unusual chains of thought, antitheses, word play and novel imagery in an intricate oratorical design replete with digressions and byways. The convoluted but coherent architecture of this species of sermon helped listeners and readers to grasp religious truths by leading them to the intended destination along unexpected paths. The *concetto* sermon, introduced into Italy via Naples, thrived well into the eighteenth century; it was popular but clearly required substantial effort to produce, and where talent was lacking it deteriorated into displays of tortuous wit and vain learning. In his picaresque novel *Historia del famoso predicador Fray Gerundio de Campazas, alias Zotes* (1758), the Jesuit José Francisco de Isla (1703–81) satirized what he regarded as the degenerate and tasteless preaching of his day. The book, which gave rise to the derogatory epithet, *gerundianismo,* for such contrived sermons, was outlawed by the Spanish Inquisition. In Great Britain – where the early development of the neo-Classical style has somewhat obscured its enduring popularity – the confessional sermon is represented above all by English Puritan and Scots Calvinist discourse. It, too, was criticized for its bits and pieces of Latin and Greek, for its play on words ('the egress, regress, and progress, and other such stuff', noted a critic in 1660),[19] and for its tedious exegesis, cumbersome style and complicated divisions.

Transformation

Eighteenth-century preachers discovered the importance of empathizing with, and adapting their discourse to articulate and educated audiences. Here, England and France were the cradles of renewal. In seventeenth-century England the neo-Classical 'plain style' had been advocated in the circles of the Royal Society; in France the *Académie Française* awarded a *prix d'éloquence* to the best sermon delivered before its members. England is connected with the name of John Tillotson, who pleaded for sensible reforms at the right time. Tillotson's attractiveness lay partly in his appeal to reason and partly in his mastery of the neo-Classical style. As a sermonizer he lived up to the expectations of a polite and informed urban public that favoured his down-to-earth discourse, destitute as it was of disconcerting emotionalism and unnecessary embellishment, and adducing a moral message in plain but elegant prose. Tillotson's avoidance of polemic and enthusiasm, his clear structure, attractive style and measured language as well as his appeal to 'reasonable religion' made him uncommonly influential in Protestant Europe. Tillotson, claimed reformers from Edinburgh to Königsberg, had all but ended the era of 'false rhetoric', affectation of learning, superfluous digression, far-fetched metaphor, appalling wit and vulgar language by heralding an age of simplicity, brevity, clarity, reasonableness, moderation, and 'natural' arrangement. As Gilbert Burnet put it, what a preacher must strive for is 'Plainness of a clear but noble Stile'.[20]

In France, a number of excellent preachers inspired by classical manuals of rhetoric set the standards of the noble style. In consequence, the French court sermon has long had the rare prerogative of ranking as an artefact of literary culture; even one as critical as Voltaire had Massillon's sermons read to him over dinner. Selecting choice pulpiteers to glorify the reigns of his own kingdom and the next, Louis XIV patronized and enjoyed the sophisticated arrangement, creative abundance, esprit, consummate style, elegant phrasing and brilliant diction of a sermon that, according to some critics, all too frequently served the orator's vanity more than it did the glory of God. The great stylist and master orator was Bossuet, who was typically extolled as 'the French Demosthenes'. Improvising at court or in the Parisian churches, Bossuet riveted audiences through the fervour, originality, clarity, and liveliness of his sermons on such subjects as Providence, church unity and the obligations of the King of France. Together with Bourdaloue and Massillon, Bossuet belonged to a French court triumvirate whose superb mastery of oratorical techniques would influence subsequent generations within and beyond France. Each had his own style. Whilst Bossuet captured his audience through profound insights and powerful rhetoric, the Jesuit Louis Bourdaloue (1632–1704) did so through logic and argument. Dubbed 'the king of preachers and preacher of kings', this dedicated moralist did not shrink from castigating ladies and courtiers given, respectively, to idleness and ambition. Jean Baptist Massillon (1663–1742), no less committed to moralizing, probed the heart and the passions, and possessed much psychological insight. The French Protestant sermon, too, flowered in the decades around 1700: a disproportionately large number of Huguenot or Walloon preachers throughout Europe were famed for their oratorical prowess. Sermonizers such as Jean Claude (1619–87) in France, Jacques Saurin (1677–1730) in the Dutch Republic, and Isaac Beausobre (1659–1738) in Berlin developed biblical themes 'synthetically', avoiding speculation and abstraction but emphasizing moral edification. Claude's *Traité de la composition d'un sermon* (1688) was as widely read in Europe as it was brief and to the point.

Around the turn of the seventeenth century, German Pietists were arguing that the aim of a sermon, rather than to moralize, was to convert, to internalize the faith and make it manifest in daily life. Its vocabulary inspired by the Song of Songs, the Pietist sermon introduced a simpler, more biblical and more practical alternative to what it regarded as the abstruse formalism, superfluous ornamentation and sterile polemicism of the reigning 'orthodox' style. The Lutheran bishop Eric Pontoppidan (1698–1764) was one among many who disseminated such ideas – in his case in Denmark. After about 1750, Spanish Jansenists, inspired especially by Bourdaloue, similarly took the lead in reforming the sermon.[21] The combined influence of Pietism and Jansenism, English and French models, literary and aesthetic developments and the steady growth of an informed, articulate and polite public, gradually led to widespread criticism of the confessional sermon. Sermons, so the reformers claimed, were not meant to affirm or confirm the authoritarian, confessional order of society, but to transfer practical information, transform behaviour and impress upon listeners and readers simple beliefs and moral knowledge. Whilst evangelicals stressed individual choice and personal experience, reformers in all European countries attempted to make concrete the scriptural message, accommodating it to the understanding of the 'people'. The sermon evolved into a vehicle of communication reflecting – and thus also propagating – in both form and content new ideas on social order, improvement and polite society. There was also a growing regard for the sermon as a literary product, as a discourse requiring literary craftsmanship in addition to professional competence; the rising medium of the periodical devoted considerable space to reviews of sermons.[22] Pulpit oratory profited from the eighteenth-century revaluation of rhetoric as a tool to study human nature, drawing specific attention to the effects of oral discourse – words and arguments and gestures – upon an audience.

The call for simplicity and clarity, and the positive appraisal of a more 'synthetic' method of preaching, thus found growing resonance among the clergy of west and central Europe. The effort to reach the audience was not limited to the use of elegant speech and the appeal to reasonableness and common sense. Sermons became shorter and pithier, while the thematic rather than analytic design prevailed. Reformers generally agreed that successful eloquence reflected the moral disposition of the orator, and that due attention had to be given to the passions as 'the springs of action'. Proponents of the 'pathetic' style gave particularly serious consideration to the emotions. They asserted most emphatically the ancient adage that a preacher must feel for himself what he intends his audience to feel; only he who speaks the language of the heart is able to touch the hearts of others. In transferring their own religious enthusiasm to their hearers, James Hervey (1714–58) and Johann-Caspar Lavater (1741–1801) employed familiarity of speech, an emotive style and such rhetorical means as monologues, exclamations, and 'sentimental' perorations.

Writers on homiletics argued forcefully that competent preaching depended more than ever on the social experience of the sermonizer and on his ability to make pertinent psychological observations. Eighteenth-century homiletic theorists believed (to paraphrase Alexander Pope) that the proper study of preachers, next to the Bible, is man. The more radical elements of the Protestant *Aufklärung* – the so-called 'neologians' – gave the sermon a distinctly moral character. They limited doctrine to knowledge of God, virtue and immortality, and hailed, as the general aim of the sermon, the inculcation of wisdom, morality and religious bliss (*Glückseligkeit*). Johann Joachim Spalding, one of many avid readers of Tillotson and the writer of the bestselling *Von der Nutzbarkeit des Predigtamtes und deren Beförderung* (1772), argued that a sermon could only be useful when it 'led the Christian to godliness and peace of mind'. Such notions were not restricted to Germany. The French literary critic Jean-François

Marmontel (1723–99) insisted that it was unnecessary to trouble churchgoers with doctrine, since the fact that they were present in church proved them to be Christians already; hence, the purpose of the sermon should be to turn loyal Christians into virtuous churchgoers.[23]

In a hermeneutics sharply criticized by, among others, Johann Gottfried Herder (1744–1803), the biblical text was seen as an historically outmoded husk in which a kernel of truth was preserved. Those verities which Jesus and his apostles had adapted to the limited understanding of their own contemporaries now had to be reaccommodated to the somewhat superior capacity of late eighteenth-century audiences. This entailed an attack on the Canaanite tongue utilized by previous generations and epitomizing its obsolescence by such unintelligible expressions as 'children of wrath', 'putting on Christ' and 'being in the letter of circumcision'. To combat this 'orientalism', a German preacher might make use of the *Wörterbuch des Neuen Testaments zur Erklärung der christlichen Lehre* (1772) by Wilhelm Abraham Teller. According to Teller's dictionary 'conversion' was simply an archaic term signifying 'self-improvement'. The preacher thus turned into the teacher and 'enlightener' of his congregation. For preachers such as Johann Friedrich Wilhelm Jerusalem (1709–89), whose sermons were widely enjoyed by educated publics throughout Europe, the sermon was a principal agency of enlightenment, moral integrity, and spiritual equanimity.

Preachers now often addressed themselves specifically to what they regarded as the atheism needlessly rampant in the higher social circles. Apologetics developed into a prominent theme, Mosheim (among many others) producing a sermon on 'The foolishness of scoffers at religion'. If sermons ought to reformulate and defend the meaning of biblical texts, they should also be useful. This emphasis on utility led some sermonizers to discuss such topics as the advantage of feeding livestock in stables (appropriately held during Christmas), the possibility of being buried alive (preached at Easter) and medical theories promising a healthier and longer life. In general, the successful pastoral response to the development of an articulate public open to moral guidance but free to pick and choose its spiritual shepherds reaffirmed the status of the sermon as a primary means of oral transmission. Preachers preferred reaching audiences effectively and publicly to endorsing traditional assumptions in institutional environments. One consequence was the growing respectability of those sermons held outside the established churches. In the twilight of the *ancien régime*, the independent sermon of the revivalist movements and missionary societies had become a valued mode of religious oratory.

Notes

1. Frank Lambert, *George Whitefield and the transatlantic revivals, 1737–1770* (Princeton: Princeton University Press, 1994), pp. 52–94.
2. Quoted in A. C. Underwood, *A history of the English Baptists* (London: Baptist Union Publishing Dept., 1947), p. 138. The reference is to the Baptist minister James Foster (1697–1753).
3. James Downey, *The eighteenth-century pulpit: A study of the sermons of Butler, Berkeley, Secker, Sterne, Whitefield and Wesley* (Oxford: Oxford University Press, 1969), pp. 8–9.
4. Rudolf Lenz, *De mortuis nil nisi bene? Leichenpredigten als multidisziplinäre Quelle unter besonderer Berücksichtigung der Historischen Familienforschung, der Bildungsgeschichte und der Literaturgeschichte* (Sigmaringen: Thorbecke, 1990), p. 20.
5. Johann Baptist Schneyer, *Geschichte der katholischen Predigt* (Freiburg: Seelsorge Verlag, 1968), pp. 259–61.
6. Edwin Charles Dargan, *A history of preaching*, 2nd edn, 2 vols. (Grand Rapids, MI: Baker Book House, 1954), vol. 2, pp. 254–5.
7. Urs Herzog, *Geistliche Wohlredenheit. Die katholische Barockpredigt* (Munich: Verlag C. H. Beck, 1991), pp. 125–49; Jacques Truchet, *La prédication de Bossuet. Etude des thèmes*, 2 vols. (Paris: Editions du Cerf, 1960), p. 24.
8. Herzog, *Geistliche Wohlredenheit*, pp. 233–41.
9. Quoted in Jelle Bosma, *Woorden van een gezond verstand. De invloed van de Verlichting op de in het Nederlands uitgegeven preken van 1750 tot 1800. Monografie & bibliografie* (Nieuwkoop: De Graaf, 1997), p. 269.
10. Quoted in Ann Matheson, *Theories of rhetoric in the 18th-century Scottish sermon* (Lewiston, NY: Edwin Mellen Press, 1995), p. 105.
11. Franz M. Eybl, *Abraham a Sancta Clara. Vom Prediger zum Schrifsteller* (Tübingen: Niemeyer, 1992), pp. 92–3.
12. Lenz, *De mortuis nil nisi bene?* pp. 14, 142.
13. Reinhard Krause, *Die Predigt der späten deutschen Aufklärung (1770–1805)* (Stuttgart: Calwer Verlag, 1965), p. 121.
14. Cf. Lori Anne Ferrel and Peter McCullough (eds.), *The English sermon revised: Religion, literature and history 1600–1750* (Manchester: Manchester University Press, 2000); Larissa Taylor (ed.), *Preachers and people in the Reformation and early modern period* (Leiden: Brill, 2001).
15. Historical overviews of sermon oratory include Joseph Romain's *Histoire de la prédication ou la manière dont la parole de Dieu a été prêchée dans tous les siècles* (1727) and Philipp Heinrich Schuler, *Geschichte der Veränderungen des Geschmacks im Predigen, insonderheit unter den Protestanten in Deutschland* (1792–94). Eighteenth-century *historiae literariae* often include sections on sermons.
16. François Brun, 'La prédication au XVIIIe siècle', in Jean Delumeau (ed.), *Histoire vécue du peuple chrétien*, 2 vols. (Toulouse: Privat, 1979), vol. 2, pp. 43–66.
17. Werner Schütz, *Geschichte der christlichen Predigt* (Berlin: de Gruyter, 1972), pp. 120–1.
18. For literature on this topic, see *Enzyklopädie des Märchens. Handwörterbuch zur historischen und vergleichenden Erzählforschung*, ed. Rolf Wilhelm Brednich *et al.* (Berlin: de Gruyter, 1975–). Vol. 10/3 contains relevant entries for 'Predigt', 'Predigtexempel', Predigtmärlein', and 'Predigtschwänke'.

19. Robert South, quoted in Downey, *The eighteenth-century pulpit*, p. 23.
20. Quoted in Rolf P. Lessenich, *Elements of pulpit oratory in eighteenth-century England (1660–1800)* (Cologne: Böhlau, 1972), p. 10.
21. Joël Saugnieux, *Les jansénistes et le renouveau de la prédication dans l'Espagne de la seconde moitié du XVIIIe siècle* (Lyon: Presses Universitaires de Lyon, [1976]).
22. Matheson, *Theories of rhetoric*, p. 1.
23. Frank Paul Bowman, *Le discours sur l'éloquence sacrée à l'époque romantique. Rhétorique, apologétique, herméneutique (1777–1851)* (Geneva: Librairie Droz, 1980), p. 13.

8

Christian education

DOMINIQUE JULIA

Literacy, reading, and faith

One of the fundamental characteristics of the Protestant and the subsequent Catholic Reformations was the assertion that no one could claim to be a Christian unless they could account for their belief. Thus, Luther viewed the catechism as 'something each Christian must absolutely know, so that anyone not knowing it will not be considered a Christian and will not be admitted to any of the sacraments'.[1] Indeed, a strong link was established between religion and teaching among Protestants and Catholics alike. This link persisted throughout the early modern period, with the catechism, a unique expression in question-and-answer form of the dogmatic truths essential to belief (the Ten Commandments, the creeds, the principal prayers) viewed as an essential work, laid out for easy memorization by children. Luther had even maintained that it should be displayed on tablets (*Tafeln*), hung both in church, and in the school and home. Based on quotations from the gospel and the Pauline apostles, the *Haustafel* defined the Christian's social obligations not only towards church authorities, but towards the prince, towards the father or master of the household, and towards the husband on the part of the wife. Over time, the compulsory nature of such religious education led to the development of writing and, more importantly, of reading skills – even if the nature of this apprenticeship varied by region and by country. In certain cases, the learning of Christian truths remained strictly church-centred and oral, memorized solely during Sunday catechism without the intermediary of books or school. This was the case, for example, in regions of Catholic France where French was not understood. Here, children learned the catechism in the local language or dialect, whether in a printed translation or as translated orally by a cleric or vicar from an official text approved by the Bishop. Many Occitan translations were made between 1640 and 1660 and catechisms existed in Basque, Breton, and Flemish. As the Bishop of Dax observed in 1752, 'the catechisms given by pastors and regents are never to teach language, but to enable religion to be understood and retained, and this can and should be done only in the language heard and spoken by the people themselves'.[2]

In Lutheran Sweden, the learning of Christian truths took place either in the church or in the family, with the family transformed through the logic of the universal priesthood into a teaching institution. Indeed, the ecclesiastical law of 1686 ruled that every individual should be able to read and understand the Bible. Even children, agricultural workers and servants should learn to see with their own eyes God's commandments in His Holy Scripture. The immense literacy campaign that lasted from the 1660s through to the beginning of the nineteenth century was based both on the *Hustlava* (a sign hung on the wall to remind the Christian of his duties and obligations) and on the Book of Psalms, which between 1695 and 1819 went through no fewer than 250 editions with a distribution of over 1.5 million copies. This massive movement focused solely on the teaching of reading, not in school but in the home. During examinations preceding communion, the pastors of Lutheran deaneries regularly checked reading ability as well as knowledge of the catechism. According to the oldest surviving registers, three conclusions may be drawn. First, the ability to read, which about 40 per cent of the Swedish population possessed around 1660, rose to 70 per cent towards 1690 and reached 80 to 90 per cent after 1750. Second, as early as the 1680s, a sequence was established where learning to read was to precede memorization of the catechism: thus individuals learned their faith from a book. Lastly, during this same period, the difference in reading ability between girls and boys in the youngest age groups largely disappeared.[3]

The well documented, if exceptional, case of Sweden leads us to speculate on the cultural frontiers running across Europe, frontiers which cannot be explained by differences in religious denomination. Studies carried out over the last thirty years in various parts of Europe document the progress in literacy in the states of north-west Europe, including England, the Low Countries, the Rhineland and north-eastern France. Clearly, the percentages obtained are not precise, since they are based on sources that are not always comparable, and they may conceal large differences within the relevant regions between town and country, men and women and among various professions. In rural areas, marked differences are apparent between the enclosed *bocage* regions – divided and isolated and with fewer major routes of communication – and the cereal-growing plains, more open both to military invasion and to the spread of the written word. Nevertheless, on the whole, north-west Europe was more advanced economically, had a denser population, and was more urbanized – factors which played a decisive role in the advance of literacy. But even though differences in literacy rates persisted within this zone, indicative of the fragility of educational institutions and the novelty of writing in certain areas, overall male literacy rates were already above 70 per cent at the end of the eighteenth century, with the proportions in many towns rising even higher. For Europe as a whole, regional patterns emerge that in fact trace long-standing cultural boundaries: such is the line between Saint-Malo and Geneva which separates the more advanced north and north-eastern France from the far less literate west and south; so too the Stralsund–Dresden line which divides east and west Germany. Even within the much less literate zone of southern Europe, the north of the Italian peninsula (Liguria, Piedmont, and Lombardy) contrasts with the largely illiterate centre and south.

In fact, uneven literacy rates were due to complex combinations of economic, social, and cultural factors. All recent studies have stressed the error of assigning one particular cause to the advance or lag in such rates. Above and beyond questions of property ownership (regions of large landed estates such as eastern Prussia and Pomerania or the south of the Italian peninsula had higher illiteracy) or the general lead of town over country (not the case, however, in the Kingdom of Naples), three points must be stressed. First, it is clear that linguistic diversity could hinder the success of educational policies: regions of Prussia with the highest concentrations of non-German speaking populations – particularly Polish – were also the most unreceptive to teaching in German. Similarly, areas of Scotland where inhabitants spoke Gaelic were those with the lowest rates of reading and writing in the seventeenth and eighteenth centuries. In southern France, where Occitan was usually the sole language spoken and understood, virtually no one knew how to read or write. Here catechisms, hymns and carols were memorized through the words of an intermediary such as the vicar, clerical school teacher, or missionary, who used printed collections or manuscripts. In general, only the elites learned French, viewing the acquisition and mastery of this language as the primary means of cultural integration. Yet the wide difference between Calvinists and Catholics in the French Midi should also be noted. The Catholic hierarchy opted for an oral ministry, based on the use of collective singing and memorization to reach the people in their own language, while the liturgical language itself remained unknown to them. In contrast, the Huguenots elected French as the sacred language for both Bible reading and the singing of psalms. It is thus not surprising that the male and female 'prophets' who appeared in Dauphiné and the Cévennes after the Revocation of the Edict of Nantes expressed themselves in French, as if, for these inspired illiterates, only that language could carry the sign of divine intervention.

A second phenomenon is worthy of note. The comparison of literacy rates between Catholic and Protestant communities does not necessarily lead to the conclusion that Protestants consistently advanced more rapidly than Catholics. To be sure, the English Puritans' belief in God's active presence in everyday life strengthened their spiritual self-examination and self-discipline and motivated a desire in the seventeenth century to write autobiographies and personal journals. So too the Quakers, who believed that individual perfection was achieved gradually through a process of daily self-discipline, were all able to sign their marriage acts by the second half of the eighteenth century, while in the rest of England two-fifths of men and two-thirds of women could not. In the coastal parishes of Lutheran Oldenburg in northern Germany, all men and women knew how to read, while 70 per cent of men and just under 50 per cent of women could write. These exceptionally high rates were due both to the large number of schools built in the different communities, and to the strict monitoring by Lutheran pastors who made frequent visits to their parishioners' homes to verify reading competency. In this instance, church policy and scholastic exigencies resulted in near total literacy.[4] Nevertheless, historians have perhaps been too quick to suggest the overall superiority of Reformed towns over Catholic towns. The differences which exist are not necessarily related to religion alone. Indeed, within the complex set of factors that account for the history of literacy, it is difficult to isolate the advantages of a particular faith, and literacy differences may derive less from religious than from socio-economic distinctions. On occasion, in seventeenth-century England, the Puritan message was better received in less literate urban environments. In the Catholic town of Koblenz in the central Rhineland at the end of the eighteenth century, 86 per cent of men and 60 per cent of women signed their marriage acts. (The gender differences seem primarily due to the movement of women from lower-class rural areas to find work as servants in the town.) The high figures resulted from both an extremely dense elementary school infrastructure (where every parish had a school and populated, widely scattered parishes had several) and near universal school attendance among seven- to eleven-year-old children – as required in the late eighteenth century by a decree of the Elector of Trier. The statistics for Koblenz are probably valid, moreover, for the whole of the Catholic Rhineland at the end of the eighteenth century, since similar attendance rates in the same years are seen in Cologne, Bonn, and Mainz. Literacy percentages for the free Lutheran town of Speyer between 1771 and 1795 (estimated males 95 per cent, females 68 per cent) are only slightly higher than those in Koblenz.[5] In any case, such figures call for a fresh look at the old notion that Catholic countries were educationally backward. The close and competitive situation in which denominations found themselves in this region of Germany may have helped advance literacy for both Protestants and Catholics. Religious frontiers forced both groups to define themselves in reference to one another, creating an ongoing process of both differentiation and mutual dependence and leading paradoxically to reciprocal imitation.

A final point is worth mentioning: the effects of the local political system may also have affected literacy. All historians have stressed the role played during the eighteenth century by certain mountain 'republics' in the advance of literacy. Networks of kinship and alliances came together to maintain continuous chains – renewed from generation to generation – of temporary and permanent migration of literate men: clergymen, school teachers, and itinerant sellers of printed material. In the Protestant Queyras, as in the Catholic Briançonnais areas of the French Alps, or in the Alpine valleys around Lake Como in Austrian Lombardy, exceptionally high rates of masculine literacy (up to 80 per cent) have been found. To explain this phenomenon historians must consider not only the nature of the local economy (land held in small plots and a strong presence of artisans who must frequently emigrate) and the density of the modes of instruction (based in hamlet schools and informal study within the family), but also the importance of collective management achieved through community meetings which dealt autonomously with juridical, economic, and financial problems. At least among boys, this unusual environment of interpersonal relationships may have prompted a desire to learn and to pursue autodidactic study outside the official school system. Similar circumstances existed in the Swiss canton of Neuchâtel, where direct village democracy, based on local political power, economic equality, and free working conditions, encouraged the development of both formal education and self-instruction within one's family and profession.[6] In this Protestant land, where Calvinism had been introduced by Guillaume Farel, examinations before first communion at ages sixteen or seventeen represented both the end of schooling and the rite of passage into adult life. The test took place in the church, before the community and its elected representatives. Not only was the pastor's teaching being judged, but a whole generation's knowledge of the dogmatic truths – truths that had been read, memorized, and understood in the family as much as at church and school, and had been integrated into the individual and collective value systems.

Primary school education

It would be impossible to enter into all the details of the development of schools in the early modern period. They differed widely in their statutes, in their funding (whether from church benefices, community contributions, individual families, or religious legacies), in their teachers (whether laymen, clerics, or members of congregations), and in the nature of attendance (state-imposed or not, co-educational or not). One should note that even in less literate parts of Europe, such as eighteenth-century Castile, surprisingly large numbers of school books were published. The *cartillas* (reading primers containing the main Christian prayers) published by the Valladolid cathedral chapter had annual print-runs of 300,000 to 400,000 copies throughout the second half of the eighteenth century. Between 1740 and 1761, the confraternity of Madrid booksellers published more than 500,000 copies of Gerónimo de Rosales's *Cáton christiano*, a religious study book also used as a primer. These printed works were presumably used for teaching in many different ways in schools, homes, and catechism classes.[7] Even though a considerable number of these works were destined for the Americas, there can be no doubt that wherever they were used, they helped achieve a certain level of minimal literacy.

Three points can be made concerning the operation of primary schools during this period. First, one should not overlook links to the general determination of political, municipal, and ecclesiastical authorities to shape Christian civility and eradicate begging and vagrancy. The general movement in the seventeenth century to create workhouses, *hôpitaux généraux*, or *Zuchthäuser* sought to remove the poor from general society and – laziness being the mother of vice – to put them to work. It was not simply a question of economic need, but a desire to create a moral order within the walls of the establishment: the obligation to work, together with penitence and a control of the emotions, would offer the poor a means to salvation. But education was also included within this scheme: schoolmasters provided the hospital's 'adopted' children with a basic schooling and religious grounding, while master craftsmen taught them practical skills. Moreover, the effort to lock-up and restrain vagabonds was accompanied by an intense effort to give instruction to the poor in general. The same devout circles (nobles, magistrates, office-holders, merchants) simultaneously supported both the workhouse 'lock-up' and free charity schools. In Catholic France from the second half of the seventeenth century, these tendencies were accentuated under the influence of the *Compagnie du Saint-Sacrement*, the Marian congregations founded by the Jesuits, and various groups associated with the Jansenists. The best-known schools were those run by the Christian Brothers, founded by Jean-Baptiste de La Salle. In northern Germany similar objectives were sought in the context of charity schools and orphanages. The Lutheran Pietists played an important role in this movement, especially under the influence of the Halle orphanage created by August Hermann Francke. The Pietists' orphanage foundation owned its own press and widely circulated low-cost religious texts. Thus, between 1720 and 1735 no less than thirty-nine editions of the New Testament and some twenty-three editions of a small format family Bible were printed.

There were, of course, differences between Protestant and Catholic Europe in the various movements to discipline and educate orphans and the children of the poor. Thus, Lutheran Pietism stressed the Bible, psalm recital, and direct contact with the Scriptures (the Bible being used for reading), and these elements, reinforced in the home, invariably strengthened a strong confessional identity. But one can also draw up a lengthy list of similarities in the educational activities of the two confessions. All such institutions, whether Protestant or Catholic, were moved by the goal of instilling in their pupils both Christian civility – the love of truth, obedience, zeal for work – and more 'practical' knowledge. Facing a growing number of students, pedagogic institutions reacted in a manner characteristic of early modern power structures in general, imposing sanctions to distinguish individuals according to ability, merit, and a quantitatively assessed 'level'. Repetitive school work to check and control learning was also integrated into a system of reciprocal and hierarchical supervision. Pedagogy came to resemble an analytical science, breaking down time and space to allow the teacher to focus on microscopic detail unhindered, and to detect immediately any individual not acting according to the rules. A highly ritualized schedule was developed in which the day was punctuated with regular lectures, exercises, and prayer so as to eliminate disorder and confusion. To strengthen the schoolmaster's authority over his young charges, a similarly ritualized system of punishment and reward was established. Separated from the outside and from the bustle of the town, a rigid procedure of study was installed inside a space divided up into particular areas for classes, within which each pupil found his allotted place. Teaching material was identical for every child at each level of the curriculum, and final examinations or continuous assessment indicated clearly a student's readiness to move to a higher level. Modern pedagogy thus emerged from the need to impose order and coherence on the undisciplined body of schoolchildren from various social classes constituting the 'people' of the towns. In the France of 1790, the Christian Brothers' schools provided 35,000 pupils with schooling in the 108 towns where they were established – an average of a quarter of all boys between seven and fourteen, rising to as high as 40 per cent in towns of less than 10,000 inhabitants. Clearly, the effects of the Brothers' method extended well beyond the institutions themselves.

A second point concerns the professionalization of teaching at the primary school level. At the beginning of the early modern period a dynastic system of teacher training still held sway, where the son succeeded the father, from whom he received his apprenticeship in the basic classroom functions and tasks. But by the end of the seventeenth century, both Protestants and Catholics began to show interest in professional teacher training. Here again, the Pietists played an important role as initiators. Among the various *seminaria praeceptorum* founded in Halle by Francke was the *Institut der Praeparandie*, created in 1717 with the aim of training future primary school teachers for the various Halle schools. The impact of this creation was felt beyond Halle, when pastors Christoph Schinmeyer and Johann Julius Hecker endeavoured to establish 'seminaries' on the same model, respectively in Stetin (1732–37) and Berlin (1748). In 1753, the latter was recognized as a 'Seminary for sacristans and schoolmasters in villages of the royal electorate domain'. It admitted both regular boarding students and poor craftsmen who attended vocational training courses for a few weeks or months outside their regular work. Nevertheless, the impact and effectiveness of such initiatives were limited, since they remained somewhat private and local, closely linked to the specific needs of the institutions that created them.[8] On the Catholic side, the secular institution for primary school teachers founded by La Salle for the Christian Brothers had two original features by comparison with religious orders: the Brothers were forbidden to study Latin or to enter the clergy. This double ban preserved a relatively 'popular' recruitment of those joining the Brothers and prevented a drift towards a form of 'secondary' teaching for the elites – as occurred with some religious orders like the Piarists towards the end of the eighteenth century. The Brothers were recruited from the best of the schools' pupils, those who were 'intelligent and of a pious disposition, and who, when judged ready to do so, were themselves prepared to enter the community'. For this teaching corps of modest origins – intermediaries between the ecclesiastical authorities and the laity who was to be instructed and edified – it was necessary to create a way of life that distinguished them clearly from the general population. The 'Rules of Propriety and Christian Civility' were written to instil in the Brothers (described as 'all laymen, uneducated and with average intelligence at best') a social behaviour which they would then transmit to their pupils: the 'modesty' demanded by Christian morality and requisite to their position; and a control of the emotions and passions so that punishments would be administered without anger or impatience, but only in a manner that was 'pure, charitable, just, appropriate, moderate, non-aggressive and prudent'.[9] Manuals produced for teachers' use, such as *Conduite des écoles chrétiennes* (1720), provided such a wealth of detail that Brothers had no need to reflect on what to do or how to do it in a given situation: their skill lay solely in carrying out the rules.

A third point concerning the primary schools relates to the more general movement among Enlightened governments to reform education. Even if this domain received less attention than reforms seeking to modernize other areas of traditional state control – the army, finance, justice – it is clear that a growing number of laws in the second half of the eighteenth century in the German states, in Austria and on the Italian peninsula sought to place the entire educational system under state control: children, it was argued, should belong to the state. At the core of such reforms was the creation of teacher-training schools, or *Normalschulen*, an initiative of Ignaz von Felbiger, provost of the Augustinian canons of Sagan. Felbiger was directly inspired by the Berlin pastor Hecker, when in 1765 he proposed his regulations for elementary schools in Silesia – following a request of the Prussian governor. As early as 1764–65, a 'model' school for the training of schoolmasters was created in Breslau. But it was especially in Austrian lands that Felbiger was able to develop his plans. The general school decree of 6 December 1774 provided for the creation in each province of a 'normal' school which was to serve as the model for all other schools and guarantee the training of teachers for Catholic schools.[10] Eleven hours per week of 'theory' were devoted to religion (the catechism, the Bible, Christian ethics), reading, writing, and arithmetic, in a course of study that might last two or three months. But the most important training came through teacher practice, in which future masters learned Felbiger's methods either in the normal school itself or in nearby institutions. The success of the teaching reforms was due to the rapid establishment of such schools not only in the Austrian provinces and in the Slavic and Hungarian domains under the Habsburg crown, but also in the Austrian Netherlands and in Lombardy – all of which helped train a large number of new schoolmasters during the final decades of the eighteenth century.[11] Moreover, the effect of Felbiger's model clearly went well beyond the Habsburg territorial boundaries. One finds elements of his method in Bavaria, in the electorates of Mainz, Cologne, and Trier, and in the bishoprics of Eichstätt and Speyer. In all of these areas normal schools would play a pioneering cultural role under the tutelage of clerics versed in the Catholic Enlightenment.

Secondary and university education

Turning to the secondary schools and the teaching of Latin, the similarities between Catholic, Lutheran, Calvinist, and Anglican institutions appear to significantly outweigh the differences. In 1650, all of these institutions shared a similar humanist heritage: from the *Schulordnungen* or *Kirchenordnungen* of Philipp Melanchthon to Jean Sturm's model *gymnasium* in Strasbourg, to John Calvin's schools in Geneva and Zwingli's in Zurich – all of which, in turn, drew on the methods established by the Brothers of the Common Life at the end of the fifteenth century. In addition, the Jesuits' *Ratio Studiorum* (1599) owed much to the *modus parisiensis* developed within the University of Paris at the beginning of the sixteenth century. On both sides of the confessional boundary one finds the same organization of studies by successive classes, lessons (*praelectiones*), and exercises (questions, debates, prose imitations); the same use of classical antiquity, in both its rhetoric and its ideals of 'rectitude and virtue', as a basis for the education of the Christian man; the same divisions into smaller groups to maintain order and avoid overcrowded classes; the same competitive emulation (compositions, prizes, public recitations) aimed at enriching school life. The same texts were also studied in the same order (in particular Cicero's *Epistles* – the model for the Latin essay – along with Virgil and Horace), although Catholics were perhaps more rigorous in eliminating classical authors considered lascivious or obscene. In the Lutheran schools, Terence was seen as one of the most useful authors for Latin conversation, whereas the Company of Jesus usually banned him completely. No doubt Greek was more frequently taught in the Protestant schools than in the Catholic, and indeed, the Greek New Testament was one of the texts most commonly read by the Protestants, second only to Isocrates's *Discourses*. No doubt also the textbooks used on the two sides of the confessional divide were not precisely the same. But here one must take into account the emerging market in school books with its own specialized authors, booksellers and printers. In Lutheran and Calvinist countries, the Greek and Latin grammar books written by the Dutch scholar Gerhard Johannes Vossius in the early seventeenth century had wide distribution in Holland and northern Germany, as well as in the French Calvinist academies. The Jesuits, for their part, remained loyal either to Father Emmanuel Alvarez's grammar book, often translated into the vernacular, or to the older manual by Despautère, revised and amended by one of the Jesuit fathers. Yet there was a clear tendency towards the standardization of textbooks, either for the sake of simplicity and clarity, or because they were favoured by a particular teaching order. It was above all on the question of religious instruction that major distinctions between Catholic and Protestant schools appeared

In their development the Latin schools, the *collèges* and the *gymnasia* were all fundamentally linked to the growth of territorial churches and the modern state. Following the devastation of the Thirty Years' War, the German Protestant princes hoped to revive Christian teaching in order to re-establish religious order and guarantee social and political stability. The education of their subjects also became an important priority as a means of supplying the administrative workforce needed by both state and church. The restoration of the Latin schools occurred particularly under the impetus and authority of the territorial churches, where local or central consistories took responsibility for the organization and good governance of the schools. Nevertheless, following the concept of Christian sovereignty the prince himself might also order a general inspection of the schools within his territory – as in Saxe-Gotha in 1642 or in the Duchy of Brunswick after 1648. From this increased surveillance and the consequent inspection reports, we can perceive the fundamental importance of the religious apprenticeship in the Latin schools. Such schools clearly played an active role in the lives of the local churches. Much school time was devoted to hymns, and particularly to the singing of psalms. Indeed, the second most important position in a Latin school was generally that of the cantor, who conducted the choir both in religious services in the church and in burial ceremonies, where pupils escorted and solemnified the procession from the deceased's house to the cemetery. In addition to Sundays and religious festivals, pupils attended church two or three times a week to sing, pray, and listen to sermons; and took communion four times a year, after having asked forgiveness of their sins before the school rector, who implored them to correct their lives. Protestant Latin schools differed from the Catholic less in the rote-learning of the catechism in the vernacular (this also happened in Jesuit schools, where pupils memorized the *Catechismus minimus* or *minor* by Pierre Canisius) than in the reading of passages from the Bible: Proverbs or Ecclesiastes for younger pupils; chapters from the gospels or the Old Testament for the older ones. Pupils memorized extracts and transcribed them into special copy books. Other works such as Sébastien Castellion's *Dialogorum sacrorum ad linguam simul et mores puerorum libri quatuor* would complete the pupil's biblical instruction.

The penetration of religion was equally pervasive in the Catholic schools. Interpretations of dogma in the catechism alternated with interpretations of the mysteries celebrated during the liturgical year: taught by the Jesuits in the vernacular in the earlier grades and then in Latin. Inevitably, emphasis was placed on the authority of the Catholic Church and on papal supremacy, with rote memorization playing an important role and public debate sharpening the pupils' competitive sense. Such religious education did not authorize direct contact with the Bible, except through commentaries given in the Sunday sermon. Nevertheless, pictures and engravings were hung in chapels and school corridors to excite the imagination. Their subjects often emphasized dogmas and scenes rejected by the Protestants: representations of the miracles of the Eucharist, depictions of the saints and martyrs attesting the necessity of good works, or celebrations of the Virgin's victories over heretics. Plays based on Old Testament stories, the lives of the martyrs, or the Jesuit saints, were performed on important feast days, thus providing visual and oral pedagogical models to be imitated. Spiritual readings and prayer books (many written by Jesuit fathers) were included as a means of reinforcing piety and encouraging pupils to pattern their behaviour on their belief. The fathers also gave spiritual guidance to pupils in their care, and Marian sodalities provided many of the boarders with additional spiritual exercises and an initiation into charitable activities. Pupils were encouraged to partake regularly in the sacraments, with monthly confession and weekly communion. An emphasis on the Eucharist was further promoted through frequent adorations of the Blessed Sacrament, the forty hours' devotion at Carnival time, and the celebration of Corpus Christi, with its grandiose town processions. The Jesuits also encouraged the worship of relics, which provided an occasion for magnificent ceremonies, particularly when the bones of saints were transported from the catacombs. In sum, the more sober and restrained worship of the Protestants was countered by a Jesuit-inspired triumphalism.

Beyond this division in the forms of religious worship, other distinctions cut across the various confessional boundaries. Everywhere, one could find a hierarchy of pedagogical institutions that broadly corresponded to the administrative, economic, and demographic importance of the towns in which they were located. In reality, the network of schools had been largely created before 1650. Thereafter, it was primarily reinforced by an expansion of teaching in the more advanced classes, providing university-level instruction, albeit without the authority to award university diplomas. In this way certain Latin schools were transformed into *gymnasia illustria*. Social demand for new schools came primarily from the elites of smaller towns who wanted their children initially to be taught close to their families, before being sent away to larger institutions. Financial limitations enabled remuneration of only one to three teachers in such towns. Inevitably, the quality of secondary schools (whether English grammar schools, German Latin schools or French, Spanish, and

Italian *collèges*) varied greatly and identical class denominations could conceal very different levels of achievement. In France it was not unusual for pupils from the provinces transferring to a Parisian *collège* to be asked to repeat or even drop back a class. In Catholic countries, uneven achievement levels were occasionally regulated through the standardization imposed by the *ratio studiorum* of a religious order or secular teaching congregation. Indeed, throughout the seventeenth century, as much to solve problems of teacher recruitment as for financial reasons, towns frequently called upon orders and congregations to manage their schools. However, inconsistencies in quality invariably appeared between the schools of different orders and congregations. The Jesuits' strategy in establishing their institutions privileged political capitals and main university and economic centres, in the professed goal of using the elites to take back areas affected by the poison of heresy. Moreover, the Society's financial requirements generally precluded the creation of schools in small towns except under very special conditions. With the aid of political authorities, the Jesuits were often able to establish a network of secondary schools centred on a university they controlled: this was the case in the Spanish Netherlands with the university college of Anchin in Douai. But this strategy occasionally met with ferocious resistance from secular university bodies (Paris, for example) which had managed with difficulty to maintain their own secondary schools. Although the Jesuits almost entirely dominated the teaching of Latin in the Catholic portions of the western Prussian territories, as well as in Upper Bavaria, Austria, and the north-western empire (the southern Netherlands, the principality of Liège, the Archdiocese of Cologne, and Westphalia), in the course of the seventeenth century other religious orders emerged to take charge of the more modest schools, notably the Augustinians, the Recollets, and the Friars Minor.[12] During the same period in France, the Oratorians and the Doctrinaires each took charge of over twenty *collèges*, most often in towns with less than 10,000 inhabitants – either because the Jesuits had refused the offers made to them, or because town councillors objected to the arrival of an order which vowed particular obedience to the pope (as in the fiercely 'Gallican' town of Troyes). In the Italian peninsula, the network of secondary schools was strengthened gradually with the arrival of the Barnabites, the Scolopes and the Somascans, who often agreed to move into more modest towns, even if the orders' central authorities remained reticent to sanction smaller schools. On occasion, certain other groups (from the Carmelites and Dominicans to the more recently created Eudists, Missionaries of Saint-Joseph and priests of the Saint-Sacrement of Valence) broadened the range of the teaching orders, particularly after the end of the seventeenth century, when smaller towns found it increasingly difficult to attract the major teaching congregations. In certain areas such as Brittany, schools remained in the hands of secular priests – frequently through the patronage of the bishops who used them in part as diocesan seminaries. As for the staffing of Protestant schools, one must be wary of the oft-repeated descriptions of a poverty-stricken and unstable corps of teachers who only retained their functions while waiting for pastoral positions to open up. A closer look at specific teaching careers reveals that masters in Latin schools remained much longer than historians previously suspected. Thus, in the Duchy of Brunswick in the third quarter of the seventeenth century, two-thirds of Latin schoolmasters stayed more than five years at the same posts and location, and four out of ten remained more than ten years.

Three additional points can be made regarding secondary schools of the period. First, the differences in the social profile of students in the various schools seem to have increased, especially through the impact of boarding schools. Such institutions, along with private tutorships, represented the social and moneyed elites' preferred methods of schooling. During the eighteenth century, a third of the English gentry and quarter of English peers received private home education. Private tutelage and boarding schools were often combined, moreover, when pupils moved into schools along with their tutors. For the privileged by the late seventeenth century it was no longer a question of uncertain lodgings in a private home or in the teachers' rooms – as had usually been the case in the sixteenth century – but of buildings specifically constructed for this purpose. The *seminaria nobilium* or *collegi dei nobili* in the Italian peninsula; the great Jesuit and Oratorian boarding schools in France (La Flèche, Louis-le-Grand, Pont-à-Mousson, or Juilly); and the nine English public schools, all offered a wide range of complementary classes. In addition to the traditional curriculum, other skills were taught, including dancing, singing, drawing, the arts of war (fencing and horseback riding), and studies of use to both nobles and tradesmen (maths, accounting, calligraphy). Boarding schools offered the privileged two key advantages. Firstly, children were guaranteed a strict moral and intellectual education under supervision; secondly, they gained significant worldly experience through a controlled elite environment. It was not by chance that a large proportion of the English elite passed through the public schools, with Eton and Westminster ranked as the most preferred.

A second point concerns the progressive differentiation of the subject matter taught during the period. The humanities curriculum devised in the sixteenth century appeared more and more out of step with the evolution of science and technology and corresponded less and less to the demands of the various social groups. The article, 'Collèges', written by d'Alembert for the *Encyclopédie* (1753), argued that a young man lost the ten best years of his life learning a dead language. He promoted rather a curriculum which included history, foreign languages, geometry, and experiments in physics. In any case, one can observe a certain 'scholarization' of the apprenticeships available to the elites. An earlier academy for nobles established at the beginning of the seventeenth century, the *Collegium illustre* in Tübingen, was cut short by the wars. But later in the century local political leaders (like those of Turin in 1678, Wolfenbüttel in 1688, or Nancy-Luneville in 1699) pushed for new academies, in which accomplishments like dancing and drawing were taught, together with martial skills (riding, fencing, military exercises with pikes and muskets) and other subjects useful for future military officers (arithmetic, geometry, the attack and defence of fortifications, history, geography, and foreign languages). Entry was usually at adolescence, following study either in a conventional Latin school or through private tutoring.[13] Recruitment to such schools long conserved two particular features: they were both international, receiving many foreign aristocrats in the course of their 'Grand Tours'; and inter-denominational, practising a *de facto* ecumenism, in which Calvinists, Lutherans, and Catholics all lived together.

In fact, alongside the traditional humanist model created at the end of the sixteenth century, a whole range of private and public initiatives developed in the eighteenth century, offering broader educational options in response to the professional needs of diverse social groups. Training which had previously consisted of lengthy practical experience under military engineers or architects, or at different commercial trading posts in Atlantic or Mediterranean ports, now took the form of instruction in specialized schools. The models for such education could be extremely varied. Some of the older grammar schools, like those in Manchester, or Newcastle, or Christ's Hospital in London, updated their courses by offering teaching in mathematics and navigation. At the same time, different forms of technical training emerged in various European countries, usually including a period of boarding, and a range of complementary classes. There were preparatory schools, often state-supported, for the technical branches of the army (marine, artillery, engineers); and soon preparatory schools emerged for civil engineers, architects, and merchants. In Catholic countries such schools were especially developed by the Christian Brothers, whose rules, as we have seen, forbade their members to learn Latin.

Seminaries for training the Catholic clergy should also be included among the specialized schools. Initially existing only as modest retreats for those about to be ordained, some gradually turned into full teaching institutions, so that only a fraction of future priests went on to the university. This development, although not general, was no doubt aided by theological conflicts, especially those related to the anti-Jansenist bull *Unigenitus*. Bishops wished to control the formation of their clergy and to be certain of the theological stance of seminary professors. Thus, in France the Lazarists and Sulpicians were particularly assiduous in following the Roman directives. In sum, two separate tracks began to emerge for secondary and higher education, with the universities broadly teaching the 'pure' sciences, while the specialized schools – like those training 'surgeons' – taught applied sciences and technical skills. Nevertheless, universities were also obliged to face social demand for specialized knowledge. This was reflected in the increase in the number of chairs – notably in German universities – in fields such as political economy, modern languages, administrative sciences, and national civil law. The growth of the percentage of students graduating, compared to the number of initial registrants, is also significant. There was a growing balance between the demand for certain specialized skills and the supply of individuals trained at the university for such professions as that of pastor, judge, lawyer, and physician.

The role of the state

Above all – and this is the third point to be stressed regarding the overall development of secondary education – the modern state increasingly tended to consider teaching as falling under its sole jurisdiction, following the principle that the church is *within* the state. To be sure, in Hanoverian England, the state actually became less interested in secondary and higher education, viewing neither as matters of state concern. The reforms which were carried out, such as university teaching of the natural sciences, were only partial, and depended mainly on internal factors (the organization of liberal arts courses, pedagogical approaches, or the university's finances). So too in the United Provinces, the resolutely federal structure of the state and the regional bases of sovereignty precluded any general reforms. Yet we have already mentioned the early initiatives towards sweeping educational transformations taken by certain German states such as Saxony-Gotha, Brunswick and Prussia, even though the results were not always equal to the ambitions. Such reforms indicate a desire both to provide the state administration with competent and loyal workers and also to establish an educational hierarchy in which the different levels worked well together.

For the Protestant regions, historians have rightly emphasized the role of the Pietist movement in the creation of the University of Halle (1694). But it should also be noted that the margrave of Brandenburg, Frederick III of Hohenzollern, was himself a Calvinist who wanted to found a Lutheran university that was clearly distinguishable from the orthodox Lutheran universities of Leipzig and Wittenberg in the neighbouring electorate of Saxony. In fact, Halle soon became the principal educational institution for officials of the Prussian church and state. The Pietist faculty of theology developed as an effective centre of resistance against Lutheran orthodoxy. But at the same time the innovative faculty of law began teaching cameralist theories of political economy, while the philosophy faculty introduced natural law. The choice of German over Latin as the teaching language also contributed in modernizing the curriculum.[14] Borrowing many features from the Halle model, the Elector of Hanover founded the University of Göttingen in 1737 as a state institution with the primary aim of training civil servants. It attracted both members of the nobility (who throughout the eighteenth century represented 10 to 15 per cent of the student population – a considerable percentage for the period) and of the rich middle classes. But it did not refuse foreign Catholic students, who were granted the right of openly practising their faith. Three factors in particular helped make Göttingen a model of the modern university. First, the traditionally privileged position of theology over the other faculties was weakened from the outset because university statutes forbade denunciation of professors for 'heretical' opinions. The curbing of the power of censorship tended less to undermine the church's authority than to eliminate theological quarrels, especially between orthodox and Pietist Lutherans. Second, the state reserved the right to nominate professors, the faculties being allowed merely to make nominations: the traditional powers of the university were thus greatly reduced. Finally, the teaching offered was substantially broadened: thus, the law faculty, the heart of the university, taught not only Roman law, but also German customary law, feudal law, constitutional law, imperial jurisprudence, and the history of law. So too the philosophy faculty, while continuing to offer first-year foundation courses, now proposed a wide range of new disciplines: empirical psychology, natural law, politics, natural history, pure and applied mathematics (including civil and military architecture), history and its related fields (geography and diplomacy), and both ancient and modern languages.

In the Catholic regions, the reform movement began in the 1720s with the sweeping decrees of Victor-Amedeus II of Piedmont which forbade all regular clergy (including the Jesuits) from teaching in secondary schools. This transformation entailed, first, a centralization which removed the control of teaching matters from the University of Turin and, second, a move towards uniformity, which sought to regulate school administration, teachers' qualifications, and the curriculum of studies. A central scholarship school, the *Collegio delle Provinzie*, was established which granted awards more objectively, according to the population density of each province. The plan was to restructure the ruling class and create a new elite of civil servants by introducing meritocratic principles and incorporating the better pupils emerging from the *ceto civile*. The idea spread rapidly and gained European dimensions with the series of state expulsions of the Jesuits: first in Portugal (1759), then in France (1764), Spain (1767), and the Kingdom of Naples (1768), followed by the complete abolition of the Company through the bull *Dominus ac Redemptor* in 1773. The suppression of the largest teaching order in Europe was experienced by several countries as a profound rupture which seriously affected the religious education and direction of the younger generation. It also provoked a fundamental re-examination and reorganization of public education. This modernization was based on three principles: firstly, the concepts of public instruction and national education emerged, along with the assumption that the entire teaching establishment belonged in the state's domain. Such demands could lead to direct conflicts with church authorities, as occurred in 1783 when Joseph II decided to create a series of 'general' seminaries where future priests would be trained independently from the episcopacy. Priests were henceforth to be seen as state functionaries charged with ensuring the local civic order. Secondly, a corps of teachers was created which differed radically in their education, allegiance, and recruitment from the members of religious congregations. And lastly, such national educational schemes brought with them the renewal of teaching programmes, marked by a revaluation of the system of the 'humanities'. It is impossible to explore here the gap that may well have existed between legislation and reality. It seems likely, however, that the driving force of this movement was to be found less in the language of its advocates – whether from ideas concerning administrative practices, or from new governmental forms of 'Enlightened' despotism – than in the long-term process by which the modern state was constructed, a process which demanded an increasing number of skilled administrators to serve it. The Catholic clergy, as the Protestant, would henceforth be treated as state administrators, a transformation that would only further accelerate during the decade of the French Revolution. (Translation by Jane Yeoman and Timothy Tackett)

Notes

1. From *Der Grosse Katechismus*, in *Martin Luthers Werke* (Weimar: Böhlau, 1910), vol. 30, p. 129.

2. See Jean Eygun, *Au risque de Babel. Le texte religieux occitan de 1600 à 1850* (Bordeaux: Association d'etude du texte occitan, 2002), p. 304.

3. Egil Johansson, 'The history of literacy in Sweden', in Harvey J. Graff (ed.), *Literacy and social development* (Cambridge: Cambridge University Press, 1981), pp. 151–82.

4. N. Norden, 'Die Alphabetisierung der oldenburgischen Küstenmarsch im 17 und 18 Jahrhundert', in Ernst Hinrichs and Wilhelm Norden (eds.), *Regionalgeschichte. Probleme und Beispiele* (Hildesheim: Lax, 1980), pp. 103–64.

5. Etienne François, 'Die Volksbildung im ausgehenden 18 Jahrhundert', *Jahrbuch für westdeutsche Landesgeschichte*, 3 (1977), pp. 277–304.

6. On the region of Neuchâtel, see Pierre Caspard, 'Pourquoi on a envie d'apprendre. L'autodidaxie ordinaire à Neuchâtel (XVIIIe siècle)', *Histoire de l'éducation*, 70 (May 1996), pp. 65–110; and 'Examen de soi-même, examen public, examen Etat de l'admission à la Sainte-Cène aux certificats de fin d'études, XVIe–XIXe siècle', *Histoire de l'éducation*, 94 (May 2002), pp. 17–74.

7. Antonio Viñao Frago, 'Aprender a leer en el Antiguo Regimen: cartillas, silabarios y catones', in A. Escolaño Benito (ed.), *Historia ilustrada del libro escolar en España. Del Antiguo Reimen a la Segunda Republica* (Madrid: Ed. Pirámide, 1997), pp. 148–91.

8. Wolfgang Neugebauer, *Absolutischer Staat und Schulwirklichkeit in Brandenburg-Preussen* (Berlin: de Gruyter, 1985), pp. 372–423.

9. Jean-Baptiste de La Salle, *Conduite des écoles*, in *Œuvres complètes* (Rome: Frères des Ecoles Chrétiennes, 1993), pp. 664–5.

10. Neugebauer, *Absolutistischer Staat und Schulwirklichkeit*, pp. 414–16. Between 1765 and 1778, over 100 schoolmasters were trained for Silesia and seventy-seven for Western Prussia.

11. Helmut Engelbrecht, *Geschichte des östereichischen Bildungswesens*, vol. 3: *Von der frühen Aufklärung bis zum Vormärz* (Vienna: Osterreichischer Bundesverlag, 1984), pp. 106, 108, 129–38, 491–501.

12. Johannes Kistenich, *Bettelmönche im öffentlichen Schulwesen. Ein Handbuch für die Erzdiözese Köln, 1600 bis 1850*, 2 vols. (Cologne: Böhlau Verl, 2001).

13. Norbert Konrads, *Ritterakademien der frühen Neuzeit. Bildung als Standesprivilag im 16 und 17 Jahrhundert* (Göttingen: Vandenhoeck and Ruprecht, 1982).

14. See Anton Schindling, 'Die protestantischen Universitäten im Heiligen Römischen Reich deutscher Nation im Zeitalter der Aufklärung', in Notker Hammerstein (ed.), *Universitäten und Aufklärung* (Göttingen: Wallstein, 1995), pp. 9–19.

9

Christianity and gender

MERRY WIESNER-HANKS

Histories of Christian groups written by their adherents during the seventeenth and eighteenth centuries often highlighted the role of women, viewing their actions as heroic signs of God operating through the least of his creatures. Gottfried Arnold, a German Pietist who published an enormous and sympathetic history of 'churches and heresies' in 1729, included a long list of 'blessed women who showed the way to the truth, or who suffered greatly, or who were amazingly gifted, enlightened or directed by God'.[1] Critiques of these same groups, written by their opponents, also noted women's power, which they regarded as proof of the group's demonic or at least misguided nature. Among the 'errors, heresies, blasphemies and pernicious practices of the sectaries' described by Thomas Edwards in *Gangraena* (London, 1646) was the fact that they allowed women to preach. Johann Feustking, a German theologian, turned his attention entirely to women in *Gynaeceum Haeretico Fanaticum* (Frankfurt and Leipzig, 1704), spending 700 pages describing, as his full title reads, the 'false prophetesses, quacks, fanatics and other sectarian and frenzied female persons through whom God's church is disturbed'.

Historians of Christianity in the late nineteenth century often attempted to be more 'objective' and 'scientific', which meant that they highlighted official institutional and intellectual developments and paid less attention to popular devotional practices or individuals outside the mainstream. Like their colleagues in the newly professionalizing field of secular history, they often left women out of the story altogether as they tried to draw a sharp line between history (including church history) and the 'softer' genres of literature and devotional writings.

Research on the history of women and gender – by which historians mean the culturally constructed, historically mutable, and often unstable system of sexual differentiation involving men as well as women – over the last thirty years has led many scholars to return to a position similar to that of Edwards and Feustking. They see the seventeenth and eighteenth centuries as a period in which Christianity in many parts of Europe – and not simply that of 'sectaries' and 'fanatics' – was feminized. Large numbers of people thought the established churches, both Protestant and Catholic, had lost their spiritual vigour, and turned to groups that emphasized personal conversion, direct communication with God, and moral regeneration. Some of these groups, such as the Levellers or the Immortalists, survived only briefly; others, such as the Quakers, became involved in social and political changes; others, such as the Jansenists or Pietists, shaped the existing Catholic and Protestant churches; and others still, such as the Moravians or Methodists, became institutionalized as separate denominations. Many of these groups were inspired by or even founded by women, and had a disproportionate number of women among their followers. Such women used the language of religious texts and the examples of pious women who preceded them to subvert or directly challenge male directives. Very few of these groups, however, explicitly broke with Christian traditions that privileged men. In almost all of them, God was still thought of as male, the account of creation was understood to ascribe or ordain a secondary status for women, women were instructed to be obedient and subservient, the highest (or all) levels of the clergy were reserved for men, and religious traditions were used by men as buttresses for male authority in all realms of life, not simply religion. Thus in these centuries, as in all Christian history, messages about gender were contradictory and ambiguous, providing ideas that supported gender hierarchy as well as gender complementarity and equality.

Protestants in Europe and North America

The period of the English Civil War (1640–60) lies somewhat outside the chronological boundaries of this volume, but it provides a unique opportunity to hear women's religious ideas, for the hiatus in censorship during the war allowed many religious works by women – and men who were not officials in established churches – to be published. Women's leadership and actions during the war also served as one example of the 'world turned upside down', which the Restoration of the Stuart monarchy in 1660 sought to set right again. That Restoration and the re-establishment of the Anglican Church led many English Puritans to immigrate, and they took their ideas about gender and sexuality as well as theology to continental Europe and ultimately to North America.

Though most Puritan writers and preachers did not break with Anglicans or continental Protestants on the need for wifely obedience or women's secondary status, certain aspects of Puritan theology and practice prepared women for a more active role. All believers, male and female, were to engage in spiritual introspection, and in particular to focus on their experience of conversion. This experience was an indication that one was among the elect, and in more established Puritan communities such as those of New England it became a requirement for membership in a congregation. A particularly dramatic conversion could give one a certain amount of power, especially if it resulted in the healing of an illness or a continuing experience of divine revelation. Women's conversion narratives are often very personal and physical, such as that of Sarah Wight published as *The Exceeding Riches of Grace Advanced* (London, 1647): 'Now I have my desire; I desired nothing but a crucified Christ and I have him; a crucified Christ, a naked Christ; I have him and nothing else . . . *I am so full of the Creator, that I now can take in none of the Creature. I am filled with heavenly Manna.*'² Though Wight appears in some ways as passive, she is discussing her own spiritual development publicly in a way that was new for Protestant women. Nuns were the only other women whose spiritual growth and trials had been viewed as important, though not even Saint Teresa of Avila's autobiography made it into print during her lifetime.

Puritans viewed prayer as an active force that could influence state affairs. Puritan women (and men) privately and publicly prayed for certain political changes, and were firmly convinced that prayer aided one's family, community, and political allies. For Puritans, who had rejected the efficacy of exorcism, group prayer was the most powerful weapon in cases of possession, and many tracts report on the efficacy of such prayers against that worst of enemies, Satan.

Women's prayers and conversion narratives often grew into more extended prophecies in seventeenth-century England, some of which were described by others (often hostile to the woman or the message) and some of which were published by the women themselves. Lady Eleanor Douglas, for example, published thirty-seven pamphlets during her life, despite frequent imprisonments for sedition. Female prophets were occasionally criticized for speaking out publicly on political and religious matters, but they had Old Testament and classical precedents for what they were doing, and were usually viewed in the way they viewed themselves – as mouthpieces of God, as, in the words of some, 'impregnated with the Holy Spirit'. Women who went beyond prophecy to actual preaching also emphasized the strength of their calling, but this was not enough in the eyes of most observers to justify such a clear break with the deutero-Pauline injunction forbidding women to teach. It is difficult to know how common female preaching actually was during the Civil War decades, for most reports of it come from extremely hostile observers such as Thomas Edwards who were in turn criticized for making up some of their accounts. Women tended to preach spontaneously at informal or clandestine meetings, and their listeners never thought to record the content of their sermons, so it is unclear how much sustained influence they exerted.

Women clearly did have an impact on the spread of more radical religious ideas through two other activities, organizing what were known as 'gathered' churches in their own homes and publishing pamphlets. Puritan women had often organized prayer meetings and conventicles in their houses during the early part of the seventeenth century, and after the Restoration they continued to open their homes to Baptists, Presbyterians, Quakers, and other groups. Post-Restoration commentators belittled such groups by pointing out the large number of women they attracted, though again we have few objective records with which to judge the actual gender balance. As noted above, political and religious pamphlets authored by women appeared most frequently during the two decades when censorship was not rigorously enforced, as part of a more general explosion of pamphlet literature by a wide range of authors. Though most female authors deprecated their own abilities and described them-selves as 'instruments of God's power', they clearly intended their works to be read by men and felt no limits as to subject matter, delving into complex theological and doctrinal matters and directly challenging the actions of the king or parliament.

A sense of urgency pervades most women's pamphlets, an urgency which occasionally led women to more overtly political actions. Several times during the Civil War decades, women petitioned parliament directly. In 1649, hundreds of women petitioned for the release of the Leveller leader John Lilburne, and 7,000 Quaker women signed a petition to parliament in 1659 for the abolition of the tithes. The language of the Leveller women clearly indicates that they felt a right to operate as political actors: 'We cannot but wonder and grieve that we should appear so despicable in your eyes as to be thought unworthy to Petition or represent our Grievances to this Honourable House. Have we not an equal interest with the men of the Nation, in those liberties and securities contained in the Petition of Right, and other good Laws of the Land?'[3] Not until the French Revolution did statements such as this, claiming political rights for women who were not hereditary rulers, emerge again in Europe.

Such actions came to an abrupt end with the Restoration, and most of the radical groups in which women had participated died out. The most important exceptions to this generalization were the Quakers, who had been the most supportive of women's independent religious actions throughout the decades of the Civil War. George Fox, the founder of the Quakers, did not advocate women's social or political equality, but did support women's preaching. Separate women's meetings, first in England and then in British North America, oversaw the readiness of candidates for marriage, cared for the poor and orphans, upheld the maintenance of decorous standards of dress, and at times ruled on other moral issues. Quakers taught that the spirit of God did not differentiate between men and women, and advocated qualities for all believers similar to those which most Protestants stressed for women: humility, self-denial, piety, devotion, modesty. These were not to make one weak in the face of persecution, however, and Quakers were the most viciously persecuted of all the radical groups, perhaps because they were the most adamant in proclaiming their beliefs. Quaker women preached throughout England and the English colonies in the New World, and were active as missionaries also in Ireland, continental Europe, and occasionally elsewhere in the world. They were whipped and imprisoned for preaching, refusing to pay tithes or take oaths, or holding meetings in their houses, and they were accorded no special treatment for age, illness, pregnancy, or the presence of young children. Quaker women also published a large number of pamphlets, most of them apocalyptic prophecies or 'encouragements' for co-believers, as well as spiritual autobiographies – all of which constitute some of the few sources we have from the seventeenth century written by middle- or lower-class women.

Margaret Fell Fox (1614–1702), who eventually married George Fox after years of organizing, preaching, visiting prisoners, and being imprisoned herself for her Quaker beliefs, published *Women's Speaking Justified* in 1669, which argued that Paul's prohibition of women's preaching had only been meant for the 'busie-bodies and tatlers' of Corinth, and provided a host of biblical examples of women who publicly taught others. Fell did not argue for women's equality in secular matters, but for Quakers spiritual matters were more important anyway. The women's meetings that she organized gave many women the opportunity to speak in public and to engage in philanthropic activities for persons outside of their own families. Though Quakers as a group became increasingly apolitical in the eighteenth century, social action by Quaker women continued. Many of the leaders of the abolitionist and women's rights movements in nineteenth-century America were women who had been brought up as Quakers.

Though many areas of Europe experienced social and political revolts in the seventeenth century (leading some historians to suggest that this was a time of 'general crisis'), female religious writers and thinkers on the continent were generally not involved in them to the same extent as Leveller and Quaker women in England. Most continental women religious thinkers were mystics and ecstatics, who might have visions of political events, but who did not work to bring these about. They tended to emphasize the inner life of the spirit and to downplay the importance of the Bible, the ordained clergy, the external ceremonies or sacraments, higher education, and sometimes reason. Antoinette Bourignon (1616–80), a French mystic and reformer, believed spiritual rebirth more important than baptism so that Jews and Moslems might also be blessed and resurrected. She refused to be associated with any group, saying that the divisions within Christianity were signs of the coming end of the world.

Several female religious thinkers both on the continent and in England drew large numbers of followers. Jane Lead (1623–1704), for example, wrote that true religious knowledge came only through turning inward and finding one's own inner light. She organized a circle of like-minded people called the Philadelphian Society, urging them to seek the 'virgin wisdom of God' and not go 'whoring after Lord Reason'. Like the Quakers, whose official name was the 'Society of Friends', she did not want to describe her associates as a 'church'. Some of the works of female religious writers went through numerous editions and translations, suggesting that they were widely read, and a few continue to be published or included on websites related to spirituality today. Most church and state officials reacted with horror to such women, however, both for their independence in expressing their ideas and for the content of what they were saying or writing. Many women and the groups they were associated with were driven from place to place seeking more tolerant political authorities. Antoinette Bourignon was forced from France to Flanders to Germany and finally to the Netherlands, which provided a refuge for Philadelphians and Quakers as well. The Netherlands was the most tolerant part of Europe so that it was also the most common place of publication for the works of these women and those of other radical religious thinkers.

Women also played a significant role in the Pietist movement of the late seventeenth and eighteenth centuries. Born in Germany and then spreading elsewhere, the movement emphasized morality, Bible study, and personal spiritual regeneration. The history of Pietism is often written as the history of its best-known leaders, Philipp Jakob Spener and August Hermann Francke, but in many ways it was a grass-roots movement of lay people who met in prayer circles and conventicles, among whom were many women. Johanna Eleonora Petersen (1644–1724) organized several Pietist circles and wrote a huge number of tracts, including a commentary on the Book of Revelations. Erdmuthe von Zinzendorf (1700–56) was largely responsible for the financial security and day-to-day operations of her husband's colony of Moravian Brethren at

Herrnhut in Germany. Count Nicholas von Zinzendorf had originally intended the Herrnhutters to be a group within the Lutheran Church that would encourage deeper religious sensibilities, but they came to be considered a separate body. Zinzendorf was banished from Germany for more than ten years and travelled to America and England to set up Moravian congregations. During this time Erdmuthe handled missionary work in Denmark and Livonia, established orphanages, and ran the home colony. Her dowry and family money provided most of the support for all Herrnhutter activities.

The most important outgrowth of Pietism in the English-speaking world was Methodism, a group in which women were also very active. Even during her son's Anglican ministry, John Wesley's mother Susanna had held unauthorized meetings with over 200 in attendance at which she read sermons and discussed religious issues. Both men and women in Methodism were encouraged to give public testimony of their conversion experiences and spiritual life and to 'exhort' others to faith and repentance. By the 1760s, Sarah Crosby (1729–1804) and Mary Bosanquet Fletcher (1739–1815) had, with John Wesley's reluctant approval, gone from less formal 'exhorting' to being leaders of Methodist 'classes', weekly meetings at which members were to give an account of their actions and discipleship. Methodism was ridiculed for allowing female preaching, and often criticized in gendered language – as 'silly women' – because of women's active role and because the testimony of all followers seemed overly emotional and sentimental. After John Wesley's death in 1791, Methodists became increasingly hostile towards a female preaching ministry, and from 1803, women were restricted to addressing other women and then only under strict conditions. Some women continued to preach anyway, however, particularly in rural, frontier, and mission areas.

Several male Pietist and Methodist leaders developed less hierarchical ideas about gender than more traditional Protestant writers. Zinzendorf, for example, thought that Adam was androgynous before the fall and that men had to recover the feminine part of their souls in order to be saved. Moravians sang hymns to Jesus' penis and Mary's breasts and uterus, which Zinzendorf defended by asserting that shame about Jesus' or Mary's sexual organs was a denial of the full humanity of Christ. For many Pietists, Christ was also androgynous; male, yes, but a virgin, so that he was not fully a man. The Pietist emphasis on devotion rather than doctrine also led some writers (including Johanna Eleonora Petersen as well as male writers) to view women as the clearest embodiment of proper piety.

This championing of female or androgynous qualities in theory did not lead to permanent female church leadership in practice, however. As we have seen, the Methodists banned female preaching, and in 1764 a Herrnhutter synod explicitly forbade women from all governing offices except the most minor, noting that this would help them control their 'desire for [masculine] power [*Herrnsucht*]'. Zinzendorf himself criticized Erdmuthe for her independence, which he called pride. His second wife was a much younger woman who had long been his travelling companion. Gottfried Arnold, a Pietist himself and one of the few eighteenth-century historians sympathetic to individuals outside of the established churches, wrote that women had to be particularly careful if they were religious individualists, since Satan could easily lead them from religious freedom to sexual license. Those Pietist and Methodist historians who included women such as Johanna Petersen, Erdmuthe von Zinzendorf, or Susanna Wesley in their histories were careful to describe them as 'helpmates'.

Shakers – officially the United Society of Believers in Christ's Second Appearing – had no such reservations. They first began in the 1740s around Manchester in England, and in 1758, Ann Lee (1736–84) joined and became the leader. Lee was a visionary and mystic, whose followers regarded her as the second coming of Christ. God, in their eyes, was both female and male, so that Christ's second coming would have to be in a female body. Her visions also told her that sexuality was depraved, and her followers swore celibacy and chastity. She and her followers were severely persecuted, and in 1774, she led eight of them to the American Colonies. Persecution continued, however, and she died as the result of beatings. Despite – or perhaps because of – their advocacy of celibacy, the Shakers continued to win followers. At their peak, about 1830, American Shakers may have numbered 6,000 people.

The Shakers were not the only radical or Pietist group to develop unusual ideas about sexuality or distinctive systems of marriage. Such groups did not regard marriage as a sacrament – most rejected the idea of sacraments completely – but they placed more emphasis on its spiritual nature than did Lutherans or Calvinists. Marriage was a covenant – a contract – between a man and a woman based on their membership in the body of believers, and thus was linked to their redemption. Because of this the group as a whole or at least its leaders should have a say in marital choice, broadening the circle of consent far beyond the parental consent required by Luther, Calvin, and other less radical reformers. Quakers who wished to marry had to produce a certificate stating that both parties were Quakers or risk expulsion. Moravians in Pennsylvania were segregated by sex until marriage. When a man wished to marry, he came to the Elders' Conference, which proposed a possible spouse. Three coloured ballots standing for 'yes', 'no', and 'wait' were placed in a box, and one was drawn, which was regarded as the 'Saviour's decision'. Along with the Shakers, a few other groups forbade all sexual relations, relying on conversion to gain new members. The 'Immortalists' in New England, led by Sarah Prentice, held that conversion had made them bodily incorruptible and that marriage was a spiritual union over which civil authorities should have no control.

Ideas such as these horrified most Protestant authorities (and Catholic, for that matter), who regarded male-headed households, in which men controlled their wives, children, and servants, as structures established by God, and believed that church and state should act together to enforce morality and order. Except during brief periods such as the English Civil War or the French Revolution, every state in Europe had an officially established church. In some parts of Europe, including most Catholic states along with England and Scotland, church courts were officially independent of state control, with their own judges and legal codes. In others, including most Lutheran areas, they were part of the state government, with their policies and procedures established as part of national or territorial law codes. Though they thus differed in their level of state control (and in some areas this level of control was contested), church courts did not differ significantly from secular authorities in their attitudes towards marriage, morals, and sexual issues. In most Protestant and some Catholic areas, parental consent was required for marriage, even if the spouses were adults. Laws regulating marriage and morals were issued more frequently, with stern admonitions about their enforcement, and investigations were held questioning pastors and lay people about their ideas and conduct.

In England divorce was only possible by act of parliament, but Protestants in some parts of Europe and European colonies did allow divorce for adultery and impotence, and sometimes for contracting a contagious disease, malicious desertion, conviction for a capital crime, or deadly assault. This dramatic change in marital law had less than dramatic results, however, at least judging by sheer numbers. In contrast to today, when divorce is a large part of all civil legal procedures, Protestant marriage courts heard very few divorce cases, because marriage was the economic and social foundation of society. The vast majority of cases involving sexual conduct actually heard by Protestant church courts in Europe and lower courts in New England were for premarital intercourse, usually termed fornication, which became evident when a woman showed signs of pregnancy. Along with punishing those found guilty of fornication, Protestant authorities also attempted to restrict occasions which they increasingly viewed as sources of sexual temptation, such as parish festivals, spinning bees, and dances. Sodomy was generally a capital crime, though the number of actual sodomy cases was very small. The

Puritans who ruled England during the period 1640–60 and New England in the colonial period were much more worried about blasphemy and illegitimacy than about sodomy.

Catholics in Europe

Catholic women as well as Protestant were active in the church in the seventeenth and eighteenth centuries, and their contributions were similarly opposed, ridiculed, or minimized. During the sixteenth and early seventeenth centuries, several women, including Isabel Roser in Italy and Mary Ward in England, had attempted to establish a female order of Jesuits, or at least a women's order similarly dedicated to work out in the world. The leaders of the Jesuit order and the popes were horrified at the thought of religious women in constant contact with lay people, and the Council of Trent reaffirmed the necessity of cloister for all women religious. Enforcement of this decree came slowly, but gradually even groups set up to educate girls, such as the Ursulines, were ordered to accept claustration. Later, on the Continent, Mary Ward attempted to circumvent this ruling by having the women in her group – termed the Institute of the Blessed Virgin Mary – take no formal vows. But her independence and popularity aroused the suspicions of the Catholic hierarchy, which in 1631 ordered the schools and houses run by the Institute to be closed, while Ward herself was imprisoned. Similar uncloistered communities of women, such as the Visitation – begun by Saint Francis de Sales and the lay woman Jeanne de Chantal to serve the poor – were also ordered to accept claustration or be closed. Most of the communities accepted the cloister, and the founders of the Visitation were eventually both canonized.

The separation of women's religious communities from the world lessened their ability to solicit funds, and the post-Tridentine emphasis on the sacraments meant that most benefactors preferred to give donations to male houses whose residents could say Mass. Many female houses grew increasingly impoverished, and more interested in the size of the dowry of a prospective entrant than in the depth of her religious vocation. By the seventeenth century, convents in many parts of Europe were both shrinking and becoming increasingly aristocratic. In Venice, for example, nearly 60 per cent of all women of the upper class joined convents. The long-range effect of claustration was not an increase but a decrease in spiritual vigour.

Beginning in the later seventeenth century, lay women in some parts of Europe were slowly able to create what had been so forcibly forbidden to religious women – a community with an active mission in the world. Leadership in this change was provided by the Daughters of Charity (now often called the Sisters of Charity) begun in 1633 by Vincent de Paul and Louise de Marillac. Though both founders privately thought of the group as a religious community, they realized that outwardly maintaining secular status was the only thing that would allow them to serve the poor and ill. The Daughters took no public vows and did not wear religious habits, and constantly stressed that they would work only where they were invited to do so by a bishop or priest. This subversion of the rules was successful, for the Daughters of Charity received papal approval and served as the model for other women's communities that emphasized educating the poor or girls. By 1700, numerous teaching and charitable 'congregations' were found throughout Catholic Europe. They explicitly used the Virgin Mary as their model, stressing that she, too, had served as a missionary when she had visited her cousin Elizabeth during Elizabeth's pregnancy with John the Baptist. The marquise de Maintenon (1635–1719), initially the governess to some of Louis XIV's children and later his (secretly married) second wife, founded a school for poor but honourable aristocratic girls at Saint-Cyr in 1686. Madame de Maintenon had been educated by the Ursulines, and saw this institution as training young women for lives of Christian virtue in the world, not in the convent. Saint-Cyr was later required to adopt the rules of a religious order, but relatively few of its graduates became nuns.

The Daughters of Charity and other such congregations were often backed by women's confraternities, whose members supported the congregation financially while also engaging in charitable works themselves. Such confraternities were patterned after those men's confraternities which had been founded by Jesuits as a means of both combating Protestantism and deepening Catholic spiritual life. Some were dedicated to spiritual practices with special meaning for women, such as saying the rosary. Both congregations and confraternities provided women with companionship, devotional practices, and an outlet for their energies beyond the household. Huge numbers of women joined them in the seventeenth and eighteenth centuries, a phenomenon which certainly contributed to women's greater loyalty to the church in a period of growing secularism. During the French Revolution, women hid priests who refused to sign oaths of loyalty to the government, attended illegal worship services, and occasionally organized prayer meetings and processions. Anne Marie Rivier (1748–1838) led worship and opened schools in her village during the 1790s, and later founded the Présentation de Marie, which became the largest teaching congregation in much of France, with over 100 houses at the time of her death. In the early nineteenth century, when boys in some parts of Europe began to receive free public education, congregations and convents often offered the only education for girls in Catholic areas, which further heightened the feminization of religion.

While many Catholic women joined confraternities or engaged in charitable activities, a few advocated a more interior form of devotion. Louise Françoise de la Vallière (1644–1710) was during the 1660s the mistress of Louis XIV, by whom she had four children. After she fell out of favour with the king and went through a near-fatal illness, she had a spiritual conversion and withdrew from Paris to a nearby Carmelite convent. She wrote a series of prayers to God repenting for her earlier life and presenting a model of redemption through direct mystical encounters, *Réflexions sur la miséricorde de Dieu*. Marguerite de la Sablière (1640–93) was a Huguenot and the organizer of a popular *salon* in Paris who converted to Catholicism in 1680 and became a solitary penitent, emphasizing unquestioning submission to the will of God in *Maximes chrétiennes* and *Pensées chrétiennes*.

The best-known female mystic of this period was Jeanne-Marie Bouvier de la Mothe Guyon (1647–1717), a French woman who was very much influenced by the writings of Saint Francis de Sales. Madame Guyon taught that one should try to lose one's individual soul in God, reaching inner peace through prayer and the pure and disinterested love of God, an idea generally termed 'quietism'. She felt herself called to spread this mystical method, and in 1685 she published *Moyen court et facile de faire l'oraison*. Her ideas attracted women and men, including High Church officials such as Archbishop Fénelon, who later wrote that he had learned more from her than from any theologian. Madam Guyon was imprisoned several times on the orders of Bishop Bossuet, the most influential French ecclesiastic of the period, who was particularly incensed that her quietism, detachment, and lack of concern for external religious structures took her in spiritual terms out of his power. If such ideas spread further, wrote Bossuet, they would lead to an intolerable lack of respect for authority. Her writings were placed on the Index of Forbidden Books, and though she always asserted she was submissive to the Catholic Church, after her death her ideas became better known among Protestants than Catholics. Her writings began to be published in Holland in the early eighteenth century, and in translation they became popular with Methodists in Britain and North America. They are available in paperback versions from many Christian publishers today, advertised for their guidance in prayer and spirituality, not as historical documents.

Saint Francis de Sales provided the initial inspiration for another group of women who emphasized personal holiness and spiritual renewal. During the early seventeenth century, he advised the abbess of Port-Royal, Angélique

Arnauld (1591–1661), about reforms to her convent. Nuns from Port-Royal became renowned for their piety, and their help was sought all over France for the reform of convent discipline. The abbey then became the spiritual centre of Jansenism in France, the movement based on the ideas of the Dutch theologian Cornelius Jansen, particularly those discussed in his posthumous work *Augustinus* (1642). Jansen advocated greater personal holiness, lay reading of and meditation on Scripture, lay participation in church services, scrupulous attention to morality, and less frequent communion for the faithful. These ideas were shared by Angélique Arnauld's brother Antoine, a priest and teacher at the Sorbonne, who published in 1643 *De la fréquente communion*, which was also an attack on the Jesuits.

Two papal bulls in 1653 and 1656 condemned some of the ideas contained in *Augustinus*, and in 1661 Louis XIV ordered all members of the French church to sign a statement indicating their adherence to the bulls. The nuns at Port-Royal refused, commenting that some (Jansenist-inclined) theologians argued that the papal bull misrepresented what Jansen had said, and that, as women, they were clearly not capable of making judgements about theological matters on which learned men disagreed. They pointed out that God's law (as stated by Paul in the New Testament) ordered women to keep silent on matters of theology, and that they were simply obeying this higher law rather than Louis' command. The nuns at Port-Royal may have learned how to use stereotypes about women's weakness and duty of obedience to their advantage from the writings of Teresa of Avila, whom Angélique Arnauld in particular greatly admired, and who had been made a saint in 1622. Louis XIV's newly appointed Archbishop Péréfix questioned the women, ordering them to sign the anti-Jansenist statement because of their duty of obedience to him and to their king. But most of them remained firm, stressing the primacy of God's law over man's law, and noting that their God-given power of reason indicated that the king and archbishop had ulterior motives. Péréfix then refused them the sacraments, exiling many of them to other convents, and placing those who remained under house arrest. A truce with the papacy quieted the debate for several decades, but in 1705 the Port-Royal nuns were ordered to accept another anti-Jansenist papal bull. They again refused, and in 1709 Louis XIV demolished the convent and banished the nuns to other houses.

The writings of the Port-Royal nuns, including reports of their interrogations by Archbishop Péréfix, became part of a body of Jansenist literature that continued to circulate, though Jansenism itself was increasingly suppressed and many Jansenist priests fled France. Jansenist laity continued to hold underground prayer meetings, and there is some evidence that women read and commented on Scripture at these meetings. Women were also imprisoned for distributing prohibited Jansenist literature. Despite its official prohibition, Jansenism continued to shape the religious life of many women in France, encouraging them not only to become literate but to become frequent readers, to develop their children's spiritual lives through family devotions, and to accept Catholic doctrine not simply as a matter of emotional commitment and habit, but through intellectual conviction.

Debates about women's duty of obedience and capacity for reason emerged not only within the context of Jansenism, but also, and ultimately more significantly, within the critical discourse of the Enlightenment. In the salons of Paris and other cities, and in letters and printed works, men and women discussed the degree to which rational abilities were shaped by gender, and whether men and women were, in their basic nature, equal or different. Those arguing for equality in reason, such as Louise d'Epinay, generally noted that men and women were also the same in exhibiting a range of propensity for virtue and vice. Those arguing for difference, such as Antoine-Léonard Thomas and Jean-Jacques Rousseau, asserted that contemporary women – especially those leading discussions in salons – were morally lax, but that in their basic nature women had more virtue.

For Rousseau in particular, whose ideas would become extremely influential, women's natural virtue was to be exhibited only in the private sphere of the household and family. Though in her role as wife and mother a woman was to be the moral centre of the family, she was still always to be obedient to her husband because, as Rousseau notes in *Emile* (1762), 'woman is made specially to please man'. Somewhat paradoxically, women's 'natural' moral capacity could be enhanced by training, and in this religious literature, especially the stories of virtuous women from the past, were especially helpful. Rousseau does not place religion *per se* within the 'private' realm of women and family, but nineteenth-century writers whose ideas were shaped by his writings often did. Those writers included Protestants as well as Catholics, and many scholars see the nineteenth century as a time when Christianity in many areas was domesticated, as well as feminized.

In terms of issues related to sexuality, during the seventeenth century more rigorous theologians, especially Jansenists, urged a greater attention to sexual sins, charging Jesuit confessors with 'laxism' and 'casuistry' when they examined the intentions and desires of confessants as well as their actions. During the eighteenth century, the bulk of the clergy took a more moderate position. The most influential Catholic writer on moral issues, St Alphonsus Liguori (1697–1787), advised confessors not to concentrate too much on sins which they had little hope of eradicating, such as lustful thoughts or fornication. In his opinion, explaining the sinfulness of acts that people would not give up simply transformed unwitting sins into mortal ones. In some respects, Liguori extended to men, or at least to common men, Rousseau's ideas about women. Both men and women are better left in a more 'natural' state, without being corrupted by too much knowledge. Such ideas were shared by many Catholic government officials, and the number of schools for children of both sexes was significantly smaller in Catholic areas than in Protestant.

In practice rather than in theory, there was more variety in patterns of marriage and sexuality in Catholic Europe than the officials at the Council of Trent hoped would be the case. Tridentine regulations and other measures of social discipline were much easier to enforce in cities and towns than in more isolated rural areas, and depended on the cooperation of secular authorities, which was not always forthcoming. In France, for example, the royal council refused to acknowledge the decisions of Trent, so royal and local church legislation became the basis of matrimonial law. Enforcement of clerical celibacy and the end of clerical concubinage were slow in coming, as were effective prohibitions of sexual relations before marriage among the laity, especially in rural areas. Prostitution was often licensed in Catholic areas rather than being prohibited as it was in Protestant areas, though reforming bishops occasionally tried to close all brothels, opening special houses, termed Magdalene houses, for repentant prostitutes and other 'fallen women'. Sodomy fell under the jurisdiction of the various Inquisitions in some parts of Catholic Europe, under episcopal courts in others, and under secular courts in still others, and regional differences emerged in both arrests and punishments. In general the severity of punishment for sodomy gradually declined, with the last execution for sodomy in Aragon in 1633 and in Castile and the rest of Catholic Europe about a century later. By the early eighteenth century in Paris, police began to track 'sodomites' using spies and informers, with punishments couched in the religious language of repentance even though the cases were handled by secular courts.

Christians outside of Europe

European colonization took Christianity around the world, and in areas colonized by the Spanish, Portuguese, and French, convents for women were generally established relatively shortly after the initial conquest – during the 1520s in the Caribbean, 1540s in Mexico, and 1550s in South America. In 1637, the same year that Jesuit missionaries in Canada established the first community for Indian converts, Marie de l'Incarnation and several other nuns established an Ursuline house in Quebec, which soon took in both native women and European immigrants. The Ursuline nuns were joined by Augustinians, and the number of convents grew. By 1725, one out of every hundred residents in New France was a nun. The numbers of women in convents in Latin America may have been even higher. One in five of the female population of Lima in the seventeenth century lived in convents, though most of these were servants, slaves, or lay sisters, not professed nuns. In Latin America, it was often difficult for upper-class women of European background to find a spouse acceptable to their families, and the convent appeared as the only honourable alternative. In the Portuguese colony of Bahia, for example, more than three-quarters of the daughters of leading families went into convents. They often took their servants and furniture with them, and paid little or no attention to the Tridentine rules on enclosure. Bishops throughout Latin America complained regularly about the number of servants employed by nuns and the number of visitors present in convents at all hours of the day.

Though the Ursuline house in Quebec took in both immigrants and indigenous women, most convents in colonial areas accepted only European women as professed nuns, with indigenous or mixed-blood women allowed in only as lay sisters or servants. The first convents solely for native women did not open in the Philippines and in Mexico until the early 1700s. Lay organizations for indigenous women and men were more common. Lay confraternities dedicated to the Rosary were established in Melaka and the south-east coast of India by Portuguese missionaries, whose members carried out charity work among the poor and sick, cared for their own members, and encouraged their members to give up non-Christian religious and cultural practices. Alexandre de Rhodes (1591–1660), a Jesuit missionary in Vietnam, set up communities of celibate men and women as catechists (the later called 'Amantes de la Croix'), who cared for the ill as well as attempting to win converts. They took vows of poverty, chastity, and obedience, but were not technically members of religious orders, so that, like the Daughters of Charity, the women among them were able to participate in an active mission out in the world. Women who were members of religious orders carried out their teaching and missionary work from within their convents. Even the most permeable Latin American convent walls allowed people in more easily than they allowed nuns out.

Among Protestants, women were not as active as missionaries in the seventeenth and eighteenth centuries as they would be in the nineteenth century. Among radical or Pietist groups such as the Quakers, Moravians, and Methodists, however, women did occasionally teach and preach to indigenous people and European immigrants. Such women were generally the wives or sisters of male missionaries, though occasionally women travelled without their male relatives. Two English Quaker women, for example, Elizabeth Hooton and Joan Brocksopp, went to Barbados and Jamaica in the 1660s and 1670s, where they read the Bible publicly and challenged ministers.

Women's independent religious activities in colonial areas were limited, as they were in Europe, by ideas about women's weaker nature and inferior status, and also by fears about the possibility of sexual contact between European women and native men. The earliest European colonizers, whether soldiers, missionaries, traders, or officials, had almost all been men, who had regularly engaged in sexual relations with indigenous women. Spanish, Portuguese, and Dutch authorities initially encouraged sexual relations and even marriage between European men and indigenous women as a means of making alliances, cementing colonial power, and increasing the population. The directors of the Dutch East India Company gave soldiers, sailors, and minor officials bonuses if they agreed to marry local women and stay in the Dutch colonies as 'free-burghers'. This policy was opposed by some Dutch missionaries, but accepted by others, who hoped marriage with local women would not only win converts but also give missionaries access to female religious rituals. The Directors of the British East India Company gave additional encouragement in 1687, decreeing that any child resulting from the marriage of any soldier and native woman be paid a small grant on the day of its christening.

There were limits to this acceptance of inter-marriage, however, often explicitly along racial lines. Rijkloff von Goens, one of the Dutch governors of Sri Lanka, supported mixed marriages, but then wanted the daughters of those marriages married to Dutchmen so that the Dutch 'race' would 'degenerate' as little as possible. In the Dutch colony of the Cape of Good Hope (South Africa), though the races were not segregated and there was much sexual contact between European men and African women, this colour hierarchy was so strong that it largely prevented inter-racial marriage. Until 1823, slaves in Cape Colony could not marry in a Christian ceremony. A man wanting to marry a slave had to baptize and free her first. Slaves marrying among themselves often devised their own ceremonies, or married in Muslim ceremonies even though Islam was not a recognized religion.

By the second and third generation, many European men preferred women of mixed race as marital partners. In Dutch and English areas, some of these women were Catholic, the children of marriages between Portuguese men and local women. Protestant church authorities worried about the women retaining their loyalty to Catholicism, raising their children as Catholics and perhaps even converting their husbands. Thus, although they often tolerated Catholicism in general, they required marriages between a Protestant and a Catholic to be celebrated in a Protestant church and demanded a promise from the spouses that the children would be raised Protestant.

The fate of children from inter-racial unions varied enormously. Some of them were legitimated by their fathers through adoption or the purchase of certificates of legitimacy, and could assume prominent positions in colonial society. For example, two of the sons of François Caron, who had worked for twenty years for the Dutch East India Company and had five children with a Japanese woman, later became well-known ministers in the Dutch church. Many more children did not get much support from their fathers, and survived by begging or petty crime.

Church policies regarding marriage and morality were often counterproductive. In Dutch colonies, for example, marriages could only be solemnized when a pastor visited, which in remote areas might be only every several years. This did not keep people from marrying, however, but instead encouraged them to maintain traditional patterns of marriage, in which cohabitation and sexual relations began with the exchange of gifts, rather than a church wedding. Protestant missionaries advocated frequent church attendance, viewing sermons as a key way to communicate Protestant doctrine. The Asian wives of European men took this very much to heart and attended church so frequently and in such great style that sumptuary laws were soon passed restricting extravagant clothing and expenditures for church ceremonies. In the Danish Lutheran colony of Tranquebar, children of European men and local women born out of wedlock were denied baptism, but they were simply baptized in Portuguese Catholic churches, clearly not the intent of the Danish political or religious authorities.

Because initially almost all Europeans in colonial areas were men, inter-racial sexual relations generally did not upset European's notions of their own superiority, for the gender and racial hierarchies involved reinforced one another. Relations between European women and indigenous men were another matter, however, which led to restrictions, both formal and informal, on European women's mobility and activities in many colonial areas. In addition, once more women began to immigrate, official encouragement and even toleration of mixed marriages involving European men and indigenous women generally ceased. Informal relations, including rape, prostitution, concubinage, and informal marriage, continued, of course, and few Catholic or Protestant clergy were much concerned about them. Half of all slave children in colonial Brazil, for example, were baptized with unknown fathers, often a white or mixed-race man. By the seventeenth century in some parts of Latin America, mixed-race individuals – termed 'castas' – were the largest population group. They rarely officially married and during the period 1640–1700 in Central Mexico, 66 per cent of births to mixed-race women were out of wedlock. Though the Catholic Church officially decried extra-marital sexuality, it never refused to baptize the children and even occasionally sponsored group weddings to regularize a number of informal unions at one time. Had they known about such practices, commentators such as Thomas Edwards or Johann Feustking would have been just as horrified as they were about European religious groups in which women played a prominent role.

Notes

1. Gottfried Arnold, *Unpartheiische Kirchen und Ketzerhistorie vom Anfang des Neuen Testaments bis auf das Jahr Christi 1688* (Frankfurt: Thomas Fritschens sel. Erben, 1729), p. 1108. My translation.
2. Quoted in Barbara Ritter Dailey, 'The visitation of Sarah Wight: Holy Carnival and the revolution of the saints in civil war London', *Church history*, 55 (1986), p. 447.
3. Quoted in Hilda Smith, *Reason's disciples: Seventeenth-century English feminists* (Urbana: University of Illinois Press, 1982), p. 55.

10

Popular religion

WILLEM FRIJHOFF

Approaches to popular religion

In historical discourse, the term 'popular religion' has long had widely differing meanings depending upon the social group, the place, the time, and even the religious context for which it is used. One of the leading contemporary historians of popular culture, Michel Vovelle – closely linked to the celebrated *Annales* school of French historiography – has usefully distinguished between four approaches to this subject taken by historians in the twentieth century.[1] The first approach considers popular religion as a sort of 'original', primitive religiosity of humankind, which over the centuries repeatedly adapted itself to the current cultural context, but remained fundamentally the same. Popular religion in this view is pre-Christian and even anti-Christian. It continues quietly to live its own life independent from ecclesiastical rules, often as a kind of underground religion, undocumented by official society. The anthropologist Margaret Murray was one of the first to make use of this powerful image in her 1921 book *The witch cult in Western Europe*. A similar approach has recently been used by certain medieval historians, who postulate the existence throughout the Middle Ages of a substantial, semi-Christianized rural and urban population which continued to embrace older religious concepts and to interpret Christian dogma and liturgy in its own essentially pagan manner.[2] The Protestant and Catholic Reformations were, in this view, massive efforts to eradicate the 'pagan' or 'magical' legacy of pre-medieval and medieval society.

A second approach to popular religion is based on social stratification theory. For the early modern period, the best example comes from the work of Robert Mandrou. He distinguishes the religious culture of three different social strata: firstly, elite piety, largely individualized and open to high levels of spiritual creativity (as, for instance, in Baroque mysticism or Jansenist piety); secondly, the institutionalized and ordered religion of the urban classes, increasingly controlled by the clergy and organized in clear institutional structures with its own system of values and obligations (including confraternities and other pious corporations, and the lay sections of religious orders); and thirdly, rural religion, strongly characterized by a syncretism between pagan relics and Christian additions. Later in his career, Mandrou applied this scheme to the witch hunt, in his influential study of the attitude of French magistrates towards persons accused of witchcraft.[3]

The problem with these first two approaches is their rather static nature. Many of the so-called 'ancient traditions' may well be inventions of later periods, meant to adapt this legacy to new circumstances, or even to create the illusion of historical continuity in order to legitimate current practices. The second approach, in particular, presupposes a kind of 'immobile' society – as eighteenth-century rural France has sometimes been called – and relies heavily on the structural analysis so popular among *Annales* historians of early modern society in the 1960s and 1970s.[4] Yet from the late Middle Ages to the early nineteenth century, rural society, and urban society still more, went through a profound cultural, social, and economic evolution.

The third approach stipulated by Michel Vovelle develops a more dynamic conception of popular religion. It assumes an essentially synchronic opposition between official religion and alternative religion. In this vision, popular religion is not in a position of dependency but of competition, a militant alternative to the established churches. It exists as a dynamic counter-culture to the church of the ecclesiastical elites, and consequently evolves as elite strategies evolve. Some scholars have gone so far as to assert that there is no popular culture without opposition to elite culture. Two books have been particularly influential for this approach: Mikhail Bakhtin's study of the notion of popular culture in François Rabelais's works, and, inspired by him, Carlo Ginzburg's presentation of the religious cosmogony and the utopian world-view of Menocchio, the sixteenth-century Friuli miller summoned before the Holy Inquisition and ultimately executed by it. In Ginzburg's view (presented in this book and in others of his works), Carnival, *charivari*, iconoclasm, the festive side of rebellion, derisive fraternities, mock liturgies, devil's cults – all must be seen as popular registers of religious belief and practice, historical indicators of an alternative social order rooted in ancient traditions but continually being adapted and reshaped, and persecuted as such by the established authorities.[5]

The fourth and final approach to popular religion looks for religious dynamism not in forms of opposition but in a historical process of acculturation between the prescribed, official religious system and the experienced, lived practice of everyday religious life. This is essentially the approach taken by the

Italian historians Ernesto de Martino and Gabriele de Rosa and by the French historian Jean Delumeau.[6] In Delumeau's view, there is no pre-established body of popular religion. On the contrary, popular practices and beliefs are historically constructed. The distinction between official and popular religion is conceived as that between the prescribed religion and the *religion vécue*, or lived religion: between religion as the church authorities would have it and religion as it was experienced in actual life. Following this thesis, the origin and the legitimacy of popular practices barely matter. On the contrary, it is the encounter and the interplay of the two worlds that constitutes the historical phenomenon of religion. According to Delumeau, early modern 'popular' religion owes its existence to the particular Counter-Reformation context, when the ecclesiastical authorities found themselves obliged to undertake a straight-forward offensive against the *religion vécue* in order to civilize and Christianize (or re-Christianize) their flock, i.e., to bring their living practice into conformity with the official, prescribed religion of the church. The result, in Delumeau's eyes, was an enormous campaign for the acculturation of the – especially rural – masses, in order to accustom the ordinary people to the rules and regularity of religious practice as ordered by the church.

Clearly, whatever approach one takes to the subject, popular religion must be seen as historically embedded in a process of interaction or negotiation, between experience and prescription, practice and institutionalization. From the top to the bottom of society, individuals work with different repertoires of forms and meanings, historically shaped and transmitted but continuously renewed in the process of appropriation itself. The early modern era appears, in this respect, as a period during which popular religious experience increasingly clashed with institutional religion, and in which the Catholic and Protestant clergies alike attempted to gain control of the popular domain, with the firm intention of confining it to the norms of the established church. Yet from one place to another, and among the major Christian churches themselves, the motives and strategies as well as the outcomes of these attempts, varied substantially.[7]

Nature, the supernatural, and the sacred

Inasmuch as religious or magical practices were a way of conjuring uncontrolled or evil forces, any recourse to the supernatural presupposed a perception of the specific relations between the natural, the preternatural and the supernatural. But during the early modern period, developments in the religious world and the advent of the scientific revolution brought fundamental changes in the perception of the universe. Initially, the material world was viewed as part of the cosmic order.[8] It was thought to represent not only physical properties but also spiritual forces, which were expressed in transgressions or subversions of the natural order. Miracles and the huge sector of magic and the marvellous (such as monstrous births, blood rains, or solar eclipses), supernatural messages or portents, as well as natural disasters (floods, great fires, volcanic eruptions), famines, plagues and other catastrophes – all testified to the need both to respect the world of nature given by God and to understand the sacred order through which these forces could be conjured and controlled by means of appropriate rituals. Indeed, during the early modern period a sharper distinction was made between the supernatural, 'wonders' and 'miracles', caused by God alone, and the preternatural forces or events, 'marvels', which depended on secondary causes (including the works of angels and demons), rather than on God's direct interference in the order of nature.[9]

An enormous variety of sacral places, persons, and objects were maintained to provide protection against various forms of evil or shelter from divine punishment. Throughout the Christian world, saints like Sebastian or Roch, and a variety of Marian sanctuaries, protected the faithful against the plague, which was symbolically represented by transfixing arrows or purulent wounds. Pilgrimage shrines with sacral objects – such as Saint Hubert's in the Ardennes – served to heal or conjure rabies, or other contagious diseases whose physical causes remained unclear. Some places seemed to acquire a sacred meaning because of their exceptional sites on mountains or islands (like Mont-Saint-Michel in French Brittany); others because of their historical connections to the history of salvation or the relics of saints or other sacred persons: Jerusalem, Rome, and Santiago de Compostella (a city at the end of the world, *finis terrae*) are the most eminent examples. During the early modern period, Loreto in the province of Ancona (Italy) emerged as a major shrine; here, according to a fifteenth-century legend, the *Santa Casa*, or home of the Holy Family in Nazareth, had been transferred by angels. Certain cities, like Rome, Cologne or Naples, were huge shrines in their entirety, with all sorts of relics and other sacred objects in a multitude of churches, chapels, and convents.

In the long run, the Reformation brought a new perception of the sacred. Protestant theology ultimately refused to recognize a sacred sphere set apart from earthly life. Since in biblical terms the whole world was considered as blessed by God, and since the principal aim of humankind was to recognize the Lord in the whole of creation, there were no specific holy places, persons, periods, festivals, or objects. In principle, all the faithful shared in the general priesthood of believers. Churches lost their sacral quality; holy objects, statues and pictures were destroyed; holy festivals were abolished or reduced to simple commemorations founded on human memory rather than on the supernatural. Protestant theology and liturgy sought to eliminate the sacred order of ritual and the supernatural and replace it by the Holy Word of God, considered to contain its own efficacious force. Orthodox Calvinists and some other Protestant communities even wanted to abolish the whole Christian calendar as superstitious and return to the Old Testament order of time, where the ancient Sabbath was the only break in the weekly rhythm of labour permitted to true Christians, who were held to observe it through stern, rigorous rituals.

Insensibly, the Protestant shift in the perception of the natural world gave birth to a new sacral order. The belief in a more or less autonomous order combining both nature and the supernatural was replaced by an intimate conviction of God's providence and omnipotence. God could and always would interfere actively in the natural world, either directly through his Holy Word or the Holy Spirit, or indirectly through the intervention of angels or demons. The reality of the immediate intervention of the devil in this world was also widely assumed. In a more learned, biblically based and socially ordered way, demonology took over the role of ancient magical beliefs and brought a huge revival of belief in witchcraft. But at the same time this new sacral order prepared the way for a more rational view of the universe during the eighteenth century – a rational view that soon came to exclude otherworldly interventions altogether. In the new, early modern mentality, such interventions by God were essentially tied to the moral order and answered to a logic of divine reward for human virtues and retaliation for human vices. This logic, in turn, could be immediately deciphered by man through the guidance of God's Word as contained in the Holy Bible. Welfare, adversity, calamities, and disasters, prodigies, portents and prophecies, were seen as so many signs of God's blessing or wrath. Sickness and misfortune were further interpreted as opportunities to purify one's spirit and bring one's attitude into agreement with the will of God.[10]

Superstition

This moralizing of the natural world had important consequences for the Protestant definition of popular religion, and the attitude of the Protestant clerical elites towards *superstition*. 'Superstition' was conceived as a capital sin against the order of God, against his honour and uniqueness, as prescribed in the Decalogue. Superstition was defined as an infringement on God's omnipotence through recourse to other supernatural powers; or, as the Catholic

Council of Malines (1607) put it: 'to expect any effect from anything, when such an effect cannot be produced by natural causes, by divine institution, or by the ordination or approval of the Church'.[11] In this sense, the word 'superstition' became a general term for all actions and beliefs that were considered contrary to God's will, as expressed by his church. In everyday idiom, however, superstition could have a variety of meanings, depending on the period under consideration and the relations between the different religious communities involved.

All the Reformers devoted a large and intellectually essential part of their work to the fight against superstition, although in actual practice ministers could take rather different attitudes towards the 'relics of paganism', as they often called it. The notion of superstition, of medieval origin, entailed a variety of beliefs and practices considered as pagan or illicit for the true believer, and viewed as sources of unruliness within a well-ordered church community. Yet, in the confessional conflicts of the post-Reformation period, superstition became a label denoting not so much a *specific* level of religious culture (less valued than official religious creed and practice), than a *different or alternative*, or at any rate an *excessive* form of religious culture. In fact, Protestant church authorities widely employed the term 'superstition' in two different ways. First, they used it to denounce all those forms of mass religious practice which did not fit into a well-ordered church community of their own conception. Second, and more broadly, they used it to denounce whole competing religious communions, especially Roman Catholicism, including the higher, well-ordered forms of Catholicism which were, in fact, rather close to their Protestant equivalents.

The intellectual rejection of magic and superstition – and also of a whole range of Christian beliefs and practices which were more or less equated with magic and superstition by Protestant theologians and ecclesiastical leaders – must not blind us to what happened in real life. In fact, the early modern world-view, whether Catholic or Protestant, was fundamentally theocentric. In their daily lives, people were prone to accept interventions from outside the natural world as real events, charged with meaning. The extraordinary, the marvellous, the miraculous, or any other event that was perceived as unnatural – these were readily interpreted as tokens, signs of some other reality, in the common understanding of the world, although specific forms and meanings evolved throughout the centuries, and although the symbolic meaning of the supernatural was more compelling than that of the preternatural. In this respect, Protestants did not really differ from Catholics – at least not until Enlightened thought changed the stakes in the eighteenth century.

Straightforward magical thinking was rejected, but not the belief in super-natural intervention as such. On the contrary, the cultural universe of both Christian communions was characterized by other-worldly semantics, even though Protestants rejected the sensory apprehension of the divine and priv-ileged the word whereas Catholics played with rituals, images, and visual symbols.[12] Stories about the involvement of angels and devils in earthly affairs continued to be presented as real events in all the churches. In Protestant as well as Catholic sources, heaven protected its chosen saints or the privileged objects of religious transmission, which were made particularly meaningful by these heavenly interventions. Stories abound about indestructible bibles, and incombustible images of Martin Luther or copies of the celebrated book of German Protestant spirituality, the *Paradiesgärtlein* of Johann Arndt (1624).[13] Bibliomantics, the semi-magical random use of the Bible for making choices or predicting future events, remained widespread among Protestants. If the range of sacral objects was different, the Protestant use of such objects largely conformed to Catholic ways of dealing with the sacred.

Until well into the early modern era, Catholics and Protestants shared a similar physical and symbolic mental universe. Their perception of natural phenomena and their stories about causalities in the earthly and heavenly worlds continued largely to support one another, despite the combative trea-tises, sermons, and warnings from controversial theologians on both sides. One need only compare their reactions to the preternatural or the appar-ent interventions of heaven in this world: magic and witchcraft, comets and eclipses, angels and demons.[14] Their experience and perception of the world were strongly dependent on a cultural order that ecclesiastical discourse only very gradually succeeded in influencing. The Calvinist theology of won-ders attempted to break from Catholic traditions, but it remained a prisoner of its own vocabulary, which continued to dominate understandings of the miraculous.[15] In other respects, religious discourse itself struggled with a cer-tain number of incongruities in the perception of the natural world that the dogmatic ukases pronounced by theologians or synods were unable to erad-icate. They were at the base of the theory of *accommodation*, according to which the Holy Ghost, while inspiring the authors of the Bible, had adapted itself, as far as natural phenomena were concerned, to the modes of percep-tion of ordinary people. This theory, put forward in the sixteenth century by Calvin, himself a disciple of Saint Augustine, was strongly revived from the second half of the seventeenth century when differences were growing between the universe of everyday perception, academic exegesis, and learned science.[16]

Thus, a community of everyday cultural perceptions and practices existed between Catholics and Protestants, strengthened by the domestic religious practices (praying, singing, reading) that were common everywhere. Periodically the intellectual elites attempted to change the situation through dogmatic or apologetic writings. But though Protestant theology might reject the intercession of saints in heaven, the models of sanctity and indeed of the good life were largely identical within the different confessions, precisely because of their rivalry in this matter: models of behaviour not only shaped group identity, but they also had to be persuasive for others, if there was to be any hope of converting those others. Indeed, the early modern sources reveal that Catholics could respect and even embrace Protestant forms of godliness or holiness and vice versa.[17] This community of values and of models for life was one of the main foundations of the interconfessional conviviality that for early modern Dutch society I have called the *ecumenicity of everyday life*. This phrase refers to the capacity of members from different confessional sectors to co-exist peacefully in everything essential to their common cultural and social life, and to reach civic concord by disregarding the ecclesiastical disputes and divisions that the growing confessionalization tried to impose on public life.[18]

This pluri-confessional community of perception realized in the Netherlands was representative of a situation existing throughout Europe: Protestants and Catholics from different German territories, and Huguenots and Catholics in France, did not behave all that differently. They all shared the same basic perceptions of nature, community, and the universe. As such, they constituted an *interpretive community*, to the extent that, for the Catholics as well as the Protestants, signs and wonders publicly revealed the intentions of God, and in this way revealed the meaning of the perceived extraordinary. Only very slowly during the course of the seventeenth and eighteenth centuries would a clearer distinction emerge among the faithful between the evidence of the religious 'sign', intimately and almost immediately embedded with meaning, and the objective 'fact' that now had to be placed in a scientific discourse in order to become relevant.[19]

There is no reason to wonder about this basic continuity of popular religious culture in space and time. Historians had formerly portrayed the passage of a local community to the Reformation as a collective event, inspired by the leaders and immediately realized in the totality of its aspects and dimensions. This image, however, has been dismantled over the last few decades as new research in socio-cultural history has become available. We now recognize that sixteenth-century people, including the local pastors themselves, were often reluctant to accept the Reformation, or hesitated to embrace it in all its intellectual and moral consequences. The complaints or 'abuses' registered in the consistorial minutes or visitation reports demonstrate that the transformation of religious culture took a long time. In fact, the transition to the new confessional faith was normally the result of tough, ongoing negotiations between the ecclesiastical authorities and the local community – a local community which had long enjoyed its own conception of religious life and the role of the clergy, and which was often unprepared to sacrifice that conception at the bidding of the authorities in church and state. This new model of the 'negotiation' of religious culture, centred on an interactive process involving a number of actors, accounts much better for the apparent anomalies of the Reformation process, and for the uneven development of its different parameters. Religious institutions, persons or objects, practices or beliefs acquired symbolic meanings that made them unassailable, precisely because they came to be embraced as elements of the local community's identity.

The reform of popular religion

During the seventeenth century, and even more during the eighteenth century, popular religion became the main target of the reform efforts directed by all the religious authorities of western Christianity, Protestant and Catholic. In order to understand the issues at stake, we must return to the period immediately following the Protestant Reformation. The Council of Trent (1545–63) had been the starting point of a huge enterprise of reform of the Roman Catholic Church. While this 'Catholic Reformation' was provoked in part by the evident success of Lutheran Protestantism throughout the Holy Roman Empire and beyond, it was equally rooted in the late medieval sentiment of the inadequacy of the established Christian order – of its devotional life, of its ceremonial cults and ethical codes – to respond to the new requirements of the Christian community and of the individual life of the faithful. With respect to popular religion, the two key concepts of the Council of Trent were reform of the clergy and education of the masses. The canons and decrees of Trent express the conviction that the Christian community should be raised to a higher level of intellectual performance and moral commitment, and that such a reform would automatically engender a better religious life for the whole community. To pursue this reform, Trent advocated an elite corps of highly disciplined and well-trained priests working for the moral, spiritual, and temporal welfare of the masses. These priests would reside in their parish, live in chastity, and cultivate themselves by reading spiritual books. In brief, they would serve as examples of saintly living for the faithful.[20]

The masses, meanwhile, would be educated by this new-model clergy, through the ceremonials of liturgy, through preaching and catechesis, and, individually, through holy confession. Generations of Catholic reformers thought that such a better-educated laity would automatically withdraw from those popular religious practices and beliefs that were now clearly defined as superstitious, unruly, and even immoral. Popular devotion would be canalized into the norms and values that corresponded to the intellectual, emotional, and moral canons of the Catholic Reformation. With this in mind, popular devotion was encouraged, and new devotions were created, insofar as they could promote a better education for the people. Miracles that served the cause of the Catholic Reformation were readily promoted among the public, and a special category of Counter-Reformation saints arose, adapted to the new requirements of the Roman Catholic Church. New religious orders were created as bearers of this movement and each of them adopted its own pastoral strategy. The Jesuits, for instance, promoted in many different ways – including the use of traditional devotional practices – the cult of the saints of their Company: the founder Ignatius Loyola and the great missionary Francis Xavier, and also John Berchmans, Aloysius Gonzaga, and Stanislas Kostka, spiritual heroes and patron saints of the young. Most important in this respect were the confraternities for young people inside and outside the Jesuit colleges, where individuals were trained to imitate the virtues of the saintly heroes.[21]

Beside the continuous efforts at preaching and catechizing – expressed in innumerable collections of sermons, preaching manuals, catechetical primers and prayer books for the laity – the Catholic Reformation was characterized by a strenuous and prolonged attempt to eradicate what was increasingly interpreted as the pagan, animistic mentality of the masses, especially in the countryside. This mentality was to be replaced by a new religious idiom, directed towards the internalization of religious experience.[22] During the seventeenth and still more during the eighteenth century, the conviction grew that the laity, at least the lower social classes, had never really been Christianized, and that forbidden, sometimes even hidden forms of popular religion preserved pre-Christian forms of pagan folklore. These all had to be excised: sexual beliefs and customs, pre-nuptial intercourse, fertility rites, midsummer bonfires meant to conjure the forces of nature, and social rituals of the world turned upside down practised during Carnival, Epiphany, and other occasions.

This 'Christianizing offensive' was a form of acculturation, conceived to transform 'pagan' peasants and townspeople into truly Christian believers, and ultimately to make the religion of the clerics the religion of the whole community. It found a marvellous and ready instrument in the visitation practice that had existed since the later Middle Ages but that had never been properly used for this target. Over the course of two centuries, Roman Catholic bishops everywhere in Europe organized on a regular, sometimes even annual basis the systematic visitation of all the parishes within their dioceses. An ever more precise and elaborate questionnaire attempted to identify the vices of the flock and permitted the bishop to follow the pastoral efforts of the parish priests and their achievements in eradicating unruly practices.[23] The many surviving copies of these questionnaires provide an illuminating view of the rich varieties of popular religion. However, they also reveal something of the Catholic Reformation paradox: while the clergy undoubtedly succeeded in eliminating many of the most blatant 'abuses' (as they were commonly called) through different forms of acculturation to the standards of the ecclesiastical elite, many other customs went underground and escaped ecclesiastical control. They surfaced again in the nineteenth and twentieth centuries as simple forms of local folklore, pertaining to the broad domain of everyday religion, but without much ecclesiastical impact.[24] Moreover, parish priests often played a mediating role between the demands of the ecclesiastical elite, on the one hand, and the faithful entrusted to their moral and spiritual care, on the other. Many priests tended to listen to both sides and to invest new forms with old meanings, or vice versa. Loyalty to their flocks often took precedence over obedience to higher authorities.

The fight against superstition was also one of the major objectives of the Protestant Reformation. Even after the effective repression of 'papist superstitions' by the coalition of public and religious authorities, the denunciation of such practices remained a favourite pastime of zealous ministers, whether they were Reformed, Puritan, Arminian, Lutheran, or Anabaptist – not to mention the various new communities in the Anglo-Saxon world, such as Quakers and Methodists. By denouncing the adversary, often through the use of fictitious epithets such as 'the Jesuits' (in many cases a general term of invective, with much the same meaning as 'Antichrist'), they delimited their territory. They confirmed their own religious, moral, and public order, and effectively affirmed their identity. Not to be outdone, and faced with this Protestant offensive, the Catholic Church developed its own cultural identity, either by rejecting superstitions, or by using them to its advantage by transforming practices of an apparent magical nature into purified and church-bound identity rituals.[25]

Mixed territories

While Protestantism rejected popular religion from the outset as an outrage against God's providence and omnipotence, Catholicism maintained a more complicated relationship with popular religion. The difference between their two confessions became obvious whenever Protestantism and Catholicism confronted one another on the same territory – for example, in the British Isles, in the Holy Roman Empire, in France before the Revocation of the Edict of Nantes (1685), in the Swiss Confederation, and in parts of central Europe on the border of western Christianity. In such mixed territories, Catholicism had to manoeuvre between the conventions of popular religion, the purity of its own teachings, the dialogue with the other confessional groups, and the requirements of apologetics. Roman Catholic Baroque culture most visibly marked itself off from Protestant religious culture by the importance it attributed to images and gestures, statues and rituals for educational aims and also by its permissive attitude towards different forms of popular religiosity. Indeed, acquiescence to popular religion became one of the most distinctive marks of Catholicism. This is indicated in the travel accounts of young Protestants who in the seventeenth and eighteenth centuries made their 'grand tour' through Europe. In the devotional practices of many Catholic churches, chapels and pilgrimage shrines of France, Germany, and above all Italy, these Protestant travellers discovered a religious culture that was radically different from their own. What they found confirmed them in their disdain for the Catholic clergy, who the travellers accused of maintaining their flocks in a state of brutal ignorance; it also confirmed their disdain for the Catholic Church, which they viewed as concerned solely with its outward ceremonials.

In this juxtaposition of several opposing forms of religious practice, the United Provinces of the northern Netherlands present an interesting case study. In that confederation, the Reformed Church was the only publicly admitted religious creed. Nevertheless, individual freedom of conscience – though not of public worship – remained guaranteed to all through the regulations in Article 13 of the founding treaty of the confederation, the Union of Utrecht (1579). This guarantee was never really challenged during the course of the early modern period, even by the most violent defenders of the public monopoly of Calvinism. This meant that several important religious groups linked to major churches, as well as many smaller local communities of dissenters, survived with the connivance and sometimes – especially in Amsterdam and in some other large towns – with the full protection of the secular authorities. The Catholics, who represented about a third of the population (and substantially more in certain regions), developed a new confessional consciousness during the seventeenth and eighteenth centuries. Within this context, popular religion became a central element in a dialectical interaction between the churches. The Reformed Church maintained its firm rejection of all forms of 'papal superstition', including under that term both the universal (liturgical and dogmatic) and the local (popular) aspects of Catholicism. However, the apparent Catholic leniency towards popular religious practices attracted many people. This in turn obliged the Calvinists repeatedly to strengthen their negative position against such practices, and even to broaden their attacks to include cultural activities that were not strictly religious. Thus certain aspects of public festivals, Carnival, and burial practices became relegated to the sphere of 'papal superstition'.

A well-known case is the festival of St Nicholas' Eve. Saint Nicholas was originally the patron saint of the Old Church of Amsterdam, and hence of the town itself. Traditionally, a fair was held on that day on the central place, the Dam, in front of the town hall. Children's sweetmeats were sold, and these played a role in the reward and punishment rituals followed by parents in the home. The painter Jan Steen (1626–79), a Catholic from Leiden, represented a family gathering and its rituals on St Nicholas' Eve in a well-known picture, just as he painted other family festivals, like Epiphany, or the religious family rituals of everyday life. For the Reformed consistories, St Nicholas' Eve was nothing more than a papal superstition, a relic of the old popular religion that had to be abolished without reserve. Yet, for the general public the meanings of the festival remained strong, both as a symbol of the town's identity and as the occasion for the most important family and children's festival in the country. Soon the cult of Saint Nicholas had evolved in two different directions: towards a secular festival, on the one hand, and towards a Catholic reinterpretation of Saint Nicholas as a saint in the devotional repertoire of the general Catholic calendar, on the other. The secular family celebration of St Nicholas' Eve continued without interruption through the late eighteenth and early nineteenth centuries, when educationalists, including liberal Protestant ministers, discovered the pedagogical possibilities of the reward and punishment ritual, and renewed their interest in the moral dimensions of the festival.

Indeed, in the early modern Dutch Republic, the Catholic community subjected all of the practices and beliefs of traditional religious culture to reinterpretation. This, in turn, had two possible outcomes: either the practices and beliefs were embraced as true elements of the Catholic faith (and put forward as such in apologetic disputations with Protestant ministers); or they were rejected as full-fledged 'superstitions', incompatible with

Counter-Reformation views of the sacred sphere. In this way everyday dialectics brought a clarification of attitudes towards popular religion: Protestants were against any form of popular religion, whereas Catholics claimed some of these forms were integral to their 'Catholic', that is, universal religion, but rejected other forms as contrary to the standards of the Counter-Reformation church. In territories with mixed confessions, individuals could take advantage of the various attitudes of the different churches towards popular practices and beliefs, and thus seek their own maximum benefit. The documents show that they did so. Catholic shrines, even after their destruction, continued to attract both Catholic and Protestant faithful, who went there to perform forbidden healing rituals against plague, cattle disease, or natural disasters.

In Holland, for instance, the miraculous Marian well at the village of Heiloo near Alkmaar, a former place of pilgrimage where Our Lady's chapel had been destroyed after the Reformation, attracted both Catholic and Protestant breeders during the bovine plague of the winter of 1713–14. People came in such numbers to draw water into barrels and bottles – even carrying them away with four-horse carts – that locals opened inns on the spot. The civil authorities did not dare interfere, fearing it would cause a riot.[26] Interestingly, the site provided another message for the better educated laity, both Catholic and non-Catholic. Since the well had miraculously started to flow again on the night of Our Lady's Immaculate Conception (8 December), the Franciscan friars used it to demonstrate the truth of this dogma both to Protestants and to unconvinced Catholics. This was typical of post-Reformation cults: on one level, they served the everyday needs of the ordinary faithful, but on another level they contained an apologetic message for the non-believers. In the post-Reformation world of western Christianity, virtually all forms of religious discourse, including popular religion, had opponents in mind and tried to define a message that might win those opponents over.

Yet this example is also indicative of the distance which existed in early modern society between dogma and the everyday religious experience of the masses. In that fundamentally religious society where everybody had need for a proper confessional identity, people invariably felt a certain measure of opposition towards other churches or religious groups. Yet whenever possible, they sought out religious practices that fitted best with their everyday needs and they lived rather peacefully together so long as the higher civil or ecclesiastical authorities did not interfere. This basic solidarity of all towards the common needs of the community may be called the 'ecumenicity of everyday life'. Indeed, such an inter-confessional *modus vivendi* always started from the unspoken assumption that, on the basis of a shared general Christian consciousness, differences of religious practice, ceremonial, church organization, or belief should be put within brackets for the sake of communal and individual well-being in a multi-confessional society. In such a situation, popular religious practices and beliefs could easily shift from the confessional order to a purely secular order, and escape any control by the ecclesiastical authorities.

Social discipline and the acculturation thesis

Raising the religious practice of the laity to a higher cultural level required a double transformation in the public space. First, in order to make people aware of the distinction between a compulsory universal religion and forbidden forms of popular religion, the secular authorities developed a series of legislative measures, coercive actions and moral incentives within the public sphere, that have been described by early modern historians as 'social discipline'. Although this process was primarily an effort by the secular state to shape a homogeneous citizenry, it was sustained in many respects by a second and similar process of the 'confessionalization' of the churches.[27] The reform of religious practice, belief, and ritual entailed the imposition, and indeed the enforcing, of new norms, morals and practices from above, by the religious and secular authorities, who were usually acting together with a common strategy. In practice, the instruments of this moral offensive differed from church to church and from territory to territory, depending on the degree of co-operation between church and state authorities. Yet, structurally the policy of intervention was the same everywhere: formal regulations were issued for public behaviour in an increasing number of places and occasions; church discipline was enforced; a system of regular, periodical visitations of parishes, communities, and even families was introduced for the enforcement of precepts and the eradication of abuses; the new rules were systematically taught to the people, specially the lower classes, in sermons, catechisms, schoolbooks, popular literature, popular prints, and any other medium available; and finally, whenever possible, mitigated, broadly acceptable versions of popular practices and beliefs were incorporated into the body of church ritual and dogma. As such, this strategy had two faces. The first was a more secular face, expressed in the control of one's behaviour in human contacts and especially in the public area, fashionable ever since the age of humanism and Erasmus's *De civilitate morum puerilium* (1530), one of the most widely printed etiquette books and school primers of the early modern era. The second was a more religious face, expressed in the so-called 'Christianizing offensive', that is, the imposition of the norms of Christian high culture onto the religious experience of the masses.

Among Catholics, the revival of even a purified traditional Catholicism could not suffice. Too many older forms of religious culture had been contaminated with false connotations and obsolete meanings. Some of the older saints – Saint Anthony, Saint Nicholas, or Saint Roch, for example – could be reinvigorated within the new militant context. But new saints, representing new values and able to give new impetus to the exercise of virtue and the devotional life had to be added to the Catholic pantheon. First of all there was Saint Joseph, Christ's foster-father. Yet even more important were those saints who possessed an exemplary value because they had experienced the difficulties of the era themselves and had found their own solutions: Teresa of Avila, John of the Cross, Francis Xavier, Roberto Bellarmino, Francis de Sales, Marie de l'Incarnation, Jean-Baptiste de La Salle, Joseph de Copertino, Rosa de Lima, Alfonso-Maria de Liguori, and Benoît-Joseph Labre, to name only some of the most significant bearers of the new values. The same holds for pilgrimages, purposely promoted in a purified form and accommodated to the new values and new spiritual claims of the church[28] – which, of course, did not prevent lay people from venerating local hermits or healing saints, or from using ancient therapeutical springs as well, mostly against the wishes of their bishop or parish priest.

The cult of the Holy Virgin was promoted under a multitude of mostly new titles, which proclaimed her qualities as a moral example and protective mother of Christendom. New Marian pilgrimage sites were created, and old sites were revitalized – including Loreto in Italy, Montaigu in the Spanish Netherlands, and Kevelaer in Germany. Devotions were centred on Christ, the Holy Family, and the mysteries of faith. The rosary, the scapular, and at the top of the devotional hierarchy, the sacraments, all received a powerful new impetus. The sacraments themselves, in particular communion and confession, were surrounded with new rituals: communion became an aggregation ritual similar to the confession of faith in Protestantism or baptism among the Anabaptists; confession became an instrument for the control of individual moral development. New methods of communal Christianization were designed, the most important probably being the 'missions' during which whole parishes were submitted to a multi-faceted spiritual barrage by a visiting team of priests, members of specialized religious orders, who worked to obtain a collective conversion to true Christian life, beliefs, and morals.[29]

Yet social discipline, however pervasive it may have been in the societies of early modern continental European, was not able to absorb the totality of popular religious practice. Several sanctuaries remained available to those who wanted to maintain their customary behaviour – even as the eighteenth-century clergy became ever more critical of disorderly forms of popular practice, and as the measure of disorder became increasingly severe. There were of course always forms of clandestine behaviour, which were more or less common depending on the strength of public persecution or law enforcement. But the forbidden practices now took place in a more or less tolerated private space, protected from the rules of public society. Eventually, during the eighteenth century, the intellectual elites discovered the persistence of these forms of popular religion outside the public domain. Indeed, the movement of western European societies towards a more general, less confessional form of Christian consciousness brought with it the realization that all churches had to cope with the same problem.

Debates

Was this acculturation successful? Jean Delumeau, Keith Thomas, and William Monter are among those historians who in their studies of the period have tried to draw up a balance-sheet of two centuries of Christianizing efforts.[30] All three concluded that there was a decline in popular superstition and witchcraft beliefs by the end of the eighteenth century. In general terms, this process began in the late Middle Ages when rather common forms of paganism and shamanism – or syncretism between magic and religion – were said to have existed among the laity. There then followed a period of the repression of such 'abuses', the purification of the ecclesiastical institutions themselves, the reformation of ritual, and an education of the various elites – whether civil, ecclesiastical, judicial, intellectual, or cultural. Finally there developed an internalization of the true Christian faith, intended to create a community of converted, pure, and 'real' Christians. The churches clearly played a role in this process, but the spread of new ideas via the scientific revolution was also critical. For many people, by the end of the eighteenth century the universe was easier to comprehend than it had been two centuries earlier.

According to Thomas, whose *Religion and the decline of magic* (1971) has been very influential in this field, magic and religion were initially disconnected from each other. Then religion took over the functions of magic and was, in its turn, by the end of the seventeenth century, dissociated from reason, science, and technology. Thomas speaks here of a 'process of disillusion', a term that mirrors Balthasar Bekker's rejection of the 'enchantment of the world'.[31] In spite of its massive erudition and broad empirical approach – though restricted, to be sure, to the English case – Thomas's study was criticized from the outset by cultural anthropologists, both for its use of a rather crude form of functionalism and for its lack of theoretical rigour with regard to magic. Thomas treated magic largely as a negative version of religion, without much coherence in and of itself.[32] Moreover, like the works of Delumeau, Thomas's book reveals both a carelessness about theory and a 'Whiggish' view of the progress of humankind that, a generation later, appears a bit naive.

One of the historical elements that is under-represented in both Delumeau's and Thomas's picture is the perception of magic by the religious elites themselves. Beginning in the seventeenth century, and increasingly in the eighteenth century, the cultured elites became aware of the existence of a more or less synthetic body of popular culture. The first efforts to describe popular religion were made in the second half of the seventeenth century, for the purpose of denouncing or resisting its practices. To be sure, certain theologians or other adversaries of popular religious beliefs or practices had previously prepared catalogues of 'popular' errors, but such works were mostly centred on specific burning issues of the day or were directed against the papacy, and they therefore lacked the necessary objectivity to be useful for historians. This was the case, for example, with the popular catalogue of papist misdeeds drawn up by Philip Marnix van Sint-Aldegonde under the title *The Bee Hive of the Roman Church* (*Den Byencorf der H. Roomsche Kercke*, 1574), translated and reprinted many times.

A century later, more fully developed descriptions of popular religious practices were undertaken almost simultaneously in several different countries. Dutch ministers prepared systematic catalogues of 'errors' or 'sins', directed less against the papists than at accusing their own flock of Roman Catholic superstitions. Examples are the *Swart register van duysent sonden* (*Black register of a thousand sins*, 1679) by the Dutch minister Jacobus Hondius and the *Almanachs heyligen* (*The saints of the almanac*, 1680) by his colleague Abraham Magyrus. In Germany, Johann Georg Schmidt published between 1706 and 1729 a dictionary depicting no less than a thousand reprehensible superstitious practices.[33] The interesting point here was not the accusatory tone of the work, but its attempt to provide a full, systematic description of such practices. We find a similar attempt in the writings of the brothers Adrian and Johannes Koerbagh, who were convicted of atheism in 1668 because of their critical assessment of many religious beliefs. On the Catholic side, this project is reflected in the work of the priest Jean-Baptiste Thiers, whose *Traité des superstitions* (Paris, 1679) was the first systematic catalogue of popular religious practices in France. Father Thiers's thoughtful reflections on the definition of superstition make his treatise a useful example of the seventeenth-century debate – a debate that was the prelude to the late eighteenth-century construction of popular religion as an object of scholarship.[34]

The whole debate was raised to a higher intellectual level by a group of contemporary critics of popular beliefs in Holland linked to the first or 'radical Enlightenment', as Jonathan Israel has called it: these included Pierre Bayle, Anthony van Dale, and above all Balthasar Bekker.[35] Bekker, a university graduate in theology and pastor in the university town of Franeker and then in Amsterdam, attempted to establish a phenomenology of the practice of magic and the belief in the intervention of the devil, by drawing examples from his pastoral experience in both towns. His two-volume synthesis *De betoverde weereld* (*The enchanted world*, 1691–93) is perhaps best known for its title, which was later immortalized by Max Weber in the famous expression 'die Entzauberung der Welt' ('the disenchantment of the world'). Bekker's richly documented work was quickly translated into French, English, and German and it provoked a truly international debate. Despite the condemnation of the book by the Synod of Holland – which denounced its ironic criticism of exegetic and theological dogmatism and its scepticism regarding any form of demonology – Bekker remained for many a beacon in the battle against superstition.[36]

Roughly a century after this phase of critical cataloguing of popular practices and beliefs, a second phenomenon changed the perception of popular religion: this was the discovery of 'the people' in the second half of the eighteenth century. Popular religion, magic, and superstition now became the object of a new kind of scholarship. The older studies of 'curiosities' by learned antiquarians developed into systematic research strategies for obtaining knowledge of popular culture, considered as the heart of 'the people' (*das Volk*), and indeed of the 'nation'. Traditionally, Johann Gottfried Herder (1744–1803) is credited with having first formulated, around 1775, theories about the identity of the people, and the opposition between popular culture (*Kultur des Volkes*) and learned culture (*Kultur der Gelehrten*).[37] Herder rightly distinguished between three accepted meanings of *das Volk*: an ethnic meaning (*populus*), a political meaning (*natio*), and a social meaning (*vulgus, plebs*). Peter Burke has characterized this discovery of the people as a 'movement of cultural primitivism in which the ancient, the distant and the popular were all equated'.[38] This may be true, yet the discovery was embedded in a broad European movement of rising national consciousness that began simultaneously in almost all of the countries of western Europe.[39] In the Dutch Republic, for instance, the Leiden scholar Johannes Le Francq van Berkhey (1729–1805) drafted a remarkable description in the 1770s of the customs of the people of Holland (*Natuurlyke Historie van Holland*, 1769–1805), including their everyday religious culture, a description which is now viewed as marking the origins of Dutch ethnology. The first chair in Europe in the field of anthropology (or *Volkskunde*, a term first used in 1782) was founded at the University of Göttingen about the same time, and the new discipline grew to maturity within a few decades. Everywhere in Europe the rising national consciousness produced a need for systematic knowledge of local populations and their culture, with particular emphasis on the difference between the elites, with their cosmopolitan outlook, and the strongly localized culture of the masses. Later, in the early nineteenth century, the churches would come to accept well-ordered popular beliefs and practices as authentic forms of religious experience, and even promote them as a remedy against the 'moral depravity' of the elites.

Notes

1. Michel Vovelle, 'La religion populaire, problèmes et méthodes', in *Idéologies et mentalités* (Paris: François Maspero, 1982), pp. 125–62.
2. Margaret Murray, *The witch-cult in western Europe* (Oxford: Clarendon Press, 1921); Ludo Milis (ed.), *The pagan Middle Ages* (Woodbridge: Boydell Press, 1998).
3. Robert Mandrou, *Introduction to modern France, 1500–1640: An essay in historical psychology*, trans. R. E. Hallmark (New York: Holmes and Meyer, 1976); and *Magistrats et sorciers en France au XVIIe siècle. Analyse de psychologie historique* (Paris: Plon, 1968).
4. Gérard Bouchard, *Le village immobile: Sennely en Sologne au XVIIIe siècle* (Paris: Plon, 1972).
5. Mikhail Bakhtin, *Rabelais and his world* (Cambridge, MA: MIT Press, 1968). Carlo Ginzburg, *The cheese and the worms: The cosmos of a sixteenth-century miller* (London: Routledge & Kegan Paul, 1980); *The night battles: Witchcraft and agrarian cults in the sixteenth and seventeenth centuries* (London: Routledge & Kegan Paul, 1983).
6. For example, Ernesto de Martino, *Sud e magia* (Milan: Feltrinelli, 1971); Gabriele de Rosa, *Vescovi, popolo e magia nel Sud* (Naples: Guida, 1971); Jean Delumeau (ed.), *Histoire vécue du peuple chrétien*, 2 vols. (Toulouse: Privat, 1979); and *Catholicism between Luther and Voltaire: A new view of the Counter-Reformation*, trans. Jeremy Moiser (London: Burns & Oates, 1977).
7. For this perspective, see Roger Chartier, 'Le monde comme représentation', *Annales. Histoire Sciences Sociales*, 44 (1989), pp. 505–20; also Joris van Eijnatten and Fred van Lieburg, *Nederlandse religiegeschiedenis* (Hilversum: Verloren, 2005); and Gerard Rooijakkers, *Rituele repertoires. Volkscultuur in oostelijk Noord-Brabant 1559–1853* (Nijmegen: SUN, 1994).
8. See R. W. Scribner, 'Cosmic order and daily life: Sacred and secular in pre-industrial German society', in Scribner, *Popular culture and popular movements in Reformation Germany* (London: Hambledon Press, 1987), pp. 1–16; and 'Elements of popular belief', in Thomas

A. Brady Jr., Heiko A. Oberman, and James D. Tracy (eds.), *Handbook of European history 1400–1600*, vol. I (Leiden: Brill, 1994), pp. 231–62.

9. Lorraine J. Daston and Katherine Park, *Wonders and the order of nature, 1150–1750*, 2nd edn (New York: Zone Books, 2001).

10. Wolfgang Brückner, *Volkserzählung und Reformation. Ein Handbuch zur Tradierung und Funktion von Erzählstoffen und Erzählliteratur im Protestantismus* (Berlin: Erich Schmidt, 1974); Fred van Lieburg, *Merkwaardige voorzienigheden. Wonderverhalen in de geschiedenis van het protestantisme* (Zoetermeer: Meinema, 2001); and Alexandra Walsham, *Providence in early modern England* (Oxford: Oxford University Press, 1999).

11. Quoted in the introduction of Helen Parish and William G. Naphy (eds.), *Religion and superstition in Reformation Europe* (Manchester: Manchester University Press, 2002). See also Kai Detlev Sievers, 'Aberglaube in der Sicht der potestantischen Orthodoxie und der Aufklärung. Entwicklungsgeschichtliche Betrachtungen', *Kieler Blätter zur Volkskunde*, 13 (1981), pp. 27–54.

12. David D. Hall, *Worlds of wonder, days of judgment: Popular religious belief in early New England* (New York: Alfred A. Knopf, 1989) analyzes Protestant popular religion in its literate, verbal dimension. See also Andrew Cunningham and Ole Peter Grell, *The four horsemen of the Apocalypse: Religion, war, famine and death in Reformation Europe* (Cambridge: Cambridge University Press, 2000); and Gábor Klaniczay, *The uses of supernatural power: The transformation of popular religion in medieval and early modern Europe* (Cambridge: Polity Press, 1991).

13. R. W. Scribner, 'Incombustible Luther: The image of the reformer in early modern Germany', in Scribner, *Popular culture and popular movements in Reformation Germany* (London: Hambledon Press, 1987), pp. 323–53; Etienne François, 'Das religiöse Buch als Nothelfer, Familienreliquie und Identitätssymbol im protestantischen Deutschland der Frühneuzeit (17.–19. Jahrhundert)', in Ursula Brunold-Bigler and Hermann Bausinger (eds.), *Hören, Sagen, Lesen, Lernen. Bausteine zu einer Geschichte der kommunikativen Kultur* (Bern: Peter Lang, 1995), pp. 219–30; and Alfred Messerli, 'Die Errettung des "Paradiesgärtleins" aus Feuers- und Wassernot', *Fabula*, 38 (1997), pp. 253–79.

14. See, for instance, Stuart Clark, *Thinking with demons: The idea of witchcraft in early modern Europe* (Oxford: Clarendon Press, 1997).

15. M. Sluhovsky, 'Calvinist miracles and the concept of the miraculous in sixteenth-century Huguenot thought', *Renaissance and Reformation*, 19 (1995), pp. 5–25.

16. Wiep van Bunge, 'Balthasar Bekker's Cartesian hermeneutics and the challenge of Spinozism', *The British journal for the history of philosophy*, I (1993), pp. 55–79.

17. Jürgen Beyer, Albrecht Burkardt, Fred van Lieburg, and Marc Wingens (eds.), *Confessional sanctity (c. 1500–c. 1800)* (Mainz: Verlag Philipp von Zabern, 2003); Willem Frijhoff, 'Witnesses to the Other, incarnate longings: saints and heroes, idols and models', *Studia Liturgica: An international ecumenical review for liturgical research and renewal*, 34 (2004), pp. 1–25; Patrick Collinson, *Godly people: Essays on English Protestantism and Puritanism* (London: Hambledon Press, 1983); Brad S. Gregory, 'Martyrs and saints', in Ronnie Po-chia Hsia (ed.), *A companion to the Reformation world* (Malden MA: Blackwell, 2004), pp. 455–70; John Exalto, *Gereformeerde heiligen. De religieuze exempeltraditie in vroegmodern Nederland* (Nijmegen: Vantilt, 2005).

18. Willem Frijhoff, *Embodied belief: Ten essays on religious culture in Dutch history* (Hilversum: Verloren, 2002); 'La coexistence confessionnelle: complicités, méfiances et ruptures aux Provinces-Unies', in Delumeau, *Histoire vécue du peuple chrétien*, vol. 2, pp. 229–57; and 'Le seuil de tolérance en Hollande au XVIIe siècle', in *Homo religiosus. Autour de Jean Delumeau* (Paris: Fayard, 1997), pp. 650–7.

19. Lorraine Daston, 'Marvelous facts and miraculous evidence in early modern Europe', *Critical inquiry*, 18 (1991), pp. 93–124. See also Geneviève Demerson and Bernard Dompnier (eds.), *Les Signes de Dieu aux XVIe et XVIIe siècle* (Clermont-Ferrand: Faculté des Lettres et Sciences Humaines, 1993); and Willem Frijhoff, *Wegen van Evert Willemsz. Een Hollands weeskind op zoek naar zichzelf 1607–1647* (Nijmegen: SUN, 1995).

20. Delumeau, *Catholicism between Luther and Voltaire*; Wolfgang Reinhard and Heinz Schilling (eds.), *Die katholische Konfessionaliserung* (Gütersloh: Gütersloher Verlagshaus, 1993); Ronnie Po-chia Hsia, *The world of Catholic renewal, 1540–1770* (Cambridge: Cambridge University Press, 1998).

21. Louis Châtellier, *The Europe of the devout: The Catholic Reformation and the formation of a new society* (Cambridge: Cambridge University Press, 1989).

22. For an important dimension of this pastoral effort, see Jean Delumeau, *Sin and fear: The emergence of a Western guilt culture, 13th–18th centuries* (New York: St Martin's Press, 1990).

23. Dominique Julia, 'La Réforme posttridentine en France d'après les proces-verbaux des visites pastorales: ordre et résistances', in *La Società religiosa nell'età moderna: Atti del Convegno studi di Storia sociale e religiosa, Capaccio-Paestum, 18–21 maggio 1972* (Naples: Guida Editori, 1973), pp. 311–415.

24. Judith Devlin, *The superstitious mind: French peasants and the supernatural in the nineteenth century* (New Haven: Yale University Press, 1987).

25. Willem Frijhoff, 'Problèmes spécifiques d'une approche de la "religion populaire" dans un pays de confession mixte: le cas des Provinces-Unies', in *La religion populaire, Paris, 17–19 octobre 1977* (Paris: Editions du CNRS, 1979), pp. 35–43.

26. Frijhoff, *Embodied belief*, p. 126.

27. Michael Prinz, 'Sozialdisziplinierung und Konfessionalisierung. Neuere Fragestellungen in der Sozialgeschichte der Frühen Neuzeit', *Westfälische Forschungen*, 42 (1992), pp. 1–25; Heinz Schilling, 'Confessional Europe', in Brady *et al.*, *Handbook of European history 1400–1600*, vol. 2: *Visions, programs and outcomes* (Leiden: Brill, 1995), pp. 641–82; Ronnie Po-chia Hsia, *Social discipline in the Reformation: Central Europe 1550–1750* (London: Routledge, 1989).

28. Philippe Boutry and Dominique Julia (eds.), *Pèlerins et pèlerinages dans l'Europe moderne* (Rome: Ecole française de Rome, 2000).

29. Jean Delumeau (ed.), *La première communion. Quatre siècles d'histoire* (Paris: Desclée de Brouwer, 1987); Louis Châtellier, *La religion des pauvres: Les missions rurales en Europe et la formation du catholicisme moderne, XVIe–XIXe siècle* (Paris: Aubier, 1993); Bernadette Majorana, 'Une pastorale spectaculaire. Missions et missionnaires jésuites en Italie (XVIe–XVIIIe siècle)', *Annales, Histoire Sciences Sociales*, 57 (2002), pp. 297–320.

30. Delumeau, *Catholicism between Luther and Voltaire*; Keith Thomas, *Religion and the decline of magic: Studies in popular beliefs in sixteenth- and seventeenth-century England* (London:

Routledge & Kegan Paul, 1971); William E. Monter, *Ritual, myth and magic in early modern Europe* (Athens, OH: Ohio University Press, 1984).

31. Thomas, *Religion and the decline of magic*, p. 774.
32. See Hildred Geertz, 'An anthropology of religion and magic', *Journal of interdisciplinary history*, 6 (1975), pp. 71–89.
33. Ingeborg Weber-Kellermann and Andreas C. Bimmer, *Einführung in die Volkskunde/Europäische Ethnologie: Eine Wissenschaftsgeschichte* (Stuttgart: Metzler, 1985), p. 13.
34. François Lebrun, 'Le "Traité des superstitions" de Jean-Baptiste Thiers: contribution à l'ethnographie de la France du XVIIe siècle', *Annales de Bretagne*, 83 (1976), pp. 443–65; Jacques Revel, 'Forms of expertise: Intellectuals and "popular" culture in France (1650–1800)', in Steven L. Kaplan (ed.), *Understanding popular culture: Europe from the Middle Ages to the nineteenth century* (Amsterdam: Mouton, 1984), pp. 255–73.
35. Jonathan I. Israel, *Radical Enlightenment: Philosophy and the making of modernity* (Oxford: Oxford University Press, 2001).
36. Willem Frijhoff, 'The emancipation of the Dutch elites from the magic universe', in Dale Hoak and Mordechai Feingold (eds.), *The world of William and Mary: Anglo-Dutch perspectives on the Revolution of 1688–89* (Stanford, CA: Stanford University Press, 1996), pp. 201–18; Robin Attfield, 'Balthasar Bekker and the decline of the witch craze: The old demonology and the new philosophy', *Annals of science*, 42 (1985), pp. 383–95.
37. Peter Burke, *Popular culture in early modern Europe* (London: Temple Smith, 1978), pp. 3–22.
38. Burke, *Popular culture*, p. 10.
39. Anne-Marie Thiesse, *La Création des identités nationales. Europe XVIIIe–XXe siècle* (Paris: Editions du Seuil, 1999).

Jewish–Christian relations

FRANCES MALINO

I am a Jew! Hath not a Jew eyes? Hath not a Jew hands, organs . . . If you prick
us, do we not bleed? . . . if you wrong us, shall we not revenge?
   I will buy with you, sell with you, talk with you, walk with you . . . but I
will not eat with you, drink with you, nor pray with you.

Strangers in foreign lands

In the *Merchant of Venice*, Shakespeare captures both the ambiguity of Jewish–
Christian relations in early modern Europe and the myths surrounding the
Jew, the blood-thirsty usurer of medieval legend, 'the very devil incarnation'.
Moreover, Shylock's oft-quoted insistence, that as a human he differs not at all
from Christians and that as a Jew he must dwell apart with his own traditions,
practices, and laws, gives voice to an enduring tension not only in Jewish
history but also in any attempt to relate to the demythologized Jew, in any
attempt to welcome Jews into the body politic.

Shakespeare probably never met a Jew, since there were no more than a
hundred living in London and Bristol. Expelled from England in 1290, they
had no legal guarantee of existence and were only semi-overt in their religious
practices. By 1609, even these few Jews had disappeared. Indeed, by the middle
of the seventeenth century, no Jews could be found in Spain, Portugal, France
and parts of Germany as well as in England.

By the end of the eighteenth century, except for the Iberian peninsula, Jews
had returned to Europe, numbering 175,000 in Germany, 70,000 in the Austrian
Empire, 100,000 in Hungary, 40,000–50,000 in France, 50,000 in Holland, and
25,000 in Britain. These numbers represented not only a demographic change
but reflected as well the beginnings of an amelioration in Jewish–Christian
relations, whose contours remained in flux throughout the nineteenth and
twentieth centuries.

For much of our period, however, Jews were viewed as strangers or exiles both by themselves and by their Christian contemporaries. They had no legal claim to acceptance or toleration. Royal permission to remain or return, moreover, did not necessarily entail the right to reside in a particular town or village, a right granted or rescinded only by local authorities. In Fürth, for example, there was a thriving Jewish community, but in neighbouring Nuremberg, a Jew could appear only during the day and only in the company of a local inhabitant. Jews were permitted to reside in Leipzig but only during the period of the great fairs. While a diverse community of Jews had lived in Buda for centuries, no Jews could remain overnight in Pesth. In Strasburg, Jews could enter the city during the day by paying a poll tax but had to leave as soon as the evening bells tolled. The Jews may have used persuasion, pressure, and financial contributions to retain and expand these contracts, but they never questioned their legitimacy.

Although subject to numerous and oppressive geographic, financial and sartorial restrictions, which often confined them to cramped quarters and ghettos, to lending money and dealing in used clothing, and to a particular dress code designed to call attention to their status and identity, Jews were also almost universally granted the privilege of juridical autonomy. Within their communities, they were free to establish charitable institutions, elect a governing body, define the curriculum of their schools, register their births, marriages and deaths, and adjudicate civil cases in their own courts of law. The communities maintained their power of discipline by the use of excommunication (*Herem*) made even more essential by the imposition upon them of collective liability.

The ghettos and Jewish quarters might have erected barriers between Jews and Christians, but they were never hermetically sealed. On the contrary, financial relations between the two communities were frequent, if not always harmonious. Memoirs and autobiographies, moreover, suggest that at least in some instances there were also cultural and theological exchanges. The Italian Rabbi Leone Modena, for example, took great pleasure in describing his homiletic successes. 'In attendance [at the synagogue] were the brother of the King of France, who was accompanied by some French noblemen and by five of the most important Christian preachers who gave sermons that Pentecost. God put such learned words into my mouth that all were very pleased including many other Christians who were present.'[1]

Traffic in the Venetian ghetto was certainly two-way since Modena often ventured outside 'to shop for books, to work in the print shop of Christians, to gamble, to visit gentile friends, to give instruction to gentile students, to appear in court at St. Marks . . .'.[2] Personal and even cordial interactions notwithstanding, however, relations between Modena and his Christian contemporaries led him to devote much of his literary work to polemical writings defending rabbinic Judaism.

Relations between Jews and Christians in the early modern period as well as the attitudes each community held towards the other defy easy generalization. Broad parameters can, nevertheless, be described and delineated. Significantly, and in spite of the trauma of a pseudo-Messianic movement of global proportions, Jews sustained their Messianic belief in an ultimate redemption and ingathering. As members of a Jewish nation to which they belonged both by birth and religious obligation, they brought meaning to their lives through Jewish tradition, law, and history. The Christian world represented literally a world apart, offering little if any temptation spiritually, socially, or morally. That Jews retained their own languages, Yiddish or Ladino, and often did not speak the language of those among whom they lived, served to reinforce the particularity of their universe just as it strengthened their ties with distant co-religionists.

Popular Christian attitudes towards Jews reinforced this estrangement. Considered a pitiless creditor and an enemy of mankind, believed to possess the magical powers of a sorcerer and the physicality of the devil, Jews were accused of ritual murder, host desecration, and the poisoning of wells. Papal decrees might refute these accusations, but never in question was the belief that Christianity had superseded Judaism and that Jews were to be physically identifiable, geographically segregated, and collectively tainted with the accusation of deicide. Although forced conversions were eschewed, churches often required the presence of local Jews at a monthly Mass. They rarely attended without first putting wax in their ears.

Within these broad parameters existed both extraordinary diversity and an ambiguity reinforced by distinctions among the Jews themselves. The most notable were those between Sephardim, whose culture and religious traditions testified to an Iberian past, and Ashkenazim, whose centuries of cultural and linguistic development took place within small German towns and villages. These distinctions led to the creation of communities as different, given their rights and obligations, as they were similar because of their Jewish identity. One need only compare the communities of Bordeaux and Alsace.

In his determination to populate Bordeaux with enterprising foreigners, Henri II chose to overlook the possible crypto-Judaism of those fleeing the Inquisition. For more than a century and a half, 'Portuguese merchants' or

'New Christians' remained titular Catholics. As such they were free to enter fully the economic and professional life of Bordeaux. By the beginning of the eighteenth century, however, these 'New Christians' began to discard their Catholic ways and by the time royal *lettres patentes* officially recognized them as Jews in 1723, they had established a tightly organized Jewish community able to oversee and discipline the activities of its members.

Emergence as Jews had, of course, placed restrictions on their lives. Prevented from participating in the chamber of commerce, the Jews of Bordeaux were also excluded from the guilds and municipal functions and were expected to pay significant sums for their privileges. But within these confines, they prospered, and wealthy shippers, brokers and bankers, many of whom owned land, could be found among them. Significantly, their willingness to live according to non-Jewish law in matters of inheritance, their emphasis on biblical rather than Talmudic Judaism, and their sensitivity to the secularized bourgeois world in which they lived, led the Jews of Bordeaux to identify as much if not more with their Christian neighbours than with their co-religionists in north-eastern France. 'A Portuguese Jew is English in England and French in France', the Jews of Bordeaux explained to the French minister Malesherbes, 'while a German Jew is German everywhere because of his customs from which he rarely deviates'.[3]

When Alsace was annexed to France (1648 and 1697 for the city of Strasbourg), there were already at least 587 Jewish families spread throughout the countryside in tiny communities. Permission to reside in the cities and villages depended on the arbitrary decision of the more than sixty-one different local authorities, authorities whose privileges the French crown had promised to affirm. The Jewish population increased dramatically throughout the eighteenth century, bringing the number of families to more than 4,000 by 1784. With this sixfold increase came greater competition over the few avenues of livelihood open to Jews and an explosive hostility between them and their peasant debtors. 'As for intolerance', a lawyer to the Council of State wrote towards the end of the eighteenth century, 'Alsace is two centuries behind the other provinces of the kingdom. By persecuting the Jews, the people there believe they are fulfilling the decrees of heaven.'[4]

The ambiguities of tolerance

Not until 1965 with Pope John's *Nostra Aetate* would the Roman Catholic Church 'absolve' Jews from the deicide charge. Almost two centuries earlier, however, modernizing monarchs, Enlightenment ideology and the breakdown of traditional communal life brought into question as well as public debate the status of the Jews, their religious practices, and their collective identity. Not surprisingly, Jewish historians weigh the historical significance of these developments differently. Yet all agree, as did many at the time, that by creating a secular and 'semi-neutral' space of interaction, they radically and permanently altered Jewish–Christian relations.

The motivations behind the Austrian Edict of Tolerance of 1782 and the French *Lettres Patentes* of 1784 differed significantly. Joseph II had in mind an ambitious overhauling of his empire, which included ensuring that all his subjects become equally productive regardless of religious opinions or influential status. Louis XVI was merely responding to an increasingly volatile situation in Alsace. Yet in both cases, the reforms concerning the Jewish population were motivated by a determination to ease humiliations and minimize distinctions. They also gave voice to similar ambiguities, contradictions and, perhaps most significantly for future events, a contingency of toleration fuelled by ambivalence.

Joseph's determination to centralize and rationalize his realm included closing monasteries and convents, abolishing serfdom, and making education universal, free, and compulsory. Military service also became a universal liability. The Edict of Tolerance as well as other decrees specific to the Jews reflected these widespread changes. Forbidding Hebrew and Yiddish in public commercial records, Joseph denied the Jews their rabbinical jurisdiction, made them liable for military service and required them to adopt German-sounding personal and family names chosen from government-prepared lists. He also permitted the Jews to discard special emblems and dress, to learn handicrafts, arts and sciences, and without restrictions to devote themselves to agriculture. The doors of the universities and academies were opened to them and the body tax, along with special law taxes and passport duties, were abolished. Full citizenship, however, was not to be extended to the Jews. They could neither settle where they liked, for example in towns from which they had previously been banished, nor were they freed from protection money.

Having abolished the body tax paid by many of the Jews in Alsace, Louis XVI sought to ameliorate the economic position of the Alsatian Jews while simultaneously controlling their numbers. The *lettres patentes* of 10 July 1784 denied the right of local authorities to expel Jews legitimately resident in Alsace, provided formal recognition of the authority of the lay leaders and rabbis, and modestly expanded their range of economic activities – for example, Jews could now rent farms and vineyards, exploit mines, engage in banking and commerce, and establish factories. The *lettres patentes* also denied Jews the right to marry without permission from the crown and required an official list of those Jews permitted to reside in the province. A subsequent decree, permanently postponed by the Revolution, announced that Jews not listed in a forthcoming census would be given one month to leave France.

Although the Jewish leadership, whose authority remained intact, generally reacted positively to these *lettres patentes*, the Alsatians fought bitterly against any extension of privileges to the Jews:

> The Jews are not able to be incorporated into any Christian nation. They regard themselves as the people of God living in exile and servitude which only the coming of the Messiah will terminate. They will never have any affection for a government which they view if not as tyrannical, then at least as temporary, precarious and unworthy of commanding them. They will never have any affection for a country which on religious grounds they will never regard as their own. Raised since infancy in horror of Christianity, speaking a particular language, following particular laws. . . . hated and despised by the nation which they hate and despise, it is impossible that they could ever become useful, zealous and faithful members.[5]

These arguments, reinforced by others suggesting that the Jews would ruin the Alsatian economy and displace the Alsatians, would reappear often during the revolutionary and Napoleonic debates. So, too, would the response they elicited from one government minister – that humanity demanded that the Jews be freed from their oppression. 'We will succeed', this minister concluded, 'despite Moses and the Talmud'. But even he agreed that if failure was to occur, expulsion of the Jews was always possible.[6]

In contrast to France, reaction to the far more radical reforms proposed by Joseph was intense and heated among the Jews themselves. For some, the edict of 1782 opened a new vista of the future. Such was the view of Naphtali Herz Wessely who, in his 1782 *Words of Peace and Truth*, urged his fellow Jews to embrace the educational and linguistic reforms of a 'great man, a saviour to mankind, an exalted emperor'. For Wessely, 'human knowledge', which included arithmetic, geometry, astronomy, history, and geography, and which, he argued, had long been neglected by the Jews, should join that of the 'Torah of God'. In so doing, it would serve both 'to mend the breaches made by preceding rulers', and allow the children of Israel 'to be men who accomplish worthy things, assisting the king's country in their actions, labour and wisdom'.[7]

Opposition to these words of 'peace and truth' ushered forth from the pens and sermons of revered rabbis. The foundations of Jewish education were to rest with the ancient sages of the Talmud, one warned, and the sciences, if to be studied at all, were merely an adornment. How can one envy the study of Torah, another asked, when an 'evil man has arisen from our own people and brazenly asserted that the Torah is not all important?' A determination to protect the integrity of their religious universe no doubt motivated these rabbis just as it did many of the Alsatians. Ironically, however, while the Alsatians argued that the Jews were inherently inassimilable, the rabbis feared the antithesis, an increasing acculturation to the non-Jewish world. That Wessely had shorn his beard and that Joseph might well have preferred their conversion, merely added grist to these rabbis' mill.

Were these fears and accusations, however, warranted? Even eighty years earlier one finds evidence to justify them. In her riveting memoir, Glückel of Hameln, a woman of great piety and extraordinary business acumen, wrote with undisguised anguish of the spiritual laxity and increasing acculturation she witnessed among Metz Jews. When she first arrived from Hamburg (1700), she wrote, 'Metz was a noble and pious community. No one wore a *perruque*, and no one heard of a man going out of the *Judengasse* to bring a case before a Gentile tribunal. No such arrogance reigned in the old days as now [1719].'[8]

Bringing cases between Jews to the non-Jewish courts of law, of course, represented a serious violation of the laws and customs of the Jewish community. Indeed, in 1710 all the members of the Metz community had taken a solemn pledge not to go before non-Jewish tribunals, and they had stipulated excommunication for those who transgressed this law.[9] This pledge notwithstanding, the next years were filled with cases of recalcitrant Jews threatening their lay leaders if they dared excommunicate them and the leaders appealing at one time to *parlement*, at another to the crown to permit the use of excommunication. 'These are questions of religion', the leaders maintained in one such case. 'Are you sure they do not concern insults to royal justice?' the *parlement* would respond.[10] 'We are obliged to appeal to your Majesty', the leaders wrote in their 1718 address to the king, 'in order to prevent ruinous disorders within our community'.[11]

The most poignant appeal occurred in the spring of 1774 when the distinguished *parlementaire* lawyer Pierre-Louis Roederer arrived in Paris. Roederer had the double task of seeking reinstitution of the *parlement* of Metz (recently abolished by the Chancellor Maupeou), and of defending the interests of the Metz Jewish community against a certain Rambac. Rambac had not only defied his own community's authority, but had gone so far as to accuse the Jewish leaders of harassment and of attempting to limit the proper jurisdiction of public tribunals. Rambac was a man given to 'dissolute conduct', these leaders argued in their memoranda to the Chancellor and the Intendant of Metz. He had dared challenge the power of the Jewish leadership to excommunicate those who 'by their bad conduct, their disdain for their superiors, and their breach of national discipline, deviated from the precepts of their religion'.[12]

These cases, and the many more which appeared before the bailliage courts and *parlement* of Metz, concern individuals who, increasingly comfortable in the non-Jewish world, were determined to assert their independence from community control. They also suggest the vulnerability of the Jewish community as a whole. None of this, of course, was unique to Metz. On the contrary, in Germany and Austria the financial ventures of a number of individuals, for example Süss Oppenheimer, the confidential advisor to Duke Charles Alexander of Württemberg, brought wealth to their sovereigns and comparable privileges to themselves and their families. Exempted from the jurisdiction of both Jewish and non-Jewish courts, accountable only to the royal court, these 'court Jews' ostentatiously and precariously balanced participation in both Jewish and non-Jewish worlds. In many areas of Europe, moreover, examples could also be found of a laxity of religious observance, a waning of the traditional valuation of religious education, and a cultivation of philosophy, science and other branches of knowledge of non-Jewish origin. Even Glückel received both a secular and religious education as did her brothers and sisters.

Enlightenment and universalism

Do these examples indicate a newly emerging, albeit no less complicated, basis for Jewish–Christian relations? Some Jewish historians suggest that this is indeed the case. Others, however, point to a later period (*c.* 1770) and to the time when Jews and Christians began to mingle both in defiance of the barriers separating them and on the basis of new concepts in contradiction to the value system of their traditions.[13] These historians focus their attention on the communities of Berlin and Königsberg and most especially on Moses Mendelssohn and his circle.

Born in Dessau in 1729, the son of a Torah scribe, Moses Mendelssohn made his living as a textile merchant in Berlin. Immersing himself in European culture, indeed becoming creative in this culture himself, Mendelssohn participated in the activities of the learned societies of Berlin, soon counting the finest minds of Germany among his friends and admirers.[14] In addition to his philosophical works, including *Phaedon* in which he set out to prove the immortality of the soul, he also oversaw the translation of the Pentateuch into German believing that for orthodox Jews it would open the door to non-Jewish culture and for the assimilated it would facilitate a return to Torah. Convinced that Judaism, defined as natural religion and a special revelation of law, could be united with the philosophy of the Enlightenment, Mendelssohn envisioned full tolerance and respect between Jews and Christians on the basis of a shared common culture. If Christianity would divest itself of its irrational dogmas, he wrote to the Crown Prince of Brunswick-Wolfenbüttel, and agree that its founder had never freed the Jews from the Mosaic law, then Judaism would recognize Jesus as a 'prophet and messenger of God', sent 'to preach the holy doctrine of virtue . . . to a depraved human race'.[15]

Mendelssohn and his fellow *maskilim* (religious Enlighteners), among whom was Naphtali Herz Wessely, believed that they were participating in a great social revolution. Not even the realization that Mendelssohn's Christian admirers assumed he would soon convert, or Mendelssohn's public confrontation with the Swiss theologian Johann Caspar Lavater, one of the important exponents of Enlightened Christianity, diminished their faith in a future community of Enlightened Jews and Christians, living together harmoniously, mutually respecting each other's religious differences. The *Haskalah* they initiated (the Jewish version of the religious Enlightenment comparable to the Protestant theological Enlightenment and Reform Catholicism), with its call for secular education and religious reform, soon attracted followers well beyond the confines of the German states.[16]

Berr Isaac Berr, among the most respected and important leaders of French Jewry, fully identified with this Berlin *Haskalah*. He subscribed to its Hebrew journal *Hame'asef*, translated Wessely's *Words of Peace and Truth* from Hebrew and secured its publication in France.[17] Moses Ensheim, a brilliant mathematician from Metz, left his wife and child to travel to Berlin, where he became tutor to Mendelssohn's family and contributor to *Hame'asef*. Isaiah Berr Bing, also of Metz, became a disciple of Mendelssohn, and translated his *Phaedon* into French. Even the official leader of the Jews of Alsace, Cerf Berr of Mendelsheim, turned to Mendelssohn for help. His plea and Mendelssohn's connections elicited Christian Wilhelm von Dohm's pivotal treatise *Über die bürgerliche Verbesserung der Juden* (Concerning the Amelioration of the Civil Status of the Jews).[18]

These personal ties notwithstanding, however, Jews from other countries rarely, if ever, appropriated in full either the positions of the Berlin *maskilim* or the principles they used to justify them. On the contrary, logically consistent arguments often bifurcated when translated into differing religious and political climates. When shaped and politicized, moreover, as they were by such French figures as Mirabeau, Jacques-Pierre Brissot and the abbé Henri

Grégoire, these arguments contributed to a rhetoric of regeneration and emancipation which defined and gave direction to Jewish–Christian relations throughout the nineteenth century.

Regeneration and amelioration

Searing events illustrating the vulnerability of Jews as well as Protestants charged the climate of the last years of *ancien régime* France. Millenarians, rationalists, and humanitarians expressed a common theme. Their motivations may have differed and their goals competed, but they all agreed that France must acknowledge its non-Catholics and grant them basic human rights. 'In France it is not at all religion, but origin which determines that one is French', the Parisian lawyer Jaladon argued in 1784. 'Atheist or deist, Jew or Catholic, Protestant or Muslim – what does it matter? If one is born in France of a French mother and French father, . . . then one is French and enjoys all the rights of a citizen.'[19]

On 25 August 1785, the Metz Royal Academy announced the subject for its 1787 competition: 'Are there means to render the Jews more useful and happier in France?' That this Academy chose to investigate the condition of the Jews could have been anticipated by its previous year's competition which dealt with the laws and opinions concerning bastards – in other words, those born of Protestant parents. This time, however, the Academy found the entries to be 'mediocre' and decided to extend the competition until the following year. In 1788, having despaired of finding an essay which resolved the 'multiplicity of doubts' concerning the Jews, the Academy agreed to crown three 'good' works.

In its published broadsheet, the Academy, and more specifically Pierre-Louis Roederer, had specified just which doubts it had hoped to see refuted.[20] Johann-David Michaelis and Voltaire, Roederer explained, portray the Jews as eternally doomed and public opinion has followed them.[21] Jean-Jacques Rousseau claims that Moses has given the Jews customs incompatible with those of other nations, and their enemies have seized upon this perhaps indiscreet assertion as truth.[22]

Roederer, of course, was not alone in signalling the impediments to integrating the Jews provided by these 'celebrated writers'. Since the eighteenth century, Jews and non-Jews alike have debated their contribution, and that of the Enlightenment as a whole, to the construction of a modern anti-Semitism predicated not merely on an antipathy towards Judaism, but also on the presumed innate and irremediable characteristics of the Jews themselves.[23] That the anti-Semitic pamphleteer Henri Labroue chose to publish in 1942 an anthology of Voltaire's quotations titled *Voltaire antijuif*, merely fuels the passion with which the legacy of the Enlightenment is debated.[24]

The essays submitted to the Metz Academy illuminate just how complex and ambiguous was the impact of the Enlightenment even on its contemporaries. Valioud, the secretary of the Agricultural Academy of Laon, for example, defended the Jews against the charge of deicide, suggested that the insulting prayers on Good Friday be modified and advocated religious pluralism. After arguing in seventeen articles that granting the Jews freedom and security were the means to insure their usefulness and happiness, however, he concluded that unless one acknowledged miracles, 'only the way we treat them will lead them little by little to convert'.[25] Paradoxically, the abbé de la Lauze argued otherwise. 'Grant both the rich and the poor citizenship and let them enjoy their property and their freedom in peace. To live subjected to the laws of the country one inhabits, to contribute to the taxes of the state in which one is domiciled without being a citizen, is to have no homeland. What! Is happiness ever the lot of a man who is a foreigner in the midst of the nation in which he was born!'[26]

The public never heard mention of Valioud, the abbé de la Lauze or a number of the other contestants. For the Academy announced only the names of the three who had shared the *palme* – the abbé Grégoire, *curé* of Embermesnil, Thiéry, Protestant lawyer to the *parlement* of Nancy and the Polish Jew, Zalkind Hourwitz. In their prize-winning essays, published and reviewed in the important journals of the capital, they advocated welcoming the Jews 'as men' into the French nation. In return, they expected the Jews to resemble the French in dress and speech and to dwell alongside them instead of in Jewish quarters.

Both Grégoire and Thiéry also made clear that they considered Judaism inferior to Christianity and the Jews in need of 'correction'. One should never lose sight, Grégoire warned, of the character of the people one proposes to correct. Hourwitz, on the other hand, vehemently denied that the faith of the Jews stood in the way of full equality, that their 'character' required *régénération*, or that they need first demonstrate their worth: 'The means to make the Jews happy and useful? Here it is, cease to make them unhappy and useless, in giving them, or rather returning to them the rights of citizenship . . . Have we such an abundance of time and enlightenment that we can prostitute them in the investigation of foolishness and barbarity?'[27]

Investigation, however, was precisely the task given by the king to the French minister Chrétien Guillaume de Lamoignon de Malesherbes. Malesherbes had originally assumed that the edict he completed in 1787, which reaffirmed the freedom of conscience of non-Catholics, granted them the rights of marrying, burial, and bequeathing their estates outside the authority of the Catholic Church, and permitted them the exercise of crafts and trades, included *all* non-Catholics. Apparently in agreement, the *parlement* of Paris registered the edict immediately. Not so the *parlement* of Metz, which refused to do so explaining that Metz would become a 'tribe of Jews'.

Pierre Louis Roederer recalled that immediately after the promulgation of the 1787 edict, the king complimented Malesherbes for his success and then said: 'You have made yourself a Protestant: now I shall make you a Jew: Occupy yourself with the condition of the Jews'.[28] Roederer, however, telescoped the events in his recollections of more than a decade later. For Malesherbes addressed himself to the question of the Jews only after the crown assured for them an even less secure status by tacitly excluding them from the edict, a fact duly noted by the Jews themselves: 'The Jew, man like all others, not only does not profit from this generous law, but must become even more degraded by this same law which, in eliminating forever intolerance towards foreigners, continues it especially and only towards the Jew'.[29]

Malesherbes left few sources untapped in his new task. He turned to his friends, to the Jews of the south-west, the east and Paris, to police inspectors, and to ministers both in France and abroad. He gathered information concerning the laws and customs of the Jews as well as reports – both solicited and unsolicited – from their friends and their enemies. He read their history and charted their settlements. He obtained a map of Alsace with the major routes and towns, all to provide him with the answer to one consuming question: could and would the Jews of France abandon their exclusiveness and particularity in return for the rights of Frenchmen? In other words, were the Jews really comparable to the Protestants – who distinguished themselves from the majority of Frenchmen only in matters of faith – or were they a permanently separate and potentially dangerous people? The more Malesherbes probed, interviewed, and pondered, the less confident he became of an answer.

In his private musings, Malesherbes dwelt on the isolation of the Jews, their determination to remain separate from all others, and the potential danger they represented.[30] At present, he noted, the Jews are not at all comparable to the Protestants. They are hated because of the 'crime' of their ancestors and their exclusive commitment to commerce. Citing the prophet Jeremiah, he called attention to the many ways in which Jews were prevented from eating and drinking with the French, engaging in the salutary world of agriculture or escaping the opprobrium of an *imperium in imperiis*.

Although publicly Malesherbes remained committed to improving the lot of the Jews, by the eve of the Revolution, government interest in the question of the Jews had lost much of its momentum, partly because of more compelling events but also perhaps as a result of Malesherbes' profound reservations. The intensive months of examination and gathering of information had produced nothing concrete. But they had succeeded in publicly linking the discourse of tolerance to the granting of civil rights to the Jews, especially now that these rights no longer depended on adherence to the Catholic faith. They had also presented the Jews of France, brought together for the first time categorically, albeit not in fact, with an urgent task of self-definition.

By the end of the eighteenth century, then, among 'Enlightened' Jews and non-Jews alike, there had evolved an image of the future in which everything pertaining to the Jews – their education, economic diversification, language, and civil status – was to be radically altered. Even the very character of the Jews was to be transformed. 'Let us cherish morality', the abbé Grégoire had written, 'but let us not be so unreasonable as to require it of those whom we have compelled to become vicious. Let us reform their education, to reform their hearts; it has long been observed, that they are men as well as we, and they are so before they are Jews.'[31]

Needless to say many challenged this image of the future, for at the very least it was predicated on a diminution of the Christian character of society and of the Jews' theological significance for Christianity. In line with arguments presented by Michaelis and Rousseau, moreover, others argued that the religion, traditions, and messianic expectations of the Jews made their integration neither possible nor desirable. Even among the Jews themselves, there was much debate about the cost of this integration, and, although welcoming an end to the oppressive regulations which constrained their life, rabbis and leaders alike struggled to retain the autonomy of their communities and the validity of Jewish tradition.

Emancipation and integration

Of the three Metz laureates, Zalkind Hourwitz alone had given voice to a new ideal of citizenship – democratic, non-corporatist, and inclusive – an ideal which found expression in the French Revolution's Declaration of the Rights of Man and the Citizen. 'Tolerance!' the Protestant deputy Rabaut Saint-Etienne exclaimed amidst the debates of August 1789: 'I demand that it be proscribed and it will be, this unjust word which represents us only as citizens worthy of pity, as guilty ones whom one pardons. . . '.[32]

It was this ideal of citizenship, in contrast to the arguments of Grégoire, Thiery and much of Enlightenment ideology, which the Parisian revolutionaries embraced when they welcomed the Jews as active participants in the Revolution – on the streets, in the cafes and clubs, and in the uniform of National Guardsmen; and when they prepared their memoirs and petitioned the Constituent Assembly in January–February 1790 on behalf of the Jews. Events in the capital notwithstanding, however, the Constituent Assembly found it necessary as early as December 1789 to test the inclusiveness of the Declaration of the Rights of Man, specifically in relation to participation in civil and military office. When an original motion specifying non-Catholics was expanded to include every male, regardless of profession or the religion he professed, a deputy from Alsace, asked 'Do you mean the Jews?' 'Yes', came the reply.

This brief exchange quickly shifted the discussion from active citizenship to one which questioned the fundamental nature of the new French state and the national identity of its Jewish inhabitants. 'To call the Jews citizens', the abbé Maury proclaimed, 'would be as if one would say that, without letters of naturalization and without ceasing to be English and Danish, the English and Danes could become French'.[33] While some deputies argued that the Jews should be excluded altogether, others suggested 'tolerating' them or even giving them 'hospitality', 'protection', and 'security'. To this Clermont-Tonnerre countered with what would soon become not only the paradigm for integration of the Jews throughout Europe but also the leitmotif of future debate on the terms of their emancipation: 'We must refuse everything to the Jews as a nation. We must grant everything to them as individuals. We must cease to recognize their judges, for they shall have only ours. We must refuse them the protection of their own laws. It is necessary that they be neither a political body nor an order. Only as individuals can they be citizens. But one will say, they do not want to be citizens. Ah well! If that is what they want, and they express it, then they must be expelled. It is repugnant that there be in the State a society of non-citizens and a Nation within the Nation. But they do not speak of this . . .'[34]

On 24 December 1789, the revolutionaries welcomed non-Catholics as full members of the body politic. They also explicitly postponed any decision concerning the Jews. Before pronouncing on this long-suffering people, Bon-Albert Briois de Beaumetz announced, 'it is necessary to know from it what it wishes to be, at what price it wishes to obtain its liberty and finally if it is worthy of receiving it'. De Beaumetz's questions may have echoed those of the Metz Academy, but they anticipated as well future discussions among the Jews themselves. In Germany, for example, in the early decades of the nineteenth century, rabbinical conferences would set as an agenda reforming the practices of Judaism in order to insure compatibility with citizenship in a modern nation state.

Twenty-five months of agitation, discussion, debate, and adjournment finally ended on 27 September 1791. (A year and a half earlier, on 28 January 1790, the Assembly had permitted the Sephardic Jews to continue to enjoy the rights they had previously enjoyed, including active citizenship.) Arguing that freedom of religion permitted no distinction in the political rights of citizens because of their faith, Adrien Duport once again specifically included the Jews: 'I believe that the Jews cannot be the only ones excepted from the enjoyment of these rights when pagans, Turks, Muslims, even Chinese, in a word men of all religions, are admitted'. This time those present (many deputies who would have objected having long since emigrated) tacitly agreed that to speak against Duport's proposal was to fight the Constitution itself.

A commitment to France, to the ideals of the Revolution and to the Constitution had led the revolutionaries to acknowledge the Jews as fellow citizens. They had done so, however, by granting citizenship to 'individuals of the Jewish persuasion', thus addressing neither the contested nature of Jewish existence in the *ancien régime* nor the definition of Judaism as more than a set of religious beliefs.[35] Not until 1806, when Napoleon convened the Assembly of Jewish Notables would these issues be confronted. In the meantime, as liberty trees were planted and ghetto walls crumbled, the French armies extended emancipation to the Jews of Italy, Holland, Belgium, and southern Germany. Since Prussia had included among its reforms a decree emancipating its Jews, and Britain had quietly permitted significant social and economic integration, only those Jews residing in the Habsburg Empire were unaffected.

With Napoleon's defeat, however, came a setback to Jewish emancipation. Restrictions were restored, and Jewish disabilities revived. In some instances, for example in Rome, the Jews were once again confined to ghettos. Although the Treaty of Vienna assured the Jews enjoyment of all rights accorded to them 'in' the several German states, a last-minute shift to the preposition 'by' left only the Jews of Prussia with these rights. Hostility to the Enlightenment, to Napoleon, and to religious scepticism fed traditional religious enmities and provided additional justification for excluding the Jews.

Ironically, however, it was not the defeat of Napoleon but Napoleon himself who eroded the rights of the Jews in France. On 17 March 1808, he approved a series of three decrees. While the first two assured them an official consistorial organization somewhat comparable to that of the Protestants, the third, known as the 'infamous decree', subjected the majority of the Jews of France, for at least ten years, to onerous economic, geographical, and military restrictions. 'The evil done by the Jews', Napoleon explained to his Council of State, 'does not come from individuals but from the very temperament of this people'.[36]

By convening an Assembly of Jewish Notables and a Grand Sanhedrin, Napoleon also raised anew the question of citizenship for the Jews. Requiring from them doctrinal as well as concrete economic guarantees, he successfully redefined their emancipation and linked it – along with that of all the Jews of Europe – to the expectations, ambiguities and contingencies articulated throughout the eighteenth century.

On 28 January 1790, the revolutionary Jacques Godard had addressed a meeting of the General Assembly of the representatives of the Paris Commune. He had come to seek active citizenship for the Jews of Paris. Moved by Godard's impassioned address, the abbé Mulot, President of the Commune, turned to the Jews in attendance. 'The distance of your religious opinions from the truths that we profess as Christians cannot prevent us, as men, from bringing ourselves nearer to you, and if mutually we believe each other to be in error, . . . we are nevertheless able to love one another'.[37] Voltaire had called himself tolerant, a leading journal would subsequently remark, but he could have learned something from the abbé Mulot.

Sixteen years later, Napoleon presented Jewish deputies from France and Italy with twelve questions. The fourth question, reversing the onus assumed by the abbé Mulot on behalf of his fellow Christians, asked if in the eyes of Jews, Frenchmen were considered as their brethren or as strangers. 'All Frenchmen are our brethren', the deputies responded, 'This glorious title, by raising us in our own esteem, becomes a sure pledge that we shall never cease to be worthy of it'.[38]

Despite a century and a half of liberalization, relations between Jews and Christians would continue to be both tenuous and vulnerable. Yet if the 'love' so eloquently articulated by the abbé Mulot was replaced by a contingency of acceptance, there was nevertheless a blunting of animus in the name of a shared brotherhood. Shylock's queries had been relegated, albeit not permanently, to the past.

Notes

1. *Autobiography of a seventeenth-century Venetian Rabbi*, ed. and trans. Mark R. Cohen (Princeton: Princeton University Press, 1988), p. 6.
2. *Ibid.*, pp. 5–6.

3. 'Mémoire présentée par MM Lopes-Dubec père et Furtado ainé', Archives départementales de la Gironde, Série I.

4. Bibliothèque Nationale, n.a.fr. 20081, Collection Coquebert de Montbret.

5. 'Coup d'œil sur la situation actuelle de l'Alsace, relativement aux Juifs', Archives nationales, H 1641, n° 3.

6. 'Fragments d'une Conversation entre un Baillif d'Alsace et M. d'A . . . m . . . f . . . de l'A . . . touchant les Juifs d'Alsace', Archives nationales F^{12} 854B.

7. Paul Mendes-Flohr and Jehuda Reinharz (eds.), *The Jew in the modern world* (Oxford: Oxford University Press, 1995), pp. 70–4.

8. *Memoirs of Glückel of Hameln*, trans. Marvin Lowenthal (New York: Schocken Books, 1977), p. 267.

9. 'Copie d'une publication faite dans la synagogue contre les juifs qui porteront dorénavant leur affaires aux juges ordinaires', [in Hebrew] Archives de la région lorraine et du département de la Moselle, 17 J 23 Jur. 15.

10. Archives de la region lorraine, Jur. 21.

11. Archives de la region lorraine, Jur. 27.

12. 'L'affaire de Saloman Rambac', Archives Nationales, 29 AP 3.

13. Jacob Katz, *Tradition and crisis: Jewish society at the end of the Middle Ages*, trans. Bernard Dov Cooperman (New York: New York University Press, 1993).

14. Lessing, for example, modelled the protagonist in his *Nathan der Weisse* after Mendelssohn.

15. Michael Meyer, *The origins of the modern Jew* (Detroit: Wayne State University Press, 1967), p. 36.

16. David Sorkin, *The Berlin Haskalah and German religious thought* (London: Valentine Mitchell, 2000).

17. Hatwic Weisly [sic], *Instruction salutaire addressée aux communautés juives* (Paris, 1790).

18. Christian Wilhelm Von Dohm, *Über die bürgerliche Verbesserung der Juden* (Berlin, 1781–83).

19. Paul Hildenfinger (ed.), *Documents sur les Juifs à Paris au XVIII siècle* (Paris, 1913).

20. *Prix proposés en 1787 par la Société royale des sciences et arts de Metz*, Archives nationales, 29 AP 6.

21. 'Herr Ritter Michaelis Beurtheilung', in [François-Marie Arouet] Voltaire, *Dictionnaire philosophique* (Basle, 1764), vol. 14.

22. Jean-Jacques Rousseau, *The government of Poland*, trans. Willmoore Kendall (Indianapolis: Bobbs-Merrill, 1972), p. 6.

23. Arthur Hertzberg, *French Enlightenment and the Jews* (New York: Columbia University Press, 1968), p. 286.

24. Roland Mortier, 'Les "philosophes" français du 18e siècle devant le judaïsme et la judéité', in Bernhard Blumenkranz (ed.), *Juifs en France au XVIIIe siècle* (Paris: Commission française des archives juives, 1994), p. 191.

25. Bibliothèque de Metz, MS 1349.

26. *Ibid.*

27. *Ibid.*

28. *Journal de Paris*, 24 (22 Frimaire An VII).

29. 'Réflexion sur l'enregistement de l'Edit des non-catholiques au parlement de Metz et projets pour rendre les juifs plus utiles et plus heureux en France', Archives nationales, 29 AP 3.

30. Archives Nationales, 154 AP II 135.
31. Mendes-Flohr and Reinharz (eds.), *The Jew in the modern world*, p. 50.
32. Léon Kahn, *Les Juifs de Paris* (Paris, 1895), pp. 17–18.
33. *Archives parlementaires de 1787 à 1860, recueil complet des débats législatifs et politiques des chambres françaises. Première série*, vol. 10 (Paris, 1878), p. 757.
34. *Archives parlementaires*, vol. 10, p. 756.
35. *Archives parlementaires*, vol. 31 (Paris, 1888), p. 441.
36. Simon Schwarzfuchs, *Napoleon, the Jews and the Sanhedrin* (London: Routledge and Kegan Paul, 1979), p. 50.
37. Jacques Godard, *Discours prononcé le 28 janvier 1790* (Paris, 1790).
38. Mendes-Flohr and Reinharz (eds.), *The Jew in the modern world*, p. 130.

12

Architecture and Christianity

JEAN-MICHEL LENIAUD

A little-known body of architecture: an overview

In their studies of early modern architecture, art historians have not been unduly concerned with questions of quantity. Yet it is clear that the shear number of religious constructions built in Europe after the middle of the sixteenth century was considerable, and that with the exception of urban and rural housing, there was probably no area of architectural activity more dynamic than the construction of places of worship. During much of this period Europe came to resemble one immense church construction site. Yet this expansion cannot be explained solely by the growth or mobility of the population, nor by the earlier destruction of churches through acts of violence, nor even by the deterioration of the stock of existing medieval churches. It was due rather to the state of religion which emerged from the Reformation. On the one hand, new denominations had particular liturgical requirements that meant they were no longer content to adapt the churches of the Middle Ages: they had to build new ones. And on the other, the Catholic Reformation's assimilation of elements of both humanism and the Protestant Reformation led to a re-appraisal of needs for liturgy, architecture, and decor. Moreover, Catholic renewal led to new forms of spirituality and pastoral activities and subse-quently to the founding of numerous religious orders, all of which required the construction of chapels for their communities.

In addition to the significant quantitative increase in construction, church building in this period was marked by an unprecedented involvement of politi-cal authority. This was a result of the strong new relationship which developed in Europe of the period between states and national churches – a relationship that entailed both restoration and modernization for the states and protec-tion for the national churches. To a certain degree, the civil administrations came to assume the powers of the ecclesiastical authorities, or at least to inter-vene in their affairs. Thus, for example, in France the crown involved itself in the reconstruction of cathedrals destroyed by the Protestants (e.g., Orléans in 1601; Valence in 1604). And this was not simply a financial involvement: multiple forces compelled both the state and the local town councils to intervene with the ecclesiastic authorities and take control of construction, so that the appointment of architects became the prerogative of the royal administration. This intrusion of the civil into the realm of the Catholic bishops went hand in hand with the use of royal power over the Protestants. Thus, the Edict of Nantes of 1598 dictated the sites and the numbers of Protestant churches to be established, while the Revocation of that edict in 1685 proceeded to order their destruction. State control over church construction became less forceful at the end of Louis XVI's reign, but the Napoleonic Concordat of 1801 and subsequent texts accorded the civil authorities considerable control over both the authorization of construction and the architectural definition of Catholic and Protestant churches as well as synagogues. A similar phenomenon of state control occurred in Great Britain. The Act of 1711 instituted a tax to finance fifty new churches to be built in the cities of London and Westminster and in suburban towns. The 'Act for Fifty New Churches' was echoed a century later by the Church Building Act of 1818. But in the latter case it was not the number of churches that was stipulated, but the grant to be made – a million pounds. Experience had taught it was not wise to become involved in financial over-expenditure.

Can one go a step further and use the characteristics of the various forms of architectural design and decoration observed in places of worship to ascertain something of the nature of religious sentiment at the time of construction? Some authors do not hesitate to do so. Thus, the 'coldness' of churches constructed after the 1818 Church Building Act is said to demonstrate the degree to which religious feeling had been replaced by the prescriptions of social convention. Contemporaries themselves sometimes tried to make similar links. In seventeenth-century France, enemies of the Jesuits did not hesitate to connect the Italian influences on Jesuit architecture – modest though they were – with what they judged to be the order's lack of moral rigour. Clearly, such links should only be made with great caution, for we are far from possessing the keys to the interpretation of architectural forms. And yet neither should we accept common place generalizations. Such is the assertion that the French of the *ancien régime* were always wary of the spontaneity of the Baroque and the Rococo – whether in Borromini's Roman churches or in the great abbey of Ottobeuren by Johann Mikael Fischer (1748–53). The historian of art can go further than this and suggest to the historian of religion that the gradual shift from a polychromatic interior decor to a white achromatism (and similarly, the increasing scarcity and abstraction of iconography) may have expressed a new intellectualization of the mysteries of faith, along with a denunciation of what the late eighteenth century called 'superstition'.

One can conclude these general remarks with a final observation. From all that precedes – the dynamism of this specific building sector, the involvement of both civil and ecclesiastical authorities, the vitality of religious feeling – it follows that church construction remained, just as it had been in the Middle Ages and the Renaissance, one of the privileged areas of architectural creativity. No important architect of the age was uninterested in such construction to one degree or another. Despite the historiographical tradition that argues for a progressive secularization of institutions, societies, and cultures, it is impossible to maintain that there was one sphere of secular art and another separate sphere for the sacred. If there was one place during the early modern period where the whole of society assembled, it was undoubtedly in the church; and, by the same token, if there was one artistic project which brought together artists in substantial numbers (aside from the construction of palaces, theatres, and opera houses), then without a doubt it was also the church. Bearing this in mind, one can understand why the construction of places of worship so appealed to architects of the period; and by corollary, one can also comprehend the enormous diversity of stylistic designs.

The flowering of styles

The first decades of the seventeenth century were characterized by an extreme distrust of the exuberance that derived from the style of Michelangelo, a strict selection from among the various ornamental forms, and an assertion of a taste for simple volumes. Certain countries, including Great Britain, had never experienced Mannerism. Inigo Jones acclimatized Britain to the Euclidean forms of Palladio's art: Saint Paul's Church in Covent Garden (1631–33) displays a vast Corinthian portico with a triangular tympanum in the style of a Tuscan temple. But Palladio's influence was most significant in Venice, as shown in the dome and façades of Santa Maria della Salute, built by Baldassare Longhena at the entrance to the Grand Canal (1631–51). In Rome, Carlo Maderno continued the construction of Saint Peter's, and produced the nave and façade (1607–12) in largely classical style with touches of Mannerist detail.

By contrast, Francesco Borromini was inspired both by Michelangelo's heritage and the spirit of originality. In 1638–42, he built the Oratory for the congregation of Saint Philip Neri according to an original plan with a curved rather than a rectilinear façade that undulated between the concave and the

Figure 1 St Peter's Basilica, Rome. The façade, with its dramatic classical style and mannerist detail, was designed by Carlo Maderno and completed in 1607–12. It would exercise a profound influence on church architecture. (Photograph by Graham Astles.)

convex, and a pediment with both arched and triangular tympana. Similarly, Sant' Ivo della Sapienza (1643–50) displayed original forms such as the hexagon in the shape of an alveolus and a shell-like triple spiral. Several architects followed comparable paths. Pietro da Cortona combined hemispherical and parallelepiped forms in the façade of Santa Maria della Pace (Rome, 1656) and created new effects with pilasters and columns. At Santa Maria in Capitelli (1663–67), Carlo Rinaldi produced two orders of columns, one in the front, the other deep-set in the wall. But the most Borrominian of them all was probably Guarino Guarini. A Theatine priest and scholar of mathematics, he created undulating façades and centred covers, their structures formed of complex stacks. Thus, in the Chapel of the Sindona in Turin, a staggered superposition of several levels of hexagons rose above a circular drum, each element not segmental but arched. A late echo of this type of structure is seen in San Gaetano, the Nice Theatines' Church, built in 1744 by B. Vittone, himself a disciple of Guarini.

Nevertheless, such bold individual creations did not correspond with the overall taste of the period. Bernini himself showed restraint in Sant' Andrea al Quirinale (1658–70) with an oval cylindrical drum flanked by small chapels, and a semi-circular portico. Between 1660 and 1670, the classical reaction became more pronounced, as shown in the façade of Santa Maria in Via Lata (Rome, 1658–62) where Pietro da Cortona renounced the curved lines he had employed in preceding years in favour of a superposition of two porticos with almost no projections. In 1662 in the Piazza del Popolo, Carlo Rainaldi designed two nearly twin churches, fronted by antique-style porticos. Carlo Fontana moved in a similar direction with San Marcello al Corso (1682).

The triumph of the grand classical style was ensured in Great Britain by Christopher Wren, who saw in the Great Fire of London (1666) an opportunity that finally led to the decision to rebuild fifty-two churches. His ideas were realized in the rebuilding of the first twenty churches, carried out as early as 1670–71. Saint Stephen in Walbrook (London, 1670) consists of an outside structure in parallelepiped form with a dome, the whole according to a central plan. Wren pursued his thinking in the reconstruction of Saint Paul's Cathedral in London, where he took Saint Peter's in Rome as inspiration. Some years later, architects in charge of implementing the 1711 Tory Act remained faithful to Wren's experiments in urban monumentalism. They included his collaborator, Vanbrugh; Hawksmoor, with his basilica plan at Christchurch, Spitalfields (1714–20), his design of Saint Mary's Woolnoth, inscribed in a square (1716–24), and Saint George-in-the-East, with almost neo-classical modenature; James

Figure 2 St Paul's Cathedral, London, frontis. The cathedral was reconstructed after the Great Fire of 1666 and work was completed in 1708. The architect, Sir Christopher Wren, took St Peter's basilica in Rome as his inspiration. (Photograph by Sam Lloyd.)

Gibbs in Saint Mary-le-Strand (1714–17) with semi-cylindrical portico and a tall spire, standing like an urban lighthouse at a crossroads, and Saint Martin-in-the-Fields (1722–25), with portico, semi-engaged columns, and steeple; John James with his Saint George's Church (1720–25); and Thomas Archer with his Saint John's in Smith Square.

The situation in France

Rejecting Italian influence because of national pride, attracted by architectural innovation yet not renouncing its Gothic tradition, fascinated above all by unity and balance: France presented the dual achievement of both quantity and diversity. Thus, in response to Protestant vandalism during the Wars of Religion, the cathedrals of Valence and Orléans were reconstructed respectively in Romanesque and Gothic style, following their original designs – with the rebuilding in Orléans continuing until the end of the *ancien régime*. Indeed, a certain taste for the Gothic was visible in the works of a number of French architects from abbé Martellange through Soufflot, and including the architecture of the Prémontré Order – with its preference for large church halls – and such theoreticians as André Félibien (1699), Michel de Millin (1702), Jean-Louis de Cordemoy (1706), and abbé Laugier (1753).

A clear transformation appeared with the façade of Saint-Gervais (1616), designed by Salomon de Brosse, where a screen with three superimposed orders was built in front of a vast Gothic nave. From the outset, critics elevated the work to the level of a national model. Among the domed churches, no doubt one of the most ambitious was the Val-de-Grâce, begun in 1645 by François Mansart at the request of Anne of Austria and continued by Le Mercier, the designer of the dome of the Sorbonne Chapel (1635). Mansart, who had already built the dome of the Chapel of the Visitation, rue Saint-Antoine (1632–33), suggested an ambitious plan to Louis XIV for a funeral chapel for the Bourbon family that combined a central plan with a cupola (1665). The chapel would have been erected in the chevet of the great abbey church of Saint-Denis. Although Mansart died in 1666 without being able to execute his project, his innovative idea of a low, open cupola, fitted into a dome to produce indirect daylight, was taken up by his nephew Jules Hardouin-Mansart in the church of the Invalides (1676).

An Italian influence is to be seen in a number of churches from different religious communities. One finds good examples in the Carmelite and Oratory churches in Paris and, slightly later, the church of Saint-Paul-Saint-Louis, the central edifice of the Jesuits in France. Inspired by the plan for Gesù in Rome (finished in 1584), the latter was constructed according to plans by Etienne Martellange (1627–41). In 1662, it was the turn of the Theatines, an order brought to France at Mazarin's request. Their chapel was erected according to Guarino Guarini's plans and combined elliptical spaces and convex and concave curves: compositions based on the diagonal with the taste for 'extravagance' that served to strengthen France's assertion of Classicism.

Figure 3 Val-de-Grâce, Paris. The church was built between 1645 and 1667. The work was commenced by the architect François Mansart and completed by Jacques Le Mercier. The cupola was designed by Pierre Mignard. (Photograph by Helen Chenut.)

Figure 4 Church of the Invalides, Paris. Interior. Begun in 1676 by Jules Hardouin-Mansart, nephew of François Mansart who had been the architect of Val-de-Grâce. A low, open cupola fitted into the dome floods the interior with a soft, indirect daylight. (Photograph by Helen Chenut.)

In 1676, Hardouin-Mansart undertook construction of the Invalides church. He employed a highly original approach and produced two successive chapels: one was for soldiers, while the purpose of the other remains a mystery, but was perhaps intended to be Louis XIV's burial-place. In front of the church façade, Mansart also had planned for a semi-circular area, marked off by two porticos. Overall, the plan expressed various ideas taken from Saint Peter's in Rome and, in France, from the Val-de-Grâce, which combined a centrally planned choir with a lengthened nave, and (so it was said) from the plan for the Bourbon funerary rotunda at Saint-Denis.

The Royal Chapel at Versailles, begun in 1698 by Hardouin-Mansart and completed in 1710 by Robert de Cotte, is interesting for the architect's choice of a deliberately archaic plan. Mansart initially proposed a central plan, but decided in favour of designs inspired by the Sainte Chapelle and the Palatine chapels of the Middle Ages. His plan aimed for distinction through its size and its links to the chateau itself, with its elongated nave and two-level elevation, and with its upper level, the crowning glory, reserved for the king. Moreover, the interior contained a markedly new, raised element: at the level of the upper chapel, the entablature-supporting columns were replaced by square piers that carried low-level arcades and formed a colonnade inspired by Claude Perrault's west façade of the Louvre. This idea for church architecture first appeared prior to 1697, in a project also attributed to Claude Perrault: an antique-styled basilica, with a colonnade beneath the entablature. The design was inspired by Vitruvius in his Fano basilica, a work reproduced by Perrault in an illustration for his translation of Vitruvius.

Any connection between Vitruvius's conception and an analogous earlier experiment – the Protestant Temple at Charenton, designed by Salomon de Brosse – is no doubt fortuitous. In any case, the impact of Vitruvius's work confirms the attraction of the oblong design. In Reformed churches examples of the central plan are found from the outset, whether circular as in Antwerp, or octagonal as in La Rochelle; but after the Revocation of the Edict of Nantes, which led to the destruction of so many Protestant churches in France, Charenton would serve as a model throughout northern Europe.

The Rococo in central and oriental Europe

The Italian monumental tradition spread northwards in central Europe due to the movements of itinerant teams of stone-masons and decorators from Lombardy and Milan, in search of new building sites. In countries where efforts were being made to restore the Catholic faith, the arts, and particularly architecture, assumed an especially dynamic role in missionary apologetics. A number of countries participated in this Baroque experimentation, conceived to win over converts through the senses before doing so through discourse: thus in Bohemia (Kilian Ignac Diezenhofer with Saint Nicholas de Mala Strana in Prague), in Hungary (Prandtauer in Melk Abbey, 1709–11), and in Vienna (Fischer von Erlach with the church of Saint-Charles-Borromeo, 1715–23).

Originating in France, the Rococo influence grafted itself onto the Italianate trunk to produce an art that was particularly voluble, optimistic, and luminous. In terms of monastic architecture, the finest examples were provided by Balthasar Neumann in Neresheim (1745–98) and Vierzehnheiligen (1745–72); by Dominikus Zimmermann in the Wies sanctuary (1745–50); by the Asams in Munich, Ratisbonne, and Freising; by Johann Mikael Fischer in Ottobeuren (1748–53); by Peter Thum in Saint-Gall in Switzerland; and indeed by the anonymous builder of Einsiedeln Abbey, also in Switzerland. Buildings by these architects privileged the curved line and juxtaposed the oval for the nave and the rectangle for the choir – as in the Wies church; they developed wide façades flanked by towers and preserved the use of generous bays from the hall church tradition to produce a profusion of light.

Forms of a similar kind, adapted to local contexts, spread to Dresden, the capital of Catholic Poland during the reign of Augustus the Strong (the court church); and to Russia, particularly Saint Petersburg, through Dominico Trezzini (the Peter and Paul Basilica, 1712–23) and Bartolomeo Rastrelli (the Smolny Convent); as well as to Rome, Naples, and Sicily. In their own particular manner, Spain and Portugal also adapted the Rococo, whether through the designs of foreign architects, such as Konrad Rudolf (Valencia), Jaime Bort (Murcia), or Johann Friedrich Ludwig; or of local masters like the Figueroas in Andalusia and the Churrigueras in Salamanca. In the following years, architecture that combined Baroque and Rococo with indigenous traits spread throughout Latin American regions (as in the Ocotlan sanctuary in Mexico, c. 1745; or the Congonhas church in Brazil).

France: the move towards neo-classic simplicity

With one or two exceptions, such as the reconstruction of the Gothic cathedral of Orléans or the great abbey of Ebersmunster in Alsace – influenced by the style of Alpine Europe – France refused to adapt the Rococo to her own

Figure 5 Einsiedeln Abbey (Benedictine), Switzerland. The lavish rococo interior contains an organ in both arms of the transept. The abbey was constructed between 1719 and 1735. (Photograph courtesy of the United States Historical Archive.)

religious architecture. In 1726, Juste-Aurèle Meissonnier proposed a façade for Saint-Sulpice (originally designed by Christophe Gamard in 1643) that was marked by Borromini's influence. But the plan was rejected. In 1732, the competition for this final portion of the church was won by Jean-Nicolas Servandoni, a decision that marked the triumph of columns and horizontal entablatures. Despite the Borrominian curves employed in the upper parts of the towers, Jean-François Chalgrin's intervention into the construction of the upper balustrade after 1770 consolidated the dominance of the straight line. This tendency was confirmed in the meantime with Soufflot's 1764 project for Sainte-Geneviève (soon renamed as the Pantheon). Here the architect's aim was to reconcile the Greek order, exemplified in France by Perrault's colonnade, with the science and lightness of Gothic construction that he so admired. A highly intellectualized design resulted, presenting no seductive artifice but consisting of a wholly calculated layout of straight lines and curves, parallelepipeds, and spheres. The plan was distinguished by an almost perfect symmetry and gridded organization.

The pronounced tendency towards abstraction was reaffirmed in another contemporary project. In the same year, 1764, Jean-François Chalgrin was charged with the construction of Saint-Philippe du Roule. Employing an exterior Tuscan porch, Ionic colonnades in both the aisle and the semi-circular choir, and a coffered vault, Chalgrin readapted the form of the ancient basilica, which quickly became the model for many subsequent decades of religious architecture. Similar layouts may be seen in the Saint-Symphorien de Montreuil, built by Louis-François Trouard in Versailles (1764–70); and in the Saint-Louis in Saint-Germain-en-Laye, begun by Nicolas Potain, once again in 1764. Potain used the same style in Rennes Cathedral, for which the plan was approved in 1764, although the construction began only in 1786. After the Revolution, virtually all French churches would conform to the style derived from Saint-Philippe de Roule, adapted to the basilica plan and with the addition of an entrance porch. (The sole exception was the Madeleine, whose design was carefully chosen by Napoleon I, more as a temple dedicated to the Glory of France than as a church for Catholic worship.) In Paris, this basic design could be seen in churches by Hippolyte Godde (Saint-Pierre du Gros Caillou, Saint-Denis du Saint-Sacrement), by Molinos (Sainte-Marie des Batignoles), and by Hippolyte Lebas (Notre-Dame de Lorette). The style was retained until the 1840s when the neo-Gothic arrived to challenge aggressively the pre-eminence of neo-classicism (in Paris, Gau's Sainte-Clotilde; in Nantes, Jean-Baptiste Lassus's Saint-Nicolas).

Furniture and fittings

The rupture of the Reformation led to different conceptions of the religious function not only of the church, but of its furniture and fittings as well. Some places of worship now excluded all sacramental functions, electing to serve as meeting-places for Scripture readings, commentaries, or prayer. Others reaffirmed their status as privileged areas of the divine presence, or sacred places for the mystery of the Eucharist and the other sacraments. As it emerged from the Reformation, the Protestant Church found the greater part of its surface area and walls taken up by pews, stalls, and galleries for the reception of the community. The table, pulpit, and occasionally the organ were situated in front. The Catholic Church, by contrast, attempted to partition a given space between the sanctuary and the priests, on the one hand, and the congregation, on the other. Significant room had necessarily to be accorded to liturgical furniture. In France, pews were not widespread in churches until after the return of religious service following the Concordat of 1801.

Central elements in the furnishings were the altar and the altarpiece. With much modification the altarpiece, a medieval inheritance, was transformed into the Catholic Reformation's principal piece of furniture. Thereafter, its main purpose was to act as adjunct to the tabernacle where the Eucharist was held – until then kept in the suspensions, wardrobes, or eucharistic towers. Iconographic practice ensuing from the Tridentine decrees saw the gradual disappearance of most historical scenes and the subjects of altar-paintings restricted to duly codified themes. Whether or not in conjunction with this type of altar-painting, a new and more abstract iconography now emerged, consisting of symbols devoted to commentary on the Trinity. Cherubs were placed here and there on the tabernacle, and above them the glorious symbol of the celestial host, the dove of the Holy Spirit, and the tetragram. As an expression of sovereignty, a canopy was positioned over the entire structure. Within the parameters of this basic schema, the majority of altarpieces attained very considerable dimensions, until a counter-movement gradually led to their suppression. By the end of the eighteenth century and especially by the beginning of the nineteenth, elements accompanying the altar were limited to the tabernacle, candelabra supports, and cherubs.

In France, the altar itself almost always backed onto the end of the choir (e.g., in the Versailles Chapel and Notre Dame in Paris). Rome innovated in this area by transporting the altar, consisting of a large table, towards the nave.

Between 1624 and 1633, Bernini installed in Saint Peter's a monumental dais in the shape of a baldaccino. Such a staging of the sacrifice of the Mass and the real presence, renewing the Paleo-Christian tradition of the *ciborium*, immediately prompted imitators in France, notably in the Val-de-Grâce (1665). But it was not until the middle of the next century that altars in the 'Roman style' and 'tomb altars' in the shape of a table were fully developed in France (e.g., in Valence Cathedral). Even then there were problems: in 1753, the chapter of Noyon Cathedral was bitterly divided over the question of the installation of such an altar, and decided to place the affair before the king's counsel – who came down in favour of those who supported innovation.

In monastic and collegiate churches that functioned as parishes, choirs were reorganized. The opaque barrier of the older medieval jube now became lighter and more transparent through the use of iron-work, and a small altar was attached to the bottom of one of the pillars at the choir entrance for celebration of the parish Mass. Such modifications were made with the intention of bringing the faithful closer to the liturgical act, particularly the consecration.

Other church furnishings also acquired new significance. The pulpit was placed in the middle of the nave to facilitate contact between the priest and his congregation. It took on monumental proportions, was provided with a sound-break to improve the acoustics, and acquired a characteristic iconography (e.g., the four evangelists, or the pelican devouring its entrails to nourish its children, as a symbol of Christ). The practice of auricular confession developed alongside missions and sermons, and a new piece of furniture was designed and installed in proportion to the number of priests serving the parish. (About this time Prague Cathedral brought back devotion to Saint Jean Népomucène, martyred for having refused to divulge a confessional secret.) Finally, organs frequently came to attain monumental proportions, with several different instruments now merged into a single panel containing several cases – the positive organ, the great organ, the choir, and the echo. The instrument's location within the church might vary. In Protestant churches it was often placed above the pulpit, but it was usually set at the back of the nave in French Catholic churches. There might even be two organs, one in each arm of the transept (as in Einsiedeln). And in large churches, an additional instrument was placed in the choir or on the enclosure to accompany collegiate or monastic services.

The visual arts and emotional arousal

Neither the evolution of architectural design nor the development of church furnishings can explain, in and by themselves, the originality of buildings of worship at the time of the Catholic and Protestant Reformations. The architect and the clergyman, whether priest or pastor, worked together towards the common goal of glorifying the church. In the medieval period, the urban church often appeared somewhat inconspicuous, prevented from standing out among its surroundings by a lack of space and the chaotic character of the neighbouring structures. Engravings of cities at the beginning of the modern period suggest that the height lent to church flèches was due more to design conventions than a desire to signal the church's location within the urban area. Saint Charles Borromeo appears to be one of the first seriously concerned with the need to separate the place of worship from its neighbouring buildings (*Instructiones fabricae ecclesiasticae et supellectilis ecclesiasticae libri duo*, 1577). Here he took into account both questions of financial security, and the right of a place of divine worship to be set apart from secular life. Accordingly, he put forward the idea that the network of urban streets should surround the building at the chevet and sides, but that the main façade should open onto a public space. Yet the architectural and urban project could not be restricted to such functional purposes. The construction of places of worship was part of a larger objective, of what the ancient Romans called the 'ornamentation' of the city. The façade now appeared as a constituent element of the urban visual complex (in the Gesù it even took the form of a triumphal arch). It was to this end that Carlo Raimondi built the twin churches in the Piazza del Popolo in Rome, for example. Similarly, Christopher Wren recommended that church towers be built tall and beautiful, so that without excessive expenditure, the architect might distinguish the place of worship from its built-up surroundings, and embellish the overall appearance of a city. In a period when urban planning was seen as a policy to construct public buildings around which residential areas might progressively develop (the Invalides in Paris, for example), the building of new churches held an important position in city design.

Within this redefined urban space, the external aspects of buildings of worship accrued the powers of a new symbolic discourse. In 1631, for example, Baldassare Longhena confirmed that his choice of a central plan for the Salute in Venice was based on the desire to design a crown for the Virgin Mary. Borromini explained that the façade of the Congregation of the Oratory of Saint Philip Neri, curved but convex in the centre, offered the image of the mystical church opening its arms to welcome believers into its heart (1638–42). Bernini adopted the same metaphorical language for Saint Peter's Square. And for Sant' Ivo delle Sapienza (1643–50), he suggested an analogy between the motif of the tiered dome with its triple-spiralled steeple and the image of the papal tiara. In a similar manner, Guarino Guarini designed the chapel of the Sindona in Turin (1667–90) according to a tripartite scheme, conceived to express the mystery of the Trinity.

In the interior, spatiality was guided by the functional goal of enabling the congregation to see and to hear. This was clearly the case for denominations that had grown out of the Reformation, but it was also so with Catholicism – despite the fact that Christopher Wren attempted clearly to distinguish Anglicanism from the Roman religion. 'Roman Catholics', he wrote, 'are able to build larger churches, because they need to hear the murmur of the mass and see the elevation of the host, but our churches must be designed for the audience'. This was the point of view that led to the elimination of the rood screens that enclosed the canons' choir in cathedrals, but it was only after the 1801 Concordat's confirmation of the cathedral's parish function – in addition to its capitular role – that the last screens were removed (as in the Cathedral of Rodez after 1823 and of Limoges in 1888).

A similar preoccupation with sight and sound led architects to widen naves and limit the function of aisles to circulation only, and to propose different relationships between the nave and choir, usually in order to elevate the choir. In Leipzig, for example, the church of Saint-Nicolas was a Gothic structure in which a space for the congregation in the shape of an ellipse was created during the eighteenth century. One may also wonder whether the mid-eighteenth-century tendency to build smaller-scale edifices and to adopt the basilica plan were not linked to similar requirements of sight and sound. Experiments conducted in concert halls in Great Britain confirm the superiority on this score of an oblong plan extended in a hemispherical gallery, with the moving of bays to the upper part of the gutter-carrying walls. Nevertheless, it remains the case that in the 1840s, when a counter-movement emerged in favour of the neo-Gothic, proponents of the medieval style (such as Charles de Montalembert and Adolphe-Napoléon Didron) opposed the basilica style precisely because of its supposed resemblance to worldly and secular concert halls. Yet despite such criticisms, the majority of neo-Gothic churches retained a volumetric unity characteristic of buildings in the preceding generation. In sum, the oblong plan, whether or not in the form of a basilica, seems clearly to have been preferred because of its acoustic qualities. However, a certain number of buildings with a circular plan on the model of the Pantheon in Rome (e.g., the Madre in Turin; or Possagno church, designed by Antonio Canova) continued to be constructed during the first two decades of the nineteenth century.

Research into questions of spatiality should not be restricted, however, to matters of function alone. Architects also invented ways to expand internal space in order to reduce any impression of the finite. The use of a dome permitted such an effect, particularly when painted with a *trompe l'œil*. In Rome, the dome of Sant' Andrea della Valle (1625–27) initiated a long run of fresco painting, which with the aid of academic studies on perspective, exploited a surface's continuous curve in order to produce the illusory effect of ascent to heaven. In France, the most significant such example is found in the dome of the Val-de-Grâce, painted by Pierre Mignard (1663–66). Similar effects in long spatial areas such as naves are more difficult to achieve, because the painter must reconcile his plan of an illusory ascent with the oblique viewpoint of a person entering the church. Pietro da Cortona (in Santa Maria in Vallicella, 1647–51) and Giovanni Battista Gaulli, known as Baciccio (in the Gesù, 1672–79), produced the first masterpieces conveying this type of effect. The *trompe l'œil* enabled the creation of an imaginary space at the centre of a constructed space, which gave the believer the sense that the boundary between heaven and earth had been removed. In the eighteenth century, Rococo architecture and decoration followed a similar path in Alpine and central Europe, as well as on the Iberian peninsula and in Latin America.

The expansion of internal space through architecture and painting was accompanied by subtle and complex research into the use of light. The aim was to create an emotional effect on the spectator by dissimulating the position of the light source, and so to accentuate the effects of mystery and unreality. This is what Bernini aimed to produce with his *Saint Theresa in Ecstasy* (1647–52) in the Cornaro Chapel of Santa Maria della Vittorio. An angel transports the saint towards the divine light on a cloud, the unattainable nature of the divine being suggested by atmospherical light reflected onto golden rays through an invisible oculus. Guarino Guarini made a speciality of creating direct or indirect light which would confer qualities of transcendence and infinitude onto an interior space. His greatest masterpiece of mathematical science was the Sindona in Turin, where he covered the dome with a superposition of octagonal structures, conceived in such a way that openings allowing light into the building remained invisible to the viewer. A light of mysterious origin, filtering through the black marble interior, seemed tinged with darkness, producing an obscure or black light – a *tenebrosa luc*. The believer who came to the Sindona to worship Christ's shroud, one of the most famous relics in Christendom, was thus led to understand that he found himself at the very core of a picture of Christ's tomb on Resurrection Day. Another fine example of this type of lighting pathos may be seen in Prague at Saint-Nicholas de Mala Strana (by Dienzenhofer) where the dome, designed as a lantern, produced a luminosity that changed in relation to the outside light. So too Hardouin-Mansart was able to create surprising effects through the use of light in the chapel of the Invalides in Paris. He dissimulated openings in the dome with an internal calotte in the centre of which an oculus spread light throughout the building

The generation from Soufflot (Sainte-Geneviève) to Boullée (the design of a revolutionary *metropole*) renounced the pathos of surprise in favour of the simpler and more contrasting effects produced by successions of dark and well-lit spaces. In his fictional work, *L'An 2440, rêve s'il en fût jamais* (1770–87), Louis-Sébastien Mercier articulated the religious and aesthetic objectives of an imaginary future, which might have been those of the end of the *ancien régime*. In his temple devoted to a somewhat pantheistic worship of the Supreme Being a dome-crowned rotunda was supported by a single line of columns and opened by four large portals; the light filtered in through transparent stained-glass windows set into the dome's summit. This lighting descended from the zenith, Mercier wrote, put the interior in contact with heaven, the elements, and the seasons.

The taste for abundant light characteristic of the French aesthetic went hand in hand with a gradually diminishing interest in architectural polychromy. In the period from the middle of the eighteenth century through the 1820s (e.g., in Notre Dame de Lorette), even while interest in colour was reviving following archaeological discoveries of painted decorations on Greek temples, places of worship remained committed to white. In Paris at Saint-Séverin from 1699, and at Saint-Merry from 1751, medieval stained-glass windows were removed and replaced with white glass. Nevertheless, these transformations in taste did not take place without discussion. In 1754, those canons of Noyon who rejected the modernization of the choir attempted to argue (in line with the thinking of Jean-Baptiste Thiers, 1688) that a desire to see and be seen was contrary to piety, and that obscurity was more appropriate for the celebration of the sacred mysteries. The king's counsel did not uphold the argument, but in the early 1780s the canons of the Sainte Chapelle in Paris successfully blocked the plans of the royal administration to replace the thirteenth-century stained-glass windows of Saint Louis with white glass. Similarly, the white-washing of interior walls could trigger debate. In the *Tableaux de Paris*, Sébastien Mercier argued against the practice of replacing age-old mysterious shadow with an atmosphere so obviously profane (as in Notre Dame in Paris, 1753). In 1806, following the Revolution, Millin would echo Mercier's thoughts.

Debates such as these allow us to perceive the complex interweaving of arguments. An increased control over the cult of images after the promulgation of the canons of the Council of Trent had led to a growing scarcity of iconographic subjects and historical scenes and, by consequence, to a decline in the use of colour. In addition, the functional and rational characteristics of the liturgy led to a rejection of the powerful effects of the seventeenth-century Italianate style, and to the production of more simply articulated white spaces. But after 1750, there emerged a simpler and more natural sense of pathos which built on the contrasts of light and shadow. In 1774, Wailly blocked up the windows of the chapel of the Virgin in Saint-Sulpice, as Boullée had done earlier in the Calvary chapel in Saint-Roch, and indeed as Quatremère de Quincy was to do at the start of the Revolution when he ordered the covering of nave windows in the Panthéon.

It would be interesting to undertake comparable studies in the area of sound. By its simplification of interior architecture, the modern period opened the way to a new spatialization of music, and perhaps even more, to a different style of composition. The polyphony which succeeded medieval monody presumed a relatively restricted and acoustically reliable space. The use of two choirs in dialogue with each other, and sometimes the use of two organs, developed to advantage the stereophonic qualities of the new spaces (as in the abbey church of Einsiedeln with two organs in the transept and a third in the choir). The significant place occupied by music during the service and in religious life generally – whether performed by the organist, the choir, the chapel, or other sources used in the *lectio divina* and its psalmody – remains to be explored. The poorly known, but no doubt considerable interaction between architecture and music needs to be examined, along with the relationship between architecture and sound more generally – where 'sound' should also include the preacher's words and the prayers of the minister and his acolytes in the many different contexts required by the liturgy and the reading of holy texts.

The new temple

The denominations that came out of the Reformation were not alone in introducing the term 'temple' to designate a place of worship. Not without reservations – similar to those of the early Christians who wanted to distinguish themselves from pagan religions – Catholics in the seventeenth and eighteenth centuries also used this term. Theologians were insistent that the Infinite Divinity could not be restricted to the dimensions of a dwelling-place made by man, and stressed that the church was above all the place of the *ecclesia*, the congregation of the faithful. However, the significance placed on the Holy Sacrament and the Real Presence led to the definition of the building in question as the *Domus Dei*, the *Janua Cœli*. On this foundation there emerged a metaphorical discourse rooted in the commentaries of the

Fathers and theologians of the Middle Ages which offered a sort of semantic representation and anchored Christianity, as purified by the Catholic Reformation, in the poetical and sacred world of biblical antiquity. This discourse was reinforced, moreover, during the early modern period through the revival of biblical studies prompted by Christian humanism, through the climate of intellectual competition between Catholic and Protestant exegetes, and through the influence of Jansenism accentuated by theological rigourism. It was hoped thus to respond to the primitivist discourse of the Reformation, which aimed at returning to the first Christians, by claiming a direct line of legitimacy from the religion of Israel to the Roman Church. Thus, the church became the 'temple', the choir was referred to as the 'Holy of Holies', and the container of the Eucharist became the 'tabernacle', framed by two cherubs with veiled faces, as they had flanked the Ark in the Holy of Holies. In a similar manner, the Eucharist in the monstrance came to be represented by the Burning Bush; the First Person, by the Hebrew tetragram in an equilateral triangle (as in the altarpiece at Karlskirche in Vienna – dedicated, moreover, to Saint Charles Borromeo); the Second Person by the letters IHS. The priest became known as the 'sacrificer'; the chasuble took the form of the 'sacrificer's apron'; and the priest's acolytes were designated 'Levites', sometimes referred to as 'the sacerdotal tribe'. Intellectuals pored over biblical texts and the *Antiquities of the Jews* of Flavius Josephus, and produced numerous recreations of temples and their contents – from Juan Bautista Villalpando and Louis Maillet, canon of Troyes, to Dom Calmet and Johann Bernard Fischer von Erlach (1721). A scholarly iconography displayed Old Testament prefigurations of the Eucharist, of the sacrificial altar, and of the altar for the bread offering to the empty throne of the Divine Presence (as in the sacristy panelling of the priory of Saints-Pierre-et-Paul in Souvigny, Allier). In sum, one is led to conclude that Roman Catholicism saw the first of its 'revivals' during the early modern period – a biblical 'revival' in advance of that which occurred from the 1830s in favour of the Middle Ages.

This interpretation of the Real Presence through Old Testament prefigurations was intended to reconcile the twin demands of transcendence and reason characteristic of Catholicism during the early modern period. It tended to de-emphasize Christ's human nature, while symbols like IHS and the lamb were given special prominence; the narrative of church history, and particularly of the saints, was also neglected. It testified to a religion that tended towards abstraction in its desire to suppress superstition. It was closely contemporary to the effort (though with considerable local variation, particularly in France) to purge places of worship of all artifice pleasing to the senses – pictures, figures, sculptural mouldings, colours, historicized repre-sentations – in order to dedicate them to the Holy Name. It is incorrect to suggest that the plans and achievements at the end of the eighteenth century were the reflection of a utilitarian conception of religion, a kind of generalized Josephinism in which the state classified religion as one of its 'public services'. This would be to see religious indifference in what, if studied carefully, was nothing other than a passion for abstraction. Boullée's plan for the interior of a revolutionary *metropole* can remind us of the power of the pathos that stimulates the religious imagination: at the top of a three-flight staircase that emerges from the end of a dark nave, at the transept crossing, lit suddenly by rays falling from a gigantic dome, and in front of the opening to a shadowy apse marked by a triumphal arch, rises an altar, placed on a pedestal of extraordinary size. On this Roman-style altar-table, a *sacrificateur* celebrates the cult of the Supreme Being, surrounded by a cloud of incense. With the priest silhouetted against the light and the crowd bowed along the length of the nave steps, the atmosphere is imposing. One is surely not far from the 'mysteries of Isis' and *The Magic Flute*, or from masonic costume and revolutionary ceremonies. Yet this magnificent intellectual theatricality, lying as it does somewhere between reason and pathos, is not unworthy of taking its place in a chapter on Bernini, Borromini, and Guarini.

In a similar manner, the Neo-Gothic Renaissance, in its retrospective regard towards the Middle Ages, would bring to the sanctuary the humanity of Jesus the evangelist, Jesus the romantic harbinger of a social discourse, along with the golden legends of medieval saints, polychromy, penumbra, and a sense of the *pittoresque* in architectural forms. Something of the Enlightenment's religion – or rather of the biblical, abstract, and rigorist conception of that religion – would remain in the nineteenth century, but the rapid renewal of architectural forms after 1830 would express without words the exigencies of a new religious sensibility. (Translation by Jane Yeoman)

PART III

MOVEMENTS AND CHALLENGES

13

Christianity and the rise of science, 1660–1815

LOUIS CHÂTELLIER

The period from 1660 to the beginning of the nineteenth century was distinguished not only by significant technical and scientific progress, but also by the spread of a new way of thinking that drew for its effectiveness on scientific reasoning. English intellectuals such as Samuel Clarke were inspired by Newton's *Philosophiae naturalis principia mathematica* (1687), while the huge impact of Leibniz's *Essais de Théodicée* (1710) was due largely to the author's mathematical knowledge. In France, the *Encyclopédie* (1751–72) represented not only an inventory of modern science, but an initiation into a new method of analysis, which was applied to the entire range of physical and metaphysical phenomena. That, indeed, was how d'Alembert, writing in his *Discours préliminaire* to the *Encyclopédie*, explained the sub-title of the *Dictionnaire raisonné des sciences, des arts et des métiers*.[1]

Christianity, in principle, was not hostile towards scientific thought. Had not Saint Augustine written in his *On Christian Doctrine*, 'All the sciences fight on behalf of the Christian religion'?[2] Many theologians – such as Nicholas of Cusa at the close of the Middle Ages[3] – had been passionate practitioners of mathematics. During the sixteenth century, all universities, both Catholic and Protestant, taught mathematics. From 1550 on, the secondary schools of the Society of Jesus, founded in the part of Europe still faithful to the Roman Church also did so, and this new religious order played an important role in the teaching of mathematics during the period of the Catholic Reformation.[4] Nevertheless, there was a boundary beyond which neither Luther nor the papacy could step: the teachings of the Bible, whether scientific or theological, could in no way be questioned. Galileo, who had attempted to establish just such a distinction between what belonged to the domain of belief and what to the secular sciences, not only had not been supported, but had been harshly condemned by the Holy Office at his second trial in 1633.[5] Such extreme severity towards a loyal Catholic had caused surprise. The decision was much discussed, and many privately speculated whether – beyond Galileo's specific case – the Roman judges were not rather targeting the new science, or indeed, emancipation from the ancient philosopher who still remained the intellectual leader inside the Catholic Church: Aristotle.

Thus, in the mid-seventeenth century the relationship between scientific thinkers and ecclesiastical authorities was marked by reciprocal mistrust. Certainly this was the case in Catholic Europe. Perhaps this was the reason for the new intellectual momentum in Protestant Europe.

From Descartes to Newton

Nevertheless, one must not overlook the case of Descartes. His reaction to Galileo's condemnation well reveals the state of crisis provoked by the trial among Catholic intellectuals. In November 1633, Descartes wrote that when he heard the news, '[I was] so shocked I almost resolved to burn my papers, or at least to keep them hidden. I simply could not imagine that he [Galileo], who is Italian, and of whom even the Pope thinks well, I believe, could have been criminalized for anything other than wishing to establish the movement of the earth . . . and I confess that if Galileo is wrong, then so are all the foundations of my Philosophy [of Physics], since he clearly uses them to support his case.'[6] As it turned out, the publication of Descartes's treatise 'Le Monde', already in finished state, was withheld until 1664, after his death.[7]

However, Descartes did not allow these events to prevent him from taking effective action to free thinking from Aristotle's grip. The *Discourse on Method* was intended to demonstrate the effectiveness of his logic in scientific reasoning; to this end, he published a *Geometry* and a *Dioptric* alongside the treatise (1637)[8]. Above all, Cartesian rationalism inspired the methods of several other great scholars. The first of these was Christiaan Huygens, who used Descartes' method in rigorously developing his own laws on the impact of bodies. Further, in the *Systema Saturnium* (1659), Huygens provided a solid argument in favour of the earth's movement, by transposing his observations of planetary satellites onto the whole solar system. The earth clearly turned around the sun, as did the moon around the earth: thus Copernicus's system was confirmed once again.[9] This kind of reasoning was to carry Huygens towards the vision of an infinite universe (the *Cosmotheoros*), where an unlimited number of planets could not fail to be inhabited in much the same way as our own world.[10]

Huygens's idea met with great acclaim at the end of the seventeenth century, and reached the general public thanks to the pen of Fontenelle, whose talents as a thinker equalled those as a writer. In his *Entretiens sur la pluralité des mondes* (1686), Fontenelle did not simply accept that other planets were inhabited, but also: 'That fixed stars are in fact as many suns, each one of which illuminates a world' (Fifth Evening). Nevertheless, an idea that seemed logical from an astronomical point of view, became unacceptable when examined by theology. How should Creation be understood? What value should be given to the Bible, when it might be nothing more than one among thousands of religious stories? And Christ who came to save us, could he not be, as some thought, just one of many Christs present somewhere in the universe?[11] Yet from another point of view, as the Swiss mathematician Jean Bernouilli maintained, it was inadmissible to conceive of the divine Almighty as finite. The Almighty was manifest as much in the infinitely small (a globule of air) as in the infinitely large (the universe and giants).[12] In this way an understanding of the world was reached not unlike that later described by Swift in his *Gulliver's Travels* – yet Bernoulli was utterly serious. Scientific progress had led to the possibility of an entirely new reading of the Bible, at precisely the moment when scholars, using philology and the comparative study of civilizations, were attempting to identify its original meaning.[13] In this sense, one wonders whether the various academies – and notably the Academy of Science founded by Colbert in 1666 – might not have been founded with the partial intention of 'disciplining' thinkers.[14]

A different path was taken in England, or at least initially. The Royal Society, the model of the *Académie des sciences*, functioned more to promote emulation than to control thinking. It also found itself with a veritable task of apologetics to fulfil towards those whose faith was wavering. 'If (as the Apostle says)', wrote Thomas Sprat, one of the first members, in 1667, 'the invisible things of God are manifested by the visible; then how much stronger arguments has he [the scientist] for his belief in the eternal power of the Godhead from the vast number of creatures that are invisible to others but are expos'd to his view by the help of experiments'. In this way, out of experiments, he found 'arguments to adore' the Deity, for 'he has always before his eyes the beauty, contrivance, and order of Gods' works'. He also pointed to the celebrated words of Francis Bacon: 'by a little knowledge of nature men become atheists; but a great deal returns them back again to a sound and religious mind'.[15] One can understand how one of the great scientists of the time, Robert Boyle, an adversary of Aristotle and Paracelsus (*The Sceptical Chemist*, 1661) and the founder of modern chemistry, thought of his research as a kind of apostolic mission. In his will, he established a foundation with the aim of challenging atheists and non-believers through the use of scientific argument.[16]

Under such conditions, it is not surprising to find that the conclusion to Isaac Newton's *Principia* soared like a hymn to the divine. 'It follows from this', wrote Newton at the end of his general commentary,

> that the true God is living, intelligent, and powerful, . . . that he is supreme, or supremely perfect. He is eternal and infinite, omnipotent and omniscient, that is, he endures from eternity to eternity, and he is present from infinity to infinity; he rules all things, and he knows all things that happen or can happen. He is not eternity and infinity, but eternal and infinite; he is not duration and space, but he endures and is present. He endures always and is present everywhere, and by existing always and everywhere he constitutes duration and space.[17]

Nevertheless, there was a difference between the conception of science held by a Robert Boyle and that held by a Newton. For Newton, science was not simply a question of awe before the wonders of Creation but rather of the representation of God's work, as if, once the scientist's research was complete, he had risen to divine heights and was able to contemplate God's work. This no doubt explains the exasperation of those such as Huygens and Leibniz, who when interrogating Newton on the universal principle of attraction, invariably received the response (through the intermediary of Samuel Clarke), that God was 'present everywhere'.[18] How could scientists know this and speak with such conviction? The future Bishop of Cloyne and author of the *Analyst*, George Berkeley, had his own explanation. For Berkeley, the scientists' certitude came from their use of the new calculus, known as infinitesimal or differential, with which Newton had been able to calculate the elliptical paths of the planets with the utmost precision.[19] But, wrote Berkeley in 1707, does man have the right to 'go beyond his notions to talk of parts infinitely small or *partes infinitesimae* of finite quantitys, and much less of *infinitesimae infinitesimarum*, and so on'.[20] Was this not to endeavour to penetrate the very mysteries of Creation and to elevate oneself, with a pride similar to Lucifer's, to the place of God? It was not just Newton and Anglicanism which were challenged. Leibniz, who disputed with Newton the honour of having first discovered infinitesimal calculus, was taken to task by the Jesuits – with whom he generally had good relations. In the second issue (May–June 1701) of their journal published in France, *Les Mémoires de Trévoux*, the Fathers of the Society of Jesus attacked Leibniz over an article on the new calculus that he had had transmitted to the journal by a friend. 'But when one reasons about the infinite', wrote the journal's editor, 'then the infinite of the infinite, then the infinite of the infinite of the infinite, and so on, without ever finding the final terms, and then applies this infinite number of infinities to finite magnitudes – then those whom one is trying to instruct or hoping to persuade will not necessarily possess the insight needed to see clearly into such profound depths'.[21] In more diplomatic form, here was a warning on the new calculus every bit as firm as Berkeley's.

At the end of the seventeenth century, in both Catholic and Protestant countries, the relationship between science and religion was marked by a certain ambiguity. Scientific progress aroused considerable interest among the general public, as demonstrated by the birth of a specialist press after the 1660s (in England, *The Philosophical Transactions*; in France the *Journal des savants*; and in Germany the *Acta Eruditorum*). Catholic and Protestant ecclesiastics usually encouraged this curiosity, considering it the best defence against scepticism, atheism, or simple religious indifference, and feeling that the wonders waiting to be discovered could lead only to the Creator. However, there came a moment towards the end of the seventeenth century and the beginning of the next, when the advances in the scientific movement and the honing of new research techniques did not lead quite so obviously towards God. Certain people felt that the prodigious development of the human mind might be sufficient to account for everything.

The problem of infinity: from Hell to Paradise

It is scarcely surprising that towards 1700 Newton's discoveries should renew the debate over the problem of the infinity of space and time. In reality, such discussions had not ceased since the writings of Epicurus and Lucretius in Antiquity. But it took on a new dimension at the time of the Counter-Reformation, with Giordano Bruno's trial and death at the stake in Rome (1600).[22] Bruno had been accused of appropriating ideas from ancient pagan and atheist authors for his celebrated work, *De l'infinito, universo e mondi* (1584). As a result of this, the very idea of infinity threw even the most learned thinkers into a state of terror. One of Blaise Pascal's correspondents wrote to him, 'I tell you that as soon as the idea of infinity enters into a question, however slightly, then the entire problem is rendered inexplicable, for the mind becomes troubled and confused'.[23] Pascal himself explained the reason for this fear in a celebrated passage from the *Pensées*: 'Unable to observe infinity', he wrote, 'men have gone recklessly in search of nature, imagining themselves to be of a similar proportion'. And he added, 'When that is truly understood, I think men will rest, each in the place accorded him by nature'.[24] A few years later, the authors of *La Logique de Port-Royal*, Antoine Arnauld and Pierre Nicole, would be even more precise. They urged their readers 'never to become involved in seeking anything above us . . . anything to do with infinity, for since our minds are finite, they become confused and lose themselves in infinity, and are overwhelmed by the mass of contradictory ideas which arise'.[25] Protestants and Catholics alike – and Jansenists as much as Jesuits – found themselves agreeing in their refusal to accept infinity as an object of study. Infinity was the domain of God alone and of His Creation. To engage with the question was tantamount to violating a taboo, or worse, to acting as if God did not exist. A direct path seemed to lead from belief in the infinity of the universe to atheism.

Thus, despite Newton's precautions and the professions of faith expressed in the *Principia*, he nevertheless had to clear himself of heavy suspicions regarding his religious belief. Perhaps in response to his critics, or simply because theology was a constant preoccupation, Newton devoted his last years to writing a work of history.[26] Although *The Chronology of Ancient Kingdoms Amended* was published in final form a year after his death (1728), the work's main tenets had been known earlier. It had been expected to challenge traditional chronology through the use of modern astronomy; it did so, but it did much more. It represented an initial outline of a calculus of probability, which the work employed to prove the accuracy of sacred history's development as taught by the Church of England. Better still, according to Newton, his method enabled him to prove the Hebrews' pioneering role in the history of civilization, well before that of the Greeks.[27] At this point, the impeccable orthodoxy of the author of the *Principia* could no longer be disputed. Moreover, the most authoritative interpreters of Newton's thought, who included his successor at Cambridge, took care to head off any possible criticism. 'The Mosaick Creation', wrote William Whiston in 1696, 'is not a nice and philosophical account of the origin of all things, but an historical and true representation of the formation of our single earth out of a confused chaos, and of the successive and visible changes thereof each day, till it became the habitation of mankind'.[28]

However, what the Master wrote was one thing, the interpretation given by the English and French Newtonians, was quite another. One of the latter, Voltaire, did much to help Newton's ideas penetrate on the continent with his *Eléments de la philosophie de Newton* (1738). Voltaire was not a mathematician and it is clear that he had not worked for fours years on the *Principia* – having what he did not understand explained to him by Newton's translator, Madame du Châtelet – only to conclude that Newton's work did not affect the church's traditional teaching. The ultimate outcome of all Newton's calculations, according to Voltaire, was something quite different. In the vastness of the universe, he wrote, the earth was merely a point. This particular point had undergone a violent disturbance, 'the cause of which is hidden, the length almost unimaginable, but which seems to guarantee the human species a scarcely conceivable duration'. 'But', he continued, 'there is every likelihood that this will be a period of one million, nine hundred and forty-four thousand years'.[29] Thus according to Voltaire, the infinity of space corresponded to the infinity of time – a problem that Newton, of course, had taken care to avoid. From this point on, both biblical chronology and sacred history more generally were relegated to the rank of a fable, the fruit of man's imagination about his origins. As for God, He presided from very far away and from a very great height over the movement of the planets He had previously created. It was in this way that 'Voltaire's religion' took shape – a religion which might best be described as a scientific deism.[30]

It was thus a veritable revolution in the history of thought, or more specifically in the history of modern Christianity, when Leibniz, far from warning against the dangers of infinitesimal calculus (which he invented at about the same time as Newton), saw it as a way to approach God and to convince oneself of the greatness of His work. 'Finally', he wrote in a 1694 article in *Acta eruditorum*, 'it is because our calculus is properly that part of general mathematics which deals with infinity, that we need it in applying mathematics to physics, since the nature of the infinite Author falls ordinarily into the workings of nature'.[31] At the end of his life, during a debate in which he opposed Newton's spokesman, Samuel Clarke, Leibniz wrote, 'God made the world through calculations'.[32] For him, theology was inseparable from mathematics, echoing in this the thinking of the greatest of Christian intellectuals, Saint Augustine. Similarly, he also challenged modern critics of the Bible and religion such as Pierre Bayle, Jean Le Clerc, and John Locke. 'Their problem', he wrote to Father Malebranche in 1711, 'was that with so little training in mathematics they were unable to fully understand the nature of the eternal verities'.[33] Thus, far from opposing religion, science in the age of Newton and Leibniz was a road which led to God.

However, the road in question took different paths to attain its goal. Newtonians thought it was the vastness of the world and its remarkable organization which proved God's existence to man – a God who could also be envisioned as the supreme principle of the universe: in other words, an abstraction. Leibnizians, on the contrary, saw God as a living Person (*'cum Deus calculat'*) whom one could reach through reason, because He was always at work 'in a perpetual *present*'.[34] In this manner, the idea of divine providence that would be put into question in the eighteenth century was not only upheld, but in fact strengthened.[35] It was clear that Leibniz's religious thought, relying on the latest advances in science, had not so much broken with Christian tradition as given it new force.

Nature alone

At a certain point, Leibniz (who was also a geologist) was asked to clarify his views on the duration of Creation.[36] Had it really happened in the space of six days, as the Bible said? Leibniz did not see the question as being of vital importance: 'I do not dare determine if the six "days" of the Creation consisted of years, or of much longer periods', he explained to a correspondent in 1698. 'I would probably share the view of those who link Genesis only to the formation of the earth's sphere, and interpret the creation of the stars as their first appearance to our sight – if I could do so without transgressing the proper use of language.'[37] However, with time, the question became much more complicated. At first the discovery of fossils seemed to support the biblical flood. But soon fossils were being discovered everywhere, leading to the idea that there had been not just one but many floods. Moreover, stories similar to that of Noah in the Book of Genesis were found to exist in a wide diversity of civilizations. There seemed no choice but to conclude that the sea had covered huge areas of the planet, perhaps the entire surface, for centuries – some even thought for hundreds of centuries.

The time came when the finest naturalists of the period were no longer satisfied with questioning the biblical chronology or various events described in the book of *Genesis*, but the act of creation itself. Buffon was a committed Newtonian who had greatly furthered his renown among French intellectuals by translating the mathematician's treatise on infinitesimal calculus.[38] Buffon also chose to place his *Théorie de la terre* (1749), freely inspired by Newton's *Principia*, at the beginning of his *Histoire naturelle* (1749–67). In the beginning, he explained, the sun had been nothing but a simple star, with its incandescence maintained, according to the laws of gravity, by the comets that circled round it. But, he continued, 'sometimes the comets go so close to the sun that some inevitably fall into it'.[39] At some point, one of them had detached part of the sun's matter, which was then projected into space and was acted on by the forces of universal gravitation. Little by little, this mass of liquid and gas cooled and became our earth.

Nevertheless, the conception of the world developed by Buffon was not materialist. In the beginning there had clearly been an 'impulsive force' which could only have been produced by 'the hand of God'.[40] In a similar vein, he occasionally interrupted the narrative of the *Histoire naturelle* with his 'Views', in which he stepped back from the text and brought together the main points of his analyses, always taking care to place God at the summit. Thus, in his 'First View', Buffon defined as he saw it the relationship between God and nature. 'Nature', he wrote,

> is the system of laws drawn up by the Creator for the existence of things and the inheritance of human beings. Nature is not a thing, for that thing would be everything; nature is not a being, for that being would be God. We may see it rather as a vital force, vast, encompassing all, animating all, and which, being subordinate to the power of the supreme being, began to act only at his command, and continues to act only with his support and his consent.[41]

This wonderful text is no doubt indicative of Buffon's state of mind when he began writing his *Histoire naturelle*. Yet, as some contemporary critics have observed, his thinking may well have evolved as his work progressed.[42] He opened his last work, *Les Epoques de la nature* (1778), with a commentary on Genesis. But after citing the first verse ('In the beginning God created heaven and earth'), he made what he felt was a vital modification to this text. The verse should read rather 'In the beginning God created THE MATTER of heaven and the earth'.[43] Thus, between the act of creation and the earth's final formation, hundreds of thousands – even millions – of years could have elapsed.[44] Indeed, the reader might even wonder about the true necessity of such a first act, and consequently, of God himself.

Even earlier, in the *Encyclopédie* edited by Diderot and d'Alembert, several authors had suggested similar ideas.[45] Some years later, in his *Système de la Nature ou des Loix du monde Physique et du monde moral* (1771), Baron Paul Henri d'Holbach was not afraid to expound publicly his materialist theses, diffusing them widely under a pseudonym.[46] In the course of his exposition, he even appeared to respond to Buffon, who had left the creation of matter in the hands of God. 'Thus when someone wants to know where matter comes from', wrote d'Holbach, 'we will reply that it has always existed. And if someone asks how matter came to move, we will reply that simply for the same reason it has moved since all eternity'.[47]

All the same, despite its renown, the *Système de la Nature* was more a materialist manifesto than a scientific work. The majority of Enlightenment scientists were much more prudent than d'Holbach. When they had doubts, they took care not to voice them publicly, and most importantly, not to allow their conclusions to appear definitive. Such authors usually retained a place for God in their thinking, even if they took care not to specify what that place might be. Even though Laplace referred constantly to Newton in his *Exposition du système du monde* (1796), he never mentioned the word 'Creator', except very discreetly in his conclusion.[48] To be sure, in his *Essai philosophique sur les probabilités* (1820), based on his course taught in 1797 at the Ecole Normale Supérieure, he cautiously left the way open for a spiritual interpretation of his research. He wrote in fact that if calculations were made on 'all the rotations and orbits of the planets and satellites', one would conclude that 'the odds are more than two hundred thousand million to one that the movements are not a result of chance'. Yet he never took a clear position on 'the original cause' of planetary movement.[49]

It is interesting to observe that while references to God tended to disappear after the second half of the eighteenth century in the well-established sciences, this was not the case in newer areas of scientific research such as botany, only recently elevated to the rank of a science by Carl von Linné.[50] In his *Philosophia botanica* (1751), Linnaeus stated as a truth of faith that 'There are as many species as the diverse forms created in the beginning by the Infinite Being'.[51] So too Georges Cuvier, the founder of palaeontology, remained faithful to biblical chronology and found no problem in incorporating the catastrophes he might observe on the earth's surface into the historical narrative of the Holy Book.[52] Such ideas were still far removed from the evolution of species and the 'transformism' that Lamarck was to introduce at the beginning of the nineteenth century.[53]

The entirely new science of electricity is of particular interest here. The English scholar and preacher Joseph Priestley saw his *History of Electricity* (1770) both as a work of science and a work of religious proselytism. Priestley viewed the new form of energy as being a sign of the 'progressive revelation [by God] of the wonders of Nature'. He expected it to bring about religious purification and a Christian revival. In 1777 he wrote, 'The rapid process of knowledge, which like the progress of a wave of the sea, or light from the sun, extends itself not in this way, or that way only, but in all directions, will, I doubt not, be the means, under God, of extirpating all error and prejudice, and of putting an end to all undue and usurped authority in the business of religion'.[54] In this way, the scientist became a prophet, the herald of a new era. Priestley's case was not unique. At about the same time, a group known as the 'electric theologians' (Oetinger, Fricker, and Divisch) were establishing themselves in central Europe. They saw electricity as a manifestation of divine power. Indeed, in their view, this mysterious 'fluid' made no distinction between Pietists and Catholics and thus, in its way, served the ecumenical cause.[55]

But the case that is perhaps most worthy of attention and that pointed most clearly towards the future, is that of Ampère, author of the *Théorie mathématique des phénomènes électro-magnétiques* (1820).[56] Brought up in the spirit of the Enlightenment, but badly shaken by two successive tragedies (his father's execution at Lyon during the Terror and the death of his young wife), Ampère was first attracted to religious militancy and then to the atheism of the *Idéologues*, before being definitively converted to Catholicism in 1817. This was the year of publication of another work with great influence on intellectuals, the *Essai sur l'indifférence en matière de religion*, by abbé Félicité de La Mennais. But beyond Ampère's conversion, it was the way in which he combined his faith with his life as a scientist which was to serve as an example. His conversion came from the depths of his being and only he and perhaps those closest to him were affected by it, but his work was in no way altered by his new beliefs. He felt that science was science; that it need not be either Christian or atheist.[57] And little by little, the conception that sought clearly to separate science from religion was to be solidly established. Yet such a separation would not come about without difficulty, as the violence surrounding the debates over Darwinism was to demonstrate.

Thus, the history of the relationship between science and religion from 1660 to 1820 came to be dominated by an ever-clearer separation between the two areas. Put differently, one might say that an increasingly radical simplification in the area of religion corresponded to an ever-greater secularization affecting all aspects of the scientist's endeavours. Step by step, the interpenetration between sacred history and natural history that had so long prevailed tended to disappear. Indeed, was sacred history even a science? Would it not better be described – depending on individual opinions – as a tradition or a mythology? Unless, that is, one came to understand over time that religion was impervious to any kind of proof, to any kind of experiment; that it belonged rather to the realm of the intimate and that it might vary depending on the individual, the historical period, and the age of life. Such a change occurred without victor or vanquished. The advance of science coincided with the beginnings of an immense transformation in religious sensitivity, a transformation in which the individual was to assume an essential position. Science therefore had not acted alone. Its effects had been expanded and amplified by such major movements as the Enlightenment and the French Revolution; and perhaps also, in equal measure, by the evolution of spirituality within the various Christian confessions. (Translation by Jane Yeoman and Timothy Tackett)

Notes

1. Jean le Rond d'Alembert, *Discours préliminaire de l'Encyclopédie*, ed. M. Malherbe (Paris: Vrin, 2000).

2. Cited by Marin Mersenne, *Correspondance du P. Marin Mersenne religieux minime*, ed. Madame Paul Tannery and Cornelis De Waard, 18 vols. (Paris: PUF, then CNRS, 1945–88), vol. I, p. 409.

3. *Horizonte. Nikolaus von Kues in seiner Welt. Eine Ausstellung zur 600. Wiederkehr seines Geburtages* (Trier: Bischöfliches Dom-und Diözesanmuseum Trier, 2001).

4. Antonella Romano, *La Contre-Réforme mathématique. Constitution et diffusion d'une culture mathématique jésuite à la Rénaissance* (Rome: Ecole française de Rome, 1999).

5. Pietro Redondi, *Galileo eretico* (Turin: Einaudi, 1988); F. Beretta, 'Le siège apostolique et l'affaire Galilée: relectures d'une condamnation célèbre', *Roma moderna e contemporanea*, 7/3 (1999), pp. 241–461.

6. Mersenne, *Correspondance*, vol. 3, p. 558.

7. René Descartes, *Le Monde, l'Homme. René Descartes*, ed. Annie Bitbol-Hespériès (Paris: Seuil, 1996), p. xlvii.

8. Geneviève Rodis-Lewis, *Descartes: Biographie* (Paris: Calmann-Lévy, 1995).

9. P. Radelet-deGrave, 'L'Univers selon Huygens, le connu et l'imaginé', *Revue d'histoire des sciences*, 56 (2003), pp. 79–112.

10. *Ibid.*, pp. 104–12.

11. Louis Châtellier, *Les espaces infinis et le silence de Dieu. Science et religion, XVIe–XIXe siècle* (Paris: Aubier-Flammarion, 2003), pp. 137–49.

12. J. Cohn, *Histoire de l'infini. Le problème de l'infini dans la pensée occidentale jusqu'à Kant*, trans. J. Seidengart (Paris: Editions du Cerf, 1994), p. 191.

13. Bernard Neveu, *Erudition et religion aux XVIIe et XVIIIe siècles* (Paris: Albin Michel, 1994).

14. Roger Hahn, *The anatomy of a scientific institution: The Paris Academy of Science, 1666–1803* (Berkeley: University of California Press, 1971); On the control of free thought in the modern period, see P. Prodi (ed.), *Disciplina dell'anima, disciplina del corpo e disciplina della società tra medioevo ed età moderna* (Bologna: società editrice il Mulino, 1994).

15. Thomas Sprat, *History of the Royal Society*, ed. Jackson I. Cope and Harold Whitmore Jones (London: Routledge, 1959), pp. 349, 351; Georges Gusdorf, *La révolution galiléenne*, vol. I (Paris: Payot, 1969), p. 41.

16. Hélène Metzger, *Newton, Stahl, Boerhaave et la doctrine chimique* (Paris: Alcan, 1930), pp. 69–71; Gusdorf, *La révolution galiléenne*, pp. 40–1; L. B. Guyton de Morveau *et al.*, *Méthode de nomenclature chimique*, ed. Bernadette Bensaude-Vincent (Paris: Seuil, 1994), pp. 43–4.

17. I. Newton, *The Principia: Mathematical principles of natural philosophy*, trans. I. Bernard Cohen and Anne Whitman (Berkeley: University of California Press, 1999), p. 941; I. Bernard Cohen, *Introduction to Newton's 'Principia'* (Cambridge, MA: Harvard University Press, 1971); Frank E. Manuel, *The religion of Isaac Newton* (Oxford: Oxford University Press, 1974); François De Gandt, 'Présentation', Isaac Newton, *De la gravitation suivi de du mouvement des corps* (Paris: Gallimard, 1995), pp. 9–108.

18. *Recueil de diverses pièces sur la Philosophie, la Religion Naturelle, l'Histoire, les Mathématiques etc. par Mrs Leibniz, Clarke, Newton et autres auteurs célèbres*, 2 vols. (Amsterdam, 1740),

vol. 1, pp. 69–70; A. Rupert Hall, *Philosophers at war* (Cambridge: Cambridge University Press, 1980).

19. P. Mancosu, *Philosophy of mathematics and mathematical practice in the seventeenth century* (Oxford: Oxford University Press, 1996).

20. George Berkeley, *The works of George Berkeley*, ed. Alexander Campbell Fraser, 4 vols. (Oxford: Clarendon Press, 1901), vol. 3, p. 410.

21. *Mémoires pour l'histoire des sciences et des beaux arts*, called *Mémoires de Trévoux* (May–June 1701), p. 224.

22. F. Monnoyeur (ed.), *Infini des mathématiciens, infini des philosophes* (Paris: Belin, 1992).

23. Blaise Pascal, *Œuvres complètes*, ed. J. Mesnard, 4 vols. (Paris: Desclée de Brouwer, 1964–92), vol. 3, p. 354; Louis Châtellier, 'La limite entre le fini et l'infini chez les savants et les théologiens du XVIIe siècle', *Le Temps des savoirs. Revue interdisciplinaire de l'Institut universitaire de France*, 3 (2001), pp. 37–51.

24. Blaise Pascal, *Pensées*, ed. Philippe Sellier (Paris: Mercure de France, 1976), pp. 128–31.

25. A. Arnauld and P. Nicole, *Logique de Port-Royal ou Art de penser*, ed. P. Clair and F. Girbal (Paris: Vrin, 1993), p. 295.

26. R. S. Westfall, *Never at rest: A biography of Isaac Newton* (Cambridge: Cambridge University Press, 1980), chap. [ ]; A. Rupert Hall, *Isaac Newton, adventurer in thought*, new edn (Cambridge: Cambridge University Press, 1996), pp. 202–24.

27. Frank E. Manuel, *Isaac Newton, historian* (Cambridge: Cambridge University Press, 1963), pp. 98 and 139–65.

28. William Whiston, *A new theory of the earth* (London, 1696), p. 3, cited in Manuel, *Isaac Newton, historian*, p. 144.

29. Voltaire, *Elemens de la philosophie de Newton, mis à la portée de tout le monde* (Amsterdam, 1738), p. 296.

30. René Pomeau, *La Religion de Voltaire*, new edn (Paris: Nizet, 1969).

31. A. Robinet, *Architectonique disjonctive, automates systémiques et idéalité transcendantale dans l'Œuvre de G. W. Leibniz* (Paris: Vrin, 1986), p. 301.

32. *Ibid.*, p. 425.

33. G. W. Leibniz, *Die philosophischen Schriften*, new edn, 7 vols. (Hildesheim and Zurich: Georg Olms Verlag, 1996), vol. 1, pp. 360–1.

34. Robinet, *Architectonique disjonctive*, p. 425, italics added.

35. Leibniz, *Die philosophischen Schriften*, vol. 6: *Essais de théodicée*, pp. 156–7.

36. C. C. Gillispie, *Genesis and geology: A study in the relations of scientific thought, natural theology and social opinion in Great Britain*, new edn (Cambridge, MA: Harvard University Press, 1996); R. Laudan, *From mineralogy to geology. The foundation of a science, 1650–1830* (Chicago and London: Chicago University Press, 1987); G. Gohau, *Les Sciences de la Terre aux XVIIe et XVIIIe siècles: naissance de la géologie* (Paris: Albin Michel, 1990).

37. L. Davillé, *Leibniz historien* (Paris, 1909), p. 372.

38. I. Newton, *La Méthode des fluxions et des suites infinies*, ed. and trans. M. de Buffon, new edn (Paris: Blanchard, 1966).

39. Georges-Louis de Buffon, *Les époques de la nature* (Paris, 1778), new edn, ed. J. Roger (Paris: Editions du Museum, 1988), pp. xlvi–xlvii.

40. Jacques Roger, 'Buffon et l'introduction de l'histoire dans l'*Histoire naturelle*', in *Buffon 88*, ed. Jean Gayon (Paris: Vrin, 1992), p. 199.

41. *Œuvres philosophiques de Buffon*, ed. J. Piveteau (Paris: PUF, 1954), p. 31.
42. Roger, 'Introduction', to Buffon, *Les Epoques de la nature*, p. cxii. Roger writes: 'I am convinced that at the end of his life Buffon no longer believed in God'.
43. In capitals in the text, Buffon, *Les Epoques de la nature*, p. 19.
44. Louis Châtellier, 'Buffon, le temps et Dieu', in *Religions en transition dans la seconde moitié du XVIIIe siècle*, ed. L. Châtellier (Oxford: Voltaire Foundation, 2000–2002), pp. 263–73.
45. Jacques Proust, *Diderot et l'Encyclopédie* (Paris: A. Colin, 1962); Jacques Roger, *Les sciences de la vie dans la pensée française du XVIIIe siècle* (Paris: A. Colin 1964); Denis Diderot, *Œuvres*, ed. Laurent Versini (Paris: R. Laffont, 1994), vol. 1, *Philosophie*.
46. Paul Heinrich Dietrich, Baron d'Holbach, [under pseudonym of M. Mirabaud], *Système de la nature ou Des loix du monde Physique et du monde moral* (London, 1771).
47. *Ibid.*, vol. 1, p. 29.
48. Pierre-Simon de Laplace, *Exposition du système du monde (1796)*, new edn (Paris: Fayard, 1984); Charles C. Gillispie, R. Fox, and I. Grattan-Guinness, *Pierre-Simon Laplace (1749–1827): A life in exact science* (Princeton: Princeton University Press, 1997).
49. P. S. Laplace, *Essai philosophique sur les probabilités* (Paris, 1820), p. 93.
50. W. Blunt, *The complete naturalist: A life of Linnaeus* (London: G. Rainbird, 1971); James L. Larson, *Reason and experience: The representation of natural order in the work of Carl von Linné* (Berkeley: University of California Press, 1971); Tore Frängsmyr (ed.), *Linnaeus: The man and his work* (Berkeley: University of California Press, 1984).
51. Carl von Linné [Linneus], *Philosophie botanique*, trans. François A. Quesné (Paris, 1788) p. 131.
52. Georges Cuvier, *Discours sur les révolutions de la surface du globe et sur les changements qu'elles ont produits dans le règne animal* (Paris, 1828); W. Coleman, *Georges Cuvier, zoologist: A study in the history of evolution theory* (Cambridge, MA: Harvard University Press, 1964).
53. G. Laurent (dir.), *Jean-Baptiste Lamarck 1744–1829* (Paris: Editions du CTHS, 1997); P. Corsi, *Lamarck. Genèse et enjeux du transformisme (1770–1830)* (Paris: CNRS Editions, 2001).
54. Jan Golinski, *Sciences. Public culture: Chemistry and Enlightenment in Britain 1760–1820* (Cambridge: Cambridge University Press, 1992), p. 81.
55. E. Benz, *Theologie der Elektrizität. Zur Begegnung und Auseinandersetzung von Theologie und Naturwissenschaft im 17. und 18. Jahrhundert* (Mayence: Verlag der Akademie der Wissenschaften, 1971).
56. J. R. Hofmann, *André-Marie Ampère: Enlightenment and electrodynamics* (Cambridge: Cambridge University Press, 1995).
57. Châtellier, *Les espaces infinis*, pp. 205–14.

14

The Enlightenment critique
of Christianity

MARGARET C. JACOB

The crisis provoked by monarchical absolutism and established churches

The period after 1660 saw the emergence of the first sustained attack on Christianity from within Europe since the triumph of the Christian Church under Constantine in the fourth century. To be sure the critics were few and the dangers great. But once unleashed, they became a radical force, never again to be silenced. A specific set of circumstances caused the anti-Christian genie to spring from a dark and angry place within minds angered by fear and persecution. Some of these circumstances were contingent on political events, but others had to do with the intellectual forces unleashed largely by the new science from Copernicus to Newton. The formal philosophical systems and discoveries of the seventeenth century – and the Baroque age will always be remembered for Galileo, Descartes, Hobbes, and Spinoza – shattered a previous certainty once given to the philosophy of Aristotle as interpreted by the Christian scholastics. In addition, in the 1680s the promotion of absolutist policies in France and Britain threatened the stability of all of northern and western Europe and the religious independence of Protestants in England, Ireland, the Dutch Republic, and potentially in the German states west of the Rhine.

In 1685, Louis XIV revoked the Edict of Nantes and declared Protestantism illegal in France; he also made clear his desire to fortify his kingdom by seizing land belonging to the Low Countries and the independent German states. The land- and slave-owning privileges of Protestants in the French colonies were also severely restricted as were the 'freedoms' offered to slaves. In the same year the Catholic James II came to the throne of England and declared his desire to secure privileges for his co-religionists. He also called in the charters of the corporations upon which rested the authority of all local and Protestant magistrates. Throughout Europe, particularly among Protestants, the equation of absolutism with Catholicism was a given. In the minds of many Protestants the equation had suddenly been rendered stark by the reality of what could only be defined as tyranny and persecution. In 1685, all signs pointed to a revival of religious warfare, in words, if not in deeds. Well over 200,000 French Protestants made the journey out of France, and those who stayed behind were imprisoned or submitted to conversion. These were the events that form the essential background to understanding the Enlightened critique of Christianity as it emerged with virulence in the period of the 1680s. From that moment onward, the critique only became more pointed, more strident, sometimes less anonymous, but always suspicious of clerical authority and often bitter. It lay at the heart of the crisis provoked by monarchical absolutism.

Not only negative factors provoked the Enlightened critique of Christianity. New and positive intellectual forces affected all Christians, and these indigenous resources were available to the disaffected from church and state. The seventeenth century had been the great age of natural philosophical enquiry that began with Galileo and ended with the publication in 1687 of Newton's *Principia*. These thinkers intended no assault on Christianity, nor implied any in their scientific writings. But adjusting the western understanding of nature in radically new directions had been perilous. Piously it was believed that the Bible said that the earth was in the centre of the universe. In 1543 Copernicus argued that mathematically it made more sense to put the sun in the centre. Fifty years later Galileo went further. He challenged the basic medieval assumption that only the earth was a real body, that all other heavenly bodies were made of a fine ethereal matter. In 1610 he trained his telescope on the moon and proclaimed that the shadows he saw were best explained as mountains. The celestial and terrestrial worlds were beginning to look increasingly like the same matter, heavy and measurable, just configured differently. These new metaphysical assumptions about nature played into the religious crisis of the 1680s, the roots of which had been festering for at least two decades.

Gradually, especially after 1685, one villain emerged as the ogre of choice among the anonymous libellers whose literary momentum surged with the renewed persecution of Protestants: Louis XIV, the Sun King, the enemy of French Protestants who in his amorous liaison with a new Catholic mistress had suddenly got pious and devout. The potential of this French king to abuse his power had been suspected as early as his coronation in 1661. The French-language press outside of France, generally located in the Dutch Republic, sometimes in Liège, was largely a Protestant operation and it wasted no time pointing out the dangers to religious liberty posed by the new king. Phoney publishers were even invented so that the message could be got out with the minimum of danger for printers and owners. Among the most famous of these false imprints was 'Pierre Marteau of Cologne', who never existed, and the imprint was probably started as early as 1661 by the Dutch publishing house, Elsevier. Soon Pierre Marteau had fictional colleagues, more precisely competitors, like 'Jean le Blaue, Cologne', 'Pierre Martheau, Cologne', 'Pierre de la Place, Cologne', and 'Jean L'Ingenu' also from Cologne. One fellow just called his publishing house '***'.

Jean L'Ingenu printed books that told about love between priests and nuns, and they were bound with yet another salacious exposé that told all about the goings on at the French court.[1] Imitators published works like *La chronique scandaleuse, ou Paris ridicule* . . . [1668], and *Relation de l'Estat et Gouvernement d'Espagne* [1667]. Because it was Catholic and absolutist with a clergy that functioned like an arm of the state, Spain and its government also came under fire from the Dutch publishers, supposedly from Cologne. Of course, the Dutch had revolted over a century earlier against the Spanish and there was no love lost on either side as a result. In the Protestant mind, a consensus formed earlier in the seventeenth century now revived: Catholic kings and the clergy who supported them were dangerous. Only unlike earlier in the century, a new alternative appeared. Perhaps the problem lay with religion itself, or at least with excessive devotion, with punctilious attention to dogma and an eagerness to believe what was said from the pulpit. Too much faith undid decency and civility, next came fanaticism.

After 1685, the attacks on the French king became menacing: the revocation of the Edict of Nantes will be his undoing, the opposition press said. Louis XIV had made an alliance with the Jesuits, but they cannot be trusted as they oppose all sovereignty but their own. Then came the moral of the story: 'eyes that are enlightened by the light [can see] that France . . . is in the grip of a Catholic fury'. The metaphor of the Enlightened owed as much to the early publishers as it did to the philosophers, and it remained a rallying cry throughout the century. Indeed the term would eventually baptize the age. The anonymous tract where it made an early appearance went on to advocate duplicity as a means of survival. Protestants must do what the Jews did. When persecuted they hid their religion but raised their children to be faithful – just look around Amsterdam to see how Judaism survived.[2] Louis XIV will have his kingdom reduced to ashes by his enemies who have been 'sent by God and the celestial powers who have been profoundly irritated against the tyrannical Government that has been established in France'. In the heat of the battle lines being drawn against absolutism and the French king, believers, as well as the impious and mocking, made common cause. After 1715, and the defeat and death of Louis XIV, few such common causes would again present themselves.

In the late seventeenth century the habits of secrecy and anonymous publishing now emerged as tools to be used against censorship or established authorities anywhere. On both sides of the English Channel, most particularly in Protestant Europe, a new republic of the mind was being proclaimed by journalists and pamphleteers. A great many citizens were excluded from this new 'republic of letters', nevertheless – so the hope went – Europeans were on the threshold of a new, enlightened age, and the abuses that have been introduced into the world will be corrected.[3] Republics, even in the mind, must be the answer; they are freer places, where prudence and 'continence . . . passed from mother to daughters as an aspect of religion' mean that the decadence of the French court could be avoided. Of course, such pieties about the virtues found among citizens of republics did not stop the publishers from describing in the same book, and in lurid detail, the mischief of kings and their mistresses.[4]

Protestantism and orthodoxy

The complex relationship between Protestantism and the earliest stirring of the Enlightenment's critique of Christianity needs to be addressed. People generally do not just wake up one morning and stop believing in God, or settle for deism when they have just been to church the previous Sunday. Rather, what appears to be happening in the lost world that Pierre Marteau partially opens, involves a gradual metamorphosis. The move went from believing in the reasonableness of the Protestant version of Christianity – vividly highlighted by the obvious irrationality of injustice and persecution as being witnessed in the 1680s – towards the belief that simply being reasonable holds the key to virtuous living. If the pilgrim got to that place the only thing to do on a Sunday morning was to read the newspaper or write letters. In the first instance, the Enlightened critique of Christianity emerged first in Protestant circles, and while plenty of Catholics could criticize their church, Protestant thinkers tended to be in the vanguard that pushed anticlericalism into open heterodoxy, finally deism, atheism, and pantheism.

Another bold impostor from Cologne allows this turning point within the international Protestant consciousness to be illustrated more concretely. *Le Jesuite secularisé* (1683) wanted the world to know how evil the Jesuits had become. Jesuits were assassins in disguise, pensioners in the employ of Spain, 'pedagogues . . . sodomites'. By comparison, Calvinists acted reasonably in their congregations, but thinking about it, so too did the Socinians, i.e., those who deny the divinity of Christ.[5] In the tract simply not being fanatical became the key to true religiosity. This anonymous author had taken a religious journey that key thinkers of the early Enlightenment in England also took. Some Protestants like John Locke would remain Christians while wanting a more rational Christianity; his exact contemporary against whom Locke sometimes wrote, John Toland, eventually left the Christian fold entirely. One tract from his pen bore the title *Socinianism truly Stated . . .Recommended by a Pantheist to an Orthodox Friend* (1705). Toland did not tell what he meant by being a pantheist – a term he coined in the tract – but he made it clear it had little to do with Christian orthodoxy.

In the 1690s, John Locke published a tract intended to bolster Christianity, *The Reasonableness of Christianity* (London, 1695), and in it he tried to pare it down to essentials. The following year, when pre-publication censorship had been removed, the deist soon to turn pantheist, John Toland, answered him with *Christianity not Mysterious* (1696). Why have religious doctrines or dogmas at all? Why not just find a set of reasonable principles founded on nature's laws on which everyone could agree? The persecutions and the efforts to impose absolutism on the unwilling put pressure on all Protestants to decide how to articulate the virtues of religious belief and practice. We now know that Locke wrote the *Reasonableness* because he had seen a pre-publication copy of Toland's manifesto for an unmysterious religiosity that had more to do with deism and the secular than it did with Christianity.[6] Both Toland and Locke belonged to the same political party. Toland had even trained for the Presbyterian ministry – briefly – at Leiden in the Netherlands. Locke, like Newton, secretly did not believe in the doctrine of the Trinity. But both Newton and Locke were horrified at where reasonableness, coupled with a grasp on the new science, could take someone like Toland, especially when combined with being angry at the high and the mighty.

Sorting out the varieties, the twists and turns that Protestantism took late in the seventeenth century, partly because of historic tensions within its diverse doctrinal groupings but largely because of the pressure put upon it by the threat of absolutism – or the fear of its return – requires nuance. It is useful to think of an emerging, conservative Protestant version of the Enlightenment that can be seen in Britain, the Netherlands and parts of Germany. Its advocates like Locke endorsed religious toleration, at least for all Protestants, and they were receptive to the new science. They had no time for deism or the bawdy so beloved by the publishers. Pierre Marteau would not have been welcomed among pious conservatives, but his type might have found a home among 'fringe' Protestant sects like the Mennonites and the Collegiants in the Netherlands, or liberal Quakers in England. All had roots in the so-called Radical Reformation of the sixteenth century where emphasis was laid upon the 'inner light' and the dictates of individual conscience. All downplayed the authority of the clergy and tended to be liberal in doctrinal matters. Being a publisher of the bawdy did not have to mean that you endorsed it as a way of life. Business can sometimes just be business, and finding a home among Quakers or Mennonites might be a solution to a troubled religious quest.

To become a seeker given to heterodoxy required first a deeply personal anger. Persecution under the policies of Louis XIV, Charles II, and James II in England – aided and abetted by their loyal clergies – put rage on the Protestant agenda. At the very least their policies made you suspicious, 'their religion is one Grand Monarchy'.[7] Jesuits, scholastics, the Machiavellian leadership of the established churches, were seen to be doing to Protestants what had been done to the Jews.[8] The only hope was to appeal to the court of 'public opinion', a term being invented in the 1680s as much out of necessity as out of the leisure and relative affluence that undergird the new sociability.[9] First writers tried preaching piety and humility at the 'les Grands'.[10] Then they lampooned the Catholic clergy and did so in ways that sold books.[11] They courted the public with mockery and satire to cut the great down to size; that seemed to have little effect on the actual political situation. They said that Louis XIV 'is a true son of the Church. The Cardinal is one of his parents.'[12] Then more sombre critics began to wonder, might not the problem be more systemic, lying deep in the European consciousness?

At the same time as the doubts surfaced about the tendency to persecute at the heart of European life, a new travel literature had begun to appear. Perhaps the imagination it unlocked suggested new systems of social or political organization. For some seekers the only place to go lay in the imagination as stimulated by tales from exotic lands. Almost simultaneously, Europeans were discovering two new worlds: one in the heavens as detailed by Copernicus, Galileo, and Newton; the other on the earth recounted by merchants, slave traders, and missionaries. They generally treated the distant as exotic, inferior, and certainly odd. But in the travel literature the discontented in Europe found another way to imagine their world by invoking an imaginary new one. All the androgynous Australians were born with two sexes inside them, and the word 'father' is unknown to them. Hence mothers and children cannot be subordinated to fathers, and 'the great empire that the man has usurped over the woman, has been rather the effect of an odious tyranny and not a legitimate authority'.[13] Once tyranny comes under attack, its definition could, with relative ease, be broadened. Once the high and mighty were seen to be sexually far-fetched, why not invest whole peoples with the power of sexual license? Travel east or west – even to Africa – and there love can be made freely, without shame.[14]

The essence of humankind, according to the Australians, is liberty, and also 'they believe that this being incomprehensible is all there is and they give him all the veneration imaginable'. They never, however, talk about religion. The Australian explicator, le vieillard philosophe, knew science. He explained that the universe is composed of atoms in motion, nothing more. In the journey to an imagined new world the passage from deism to materialism had become virtually effortless. Journeying at precisely the same moment to Tartary, an anonymous English traveller discovered 'Death to be nothing else but a Cessation from the Motions of Action and Thought'. If anyone asked about religion say only that you are a shepherd.[15] The genre of utopian travel literature intended to teach irreligion and to open up new vistas of disbelief originated among countless anonymous authors writing late in the seventeenth century. Only in the 1720s did the great philosophers like Montesquieu and Voltaire take up the genre, and given their literary and imaginative skill, elevate it to great and canonical status. From its humble origins onward, utopian travel literature never ceased to be a vehicle for critiquing the Christian clergy, their rigid doctrines, and habits of intolerance.

Spinozism and the radical Enlightenment

The new science from Galileo onward gave a profoundly new definition of matter as atomic, moved by contact action between bodies, as measurable, as knowable through its velocity and weight. It left unsolved the exact role that the deity played in this new mechanical universe. Of the major natural philosophers after Galileo, only Descartes tried to offer an entire philosophical synthesis that placed God in charge of creation through an act of his will while leaving nature to be a configuration of mechanisms, of constant push and pull among and between bodies. The planets stayed in their orbits held in place by a fine ethereal medium and these vortices of whirling ether filled the celestial world as imagined by Descartes. It was inevitable that someone would seek to unify Descartes' universe and resolve the dilemma of God's role in it. This Spinoza undertook by conflating God with Nature and pantheism, as Toland called it, became a viable creed. In the lifetime of Spinoza and beyond, spinozism had many meanings. All of the meanings were bad in the eyes of the devout.

Spinoza was an Amsterdam Jew who got expelled from his synagogue, probably for his heretical views. He wrote in Latin, first in his *Tractatus Theologicus Politicus* (1670) but quickly his ideas and text were translated – heretical Protestant circles in the Dutch Republic being among the first to take up his ideas – and then spinozism made its way into numerous anonymous books and manuscripts. The most famous and infamous became the *Traité des trois imposteurs* (1710–11). It began with a translation from part of Spinoza's *Tractatus* and then went on to label Jesus, Moses, and Mohammed as the three great impostors. Everything we know about the creation of this outrageous tract traces it to renegade Protestant circles in the Dutch Republic.[16] All knew John Toland well, and many went on to have masonic associations.

By the 1720s and on both sides of the channel – and writing in many languages – the Christian clergy of whatever church were genuinely alarmed. In England in just that period a periodical, *The Freethinker*, took up the cause of irreligion. It said that freethinking was the 'foundation of all human liberty: remove the one and the other cannot stand'. What most clergymen did not know was that its sponsors lay in the highest circles of the Whig government.[17] The situation was grave, and all the more so because it seemed as if the authorities had lost control over the printing presses. This was especially true also in France where a vast French language press operated north and west of its borders, in the Dutch Republic and Switzerland.

The publishing freedom of the 1720s gave the young Voltaire his start. He had been unfairly imprisoned in Paris, left for the Low Countries where he sought a publisher for his long poem in praise of Henry IV, the king who had in the 1590s given France its first taste of religious toleration. He gravitated to the same publishing circles involved in bringing out the *Traité des trois imposteurs*. Having no success, he ventured to England and fell in love with its relative freedom and its science. His *Letters on the English* (1733) made his literary career and gave Europe justification for a rabid Anglophilia that affected Enlightened circles. Voltaire never embraced the radicalism of the freethinkers; he never became a republican or a materialist. But his iconoclastic style owes much to that pioneered by the anonymous journalists and radical Whigs of an earlier generation.

1720s and 1730s: retreat and Christian renewal

Science proved a faithful ally to both sides in cultural war about orthodoxy; if anything it served the pious more faithfully. Newton's immediate followers of the 1690s and beyond had been deeply pious and had risen in the London pulpits to defend Christianity by recourse to new arguments drawn from the harmony and design imagined in nature. In Protestant Europe, on both sides of the channel and eventually on both sides of the Atlantic, a new theology emerged, given the somewhat ungainly title, physico-theology, namely a theology that drew its examples from natural philosophy, in particular Newtonian physics. The very vastness of the spacing of the heavenly atoms, Richard Bentley said in the opening Boyle lectures, proved God's providential barrier against matter being able to group and form under its own power. The danger of materialism lurked in the heresies unveiled by Spinoza, Hobbes, and their many followers. Newtonian science offered an infallible antidote, so said his clerical followers.

In the Dutch Republic the pious Bernard Nieuwentyt produced in Dutch in 1715 *Het Regt Gebruik der Werelt Beschouwingen* ('On the Correct Use of World Views') and it made its way into English as *The Religious Philosopher*. Its translator told John Toland the book was meant as an antidote to his writings. It sought to show at every turn God's mastery over creation, his power and majesty affirmed by the order and design displayed by creation. The Newtonian, Jean Desaguliers was instrumental in having the book translated into English. In France the pious abbé Noel Antoine Pluche wrote a long (and to our eyes) tedious work, *La Spectacle de la Nature* (1732) that made its way into multiple French editions and into nearly every European language. It too affirmed God's total dominion, only in the French monarchical context Pluche added the twist: that the king's power imitated the divine. There were probably far more French followers of Pluche than there were proponents of Voltaire. Certainly Bentley enjoyed more public approval than Toland.

The Spectacle of Nature expressed far more closely the majority sentiments of the age than did the heretical musings of the spinozists. As Pluche, Nieuwentyt, Bentley, and others would have it, God is the only active, self-moving, self-willing, self-sufficient, and eternal being. Matter, by contrast, is passive, inert, determined by God's will, contingent upon His nature, and finite. Matter in motion is not due to some inherent property called motion that matter possesses, but rather to God's acting on matter so that it conforms to His will. The stage of history can be dominated by those whose power imitates that of the creator although in the Dutch and English case, they cannot be absolute monarchs. No numbers can ever be given to show how many people subscribed to such views, pious or materialist. But the sheer number of editions for which the pious of the 1730s and 1740s could take credit suggests that for a time at least, they were making the louder noise.

The mid-century materialist and
pornographic crisis

The 1740s found continental Europe at war. Prussia took Silesia from Austria in an act of naked aggression. Once again the French invaded the Low Countries. The War of Austrian Succession (1740–48) brought little advantage to the French and among its intellectuals by the end, disillusionment with king and army was palpable. At the same time, Dutch military weakness was exposed and the British engineered a revolution there in 1747–48 that brought in a new *stadholder*, William IV, whose wife was the daughter of the British monarch. It ultimately failed to address the Republic's many problems. Eventually, even its Austrian allies despaired, and in 1756 effected a diplomatic revolution, breaking over half a century of alliance with the Dutch and the British in favour of the French. In short, by the late 1740s a new instability appeared in Europe and rivalry between Britain and France in the old and new worlds became more pronounced and more dangerous.

No simple linkage can or should be claimed between national political or international contexts. Yet at just the moment of the late 1740s when political stress and instability returned to the European scene, so too did the virulence of philosophical heresy. The leading characters in the unfolding drama were the Dutch trained medical doctor, Julien La Mettrie at one end, and the independently wealthy philosopher and freemason, Claude Helvétius at the other. In the supporting cast lay dozens of minor characters, some anonymous, like Diderot, who went on to become quite famous, others whose masks will probably never be removed at this great distance. Diderot contributed a materialist and pornographic novel, *Les bijoux indiscrets*, for which he served time in the Bastille, and indeed the materialist crisis brought that genre into its own with the classic novel by John Cleland, *Fanny Hill*, published in 1748–49 and the anonymous, *Thérèse philosophe* also of 1748 and almost certainly by the spinozist, the Marquis d'Argens. Fanny Hill, the most memorable recreation bequeathed to us by the freethinking pen, was passive when in love but active when being sexual. She was also quite the philosopher: 'The fire of nature, that had so long lain dormant, or conceal'd began to break out, and make me feel my sex for the first time . . . I should stop; but I am so much in motion . . . Natural philosophy all resided in the favourite centre of sense [i.e., her vagina] . . . All my animal spirits then rush'd mechanically to that centre of attraction, and presently, inly [*sic*] warm'd, and stirr'd as I was beyond bearing, I lost all restraint, and . . . gave down, as mere woman, those effusions of pleasure, which in the strictness of still faithful love, I could have wish'd to have up.'[18] By 1750, materialism had become entertaining as well as remaining philosophically intense.

La Mettrie's opening salvo, *L'Homme machine* (1747), appeared anonymously in Leiden, the spot where La Mettrie's materialist's views had forced him when he was dismissed from his medical post in France. Leiden had been his student home and that of his revered teacher, Boerhaave. In La Mettrie's view, man is a machine and the spiritual state results from the rearrangement of matter that is self-moving and sensitive. Thought, feeling and moral sentiment lie in the stuff of matter. This was too much even for the States of Holland. La Mettrie was forced to flee to Berlin, the last refuge of contemporary heretics. Frederick the Great gave them a place at his court provided they did not criticize his bellicosity or his military. Even La Mettrie's Dutch publisher had to issue a lengthy tract justifying his right to publish books with which he violently disagreed.

The books of heresy and sexual bravado that also preached materialism now seemed unstoppable. In English and French a new body of pornographic literature arose and in fictional form it gave life to the materialist credo. From its earliest appearance in the 1650s as a part of the new French genre of fictive realism, pornography sought to arouse by presenting the sexually libertine in graphic detail; indeed, that was its primary purpose. But in the same anonymous texts lurked heresy and irreligion as well as a subversive stance towards established authority. The clergy were uniformly despised, but aristocrats and kings did not fare much better in works like *Thérèse philosophe* and *Fanny Hill*. Indeed these still-read fictions sought to titillate by depicting the high and the mighty as knowing no moral restraint. Only their hypocrisy kept them from admitting that living like a libertine required heresy as its necessary companion. The actual preaching of materialism, along with contempt for established authority, came from the mouth of honest libertines like Thérèse, the true philosophe, or prostitutes like Fanny Hill. Such literature may have encouraged loose living; it also fostered free-thought and heterodoxy. Pornographic texts circulated on the same clandestine circuits used by the heterodox, and without exception materialism graced both genres of literature.

Generally, freethinking as we find it among John Toland, Anthony Collins, and their friends who made the term famous in 1713, often included a distinctive set of metaphysical beliefs. From Collins and Toland to Erasmus Darwin in England, or from Dutch spinozists to the Baron d'Holbach in Paris, freethinkers generally embraced a pantheistic materialism which located motion in matter or spirit in Nature and undermined the necessity for divinity as the source of movement and change. An anonymous and clandestine tract predictably from the 1740s and dedicated to the memory of Anthony Collins put the position succinctly. *Le Philosophe* – and it is from this tract that we get the French word for 'philosopher' first used for the philosophically radical proponents of the Enlightenment – knows that 'the existence of God is the most widespread and deeply ingrained of all the prejudices'. In its place the philosopher puts civil society; 'it is the only divinity that he will recognize on earth'.[19] With this posture the freethinker was ready to embrace the world, to revel in its pleasures, to live only for the here and now.

Indeed the naturalism in the Enlightenment, of which pantheistic materialism was only the most extreme and philosophically coherent version, accorded with sexual liberty. As the late Roy Porter put it, 'there was a close alignment between sexual permissiveness and endorsement of other Enlightenment outlooks'.[20] Christian apologists had known it all along. Heresy could only lead to loose living. In the 1690s, Anglican clergy saw freethinking as not primarily a disease of books, but rather one of mores. Bentley said about his famous Boyle lectures that they were aimed not at books but at mores. It is also in this period that the word 'obscene' acquires its specifically sexual connotation.[21] Predictably the pious speculated endlessly about what produced infidelity. The Newtonian, freemason and antiquarian, William Stukeley, was convinced in the 1720s that the learning of his age, and excessive attachment to it, produced infidelity or heterodoxy. 'Thus a mathematician or philosopher who has spent his whole life . . . making experiments in natural knowledge grows so delighted with his science, with the truths he discovers that he begins to despise all other studies, divinity among the rest'. Despite his dedication to the new philosophical learning, Stukeley was convinced that with it one only sees 'but the backparts of God', while with divinity one 'converses with him as a man with his friend face to face'.[22] Yet Stukeley was being shrewd when he argued that there was an emotional side to heterodoxy; he saw the alienation as a distancing of the self from God brought about by too much science and philosophy.

If in the 1720s the provincial armchair philosopher Stukeley thought there was too much philosophizing that led away from God, he would have been horrified by what the French produced in the 1750s. Aside from the towering figure of Spinoza in the 1670s, and the less philosophically original Toland writing in the early 1700s, no one until Helvétius laid out a philosophically elegant account of materialism and all of its implications. *De l'esprit* (1758) unabashedly presented the philosophical principles of a complete atheism. But it did more than that. It assured its readers that republics bring more virtues to their citizens as well as a luxury that would not corrupt. These homilies occurred amid learned discussions of Locke and Descartes while at every turn the reader was assured that 'the spirit' comprised a bundle of nerve endings. The ancient stoics and the modern natural philosophers received singular praise.

Helvétius had little interest in the libertine or the salacious, nor did most of the major philosophers who graced the French Enlightenment and were materialists. Diderot, d'Holbach and his friends, Mably, and many of the minor figures who wrote for the great *Encyclopèdie* that first appeared in 1751, gave the philosophical principles, once so turgidly laid out by Hobbes or Spinoza, a new life. Diderot's great encyclopaedia sought to encompass all the learning of the age, but in the margins of essays like the one on the soul, written by the abbé Claude Yvon, the article inserted the virulent heresy of the age. By 1752, Yvon was in deep trouble with the French authorities and fled to the Dutch Republic, predictably then to Berlin. One of the few glimpses we have of him comes from the records of an Amsterdam masonic lodge where he orated on the virtues of the philosopher. Even if on the run, men were finding ways of living as secular materialists. New ways of thinking, and not being Christian, were producing new kinds of people. Some of them found comfort in the masonic lodges where religious toleration stood high on the list of values.

Secular stances, 1770s to the 1790s

> I need not tell you the sorrow our parting gave me . . . There I see my dear Wilkes! What a Hurry of Passions! Joy! fear of a second parting! What charming tears, what sincere kisses! . . . but time flows and the end of this Love is now as unwelcome to me as would be to another to be awakened in the middle of a Dream wherein he is going to enjoy a beloved Mistress; the enchantment ceases, the delightful images vanish, and nothing is left to me but friendship.[23]

This passionate letter arrived in England in 1746 sent from the Dutch university town of Leiden by the young Paul Thiry, baron d'Holbach, to his special friend and fellow student, John Wilkes. Now back home, Wilkes was on the verge of announcing his engagement to be married. But separated from him, d'Holbach exclaims that his friendship 'has no bounds'. He wishes Wilkes well as a suitor and in his engagement; as d'Holbach puts it: 'may the paths of love be spread over with flowers [;] in one Word that you may not address [her] in vain . . . I am almost attempted to fall in love with the unknown beauty, 't would not be quite like Dom Quixotte for your liking for her would be for me a very strong prejudice of her merit . . .' D'Holbach did not fall in love with Miss

Meade, Wilkes's wife to be. In his loneliness d'Holbach sought the consolation of philosophy. He writes to Wilkes: 'I need not tell you the sorrow our parting gave me, in vain Philosophy cried aloud [;] nature was still stronger and the philosopher was forced to yield to the friend, even now I feel the wound is not cur'd'. Not even philosophy and science – for he is also reading physics – could distract the young d'Holbach from his passionate friendship for Wilkes. Yet only philosophy vies in intensity with those feelings: 'idleness renders me every day more philosopher [;] every passion is languishing within me, I retain but one in a warm degree: viz. friendship in which you share no small part'.[24] The letters, and now other information that has come to light about a student club in Leiden to which Wilkes, d'Holbach, Dowdeswell, and others belonged, suggest a coterie of young men whose manner and ambience can be plausibly described as homoerotic.[25]

Twenty years after Wilkes and d'Holbach had been students together at Leiden, they would be famous, some might say infamous. Wilkes acquired fame for heterosexual libertinism, heterodoxy and for oppositional politics with strongly republican tendencies; d'Holbach became a philosopher, a Parisian atheist who ran a salon (that excluded women) where every heresy was on the agenda. In the 1770s, d'Holbach also anonymously burst into print with materialist writings and eventually with arguments for finding a philosopher king who would weed out corruption and reform society and government from top to bottom. What the private writings and lives of Wilkes and d'Holbach suggest is that by 1750, on both sides of the English channel, heterodoxy meant more than a set of philosophical ideas. It could also mean a way of life that tested the boundaries of respectability, that was experimental and sometimes outrageous.

By the second half of the eighteenth century a new linkage was established between and among three elements: the sexually free, the philosophically heterodox, and oppositional politics, either with republican tendencies or overtly republican. Despite this new linkage, being the one or the other did not always mean practising all three. Older, stoical forms of freethinking or heterodoxy, often quite repressive or moralizing on matters sexual and insisting that passion be confined to the boundaries of heterosexual marriage, continued.[26] And there were still plenty of straitlaced republicans. Of course, one could also be a mindless libertine, practice sexual license, try to be pious (even if subject to occasional fits of guilt), and have nothing but adoration for kings and courtiers. Indeed courts had long been associated with just such libertines.

But the eighteenth century invented a new cultural style of heterodoxy, one that fused illicit passion with non-Christian philosophy and republican politics. While the affect of the heterodox free-liver would change markedly from 1700 to the 1790s – in the process move away from the rough masculinity of the rake and the showmanship of the courtier – nevertheless the free-living, freethinking radical came into being several decades before the more extreme Romantics like Lord Byron made him, or her, famous. Early in the century, Toland's circle, particularly his continental associations with the coterie around Eugene of Savoy, had the scent of the libertine, the heterodox, and the republican about it;[27] in the 1760s, there was Wilkes and his cronies, and then in the 1790s we have the life of Mary Wollstonecraft. She combined free-living, republicanism and her version of deism; by the children she bore out of wedlock, she managed to shock even upstanding republicans.

Various prominent British families provide examples of the new secularism to be found after 1750. The Watts of steam engine fame came from good commercial and Scottish stock who were the soul of respectability. By the 1790s, they were also immensely wealthy and famous. In the letters from family members, mother to son, husband to wife, brother to brother, there is barely a mention of the deity, not a prayer or invocation. Watt Sr. thought of funeral services as 'a ceremony which can be of no avail to the deceased, nor even to the survivor'.[28] Even in bereavement he did not mention God; indeed the word seems barely a part of his vocabulary. Watt's will of 1819 left not a shilling to church or chapel.[29] A similar set of lacunae appear in the letters of the famous industrialist Strutt and his family in Derbyshire. They were also involved in the circle of Erasmus Darwin who, of course, knew the Watts and Priestley. Darwin's pantheistic materialism and his free-living are well known, as is the radicalism of his own Derbyshire Philosophical Society during the 1790s. As members of the Society the Strutts evince no interest in the deity, churches, chapels, or clergymen. A letter of condolence from Elizabeth Darwin to William Strutt in 1804 never mentioned God or providence, and there was little to suggest that Strutt would have found that odd. When the radical Irish poet Thomas Moore visited the family in 1814 he found them 'true Jacobins'.[30]

In the second half of the eighteenth century in France and the Netherlands a similar process of secularization has been observed. Wills by both men and women begin to show fewer requests for Masses to be said for the repose of the soul. People of eighteenth-century France had begun to see 'death not as a mystery but as a fact'.[31] The number of men seeking ordination to the priesthood dropped markedly, and where once in the provinces men flocked to the confraternities, now they joined masonic lodges. In the Low Countries a similar trend appears. In the southern Netherlands where the Catholic clergy had ruled with a heavy hand, by the 1770s freemasonry is visible in almost every town. In the Dutch Republic with its Protestant elite clubbing took a markedly reformist direction after the 1760s, and societies dedicated to *Het Nut*, the useful, sprang up in every town.

All these changes augured a discontent with authority. The democratic revolutions that breakout late in the 1780s in Amsterdam, Brussels, and most spectacularly in Paris, await a separate treatment. But the process by which Christianity lost its lustre and its clergy fell from the highest pedestals has to be factored into that central political transformation into the modern age. The possibility to think outside of any reference to Christian doctrine made an appearance in the second half of the seventeenth century, in a movement some historians have characterized as the radical Enlightenment. By late in the eighteenth century it had made possible a world where statesmen like Thomas Jefferson could rewrite the Bible to expunge its mysterious elements, scientists like Darwin in England and Laplace in France could dispense with God, revolutionaries in Paris could empty the churches of crosses and statutes and make them into temples of reason.

Notes

1. On the French court, see *Nouvelles de l'Amerique*, in Wolfenbüttel Library, Qu N 1080a, bound with *Le Berger gentil-homme par Chavigni* (Cologne: Pierre Gaillard, 1685) and *Mademoiselle de Benonville. Nouvelle Galante* (Liège: chez Louis Montfort, 1686).

2. *Histoire de la decadence de la France prouvée par sa conduite* (Cologne: Pierre Marteau, 1687), p. 20: 'les yeux à la lumière qui l'éclaire, que la France soubs les belles & trompeuses esperances qu'on lui a fait consevoir, à laché la bride à la fureur Catholique . . . '. On Louis XIV, see pp. 24–5; for the Jews, see p. 181.

3. *La Reform dans la republique des lettres. Ou Discours sur les pretentions ridicules des demi – Scavans* . . . (Cologne: chez ***, 1695), p. 41: 'Il est vray que ce m'est présentement quelque chose de bien glorieux, de pouvoir corriger les abus qui se sont introduits parmi nous. . . '. On exclusion, see pp. 28–9.

4. *Amours des Dames illustres de Notre Siècle* (Cologne: [Jean Le Blanc], 1681), pp. 171–3.

5. [Claude Dûpré], *Le Jesuite secularisé* (Cologne: Jacques Vilebard, 1683), pp. 187–90; on the Jesuits, see pp. 223–4. Cf. Sylvia Berti, 'The religious sources of unbelief', *Journal of the history of ideas*, 56 (1995), pp. 555–75.

6. Margaret C. Jacob, *The Newtonians and the English Revolution, 1689–1720* (Ithaca: Cornell University Press, 1976), pp. 214–15.

7. *Le Cabinet Jesuitique*, p. 25, in Wolfenbüttel Library, Tq 1399; written by a pious Huguenot. On the number of the Beast, see p. 225.

8. *Relation de l'Accroissement de la Papacité et du Gouvernement Absolu en Angleterre* (Hambourg: Pierre Pladt, 1680), in Wolfenbüttel Library, Qu N 895u; aimed against Charles II. On the scholastics, see [Le Noir, Jean], *Les nouvelles lumieres politiques Pour le Gouvernement de l'Eglise, ou l'Evangile Nouveau du Cardinal Palavicin*, new edn (Cologne:

Pierre Marteau, 1687), p. 263, in Wolfenbüttel Library, Qu N 895r, bound together with *Rome anti-Chretienne* (1687) and *Le Paralelle de la persecution d'Antiochus l'Illustre contre les juifs, avec celle qu'on exerce à present en France contre les Protestans* (1687).

9. For an extremely early usage of 'the public' in French, see *L'autheur du Moine secularisé se retractant, et faisant Amande-honoraire* (Cologne: Pierre Martheau [*sic*], 1686), p. 6 ff. in Wolfenbüttel Library, Tq 54.

10. For the very earliest of the Pierre Marteau books which do just that, see *Les Devoirs des Grands* (Cologne: Pierre Marteau, 1666) and *Recueil de plusiers pieces servans a l'histoire moderne* (Cologne: Pierre du Marteau, 1663).

11. For a heterosexual, bawdy anticlerical yarn, see *Le Convent . . . des freres pacifiques. Nouvelle Galante et veritable* (Cologne: Pierre le Blanc, 1685).

12. *La chronique scandaleuse, ou Paris ridicule de c.le petit* (Cologne: Pierre de la Place, 1668), in verse.

13. Jacques Sadeur, *Nouveau voyage de la terre australe* (Paris: Claude Barbin, 1693) [almost certainly a false imprint], pp. 70–2, in Wolfenbüttel Library, Qu N 1013.2. Next to the Australian voice in the text someone wrote in 'Gabriel de Foigny'. This text is bound with tracts published by 'Pierre Marteau', *Voyage d'Espagne* (1667) and *Relation de l'Estat et Gourvernement d'Espagne* (1667); also, in the same volume, Madame d'Aunoy, *Memoires de la Cour d'Espagne* (The Hague: Moetjens, 1695).

14. *L'Infidelité convaincu, ou les avantures amoureuses* (Cologne: Pierre Marteau, 1676), in Wolfenbüttel Library, bound with *Hattige ou les Amours du Roy de Tamaran nouvelle* (Cologne: Simon l'Africain, 1676) (attributed to Gabriel Brémond).

15. [M. Heliogenes], *A Voyage into Tartary* (London: T. Hodbkin, 1689), p. 60.

16. Margaret C. Jacob, *The radical Enlightenment: Pantheists, freemasons and republicans*, 2nd edn (Morristown, NJ: Temple Publishers, 2003); also Justin Champion, *Republican learning* (Manchester: Manchester University Press, 2003).

17. Champion, *Republican learning*, pp. 156–7.

18. John Cleland, *Memoirs of a woman of pleasure*, ed. Peter Sabor (Oxford: Oxford University Press, 1985), quoting from pp. 102, 80, 64.

19. *Nouvelles libertés de penser* (Amsterdam, 1743): 'Le philosophe' is one of five tracts printed in this collection; cf. J. O'Higgins, S. J., *Anthony Collins* (The Hague: Nijhoff, 1970), pp. 216–17.

20. Roy Porter, 'Mixed feelings: The Enlightenment and sexuality in eighteenth-century Britain', in Paul-Gabriel Broucé (ed.), *Sensuality in eighteenth-century Britain* (Manchester: Manchester University Press, 1982), p. 15.

21. The *OED* has this happening in English after 1660. In French 'obscene' was coming to express the specifically 'impure' in the 1690s: see [Audry de Boisregard], *Reflexions sur l'usage present de la langue françoise* (Paris, 1692), p. 242.

22. 'Commonplace Book of William Stukeley', preserved in the Spalding Gentlemen's Society, Spalding, Lincolnshire: the quotation from the entry under 'infidelity'. Cited with gratitude to the curators. Other Stukeley manuscripts are at the Freemasons' Hall, London and date largely from the 1720s and 1730s. Stukeley regularly attended the Royal Society during Newton's presidency and long after.

23. British Library, MSS ADD 30867, 9 August 1746 from the Baron d'Holbach to John Wilkes, written from Leiden.

24. They are now published in Hermann Sauter and Erich Loos (eds.), *Paul Thiry Baron d'Holbach. Die Gesamte Erhaltene Korrespondenz* (Stuttgart: Steiner, 1986), pp. 9–10.

25. G. S. Rousseau, 'In the house of Madam Van der Tasse, on the long bridge: A homosexual university club in early modern Europe', in Kent Gerard and Gert Hekma (eds.), *The pursuit of sodomy: Male homosexuality in Renaissance and Enlightenment Europe* (New York: Harrington Park Press, 1989), pp. 311–48.

26. The Third Earl of Shaftesbury would seem to fall into that older category, although clearly he is struggling with matters sexual; see Lawrence E. Klein, *Shaftesbury and the culture of politeness: Moral discourse and cultural politics in early eighteenth-century England* (Cambridge: Cambridge University Press, 1994). See also the opening comments of Peter N. Miller, '"Freethinking" and "freedom of thought" in eighteenth-Century Britain', *The historical journal*, 36 (1993), pp. 599–602. There were also supporters of freedom in thought who could not be described as remotely freethinking – as the age understood the term – or as libertine or republican. For the first usage of the term 'freethinker' see Sebastian Smith, *The religious impostor on the life of Alexander, a sham-Prophet, doctor and fortune-teller: Out of Lucian* (Amsterdam, 1691).

27. See the papers of the court at the Österreiche Nationalbibliothek, Vienna, with erotic manuscript poems.

28. James to Annie Watt, 4 April 1792, Birmingham Public Library, Watt MSS, MII/4/4/17.

29. Watt MSS, MI/6/12, 7 July 1819.

30. Information found in 'William Strutt – Memoir', Derby Local Library, p. 60. See also their letters at the Fitzwilliam Library, Cambridge, Strutt MS 48–1947. And see Eric Robinson, 'The Derby Philosophical Society', *Annals of science*, 9 (1953), p. 360.

31. Daniel Roche, *France in the Enlightenment*, trans. Arthur Goldhammer (Cambridge, MA: Harvard University Press, 1998), p. 585.

15

The Christian Enlightenment

HELENA ROSENBLATT

The term 'Christian Enlightenment' no longer raises eyebrows; but this is a relatively recent phenomenon. A widespread consensus used to exist that the very essence of the Enlightenment – what made the Enlightenment 'enlightened' – was its attack on religion. According to Paul Hazard's influential interpretation, the express aim of the Enlightenment was to 'put Christianity on trial' and even to annihilate 'the religious interpretation of life'; similarly, Peter Gay described the Enlightenment as a 'war on Christianity'.[1] Many scholars before and after agreed with this point of view. They described the Enlightenment as being – by its very nature – anti-Christian, anti-Church and even anti-religious.

We now know, however, that the relationship between Christianity and the Enlightenment was far more complex and interesting. We realize that these previous interpretations were overly focused on France, and erroneously tended to posit a single Enlightenment. Over the past few years, scholars have been 'pluralizing' the Enlightenment, the result being that we now see it not so much as a unified and Francophone phenomenon, but rather as a 'family of discourses'[2] with many regional and national variations across Europe and in America. It has become clear that earlier interpretations were based on an impoverished view of religious traditions and perhaps even an outright disdain for them.

That the Enlightenment in Germany was a profoundly Protestant phenomenon has long been recognized. Now, however, it is becoming increasingly evident that in a great many other places in Europe, the Enlightenment was also not at war with Christianity. Rather, it took place *within* the Christian churches themselves. Scotland is a case in point. There, the church leader, university principal, respected historian and clergyman, William Robertson, espoused a 'broad, world-affirming theology' characteristic of the Christian Enlightenment as a whole.[3] To him as to many other Christians across Europe, the Enlightenment was more about reinvigorating and redefining religion than destroying it. Indeed, a growing scholarship is now showing that there existed a vibrant network of enlightened Protestants who subscribed to similar beliefs and employed a similar language. Moreover, they were joined by many Catholics who also felt that they could be religious and enlightened at the same time.

Enlightened Christians, wherever they were from, shared a commitment to a few central ideas and values. They sought ways to reconcile their faith with the new sciences emerging in Europe. They advocated 'reasonableness' in all things, including religion. It was in the name of this reasonableness that they championed a simpler, clearer, more tolerant and morally efficacious religion. They subscribed to a relatively optimistic view of human nature and had a generally positive attitude towards both reform and progress. Perhaps most importantly, they saw themselves as moderates charting a middle course, what one called 'a wise, enlightened and reliable piety',[4] equidistant from fanaticism and superstition on the one hand, and irreligion on the other.

Recognizing the existence of this Christian Enlightenment forces us to abandon the widespread assumption that the influence of religion on other realms of thought is always conservative or retrograde. Throughout history, Christian writings have served as vehicles for progressive political and social ideas. This is certainly true of the eighteenth century. However, it is also true that Christians of varying orthodoxy could be found on different points of the political spectrum. Evidence shows that the Christian Enlightenment frequently allied itself with the state, thereby providing a valuable buttress to the political status quo. In other words, the politics of the Christian Enlightenment were varied and its implications ambiguous.

In one short chapter, it will be impossible to do justice to what is now a rapidly growing field. Rather, this essay will concentrate on a few key Protestant and Catholic examples in England, Geneva, Germany, and France in order to highlight some of the movement's distinguishing features and most salient characteristics. It will then suggest some of the ways in which these characteristics were transformed over the course of the eighteenth century. The goal will be to show how Christian theologians and clergymen across Europe shared in, and contributed to, many aspects of the complex intellectual and cultural movement we refer to as the Enlightenment.

The Protestant Enlightenment: a reasonable and useful Christianity

England's role in the elaboration and dissemination of the Christian Enlightenment was seminal. Theological developments there show how wrong it is to see the Enlightenment's relationship with religion as simply adversarial. Late seventeenth- and early eighteenth-century English Protestants were not the hapless victims of a secular and rationalist onslaught. They were at least as worried about what they called religious 'enthusiasm'[5] as they were about any supposed 'war against Christianity'.[6] Tired of internecine Protestant warfare, and convinced of the need to protect civilized society from it, an influential group of English thinkers favourably disposed towards Dutch Arminianism began to view reason as a valuable ally against the resurgence of religious fanaticism and sectarianism. From the Cambridge Platonists and Latitudinarians to moderate Anglicans like William Warburton, these English Protestants elaborated an Enlightened religion which they then exported to the rest of Europe.

Their message was that the Christian religion was an eminently reasonable one. Reason and revelation could be reconciled by identifying and emphasizing the moral *essentials* of the Christian faith. Believing that such an approach would serve to unite Protestants, they also thought that the religious essentials could be confirmed by the study of nature. Thus they were among the earliest disciples of Newton and played an important part in the dissemination of his work. Many became enthusiastic proponents of physico-theology. It should be stressed that these Enlightened Protestants started out convinced that their religion would be strengthened, not weakened, by its association with science and reason. Following the English example, Enlightened Protestants elsewhere came to believe that reason could and should be adopted as an indispensable aid to religion in its fight against 'enthusiasm' and superstition on the one hand, and deism or atheism on the other. To them, Locke's *Reasonableness of Christianity* (1695) provided invaluable tools, in fact often serving as a kind of unofficial lexicon of the Christian Enlightenment.

Geneva provides a good case study of the Christian Enlightenment. Confronted with many of the same challenges as their English colleagues, Genevan theologians of the late seventeenth and early eighteenth centuries were anxious to defend the 'reasonableness' of their faith. The two most important Genevan theologians of the eighteenth century, Jean-Alphonse Turrettini (1671–1737) and his disciple and successor, Jacob Vernet (1698–1789), were central to this development. Turrettini argued that Christian doctrines could not contradict reason, even if they did, at times surpass it. 'Reason is even more necessary in theology than in human jurisprudence', he claimed, 'because it is possible that men make unreasonable laws that contradict one another, but it is not possible that God teaches us things that make no sense, or things that are contradictory'.[7] In any case, not all dogmas were equally important and, according to Turrettini, the church would do well to concentrate on Christianity's 'fundamental articles' or 'essential truths', respecting the Cartesian criteria of order, precision, and clarity. Like his English colleagues, with whom Turrettini was on friendly terms, he hoped that such an approach would help to reunite Protestants. Turrettini's was thus a moderate Christian rationalism close to that of John Locke and the English Latitudinarians. Again like the English, Turrettini's endorsement of reason's role in religious matters had much to do with his desire to put an end to the proliferation of individual revelations of the enthusiastic kind.

But Turrettini worried also that Calvinism was losing ground because it had become too dry, too pessimistic, formal and dogmatic. To address this problem, he stressed his religion's moral and practical aspects. He softened and played down the doctrines of predestination and original sin. It was under Turrettini's guidance that Geneva withdrew its support for the strict formula of Calvinist orthodoxy called the *Formula Consensus*. Soon thereafter, in 1725, the city's Venerable Company of Pastors asked that contentious matters of dogma be avoided in sermons. The pastoral corps now agreed that such things 'were not very important' and, in any case, 'not essential for salvation'. Most significantly, they felt that the disputed doctrines had 'no influence on morals'.[8]

Clearly, Enlightened Christians like Turrettini saw themselves as fighting not just *one* enemy, but in fact *three*. On the one hand were the religious 'fanatics' – the Pietists or 'enthusiasts' whose view of religion was dangerously subjective and therefore subversive to both church and state. On the other, was a growing number of deists and materialists. Actually, these could be seen as 'enthusiasts' as well, since their view was also dangerously subjective and disrespectful of authority and tradition. In fact, it was not at all clear to early eighteenth-century Christians which of these constituted the greater threat. The third enemy, who was thought to be particularly responsible for the predicament Christianity found itself in, consisted of the old-fashioned orthodox and scholastic dogmatists who had dominated the church, and whose religion was too pessimistic, too formal, rigid, and dry, and therefore out-of-touch with modern sensibilities. The effort to enlist reason and reasonableness, and to stress 'the [moral] essentials' of the Christian religion, was part of the larger project of Enlightened Genevan Calvinists to confront these *three* challenges.

The rationalizing and moralizing tendencies, instigated by Jean-Alphonse Turrettini, were furthered by his disciple Jacob Vernet, the very model of an Enlightened Christian. According to Vernet, two harmful extremes in matters of religion should be avoided at all costs: one was outright irreligion, the other superstition. Vernet had only disdain for what he called 'credulity'. A religion was patently false, he argued, when it was 'founded on fables' or when it proffered 'false ideas of the Divinity and bad ways of honouring him'. The Protestant religion, he insisted, was not a 'blind faith'; rather it was a 'reasonable doctrine'. Indeed, Vernet characterized it as a 'very enlightened faith'.[9]

Associated with this new and reasonable doctrine was a new and reasonable view of Jesus. In line with the general tendency of the Enlightenment as a whole, eighteenth-century Genevan Calvinists humanized Jesus. Increasingly, he was portrayed less as a supernatural redeemer, and more as a teacher and moral guide. Man, it was suggested, would be reconciled with God not so much through Jesus' sacrifice, but through his precepts. And these precepts, it was often repeated, were eminently reasonable and practical. Enlightened Genevan Calvinists felt it necessary to emphasize that Jesus was no 'fanatic'; he was no 'enthusiast'.[10] Of course this view of Jesus accorded well with a certain political agenda. In times of political confrontation, numerous in the eighteenth century, Genevans were reminded that Jesus was a *moral*, and not a *political* reformer. A politically submissive and obedient person, he never wished to disturb the political order. No wonder, then, that spokesmen for the Genevan church, which was closely tied to the city's patrician government, found their religion so *useful*, a point they made repeatedly. The Christian religion was useful because it inspired 'all the sociable virtues': it made people obedient and law-abiding.[11] It was an effective bridle to all the unsociable passions.

Like the Enlightenment in England and in Geneva, the German *Aufklärung* should be seen as a movement of reform within the churches rather than an attack on them from the outside. Here the philosophy of Christian Wolff (1679–1754) played a comparable role to that of Locke elsewhere. Like Locke, Wolff distinguished between those truths that could be apprehended by reason (such as the existence of God and his perfection), and those that were 'above reason' and therefore had to be supplied by revelation (such as the mysteries of the Trinity, grace, and atonement). He held that no truths contrary to reason should be admitted by Christians. The general view that Christianity was a reasonable religion was thereafter propagated by Wolffian theologians such as Siegmund Jacob Baumgarten (1706–57) and, then, by the so-called neologists.

Like Enlightened Christians elsewhere, German *Aufklärer* saw themselves as moderates charting a middle course between religious extremes. They abhorred both the 'enthusiasm' of radical Pietism and the sterile dogmatism of Lutheran orthodoxy. They were equally adverse to superstitious credulity on the one hand and excessive scepticism on the other. Instead they advocated a simple, clear, and reasonable religion whose true end was ethical action rather than empty speculation. Theirs was a tolerant and irenic religion, open to science, and optimistic about both human nature and reform.

One of the most creative contributions of the German Enlightenment was in the realm of history. It is noteworthy that the main innovation came from two theologians: Baumgarten and his student and successor Johann Salomo Semler (1725–91).[12] These two Enlightened Protestants broke new ground, both in their interest in history and their approach to it. They insisted on rigorous historical methods. They argued that texts, even biblical texts, should be interpreted as products of their place and time. Adopting and reworking the well-known exegetical principle of accommodation, they seized on the idea that 'religion', which was moral, timeless and true, was something separate from 'theology', which was bound to a particular time and place, and therefore could be false. They came to the idea that religion, even Christianity itself, was evolving and, indeed, *improving* over time. Semler eventually developed this into a fully articulated notion of 'progressive revelation', which would go on to inspire pivotal thinkers as diverse as Gotthold Lessing and Benjamin Constant.[13]

It is important to note that the intentions behind these Enlightened break-throughs in the field of historical scholarship were, in fact, *religious*. The historico-critical method, with its relatively new view of religion, was devised by sincere and committed Protestants with the express aim of better articulating and defending their religion. Once again, then, new and Enlightened ideas were generated for essentially confessional reasons. Both Baumgarten and Semler wished most of all to surmount the divisions within German Lutheranism and to refute deism. In essence, they tried to save revelation by historicizing it.

The Catholic Enlightenment

A growing number of studies offer evidence that the eighteenth century also witnessed a Catholic Enlightenment. This relatively widespread movement has been described in geographic terms as forming 'a southern crescent from the Catholic Germanies in the southeast through the north central Italies including Rome in the centre and on through the Iberian peninsula in the

West'.[14] Allowing for some regional variations and other particularities, it displayed characteristics remarkably similar to its Protestant counterpart.

The Catholic Enlightenment was, first of all, an effort at intellectual renewal, a concerted attempt to rearticulate Catholic beliefs and traditions using the language and tools of the Enlightenment. Once again, moderately rationalist clerics, aiming to steer a middle course between religious extremes, tried to reform and renew religion from within. Reacting to the excesses of both Baroque Catholicism on the one hand and rationalist scepticism on the other, they advocated a return to clarity and simplicity in religion. Like their Protestant colleagues, they argued that the true end of theology was practical. They tried to propagate the image of a church at the service of the people, and of a faith that was both reasonable and useful to society. Thus they shifted much attention away from dogma and on to matters of education and reform, which they often undertook in conjunction with the state.

Enlightened Catholicism drew on many intellectual currents, including various local forms of Jansenism. Particularly noteworthy, however, is the extent of its borrowings from Protestant thinkers like Wolff and Locke. Newtonian natural theology was also popular, enabling Enlightened Catholics to reconcile their faith with the methods and aims of the new science. Finally, a more modern and critical awareness of history may very well have come from Protestant sources as well.

At first glance, France would seem a most unlikely place for a Christian Enlightenment to develop. It was there, after all, that the Enlightenment distinguished itself by its profoundly anticlerical and even anti-religious character. It was in France that the *philosophes* adopted a particularly virulent anti-Catholic tone, summed up by Voltaire's often-cited battle cry 'ecrasez l'infâme' ('crush this infamous thing [the church]'!). This view of a France cleaved into two hostile camps has been restated recently by Darrin McMahon, whose book describes an intellectual climate polarized by secular *philosophes* and religious *anti-philosophes*. Thanks to important work on Jansenism, its hard-fought battle with the Jesuits, and its fascinating but paradoxical relationship with the Enlightenment, we also know that French Catholicism itself was deeply divided.

The truth is, however, that this tendency to focus on religious extremes and to posit stark polarities in French religious history has distorted our understanding of French Catholicism. It has diverted our attention from the development of a distinctly French version of the Christian Enlightenment. The existence of this French and Catholic Enlightenment invites us to discard the oversimplified and bipolar view of eighteenth-century French religious history and to realize that the boundaries between Enlightenment and counter-Enlightenment were, in fact, often blurred.

Over forty years ago, R. R. Palmer pointed the way when he wrote of the many educated men in the French church who were willing to give a sympathetic hearing to the new ideas circulating in Europe. They were favourably inclined to the sensationalist theories of Locke and Condillac. They were open to science and optimistic about human nature. Although they did not advocate an official policy of religious toleration, they were 'inclined to a *kind* of tolerance'. Deploring 'fanaticism', 'superstition', and 'vain [theological] disputes', they often maintained cordial relationships with leading members of the secular Enlightenment. It was undoubtedly thanks to men like these that, well into the eighteenth century, many, if not most, French Catholics felt that it was very possible to be Christian and Enlightened at the same time. In the words of Palmer, 'the line that separated the orthodox from the philosophical was indistinct'.[15]

It is not difficult to find evidence of the Christian Enlightenment in eighteenth-century France. Many French Catholics were receptive to science and physico-theology, as the very popular works of the abbé Pluche show. In France, as elsewhere in Enlightened Europe, sermons focused increasingly on moral edification, rather than on doctrinal instruction. Religious writings in general displayed a marked decline in taste for dogma and a rising interest in the so-called 'advantages' of religion. More and more frequently, one heard the argument that Christianity was a useful religion. It was useful because it contributed to social and political order. It was a bridle to all the unsociable passions. As the French admirer and translator of Bishop Warburton explained in 1742, the idea that Christianity was useful to society was heard so frequently in France that it was becoming hackneyed.[16] Nevertheless, the French clergy reiterated the point in its General Assembly of 1775. Its official *Avertissement* stated succinctly: 'Our God is a God who teaches useful things'.[17]

Enlightened French Catholics repeatedly made the point that the faith required of a Christian was not blind; rather it had strong foundations in reason. The abbé Bergier (1718–90), for example, who was one of the most important apologists of the period, and whose prolific writings were subsidized by the French church, stated unequivocally that 'Far from forbidding reason to examine the proofs of revelation, the Christian religion teaches it as necessary'.[18] Another popular Catholic writer, the abbé Gérard, declared starkly that 'To believe without reason, or against reason, is the lot of idiots'. It was what 'superstitious' or 'fanatical' people did.[19] Thus the frequently re-edited and copied *Christian Religion Proved by Facts* (1722), by the abbé Houtteville, purported to supply 'solid foundations' based on clear 'rules of evidence' and logical 'demonstrations'. Likewise, the abbé Gérard aimed to convert people to Catholicism by using 'clear' and 'evident' principles and 'reasonable' arguments;[20] he took pains to answer the attacks of deists and atheists point by point. He tried to prove that it was *they* who were unreasonable, *they* who offered illogical and contradictory arguments, *they* who had fallen prey to their 'bizarre imagination[s]'.[21] The Christian religion might contain things that were 'above reason', but they were never 'against' reason. Mysteries could at times appear 'obscure', but they were never 'absurd'.[22] Any reasonable person who examined the many historical proofs, logical demonstrations and reasonable arguments provided by sincere and knowledgeable Catholics would necessarily convert to their religion.

Thus Enlightened French Catholics used a similar language to that of their counterparts in the rest of Europe. Not surprisingly, they also read and admired the writings of Enlightened Protestant apologists such as Jacques Abbadie, William Warburton, Turrettini, and Vernet. It was perhaps with the aid of such Protestant writings that an Enlightened Catholic like the abbé Bergier acquired a greater interest in history and learned to appreciate the uses of accommodation theory. Indeed, in greater numbers and with increasing emphasis, Enlightened French Catholics turned to history to validate their religion and to provide empirical proofs in support of revelation. Then, at mid-century, another, more interesting and novel argument came to the fore. Stated powerfully by Anne-Robert-Jacques Turgot, this argument held that Christianity was not only *compatible* with reasonable and Enlightened values; it was *conducive* to them. Over the course of history, Christianity had served as an agent of progress, furthering all the things modern men held dear: philosophy, justice, equality, and good government. Following Turgot, this idea became fairly common in Enlightened Catholic writings. According to the abbé Gérard, for example, it was Christianity that, over the centuries, had done the most to

> destroy tyranny, soften manners, humanize princes, civilize the most barbaric peoples, abolish slavery, diminish the horrors of war, weaken the spirit of conquest, render peace more constant and secure, and bind all nations by a more human, more moral and more extensive law of nations.[23]

Christianity, then, was not just a 'bridle' to the unsociable passions; it was also a 'spur' to the civilizing process.

Mid-century dilemmas and the turn to sentiments

By mid-century, Enlightened Christians faced an increasingly obvious problem. Deism and even atheism were growing at an alarming rate across Europe, but particularly in France. Flagrantly anti-religious writings were proliferating. It was becoming more than evident that enthusiasm of the rational kind was the major problem confronting mainstream churches. Furthermore, scandals like the affair of the abbé Prades[24] deeply embarrassed the French church, seemingly suggesting that the rationalist enemy was within. *Philosophe* writings like Diderot's *Pensées Philosophiques* showed the apologetic limits and even dangers of church rationalism: if Christianity was true because it conformed so well to reason, did that not mean that reason alone was enough?

D'Alembert's article 'Geneva' for the *Encyclopédie* illustrates well the difficulties confronting Enlightened Christians at this sensitive point in time. In it, d'Alembert gave the Genevan church a very backhanded compliment. So enlightened had Geneva's pastoral corps become, he wrote, that they no longer believed in the divinity of Christ, they no longer subscribed to the idea of hell, nor to anything contrary to reason. In fact, very little distinguished them from deists. Embarrassed by this article, which could only have been meant as a deliberate provocation, Geneva's pastoral corps scrambled to defend their orthodoxy; but the damage had already been done.

Clearly, Enlightened Christians faced a serious dilemma. By mid-century the intellectual climate had changed, and their rationalism no longer appeared useful or even appropriate. It became imperative for them to adopt a new approach, and a new language with which to express their faith. Thus they began to use with greater frequency and urgency another vocabulary. It should be noted, however, that this relatively new vocabulary was equally integral to the Enlightenment. Having earlier embraced the language of reason and reasonableness, Enlightened Christians now increasingly turned to the discourse of sentiment and sensibility. Broadly speaking, if Enlightened Christians sounded much like Locke in the early part of the century, they sounded more like Rousseau towards the end.

Recent scholarship on the Enlightenment has shown that the eighteenth century was not just the Age of Reason; it was also the Age of Sentiment. This scholarship reminds us that the optimism about human nature so central to the Enlightenment was only in part based on a newfound confidence in the power of human reason. It was also predicated upon the discovery of certain natural sentiments with which every human being was seen to be endowed. Some scholars have gone so far as to suggest that perhaps sensibility – *sensibilité* – rather than reason was the key term of the period. Sensibility denoted that peculiarly human faculty of feeling, a capacity for refined emotion and an inherent ability to experience compassion for others. Over the course of the century, it was increasingly argued that human beings would be moralized and social progress attained, not just through the faculty of reason, but through these natural sentiments.

Locke's pupil, the third Earl of Shaftesbury (1671–1713), is often considered a founder of the sentimental philosophy. It is important to realize that although Shaftesbury deliberately divorced himself from the Christian tradition, many of those whom he inspired did not. In fact, Shaftesbury's terms and ideas were reinterpreted and incorporated by followers such as Joseph Butler and Francis Hutcheson into an eclectic kind of Christian Shaftesburianism. But the most important vehicle for sentimentalism in the eighteenth century was undoubtedly the novel, in particular, the novels of Laurence Sterne (who was, of course, himself a clergyman), Samuel Richardson and, at mid-century, Jean-Jacques Rousseau.

French-speaking Switzerland was very receptive to these Enlightenment trends. Literary scholars have noted that the sentimental novel experienced great success there, following the hugely popular works of Sterne and Richardson, which were translated, read, and imitated throughout the century. And Jean-Jacques Rousseau caused a veritable sensation with his *Nouvelle Héloise* and *Emile*. However, what has not been noted is the extent to which Calvinist theologians and preachers also adopted the language of the sentimental novel. If, by the early part of the eighteenth century, they had absorbed the Huguenot, latitudinarian and Lockean language of reasonableness, by mid-century they were increasingly receptive to the language popularized by Shaftesbury's Christianizers. Their very 'reasonable' religion was rapidly turning into a very 'sentimental' one as well.

In 1750, Jacob Vernet, the great advocate of a reasonable religion, promoted the publication of a work entitled *Théorie des sentimens agréables*. In the preface to this book, Vernet makes a few very interesting statements. God had endowed human beings with several faculties, he writes, all of them with the aim of leading them to happiness. Besides the intellectual faculties, there are bodily (*corporelles*) ones as well. God created man this way because He wanted to guide us 'not just by way of reasoning, but by way of instinct and sentiment, which is a more prompt and efficient spur [*ressort*]'. We learn from this preface that by 1750 Vernet had become convinced that what he called 'proofs of sentiment' would be more effective than 'useless arguments' against the un-Christian arguments of people like Pierre Bayle.[25] This is undoubtedly why he urged his younger colleague, Guillaume Laget, to translate Hutcheson.

Guillaume Laget (1710–70) was part of the next generation of Genevan-educated pastors who came of age around mid-century. Their sermons, published in the 1770s and 1780s show how deeply immersed they had become in the language of sentiment. The preface to Laget's published sermons tells us that as a young man, he not only translated Hutcheson at the behest of Vernet, but he also liked to read 'the very touching novels of Richardson' and advised his congregation to do the same. Laget, we are told, was a 'very sensitive [*très sensible*]' man. He 'moved' his congregation with his sermons.[26]

The preface to the sermons of Laget's colleague, Pierre Mouchon (1733–97), is equally illuminating. It speaks of Mouchon's great love of science and sensitivity to nature, which only made him love God more. We are told that when Rousseau's novels *La Nouvelle Héloise* and the *Emile* came out, this Calvinist preacher shared in the 'almost universal enthusiasm' that these novels provoked. Mouchon was 'smitten' by the 'eloquence and originality' of Rousseau.[27] Whether one speaks of the sermons of Guillaume Laget, Pierre Mouchon, Daniel de Rochemont (1719–?), or Jacob Vernes (1728–91) – all Genevan-educated Calvinist preachers of considerable repute – one notes the change of tone that had occurred by mid-century. The Scriptures are now described not only as reasonable and intelligible to the thinking mind, but, more importantly, as beautiful and appealing to the sensitive heart. Sermons are composed with the express aim of stimulating the 'inner sentiments' of the reader. Good sermons are those that 'move' and 'transport' us.

It is not that these Enlightened pastors completely severed the connection between religion and reason. According to Daniel de Rochemont, for example, the Christian religion was a religion of 'common sense'.[28] But the point he was most anxious to make was that religion was in fact superior to reason and philosophy. What made religion superior was that it appealed not only to reason but also to 'sentiment'. And sentiment was a 'much more powerful force'. Reason and philosophy were 'cold'. In contrast, because it appealed to inner sentiment, religion conveyed 'warmth' as well as 'light'; it was both 'instructive' and 'moving'. In short, religion appealed to both the heart and the mind.[29]

Similarly, Jacob Vernes explained that reason often operates in a manner that is 'too cold' or 'too slow'. It was for this purpose that God had endowed man not just with reason but with 'secret instincts', 'active and powerful spurs' that propel human beings towards the good. God had given men 'sensitive hearts' and the capacity to feel an 'inner religious sentiment'.[30]

While at the beginning of the eighteenth century, Turrettini and his disciples were keen to argue that Christian revelation was a necessary buttress to the findings of natural reason – in other words, that revelation confirmed and supported natural religion – by mid-century we find with increasing frequency the argument that revelation is necessary to buttress 'inner sentiment'. At about the same time, a new view of Jesus also emerged. Jesus had earlier been portrayed as a reasonable person, a moral teacher and guide, whose precepts were intelligible to thinking people and useful to society. Now we are told that Jesus speaks not so much to our reason as to our hearts; he speaks to us not just as intelligent creatures, but as sensitive souls. He is described as a generous and tender 'friend' who moves people to tears of compassion.

The sermons of this new crop of Genevan pastors are full of what we might call Enlightened Christian sentimentalism. They celebrate the 'sweet communication of sensitive hearts' that are 'the charm of society'.[31] Insensitivity, rather than irrationality, is now the main problem in society. Insensitive people are unsociable people; they are 'hard' and 'cold'. They calculate rather than feel. They are unmoved by tender scenes, untouched by the sweet tears of compassion. While Christianity is useful to society because it functions as a 'bridle' to the passions, it is equally so by providing a 'spur' to the generous emotions.

The language of these sermons could be surprisingly sensual. The contemplation of the divine causes 'delicious' sentiments, pleasurable 'sensations', 'warm' feelings, overwhelming 'impressions'. Speaking of the experience triggered by reading the New Testament, Rochemont explains: you can 'feel' it 'penetrate' and 'warm up the heart'.[32] Contemplating the divine stimulates and heightens all the natural penchants and inner sentiments implanted in human beings by God. 'Religion', we are told, 'only asks of you that you follow the sweetest and most beautiful of your natural penchants . . . [It] is the most beautiful privilege that could ever be given to reasonable *and sensitive* beings.'[33]

The language of Christian sentimentalism also became widespread in France during the latter half of the eighteenth century. There, too, a rationalist apologetics gradually gave way to a sentimentalist one. Thus, one finds that a popular manual on preaching advised priests to appeal more to the hearts of their parishioners. It was not enough to 'instruct' them; one had to 'move' them as well. Proofs of reason were simply inadequate without an appeal to 'the sentiments'. 'The multitude' was unswayed by intellectual arguments; they needed to be 'swept away' by their emotions. Man was much like a 'machine', predisposed to be 'affected' by 'the sentiments' of others. At the pulpit as at the bar, effective speakers therefore should address themselves to the 'heart'.[34]

This new strategy helps to explain why one of the most important Catholic apologetic works of the eighteenth century, *Le Comte de Valmont*, by the abbé Gérard, was written in the form of a sentimental and epistolary novel. Like other such eighteenth-century novels, it uses the full retinue of sentimental devices and is, for example, replete with references to weeping, trembling, blushing, and fainting. The influence of Rousseau is more than obvious. But in the case of this Christian novel, all such techniques are geared towards bringing people back to the fold.

Gérard expresses aversion to 'theological discussions'.[35] He does not want his book to be 'pedantic' and 'dry'; rather, he wants it to be 'charming'. He wants to speak of God in a way that renders religion 'lovable'. He will counter the dangerous and 'discouraging doctrines' of the deists and atheists by show-ing how 'ennobling' and 'uplifting' the Christian religion truly is. His novel will supplement reasoned argumentation and logical demonstrations with 'touching scenes' and 'benevolent spectacles' meant to 'touch' and 'move' the reader.[36]

The usual arguments encountered in earlier Enlightened Christian writings are all still present. Catholicism is a reasonable and useful religion. It makes perfect sense to anyone who cares to consider its tenets carefully and honestly. Moreover, without it, all morals would disappear. Families would fall apart and society would dissolve. Authority and justice would be overturned; 'chaos' and 'anarchy' would reign.[37] A new emphasis is added, however, when Gérard suggests that the value of religion would be immediately obvious to all people who sincerely consulted their own hearts. If they did so, they would 'find there the need for the Christian religion'. This need was an 'inner cry' that any honest person who consulted his own sentiments could not ignore.'[38]

Somewhat paradoxically, the sentimentalism espoused by Enlightened Christians like Gérard opened the door to a kind of 're-enchantment' of both religion and society. This is where the boundaries between Enlightenment and Counter-Enlightenment become particularly blurred. This is also where the influence of Rousseau is most keenly felt. Perhaps taking a cue from Julie's wedding ceremony in the *Nouvelle Héloïse*, Christian apologists of the second half of the eighteenth century no longer felt it so necessary to argue that reli-gious ceremonies and theological dogmas were intelligible and reasonable; it was enough that they were beautiful and moving. Rousseau's Julie could almost 'feel' herself being converted through her eyes and her ears.[39] 'Man', abbé Bergier explained, 'is always guided by his senses'. Therefore, he had a natural need for an 'exterior cult' or church ceremonies.[40] Replete with mysterious dogmas and elaborate rituals, the Christian religion was perfectly adapted to human nature. As Bergier further explained, 'you need spectacles to retain the attention of the people [*attacher le peuple*]'. A religion deprived of 'all ceremonial [*appareil*]' would simply not work. Such a religion would neither 'affect' nor 'instruct' anyone.[41] Rituals were 'touching' and 'consoling'; thereby they responded to a deeply felt human need. Catholicism was 'sweet and compassionate';[42] according to Gérard, it was also psychologically healing since it 'calmed the passions' and both 'sustained' and 'fortified' man's otherwise flighty character.[43]

More research is needed on this sentimentalist vein within the Christian Enlightenment before definite conclusions can be drawn about its currency and historical significance. We need to know how widespread it was in other parts of Europe. English and German Protestantism seem to have followed somewhat different trajectories from the one described here. The German *Aufklärung*, though receptive to both Scottish moral sense theory and the notion of religious sentiments, appears to have retained a more intellectual interpretation of faith, perhaps in reaction to what was perceived as a continuing Pietist threat. Similarly, Shaftesbury's English 'Christianizers' had to contend with Methodism and an often hostile reaction from the established church. Enlightened Protestants like William Warburton and Joseph Butler were horrified by what they saw as Wesleyan 'enthusiasm' and thus shied away from excessive appeals to feelings and emotions. Nevertheless, some scholars have found evidence of an 'affectionate religion' in England as well. More work is needed before its career in the eighteenth century can be evaluated. One thing is clear: throughout Europe and over the course of the long eighteenth century, the Christian Enlightenment was heavily influenced by the type of 'enthusiasm' it saw itself as combating. Indeed its proponents often seem to have tried to use the language of one type of enthusiasm against the other.

Some political implications of the Christian Enlightenment

The political implications of the Christian Enlightenment are difficult to ascertain. It may very well be that it had a contradictory influence on political ideas and events. 'Reasonableness' and 'usefulness', toleration, reform and compassion for others: these were all positive, progressive, some might even say democratic, values that the Christian Enlightenment helped to disseminate.

However, as mentioned earlier, Enlightened Christians could espouse very different political beliefs. Many wished to work in partnership with the state to promote their favourite reforms. In France, some evidence has been found of a reaction against Enlightened politics towards the end of the century. Fearful of the growing popularity of the secular Enlightenment, some Enlightened Catholics may have felt a need to sacralize the monarchy. At the same time, however, they appear to have become more sensitive to social issues. Emphasizing the social rather than political benefits of religion, they increasingly stressed Jesus' charity, egalitarianism and benevolence towards the poor. In the end, both abbés Gérard and Bergier advocated political absolutism. Gérard specifically attacked 'republican principles'[44] that were said to be circulating in France. But he also exposed problems in the socio-political order, such as the endemic corruption at court, and he advocated a much greater concern for the plight of France's poor.

If additional research confirms that Christian sentimentalism was more prevalent and intense in France than elsewhere in Europe, it might invite us to consider the political implications of the Christian Enlightenment from another angle. Recently, historians like Sarah Maza and William Reddy have exposed an ominous side to sentimentalism. They have called attention to its manichaeism – its tendency to encourage stark moral judgements of others and, related to this, its promotion of a peculiar kind of political intransigence. Sentimentalism encouraged the idea that reasonings, discussions, negotiations, and proofs were less important than the purity of a sincere heart. It helped foster the notion that one man, by simply looking into his own heart, could find there the voice of the people, an idea that would have tragic consequences during the Terror.

Christian sentimentalism may very well have contributed to this way of thinking. Indeed, some of the pronouncements of Enlightened Christians are, in retrospect, quite disturbing. While the sermons of Laget speak glowingly of the 'sincere and undisguised communication between sensitive and pure hearts', they also refer to the existence of 'bad men' in society who disguise their malignity with 'vain reasonings' and 'elegant speeches'. Such 'hypocrites' are a danger to society. God's gaze will penetrate into their hearts and punish them. Laget also intimates that hypocrites can be identified by the way they speak; presumably, they don't display the right kind of sentiments.[45]

Another troubling insight is provided by Jacques Necker, Genevan banker and finance minister to Louis XVI. Few people know that this Enlightened reformer wrote two apologetic works on the Christian religion: *L'importance des opinions religieuses* (1788) and *Cours de moral religieuse* (1800). Even fewer people know that these works are suffused with the language of Christian sentimentalism. At a critical point in Necker's first treatise, in which he extols the benefits of religious sentiment, he suggests that the French judicial system would work better if judges would stop abiding by the strict letter of the law and just consult their 'inner sentiments'. 'Innocence' would be better protected by 'the clear conscience' and 'sensitive clairvoyance' of an upright judge.[46] The example of Necker thus points not only to the wider diffusion of Christian sentimentalism, but also to how it might have insinuated itself into the language of politics. Indeed, the sermons and writings of Enlightened Christians are another way that 'Rousseauean' sentimentalism was spread throughout France in the years leading up to the Revolution.

Notes

1. Paul Hazard, *The European mind, 1680–1715*, trans. J. May (New York: World Publishing Co., 1963), pp. xviii, 44–50; Peter Gay, *The Enlightenment: The rise of modern paganism* (New York: W. W. Norton & Company, 1967), p. 203.

2. J. G. A. Pocock, 'Enthusiasm: The antiself of Enlightenment', in Lawrence E. Klein and Anthony J. La Vopa (eds.), *Enthusiasm and Enlightenment Europe, 1650–1850* (San Marino, CA: Huntington Library, 1998), p. 7.

3. Stewart J. Brown, 'William Robertson (1721–1793) and the Scottish Enlightenment', in Stewart J. Brown (ed.), *William Robertson and the expansion of empire* (Cambridge: Cambridge University Press, 1997), p. 9.

4. As quoted by David Sorkin, '"A wise, enlightened and reliable piety": The religious Enlightenment in central and western Europe, 1689–1789', Parkes Institute Pamphlet 1, University of Southampton, 2002, p. 12.

5. Klein and La Vopa (eds.), *Enthusiasm and Enlightenment*; and Michael Heyd, *'Be sober and reasonable': The critique of enthusiasm in the seventeenth and early eighteenth centuries* (Leiden: E. J. Brill, 1995).

6. Gay, *The Enlightenment*, p. 203.

7. Quoted by Maria-Cristina Pitassi (ed.), *Apologétique 1680–1740: sauvetage ou naufrage de la théologie?* (Geneva: Labor et Fides, 1991), p. 101.

8. Maria-Cristina Pitassi, *De l'Orthodoxie aux Lumières: Genève 1670–1737* (Geneva: Labor et Fides, 1992), pp. 53–5.

9. Jacob Vernet, *Instruction chrétienne* (Geneva: Henri-Albert Gosse & Comp., 1756), pp. 11–12, 110.

10. Olivier Fatio, 'Le Christ des liturgies', in Maria-Cristina Pitassi (ed.), *Le Christ entre Orthodoxie et Lumières. Actes du colloque tenu à Genève en aout 1993* (Geneva: Droz, 1994), pp. 11–30.

11. Helena Rosenblatt, *Rousseau and Geneva: From the first discourse to the social contract* (Cambridge: Cambridge University Press, 1997), esp. pp. 135–41 and 155–7.

12. David Sorkin, 'Reclaiming theology for the Enlightenment: The case of Siegmund Jacob Baumgarten (1706–1757)', *Central European history*, 36 (2003), pp. 503–30; and Eric Carlsson, 'Enthusiasm, freethinking, and the Aufklärung's historical turn: Critical history as

religious apologetic in S. J. Baumgarten and J. S. Semler', paper presented at the Minda de Gunzburg Center for European Studies, Harvard University, 11 April.

13. James Lee, 'Benjamin Constant: The moralization of modern liberty', Ph.D. dissertation, University of Wisconsin-Madison, 2003.

14. James Bradley and Dale Van Kley (eds.), *Religion and politics in Enlightened Europe* (Notre Dame: University of Notre Dame Press, 2001), p. 15.

15. Robert R. Palmer, *Catholics and unbelievers in eighteenth-century France* (New York: Cooper Square, 1961), p. 124.

16. William Warburton, *Dissertation sur l'union de la religion, de la morale, et de la politique: Tirées d'un ouvrage de M. Warburton*, 2 vols. (London: Guillaume Darrés, 1742), vol. 1, p. 3.

17. *Avertissement de l'Assemblée-générale du clergé de France* (Paris: Guillaume Desprez, 1775), p. 7.

18. [Abbé] Nicolas-Sylvestre Bergier, *Apologie de la religion chrétienne contre l'auteur du Christianisme dévoilé & contre quelques autres critiques*, 2nd edn, 2 vols. (Paris: Humbolt, 1770), vol. 1, p. 143.

19. [Abbé] Philippe-Louis Gérard, *Le Comte de Valmont ou Les égaremens de la raison*, 5 vols. (Paris: Moutard, 1774), Letter 28.

20. *Ibid.*, vol. 1, p. xii.

21. *Ibid.*, Letter 4.

22. *Ibid.*, Letter 31.

23. *Ibid.*, Letter 50.

24. The French clergyman's doctorate in theology was revoked after he made a very controversial contribution to the *Encyclopédie*.

25. Louis-Jean Levesque de Pouilly, *Théorie des sentimens* (London: Jacques Brakstone, 1750), pp. vi and 3.

26. Guillaume Laget, *Sermons sur divers sujets importants*, 2 vols. (Geneva: Berthelemi Chirol, 1779), vol. 1, pp. xi–xxii.

27. Pierre Mouchon, *Sermons sur divers textes de l'Ecriture sainte par M. Pierre Mouchon, Pasteur de l'église de Genève* (Geneva: Bonnant, 1798), p. xviii.

28. Daniel de Rochemont, *Sermons sur differens textes de l'Ecriture Sainte par feu Mr. Daniel de Rochemont, Ministre du St. Evangile* (Geneva: Claude Philibert & Bart. Chirol, 1772), p. 119.

29. Rochemont, *Sermons*, p. 119.

30. Jacob Vernes, *Sermons prononcés à Genève par Mr. Le Pasteur Vernes* (Lausanne: Jean Mourer, 1790), p. 6.

31. Laget, *Sermons*, vol. 2, p. 11.

32. Rochemont, *Sermons*, p. 10.

33. *Ibid.*, p. 85 and 119, italics added.

34. Abbé Dinouart, *L'Eloquence du corps, ou l'action du prédicateur ou l'action du prédicateur*, 2nd edn (Paris: Desprez, 1761), pp. 33–5 and 39–41.

35. Gérard, *Valmont*, Letter 52.

36. *Ibid.*, vol. 1, pp. vii, xv, 16, 33, 42, 106.

37. *Ibid.*, Letter 24.

38. *Ibid.*, Letter 23.

39. Jean-Jacques Rousseau, *Julie, ou la nouvelle Héloise*, in *Œuvres complètes*, vol. 2, ed. Bernard Gagnebin and Marcel Raymond (Paris: Gallimard, 1964), pp. 353–5.
40. Bergier, *Apologie*, vol. 1, p. 410.
41. *Ibid.*, vol. 1, p. 416.
42. *Ibid.*, vol. 1, pp. 413–14.
43. Gérard, *Valmont*, Letter 28.
44. *Ibid.*, Letter 53.
45. Laget, *Sermons*, vol. 2, pp. 6, 11, 30–3.
46. Jacques Necker, *De l'importance des idées religieuses* (London, 1788), pp. 88–9.

16

Jansenism and the international suppression of the Jesuits

DALE K. VAN KLEY

Founded by Ignatius Loyola, the Society of Jesus won papal recognition in 1540, just a few years before the first meeting of the Council of Trent where Jesuit theologians first came to Catholic attention as champions of papal primacy and the most formidable foes of Protestant 'heresy'. More than two and a half centuries later, in 1814, the papacy re-established the society as an institutional antidote to the unbelief and republican ideology bequeathed by a revolution that had marked the parting of the paths between Catholicism and modernity in political form. Yet the same papacy that restored the society had dissolved it as a source of 'troubles and dissension' only forty years before, in 1773.[1] Indeed, little in the history of Christendom between the first session of the Council of Trent and the French Revolution is more surprising than the international expulsion of the Jesuits in the third quarter of the eighteenth century.

While the papacy in the person of Clement XIV hardly acted of its own accord in 1773, the initiative against the Jesuits came from incontestably Catholic quarters. The first state to strike out against the Jesuits was the ultra-Catholic kingdom of Portugal where the 'most faithful' Joseph I expelled them from both the metropolitan mainland and the South American and Asian colonies in September 1759. The next scene of action was Bourbon France where the impetus came from the royal law courts or *parlements*, which manoeuvred the 'most Christian' king Louis XV into dissolving the society in November 1764 instead of bodily expelling all the Jesuits as had Portugal in 1759. But the Bourbon Spain of Charles III preferred the Portuguese model, and so the 'most Catholic' king expelled all the Spanish Jesuits from Spain's Asian and American colonies as well as from metropolitan Spain itself in April 1767. The Bourbon dynasty's Italian outposts of Naples and Parma soon followed suit at Spanish prompting at the end of the same year. Whereupon the united Bourbon powers, having obtained the election of a compliant pope in the conclave of 1769, put pressure on Clement XIV until he formally dissolved the society with the bull *Dominus ac Redemptor* in 1773. The papal dissolution of the society entailed in turn the end of the Jesuits everywhere, including the Catholic German states and ecclesiastical principalities, the scattered possessions of the Austrian Habsburgs, and all that remained of their missions around the world.

By the time the expulsions and dissolutions were over, the Italian Father Gabriel Malagrida had suffered trial and execution, others like the general Lorenzo Ricci had spent years in prison, while hundreds had died during the long voyages from the colonial missions back to Europe. Scores of elite colleges had also to find entirely new professorial staffs, the vast Catholic mission fields around the world lay long untended, and thousands of Jesuits faced displacement from their homelands or colonial countries of adoption to Corsica or the Papal States. And all of the Jesuits – more than 22,000 in sum – sustained 'secularization' to one degree or another, sometimes voluntarily so but in most cases not. The plight of so many displaced Jesuits even elicited sympathy from rival Christian confessions and non-Catholic states such as in Protestant Prussia, where Frederick the Great employed them in conquered Catholic Silesia, and in Orthodox Russia, where Catherine the Great used them in parts of former Poland.

Since the event so closely preceded a revolution that gave rise to an explicitly anti-Catholic nationalism, it was hard for generations that lived through both events not to view the suppression of the Jesuits in the light of the French Revolution and, reasoning *post hoc ergo propter hoc*, to draw causal connections in accord with the chronological ones. Were not the staunchest foes of the Revolution the same protagonists who, as erstwhile Jesuits – Augustin Barruel and Francois-Xavier de Feller, for example – had been the greatest obstacles to the spread of an anti-religious Enlightenment? By nationalizing church property and dissolving the Gallican church as an order, had not the revolutionary National Assembly done to the whole French clergy exactly what the enemies of the Jesuits had earlier done to the Society of Jesus? Were not the pre-Revolutionary enemies of the Jesuits the very same as those who later plotted and perpetrated the Revolution, *encyclopédistes* and *philosophes* all?

This case was easiest to make in France where, on the very morrow of the end of the Jesuits, *philosophes* themselves claimed credit for the victory. It was Enlightened 'philosophy', proclaimed Voltaire's friend Jean Le Rond d'Alembert, which had really judged the Jesuits, apart from the role of 'solicitor' in the trial.[2] Elsewhere in Catholic Europe this causal line was harder to draw, since it had been the Catholic crowned heads and their councillors who acted as both judges and solicitors in the affair. Yet the connection was commonly thought to have been effected via the influence of regalistic councillors such as the first minister Guillaume Du Tillot, the architect of the expulsion of the Jesuits in Parma. Influenced by 'filosofi' – so argued the Italian counter-revolutionary pamphleteer Giovanni Marchetti – perfidious councillors had flattered princes with the prospect of an indefinite extension of their power at the expense of the pope, the Jesuits – indeed the whole clergy – as rightful compensation for the clerical usurpation of public functions during the medieval centuries of 'feudal ignorance'.[3]

The historiography of the expulsions has consisted largely of variations on these already contemporary themes: the influence of the Enlightenment and the extension of secular authority. The themes are not unrelated to each other. For the suppression of the Jesuits aided and abetted the extension of the state's authority over education and the conduct of missions, and thus also the subordination of hitherto 'spiritual' functions to secular ends that the cause of 'Enlightenment' generally stood for. Nor are these themes wrong as far as they go. In acting as they did, the 'Enlightened' absolutists of eighteenth-century Europe indeed aspired to extend their putatively God-given secular power at the expense of the church, while what they did also elicited the applause of would-be Enlighteners, not a few of them princely councillors and advisors themselves.

That secular power was also thought to be God-given, however, points to the presence of a kind of Christian secularization at work in the expulsions in the form of a group of actors traditionally given less play in the story. These actors are adherents to a Jansenist movement – the Jesuits' old French nemesis – that had crossed French boundaries and gone 'international' in the second half of the century of lights. In its baggage, Jansenism took a Gallican ecclesiology that, while seemingly limited to France by definition, also acquired an increasingly international vocation in the eighteenth century. The 'solicitor' spelled out in d'Alembert's text was 'Jansenism', while Jansenists, along with the inevitable *philosophes* and freemasons, figure prominently in the plot diagnosed and denounced by Marchetti that had brought about the French Revolution.

This finger pointing is not totally off the mark. The international expulsion and suppression of the Jesuits was, among other scenarios, one of the last encounters in the multi-secular conflict between Jesuits and Jansenists. That is also to say that the story may be told not only prospectively as announcing the French Revolution – the more standard story – but also retrospectively as one of the last battles over the legacy of the Council of Trent. Yet the retrospective version of the story inevitably intersects with the prospective one, complicating the question of the origins of the French Revolution.

Unoriginal sins

The enmity between Jansenists and Jesuits began as a Reformation-vintage doctrinal controversy that dates in some sense to the Council of Trent, especially to its attempt to define the Catholic doctrine of justification in response to the challenges of the Protestant Reformation and, to a lesser degree, Erasmian humanism. Although Saint Augustine's doctrines of divine predestination and efficacious grace did not entail Martin Luther's doctrine of justification by grace through faith alone, that doctrine did indeed entail the doctrines of efficacious grace and predestination. For if not even faith could be regarded as an independent human contribution to the work of salvation, it seemed to follow that it was a pure 'grace' or gift of God, predestined by him for some but not for others. Luther himself spelled out these implications in a polemical exchange with Erasmus on the subject of free will in 1524, well before the doctrine of predestination acquired greater prominence in the theology of Jean Calvin. The legacy of Augustine's vindication of divine grace against Pelagius thus fell under suspicion by association with Protestant 'heresy' in addition to running against the grain of the Renaissance rehabilitation of human nature.

The first and most delicate task of the Council of Trent when it convened in 1545 was therefore to assert the principle of human responsibility against the Lutheran theses of the irreparable nature of original sin and justification by faith 'alone' while preserving room for the Catholic Saint Augustine's insistence on the exclusively divine authorship of salvation. The result was a tortuous series of affirmations and anathemas that pitted the principle of divine initiative or grace against a limited role for free human choice in a delicate balance that predictably failed fully to satisfy either pole of Catholic opinion, even as represented at the council itself.[4]

When, already reacting to Jesuit humanism, a theologian at the University of Louvain named Michel de Baye, or Baius, raised a ruckus in 1560 by laying down a series of 'hard-line' Augustinian propositions in defence of divine grace, he had only to avoid the doctrine of justification by faith alone in order to be able to appeal to the authority of the Council of Trent which he himself was soon to attend as a delegate from the Spanish possessions. Yet so too could the Spanish Jesuit theologian Luis Molina who, already reacting to 'Baianism' as well as Calvinism, tried in 1588 to reconcile divine control and human agency to free will's advantage by reducing 'predestination' to a kind of 'middle' knowledge or foresight of what human agents would choose to do with the help of a merely 'sufficient' grace vouchsafed to them in advance of every future contingency. The result was another ungracious set-to over grace, ending in a standoff between Jesuits on behalf of Molina and Dominicans defending the theology of Thomas Aquinas – and also a stillborn bull against Molina drafted under Paul IV that his successor Paul V declined to promulgate. But by the turn of the century when this controversy called *de auxilliis* took place, it would have already been hard for the papacy to change course. For meanwhile the Holy See had taken the Jesuits' side against Baius, condemning sixty and some of his propositions with one qualification or another.

So when, in 1640, yet another book by a former University of Louvain professor appeared directed against the Jesuits' 'Pelagianism' and claiming to sum up Augustine's theology of grace – *Augustinus*, it was entitled – it fell on nothing if not well-prepared ground. Its author, Cornelius Jansen, or Jansenius, had died two years earlier as Bishop of Ypres, remaining safely beyond the fray. But the Jesuits and their allies lost no time in falling on it and on its partisans in France, where Jansen's lifelong friend and fellow would-be reformer Jean Du Vergier de Hauranne, abbé de Saint-Cyran, had won adepts for the new Augustinian spirituality through his connections to the tentacular Arnauld family and as spiritual director to the reformed Cistercian convent of Port-Royal. As translated into penitential theology by Saint-Cyran and the Sorbonne theologian Antoine Arnauld, Jansen's ruthless reduction of the world of human volition to only two possible 'delectations' (one 'concupiscent' or self-interested and the other 'charitable' and directed towards God) entailed a deferral of absolution in the sacrament of penance until signs of a true turnaround motivated by charity had become evident.

Although in this doctrinal system – and in contrast to Calvinism – 'good works' rather than faith alone were necessary for salvation, the 'charitable' disposition that made them possible could be conferred by grace alone. And although the rarity of the Jansenist distribution of charity would seem to have confined the movement to a small elite, that elite was able to exploit the territorial resentments of groups adversely affected by the growing power and influence of the Society of Jesus in higher education and the confessional. By the time the great Blaise Pascal wrote his *Provincial Letters* in defence of Antoine Arnauld in the Sorbonne and memoranda for Parisian priests appalled by the Jesuits' 'lax' confessional conduct, Jansenism had found considerable support in both the academic and non-monastic clerical communities to say nothing of the lay judicial and lower office-owning milieu from which both Arnauld and Pascal himself had come.

To Jesuits on the contrary, the prominence given by what they pejoratively called 'Jansenism' to the Augustinian doctrines of predestination and 'efficacious' grace smacked of 're-boiled' Calvinism, while the retention of all the Catholic sacraments made the Jansenist 'heresy' even more dangerous because it came disguised as Catholicism. Tantamount to an attempt to alienate the faithful from the Eucharist and the sacrament of penance, Jansenism was in the Jesuit imagination no less than a plot to destroy Catholicism from within, a plot denounced as such as early as the 1640s by the Jesuit François Pinthereau and as late as the French Revolution by Marchetti.[5]

For their part, Jansenists were no less convinced of the existence of a plot, this one perpetrated by Jesuits to eliminate all their competitors in the field of education and the confessional by inventing a heresy called 'Jansenism' with which to incriminate them in the eyes of the spiritual and temporal powers of the day. Jansenists never tired of maintaining that 'Jansenism' was an 'imaginary' heresy invented by the Jesuits in order to discredit all who would not bow the knee to them within the Catholic Church. The only real heresy afoot within the church in the Jansenist imagination was that of Augustine's fifth-century foe Pelagius as rehabilitated by the Jesuits who, modernizing it as Molina's 'Molinism', made salvation dependent on the human will and scaled down the moral demands of the gospel in order to accommodate this unconverted will. Contenting themselves with only fear for the wages of sin instead of the contrition required by the gospel, the Jesuits were able to woo fundamentally unrepentant 'penitents' into their confessionals, from the level of the parish where they usurped the priest's functions to the royal court where they used their influence to persecute and dominate.

For Jansenists always professed to believe that the Jesuits espoused Pelagianism not for its own sake but as a doctrinal instrument of domination. Even the unique fourth vow of obedience sworn by professed Jesuits to the papacy was to the purpose of constructing their own 'universal monarchy' under the cover of papal authority, not to do the real work of the Holy See. The ultimate heresy at work was thus the 'desire to dominate', denounced in the very first pages of Augustine's *The City of God*.

Dominate the Jesuits did, at least until the mid-eighteenth century. In the competition for the favour of a divine-right and ever more 'absolute' monarchy, a society whose theology defended the prerogatives of the human will and countenanced the possibility of courtly incarnations of the divine enjoyed advantages over a religious movement that saw pomp as concupiscence and whose similarity to Calvinism conjured up nightmares of the recent religious civil wars. Yet Jesuits also evoked the traumatic memories of this conflict, associated as they were with the ultra-Catholic side of it and with theories that justified the assassinations of supposed 'tyrants', especially when the papacy declared them to be 'heretics'. Had not Henry IV had to expel the Jesuits from France after a Jesuit-inspired attempt on his life in 1594?

But by the mid-seventeenth century the papacy was no longer the kind of threat to this monarchy that it had represented from the Flemish wars through the civil wars of religion. To the contrary, the monarchy in the person of Louis XIV now perceived the papacy as an indispensable ally in its action against the 'republican' threat supposedly posed by a Jansenism that, like Protestantism, he readily associated with civil war, in the Jansenist case with the mid-century uprising known as the Fronde. From the arrival of Pierre Coton at the Louvre as Henri IV's confessor in 1604, the Jesuit confessor and preacher became part of the Baroque furniture at the Bourbon court.

It was hence a Bourbon monarchy constantly counselled by Jesuits that took the field against the new religious threat, successfully soliciting from the papacy a series of condemnations of 'Jansenism' beginning with *Cum occasione* in 1653 and culminating in *Unigenitus* in 1713. The first of these condemned five propositions reputedly extracted from *Augustinus* but that were really un-nuanced summations of the book's principal tendencies – that 'Jesus Christ did not die for all men', for example – while the last singled out 101 word-for-word statements from Pasquier Quesnel's *Réflections morales* on the New Testament. Along with this bull, the most effective instrument of persecution was the Formulary obtained from Pope Alexander VII and made French law that required all would-be benefice-holders to swear that the five propositions were to be found in *Augustinus* as well as in the 'heretical' sense in which they had been condemned.

The result was a religious-political set-to embroiling clergy, monarchy, and royal courts of law that reached its apogee around 1730, just when religious conflict was on the wane everywhere else in Enlightenment Europe. By the time the Jansenists got their long-sought revenge in the early 1760s, they had witnessed the destruction of their spiritual home of Port-Royal in 1709, replaced Protestants as the single most numerous habitués of the Bastille, and sustained the sting of at least 40,000 *lettres de cachet* and a systematic purge of their presence from the clergy, religious orders and congregations, and sundry seminaries, colleges and universities beginning with the Sorbonne by stages. Not even laypeople escaped the crossfire because, in contrast to anywhere else in Catholic Europe, Jansenism put down substantial lay roots in France, especially in Paris and other northern cities like Troyes and Auxerre. In one of the most unedifying phases of the controversy occurring just before the suppression of the Jesuits in France, dying laymen and women found themselves the targets of the public refusal of the sacraments of the viaticum and extreme unction along with nuns and clergymen who had appealed the bull *Unigenitus* to a future general council.

It goes without saying that this campaign was far from the work of Jesuits alone. Yet this consideration does not suffice to efface the conspicuousness of Jesuits at all stages of the process of condemnation and persecution, from the influence of Etienne Dechamps and François Annat in the coming of *Cum occasione* to the role of Louis XIV's confessor Le Tellier in the promulgation of *Unigenitus* and the destruction of Port-Royal. When, in the 1750s, the government of Louis XV finally tried to back away from the Archbishop of Paris's campaign to deny Jansenists the last sacraments, the Paris lieutenant of police sent observers to stake out the archiepiscopal palace and found to no great surprise that Jesuits were most prominent among his visitors. The perception of the Jesuits as the movers and shakers in the condemnation of Jansenism reinforced their image as un-French agents of a 'foreign' power, overshadowing their well-deserved reputation as educators and missionaries.

Although largely assembled by Jansenists, the elements in this image are of diverse derivation, reflecting the changing character of Jansenism itself. As early as the 1630s, Saint-Cyan had embraced the cause of episcopal authority in Protestant countries like England where a largely Jesuit 'missionary' clergy took its orders from Rome and tended to undermine the jurisdiction of the 'ordinaries'. In the 1650s, Pascal and Arnauld used their campaign against Jesuit casuistry to extend this stance in favour of the secular clergy to Parisian priests – another of Jansenism's mainstays – in competition with the Jesuit chapels for their parishioners. While claiming fidelity to the spirit of Trent, which had similarly aspired to make the parish the centre of worship, Jansenists also thereby took up position in favour of the 'liberties' of the Gallican clergy, liberties that had always stood in the way of the full acceptance of the Tridentine decrees in France. For the pro-papal aspect of a few of Trent's ecclesiastical decrees contradicted the Gallican liberties, which, as laid down by the General Assembly of the Clergy as recently as 1682, were held to include the right of the Gallican clergy to concur with the doctrinal judgements of Rome as well as of the entire church to decide doctrine, even against Rome if need be.

The principle of the superiority of the general council over the papacy in defining dogma became more important for Jansenism as condemnation followed condemnation, especially after four Jansenist bishops and most of the Parisian clergy formally appealed *Unigenitus* to a future general council in 1717–20. Making Jansenists into 'appellants' and anti-papal ecclesiastical constitutionalists, the movement's elision with Gallicanism further recommended the Jansenist cause to the *parlement* of Paris, which – long the chief obstacle to the acceptance of Trent in France – hardened its defence of the anti-papal aspects of Gallicanism in proportion as an anti-Jansenist monarchy grew soft on them. It was within the judicial milieu generally and the *parlement* of Paris in particular where Jansenism acquired its most politically potent 'party', just as it was the *parlements* alone (besides stray Jansenist bishops here and there) that afforded Jansenists a degree of protection against the combined assaults of monarchy and episcopate during the refusal of sacraments controversy. Not unpredictably, Jansenist barristers and publicists became the most influential advocates of the *parlement*'s putative place in the historical 'constitution'. In relation to the monarchy, this role resided chiefly in the right freely to 'register' the crown's legislative initiatives and to resist them in the name of the 'nation' if they did not conform to the parliamentary version of constitutional or 'fundamental' law.

Not the least of the paradoxes of eighteenth-century French 'political' Jansenism is that the same claims that made Jansenists into anti-absolutist constitutionalists in relation to the monarchy as well as the papacy also made them into advocates of the state's 'absolute' power in relation to the church. Because, as interpreted by the *parlements*, the Gallican liberties that protected the French church from papal domination also empowered the king's judges to make good the crown's (that is, the state's) rights over all public and external aspects of the church – even against the king if he failed to defend these rights. It was in this paradoxical role as vindicators of regalian rights over the church in spite of and even in opposition to the king that the royal judges claimed the right to intervene in so 'spiritual' a matter as the public refusal of sacraments to Jansenists. The same rationale would justify the secular courts' decision to dissolve a religious society despite the solemn vows taken by its members before God.

Although both Gallicanism and the *parlements*' constitutionalism antedate the appearance of Jansenism, Jansenists so monopolized and inflected these traditions in the course of the century that it is hard to understand them without reference to the religious conflict. And although hostility towards the Jesuits also predated Jansenism, it was the Jansenists who shaped the Jesuit into a coherent image of all that stood opposed to things free, French, and constitutional as well as to the truths of efficacious grace and the predestination of the elect. Eighteenth-century Jansenism's crowning touch to this image was that of the Jesuit as the simultaneously slavish and domineering embodiment of 'despotism', not only on account of the untrammelled power that he allowed his general to exercise over him, but also to the very marrow of his moral – or rather immoral – bones. An advocate of free will with no real will of his own, the Jesuit conspired by definition and in the service of no other despotism than his own. For while foisting despotism on both papacy and monarchy, the Jesuit was always also the assassin of popes and kings alike.

The projection of this image was largely the work of a press that, aside from the *parlement* of Paris in the 1760s, was Jansenism's only offensive weapon in its armoury. From Pascal's *Provincial Letters* in the 1650s to the launching of the weekly *Ecclesiastical News* in 1728, Jansenists pioneered the craft of clandestine publication and the currying – even creating – of a 'public opinion' in their favour. Out-publishing the Jesuits by a factor of at least five to one, Jansenists directed much of this print towards the Jesuits who occupy no less than 200 pages for the thirty-two years covered by the *Ecclesiastical News'* index published in 1760.[6] So hated had the Jesuits become in Paris by this point that when, in a case that anticipated that of the 1760s, the Jansenist barrister Jacques Aubry described the 'details of their political and monarchical government' to defeat the Jesuits' attempt to validate a contested will bequeathing them some very valuable paintings, it was 'not possible', according to a police observer, 'to express the joys of the public, particularly those who heard the reading of the sentence'.[7]

So effective, moreover, was the Jansenist press in the politics of public opinion that when, on the eve of the Jesuits' dissolution, an unbalanced and unemployed domestic servant named Damiens who had been at least indirectly influenced by this press tried to convey a non-verbal remonstrance to Louis XV by stabbing him with a penknife in 1757, this same press managed to feature the lackey as the agent of the Jesuits and reinforce their image as would-be assassins of kings.

An ironic reparation

By 1757, some Roman enemies of the Jesuits like Cardinal Passionei voiced concern that the Damiens affair would rebound against the *parlement* of Paris and therefore in favour of the Jesuits. For by that time the capital of Catholic Christendom had become host to a nest of Italian Jansenists headed by Giovanni Gaetano Bottari, first guardian of the Vatican Library and confidant of the Cardinal Neri Corsini, in whose palace he regularly met with a group of like-minded prelates known as the Archetto. Like Passionei, Bottari had been in correspondence with French appellants since the early 1750s, in particular with the abbé Augustin-Charles Clément de Bizon, canon and treasurer of the cathedral church of Auxerre and brother of several equally Jansenist magistrates, most importantly Clément de Feillet, a councillor in the *parlement* of Paris and a linchpin of the *parti janséniste* there.

It was as unofficial ambassador of the *parlement* of Paris including its first president Mathieu-François Molé that Clément undertook a trip to Rome to meet the Italian correspondents towards the end of the pontificate of Benedict XIV in 1758. Although all parties to the hoped-for negotiations knew that a putatively infallible papacy could never explicitly disavow its own anti-Jansenist Formulary or bulls, some like Clément dared to hope that the irenically disposed Benedict XIV might be persuaded to issue a statement of dogma that would protect appellants willing to adhere to it from further harassment, thereby also restoring the doctrinal balance he thought had been lost during the two centuries following Trent. Although the original model of such a statement had failed to accommodate the doctrinal antagonists when floated by the Regency government in 1720, the times now seemed more auspicious. Only two years earlier, Benedict XIV had proved willing to stand by Louis XV's declaration that *Unigenitus*'s status fell short of that of a 'rule of faith'. At the same time, the French secretary of foreign affairs and *de facto* first minister abbé de Bernis, who was not unaware of Clément's mission, wished for nothing more ardently than to bring religious peace to the realm as France stumbled into what became the disastrous Seven Years' War.

None of these signs, alas, pointed towards anything permanent. Benedict XIV died before Clément had even departed for Rome, and the few fragile hopes raised by the initial comportment of his successor Carlo Rezzonico as Clement XIII went to the grave with the papal secretary of state Alberico Archinto, whose death brought the pro-Jesuit Ludovico Maria Torregiani to power. Upon his return to France, Clément received unanimous advice from his many Italian Augustinian friends and best articulated by Bottari: that since no doctrinal help was for the moment forthcoming from Rome, 'your writers' must 'attack the Jesuits from every side except that which concerns the bull [*Unigenitus*] . . . because the Jesuits will then be able to sally forth under the ensign of the defenders of Rome and undertake demarches in view of defending it in appearance while only acting in their own defence in reality'. The point 'in sum' was 'to separate the cause of the Jesuits from that of the Court of Rome' until the Jesuits 'will have lost all of their already sinking credit, at which time it will be possible to go backwards and find remedies for past wrongs'.[8]

This advice was decisive; the immediate origin of the dissolution of the Society of Jesus in France lies here. The advice meant postponing the campaign against *Unigenitus* the better to eliminate those using it as a means to invent 'Jansenists'. Yet it also entailed an attempt to pre-empt a putative plot by Jesuits by engaging in a quite real one against them. That Clément took the advice very seriously is evident from the French translations of the letters he made for his friends in the *parlement* of Paris including of course his brother and the Jansenist barrister Louis-Adrien Le Paige, *éminence grise* of the *parlement* and trusted consultant to the most influential magistrates.[9] Although it is also evident from Clément's response to these letters that he and the French appellants placed more stock in the prospect of eventual doctrinal rectification than did the Italians – they knew the ways of Rome far better – the French Jansenist *état major* clearly convinced itself of the short-term validity of the Italians' more Machiavellian strategy and, what is more, prepared for action.

And act they did. While the *Ecclesiastical News'* New Year's editorial in 1758 still castigated *Unigenitus* for the 'mortal blow' it had 'dealt to several capital verities of Christianity' – saving the ritual flagellation of the Jesuits until the end – the year 1759's inaugural editorial devoted its energy entirely to the project of purging Christendom of the accursed 'descendants of Esau', as did those of the next six years.[10] Hard upon this change in editorial direction there followed a spate of minor judicial reverses sustained by the Jesuits – against the union of Benedictine benefices to their colleges in the provinces, against their right to sell drugs in Paris – the latter sentence greeted with wild applause by the public, and all involving Jansenist barristers in one capacity or another.

No amount of plotting and planning, it is true, could have arranged for the Achilles' case: the bankruptcy of the Jesuits' mission in the French West Indies due to the English seizure of some of its merchandise en route to Europe during the Seven Years' War, plus the astonishing decision by the French Jesuits to appeal a series of adverse decisions in the matter by consular courts to the *parlement* of Paris. But from the moment in 1760 that the Jansenist barrister Charlemagne Lalourcé assumed legal direction of the mission's bankrupt creditors in Marseille and advised them to proceed against the entire society in France rather than against the mission only, the conduct of the case against the Jesuits remained in the hands of Jansenist barristers and magistrates in the *parlement* of Paris until the provincial *parlements* entered the fray in force in 1762.

Once the Jesuits had taken the bait by allowing the case to go to the *parlement* of Paris, it was but a short step for the judges to demand to see and examine the society's constitutions to which all parties had appealed but which, like the decrees of Trent, had never been legally accepted in the land of Gallican liberties. The *parti janséniste* also adeptly circumvented the predictably moderate recommendations of the 'king's men' that these constitutions be reformed along Gallican lines. Alleging, with the authority of Pascal, that the society was morally vicious to the core, this caucus obtained a provisional sentence that began the process of dissolution by forbidding more novices or further vows and setting a date for the closure of the Jesuit colleges. By the time help for the Jesuits finally arrived from the royal council in the form of an edict of reform in the spring of 1762, the reform had been disavowed on high by both Clement XIII and the Jesuits' general as well as undermined from below by Le Paige and his cohorts, who had meanwhile leveraged their cordial connections with the *parlement* of Normandy into the first definitive judgement against the society. The stillborn edict itself obliged those provincial *parlements* that had not yet taken up the Jesuits' case to do so, which with very few exceptions they proceeded to do on the model of Paris or Rouen. When in November 1764 Louis XV belatedly issued a royal declaration dissolving the society in France while allowing former Jesuits to remain there as 'particulars', it was clear that he was only salvaging the principle of royal authority and that his hand had been forced.

What made the royal hand of justice so vulnerable to pressure from the *parlement* was the monarchy's desperate need for the *parlements'* registration of its fiscal declarations during a time of catastrophic war along with deep disunity within the ministry where Etienne François, duc de Choiseul, who had taken Bernis' place as secretary of foreign affairs, was at best indifferent to the fate of the Jesuits and in confidential contact with the key councillors in the *parlement*. Having taken advantage of these general circumstances in order to prevail in the refusal of sacraments controversy in the wake of the Damiens affair in 1757, the *parlement* of Paris only extended this advantage to its offensive against the Jesuits and to the making of religious policy in general.

Along with the charge of structural 'despotism' and incompatibility against Gallican liberties, what is unique about the case against the Jesuits in France as compared with elsewhere in Catholic Europe is its generation from 'below' in the company of popular passions, religious and proto-patriotic mixed. Although allowing individual ex-Jesuits to remain in France at royal insistence, the *parlements'* action was conceptually more drastic than the literal expulsions in Spain and Portugal, having simply dissolved a religious society as 'impious' on its own secular authority as well as invalidating its members' religious vows. And while ultimately rooted in religion – and in the unfinished business of the Council of Trent – these unique characteristics of what happened to the French Jesuits anticipate salient features of the French Revolution's dissolution of contemplative orders along with the whole clergy as a property-owning corps.

However singular, France was not the first Catholic country to act against the Jesuits – a dubious distinction that belongs to the Portugal of Joseph I and his mighty first minister Sebastião José de Carvalho e Melo, later the conde d'Oeiras before ending his career as the marqués de Pombal. Becoming a royal minister with the accession of Joseph I in 1750, Carvalho was the archetypical Catholic 'Enlightened' reformer who set out to enhance state power at the expense of the international authority of the post-Tridentine papacy symbolized by the papal nuncio and the regular orders – above all, the Jesuits – perceived as a cause of the country's cultural isolation and economic stagnation. For nowhere indeed were the Jesuits more strongly entrenched than in this Iberian laboratory of the Tridentine reformist policy where they acted as royal confessors and preachers, largely staffed the missions in Goa, Macao, and South America, and governed a university and ten colleges as well as having access to the professional faculties of the University of Coimbra by means of its college of arts which they dominated directly. Although the Portuguese monarchy already enjoyed the right to name to most secular benefices via the right of *Real Padroado* granted to it by the Renaissance popes, the post-Tridentine papacy had reasserted control over the mission field by means of the mendicants and the Jesuits, while, in Portugal itself, the Jesuits' hold on higher education enhanced their credit within the Portuguese nobility in the form of favourable court factions.

The Jesuits began to impinge upon Carvalho's annoyed attention around 1756 by way of reports from his brother Mendonça Furtado, governor of Maranhão, who blamed Jesuit missionaries in South America for native resistance to the implementation of the Treaty of Madrid. Negotiated by Portugal and Spain in 1750, this treaty settled the territorial disputes between the Iberian colonial powers in South America, incidentally dispossessing more than 30,000 Guaraní Indians in Jesuit missionary 'reductions' by transferring Uruguayan territory from Spanish to Portuguese control. The discovery of gold and diamonds in southern Brazil had opened the area to further exploration – and the converted Indians to exploitation. Thus began a trickle of individual Jesuits to the metropolis to face charges ranging from profiteering to sedition. In Portugal, the case of the Jesuit missionaries intersected with growing jurisdictional jockeying for position between the Curia represented by the nuncio on one side and secular royal prerogative courts championed by Carvalho on the other.

A dispute over the right to reform religious orders in general was already bringing this issue to a head when an apparent attempt on the life of Joseph I on 3 September 1758 resulted in the arrest and execution of prominent members of the noble Aveido and Tavora clans. This event afforded Carvalho the opportunity of framing the Jesuits as the secret animators and spiritual co-conspirators. When, in the summer of 1759, the pro-Jesuit papacy of Clement XIII repeatedly refused to grant the royal Tribunal of Conscience, or Mesa da Consciência, a blanket right to try members of the regular clergy, Joseph I and Carvalho retaliated by confiscating all Jesuit property and, in September, by literally loading most Portuguese Jesuits on ships bound for Civittavecchia on the coast of the Papal States. The increasingly isolated and repeatedly insulted papal nuncio, Filippo Acciaiuoli, soon followed the Jesuits in 1760, beginning a *rotura*, or nine-year break in relations between Portugal and the Curia that lasted until the pontificate of Clement XIV.

Events in Portugal were perforce among the several factors figuring into Jansenist grand strategy during the same decisive year of 1759. On the one hand, Carvalho's case and publicity campaign against the Jesuits could not but have given Jansenists grist for their polemical mill, providing the *Ecclesiastical News* with endless anti-Jesuitical copy in the form of reviews of the *Interesting News about . . . the Attempted Assassination [of] . . . the Most Faithful King of Portugal* and its endless *Sequels*.[11] The Portuguese ambassador to France also plied Choiseul with Carvalho's version of events, possibly prompting Choiseul's own resolve to act similarly if more covertly in France. A source of Jansenist hope on the one hand, events in Portugal were also reason for the fear on the other hand that, badly goaded in Portugal, the Jesuits would harness the profoundly pro-Jesuitical pontificate of Clement XIII the better to charge their enemies as never before.

What is more difficult to appreciate is that, however miniscule the Jansenist presence in Portugal, the international Jansenist influence was at work in Portugal as well as the other way around. The Jansenist campaign to revive the charge of regicide against the Jesuits on the occasion of the Damiens affair in 1757 suggested to Carvalho the possibility of tarring the Jesuits with the events of 3 September 1758. In an attempt to convince European public opinion of Jesuit complicity, Carvalho was able to count on French Jansenist publicists. These included the defrocked Dominican Jean-Pierre Viou, the anonymous author of the *Interesting News*; the Parisian canon lawyer Pierre Olivier Pinault, French translator of Carvalho's own published statements of his case against the Jesuits; as well as the sometime Capuchin friar Pierre Parisot alias Père Norbert and later still as the abbé Platel, who pitched his tent in Lisbon in

1760 and cranked out anti-Jesuit literature in Carvalho's service.[12] Which is to say that if events in Portugal resounded in Gallican France, they did not do so without French Jansenist help.

Aside from like publicists, one of the chief sources of Carvalho's anti-Jesuitism consisted of the reports of his cousin Francisco de Almeida e Mendonça, the Portuguese ambassador to the Curia, who himself derived much of his information from the same Roman Augustinians – Bottari, Passioinei, etc. – who were advising the French through abbé Clément.[13] Indeed, the printer Niccolò Pagliarini, employed by Almeida to publish Carvalho's *Brief Account* of his case against the Jesuits, underwent arrest and ruin in Rome by reason of publishing Jansenist literature there. When he resurfaced in Lisbon as the official printer of the Most Faithful King of Portugal, he had less the Almighty than Almeida to thank.

As the arrest of this Roman printer eloquently testifies, neither Clement XIII nor his secretary of state Torrigiani were swallowing Carvalho's version of events. Ever more convinced of the Portuguese Jesuits' corporate innocence, they dug in their heels in defence of the besieged society, braving rupture with the Portuguese court on its behalf. Nor did the *parlements'* anti-Jesuit offensive in France succeed in daunting this papal defiance. To the contrary, Clement XIII seized this occasion to rise publicly to the defence of the maligned society, addressing briefs to this effect to both Louis XV and the French bishops in their General Assembly meeting in June 1762. While the papal plea had little effect on the weak-willed king, it found in the Gallican episcopate a more resonant reception. Having long been nominated by the monarchy on account of their support for *Unigenitus*, the Gallican bishops had already sounded off in favour of the threatened society when consulted on its 'utility' by the monarchy in September 1761; they were to do so again in response to Clement XIII's *Apostolicum Pascendi* in defence of the Jesuits in 1765. In good part the product of the Jansenist controversy, this stance in favour of the Jesuits – and apparently against their king – of the overwhelming majority of Gallican bishops is yet another structural difference between France and the rest of Catholic Europe where, with few exceptions, the national episcopacies sided with their monarchies against Clement XIII and Torrigiani.

By 1761, it was already becoming clear that international Jansenism's grand strategy of concentrating all its fire on the Jesuits in order later to persuade the papacy to revisit some of the contested doctrinal sites was badly boomeranging if not backfiring. Far from driving a wedge between the Jesuits and the papacy, the anti-Jesuit offensive was so far bringing them closer together. The worst Jansenist fears on the doctrinal front were to be realized in July 1761 when Clement XIII cut the knot of a sharply split Congregation of Cardinals of the Holy Office, and, with Torrigiani's help, fulminated a brief condemning the French Jansenist François-Philippe Mésenguy's *Exposition of Christian Doctrine* on the occasion of its publication in Italian translation in Naples. 'It is finally consummated, this mystery of iniquity', reacted Bottari apoplectically if not apocalyptically in the wake of Cardinal Passionei's literally apoplectic seizure upon being obliged to subscribe to the brief as a member of the congregation. The first papal judgement against Jansenism that France had not asked for – and another factor in Choiseul's animus against the Jesuits – the brief against Mésenguy's catechism was, in Bottari's estimate, the *Unigenitus* of Italian Augustinians, evidence that 'the Jesuits were determined to use that book, as they did that of Quesnel, in order to light the fire [of discord] in Italy'.[14] A self-confirming judgement this was, inasmuch as it caused Bottari and other Italian Augustinians to cut their losses with the Curia and refashion themselves as full-fledged Jansenists in the radicalized Gallican mode.

While the effect of anti-Jesuit action and curial reaction was to transform Italian Augustinians into Gallican Jansenists in Italy, the immediate effect in France was further to transform Gallican bishops into ultramontanist defenders of the Jesuits in the absence of the relatively Gallican French Jesuits themselves. '[S]o long as the [French] bishops remain Molinists, France will know no peace', observed an ever more exasperated Bottari, who, seeing his anti-Jesuit strategy go astray, announced himself fully prepared to see 'the upcoming Assembly of Gallican Clergy [of 1765] endorse the [probabilistic] propositions that it had condemned in 1700'.[15] Worse yet, the 'curialization' of the clergy so deplored by Bottari in France began to spread by degrees to the rest of Catholic Europe and to Italy in particular in reaction to the campaign against the Jesuits. For events in the 1760s were to prove decisive in the transformation of hitherto reformist and philo-Jansenist prelates – Christoph Bartholomäus Migazzi in Austria, Carlo Amadeo Vittorio Delle Lanze in Piedmont, Johann Heinrich Frankenberg in the Austrian Netherlands, to name just a few – into determined defenders of papal authority and the future militants in an anti-Jansenist (and later still, anti-revolutionary) counter-offensive. To be sure, the end of the Jesuits was eventually and temporarily to bring religious 'peace' of a sort to France – a 'peace' born of fatigue and religious indifference, however, rather than the one the Jansenists had hoped for. But for the rest of Catholic Europe, the effect of the campaign against the Jesuits was ironically to import the hitherto mainly French 'fire of discord', as a Jansenist International squared off against an increasingly militant Ultramontanist International in the decades preceding the French Revolution.

Spain, the Bourbon family pact, and the end of the Jesuits

The religious polarization resulting from the anti-Jesuit campaign in France and Portugal began to affect Spain directly shortly after the accession of Charles III when, in 1761, the Spanish Grand Inquisitor published the Roman Congregation's condemnation of Mésenguy's Jansenist catechism without royal authorization. Whereupon the newly crowned King Charles III obliged the inquisitor to rescind the publication and to submit himself to a humiliating apology. What was at issue was less Jansenism – a Jansenist movement was less a cause than a product of the expulsion of the Jesuits in Spain – than the principle of royal versus ecclesiastical authority and the independence from Rome of the Spanish Inquisition. In defending Mésenguy's catechism, Charles III was defending his former tutor, Bernardo Tanucci, who had sponsored the Italian translation of Mésenguy in Naples and who now acted as chief minister for Charles's son Ferdinand IV who had taken his father's place as king in this Bourbon outpost. While not exactly a Jansenist either, Tanucci corresponded constantly with Bottari about the Jesuits, detesting them as agents of curial power. Although no longer Charles's tutor, he remained one of the Spanish king's most trusted and influential confidants.

The tide of anti-Jesuitism was thus not even to spare Spain, the birthplace of Ignatius Loyola himself, as the impact produced by the anti-Jesuit campaign widened to include other Catholic kingdoms in their turn. This was despite a concordat negotiated by Charles III's predecessor Ferdinand VI in 1753 that gave the Bourbon crown as much control over the Catholic Church in Spain as the Gallican rights gave the same dynasty in France. As in Portugal, however, the society's presence in Spain seemed unassailable, beginning with the confessors at the royal court and the stranglehold on the education of the upper nobility and promotion to the higher echelons of royal service. (Resentment by recently promoted university-trained *manteistas* in the royal councils against the entrenched blue-blooded Jesuit-educated *colegiales* was not the least of the unannounced causes of the Jesuits' downfall in Spain.) While the Jesuit leadership in Spain tended to be as regalist as in France – even supporting the concordat of 1753 – the society remained a symbol of papal power all the same. Nor were Spanish Jesuits any less hostile to the Treaty of Madrid than their colleagues in Portugal, since the missions most affected were Spanish rather than Portuguese.

It was the popular uprising known as the Hat and Cloak Riots of 23–25 March 1766 in Madrid that provided the occasion for the expulsion of the

Jesuits in Spain. Touched off by an unpopular decree banning the wearing of Spanish sombreros and capes that facilitated theft, the violence vented itself against the drought-driven high prices of foodstuffs, against the mercenary Walloon Guard, and against unpopular Italian ministers in the Council of Castile, especially the marqués de Squillace, minister of war and finance. While this uprising had similar sequels in cities in the provinces, the one in Madrid stood out by virtue of evidence of planning and participation by segments of the political class and their clients. Fleeing Madrid for the security of a royal residence in Aranjuez, Charles III granted a series of demands by the rioters only to rescind some of these concessions as soon as the conde d'Aranda, the new President of the Council of Castile, had re-established royal authority. With Aranda in power, the quest for hidden culprits began in earnest. Although none of the initial reports on the uprising pointed towards Jesuits in particular, by June Tanucci's letters bristled with accusations against them, as did those of one of his correspondents, Manuel de Roda y Arrieta, Charles III's Minister of Grace and Justice since 1765.

Charles entrusted the investigation of the 'origin, the instruments, and the promoters of the uprising' to an Extraordinary Council headed by the regalist or Spanish Gallican, Pedro Rodríguez Campomanes, since 1762 one of two 'fiscales' on the Council of Castile. The Extraordinary Council worked in secrecy through the summer and autumn of 1766, finally adopting Campomanes's report with royal permission on 29 January 1767 and recommending a course of action to yet another specially constituted body, or Junta, consisting of Roda and Aranda among others on 20 February 1767. Yet it could hardly have come as a surprise when, for 'urgent, and equally just and compelling causes', Charles III promulgated a decree expelling all Jesuits from his dominions dated 27 February 1767.[16] The decree remained a secret of state until Aranda executed it with military precision, in Madrid on 30 March, in the rest of Spain on 2 April, and in the colonies as the winds and tides permitted. Although the decree provided the exiled fathers with a pension, their fate was to be even more lamentable than that of their Portuguese counterparts, given that Clement XIII refused to accept more Jesuits in the papal states while neither Genoa nor France could adequately provide for them after Spanish boats began unloading them on a Corsica even less hospitable than usual on account of an ongoing civil war.

That the Spanish Jesuits played the role of scapegoats for the Riot of the Hats and Cloaks is certain. Connections to Jesuits was the one all too convenient common denominator between otherwise disparate noble, clerical and pro-French opponents to the composition and policies of Charles III's reformist ministry. But that individual Jesuits may have compromised themselves in the revolt by composing broadsides seems quite probable if not certain. In the only one of Charles III's 'hidden causes' to sustain judicial light of day, a certain Benito Navarro, a member of a Jesuit confraternity, pleaded guilty to an attempt to frame someone educated by the rival Scolopian congregation for the authorship of anti-ministerial pamphlets composed by Jesuits to whom he felt beholden.[17] In his personal correspondence with his cousin Louis XV, Charles III professed to be unalterably convinced of Jesuit involvement in the uprising, becoming the most adamant Bourbon advocate of the total dissolution of the society.

More impersonal causes provide grist for each and every historiographical mill. A quest for the influence of an anticlerical 'Enlightenment' would highlight the role of Aranda, military student of Frederick the Great and devotee of Voltaire and d'Alembert, whose admiration for French 'lights' survived the ultimate test of the French Revolution. The absolutist motivation to eliminate a Tridentine estate within the state finds its perfect embodiment in the *fiscale* Campomanes, whose two highly regalist treatises elicited from Jean-François Le Blanc de Castillon, advocate-general of the *parlement* of Aix and friend of the abbé Clément, the ultimate compliment of having 'naturalized the articles of the [Gallican] clergy of 1782 in Spain'.[18]

But the Spanish expulsion best illustrates the domino effect of action and reaction, as Spain reacted to the pro-Jesuit papal action in reaction to originally Augustinian action against the Jesuits. And here the Jansenist connection is most crucial, finding its best embodiment in the Minister of Grace and Justice Manuel de Roda, a faithful correspondent of the Jansenist diocese of Utrecht who, as Spanish envoy to Rome in the early 1760s, had come under the sway of the same nest of Roman Augustinians that had hosted the abbé Clément in Rome in 1758 and persuaded French Jansenists to postpone the doctrinal issue in favour of pursuing the Jesuits after the death of Benedict XIV. It was to Roda more than anyone else that Roman Augustinians such as Mario Marefoschi and Francisco Xavier Vasquez credited the demise of the Jesuits in Spain, as it was to Roda that the Extraordinary Council delegated the delicate task of 'refuting' Clement XIII's ultimate plea to Charles III on behalf of the doomed society in 1767.[19]

The cycle of anti-Jesuit action and curial reaction reached another level when the expulsion of the Jesuits came to the Italian peninsula itself. Satrapies of Bourbon Spain under the rule of Charles III's son and nephew respectively, the Kingdom of Naples expelled its Jesuits in November 1767 followed by the Duchy of Parma in February 1768, even though no incident could be alleged against the Jesuits such as the uprising in Madrid or the failed assassination attempts in Portugal and France. In addition to pressure from Spain, the combination of 'Enlightened' and Jansenist justification is evident in either place, in Parma in the persons of Duke Ferdinand's first minister Guillaume Du Tillot, admirer of the French encyclopaedists, and the Jansenist Theatine monk Paolo Maria Paciaudi, Duke Ferdinand's librarian, from whom Du Tillot acquired his anti-Jesuit animus. Hard pressed on all sides, Clement XIII reacted violently when Parma promulgated a Gallican-like pragmatic requiring royal permission for all decrees emanating from ecclesiastical authorities – the papacy claimed Parma as a feudal fief – fulminating a brief not only annulling this and like measures as 'iniquitous' and 'temerarious' but also excommunicating all who had advised or implemented them.[20] The anachronistic spectre of a papal interdict and the exercise of indirect power over temporal states reactivated the Bourbon powers now acting in concert, resulting in the French occupation of the papal enclaves of Avignon and Comtat Venaissin along with the Neapolitan seizure of Benevento and Pontecorvo.

Although the so-called third Bourbon alliance or 'family pact' between France and Spain did not begin to weigh as a factor against the Jesuits until after the expulsion from Spain, the idea of a concert of Catholic powers for such a purpose first appears in the correspondence of Bottari who, writing to the abbé Clément in 1759, opined that 'the only remedy is that France and Vienna unite with Portugal and Spain and ask the papacy for the suppression [of the society, as was done] in the case of the Templars'.[21] As one of the purposes of the Jansenist epistolary network was to influence Catholic court policy, and as Bottari was in at least indirect contact with all of Jansenist Europe, the idea could not have failed to make the rounds including magistrates such as Clément's brother in the *parlement* of Paris.

Bottari returned to his project of a French-led alliance against the Jesuits in early October 1765 and again on 29 April 1767 in the wake of the expulsion in Spain. If successful, such a project, he thought, 'would free the church of God from one of the fiercest and most damnable persecutions she has ever endured'.[22] Whereupon the abbé Chauvelin, one of the original architects of the suppression in France, persuaded the *parlement* of Paris to reiterate its call for such a crusade on 9 May 1767 while two days later Choiseul broached the idea with Louis XV in the Council of State, opining that 'what . . . would suit us best is if [His Majesty], the King of Spain, the Empress Queen [Maria Theresa] and the King of Portugal would unite in order to engage the Pope to dissolve the order of the Jesuits . . . so that the said society no longer has either a general or members and that all these individuals return to the common law of their birth'.[23] Enjoining secrecy, Guillaume Lambert, a Jansenist councillor in the *parlement* of Paris in regular contact with Choiseul, wrote to the abbé Clément a few days later in search of canonical advice about how the papacy might be able to annul a general's authority over an order as well as its members' solemn vows, and then seven weeks later to announce the arrival of a dispatch from Madrid 'in view of establishing a correspondence between the courts of Spain and France to obtain a bull from Rome against the Jesuits'.[24] Whether in this case the cause of international Jansenism was being manipulated by Choiseul or vice versa is a pointless question; the two were obviously pursuing perceived religious and dynastic advantage, using each other among other means.

While Charles III fully endorsed the idea of concerted action – both noticing and lauding the relevant clause in the *parlement*'s judgement of 9 May – his council came up with no plan for the papal 'diplomacy of the extinction' until it sketched out a scenario whereby France and Naples would join Spain in asking Clement XIII for the complete dismissal of his 'Janissaries' in late 1768.[25] Nor, as things turned out, did France and Spain wish to associate too closely with Pombal's pro-English Portugal or ever succeed in enlisting the Austrian empress as more than a benevolent bystander in the anti-Jesuit cause despite the Habsburg alliance with France after 1756 and dynastic marriages with the Bourbon rulers of both Naples and Parma.

Although Choiseul was indeed the main architect of the anti-Jesuitical addition to the Bourbon family pact – the Jesuits proved easier to defeat than the English – the France of Louis XV was to be a less than enthusiastic partner in the enterprise after the fall of Choiseul from power in December 1770 and the purge of the *parlements* in its wake. If, in the end, the French king stayed the course, he did so only out of personal loyalty to his cousin Charles III while permitting the Archbishop of Paris to employ ex-Jesuits much to Spanish as well as Jansenist chagrin. And although the Bourbon powers spurred by Spain were indeed to pressure Clement XIII's successor Lorenzo Ganganelli as Clement XIV into dissolving the Society in July 1773, Choiseul's plan to generalize the French model by allowing all ex-Jesuits to return home as secularized 'citizens' did not prevail. Thus those Jesuits literally expelled from their countries would mainly remain so until the turn of the century when Pope Pius VII recognized the continued existence of the society in Russia and even Spain began to let its ex-Jesuits come home to die. In the era of the Napoleonic phase of the French Revolution, those Catholic dynastic states still standing faced rather larger threats than those posed by a few thousand aging ex-Jesuits from the Iberian peninsula plus Parma and Naples.

But if the dynastically induced demise of the Jesuits did not occur precisely as conceived by Choiseul in 1767, the existence of such an evolving plan, even far earlier than in 1767, is no more subject to doubt than that of a very specific kind of Augustinian-Jansenist complicity from the very beginning of the anti-Jesuit campaign in late 1758 until the end.

While the Bourbon and Portuguese envoys and so-called Crown Cardinals never succeeded in imposing any specific conditions for their support of Cardinal Ganganelli's candidacy for the papal Tiara in the conclave during the spring of 1769, Charles III contrived to extract from him a written promise 'to justify to the whole world Your Majesty's wise conduct in expelling the restive and rebellious Jesuits' as early as 30 November of the same year.[26] Thereafter only sudden death could have released Clement XIV from an obviously conscience-encumbering obligation, although he delayed its execution for three years by alleging now the appeals of a pro-Jesuit French clergy, now the opposition of the other Catholic states – even the opposition of Protestant Prussia and Orthodox Russia. It was not a very edifying sight when the Spanish envoy José Moñino, later the Count of Floridablanca, virtually dictated the text of the brief *Dominus ac Redemptor* dated 21 July 1773 while generously distributing Spanish gold to the pope's inner circle in order to get the better of his final scruples.

A Roman triumph for the Jansenist International, the papal dissolution of the Society of Jesus was to be its passion week as well. The spectacle of the humiliation of the papacy – and one of Italy's few native states – at the hands of the Bourbon dynasty with Habsburg acquiescence was to transform many philo-Jansenist and reformist Italian clergymen into ardent advocates of papal prerogatives and purveyors of an allied neo-Baroque spirituality, while the dissolution of the Jesuits added numbers of talented angry ex-Jesuits to the ranks of an ever angrier Ultramontanist International. Against such polemical periodicals as the Florentine *Ecclesiastical Annals* and the Viennese *Church News* that modelled themselves on – and borrowed copy from – the increasingly international Jansenist *Ecclesiastical News*, ex-Jesuits took up positions as editors of militantly pro-papal periodicals such as Francescantonio Zaccaria's *Ecclesiastical Journal of Rome* and François-Xavier de Feller's *Political and Literary Journal*. Meanwhile the infernal cycle of action and reaction produced the anti-Jansenist pontificate of Pius VI in 1775. Coming hard on the heels of that of Clement XIV, this pontificate further alienated Italian Augustinians, driving Jansenists into anti-papal alliances with dynastic states in need of a theological justification for Gallican-like extensions of regalian rights such as those exemplified by 'Josephism' in Austria and the Duke Peter Leopold's Jansenist-inspired Synod of Pistoia in Habsburg Tuscany.

This ever-more polarized Catholic *fin-de-siècle* precluded any productive pursuit of other more important items on the Augustinian reformist agenda, even supposing that Clement XIV had not died soon after the dissolution – if not by poison administered by Jesuits, as Jansenists everywhere believed, quite probably in chagrin. Although the primacy of the politics of anti-Jesuitism was supposed to have produced a papacy more open to a doctrinal course correction in an Augustinian direction, the effect was the opposite, producing in Pius VI a pontificate that would see the whole French Revolution through anti-Jansenist lenses. Among the casualties of the politics of postponement were such causes as the canonization of the seventeenth-century Spanish (and anti-Jesuit) bishop Juan de Palafox, the reunion with Rome of the appellant diocese of Utrecht, the revival of the Tridentine call for frequent councils and synods – and of course the abbé Clément's plan for a papal bull that would rid the church of the legacy of the Formulary and *Unigenitus*.

Having successfully exported her hitherto unique religious and political divisions to the rest of Catholic Europe at Italian invitation, France herself now embarked on new ones apropos of the Revolution's reform of the Gallican church known as the Civil Constitution of the Clergy. For the oath to it required by the National Assembly of all beneficed clergy in the new order was to divide the French clergy more evenly than had the Formulary and *Unigenitus*, as well as to set the episcopate more resolutely against the state than parliamentary policy in the refusal of sacraments controversy and the trial of the Jesuits had done. The split became irreconcilable after Pius VI condemned the Civil Constitution as 'heretical' in 1791. While new enough, this rift nonetheless refracted pre-existent divisions over Jansenism that had not yet entirely disappeared and that, while now widespread in Catholic Europe, had still distinguished the Gallican clergy from most others during the campaign against the Jesuits. And although the Gallicanism at work in the formation of the Civil Constitution was more draconian than any pre-revolutionary precedent had been, the National Assembly nonetheless preferred the *parlements*' example of an internal secularization of an ecclesiastical corps as opposed to the external expulsions on the Iberian model. Except that in this case it was the dissolution of all contemplative monastic orders and the entire secular clergy as a corps.

Although parts of this reform were genuinely Jansenist in inspiration as well as being perceived as such by the Ultramontanist International, the Civil Constitution overshot the Jansenist agenda in several symptomatically 'encyclopaedic' ways, and came to divide what remained of the Jansenist community almost as badly as the Gallican clergy as a whole. The result was a cycle of clerical reaction and revolutionary anticlericalism that did not end until the

Revolution had experimented in 'de-Christianization' and much of the 'refractory' portion of the Gallican clergy had found no refuge except in the Italy of
a very anti-Gallican papacy – a papacy that, not content with their rejection
of the Civil Constitution, persisted in imposing on even such refugees the
signature of the Formulary and acceptance of *Unigenitus*.

It was not until after the Terror that a reconstituted 'constitutional' church
cut loose by the state as well as anathematized by the papacy was able to
take up some of the reforms postponed by the priority given to the campaign
against the Jesuits. And it was then and only then that an aged but indomitable
abbé Clément, recently elected bishop of the new diocese of Versailles, was
able to persuade a Catholic Church to put the matter of Molinistic 'errors since
the Council of Trent' on its official agenda, submitting doctrinal statements
on the subject to this church's two national councils in 1797 and 1801.[27] With
the need for councils themselves on its agenda, the National Council of 1801
also appealed its case to a future general council – the last such appeal in the
history of Christendom.

But by the time of this appeal, Napoleon Bonaparte was interring the constitutional clergy by means of a concordat with Pius VII that would give
the papacy the unprecedented power to abolish and reconstitute the entire
Gallican episcopate. In the same year, at the behest of Tsar Paul I, Pius issued
the brief *Catholicai fidei* canonically sanctioning the *de facto* existence of the
Society of Jesus in Russia.

Notes

1. Phrase from the text of the papal brief *Dominus ac Redemptor*, translated into French
   by Jacques Crétineau-Joly, *Histoire religieuse, politique et littéraire de la Compagnie de Jésus
   composée sur les documents inédits et authentiques*, 6 vols. (Paris: Mellier Frères, 1844–46),
   vol. 5, p. 284.

2. Jean Le Rond d'Alembert, *Sur la destuction des jésuites en France, par un auteur désintéressé*
   (n.p., 1765), pp. 96–7.

3. Giovanni Marchetti, *Che importa ai preti ovvero, l'interesse della religione cristiana nei grandi
   avvenimenti di questi tempi*, third edn (Cristianopoli, 1798), pp. 25–7.

4. Alain Tallon, *Le concile de Trente* (Paris: Editions du Cerf, 2000), pp. 45–63.

5. François Pinthereau, *Les nouvelles et anciennes reliques de Messire Jean du Vergier de Hauranne,
   abbé de Saint-Cyran, extraites des ouvrages qu'il a composés et donnés au public et des informations
   de sa vie et de sa doctrine* (Paris, 1648), pp. 5, 246–7; Jean Filleau, *Relation juridique de ce
   qui s'est passé a Poitiers touchant la nouvelle doctrine des jansenistes* (Poitiers, 1654); [Louis
   Patouillet, alias La Croix], *Le progrès du jansénisme* (Quiloa, 1757).

6. 'Table raisonnée et aphabétique', *Nouvelles ecclésiastiques, ou Mémoires pour servir a l'histoire
   de la constitution Unigenitus* (Utrecht: aux dépens de la Compagnie, 1728–1803), 1ère partie,
   pp. 660–868.

7. Bibliothèque de l'Arsenal, Archives de la Bastille, MS 10189, fol. 250, 15 July 1729.
8. Bibliothèque de l'Arsenal, MS 11,883, fols. 151–152, Bottari to Clément, 12 and 20 December 1758.
9. Bibliothèque de Port-Royal, Collection Le Paige, MS 549, fols. 30–31.
10. *Nouvelles ecclésiastiques* (2 January 1758), p. 3; (January 1759), p. 7.
11. [Viou], *Nouvelles intéressantes au sujet de l'attentat commis sur la personne . . . de S.M. . . . le Roi de Portugal*, reviewed in *Nouvelles ecclésiastiques*, **1759**: 6/2; 6/3; 3, 10, 17/4; 1, 8/5; 26/6; 17/7; 4, 11/9; 16/10; 13/11; 13, 22/12/; **1760**: 2, 9, 23, 30/1; 12/3; 16/4; 9/7; 20/8; 3, 10/9; 22/10; 5, 12, 19/11; 10/12, etc.
12. On Viou, see Christine Vogel, 'Der Untergang des Gesellschaft Jesu als Europäisches Medienereignis', Inaugural-Dissertation zur Erlangung des Doktorgrades des Philosophie des Fachbereiches 04 der Justus-Liebig-Universität Giessen, 2003, pp. 66, 93, 96–100. On Norbert/Platel, see Michèle Janin-Thivos, 'La mémoire de l'exécution du père Gabriel Malagrida', in Régis Bertrand and Anne Carol (eds.), *L'exécution capitale: une mort donnée en spectacle, XVIe–XXe siècle* (Aix-en-Provence: Publications de l'Université de Provence, 2003), pp. 109–27; and *Nouvelles ecclésiastiques* (20 Feb.–6 March 1745), pp. 29–38.
13. Samuel J. Miller, *Portugal and Rome, c.1748–1830: An aspect of the Catholic Enlightenment* (Rome: Università Gregorianna Editrice, 1978), pp. 51–106.
14. Bibliothèque de l'Arsenal, MS 11,883, fols. 257–258, Bottari to Clément, 3 and 17 July 1761. For a look at Choiseul's raw reaction to this event, Archives des Affaires Etrangères, Correspondance politique, Rome, MS 831, fols. 159–160, Choiseul to Bishop of Laon, 7 July 1761; and for evidence of its connection to the fate of the Jesuits in France, see Laon's account of his conversation with Torregiani in fols. 253–254, 2 September 1761.
15. Bibliothèque de l'Arsenal, MS 11,882, fols. 107, 130, Bottari to Clément, 5 June and 12 December 1764.
16. Text in French translation in *Nouvelles ecclésiastiques* (11 May 1767), p. 77.
17. Coverage of this case is in *Nouvelles ecclésiastiques* (6–13 June 1768), pp. 89–96. See also Archives des Affaires Etrangères, Correspondance politique, Spain, MS 550, fol. 161 ff., Ossun to Choiseul, Escurial, 26 October 1767.
18. Bibliothèque de Saint-Sulpice, MS 1289, fol. 99, Le Blanc de Castillon to Clément, 29 July 1768, with a copy of a letter from Le Blanc de Castillon to Camponannes, n.d.
19. Ludwid Freiherr von Pastor, *The history of the popes from the close of the Middle Ages*, trans. E. F. Peeler (London: Routledge and Kegan Paul, 1949–52), vol. 37, pp. 85–90, 125–7, 150–7. Although resident in Rome as General of the Augustinian Order, Vasquez was actually Spanish.
20. Text in Gustave-Xavier de La Croix de Ravignan, *Clément XIII et Clément XIV*, 2 vols. (Paris: Julien, Lanier et Cie, 1854), vol. 2, pp. 549–52.
21. Bibliothèque de l'Arsenal, Archives de la Bastille, MS 11,883, fol. 164, Bottari to Clément, 21 March 1759.
22. Bibliothèque de l'Arsenal, Archives de la Bastille, MS 11,882, fol. 192, Bottari to Clément, 29 [April] 1767. The month of April has been arrived at on internal textual evidence, the location of this letter *vis-à-vis* the others, and by eliminating all other alternatives.
23. Archives des Affaires Etrangères, Correspondance politique, Spain, MS 548, fols. 404–407, Choiseul to the marquis d'Ossun, Marly, 11 May 1767. For the abbé Chauvelin's speech of 29 April and the text of the *parlement* of Paris's *arrêt* of 9 May, Bibliothèque

nationale, Collection Joly de Fleury, MS 1611, fols. 111–114, 148–153; and *Nouvelles ecclésiastiques* (18 May 1767), p. 84.

24. Bibliothèque de l'Arsenal, Archives de la Bastille, MS 11,882, fol. 200, Lambert to Clément, 12 May 1767; and fol. 203, 4 July 1767.

25. The Extraordinary Council of Madrid approved the plan on 21 March 1768. See Enrique Giménez López, 'La extirpación de la mala doctrina. Los inicios del proceso de extinción de la compañnia de Jesús (1767–1769)', in *Expulsión y exilio de los jesuitas españoles*, ed. Enrique Giménez López (Alicante: Universidad de Alicante, 1997), pp. 251–5.

26. Quoted in Pastor, *The history of the popes*, vol. 38, p. 170.

27. *Actes du second concile national de France, tenu l'an 1801 de J[ésus] C[hrist] (an 9 de la Répubique française) dans l'église métropolitaine de Paris*, 3 vols. (Paris: Imprimerie Chrétienne, 1801), vol. 1, pp. 68, 463.

17

Evangelical awakenings in the North Atlantic world

W. R. WARD

The first great Protestant awakenings arose from an interweaving of Pietism, revivalism, and politics. Revivalism was distinct from Pietism but political circumstances ensured that it never had an entirely independent history. Pietism in the narrow sense of the word was a party (there were others) born of the continent-wide movement for piety early in the seventeenth century, but taking its peculiar shape from its creation within an atmosphere of conflict with Lutheran Orthodoxy; the Pietist party was Phillip Jacob Spener's answer to the disappointment of his hopes of achieving a consensus for renewal and reform. It was an answer to the problems of religious establishments in the doldrums. Revival began among the vast number of Protestants in the triangle between Transylvania, Poland and Salzburg, those who had been abandoned and left with little defence by the peace settlements of Westphalia, and hence those who (outside Hungary) had no church system to renew. The experience of these abandoned Protestants shaped the whole history of revivalism. The original compulsion among the Protestant minorities to get results quickly ensured that there was always an ethos of desperation about revivalism. Because, for these Protestant minorities, the old ways were not normative and mostly not available, they had both freedom and compulsion to experiment. Not that old ideas were of no account, for, like Pietism, revivalism grew out of the Lutheran Orthodox tradition. The revivalist theory that at the bottom of everyone's mind and conscience were fragments of belief which could be revived and made effective reflected the experience of the Protestant minorities in Silesia and the Habsburg lands long before the theory was formulated. Long deprived of the ordinances, these dispossessed minorities preserved a memory of what they were. Their secret worship in farm kitchens generated an intensity of *koinonia* uncharacteristic of the old establishments. The gatherings of peasants and miners of the Habsburg lands bore the whole weight of Christianizing successive generations.

Pietism, or in Anglo-Saxon parlance, evangelicalism, was a mixture of attitudes not primarily revivalist, few of which were shared by all evangelicals, or which were exclusive to them, and which changed steadily in time. The roots of Pietism lay in the presumption common to both Catholic and Protestant in the early seventeenth century that the way to enliven a Christian practice dulled by habit, or shrivelled by polemic, was by encouraging individual meditation. Much of the new literature was generated by the Counter-Reformation in Italy and Spain, but there were strenuous Protestant efforts to get the devotional literature of the cloister into the home. The first three books of the Lutheran theologian Johann Arndt's *True Christianity* (1606) correspond to the classical stages of the mystical way, the *via purgativa*, the *via illuminativa*, and the *via unitiva*. Indeed, in one of the most successful publishing enterprises of the modern period, Arndt subjected the medieval literature to a Lutheran editing. In 1650, the English Presbyterian Richard Baxter, echoing the Puritan bestsellers of the previous generation, complained that meditation 'is confessed to be a duty by all, but practically denied by most'. Spener's programme, the *Pia Desideria,* was written as a preface to Arndt's lectionary sermons, and Spener's class-meeting, the *collegium pietatis*, was envisaged as an intermediate stage between public preaching and private meditation, which would be to the advantage of both. Spener's hopes for the class-meeting, to be sure, were not entirely fulfilled; but henceforth evangelicalism would be characterized by emphasis upon the general priesthood fostered in the fellowship of small groups.

Spener also distinguished himself from the general movement for piety by his eschatology. The Lutheran Orthodox had become convinced that the end of the world was at hand and they drew from this two main inferences: first that this knowledge of the imminent end gave them a leverage upon the consciences of their hearers (who must repent while there was yet time); and second that the missionary task of the church was virtually finished. For Spener, however, his belief that church renewal would come through the leaven of a spiritual elite meant that he also believed that the Last Days would be deferred into the middle distance, that is, until all God's promises to the church had been fulfilled. Spener called for a dramatic revolution in pastoral strategy; instead of demanding that men be converted in time for the apocalypse (and one that was being continually postponed), the pastor should invite Christians to lives of service, on the assurance that they could make a genuine improvement in the world, and even contribute to the return of Christ himself. No one, moreover, was being asked to wait forever for the second coming. Johann Albrecht Bengel (1687–1752) whose biblical study of these questions so impressed Wesley, predicted that the millennial age would begin as early as 1836. And when late in the eighteenth century Protestants residing along the North Atlantic coastlines gained freer access to the non-European world, eschatologies like that of Spener were very heavily pressed in the cause of overseas missions.

All the evangelical movements saw in an emphasis on 'system' one of the roots of fruitless polemic; system was Aristotelian and all evangelicals were anti-Aristotelian. Here they were in the tradition of Arndt who in the fourth book of *True Christianity* confessed himself drawn to the doctrines of the sixteenth-century Swiss physician and Neoplatonist, Paracelsus: Arndt suggested that the inner light which is in every man signified the art of magic, and he viewed the Kabbala, the Jewish medieval mysticism, to be a great effort to recover the hidden mysteries under the letter of scripture. 'Where magic ceases', he declared, 'the Kabbala begins, and where the Kabbala ceases there true theology and prophetic spirit begins.'[1] The vitalism which characterized the alchemical tradition had an obvious appeal to men who were themselves seeking to recover religious vitality, but there seemed to be a strong scientific basis for it too. Both Spener and Francke dabbled in the science and mysticism of Paracelsus, and Paracelsianism remained dominant in Germany and the north throughout the eighteenth century.

Any perception of a harmonious syncretism in this Lutheran devotion to the Kabbala and Hebraic studies was mocked by the general belief that Romans 11 promised that the immediate preface to the Last Days would be the conversion of the Jews. Orthodox Lutheran expectations were encouraged by the outcome of the dreadful pogroms in Poland in 1648. While these revived the messianic hopes of many Jewish congregations for the imminent return of the Messiah based on the Kabbala, the pogroms led also to the conversion of many thousands of Jews to Catholicism. This was not, to be sure, quite the outcome suggested by the exegetes. Nonetheless, so long as many Protestants had no perspectives upon the world other than those of the Bible and the ancient classics, the Jews were bound to be a central preoccupation for them. The Quakers perceived the Delaware Indians as the Lost Tribe of Israel; sixty years later Zinzendorf took much the same view, and in between Cotton Mather and Jonathan Edwards concluded even more pejoratively that the Indians were not Jews but Canaanites, or that they had been brought over from Europe by the Devil himself to be his peculiar people untouched by Christian influence. Spener had his own Jewish problem. From 1666 to 1686 he was senior pastor of Frankfurt, a town of very mixed religious allegiance with the biggest Jewish ghetto in Germany. He began working for the religious and moral improvement of the town in the traditional Lutheran way by seeking reform from the top through action by the town council, and predictably failed. He then sought to develop a spiritual leaven for improvement through the means of his *collegium pietatis*, and in his celebrated short work, *Pia Deside-ria*, he described a programme of reform which did not rely upon state action. His new approach included the belief that the Jews were deterred from their millennial role by the decayed state of the church. Renew the church and they would come in. There was, to be sure, little evidence for this view, but it con-tributed crucially to the development of the evangelical mind by enabling it to postpone its obsession with Jewish questions in favour of mission in general. The conversion of the Jews, in any event, proved a very slow business. Spener's successors took to preaching to Jews as individuals and they gave the process institutional backing at Halle. Count Nicholas von Zinzendorf, founder of the Moravian Brethren, invested far more energy into converting Jews than the results ever warranted, and insisted that since technical millenarian questions had formed no part of the original apostolic preaching, the Moravians should follow suit. Thus he too escaped from the constrictions which the Orthodox Lutheran theologies had placed upon both space and time, and he instilled new energies into mission. The same slow progress is revealed in the English evangelist, John Wesley. He could write about the Jews in almost the old style; but when he became excited about the progress of the revival, he would use the conventional post-millennial language about the latter-day glory with all the optimism of Jonathan Edwards. Moreover, both Wesley and Zinzendorf had learned from the German Pietist, August Hermann Francke (whose edu-cational and philanthropic institutions at Halle were institutions of neither church nor state) that it was possible to apply a principle of contract to the kingdom of God, and without it the missions which were eventually launched from Herrnhut, Basel and London would never have set forth at all. The latter years of the eighteenth century, which saw the original evangelical mixture falling apart, also saw another generation of evangelicals becoming obsessed with the millennium, and creating new battering-rams against the Jews; the liberation afforded by Spener's 'hope of better times' had its limits.

The final feature of the evangelical mind might be inferred from its roots in Arndt and the vogue of meditation, that is, its commitment to mysticism. There had always been an undercurrent of mysticism in the Christian world, and now when Lutheran Orthodoxy was in the toils, its influence dramat-ically increased. A Protestant historical pedigree for 'the mystical theology' was created by the radical German Protestant theologian, Gottfried Arnold, and upheld by Spener against the Lutheran Orthodox. Francke translated the seventeenth-century Spanish Quietist, Miguel de Molinos, into Latin for academic purposes, and Molinos and Arndt were significant in his conversion. Makarius the Egyptian was not just one of the more implausible pieces of baggage taken by Wesley in 1735 to Georgia, he was a major item in the Protestant rediscovery of mysticism. Much the same can be said of the *Lives* of M. de Renty and Gregory Lopez, versions of which Wesley published, and to which he was deeply indebted. If Wesley could never quite swallow the mystic way whole, he could also never spit it out. The clashes with church authority suffered by the Flemish mystical writer, Antoinette Bourignon, and French Quietist author, Madame Guyon, attracted the attention of the whole Pietist world to the Quietists. The French Protestant student of mysticism, Pierre Poiret, produced comprehensive editions of both authors, as well as collecting the Counter-Reformation materials which the German Pietist, Gerhard Tersteegen, turned into three volumes of *Select Lives of Holy Souls* (1734–56). Molinos's message that Christianity must be simpler than the endless multiplication of devotions created during the Counter-Reformation, and the insistence of the Quietists (who were all philosophical voluntarists) that the fundamental problem was that of harmonizing the will of man with the will of God, even engulfing the one in the other, sank deep. Jonathan Edwards's great effort to incorporate creation into the work of redemption was aided by his mystical devotion to beauty. Edwards's saint, like that of every other Reformed theologian, is a pilgrim, but not a 'pilgrim through this barren land'. The saints, he declared, 'do not first see that God loves *them,* and then see that he is lovely; but they first see that God is lovely, and that Christ is excellent and glorious; their hearts are first captivated with this view'. Genuine and gracious affections have 'beautiful symmetry and proportion' as they did in David Brainerd, and as they emerged in the New Birth.[2] The evangelical peddlers of Catholic spirituality were not acting as middlemen between Catholic and Protestant; rather, they were feeding an unsatisfied Protestant market with Catholic fare. The implication of this was that the future of mysticism within evangelicalism could not be severed from its fate in the Roman Catholic Church. Unfortunately the unholy alliance between Louis XIV and the papacy to put down Jansenism which radically undermined the entire system of the *ancien régime* in France also produced the papal condemnations of Molinos; and the spiritual writer, François Fénelon, Archbishop of Cambrai, put the Quietists through the mill, and made it impossible in France to produce books with the word 'mysticism' in the title. A movement now in mortal decline no longer produced durable accounts of religious experience, but encyclopaedias, treatises, manuals, which were given a scientific character by appearing in Latin; the declining field was propped up by the creation of chairs in Carmelite colleges, and the holders of these chairs produced *summas*. Barred from university and church, mysticism sought refuge in informal gatherings, class meetings, lodges, Temples of Wisdom. Thus the evangelicals, especially those in the west who drew heavily from the more recent mystical and Quietist literature, were deriving nourishment from a movement in decay, a movement now 'textbookized' so thoroughly that it had lost its earlier appeal as a dynamo of red-hot religious experience.

For Protestants there were two other concerns. First, professional mysticism was a product of the leisure industry, and leisure was somewhat abhorrent to evangelicals. Jonathan Edwards spoke for them all, when he insisted that holiness 'consists not only in contemplation and a mere passive enjoyment, but very much in action'.[3] Though Wesley recommended the Quietist writers (especially to ladies) he would warn against their dangers in the same breath, and at the end of his life he was purging 'mysticism' from his brother's hymns. Second, there were doctrinal difficulties. Mystical union with God, even the dialectical relation envisaged by the Lutheran mystic, Jakob Böhme, did not satisfy the need for atonement. The young Anglican evangelical, Henry Venn, an adept of the Behmenist William Law, repudiated him violently when 'he came to a passage wherein Mr Law seemed to represent the blood of Christ as of no more avail in procuring our salvation than the excellence of his moral character'.[4] Böhme, it seemed, might win liberation from Orthodoxy at too high a price; and, after Wesley's death, it became clear that the large dose of empiricism in his kind of evangelicalism created difficulties regarding the doctrine of the Holy Spirit.

Thus at the moment when evangelicalism was about to enter on its period of greatest influence the evangelical syndrome was coming apart, and it was doing so in central Europe as well as the west. The Pietist Friedrich Christoph Oetinger endeavoured in the mid-eighteenth century (despite the original evangelical hostility to 'system') to construct a system out of kabbalism, Paracelsianism and Bengel's eschatology, using the doctrine of correspondences developed by the Swedish visionary Emanuel Swedenborg. This alliance of Oetinger and Swedenborg proved ill-fated. Both partners were subject to disciplinary proceedings by their own churches. Oetinger, moreover, was wedded to Bengel's system of realistic scriptural exegesis, not the spiritual, hieroglyphic interpretations of the Swedish visionary. In the event, Oetinger decided that Swedenborg's *True Christianity* (1771) was not true at all. Wesley also violently repudiated the Swede, even though this was at the cost of a small secession from his Methodist movement. Johann-Caspar Lavater, the famous preacher of Zurich, was also attracted by the doctrine of correspondences. He believed that a man's features were a product of his spiritual state; the true face beneath the mask would be revealed on the day of judgement but meanwhile some insight could be obtained by the study of physiognomy. Lavater had a remarkable gift for persuading men of goodwill that they agreed with him, and he never lost touch with the Pietist *Stille im Lande*; but what he exemplified was the disintegration of evangelicalism.

The increasing dependence of evangelicals upon empiricism increased their ability to absorb revivalism, a very different thing. The first in the field, the Silesians, moreover, found the *rapprochement* of revivalism with church Pietism eased by the supply of preachers, literature and the backing of the remaining local Protestant aristocracy, all organized by Francke. Silesian Protestantism, outside Breslau, seemed in the late seventeenth century to face the same kind of annihilation as that in Bohemia and Moravia after the Protestant defeat in the battle of White Mountain. The miners and shepherds in the Silesian hills, however, were not entirely helpless, for they could count on the support of the Berlin government which had long-term ambitions in Silesia; and in 1707, Sweden's attempt to break the mould of international politics brought additional relief. In that year, by the Peace of Altranstädt, Charles XII obtained the return of 120 Protestant churches in the indirectly governed principalities; moreover, six new 'Grace' churches were to be built in the Habsburg family lands, and to these 'Grace' churches and to some other churches schools were to be attached. But already the situation had changed. For lack of churches the Swedish troops had held their church parades in the open air, and when they withdrew, the children of Glogau gave a new meaning to the word 'camp-meeting' by following suit, gathering round their elected leaders in prayer and singing, often against parental opposition. The hazard of this 'uprising of the children', as it was called, was that the object of their intercessions, the return of Protestant churches and schools, was politically very sensitive. The Pietist publicist, August Hermann Francke, however, made the best of the story in the European press, and got the most important of the 'Grace' churches erected in Teschen in Upper Silesia. Here institutional Protestantism had gone to pieces, but there was thought to be a congregation of about 40,000 in the hills round about. For the Teschen project Francke recruited some of his ablest assistants. They first built not a church, but a large house with cellars for the wine trade, a ground floor for a bookshop and stock room, a first floor with accommodation for three preachers, and a second floor with a seminary for nobles, in short a miniature Halle, uniting propaganda and commerce at the point of greatest threat to confessional survival. The key figure was Johann Adam Steinmetz (1689–1762), a successful revivalist from

Münsterberg, who assembled a very strong team, with assistants trained in Halle, for the Czech and Polish preaching. Circumstances pushed the Teschen Pietists into revivalism. German confessions began at six on a Sunday morning, and communions, confessions and preaching would go on all day, while the crowds arriving from a distance would spend their time in enthusiastic hymn-singing. And the Teschen staff were less like ordinary parish pastors than circuit riders, dividing up their duties by rota: one week devoted to public prayer meetings and ministerial duties, the second week travelling out to the sick, the third week rest, and the fourth riding out to support the travelling preachers.

The story played out in Silesia was repeated with local variations wherever the Habsburgs tried to suppress Protestant populations. The damage to Protestant faith and practice had gone much further in Bohemia and Moravia than in Silesia, and since flight now seemed the only resort for the Protestant labouring orders, the Catholic authorities shackled the labour force more firmly to the soil. A series of peasant revolts followed and in the 1720s this resistance blended with revival under the preaching and literary propaganda of Teschen. The King of Prussia was anxious to attract Bohemian Protestant labourers, but the revolts encouraged by the Teschen propagandists were savagely put down by the Habsburgs. The most successful illicit poacher of labour across the border was Johann Christian Schwedler, the revivalist minister of Niederwiesa, who became expert in stocking the estates of the Lusatian gentry, including Zinzendorf's grandmother, with Protestant labour smuggled out through Silesian villages where the revival had given him a hold. A rootless refugee population in Lusatia was a prime target for the revivalists, and when Zinzendorf established toleration on his estate at Berthelsdorf, many settled there. There was now an open contest for the religious roots of Czech nationalism. The Habsburgs promoted the veneration of a fourteenth-century Bohemian, John of Nepomuk, obtained his canonization in 1729, and pressed the cult on a great scale. In reply, the Moravian Protestants at Herrnhut brought about one of the most famous of all revivals which beat the canonization of John of Nepomuk by a short head, and considerably outdid him in international significance. Each side now had its icon.

Meanwhile, trouble had been brewing outside the Habsburg lands but within their sphere of influence. There were, it was thought, a few thousand Protestants in the diocese and principality of Salzburg, some informally tolerated in the mines, some settled in the hills as peasants. A crisis was brought on by the election of Baron von Firmian as a reforming archbishop. He turned the Jesuits upon the Protestants residing in the principality, expelling them from their homes in a manner that astounded the whole of Europe. The first two peasants expelled made straight for the Imperial Diet at Regensburg, with a petition for the free exercise of the Protestant faith bearing 18,000 signatures. Support for the Protestant cause was swelled by revival, a coarser version of what had happened in Silesia and was to happen again in America. In November 1731, the archbishop expelled all Protestants over the age of twelve virtually without notice. Protestant Salzburgers left in huge numbers to be picked up at various points in Swabia by Prussian agents, marched by different columns to the north-east, paid a daily subsistence allowance, and after occasioning 'moving awakenings' on the way, settled in domestic service or on peasant lots between Berlin and Livonia. The operation cost the Prussian government half a million thalers, but they got 20,000 settlers. All the Protestant powers subscribed and took their share of expelled Salzburgers, the British receiving a first instalment of 200 who were settled by the Georgia trustees near Savannah with two ministers from Halle, and put under the general spiritual oversight of the Wesley brothers.

The Salzburg upheaval contributed greatly to the spread of revival. Very many people, even in Oxford common rooms, were drawn into the rescue operation, and the propaganda warfare reached levels last seen at the time of the Revocation of the Edict of Nantes. The evidence of what the ordinary faithful could do for themselves without a church system was a shock to the Protestant Orthodox. Unsettlement in the Baltic area contributed to a vivid Moravian revival there. And deep within the Habsburg Empire, in Carinthia, Styria and the Tyrol, Protestants were encouraged (and continually exhorted by Salzburger propagandists) to think that they might repeat the Salzburg miracle. What was surprising was that the Protestantism of the revivals did not affront the scruples of the evangelical syndrome. The chief exception was in Hungary where the Protestants retained their church systems despite extreme pressure, and with these church systems they also retained a foothold in those social strata which traditionally held access to political power. Nevertheless, even within Hungarian Protestantism, the greatest growth occurred within the so-called 'widowed' congregations without a pastor, which numbered about a thousand at the time of the Toleration Patent of 1781. In short, the priesthood of all believers was realized in Hungary too.

In the large towns of Switzerland and the west, the urban patriciates put up a strong fight for Orthodoxy (not always successfully), but in the great Reformed reserve of the United Provinces, the pastoral problem was quite different. Here one-third of the population remained Catholic, and many more were devoted to riotous living. Assimilation was made more difficult by giving hospitality to huge numbers of refugees and by receiving intellectual currents from else-where. Thus the Dutch escaped the dominance of a Reformed Orthodoxy and eased their way into a range of views with a minimum of separatism, while they ensured toleration for foreign Dissenters such as Moravians. All parties had to make their way on a basis of persuasion. This became clear in the ministry of Theodor Untereyck (1635–93), regarded as the Spener of Reformed Germany. He managed to seal off the late seventeenth-century Labadist secessions from Reformed Orthodoxy by a combination of thunderous Voetian preaching (fol-lowing the stern Calvinist teachings of Gisbert Voetius) and seeking to turn every household into a house-church. In short he was halfway to revivalism; and the evolution was taken further by his successor Friedrich Adolf Lampe (1692–1729). Admitting that the church could not consist entirely of the elect, Lampe required the elect to stand at the conclusion of the sermon and receive a special message. This was termed 'discriminating' preaching, and it shows how the necessities of the churches were driving the ministers towards revival-ism. It was this tradition which Theodorus Jacobus Frelinghuysen, a minister in East Friesland recruited by the Amsterdam *classis* for service in New Jersey, took to the New World and which enabled him to bed comfortably with the revivalist Tennent family.

The hero figure of Rhineland spirituality was Gerhard Tersteegen (1697–1769), the most celebrated of Protestant mystics. A lay witness who abstained from the Reformed sacraments, but was not a Quaker, Tersteegen built on the legacy of Poiret; his faith consisted in the love of God and the denial of self, and began predictably with withdrawal from the world. But revival was in the air in and about his stamping ground in the Duchy of Berg. Amid a series of revivals between 1720 and 1760, revivalists found themselves overwhelmed and called on his help. He gave up his lay calling and devoted himself to personal contact, correspondence and preaching with a great range of house-groups and individuals between Switzerland and the United Provinces. He became a revivalist because his public would not let him escape, and his hymns caught on quickly everywhere.

Watching briefs for America were kept for the Reformed by the Amsterdam and Heidelberg *classes*, and for the Lutherans by Halle. The former did not try to propagate the high Orthodoxy of the Dutch Reformed in New York, which was not much use to the Dutch diaspora in New Jersey, still less to the assimi-lated Huguenot and Palatine settlers who threw in their lot with them. These Reformed groups in the New World were provided for by Guiliam Bartholf, a Voetian from Sluis, and by another Voetian from East Friesland, Theodorus Jacobus Frelinghuysen. They were the real founders of the Dutch Reformed

Church in America. Greater doctrinal confusion developed among the German settlers in Pennsylvania who by the time of the War of Independence numbered almost half the population of the colony. The early settlers had been refugees from European persecution, but the bulk had gone to America in search of prosperity, and these economic refugees had no objection to re-creating the Lutheran and Reformed churches they had left behind. The problem was that they had come from many different Lutheran and Reformed churches, and spoke many different dialects, which they grafted variously on to a pidgin English. Confessional identity collapsed; almost half the churches built were union churches and their clergy tended to be appointed on free-market principles. Yet the Lutheran and Reformed churches in Pennsylvania withstood revival, when it came, better than the establishments in Europe, and even better than their English-language counterparts in America, the Anglicans and Presbyterians. Everyone from Whitefield onwards regarded the fragmented Pennsylvania Germans as a single cultural entity ripe for unification. In December 1741, Zinzendorf arrived in Philadelphia, ostensibly to take up a pastoral appointment, but actually to offer his own Moravian Brethren movement as a catalyst for unity. The German settlers were not susceptible to Zinzendorf's seigniorial attitudes. Francke's son, meanwhile, had been given an unmistakable signal to find money for an American mission. As well as money, Francke also sent a clergymen, Henry Melchior Mühlenberg, who came straight from running the Orphan House created by Zinzendorf's estranged aunt, Henriette von Gersdorf. Tough rather than theologically refined, Mühlenberg understood that his business in America (like that of the Pietists at Teschen in Silesia) was to revive a faith which had been neglected or perverted – and to do so with the usual accompaniments of heightened emotion and tears, and by the sort of itinerant ministry that was obligatory in America for all clergy outside New England. His reward, a total of 126 congregations gathered by 1776, would not have disgraced a revivalist anywhere. And largely because his friends in Halle maintained a supply of clergy of monochrome Hallesian views the church did not experience division or schism as a result of its revival. The *classis* of Amsterdam, meanwhile, followed suit by sending an energetic Swiss, Michael Schlatter, to organize and revive the Reformed Church in America.

The cantankerous Scots-Irish who flooded into the Pennsylvania backcountry were less easily settled. In Ireland, revival had emerged in the 1620s among Scottish settlers in Ulster as a Presbyterian response to early Stuart policies aimed at achieving religious uniformity under the Anglican establishment. The revival had been exported back to Scotland by 1625. The Ulster revival also reflected a Calvinist hankering for a godly commonwealth, a single communal profession of religion on the basis of Reformed standards, and this too was exported back to Scotland. Here, perhaps alone in Europe, revival and Reformed Orthodoxy were not easily separated in anyone's mind. By the early eighteenth century, however, both revival and Orthodoxy had waned among Irish Presbyterians. Irish Presbyterian ministers educated in Glasgow began to respond to the Age of Reason, and in 1726 they formed in Ireland a schismatic Antrim Presbytery, which refused to subscribe to the Reformed Orthodoxy of the Westminster Confession of Faith. The Orthodox Irish Presbyterians bitterly opposed these non-subscribing Presbyterians, many of whom were Arians, embracing a rational faith emphasizing morality and moderation. They insisted that Presbyterian ministers must subscribe to the Westminster Confession. This conflict in Irish Presbyterianism was speedily replicated in Pennsylvania, where it became complicated by the famous feuds fought by the Tennent family of Irish Presbyterian revivalists, the most important member of whom, Gilbert Tennent, had been decisively influenced by Frelinghuysen. The American Presbyteries on the whole had adopted a lax attitude to the Westminster Confession of Faith by the early eighteenth century. However, in response to the unrest stirred by the Tennents, many moderate Presbyterians in the Philadelphia Synod now hoped that required subscription to the Westminster Confession might be used to contain the revivalists and preserve unity within the church. Any hope of this was destroyed by the great revival led by Whitefield in 1739–40, and Gilbert Tennent's ferocious attack on unconverted ministers. The Philadelphia Synod broke up in 1741, the revivalist 'New Side' forming their own New York Synod. At this point Zinzendorf arrived in America, frightening Tennent, who then began to broach the possibility of Presbyterian reunion. In 1758, the severed wings of the Ulster tradition were reunited as communion was restored between the synods of New York and Philadelphia.

New England, the home, *par excellence*, of the Great Awakening, faced its religious problems with self-conscious assertions of its European character. Continued English immigration brought the Church of England on the eve of the American Revolution to its peak strength, and hoary rumours that a bishop was to be created for America excited unpleasant *frissons*. Anglicanism was attractive to those who thought that American disorder required the wholesale adoption of metropolitan institutions, and those who were tired of the 'insufferable enthusiastic whims' of the Whitefieldites. And there was a palpable threat from England's European enemy, France, and its client Indians. There were also pastoral problems. A church polity that had originally been designed to exclude all but the saints now simply ensured that church membership fell to very low levels. Children (who had often been the ringleaders in revival in Europe) were in America perceived as a special problem. Jonathan Edwards targeted this group in revival, but when he was dismissed from his parish in 1750, large numbers of the very young people he had admitted to church membership turned against him.

As far back as 1662, a solution had been attempted by a Massachusetts synod when it decided to restrict church membership to 'confederate visible believers . . . and their infant seed', but which also created a class of 'half-way members', subject to church discipline, and capable of transmitting baptism, but excluded from the Lord's Supper and from voting in church affairs. These half-way members had simply to 'own' the covenant, and they did so in great numbers during the late seventeenth century. This arrangement exposed the difference between those, especially of the Presbyterian tendency, who stressed the role of Christian nurture in regeneration, and those who looked to conversion. Despite this half-way covenant, however, the New England parish system continued to go downhill. Another route was taken by Solomon Stoddard (1643–1729), minister of Northampton, Massachusetts. He discarded the whole notion of covenants and adopted the ideal of a national church like the Church of Scotland. He admitted all respectable adults to communion, and put his faith in powerful preaching. He was rewarded by five separate harvests of souls, the last one being posthumous, after his parish had passed to his grandson, Jonathan Edwards, who described it in the most famous tract of the revival, the *Faithful Narrative of the Surprising Work of God*.[5] This tract, first published in England in 1737, and rapidly put into German by Steinmetz, spoke to hopes and fears widely held.

There would not be a bigger outbreak of revival in New England until the heavy hand of the Reformed ministry was loosened. This loosening was achieved by two visitors from the Middle Colonies, George Whitefield and Gilbert Tennent. Whitefield was already a master of the arts of advertisement when he arrived in New England in 1740. Despite liberally abusing unconverted New England ministers, he at first received the support of most of them because they knew that if he succeeded with his conversions the demands of the half-way covenant in those parishes which maintained it, and the objects of preaching in the Stoddardean parishes, would both be satisfied. Whitefield offered a kind of liberation by inverting the jeremiad, and implying that the trouble with New England was not an unregenerate people but an unconverted ministry. The great crowds he assembled made 'distinguishing' preaching in Frelinghuysen's style impossible; rather, Whitefield effectively dramatized the message of the New Birth, pruned of the laborious Puritan morphology of conversion, in the languages of the Bible, the market-place and human emotion. When the Holy Spirit grasped a man's soul it was a great and self-validating experience. Thus abnormal psychological phenomena which had been marginalized as enthusiasm in the old Puritan system might now be regarded as evidence of spirit-possession.

In response to these phenomena, church authority made its comeback. James Davenport, who on the authority of Acts 19:19 burnt religious books, was twice judicially found insane; Jonathan Edwards began insisting that those applying for church membership must give a strict testimony to the work of grace, and in 1750 he was thrown out of his parish. Whitefield, unable to rally the same breadth of ministerial support, never again enjoyed the same preaching success. By 1744 the awakening in New England was virtually over.

The awakening, however, experienced a second and prolonged period of life on the other side of the Atlantic, in the United Kingdom and the United Provinces. A central role in the propaganda for this stage of the revival was taken by a group of Church of Scotland ministers. John Gillies, Church of Scotland minister of the College Church in Glasgow, updated the Acts of the Apostles in his *Historical Collections of Accounts of Revival*, published in four volumes between 1754 and 1786.[6] But it was Whitefield who helped to unify both the friends and enemies of the revival by focusing the division of spirits on himself.

In England as on the continent the refugee question had left its mark. The Dissenting divine and hymn-writer Philip Doddridge was the grandson of a Bohemian refugee and had a hot line to Johann Adam Steinmetz of Teschen who had Doddridge's *Family Expositor* translated into German as an antidote to Moravianism. Huguenots gathered round Wesley and were thickly clustered in parts of the East End and old West End of London where his work had begun. In the French-speaking Perronet family he picked up victims of Swiss High Orthodoxy. Among the Palatines, who had been planted in the south of Ireland early in the eighteenth century, Wesley found an almost Silesian situation. Deprived of their church, but clinging to the Luther Bible, the Palatines in Ireland rallied enthusiastically to him, and they later took their Methodism to America. The British shared with their co-religionists abroad a fear of 'atheism', and a panic at the prospect of a final Armageddon between Catholic and Protestant, with evangelicals prominent among the propagandists. Wesley had come out of the narrowest of Jacobite stables, while Whitefield was patronized by William Pulteney, Earl of Bath. The Georgia enterprise which first brought them into public life was conducted by a nest of Jacobites. Wesley returned home from Georgia with a broad world-view and a knowledge of the continental church-situation which he had not had before. Once back in England, he encountered the most public of the policy failures of the eighteenth-century church – Bishop Edmund Gibson's humiliating repudiation of his alliance with the Whig party. Only private enterprise, it seemed, could now save the Church of England, and only the Tory–country–party alliance, bent on circumscribing the powers of the Hanoverian court, could provide a sympathetic political milieu. Wesley had taken a great deal of high-church and mystical baggage with him to Georgia in 1735, and had there initiated himself into the practical theology of almost every Lutheran school and of Tersteegen as well. He could only prune this excess of devotion by conversion; the pattern to hand was that of Moravianism, and the occasion was likely to be 'while one was reading Luther's Preface to the Romans' as was now nearly compulsory on the continent. It took time for even conversion to see Wesley through the maze. He quickly broke up the Fetter Lane society where he had been converted, and took the side of Halle in the great European conflict with Moravianism; so did Whitefield with his practical interest in orphan-house management. Both were drawn into the Methodist circle around the Countess of Huntingdon, who hoped for a fundamental reform of church and state once the present court of George II was succeeded by the Leicester House entourage of Frederick, Prince of Wales. This dream was ended by the accidental death of Frederick in 1751.

The British revival began first in Wales, where a sustained campaign by the Society for Promoting Christian Knowledge (SPCK) to assimilate Wales to the English language, culture and religious establishment, generated by reaction a religious revival which ended by being Welsh, evangelical and Dissenting. A key figure in the Welsh revival was the Anglican rector of Llanddowror, Griffith Jones, who recognized that as any such Welsh assimilation was only conceivable in the very long term, it was futile to make the Welsh drag through their devotional exercises in English. So he trained schoolmasters in his parish at Llanddowror, and circulated them around Wales during the winter season of slack employment to teach pupils to read the Welsh Bible and learn the church catechism. Jones's scheme (publicized under the Hallesian title of 'Welch Piety') was an instant success, and by the time Jones died, 3,495 circulating schools had been set up in Wales, and over 158,000 scholars had passed through them. The SPCK also poured an immense quantity of literature, mainly devotional, into Wales. Most of this was targeted at heads of families. In 1695, some 44 per cent of the Welsh population were reckoned to be under the age of sixteen, so the heads of families occupied a priestly position of immense potential importance; the evangelicals exploited it to secure 'tribal' adhesions on a great scale.

Daniel Rowland (1713–90) and Howel Harris (1714–73) each have some claim to be the father of the Welsh revival. Rowland, curate of Llangeitho, moderated Griffith Jones's denunciatory method to become a successful revival preacher. Harris, an irascible and complex character, became the archetypal unordained exhorter, warning the flock to flee the wrath to come. Although very Welsh, he wrote almost exclusively in English, attracted into Wales the whole English evangelical circus, and helped to make Whitefield the leader of Welsh Methodism. In touch with Halle, Herrnhut and New England, Harris was also linked with the Scots revivalists and with the Prince of Wales's court at Leicester House. By the time he parted company with Rowland in 1750, there were 433 religious societies in Wales and the borders, and nineteenth-century Welsh religious life was already beginning to take shape. The Calvinistic Methodists were much the largest of the Welsh movements, and these movements had already made their compromises with the tribal structure of Welsh society. Pembrokeshire was the stamping ground of Howel Davies, but its substantial English population also attracted Wesley, Whitefield and the Moravians. Cardiganshire and Carmarthenshire were pre-eminently the territories of Rowland and William Williams of Pantcelyn. Radnor, Montgomeryshire and Brecknock were the mission field of Howel Harris. Glamorgan and Monmouth were the most densely populated, and felt the power of the revival most deeply, partly because they attracted English as well as Welsh revivalists.

The Scottish problem was singular. By the Act of Union with England in 1707, the Kirk had received every conceivable guarantee, but it had to fight its way into the Highlands, and in the Lowlands where patronage issues were sore it was suspected of being an agent of English assimilation. The Scots Orthodox, like the Reformed Orthodox elsewhere, bewailed the degeneracy of the times, but their peculiar yardstick was the recollection of mass revival in early seventeenth-century Ulster and the West of Scotland. In the Highlands there was a stark struggle against armed Jacobites and often violent Catholics and Episcopalians. John Balfour, minister of Nigg in 1730, found a way to penetrate Gaelic society. He formed a fellowship meeting of his elders and a few others, which enabled them to acquire real expertise in prayer, the exposition of the Scriptures and experiential religion. This enabled them to establish public benchmarks for Highland religion, and to determine who might be admitted to communion. This system of fellowship meetings issued in deep and lasting revival, and opened the way to an evangelical conquest of the Highlands of a kind the English church could never achieve in Wales. The

Lowlands, however, were strategically decisive, and here patronage questions were crucial. The Erskine brothers seceded from the Church of Scotland in 1733 over their objections to both patronage and what they perceived as the dominance of rationalism and moderatism in the church. Within thirty years their Secession Church had gathered over a hundred congregations. In 1741 they invited Whitefield himself to join the work. The Erskine's movement looked like revival but was actually the old Presbyterian way of reform by secession and discipline. Upon his arrival in Scotland, Whitefield instantly found himself denounced by Cameronian hotheads, and he soon distanced himself from the Seceders and won his greatest triumphs in the established Church of Scotland, in the company of Leicester House forces who were seeking to change the balance in the Scottish church. In the troubled parish of Cambuslang, its minister, William McCulloch, had been labouring without significant impact since being installed in the parish in 1731. Then in 1741, the parish became the centre of a large-scale revival; with Whitefield's assistance the revival spread to other parishes by contagion and personal connection. The Last Days seemed at hand, but as in New England, the Cambuslang revival in Scotland bloomed but for a day.

However irascible at home, Harris was a peacemaker in Methodism outside Wales. There was indeed a British Methodism, which was a movement and never became a denomination; and there were others who helped to keep differences within bounds, to sustain networks which extended from eastern Europe to America and to preserve a common, unifying 'myth' about the regenerating work of Halle. All the main figures were establishment men who did not want to organize a new denomination – even in Presbyterian Scotland the Episcopalians Whitefield and Wesley tried to act within the established church. In London the religious societies had created a consolidated market ripe for the evangelists even before Whitefield arrived. These societies provided a springboard and a model for advances elsewhere, but they also showed that the sort of community revival aspired to in New England was not possible in London. Even Moravianism established its headquarters in London between 1749 and 1755, Zinzendorf competing with Wesley for political advantages from the Tory and Leicester House connexions. It was hard for English Dissenters to enter the Methodist company. Abiding loyalties to the Whigs had kept them from a Tory and Jacobite milieu, at least until their disgust with the Whig prime minister, Sir Robert Walpole, had sunk deep; by the mid-eighteenth century, the universal pledges of Protestant loyalty to the British state expressed during the 1745 Jacobite rebellion made unity between Methodists and English Dissenters easier. Philip Doddridge in particular became a 'Methodist' in the sense that he was drawn into the movement for revival and reform, and entangled in the web of the Countess of Huntingdon and Frederick, Prince of Wales. It needed friends and contacts in New England to convince the English Dissenter and hymn-writer, Isaac Watts, that the revival promoted by Jonathan Edwards was actually in the spirit of the moderate seventeenth-century Puritan, Richard Baxter, and thus to allay Watts's suspicions of the whole movement.

By 1750, the revivals in America, in the Baltic and most of Europe were over, and the days were numbered for the Methodist coalition in England. Doddridge died in 1751; so did Frederick, Prince of Wales. Frederick's death and untimely breaking of the normal cycle of British politics ensured that Whitefield would never be made a bishop and that the revival would never be more than a movement in the country. In 1753, Wesley himself was seriously ill and wrote his own epitaph; he survived, but his confidence in creating a religious society within the established Church of England was at its lowest ebb. He was at his sourest towards many old friends. In Wales, meanwhile, Howel Harris had fallen out with Daniel Rowland. The Moravians faced bankruptcy. Whitefield could not repeat his early successes in New England and Scotland. Circumstances came to the rescue. The Seven Years' War broke out in 1756, apparently heralding the long-delayed day of reckoning between Catholic and Protestant, and evoking new revivals in both England and Wales. The national rally evoked by the elder Pitt's victories brought old irreconcilables back to court; more returned with the accession of George III, and still more (including Wesley himself) with the outbreak of colonial revolt in America and Ireland. All the time relations between the political authorities in Britain and Wesley's followers got easier, until, after his death, and in the shadow of bitter differences about the French Revolution, the political authorities and Wesley's followers again mostly separated. Then the problem of authority *within* Methodism surfaced for another century. Methodism in America thrived famously on the opportunity it afforded to the English there to affirm their ethnic origin on an anti-Anglican basis – almost the inverse of the original intention. But Wesley did contribute an intensity and regularity of action which was something new. In England, he took over small connexions in the Midlands and the north that had been created by others, and these, together with the work which Wesley and his brother Charles initiated in the Newcastle region, got them off the original unadventurous London–Bristol axis and launched them into every part of the United Kingdom. Many of Whitefield's English converts emerged as Independent ministers and evangelists in their own right, transforming the size, ethos and administrative assumptions of the community they joined.

In Wales, Harris and Rowland patched up their differences, and the revival regained its momentum.

The revival thus began almost everywhere in resistance to a real or perceived threat of assimilation by the modern state, and its timetable even in the west was set by the timetable of the Protestant crisis in eastern and central Europe where the threat was most crude. But what had begun as an effort to revive the smouldering embers of religious faith in the absence of the ordinary ecclesiastical mechanisms, a testimony to the priesthood of all believers, changed as it moved westwards into a clerically managed device for solving intractable pastoral problems; most dramatically in America it issued in the creation of vast bureaucratic machines on a scale unknown in the Old World. Nowhere, except perhaps in Wales, were the hopes of reform in church and nation realized, but both church and nation were changed. Theological pluralism became the normal condition of the churches, and in the Habsburg Empire Joseph II's Toleration Patent (1781) showed that even the New Leviathan was pursuing assimilation more cautiously.

Notes

1. Dalter Nigg, *Heimliche Weisheit. Mystische Leben in der Evangelische Christenheit* (Zurich and Stuttgart: Artemis Verlag, 1959), p. 137.
2. *The works of Jonathan Edwards*, ed. S. E. Dwight and E. Hickman, 2 vols. (1834; repr. Edinburgh: Banner of Truth Trust, 1974), vol. 1, pp. 276, 309; A. Heimert, *Religion and the American mind from the Great Awakening to the Revolution*, 2nd edn (Cambridge, MA: Harvard University Press, 1968), pp. 42–3.
3. *Works of Jonathan Edwards*, vol. 2, p. 31.
4. John Venn, *The life and a selection of letters of the late Henry Venn*, ed. H. Venn (London, 1834), p. 18.
5. *Works of Jonathan Edwards*, vol. 1, pp. 344–64.
6. Repr. Edinburgh: Banner of Truth Trust, 1981.

18

Toleration and movements of Christian reunion, 1660–1789

JAMES E. BRADLEY

The peoples of early modern Europe assumed the necessity of a single, state-sanctioned church that supported and legitimized civil authority. Political order in both Catholic and Protestant countries was firmly grounded upon religious foundations; lines of political authority devolved from emperor, king, or magistrate and then extended outwards through a Catholic, Lutheran, Reformed, or Anglican church and clergy. The theory called upon to enforce such confessional uniformity was fundamentally the same in all European nations. The Peace of Westphalia (1648) had aimed to reduce confessional conflict between states by recognizing the territorial ministry of religious establishments dating from 1624, but the terms of the settlement proved difficult to apply in practice. While Westphalia granted freedom to adherents of the three recognized confessions to immigrate from a principality unmolested, these liberal terms were sometimes used to get rid of unwanted minorities. Westphalia made no provision for the Jews, and it gave no rights to Protestant sects, whether old (Anabaptist and Socinian) or more recent (Pietist and Moravian). Hence, under the pressure of a resurgent Roman Catholicism on the one hand, and the growing claims of religious minorities on the other, the settlement of Westphalia soon appeared to be unworkable and temporary.

The confessional warfare between Catholic and Protestant states in the seventeenth century gradually gave way to intra-confessional conflict within states during the eighteenth century. The religious fissures that were to have the most influence on toleration were those opened by dissenters within the boundaries of early modern states. In each of the major confessions, whether Catholic, Lutheran, Reformed, or Anglican, it was the new forms of religious dissent – Catholic Jansenism, Lutheran Pietism, Dutch Arminianism, English Puritanism, and broadly, an 'awakened' Protestantism – that propelled the arguments and social movements towards more robust expressions of religious liberty. As the permanence of minority religious groups was gradually acknowledged, most governments came by slow degrees to adopt official policies of toleration, legally defined positions that allowed some diversity in religious expression at the same time that they maintained the privileged status of an established church. Toleration was thus a compromise that modified the long tradition of territorial and enforced religious uniformity, and while specific policies varied from state to state, some form of toleration preceded the practice of full religious equality, which in general was not attained until the nineteenth century (the only exceptions being several British colonies in North America).

The subjects of toleration and religious liberty are particularly vulnerable to teleological treatments that link human progress to the growth of freedom and secularization. Recent scholarship has sought to avoid this teleological tendency by demonstrating the episodic, halting, and incomplete progress of toleration and by balancing the theory of toleration against the equally plausible theory of a unitary, confessional state. Recent studies have also examined the interplay between the conceptual development and the actual practice of toleration, and they have employed comparative methods that examine ideas in the context of widely different cultures and historical circumstances. Attention has also been given to the specifically Christian sources of early toleration theory and to the local congregations that nurtured these ideas, while the well-known, canonical texts authored by religious sceptics and non-believers are placed within the broader religious and social framework.

Confessional states and toleration in France, Austria-Hungary, and the German lands

Since the early 1660s, the religious freedom of Reformed Protestants in France had been progressively reduced by Louis XIV, and his long-standing quest for religious uniformity culminated in the Revocation of the Edict of Nantes (1685). Calvinist church buildings were razed, the laity was forbidden to assemble, their children were to be baptized and educated by Catholics, and Reformed ministers were given two weeks to conform or leave the country. The harshness of the law produced widespread conformity, even among ministers, but it also led to the most extensive forced migration in early modern Europe, producing by the turn of the century some 160,000 Calvinist refugees. Jews, who were already severely restricted as to where they could reside in France, suffered from a similar policy when they were exiled from the French colonies. Active suppression of Protestants by the government did not extend far into the eighteenth century, although an edict of 1724 did reaffirm the anti-Protestant legislation of the previous century, and local officials initiated sporadic attacks, particularly in the south of France where Protestants were numerous.

Forms of Catholic dissent were also discriminated against, though without the harshness directed against Protestants. The papal bull *Unigenitus* (1713) condemning certain tenets attributed to Jansenism had the French crown's blessing and substantial, if mixed, support from the French episcopate. Towards the mid-eighteenth century, depending on the position taken by local bishops and parish priests, some Jansenists even found themselves restricted in their access to the sacraments and effectively transformed into a community of suffering not unlike that of the French Calvinists.

From the mid-1750s onwards, however, growing royal indifference to Protestants at home and diplomatic relations with Protestant countries abroad converged with favourable changes in elite public opinion to diminish the severity of religious persecution. Despite several notorious executions of Protestants in Toulouse (the case of Jean Calas was made famous by Voltaire's *Treatise on Tolerance*, 1763), these decades witnessed a tacit recognition by the government of the right of Protestants to exist, and in this freer atmosphere, Protestants and dissident Catholics alike began to flourish. Protestants grew bolder in the organization of regional and national synods, while by mid-century French Jansenists were largely free from the discriminatory effects of *Unigenitus*, particularly with respect to their freedom to receive the sacraments. In their struggle against the Roman Catholic imposition of sacramental uniformity, both Jansenists and *philosophes* appealed to traditional Gallican liberties and the rule of law that respected individual conscience. Though Jansenists were troubled by the religious indifference of the *philosophes*, concern over the suffering of Protestants helped forge unexpected alliances. For example, the abbé Jacques Tailhé and Gabriel-Nicolas Maultrot in their *Questions on Toleration* (1758) adopted aspects of Montesquieu's *The Spirit of the Laws* (1748) on natural law while elaborating their own Jansenist arguments.[1] Writings supporting civil toleration for French Protestants appeared frequently after the late 1750s, and culminated in the Edict of Toleration signed by Louis XVI in 1787. The edict did not allow Protestants freedom of public worship or recognize Reformed ministers, but it did grant Reformed Protestants civil authentication of births, marriages, and burials, and it promised them freedom to pursue business without disturbance, thereby securing them a measure of legal and social legitimacy.

Similar impulses towards religious uniformity were found in the absolutist Habsburg Empire. The Habsburg emperor traditionally saw himself as the leader of Catholic Europe. Moreover, with the threat of further Ottoman advances into Europe, the need for a strong Catholic political and military order in Hungary, Austria, and the lands bordering Bavaria and Saxony seemed compelling. But there were many Protestants in these Habsburg dominions; indeed, in Silesia Protestants were the majority and they remained numerous in eastern Hungary, where even the most liberal forms of Protestantism had been tolerated from the early seventeenth century. In the principalities of Salzburg and Tyrol, a revived Protestant movement provoked the local authorities to expel many Protestants forcibly in the mid-1680s, while in Hungary, Habsburg policy in the 1690s sought to reduce Protestant rights to private worship only, mirroring contemporary policies in France. Religious repression, however, paradoxically contributed not to the demise of Protestantism, but to its awakening. Protestant religious revival in Salzburg, on the one hand, and an aggressive archbishop, on the other, culminated in a crisis in 1731 when the archbishop expelled some 20,000 Protestants from the principality. Many refugees found a home in Prussia, and the episode became a *cause célèbre*, with newspapers, sermons, and pamphlets denigrating the archbishop and calling for greater toleration. The unifying instincts of Charles VI, however, only hardened into a yet more repressive policy. An imperial resolution of 1733 denied the right of free emigration which had been given to religious minorities by the Peace of Westphalia, and it mandated military service, forced labour, and forcible transportation of Protestants as the means to control, if not to suppress, religious dissent.

Maria Theresa carried the repressive policies of Charles VI well into the second half of the century, even extending them by persecuting the Jews of Bohemia and Moravia. With the co-regency of Joseph II, however, a move towards greater tolerance became clearly discernible. The lessons of the widespread protests over Salzburg had not been lost on Joseph, and with his Patent of Toleration (1781) Lutheran and Reformed Protestants as well as Greek Orthodox Christians were granted the right to form congregations and erect church buildings, though towers and church bells were forbidden and non-Catholics were required to pay customary fees to Catholic priests. Protestants also gained property and civil rights, and Jews acquired freedom of worship in private, with further rights (of residence and education) extended to the Jews in 1782. Under these new conditions of freedom, Hungarian Protestants contributed to the renewal of Protestantism in Bohemia and Moravia. However, as Joseph sought to protect the privileged status of the Catholic Church (even as he abolished religious orders and held Rome at arms length), the new spirit of toleration remained fragile. When, in 1783, a few hundred peasants in Bohemia denied the Trinity, the Emperor promised them a 'sound beating' if they professed their beliefs publicly. Under the successors of Joseph II, even this limited toleration did not survive.

More coherent and long-lasting expressions of religious toleration can be found outside France and the Holy Roman Empire. In northern Europe, the Elector of Brandenburg, a member of the Reformed Church, ruled over a state that was predominantly Lutheran, and here, as elsewhere, such an anomalous relation between ruler and ruled served to promote religious toleration. From early in his reign, Frederick William, 'the Great Elector', sought to foster understanding and peace between Calvinists and Lutherans in his realm. Brandenburg-Prussia had been seriously depopulated by the wars of religion, and the need to attract settlers provided another powerful incentive for toleration. Thus, Frederick William welcomed the Jews expelled from Vienna in 1670, and within weeks of the Revocation of the Edict of Nantes, he issued the Potsdam decree which guaranteed the French Protestants legal rights in Brandenburg and offered them government subsidies. Pietists exiled from Saxony in 1690 also found a home in Prussia, with important implications for the future of toleration.

Frederick William I, King of Brandenburg-Prussia (ruled 1713–40) not only welcomed the exiles from the principality of Salzburg in the fiasco of 1731–32, he also arranged safe passage for the refugees, provided for their care on the way, and offered them support when they arrived in East Prussia. By mid-century, as rationalism at the University of Halle gradually supplanted the university's earlier ethos of Pietism, the new forms of thought gained the support of Frederick II 'the Great' of Prussia (1740–86). However, Frederick's well-known patronage of Enlightenment figures, his personal indifference to religion, and his much publicized promotion of the rights of private judgement need to be viewed in light of his more traditional, pragmatically oriented policy on toleration. To be sure, the seventeenth-century works of Samuel Pufendorf and the later writings of Gotthold Ephraim Lessing, for example, *Nathan the Wise* (1778), undoubtedly contributed to the atmosphere of toleration in Brandenburg-Prussia. But public peace, order, and military strength were paramount for Frederick. His general regulation for the Jews of 1750 was repressive, with restrictions about where Jews could live and build synagogues. Moreover, his welcoming of religious dissenters in 1763 did not extend to the unfettered freedom of public worship. The first general Prussian edict on toleration (1788) was promulgated only after Frederick II's death. It guaranteed private liberty of conscience; it extended state protection for private worship to Jews, Mennonites, and Moravians; and it sought to regulate public proselytizing, since missionary activity bore directly on the question of public peace and order.[2]

At the same time, the edict assumed a privileged place for Christianity; the church in Prussia was clearly to remain in the service of the state.

In the central German lands, many smaller principalities remained confessionally divided, both at the level of principality and city, especially in the northwest and the lower Rhineland. Two experiments in toleration that attained some notoriety emerged in the upper Rhineland and in Saxony. In the Wetterau, a group of Reformed principalities to the north and east of Frankfurt, religious dissenters were welcomed from 1712. Here, refugees for conscience sake were admitted, provided they were willing to pay a fee and promised to become hard-working and orderly citizens; the Wetterau provided some security for Protestants from the Cévennes region of France as well as for Pietists. On a smaller scale, Count von Zinzendorf, who had himself avidly studied the works of Pierre Bayle, founded a religious refuge on his estate of Herrnhut in Saxony. In the 1730s, Herrnhut attracted persons persecuted for their religious beliefs from neighbouring Bohemia and Moravia, but Zinzendorf's innovative inter-confessional vision made him anathema to the authorities, both Lutheran and Catholic, and when forbidden to return to Herrnhut, he experienced an unsettled, peripatetic existence until he left Europe for the New World.[3] Beyond the Wetterau, Herrnhut, and Brandenburg-Prussia, the greatest promise of toleration and security for Protestant Dissenters (including Moravians and Pietists) lay in the Netherlands, England, and the New World.

Confessional states and toleration in the North Atlantic before 1700

The first extended public debate over toleration in Europe occurred amid the upheavals of the English civil wars. At about the same time, the most innovative experiments in religious liberty were attempted in the New World. Colonists from England and the Netherlands put in place several practical schemes of toleration that illustrated the halting development of religious freedom. The Catholic George Calvert, First Lord Baltimore, obtained a grant for Maryland and primarily for pragmatic reasons he granted freedom of worship to non-Catholics (1632). Maryland's Act of Toleration in 1649, however, did not prevent the return of intolerance following the establishment of Anglicanism there in 1692. Not content with merely a Christian toleration, Roger Williams wished also to grant freedom to Jews in the settlement of Rhode Island from 1644. English advocates of toleration, including Williams, had already appealed to the example of religious freedom in the Netherlands, and not surprisingly, the patterns of the Old World prevailed in New Netherlands, with the Dutch granting indulgence to dissenting religious groups before the English took over the colony in 1664. Experimentation, however, was by no means universal in the New World: the Anglican and Congregational colonies of Virginia and Massachusetts reflected the ideals of the Old World confessional regimes, and in Massachusetts in particular, where Congregationalists were established as firmly as the Presbyterians in Scotland, no dissent in religion was tolerated before the late 1670s.

In the United Provinces, freedom of conscience was guaranteed to the individual, but the practice of toleration varied from region to region. The Dutch Reformed Church possessed a privileged status as the established church, with ministers' salaries paid by the state and church members possessing sole right to hold public office. Roman Catholics were susceptible to persecution because of the perception that they would promote political rebellion. Catholic public worship was outlawed and the rights of citizenship were often denied to Catholics in the eastern regions of the Republic, though Catholic rights were consistently recognized in Holland. Catholics adopted practical strategies of accommodation that allowed a more or less peaceful co-existence, though strong anti-Catholic sentiment at the local level was an abiding threat.[4]

Trinitarian Protestant dissenters, such as Remonstrants (or Arminians), Mennonites and Lutherans, were also tolerated. The Dutch authorities rejected a strict one-state, one-confession principle early in the seventeenth century when they accommodated the Mennonites on matters of oath-taking, pacifism, and marriage. Even the building of Mennonite churches was allowed, though not on main streets. No formal legal document was issued pertaining to the Jews, but the fact that they were a clearly defined immigrant group with well-guarded communal boundaries encouraged the civil authorities to exercise great lenience towards them, especially in Amsterdam. Jewish synagogues, unlike Mennonite churches, were prominent, but the Jews were consistently excluded from the guilds. Socinianism (the denial of the essential divinity of Christ) and atheism were outlawed, with those who publicly denied accepted Christian doctrine risking fines and imprisonment for blasphemy.

Following the Restoration of the Stuarts to the throne of England in 1660, religious minorities in England experienced far greater difficulties than did orthodox dissenters in the United Provinces. Initially the Puritans had the promise of Charles II that they would be treated fairly (indeed, Presbyterians had assisted in his Restoration), but in the parliament of 1661 they faced a disciplined corps of Anglicans determined to place Anglicanism on such a secure foundation that it could never again be overthrown. The Act of Uniformity (1662) required episcopal ordination and the use of the Book of Common

Prayer. Between 1660 and 1662 some 2,000 clergy, lecturers, and fellows were ejected from their livings and became thereby Nonconformists.[5] Additional restrictive laws were designed to enforce religious uniformity, and these laws bore upon Presbyterians, Congregationalists, Baptists, and Quakers alike. The Corporation Act (1661) specified that candidates for local office must take the sacrament of the Lord's Supper according to the rites of the Church of England at least one full year *before* such election. The Test Act (1673) accomplished for high government office what the Corporation Act did for the municipalities, though it was intended specifically to exclude Catholics and allowed the sacrament to be received within at least three months of admission to office. The Conventicle Act and the so-called Five Mile Act effectively dispersed the Nonconformist laity and silenced their clergy.[6]

The harshness of the law was sporadically mitigated by short-lived Declarations of Indulgence issued by Charles II and James II. These temporary Indulgences, however, were hardly satisfactory from the perspective of the Nonconformists. Recent investigations in local history have shown that persecution, though sometimes meliorated by lenient local magistrates, was both harsh and extensive, particularly against Quakers.[7] Opponents of the Anglican establishment were forced underground, and while numerous challenges to religious policy found their way into print, authors and publishers of these pamphlets laboured under considerable hazard. William Penn's imprisonment, however, combined with his connections in high government circles, had a salutary effect by promoting the founding of his holy experiment of Pennsylvania (1682). Penn's remarkable policy of religious liberty for all persecuted groups led to a flood of emigrants from the Old World and produced a religiously diverse population. But even in Pennsylvania, as the Keithian schism of 1691–93 amply demonstrated, religious freedom had its limits.[8] The Quaker George Keith was disowned by the American Quakers over his criticisms of their teaching and discipline, and departed with his followers.

In Scotland, episcopacy was forcefully reintroduced with the Restoration. Roughly mirroring events in England, royal indulgences in Scotland allowed some Presbyterian ministers to function pastorally, but there were also Presbyterian rebellions, and government policy turned against the toleration of dissent after 1674, leading to the progressive suppression of Presbyterianism and to the 'killing time' of the 1680s. In Ireland, on the other hand, Charles II's policy was to re-establish Anglicanism, but to be lenient towards Presbyterians and Catholics. James II went a step further, favouring Irish Catholics and promoting their interests. The king's tolerant religious policy in Ireland helped galvanize the opposition to his reign and contributed to his downfall.

In England, the Revolution of 1688–89 shaped a new political context in which Whig leaders in parliament were able to construct a more moderate solution to the religious problem. The Act of Toleration (1689) exempted Trinitarian Dissenters from the penalties imposed by the former legislation, provided they took oaths of allegiance and supremacy. It permitted them freedom to worship if their ministers subscribed to thirty-four of the Thirty-nine Articles.[9] The Dissenters, however, were required to meet in unlocked buildings, pay tithes and church rates, and register their places of worship. The Act of Toleration did not permit any church or group of churches to set itself up as a rival to the established church, and it did nothing to relieve the consciences of Catholics, Jews, and non-Trinitarians. While the Revolution of 1688–89 was a new beginning in one sense, for English Dissenters it continued what was begun in 1662 by forcing them into a separate and politically inferior status, though, to be sure, without a great deal of active repression. Roman Catholics fared far worse: the laity was allowed to worship in private, but they were vulnerable to double taxation, their priests were proscribed, and the threat of harassment and imprisonment was ever present.

While the Revolution indicated that a single ecclesiastical establishment for all three kingdoms was unworkable, moderate solutions for Scotland and Ireland proved elusive. Following the Revolution of 1688–89, episcopacy in Scotland was abolished and between two and three hundred episcopal priests were driven from their parish churches. In June 1690, the Presbyterian Church was established by law. The General Assembly harassed episcopal clergy throughout the 1690s, alleging their disloyalty to the crown.[10] Most Scots episcopalian clergy were indeed Jacobite in sympathy and they became increasingly so under the pressure of a Scottish Presbyterian state. In Ireland, under the conditions of an enforced exile, James II enjoyed a fleeting moment of triumph. In May 1689, with the Catholics in firm control of the Irish legislature, the legislature granted freedom of worship to Catholics, though it did not disestablish the Church of Ireland. This Catholic moderation did nothing to soften the severity of the Protestant reaction after James's Irish supporters were finally defeated in 1691, and by 1697 little was left of the toleration William III had originally envisioned for Ireland.

The theory and practice of toleration prior to the Bangorian Controversy (1717)

By 1689 there was a considerable literature on the subject of toleration. Baptists and Congregationalists had published significant treatises during the period of the civil wars and Commonwealth; thinkers in the humanist tradition, such as John Milton and those in the circle at Great Tew, had contributed a great deal in support of toleration, as had the Cambridge Platonists. Anglican Latitudinarians, who placed relatively little importance on dogma, ecclesiastical organization or liturgy, were ambivalent about toleration because they insisted upon a national church and would not allow the idea of liberty of conscience to extend to the point of separation from the established church.[11] Deists, however, consistently favoured toleration, and Commonwealthmen of both the orthodox and heterodox variety, who cherished the egalitarian ideals of the mid-seventeenth-century Commonwealth, would sustain and develop these views through the end of the eighteenth century. In the Dutch Republic, the toleration debate in the late seventeenth and early eighteenth centuries was advanced by well-known intellectuals utilizing the traditional scholarly vehicles of learned treatises and periodical essays written mostly in Latin.[12] The thought of Simon Episcopius (1583–1643) and Hugo Grotius (1583–1645) was deepened and extended by Philip van Limborch and Jean Le Clerc who advanced Dutch Arminian theories with their insistence upon the salvific efficacy of human free will and its compatibility with divine sovereignty. John Locke and Pierre Bayle were nurtured by their Dutch friendships and associations, but the two émigrés worked independently of each other. Early Dutch authors on toleration tended, like English Latitudinarians, to be Erastian in outlook (that is, tending to allow the ascendancy of the state over the church in ecclesiastical matters) and generally favoured a national church provided it was sufficiently broad and open.

Various classifications for the arguments in favour of toleration have been constructed – theological, philosophical, and political. In this period, however, theological arguments had unavoidable political overtones, and philosophical arguments about the will or the conscience or the limited nature of all human knowledge were almost without exception grounded in the Bible. Broadly speaking, the key to the early debate hinged on biblical interpretation and the extent to which the new covenant of grace could be separated from the old covenant of law. One dominant theme was that the New Testament era brought an end to the theocratic ideal, and that from Christ forward there was a clear distinction between spiritual and temporal authority which dispensed with the need for coercion in religious matters.

John Locke's *A Letter Concerning Toleration* (1689) built on this religious foundation and argued for an expanded toleration in a latitudinarian Anglican idiom. True belief, he said, is brought about not by compulsion, but by reason working through persuasion, and he grounded his arguments on the gospel principle of love for others. But while Locke wished to abolish the Test Act, he remained sympathetic to some form of comprehension, and like most Anglicans and Dissenters he was reluctant to grant full toleration to Catholics. The question of Locke's impact on the eighteenth century is the subject of ongoing debate; the Nonconformists frequently appealed to him, even as they relied upon their own apologists. The essential theoretical defence of full religious liberty came from the Presbyterian Edmund Calamy, Jr., who, while conversant with Locke, argued in his influential *Defense of Moderate Non-Conformity* (1703–05) that the *raison d'être* of Nonconformity was the refusal to allow civil or religious authority to exercise any power over an individual's conscience. Calamy understood the two defining principles of English Nonconformity to be: (1) the right of private judgement (Christ as the sole lord of conscience) and (2) the spiritual and therefore voluntary nature of the church (Christ as sole lawgiver in his own kingdom).

The practice of Nonconformity, however, is as important as its theory for understanding the history of toleration. Within a year of the Revolution of 1688–89, almost 800 temporary and 143 permanent places of Dissenting worship were licensed in England. These separated congregations embodied a physical and social reality of the first importance. The English Nonconformists comprised a religious minority that, by 1715, numbered approximately 6 per cent of the population, and this alternative religious culture, including corporate meeting places, an articulate intelligentsia, and a separate educational system, provoked a significant reaction. The entire Nonconformist tradition came under the probing criticism of both High Churchmen and Latitudinarians. Such authors argued that right belief, just like moral behaviour, ought to be encouraged by the state and that compulsion could redefine a people's understanding and render them more docile. Anglican apologists were motivated as much by genuine pastoral and educational concerns as they were by political and social issues of good order and deference.[13]

During the reign of Queen Anne (1701–14), a serious High Church effort was made to reverse the religious settlement shaped by the Act of Toleration, and return to the more repressive policy of the period before 1689. These were pivotal and defining years for English Nonconformists. From the later seventeenth century, Nonconformists had been increasingly utilizing a loop-hole in the Corporation Act, and by occasionally receiving the Anglican sacrament of the Lord's Supper at a parish church, they were technically qualifying themselves for political office. In 1702, this 'occasional conformity' became the subject of heated debate in parliament. High Church Anglicans viewed the practice as a devious attempt to undermine the proper social and electoral influence of the church and as a quasi-blasphemous abuse of holy communion. A second issue centred upon the Dissenters' educational institutions. A move in 1704 to wrest the Dissenters' academies from them cut to the heart of their legitimacy, for the Schism Bill, as it came to be called, threatened to destroy an educated Dissenting ministry. The political resurgence of the Tories gave the High Anglicans a temporary victory with the successful passage of both the Occasional Conformity (1711) and the Schism Acts (1714).

The accession of George I and the failure of the 1715 rebellion brought the Whigs back to power. The Whig victory was grounded in part upon a convergence of electoral interests between Low Church and Latitudinarian Anglicans, who sympathized with the Dissenters, and the Dissenters themselves. This alliance was nurtured on the Anglican side by Benjamin Hoadly, who became Bishop of Bangor in December 1715, and who grew increasingly critical of the use of the church's civil authority even as he advanced in its ranks. According to Hoadly, one could only believe what one sincerely considered to be right, and coercion in matters of faith and conscience was wrong. Hoadly's sermon 'The nature of the kingdom, or Church of Christ' provoked a strong High-Anglican reaction, but by 1717 there was considerable public support in favour of further relief for the Dissenters. Hoadly's arguments, while relying upon Locke, were framed in a more distinctly religious language that arguably had greater resonance with Dissenters and most Anglicans. With Whig majorities in parliament, both the Occasional Conformity and Schism Acts were repealed in 1719, and in the same year parliament passed an act that allowed Dissenters to retain local office if they were not challenged within six months of their appointment. As a result, many English Dissenters held municipal office, though their complaints against legal disabilities continued unabated.

The treatment of non-Trinitarians and Catholics under the Toleration Act in England demonstrated the abiding hegemony of the Anglican confessional state. While the Licensing Act was allowed to lapse in 1695, unshackling the freedom of the press, the Blasphemy Act of 1698 made non-Trinitarians liable to imprisonment for propagating their views. The law obviously had profound implications for Socinians and Jews. Those who published non-Trinitarian views or who openly questioned the miracles of Christ faced fines and imprisonment. Catholics were not uniformly persecuted by the government, and after the uprising of 1745 the attitudes of the political elite gradually softened, but popular anti-Catholicism could easily resurface and was rekindled with terrifying effect later in the century.

The Act of Union between England and Scotland in 1707 guaranteed the legal establishment of Presbyterianism in Scotland and thereby effectively established two churches under a single government. But in 1712 a Tory majority in the British parliament was able to pass the Scots Toleration Act which permitted public worship by Scottish episcopalians, provided their clergy took the oaths of obedience to the reigning monarch and abjuration of the Stuart claimant. The Act met with strong Presbyterian opposition in Scotland. The Toleration Act was followed immediately by the Patronage Act which restored ecclesiastical patronage to lay owners of livings, many of whom were episcopalians. When local congregations or presbyteries resisted the installation of patron's candidates into parish livings, the General Assembly felt obligated to instruct the presbyteries to install them according to the civil law. By the 1720s, patrons were becoming aggressive, abuses increased, and opposition to what many perceived as the General Assembly's growing power and influence eventually became the catalyst for the first theoretical defences of religious liberty in Scotland. Dissent in these circumstances took the form of Presbyterian secessions from the established church, but because the seceding congregations posed no political threat, no civil sanctions were pressed against them.

With the Church of Ireland comprising only about 10 per cent of the population, Ireland presented the anomalous situation of a minority religious body established by law. Protestants in Ireland were not happy with William III's lenience towards Catholics, and when they gained the upper hand in the mid-1690s, anti-Catholic legislation banished Catholic bishops and clergy living under rule. The confiscation of Catholic property followed in stages, and when combined with the denial of education, the franchise, and office-holding, these laws soon reduced Catholic political influence in Ireland to insignificance.[14] A flood of immigrants from Scotland in the 1690s meant that by the beginning of the eighteenth century Presbyterians in Ulster were more numerous than Anglicans. To address this situation, a Sacramental Test for office-holding was imposed by the Irish House of Commons in 1704 in terms almost identical to the English Law. About the same time, the legitimacy of Presbyterian marriages came under attack by the Church of Ireland, leading to prosecutions and even occasionally to prison sentences.

In 1705 the Synod of Ulster, the highest ecclesiastical court for Presbyterians in the north of Ireland, enacted a measure making subscription to the Westminster Confession compulsory for licentiates to the ministry. Toleration in Ireland was not connected to subscription to the Thirty-nine Articles as it was in England, and the subscription issue was an internal matter within Presbyterianism. The leader of Irish Presbyterian anti-subscription sentiment, John Abernethy, preached a sermon in 1719 entitled 'Religious obedience founded on personal persuasion' and thereby provoked a controversy among

Presbyterians that lasted nearly a decade. Faith is essential for salvation, said Abernethy, and by its very nature it must be deliberate, arising from the freest exercise of our understanding. Another Irish Presbyterian anti-subscriptionist, Thomas Nevin, based his arguments, like Hoadly, upon the spiritual nature of the church, criticized the law against blasphemy and boldly championed complete religious freedom for the Jews.

Movements for Christian reunion

Paradoxically, while toleration was one of the most divisive of political issues, its history was linked with efforts at Christian reunion, in both practical and theoretical terms. The best-known early modern theorists of Christian reunion were also ardent defenders of toleration: Hugo Grotius, Johannes Comenius, and the Scottish divine, John Dury. A serious theoretical attempt at broaching the Protestant–Catholic divide was explored in the extended correspondence between Gottfried Wilhelm Leibniz and Jacques Bénigine Bossuet between 1683 and 1700. When William Wake became Archbishop of Canterbury in 1716, he energetically set about to foster cordial relations and possible reunion with the Catholic Church in France. Wake commenced an extensive correspondence with L. E. Du Pin that led to theologians at the Sorbonne actually approving a remarkable proposal which, from the Catholic side, conceded such things as worship without the use of images and communion in both kinds. Wake's efforts with foreign Protestants were equally energetic, but both projects ultimately failed through lack of support from the civil authorities. Church politics also complicated efforts at reunion. In their quest for legitimacy, a few English and Scottish non-juring bishops made very tentative negotiations with the Greek and Russian Orthodox churches in 1716–22, but these efforts were of necessity conducted outside of the Anglican communion and hence were opposed and finally repudiated by Archbishop Wake himself.[15]

Most writers in the irenic tradition, however, aimed to secure the reunion of Protestants within a single national framework, and with few exceptions, the ideal of religious unity was connected to the assumed importance of a unified confessional state. In Brandenburg-Prussia, for example, Elector Frederick III (later King Frederick I) dedicated himself to the calming of religious conflict between the Lutherans and the Reformed, and he embarked on an ambitious plan to unite the two churches within his realm. He employed the court preacher Daniel Ernst Jablonski to promote religious compromise, and in an effort to find a suitable middle ground, he championed the use of the Anglican Book of Common Prayer (translated into German in 1704). In 1711 he even sought to obtain Anglican training for Prussian students of theology in the English universities, though without success. In the meanwhile, he promoted Pietism at the new University of Halle in an explicit effort to popularize the kind of inward piety and practical religion that could build bridges between confessional factions in the realm. Similarly, in the Netherlands, the established Reformed clergy were broadly sympathetic to dialogue with Lutherans, motivated in part by the desire to strengthen Protestantism in the face of Catholicism. Late seventeenth-century efforts between Reformed and Lutheran leaders foundered on theological differences, but in 1729 interest in reconciliation between Dutch Calvinists and Lutherans was restimulated by the writings of Johannes Mommers, and in 1747 these ideas were developed by Anthonie van Hardeveldt.[16]

In late seventeenth-century England, the principal aim of many Anglican churchmen was the comprehension of all English Protestants within a single established church. The desirability of union was felt all the more keenly in the wake of resurgent Catholicism abroad and the possibility of a Catholic king at home. In 1667–68, and again in 1680 and 1689, attempts were made to deal with the difficult question of reordination, and while these efforts ultimately failed, they did influence the terms of the Toleration Act. Following the Revolution, the idea of comprehending all Protestants within the established church did not attract wide discussion, but the ideal survived in the thought of Low Churchmen and pre-eminently in the person of Benjamin Hoadly, whose goal was to induce conformity by encouraging Dissenters to receive communion frequently at the parish church. Hopes for reconciliation between Anglicans and Nonconformists were set back by the events of Queen Anne's reign, although continued fear of a Catholic-supported Jacobite invasion kept the idea alive.

More was accomplished in practical terms of denominational cooperation through the Society for Promoting Christian Knowledge, founded in 1698. This Anglican organization provided support to numerous Lutheran missionaries during the eighteenth century. In the 1740s, Nonconformists Philip Doddridge and later Samuel Chandler proposed reunion with the established church and initiated talks with several bishops, including the Archbishop of Canterbury, Thomas Herring. The extent of Chandler's proposed changes to creed and liturgy probably doomed the effort from the outset, and in any case, the bishops were still thinking in terms of a comprehension that was unacceptable to many Dissenters.

What Anglicans and Nonconformists could not accomplish through direct methods was attained in limited ways through the unintended consequences of the Toleration Act. There were tensions between the three Nonconformist denominations (Presbyterians, Congregationalists, and Baptists), and between them and the Quakers, throughout the period. However, after 1689 it became appropriate to speak of a single Dissenting interest. The sacramental test for public office, the burdensome laws concerning marriage, and the onerous conventions regarding education put Dissenters of all varieties on an identical footing. Perhaps the most successful of all interdenominational associations was formed in London in 1732 for the common protection and defence of the civil rights of Presbyterians, Congregationalists, and Baptists. The Protestant Dissenting Deputies were intimately involved in the agitation for repeal of the Test and Corporation Acts, raising the funds for the legal defence of Dissenters, and providing legal counsel for a wide variety of subjects.

Toleration in the United Provinces, Britain, and Ireland, from the mid- to late eighteenth century

In the eighteenth-century Dutch Republic, most defenders of toleration continued to be drawn from religious bodies that dissented from the public church. For example, the Remonstrant Johannes Drieberge (1686–1746) advanced the views of his more famous Arminian predecessors, and the Mennonites were well represented by Herman Schijn (1662–1727), who not only argued for the legal recognition of Baptists, but also urged unity within their own ranks. In the Franeker school, however, the public church possessed a handful of advocates of a broad toleration who took issue with the privileges accorded the ecclesiastical authorities.[17]

A popular, rancorous, and public debate emerged in the United Provinces in the 1740s, and toleration remained a volatile political issue even after the formal separation of church and state in 1796. The spark for this long-standing debate was provided by the Mennonite minister Johannes Stinstra who pled for freedom of conscience in Friesland. Stinstra's association with Socinianism resulted in his suspension from the ministry, and in the aftermath of the Stinstra affair, the Frisian states, rather than growing more tolerant, actually became more repressive. After mid-century the debate engaged a wide public and began to address more controversial matters, such as natural law and virtue, with writers entertaining the possibility of salvation without the knowledge of Christian rudiments. The so-called Socratic War, a nationwide debate that lasted from 1769 to 1780, introduced the question of the superiority of non-Christian ethics and the desirability of a civic virtue divorced from revealed religion. The subsequent flowering of literature on toleration was accompanied by the appearance of an unprecedented number of vernacular publications, by the founding of new periodicals, and by the formation of societies. This literature was generally anticlerical in tone and tended to move towards an advocacy of equal rights for all. By the 1790s, religious diversity as a positive value began to prevail as the public status of religion gradually moved away from the traditional, confessional basis of control to an emphasis on an inward-looking, personal religion, which became viewed as sufficient to maintain social order and preserve the moral basis of society.[18]

In Hanoverian England, practical efforts to extend toleration under the Whig ascendancy engaged the best efforts of the three denominations, the Quakers, and the Jews in separate movements. From 1732 to 1740, the Dissenting Deputies co-ordinated the first extended agitation for repeal of the Test and Corporation Acts. The repeal movement created a vigorous, probing literature on both sides of the debate, extensively canvassing the issues of civil and religious liberty and bringing them before the public. The controversy over the Quaker's Tithe Bill overlapped with the first agitation for repeal and carried public debate on the nature and threat of Dissent into the early 1740s. The efforts of both the Deputies and the Quakers, however, were unsuccessful. The bill to naturalize the some 8,000 Jews residing in England, most of whom were foreign born and none of whom possessed the right to hold land, proved unusually divisive. The bill actually passed both houses of parliament in May 1753, but under extreme Tory opposition it was repealed the following December. In this debate, both secular humanitarian arguments for an expanded toleration for the Jews and arguments based on Christian theology were advanced.[19]

In the context of the American Revolution, opponents of established religion typically connected their criticism of the established church with radical Dissent in politics and disapproval of the government's policies abroad. In the Stamp Act crisis and the debate over American bishops there was a discernible quickening of the pace for expanded religious toleration at home. For example, Joseph Priestley's *An essay on the first principles of government* (1768) had more to do with religious liberty than with political reform. Adopting the language of both Calamy and Hoadly, Priestley argued that atheists should be freed from penal laws, while he questioned the need for religious establishments. Growth of theological liberalism in Arian and Unitarian directions prompted fresh opposition to the requirement to subscribe to the Thirty-nine Articles. Nonconformist Andrew Kippis observed that the Test Act deprived Dissenters of the enjoyment of certain civil honours and preferments, but the penal laws against non-Trinitarians deprived them of the common rights of human nature and of Christianity, and this harsher reality undoubtedly accounts for the greater volume, proportionately, of Arian and Unitarian writings on religious liberty.[20] Prompted by Archdeacon Francis Blackburne's *The Confessional* (1766), and led by Blackburne and Theolphilus Lindsey, the liberal Anglican anti-subscription movement of 1772, supported by the so-called Feathers Tavern petition, was launched and defeated in the same year. Only a few months after the defeat of the Anglican bill, the Dissenters made a similar, though unsuccessful, attempt to relieve their ministers and schoolmasters from the requirement of subscription. The Dissenting movement was a genuinely national effort; their petition bore the signatures of more than 850 Dissenting ministers, most of them orthodox Trinitarians. In the ensuing flurry of pamphlets and books, the number of orthodox authors who wrote in support of the anti-subscription cause equalled the number of heterodox authors.[21]

Two significant advances in toleration were made in England in the late 1770s. The Catholic Relief Act of 1778 repealed laws relating to Catholic schoolmasters and allowed Catholics to own property. Catholics were still debarred from public offices and the universities, however, and could not vote. In 1779, Trinitarian Nonconformist ministers and schoolmasters were exempted from subscribing to the Thirty-nine Articles provided they declared their belief in Scripture 'as the revealed will of God'. Non-Trinitarians, however, were still subject to the penalties of the Blasphemy Act. From 1787 through to 1790 there were three unsuccessful attempts to repeal the Test and Corporation Acts, and these campaigns provoked some of the most famous debates over religious liberty in the history of the House of Commons. In the midst of the first repeal effort in 1787, Priestley worked against the Blasphemy Act, not only for the sake of fellow Unitarians, but also on behalf of the Jews, but to no avail. By March 1790, the third repeal bill was doomed by the growing fear of the Revolution in France, as was any significant move towards toleration in general. C. J. Fox agreed to bring in a bill to repeal the penalties against Unitarians in 1791, but the effort failed.

Eighteenth-century Scotland presents no movement for religious equality comparable to that of England, but new claims for religious self-determination can be traced to the Presbyterian seceders. In the early 1730s, Ebenezer Erskine broke away from the Church of Scotland over the issue of patronage in a secession that took the name of the Associate Synod. Erskine and his colleagues insisted on the divine right of male communicants to choose their own pastors, and like their Dissenting contemporaries in England, they emphasized the right of private judgement and the spiritual nature of Christ's kingdom.[22] Another group of anti-patronage Presbyterians remained within the established church and came to be known as the Popular Party. Meanwhile, the moderate literati of Edinburgh, who controlled the General Assembly and exercised influence over church patronage, developed theories of civic virtue and unfettered public discourse, but strictly within the framework of a religious establishment. It was left to the seceders to challenge the dominance of the established church with respect to the rights of private conscience. During the period of the American Revolution both the Scottish Presbyterian seceders and the Popular Party expressed their dislike of an American episcopate; they also opposed the Quebec Act and the granting of relief to Catholics in England. The anti-Catholic perspective of Scottish seceders and the Popular Party paradoxically favoured greater religious freedom and was rigorously logical: popery was tyranny; clericalism among Protestants was a remnant of 'popery' and therefore to be resisted. In the 1790s, the seceder William Graham harked back to Hoadly's appeal to John 18:36 ('My Kingdom is not of this world') and produced one of the first comprehensive comparative critiques of religious establishments in Europe.[23]

Irish Presbyterians were comparatively successful in their century-long campaign for toleration. By the Toleration Act of 1719 they were granted a legally tolerated status; though the Test Act remained in place, it was little enforced. A relief act of 1737 legalized marriages performed by Presbyterian clergy. In the late 1770s, Presbyterian pressure to remove the sacramental test (and Presbyterian participation in the volunteer militia) contributed to the Toleration Act of 1780 by which the Irish House of Commons repealed the Test Act.[24] These successes can be attributed to both structural and demographic factors: Irish Presbyterians worked from a position of strength in that they were well organized and were approximately equal in numbers to members of the Church of Ireland. Because of the Catholic majority, a kind of practical toleration of Catholics prevailed; as early as the 1730s Catholics were beginning to build stone churches in the towns. As Irish Catholics did not participate in the Jacobite risings, government policy towards Catholics gradually eased from the mid-eighteenth century. The Catholic Relief Act of 1778 allowed them to own land and obtain an education; in 1793 they were granted the right to vote and admitted to the universities.

Interest in toleration forged a kind of international affiliation of like-minded people which served to promote church unity. The close interplay between Dutch and English defenders of toleration has recently been studied in detail, demonstrating a collaborative effort that went considerably beyond the influence of William III or the well-known friendship of Limborch and Locke. The eighteenth-century Dutch were thoroughly versed in the writings of Anglican latitudinarian divines, especially those of Samuel Clarke and Benjamin Hoadly. The English Dissenting tradition, mediated principally through the works of Isaac Watts and Philip Doddridge, was also important to Dutch tolerationists; Watts and Doddridge contributed to toleration in the United Provinces by providing a form of individualized piety that undermined confessional authority. The Dutch cited the English (and Swiss) defenders of religious liberty, not because their arguments were novel, but to give their views an added moral authority that was located outside the United Provinces.[25]

During the debate over introducing Anglican bishops into the North American colonies, English Nonconformists corresponded avidly with Congregationalists in New England. In Ireland the Presbyterian struggle against the Test Act drew inspiration from English Nonconformists. Some tenuous links have been discovered between the Scottish seceders, the Cambuslang revivals, and defenders of toleration in the United Provinces. During the American Revolution, Old Light and New Light Presbyterians (known formerly as 'non-subscribers' to the Westminster Confession) united with Old Light Presbyterians in support of American independence, and from 1791 Ulster Presbyterians also contributed to the short-lived alliance between Irish Protestants and Catholics for an independent Irish republic. In addition, there is considerable evidence of fraternal regard among the denominations at the local level in England. But none of these efforts actually resulted in the forging of formal institutional ties. Indeed, with the advent of Methodism and the growth of the Unitarian movement, Nonconformity in England became increasingly fragmented.

Toleration in the North American British colonies

In the British colonies at the time of the American Revolution, only Rhode Island, Pennsylvania, New Jersey, Delaware, and parts of New York legally guaranteed religious liberty. Pennsylvania still required a religious test for office-holders, while Rhode Island withheld the franchise from Jews. Eight colonies had some form of religious establishment at the onset of the war, and three New England states retained Congregational establishments well into the nineteenth century. In four of the five southern colonies, the Revolution undermined an already weak Anglican establishment. In the fifth, Virginia, the protracted debate over religious liberty between 1776 and 1786 had far-reaching implications because it bore directly upon the national government and the Constitution of the United States.

Presbyterians and Baptists in Virginia had enjoyed substantial growth during the later stages of the Great Awakening, while the conflict with England worked great hardship on the Anglicans. By 1776, the Anglicans were in an embattled position, even though they continued to control the colony's legislature. Under pressure from the dissenters, the Virginia Convention of 1776 declared, under its Declaration of Rights, all persons entitled to the free exercise of religion according to the dictates of conscience. But this declaration left the privileges of the Anglican Church and clergy untouched. Popular opposition to these limitations on toleration arose immediately from the Baptists and from the Presbyterians of Hanover County, bodies that had grown substantially during the Awakening and that were providing staunch support for the Revolutionary cause. The dissenters pressed their case under the expert leadership and guidance of James Madison and Thomas Jefferson, and during the next ten years they won successive debates concerning the issues of tithes, marriage, a general assessment for the support of religion, and the control of public charities. Jefferson's Bill for Establishing Religious Freedom was debated from 1779 to 1785 and finally became law in January of 1786. It stated that all persons shall be free to profess their opinions in matters of religion, and that the same shall in no wise diminish, enlarge, or affect their civil capacities.[26]

The debate in Virginia concluded on the eve of the Constitutional Convention in Philadelphia, and in the course of the nationwide debate over the Constitution it became clear that the goal of a stronger national government could not be realized without a Bill of Rights that would guarantee the separation of church and state at the federal level. The establishment clause of the First Amendment, ratified in 1791, forbade Congress from making any law 'respecting an establishment of religion, or prohibiting the free exercise thereof'.[27] But since powers not specifically delegated to the federal government remained with the states, the Congregational establishment was retained in three New England states until the first decades of the next century and then abolished only after fierce and costly struggles.

Most of the states of Europe and the North Atlantic witnessed some movement towards greater toleration in the eighteenth century which would eventually lead to full religious equality, but it was a movement that progressed in patterns both unpredictable and uncertain. The arguments of Enlightened thinkers, from Limborck to Locke to Jefferson, did anticipate the practice of religious freedom. But in every case in which we find substantial social and political change, the arguments for religious freedom were accompanied by the unremitting claims of religious minorities. This complex interplay between intellectual defences of toleration, the claims of dissenters, and the durability of the confessional states accounts for both the progress of toleration and the halting and incomplete nature of that progress.

Notes

1. Charles O'Brien, 'Jansenists on civil toleration in mid-eighteenth century France', *Theologische Zeitschrift*, 37 (1981), pp. 80–3.

2. Nigel Aston, *Christianity and revolutionary Europe, c.1750–1830* (Cambridge: Cambridge University Press, 2002), pp. 197–8; compare Ian Hunter 'Kant's religion and Prussian religious policy', *Modern Intellectual History*, 2 (2005), p. 8.

3. W. R. Ward, *The Protestant evangelical awakening* (Cambridge: Cambridge University Press, 1992), pp. 118–23.

4. Christine Kooi, 'Paying off the sheriff: Strategies of Catholic toleration in Golden Age Holland', in R. Po-Chia Hsia and H. F. K. van Nierop (eds.), *Calvinism and religious toleration in the Dutch golden age* (Cambridge: Cambridge University Press, 2002), pp. 88–9, 99–100.

5. 14 Car. 2, c. 4. *The Statutes,* rev. edn, 15 vols. (London: Eyre and Spottiswoode, 1870–78), contains the statutes referred to hereafter.

6. 13 Car. 2, stat. 2, c. 1 and 25 Car. 2, c. 2; 16 Car. 2, c. 4 and 17 Car. 2, c. 2. A second Conventicle Act (1670) softened the penalties but gave wider powers of enforcement.

7. Jeremy Gregory, *Restoration, reformation and reform, 1660–1828: Archbishops of Canterbury and their diocese* (Oxford: Clarendon Press, 2000), pp. 181–206. Compare Craig W. Horle, *The Quakers and the English legal system 1660–1688* (Philadelphia: University of Pennsylvania Press, 1988), pp. 279–84, with Adrian Davies, *The Quakers in English society 1655–1725* (Oxford: Clarendon Press, 2000), pp. 169–90, for evidence of local integration.

8. Andrew R. Murphy, *Conscience and community: Revisiting toleration and religious dissent in early modern England and America* (University Park, PA: The Pennsylvania State University Press, 2001), pp. 165–207.

9. 1 W. & M., c. 18.

10. Tim Harris, 'Reluctant revolutionaries? The Scots and the revolution of 1688–89', in Howard Nenner (ed.), *Politics and the political imagination in later Stuart Britain: Essays presented to Lois Green Schwoerer* (Rochester, NY: University of Rochester Press, 1997), pp. 99, 104, 107–8.

11. Richard Ashcraft, 'Latitudinarianism and toleration: Historical myth versus political history', in Richard Kroll, Richard Ashcraft, and Perez Zagorin (eds.), *Philosophy, science, and religion in England, 1640–1700* (Cambridge: Cambridge University Press, 1992), p. 155.

12. Ernestine van der Wall, 'Toleration and Enlightenment in the Dutch Republic', in Ole Peter Grell and Roy Porter (eds.), *Toleration in Enlightenment Europe* (Cambridge: Cambridge University Press, 2000), p. 114.

13. Mark Goldie, 'The theory of religious intolerance in Restoration England', in Ole Peter Grell, Jonathan I. Israel, and Nicholas Tyacke (eds.), *From persecution to toleration: The Glorious Revolution and religion in England* (Oxford: Clarendon Press, 1991), pp. 346–8.

14. D. W. Hayton, 'The Williamite Revolution in Ireland, 1688–91', in Jonathan I. Israel (ed.), *The Anglo-Dutch moment: Essays on the Glorious Revolution and its world impact* (Cambridge: Cambridge University Press, 1991), pp. 208–10; S. J. Connolly, *Religion, law, and power: The making of Protestant Ireland 1660–1760* (Oxford: Clarendon Press, 1992), pp. 263–74.

15. Judith Pinnington, *Anglicans and Orthodox: Unity and subversion 1559–1725* (Leominster: Gracewing, 2003), pp. 156–97.

16. Joris van Eijnatten, *Liberty and concord in the United Provinces: Religious toleration and the public in the eighteenth-century Netherlands* (Leiden: Brill, 2003), pp. 4–5, 119–40.

17. Johannes van den Berg, *Religious currents and cross-currents: Essays on early modern Protestantism and the Protestant Enlightenment*, ed. Jan de Bruijn, Pieter Holtrop, and Ernestine van der Wall (Leiden: Brill, 1999), pp. 253–67.

18. Van der Wall, 'Toleration and enlightenment', pp. 120–6; van Eijnatten, *Liberty and concord*, pp. 6–7, 9–11, 165, 295, 301, 363, 398–424.

19. Mel Scult, *Millennial expectations and Jewish liberties: A study of the efforts to convert the Jews in Britain, up to the mid nineteenth century* (Leiden: E. J. Brill, 1978), p. 67.

20. Stuart Andrews, *Unitarian radicalism: Political rhetoric, 1770–1814* (Basingstoke: Palgrave Macmillan, 2003), pp. 88–90, 108.

21. Anonymous, 'A view of English Nonconformity in 1773', *Transactions of the Congregational historical society*, 5 (1911–12), pp. 267–70.

22. John Graham, *The religious establishment in Scotland examined upon Protestant principles* (London, 1771), p. 275; also 61, 70, 166–7.

23. William Graham, *A review of ecclesiastical establishments in Europe* (Glasgow, 1792; 2nd edn. 1796), pp. vi, 73–86, 175.

24. J. C. Beckett, *Protestant dissent in Ireland 1687–1780* (London: Faber and Faber, 1946), pp. 49, 71, 76–8, 86–7, 102–4; compare Connolly, *Religion, law, and power*, p. 166. I. R. McBride, *Scripture politics: Ulster Presbyterians and Irish radicalism in the late eighteenth century* (Oxford: Clarendon Press, 1998), pp. 124–31, 146–8.

25. Van Eijnatten, *Liberty and concord*, pp. 90–102, 156–6, 201–3, 216, 440–6.

26. Rhys Isaac, *The transformation of Virginia 1740–1790* (Chapel Hill: University of North Carolina Press, 1982), pp. 147–54, 161–77, 279–85.

27. Thomas J. Curry, *The first freedoms: Church and state in America to the passage of the First Amendment* (New York: Oxford University Press, 1986), pp. 194–200.

PART IV

*

CHRISTIAN DEVELOPMENTS IN THE NON-EUROPEAN WORLD

19

Christianity in Iberian America

JAMES D. RILEY

In the second half of the seventeenth century, colonial Catholicism came of age in the Iberian New World. Magnificently ornate churches physically marked cities and towns in both the Spanish and Portuguese dominions, while flamboyant religious festivals, processions, and elaborately constructed displays of religious drama marked them culturally. As in much of Europe, piety and popular devotion were centred on the cult of the saints, devotions to miraculous images, and displays of penitential rigour.

Relations between church and state had stabilized, as well, in both empires. Priests and bishops functioned as royal bureaucrats, with privileges, salaries, systems of promotion, and responsibilities defined in law. While there were conflicts – the sixteenth-century struggles in the Spanish Empire between the religious orders and the episcopacy never went away – clergy, in general, lived in a universe marked by social respect, security and unwavering routine.

The new ideas of the eighteenth century challenged these Baroque structures intellectually and politically. Rational individualism attacked the emphasis on mystery and community, and physiocrats attacked the utility of the political partnership. The governments of Charles III and Charles IV (1755–1808) of Spain translated these ideas into policy in an effort to transform the Habsburg Empire into a Bourbon state. They took numerous steps to reshape the administration of the church and officially discouraged Baroque spirituality. In Portugal, as well, the government of Joseph I (1750–77) and his chief minister, the Marqués de Pombal, pursued similar measures. But how much did these monarchs achieve administratively in the colonies? And what effect did official attitudes have on the role of religion in colonial culture, as well as on the continuing process of evangelization on the mission frontiers? Those are the issues that this chapter will examine.

The Spanish state and the church in the New World

The reports on the church in the New World and the analysis of Bourbon ministers provide us with an unremittingly hostile critique of the physicality and emotionalism of the colonial religious experience, of the morality of conventual life, and of the excessive numbers and weak preparation of diocesan priests. While one can find these elements in official attitudes much earlier, what makes the Bourbon period distinctive is that in the 1750s royal support shifted sufficiently to permit officials to influence policy towards religion and the church. To paraphrase the pithy comment of one historian, reforming ministers were given leave to make the Indies a laboratory for liberal social reform.[1] As part of this effort, officials attempted to replace Baroque religious ceremonies with a more sedate set of religious performances and substitute a more rational and private religious foundation for what reformers considered pious nonsense in individual beliefs. In the interest of efficiency, the reformers also sought to reduce the number of clergy, end their independence from the direct control of the state, and change their role from that of collaborators in royal administration to that of salaried spiritual advisors.

The irony of the period is not that the Spanish reformers accomplished so much, but that they accomplished so little that was permanent. The only result of their attempts to suppress Baroque practices was to create a climate of hostility and a gulf between the culture of the educated elites and the mass of the population that would help bring about major difficulties in the nineteenth century. With regard to the institutional life of the church, in only two areas did crown policy have profound consequences: in the economic relationship between the church and the laity, and in the role of the regular orders in the life of the church. Bourbon policy also deeply affected the status of diocesan priests and, although the institutional changes were minimal, alienated this very important support of the crown.

The most important structural change resulting from Bourbon policy was its impact on the economic position of the church. Because of the prevailing piety, pious bequests and donations to support charitable activities and religious services had accumulated between the sixteenth and eighteenth centuries, allowing church institutions to amass substantial endowments. Unlike the situation in Spain, however, the mass of these funds had not been used to purchase land but consisted rather of liens on urban and rural property (called *censos perpétuos* because they had no fixed term for repayment) and cash that was loaned at interest (through a mechanism called *depósitos irregulares*). When the income from this liquid capital was combined with the regular revenues generated by the tithe, parish fees and other sources, it gave church institutions considerable financial independence from the crown and a substantial base of funds to support charitable activity.

Reformers, however, did not believe that the church's control of these assets served any productive economic purpose and were convinced that the tithe and other taxes, as well as the church courts' absolute control over litigation arising out of these matters, limited entrepreneurial activity. Thus, between the 1750s and 1800, Bourbon ministers took a number of steps to deal with these issues. They subjected church property to regular taxes, made the solicitation of loans and 'gifts' to the state from church institutions a routine practice, and severely limited the ability of ecclesiastical courts to handle economic litigation involving church-controlled assets.

As important as these legal and fiscal measures were, however, they merely set the stage for the most important assault on church resources. In 1804, the crown issued a decree requiring that practically all assets belonging to ecclesiastical institutions be liquidated and transferred to the state to be invested in royal bonds paying 4.5 per cent interest. This measure, the *Consolidación de Vales Reales*, required that owners of property subject to liens redeem them within a brief period of time, and that all debtors repay their loans when they came due. Despite enormous local protest and resistance, it is estimated that between 1804 and 1809, royal officials successfully collected 10.5 million pesos from Mexico alone.

It appears that the immediate economic impact of this appropriation of capital was not as severe as contemporaries argued. Private capital quickly took the place of ecclesiastical capital in the credit markets. But its impact on religious functions was enormous. In the short term, ecclesiastical organizations in Mexico saw their income reduced by 10 per cent, and after 1811 they lost their incomes entirely. The long-term consequences were even more devastating. The crown seizure of such funds greatly reduced the practice of pious bequests and severed the economic ties that had bound political and economic elites to the church throughout the Colonial period. Thus, the Bourbon measures prepared the way for the increasing secularization of society in nineteenth-century Mexico and the church–state conflicts that plagued the country. Whether or not the *Consolidación* had the same impact on the rest of Latin America remains to be tested, but enough evidence exists to suggest that many other parts of the Spanish Empire had a similar experience.

A second area where Bourbon policy had a major impact on the institutional life of the church concerned the changing role given to the religious orders in the New World. During the Habsburg era, the Franciscans, Dominicans,

Augustinians, Jesuits and Mercedarians played a fundamental part in the expansion of Christianity and in the maintenance of religious and cultural life. As late as the middle of the eighteenth century, regular orders controlled approximately one-third of the parishes in the New World – mostly in rural communities – dominated formal educational institutions, and were important allies of the monarchy in the expansion of the empire through their work in mission territories.

Yet while they were intimately connected to the Habsburg system, the regular orders were not seen as agents of the state in the popular mind. Local communities did not perceive religious priests as outsiders – as they did often view bishops and diocesan clergy – primarily because the regulars encouraged the Baroque popular religiosity that provided an underpinning to local identity. Thus, the orders themselves remained popular, even when local communities complained about the conduct of individual friars. The Jesuits, moreover, were held in special esteem among Creole elites because they trained many of the Creole diocesan priests, priests who became the elites' most ardent supporters in any controversy.

In the minds of the king's ministers the regular orders had a fundamental flaw: their superiors were beyond the control of the Spanish monarch. While the Habsburgs had been disposed to live with this situation, the Bourbons were not. The institutional independence of the regular orders was at odds with Bourbon absolutist policies, their support of Baroque religiosity was intellectually offensive to Enlightened elites, and their control of education and their paternalistic relationship with indigenous populations were viewed as a major obstacle to programmes of modernization. To add passion to this intellectual analysis, there was also the well-publicized issue of the decline in morality and religious observance of the orders, a decline that, in the ministers' view, threatened the good order of society.

The aspect of the crown's assault on the regulars most studied by historians was the decision to expel the Jesuits in 1767. But while that expulsion shocked local populations and was very unpopular, its consequence for religious practice was more psychological than physical. Franciscans and Dominicans took over the Jesuit mission territories without major disruption and a number of different groups came forward to replace them in educational and cultural structures. Far more serious consequences ensued from an earlier decree of 1749 that ordered the secularization of all parishes controlled by religious orders.

This decree resulted from a hasty investigation organized by the king's first ministers in 1748 concerning charges that the religious priests administering

Indian communities had abused their parishioners and that the regular orders were morally lax. Accusations of this sort were quite common throughout the seventeenth and eighteenth centuries, but until this point the king had never taken official note of them. What seems to have changed the king's mind were the simultaneous reports, received from the viceroys of both Mexico and Peru, that portrayed the situation as a crisis. When the investigating committee concurred, the king acted. In October 1749, he issued an order requiring all regular clergy to transfer their parishes immediately to diocesan clergy and to close all rural priories – which were in any case illegal.

Representatives of the regulars immediately protested that the decree would be disastrous, since there would be no room in urban priories for the displaced friars and no way to support them. They also argued that the Indians would be ill served because of the lack of diocesan priests who knew the Indian languages. The subsequent debate delayed implementation of the decree in order to take account of practical difficulties. But the measure was never withdrawn and the king's ministers added a further amendment in 1757 requiring the orders to cease accepting new novices until they had the resources to support them. Although the implementation process moved slowly and continued through the end of the colonial period, regular clergy now served in parishes at the convenience of bishops, not under the control of their own superiors, and their role in religious life among the indigenous communities outside of mission territories was severely circumscribed.

The rural communities themselves probably received the most damage from the measure. Bishops constantly complained about their inability to find enough priests to provide ordinary services for the vast majority of the population. The number of priests serving the most isolated areas declined and conditions for diocesan priests assigned to these poverty-stricken regions were abysmal because the communities could not support them. The low morale of the priests and the hostile relationship between the communities and their pastors frequently led to conflicts. On the other hand, there are indications that the number of priests from indigenous and mestizo backgrounds increased because of the desperate need for clergymen who knew the native languages.

Historians generally suggest that the orders themselves suffered from an inexorable decline after secularization. No doubt they did suffer from reduced revenues and a crisis of morale, since the loss of their parishes and priories pushed the regulars out of the rural areas with which they had been identified since the sixteenth century and in which they had powerful support. There is evidence that vocations declined as a result. Although figures are some-what unreliable, the total number of religious priests may have fallen from approximately 15,000 in the first half of the eighteenth century to approximately 12,000 at the time of independence.

But despite these losses, not all of the orders suffered equally. Those with substantial endowments, such as the Dominicans, the Jesuits (until their expulsion) and the Augustinians refocused their efforts on education and continued to be a force in urban areas where they had always been strong. The Franciscans, on the other hand, lacked any endowments to cushion the financial blow. In 1786, the Commissary General of the Order, visiting the Mexican provinces, reported that friars in the urban convents had little to occupy their time and lived in barbarous conditions. Low morale, he noted, had led to a decline of vocations.

Yet not even all Franciscan provinces declined equally. While research demonstrates that the Franciscan order in Peru had almost disappeared by the time of independence and that vocations declined precipitously in Central Mexico, the western Mexican provinces of Jalisco and Michoacán, where the *colegios* of *Propaganda Fide* were located, recovered their numbers and were opening new urban priories by the end of the eighteenth century. As a result the total number of Franciscans did not decline dramatically until the very end of the colonial period.

The Pombaline reforms in Brazil

Although the church functioned in Portugal much like its counterpart in Spain, the Portuguese experience in Brazil differed in fundamental ways from the Spanish experience. The most important distinction was that the church remained a missionary church in Brazil for much longer than it did in Spain's colonies. A combination of low numbers of local vocations that kept the diocesan church dependent on priests from Portugal, the appointment of bishops from Portugal, and a relative lack of urban settlement, kept diocesan structures poorly developed. The Inquisition, for example, was never established in the colony and no inquisitors sent from Portugal investigated religious conditions between the early seventeenth century and 1763.

In this environment the religious orders, particularly the Jesuits, dominated both the mission fields and the religious culture of urban Brazil. Thus, when the spirit of reform touched the ministers of the Portuguese monarchs, it was directed almost entirely at the regular orders, with a particular focus on the Jesuits themselves. This reform movement coincided with the reign of Joseph I (1750–77) and his chief minister, the Marqués de Pombal. Pombal saw Jesuit resistance to royal policy, particularly their overt hostility to the Treaty of

Madrid in 1750, as a challenge to the power of the state. He also gave a sinister interpretation to the control exercised by Jesuit confessors and preachers over the formation of the king's conscience, and considered as credible the rumours of vast Jesuit wealth in Brazil hidden from the crown.

For these reasons, he made it his goal to crush the Society. He succeeded during a two-year period between 1757 and early 1759. With the support of the Portuguese episcopacy and the tacit consent of the papacy, the Jesuits were charged with complicity in political movements against the crown. They were first exiled from the royal presence in 1757, then deprived of their licenses to preach and confess in Portugal in 1758, and finally, in January 1759, expelled from the Portuguese dominions.

The results for religious life in Brazil were devastating. The missionary efforts among the indigenous populations collapsed, and Jesuit educational facilities in the cities were closed. Later in the 1760s, the crown also effectively confiscated the economic assets of other religious orders such as the Dominicans, Benedictines, and Mercedarians, and the cultural influence of these orders was further eroded. Since the crown made no effort to strengthen diocesan structures, the net result was a substantial marginalization of the church. Thus, Pombal succeeded where the Bourbons had failed, with policies that helped produce a much more secular society.

Popular religiosity

One does not have to look very far into the reports of bishops and diocesan priests in the late colonial period to realize their generally low opinion for the religious beliefs and practices of their communicants. It was a rare official who commented favourably on the piety and orthodoxy of the ordinary faithful. 'Ignorant', 'superstitious', 'debased', were the more common descriptions. Yet the vast majority of observers did not use the term 'idolatry'. They considered their flocks to be Christians, albeit poor Christians.

The reports thus highlight one important element of popular religiosity. It did not conform to Enlightened perspectives on proper religious behaviour, but for the most part evangelization had been successful in introducing a Christian world-view. To be sure, a few isolated groups did reject Christianity entirely, and some cultures such as the Maya of Yucatan continued to use a Christian veneer to conceal the perpetuation of older traditions. But for most cultural groups the question was never as simple as acceptance or rejection. Rather, they pondered the new religious ideas and created an amalgam that combined the old and new cultural principles in a way that provided a satisfying and effective explanation of the universe and how to deal with it. To paraphrase one recent historian, whether they knew it or not (the strong inference is that they knew it), parish priests and missionaries from the sixteenth through to the eighteenth centuries were engaged in conversation, not conversion.[2] But it was not a conversation that ended with Baptism. The dialogue continued throughout the colonial period.

The development of the cult of the Virgin of Guadalupe illustrates this process. In 1555, the Franciscan provincial of Mexico City attacked the cult as the idolatrous worship of a man-made image. But by the mid-seventeenth century, when the apparition had been recorded in a written Nahuatl version (the *Nican Mopohua*), the story and the iconography of the Virgin had come closely to parallel accounts of Spanish Marian apparitions. At the same time, the popularity of the Virgin of Guadalupe crossed cultural boundaries. After 1648, the cult spread most quickly among Creoles, while indigenous communities outside of the Valley of Mexico ignored it. But by the middle of the eighteenth century, it was firmly grounded in all ethnic communities throughout New Spain.

The evolutionary process involving the Virgin of Guadalupe was typical of all manifestations of the cult of the saints in Central Mexico. At the end of the sixteenth century indigenous peoples may still have used medieval Christian conceptions of the intercessory roles of the saints to mask traditional Nahua understandings of the need to appease the gods and seek protection from a pantheon of household deities and higher spiritual powers. By the eighteenth century, however, knowledge of the traditional deities and their traditional characteristics had been lost. Like rural believers in sixteenth-century Spain, those in Central Mexico now saw the Christian devil and his minions as the source of ill fortune, even though the world was ultimately under God's control. They believed that the intercessory powers of the Christian saints derived from the saints' relationship with God, not from any independent authority.

Some Bourbon bishops and priests in the vice-royalty of New Spain remained suspicious that the emphasis on the cult of saints in rural communities hid crypto-pagan practices. But it would seem that, in large part, their concerns were due to the fact that few diocesan priests (and no bishops) could speak local languages well enough to understand the content of religious devotions or to speak with their parishioners about them. The clergy was also no doubt unhappy with the control exercised by the laity over such local devotions. Priests thus found their own role severely circumscribed – a situation that was all the more serious in that their own remuneration depended on lay generosity for their services. There was also a cultural divide occasioned by the eighteenth-century shift in Europe to the image of a more compassionate and accessible God who could be approached directly. Rural villagers found such an image unpersuasive. They lived in a world fraught with perils and in which patrons were deemed necessary. Access to the intercessory powers of the saints, then, was extremely important both at an individual and a community level.

The cult of the saints was also strong in the Andean highlands, and the popularity of Our Lady of Copacabana in Bolivia paralleled that of the Virgin of Guadalupe. But here much more of the pre-conquest religious traditions seem to have been retained. Ecclesiastical authorities were deeply concerned with the perpetuation of the cult of the *huacas* (ancestor spirits who were critical to communal life), and a much publicized campaign to extirpate them peaked in the third quarter of the seventeenth century. Although these efforts declined significantly thereafter, there is good reason to believe that the practices that occasioned them did not. After 1671, the prevailing tendency was to define the persistence of native religious practices as superstition resulting from ignorance rather than apostasy.

An account of a festival honouring a local saint in a village near Cuzco in 1767 provides an example of the problems of interpreting indigenous religious behaviour. The pastor reported that the festival began (as all did) with a Mass in the parish church. After Mass, the priest moved the image of the saint to the door of the church where villagers venerated it. The people also asked the saint's help in dealing with problems and left offerings of goods, animals, and money. When they had finished, the priest blessed the offerings and the villagers began a village festival, observed by the saint's image which stayed at the door of the church. At the end of the day, the priest took the offerings for himself.

This description of prayers and offerings to a village saint echoed descriptions of indigenous practices involving *huacas* that inspectors defined as idolatrous during the heyday of the extirpation movement. To be sure, the ceremony was now preceded by a Mass, the image had been given a saint's name, and the priest was intimately involved through his blessing of the image. But were such changes sufficient for the people to see themselves as orthodox Catholics and for the practices to be considered 'Catholic'? Members of the community themselves have left us no commentaries.

It is also clear that by the eighteenth century religious practice divided more along rural–urban lines than along an indigenous–Spanish continuum. As in pre-Enlightenment Europe, processions displaying saints' images and religious dramas celebrated on the great feast days and in times of trouble were critical components of urban life as well as rural life, serving both corporate and private purposes. Seventeenth- and eighteenth-century celebrations of Corpus Christi in Cuzco and Mexico City, for example, joined all ethnic elements in active collaboration for the common communal purpose and gave religious affirmation to the hierarchies of both the individual ethnic orders and colonial society as a whole.

Celebrations were just as colourful and multifaceted in the towns as they were in rural areas. The main difference was that priests and ecclesiastical institutions had greater control over urban religiosity. Ironically, when Bourbon bureaucrats attempted to suppress these urban celebrations in the later eighteenth century, they never described them as 'pagan Bacchanalia' – a term commonly used for the rural equivalent – no doubt because Hispanic elites were prominent participants in the towns. Rather, they emphasized the disorders they caused and the unproductive expenditure of money by the poor that could be better spent on feeding families. The attacks on urban processions and festivals, however, led to an unexpected response. In the very late colonial period, Creole religious and social elites turned the defence of processions and communal religiosity into a form of political resistance.

Indigenous political movements, likewise, mobilized support with appeals to Catholic religious sentiments. The Kuraka leader, José Gabriel Tupac Amaru, whose revolt against Spanish rule in Central Peru (1780–82) has been considered one of the most serious upheavals of the late colonial period, used Christian concepts of justice in an attempt to unite Creole and indigenous elites behind his cause. He also compared his movement to the revolt of the Israelites against the Egyptians. His conduct towards the church, moreover, was so deferential that after the revolt was suppressed, the crown exiled the Creole Bishop of Cuzco to Spain because of suspicions of collaboration.

The lack of a racial or cultural divide in religious practice and belief is also apparent in other areas of individual and corporate piety. Inquisition archives provide examples in which *hechicería* (a pre-columbian healing practice) was described as 'witchcraft' when it involved rural villagers, and as 'superstition' when urban Hispanic elites were the object of investigation. In fact, urbanized Indians and mestizos accepted European spiritual models and institutions in a manner little different from that of the Creole elites. The Creole mystic, Saint Rose of Lima, for example, inspired a whole range of men and women from all ethic groups in Lima and elsewhere. The pursuit of ascetic rigour as an avenue to mystical experience drew Inquisition attention both to the wives of Creole bureaucrats and to illiterate indigenous *beatas* (holy women). Even after these practices fell out of favour with Enlightened administrators and ecclesiastical leaders, they remained popular with Creoles and indigenous groups alike into the late eighteenth century. The cults of local *beatos* (holy men), such as the Lima mulatto Martín de Porres (beatified in the nineteenth century) who combined ascetic rigour and charitable activity, continued to flourish much to the dismay of peninsular archbishops such as Francisco de Lorenzana of Mexico. Even the popular hagiography surrounding officially accepted holy people such as Saint Rose of Lima continued to stress the mystical union with Christ through the denial of the body.

In their pursuit of Spanish models of perfection, however, non-Hispanics encountered many roadblocks. Hispanic values emphasized that the proper avenue for those with deeper religious callings was entry into the secular priesthood and religious orders for men, and into formally organized cloistered convents for women. Bishops and the Inquisition looked with great suspicion on *beatos* and *beatas* who pursued sanctity outside these corporate structures. And racial and social prejudices excluded non-Hispanics from full participation in ecclesiastical institutions. Not until 1769 did the crown give official encouragement to non-Hispanic men to enter the diocesan priesthood or the regular clergy, and the move was opposed vigorously by the religious orders, in particular. In the end, few indigenous men, other than the totally acculturated sons of Indian caciques, were able to take advantage of the new official policy of openness. High dowries and racial prejudice likewise restricted full participation in the *conventos grandes* (the formally endowed convents following an established European rule) to elite Creole women. Indigenous women were allowed to live in these convents, but only as servants, never as the equals of the Creole nuns. The eighteenth-century establishment of a few convents controlled by indigenous women in Mexico did very little to change the overall picture.

Blocked from full access to the most important institutions, both men and women found alternatives. Lay communal organizations such as *Cofradías* provided alternatives for indigenous and mestizo men. Poor and middling women of all ethnic groups could pursue the ascetic ideals of cloistered life through institutions known as *beaterios*. In Lima alone, between 1669 and 1704, wealthy laymen provided endowments for ten such houses. One of these, founded by the Dominicans in 1669 to honour the newly canonized Saint Rose, was intended for Hispanic women. Two other very prominent houses, however, both founded in 1677, catered to women of other groups. Kurakas endowed the *beaterio* of Nuestra Señora of Copacabana for their daughters, and the Indian *beato*, Venerable Nicolas de Allyón, and his mestiza wife, Maria Jacinta de Montoya, founded Jesús, María y José for non-Hispanic women. Both institutions remained important spiritual centres in Lima for the remainder of the colonial period.

The *beaterio* of Jesús y María y José illustrates the spirituality involved in its creation, as well as the breadth of its acceptance by non-Hispanics. In 1672 María Jacinta and Nicolas gathered seven unmarried women in a residence where they lived according to the ascetic models of Saint Teresa of Avila and Saint Ignatius, while working as volunteer nurses in the Hospital of La Caridad and performing other charity. Their reputation for sanctity grew and in 1685, as a result of patronage from the viceroy, the Archbishop of Lima raised the house to the status of an officially approved cloistered *beaterio*. Alms from wealthy residents of Lima allowed Maria Jacinta and Nicolas to construct a new building for their cloister.

Their model for cloistered life in the *beaterios* was similar to that pursued by nuns in the regular convents, but it also differed in significant ways. First, *beaterios* were subject to direct episcopal authority and established with little endowment. The bishop assigned priests to supervise them closely. Moreover, these institutions supported themselves with alms or fees for work performed, and both their poverty and their rules prevented them from taking in servants. The members performed all labour for themselves and gave little attention to the contemplative life or to the liturgy (one of the rationale for having servants in the regular convents). This lack of servants made them particularly unattractive to the elites. Although many *beaterios* acquired endowments over time, and although some were even raised to the status of convents, most remained obscure, important primarily to the local communities in which they served.

A number of indications suggest a resurgence of piety and religious zeal in the course of the eighteenth century. Despite the rhetoric of the Bourbon administrators and their general disdain for conventual life, local elites supported the foundation of a number of new convents in their communities. In Mexico, numerous houses of Capuchins, Poor Clares, and Discalced Carmelites were established. These foundations suggest that personal asceticism and the most rigorous form of cloistered life were considered important to provincial communities, whatever the views of the Enlightened elites. There was also support for new female establishments with different objectives, including the Institute de la Enseñanza founded in Mexico in 1752. Its purpose was to establish schools to provide rigorous academic training for women and it continued to expand until the end of the colonial period.

Also of importance was the Oratorian movement, intended to train and support diocesan priests who wished to practise the communal life. Following the rule of the Institutes of Saint Philip Neri, the first of these establishments opened in Peru in the 1670s. The oratory of Saint Michael founded in the Mexican town of San Miguel de Allende in 1734 provides us with an example of their impact. It became a popular centre for lay retreats and in 1743, spawned the school of Saint Francis de Sales which became a centre for educational innovation in the latter eighteenth century.

Another aspect of the eighteenth-century religious resurgence was the promotion of retreats and parish revivals intended to re-evangelize the laity. Many groups participated in the lay retreat movement, including the Oratorians, but the most publicized promoters were undoubtedly the Jesuits. At the beginning of the eighteenth century, the Society of Jesus introduced lay retreats based on a modified version of the Ignatian spiritual exercises. The retreats proved so popular that the Jesuit province in Mexico opened endowed houses devoted entirely to them in Puebla in 1727 and in Mexico City in 1750. Others were about to open in Morelia, Michoacán and in Guatemala at the time of the Order's expulsion in 1767. Indeed, it appears that the Jesuit retreats were an empire-wide phenomenon. In 1757, the Jesuit procurator of the province of Chile reported that he considered this activity to be one of the most important elements of the Society's work because of its impact on family life. In fact, in 1756, 120 women participated in retreats in the very small community of San Juan in the province of Mendoza, Argentina. After the Jesuit expulsion, townspeople lobbied the bishop to have the retreats continued, and when they were restarted using secular priests in 1775, 103 men and 115 women took part.

A development about which we know little is the movement for parish-wide missions. Particularly identified with the Franciscan *colegios de Propaganda Fide* first established in Mexico in 1683, these missions resembled the tent revivals of the twentieth-century United States and were intended to promote moral reform among the laity. A report of one such event in Cuzco in 1739 suggests their flavour. It described a three-week event conducted by Franciscans, filled with daily catechism lessons, preaching on the themes of divine judgement and the need for personal repentance, singing, bells, and public processions of the image of the Señor de los Temblores through the streets of Cuzco, accompanied by large numbers of flagellants. One preacher was reported to have set fire to his arm during his sermon in order to terrorize the packed church; another flagellated himself with an iron chain as part of his sermon;

and a third friar used a skull as a prop and prophesied that God would send a great plague by the following Easter if the people did not repent their sins.

Although this type of spiritual activity has been barely studied, we know that Franciscan convents throughout the northern hemisphere used parish missions to support themselves in the later colonial period. The popularity of these revivals in rural areas led one pastor in western Mexico to obtain permission from the bishop in 1797 to build a hospice as a base for travelling Franciscan preachers. To emphasize the impact of these events, another enthusiastic pastor reported that the powerful preaching and austere example of the missionaries brought down from the hills Indians living completely outside of parish control and disdainful of the sacraments and returned them to the practice of their faith.

Black religiosity in Brazil

The third ethnic and cultural group in the Americas, after the Europeans and the indigenous Indians, were the descendants of the slaves imported from Africa. In Spanish America, the small numbers of Africans and a general process of assimilation made black religiosity culturally indistinguishable from the practices of the surrounding indigenous and hispanicized populations. But in Brazil, a distinct black religiosity developed which has persisted to the present day. This syncretic tradition combined Christian revelation and the use of Christian institutions and symbols with African beliefs in continuous revelation via the use of mediums and contacts with ancestors. It seems to have been imported into Brazil by slaves from Central Africa who had had long exposure to Christian missionaries. Portuguese law required that owners baptize all slaves immediately after they entered Brazil. But in the absence of a significant church presence in rural areas, and abetted by Portuguese slave owners who had little interest in evangelization or continuing education beyond the minimum requirements of the law, this syncretic tradition – though illegal – flourished. Indeed, it seems that masters turned to black freedmen to initiate the newly arrived *bozales* – unacculturated slaves brought directly from Africa – into the existing community and that these freedmen also incorporated the newly arrived blacks into the existing religious organizations. Baptism was an important element in this syncretic tradition because God-parentage created bonds of fictive kinship that substituted for the biological family that could not be re-created.

The tradition generally followed Central African cosmological structures but lacked any dogmatic principles that would have brought it to the attention of the authorities. Black religiosity revolved around the use of charms and amulets thought to bring good fortune and ward off evil and thus to give the slaves some control over the exigencies of their everyday life. The cross, for example, was a popular religious symbol among slaves because it reflected both a Christian iconography and was a representation of a central African view of the cosmos that gave believers access to spiritual power. The slaves also associated charms and spiritual power with the images of the saints. Travellers' accounts, which provide our main source of information regarding these practices, continually noted the importance of the devotion to saints. But in this case, unlike the saints' cults practised by indigenous populations in Spanish America, the saints were incorporated into the African traditions. Since lay-run Christian brotherhoods (hermandades) were already a very important aspect of religiosity in Brazil because of the lack of priests, slaves found it possible to publicly manifest their religiosity through their own brotherhoods while avoiding the suspicions of authority.

Another important element of black religiosity was the emphasis on burial rituals. African tradition placed great stress on the use of such rituals to keep separated souls from wandering among the living and plaguing them. Here again, Catholic institutions provided the slaves with a cover, as well as with a set of rituals, to meet their traditional concerns. Black hermandades functioned primarily as burial societies and guaranteed that slaves would be interred in consecrated ground and with rituals that would facilitate the soul's movement into the spiritual world.

The eighteenth-century missions

While efforts in the settled areas focused on re-evangelization, missionaries were also proselytizing among new groups during the late seventeenth and eighteenth centuries. Even after 1767, despite the stress of having to assume territories that had been under Jesuit supervision, Franciscan, Dominican and Mercedarian friars opened new missions in upper California, Texas, southern Chile, the Amazonian regions of Ecuador, Peru and Colombia, northern Colombia, the Chaco regions of Bolivia and northern Argentina, and Patagonia.

The work itself also grew exponentially more difficult. The groups encountered generally were not sedentary farmers with sophisticated social or political structures. Thus, the cultural distance between the indigenous populations and the missionaries was much greater than in the period of early evangelization, and overt hostility was more common. Some groups, such as the Guajiros

Figure 6 Church of Parinacota, Chile. Completed in 1789, this New World church employs rustic materials and craftsmanship, and achieves a unified and flawlessly tasteful effect. The interior of the church is decorated with primitive frescoes. (Photograph in the Butler Collection, Centre for the Study of Christianity in the Non-Western World, University of Edinburgh.)

of northern Colombia and the Chiriguanos of Bolivia, repeatedly destroyed mission settlements when they were established and successfully resisted the efforts at evangelization.

Other groups accepted or could not prevent the establishment of missions and suffered devastating consequences. This was particularly true in the Brazilian Amazon and in the Californias. In Maranhão and in the Amazon territories, the Jesuits fought a constant battle with the settler population over the issue of the freedom of the evangelized populations and, despite crown support in the late 1680s, they were never really able to suppress the enslavement of the mission Indians. In these areas the appearance of the missions led to the disappearance of the indigenous cultures.

Jesuit and Franciscan missions in the Californias had a similar tragic result, though for different reasons. In the Californias, the issue was not exploitation, but misguided humanitarianism. The missions in Lower California were opened in 1697, and the crown agreed to give the Jesuits authority to close the territory to Hispanic settlers. The Society intended to show that it was possible to bring an area under the authority of the crown and Christianize it peacefully, without lay interference. But the missions ultimately failed because the Jesuits tried to make the indigenous inhabitants farmers and artisans living according to a European lifestyle in an environment that could not sustain it. Agricultural communities proved almost impossible to establish in the waterless expanse of the peninsula. Forced to live in the missions and confronted with frequent crop failures that led to malnutrition, the native population almost totally disappeared.

The Franciscans who established the missions in upper California after 1767 made similar cultural blunders, and the situation was exacerbated here because the missions were required to support a Spanish military presence in the region. Disease, malnutrition and cultural despair occasioned by forced residence in the missions and the disappearance of traditional life styles, all combined to produce a demographic catastrophe that severely reduced the populations of California and reduced to destitution groups that had prospered before the Spanish arrival.

While the horrors of mission life were undeniable for indigenous populations in lower and upper California and in the Brazilian Amazon, it is unclear to what extent the experience of these regions was typical. In northern Mexico, for instance, the adoption of Spanish agriculture and livestock herding improved the nutritional intake of native peoples and contributed to their demographic survival rather than to their demise. Moreover, in almost all areas other than those previously mentioned, Spanish culture did not overwhelm the indigenous populations and those changes that did occur were commonly the result of rational decisions made by the indigenous communities themselves. It seems, for example, that the Guarani were attracted to the Jesuit reductions in Paraguay because they could serve as a refuge where the indigenous groups could resist the forced loss of their culture. Acknowledging that the Spanish were never going to leave, they concluded that the mission environment would enable them to learn the Spanish ways they needed to survive without losing those elements of their traditional culture that they prized. Mocobí groups in the Chaco made similar judgements in the 1770s. In making the decision to request missionaries, the Mocobí clans understood that their life would change. But for them mission culture was a means of gaining knowledge that they could use to survive against other competing groups.

It can be concluded then that for most groups in eighteenth-century Spanish America, participation in mission life was essentially voluntary. Missions attracted people because of the advantages they offered and these people remained because of a rational decision that life in the mission was better than life away from it. But changes in traditional lifestyles had to occur. In the case of the Mocobí, receiving the benefits of mission life required them to accept the new social and political structures imposed by the missionaries, along with the public aspects of Christianity such as the Mass, the Christian calendar of feast days, and the sacraments. After they became mission Indians, they readily adopted Christian models of ascetic piety (in missionary eyes they went to extremes), but while they understood Christian moral expectations, they ignored the more abstract ideas of sin and virtue because they clashed too heavily with their traditional cultural conceptions. Their understanding of the sacraments, likewise, was not as the European priests intended it. A decade after the coming of the friars, baptism and burial rites were accepted and understood, marriage less so, and confession and the Eucharist, least of all.

This is not to say, however, that their conversion was superficial. Over time, mission Indians throughout the Americas internalized the mission structures as their own and made Christian rituals and behaviour the centrepiece of their public communal existence. Even harsh recent critics of the mission system acknowledge that indigenous communities ultimately accepted the resulting cultural amalgam. After a few generations, the Indians considered themselves Christians.

Missionaries understood this evolutionary process and accepted it. Perhaps, over time, the understanding of European religious culture by the peoples converted in the late colonial period would have come to resemble that of groups evangelized in the sixteenth and seventeenth centuries. But the question is unanswerable, because the process was cut short. The wars of independence would fatally damage the mission system in all parts of the empire.

The wars of independence in Spanish America

In their efforts to build a state, the Bourbons severed the bonds that had justified and held together the Habsburg Empire in the New World. Baroque religious ceremonies and festivals linked elites and commoners and expressed a system of shared beliefs and symbols that ultimately provided ideological support for the king himself. The attacks on popular religious practices, then, created a gulf between the leaders of society and the mass of the colonial population.

But the issue that most concerned bishops at the end of the colonial period was the growing disaffection of the diocesan clergy. Throughout the Habsburg era, the diocesan priesthood had been both a profession and a vocation. The Bourbons set out to diminish the professional aspects of the sacerdotal state in hopes of rekindling the vocation. In the eyes of the crown there were too many unemployed priests who were attracted more to the status and privileges accorded to priests, than to a life of service. Certainly, they had a point. In 1790, in Mexico City there were only 59 positions in parish service while 517 secular priests lived in the city. Those without positions, it could be argued, lacked a proper vocation. But whatever the condition of their vocation, they were still an important social group and by the end of the eighteenth century the Bourbons had forfeited their loyalty. The redefinition of the role of pastors in local communities, the attacks on legal immunities, and the contemptuous behaviour of royal officials threatened all priests. The crown's virtual expropriation of the endowments of their chantries in 1804 ultimately stripped many of a major source of income, and crown social policy after 1770, which encouraged bishops to consider mestizos and Indians for the priesthood, offended their sense of racial order. Many Creole priests, then, rejected the Spanish state and identified themselves as American when the crisis of the revolutions began. As a result, diocesan priests played an important role in the formation of the new nations.

But the cumulative effect of the Bourbon period had another consequence. Soon after independence, the number of regular clergy and diocesan priests declined sharply and fell below the level necessary to maintain the cult. The lack of personnel, combined with the hostility of the lay leadership of the new nations and the universal suspicion of the Bourbon bishops who almost to a man had supported the monarchy until the very end, greatly reinforced the secularizing tendencies of the nineteenth-century states. A church that had organized and sustained colonial culture was now brought low.

Notes

1. D. A. Brading, *Church and state in Michoacán, 1749–1810* (Cambridge: Cambridge University Press, 1994), p. 167.
2. Erick Langer and Robert H. Jackson (eds.), *The new Latin American mission history* (Lincoln, NB: University of Nebraska Press, 1995), p. 28.

20

British and French North America to 1765

MARK A. NOLL

The expansion of Christianity to North America long remained a thoroughly colonial affair. Not until after the Seven Years' War (or French and Indian War) of 1754/56–1763 did the idea even begin to emerge that new-world colonies could be anything but extensions of their mother countries, for religious as for all other purposes.[1] Huguenots, the party of Reformed Protestants in France, for instance, could play a role in the early settlement of Quebec and Acadia because a French monarch, Henri IV (ruled 1589–1610), who had once been a Protestant, had expanded their liberty with the Edict of Nantes in 1598. But after 1627, Cardinal Richelieu succeeded in banishing the Huguenots from New France as well as constricting their freedom at home. The very names of English colonies reflected a different kind of old-world presence. Virginia, for example, was named in honour of the Protestant Elizabeth who had ruled England as the virgin queen (1558–1603), and Maryland, after Henrietta Maria, the Catholic queen of Charles I (1625–49) and sister of the French monarch under whom Richelieu banished the Huguenots. Yet despite these intentions simply to replicate inherited patterns – intellectual, political, and social, as well as religious – new environments consistently forced the colonists to innovate.

From the old world, Catholics and Protestants both carried intense suspicion of the other. That antagonism, especially when exacerbated by competitive alliances with Native Americans, defined the wider horizons of formal religion for the entire period. Early on it was responsible for a rare bit of humour: on board ship to Acadia in 1604, a Catholic priest and a Huguenot minister had combated each other so vociferously that when they both died within the year, sailors of Samuel de Champlain buried them in the same grave that they might continue their arguments into eternity. Much more typically, Catholic–Protestant contention was taken in deadly earnest, as when during the French and Indian War a Virginia preacher warned that 'Our religion, our liberty, our property, our lives, and everything sacred to us are in danger', especially of being 'enslaved' by 'an arbitrary, absolute monarch' enforcing conformity to 'the superstition and idolatries of the church of Rome'.[2] The story of Christianity in colonial North America is the story of old-world religion taking on a life of its own in the contingencies of the new world.

Beginnings

The first French and English settlements in the new world lagged considerably behind the Spanish – more than a century after Christopher Columbus set sail in 1492 with the hope of converting the Indians, and decades after Bartolomé de las Casas began his Christian attempt to mitigate the Christian destruction of the Indians. Two bands of Huguenots did attempt settlements in the early 1560s on the Atlantic coast, but they were soon wiped out by a Spanish force from St Augustine, Florida.

Permanent settlement of what became the United States and Canada began only in the first decade of the seventeenth century: 1604 with the French in Acadia (the Atlantic provinces of modern Canada); 1607 with an English colony at Jamestown in Virginia; and 1608 with the establishment of Quebec by the French explorer Samuel de Champlain. Soon thereafter the Récollets, an order of reformed Franciscans, were active in the French settlements, and in 1625 they were joined by the Jesuits. Early religious life in Acadia and Quebec featured attempts at reaching the Indians and persistent difficulties in controlling French trappers and traders. The number of colonists with families remained small.

In the British colonies, by contrast, settlement that displaced the Indians and a religious life that was centred on the settlers constituted the norm. Virginia experienced great difficulties in its first years, but the colony's governors did succeed in planting the Church of England and providing it with a meagre supply of clergyman. The established Anglican presence in Virginia was later replicated in other southern colonies and the West Indies. New-world Anglicanism was eventually bolstered by two societies created under the leadership of Thomas Bray, who served as a minister for a short period in Maryland – the Society for Promoting Christian Knowledge (SPCK, 1698) that provided books for colonial ministers, and the Society for the Propagation of the Gospel in Foreign Parts (SPG, 1701) that carried out missions among Native Americans but eventually sent more missionaries to colonies (like Massachusetts) where the Church of England was weak. Despite the commendable work of these societies, colonial Anglicanism could never fully overcome a debilitating series of obstacles. The immense size of parishes posed problems for which church life in England provided little guidance. The colonial American south was also dominated by a culture of personal honour, including duelling and exalted notions of patriarchal prerogative that undermined Christian ideals. The enslavement of kidnapped Africans complicated all interpersonal relationships, including those of church and people. And because of imperial unconcern combined with colonial political resistance, it was never possible to secure a bishop, and so colonial Anglicans always lacked essential components of their church's traditional life.

A different Protestant establishment was carried to the new world in five Puritan colonies created by the precise Calvinists who had been frustrated in their efforts at completing the Reformation in England: Plymouth (1620) and Massachusetts Bay (1630), which were united as the Commonwealth of Massachusetts in 1691; Connecticut (1636) and New Haven (1638), which were consolidated as the colony of Connecticut in 1662; and New Hampshire, which separated off as a separate government from Massachusetts in 1680. Because of its enduring importance, New England Puritanism receives separate treatment below.

As an indication of the instant variety of new-world Christianity, two more foundations were also in place early on. New Amsterdam was created as a Dutch outpost at the mouth of the Hudson River in the mid-1620s. It enjoyed the services of several Dutch Reformed ministers, but they were always hamstrung by a lack of settlers from Holland and the heavy-handed mismanagement of the colony's governors. In 1664, New Amsterdam was taken over by the English and renamed New York. From 1693, the colony's new elite tried to constitute the Church of England as the established church in New York City, but by that time there were simply too many different religious groups in the colony to make an establishment work.

From the other end of the European religious spectrum, Maryland was established in 1634 as a refuge for English Catholics. Its founders, George Calvert and his son Cecilius, had converted to Catholicism after service to James I, who with his son Charles I awarded them the colony in gratitude. Protestants always made up the bulk of Maryland's settlers, and after the Catholic James II was deposed, the colony in 1691 came under Anglican rule. Yet throughout the colonial period, Maryland offered an unusual sanctuary for Catholics in a British world marked by extreme prejudice against Rome.

As colonization expanded during the second half of the seventeenth century, institutionalized Christianity grew somewhat more secure. Significantly, the strongest churches – Puritan Congregationalism, Virginia Anglicanism, and the Catholicism of New France – retained the European ideal of a comprehensive, established state church. All sought the protection of government, assumed a duty to influence the state, treated each others' missionaries as civil threats, and opposed efforts by other Christians to move into their colonies.

In the province of Quebec along the St Lawrence River, French settlement proceeded more slowly than among the English. The arrival in 1659 of the first resident bishop, François-Xavier de Montmorency Laval, marked a transition in emphasis from missions among the Indians to civilization-building among the immigrants. By recruiting priests and other religious in France, by expanding the Seminary of Quebec as an active agent of clerical formation, and by institutionalizing the tithe (eventually fixed at 1/26 of the value of agricultural produce), Laval constructed the basis for an enduring Catholic culture. But by quarrelling with the leaders of local and French religious orders and with lay governors, he also established a pattern of institutional contention that his successor, Jean-Baptiste de Saint-Vallier, carried to new depths. Spiritually, New France was inspired during the second half of the century by a number of highly respected women religious. Marie Guyart, who took the name Marie de l'Incarnation after she was widowed and entered the Ursuline order, came to Canada in 1639 and immediately became a force through the schools she founded for French and Indian girls and through her mystical piety. Marguerite Bourgeois, who arrived at Montreal in 1653, not only organized the first church in this frontier outpost but also founded the Congregation of Notre Dame that would go on to long and influential service in teaching, health care, and much else.

Although it was not obvious at the time, the tide of colonial empire was flowing towards the British, in large part because they induced more colonists to emigrate than either France or Spain. One of the main reasons for that success was the space that minority religious groups found in the English colonies. Already before the end of the seventeenth century, the Society of Friends (or Quakers) had come to many North American locations. The Quakers had soon shed the radicalism of their founding period during the English Civil War and were consolidating rapidly under George Fox (1624–91), who visited the colonies in 1672–73. Besides providing forceful teaching about the Inner Light of Christ and the virtues of Christian pacifism, Fox also offered useful information about North America to one of the Quaker's most important converts, William Penn (1644–1718), the son of a famous British admiral. When in 1681 Penn acquired a huge tract of land in the New World and in 1682 laid out the city of Philadelphia, he set the stage for a further migration of Quakers.

By the time Quakers were moving to Pennsylvania, Dutch Reformed congregations in New York were prospering in ways not possible under the oppressive interference of Dutch colonial officials. The first settlers from Scotland, or from Scotland by way of Ireland, were founding Presbyterian churches in Pennsylvania, New Jersey, and on Long Island. These churches were brought together into the first American presbytery in 1706 through the work of Francis Makemie, who was born in Ireland, educated in Scotland, and commissioned in Northern Ireland to serve as a missionary in North America. At about the same time, several different kinds of Baptist churches were taking root in New England, New York, and points further south. The creation in 1707 of the Philadelphia Association of Regular Baptists was the first of the many significant Baptist organizations in America.

The Pietist movements that took shape in Europe during the last third of the seventeenth century also began to establish a presence in America through German migrations from late in the century. The 120,000 German-speaking immigrants who came to North America over the next hundred years included some Mennonites, Moravians, and Brethren, but most were associated with the Lutheran and Reformed state churches. After the arrival of Henry Melchior Mühlenberg, who came to Pennsylvania from the Pietist centre of Halle in 1742, Lutheran church organization proceeded rapidly.

By the middle years of the eighteenth century, even more Protestants – Sandemanians, Shakers, Free Will Baptists, and Universalists, among others – had appeared on American shores. Especially in the middle colonies of New York, New Jersey, Pennsylvania, and Delaware, a functioning plurality of religion developed with no exact counterpart in Europe. Governor Thomas Dongan of New York in 1687 made an observation about New York City that would soon be apt for other areas as well: 'Here bee not many of the Church of England; few Roman Catholicks; abundance of Quakers preachers men and Women especially; Singing Quakers, Ranting Quakers; Sabbatarians; Antisabbatarians; Some Anabaptists; some Independents; some Jews; in short, of all sorts of opinions there are some, and the most part [are] of none at all.'[3] Although almost no one embraced religious pluralism as such, the European ideal of a unified Christendom was nonetheless breaking apart.

Movement beyond the spaces of that Christendom pushed new-world settlers to rethink questions of toleration. Roger Williams, a Calvinist separatist who tormented the Puritan establishment in Massachusetts until it expelled him in 1635, founded the colony of Rhode Island on the principle that government should not coerce religious practice or belief. On a visit to England during the early days of the Puritan rebellion against Charles I, Williams published his famous tract, *The Bloody Tenent of Persecution for Cause of Conscience Discussed in a Conference Between Truth and Peace* (1644). Its argument was far ahead of its time: '*God* requireth not an *uniformity* of *Religion* to be *inacted* and *inforced* in any *civill state*; which inforced *uniformity* (sooner or later) is the greatest occasion of *civill Warre, ravishing* of *conscience, persecution* of *Christ Jesus* in his servants, and of the *hypcrisie* and *destruction* of *millions* of *souls.*'[4]

Colonial conditions rather than abstract principles stimulated two similar experiments. After the forces of parliament and Puritanism had gained the upper hand in England's Civil War, Maryland's Catholic leaders passed an Act of Toleration in 1649 in the hope of preserving a space to practise their faith. Although it was soon repealed, Maryland's declaration marked a new stage in the conception of civil peace. In Pennsylvania, William Penn followed his Quaker convictions to a startling conclusion. In such works as *The Great Case of Liberty of Conscience* (1670), he extended the Quaker sense of individual religious competence into an argument against state mandates for religion. As Penn put these principles to work in New Jersey and, especially, Pennsylvania, he established what was, after Rhode Island, the most tolerant civil government in the Christian world. In the European colonies of the seventeenth century, toleration was mostly an experiment. Yet as with other spheres of practical Christianity in the new world, the experiment was also a harbinger.

The Puritans

The effort by New England Puritans to create a purer Christian civilization than they had known in England represented North America's most comprehensive and influential religious experiment. The English Puritans, who attempted in old England to reform the lives of individuals, the practice of the national English church, and the structures of their society, were frustrated first by royal opposition and then by the ambiguities of their own temporary success in the Civil War. In the new world, by contrast, Puritan colonists were able actually to implement the principles for which they had long struggled.

Led by unusually capable minister-theologians like John Cotton (1594–1652) and Thomas Shepard (1605–49) in Massachusetts, Thomas Hooker (1586–1647) in Connecticut, and John Davenport (1597–1670) in New Haven – as well as by laymen like Gov. William Bradford (1589?–1657) of Plymouth and Gov. John Winthrop (1588–1649) of Massachusetts – the 'Puritan way' became a laboratory for testing whether their conception of Christianity could flourish in an environment with external enemies removed. (Disease had greatly reduced the Native American population, and New England contained too few natural resources for it to attract intervention by other European mercantile powers.) Bradford phrased starkly the challenge that faced the Plymouth pilgrims in the autumn of 1620: 'they had now no friends to welcome them nor inns to entertain or refresh their weatherbeaten bodies; no houses or much less towns to repair to, to seek for succour . . . What could now sustain them but the Spirit of God and His grace?'[5] Winthrop, coming over ten years later with more colonists and more financial backing, was able to indulge a dream that, since New England had publicly announced its intention to follow God in seeking 'out a place of Cohabitation and Consorteshipp under a due forme of Government both civill and ecclesiastical', the Puritans would 'be as a Citty upon a Hill, the eies of all people are upon us'.[6] These apprehensions and dreams took shape in the organization of society around the biblical theme of covenant.

This variety of European Calvinism held that the basis for individual salvation was God's covenant-promise that he would redeem those who placed their trust in Christ. Puritans explained that promise as the outworking of a covenant within the Godhead whereby the Father chose those who would be saved, the Son accomplished their redemption, and the Spirit made it effective. Although internal differences about the meaning of the covenant for the visible church spurred the collapse of English Puritanism, among New Englanders there was agreement on a congregational basis for church order: thoroughly reformed churches did not need the presence of a bishop or the actions of a presbytery, but only the commitment of a local congregation to God and to each other. In turn, Puritans believed that the basis for health in society was the promise made by God to his covenanted people as a whole.

The key to constructing a Puritan social order was the ability to combine personal belief, ecclesiastical purity, and a godly social order into an interlocking covenantal system. With religious enemies scarce in the new world, internal spiritual realities replaced a willingness to suffer external opposition as the criterion for church fellowship. New Englanders asked those who wanted to join the church to testify before the assembled congregation that they had undergone a saving experience of God's grace. Such a profession then entitled men to become freemen (or voters) in the colony as well as members of a church. It also provided women, who did not vote, with the potential for unusual spiritual influence (as illustrated by the wife of a seventeenth-century Massachusetts governor, Anne Bradstreet, who wrote widely noticed poems). New England public life could then fulfil the social covenant with God, if freemen selected godly rulers and put laws in place that honoured God's written word.

Under this general system Puritans overcame considerable practical and intellectual obstacles. Protests arose from mavericks like Roger Williams, who asked where Scripture sanctioned the coercion of conscience as required by the

Puritans' unitary system, and Anne Hutchinson (1591–1642), who argued that stress on a visible profession of faith promoted hypocrisy and undercut trust in divine grace. Because England paid little attention to New England, the Puritan leaders were free to handle dissent their own way: Williams and Hutchinson were banished, a few Baptists were fined or whipped, and near the tumultuous end of Puritan rule in England the Massachusetts authorities hung four recalcitrant Quakers (1659–61).

It was never the case that all ordinary New Englanders subscribed fully to the system. But on balance, the experiment as guided by the leading magistrates and ministers worked well. New England was often at peace, the pious revelled in a steady diet of carefully prepared biblical sermons, and (despite moments of strife) the political order functioned efficiently and with more public support than any other seventeenth-century European regime. Moreover, the necessary intellectual infrastructure was put in place early on: Harvard College, founded in 1636 to provide future ministers and magistrates an education in Christian liberal arts, and a printing press (located, like the college, in Cambridge), to provide the sermons, treatises, and miscellaneous learned literature that was lifeblood for the enterprise.

The one unavoidable difficulty was the passage of time. Increasingly, sons and daughters of first-generation settlers failed to experience conversion. Consequently, fewer and fewer of the second generation presented themselves for church membership. Steadily the fear grew that the Puritans' interlocking covenants would unravel. No new converts, no covenanted church; no covenanted church, no godly society. In the face of crisis, Massachusetts' leaders proposed an ingenious expedient. Meeting as a Synod in 1662, the ministers established what later historians have called the Half-Way Covenant. Under this plan, baptized individuals of good behaviour could present their children for baptism, but neither they nor their children could take the Lord's Supper unless they made a personal profession of faith. The framers of the Half-Way Covenant hoped to preserve both the integrity of local congregations as the gathering of the elect and the participation of as many people as possible in the Puritan system. They succeeded, at least in part, but time was taking its toll. A theology forged in the crucible of English religious strife had to be modified in order to survive in the greatly altered conditions of America.

These altered conditions included a series of shocks towards the end of the century: warfare with Native Americans in 1675–76 that left twelve towns levelled and 2,000 settlers slain (but that also destroyed the Indians as a factor in the region); hysteria over witchcraft in the early 1690s culminating in twenty executions at Salem Village; the imposition upon Massachusetts in 1695 of a new charter that reduced the legal role of the churches; and, by the start of the eighteenth century, the growth of luxury and a new desire to imitate the ways of the English upper classes, especially in Boston. Despite concern over declension, expressed in fervent sermons appealing for colony-wide repentance, Massachusetts and the equally Puritan Connecticut remained the most cohesive, most religiously self-assured colonies in the New World.

For the Puritans, formal theology was also important. And there was a lot of it, from the early immigrant preacher-theologians and from later pastors trained entirely in America, including the Boston minister, Samuel Willard, who produced a massive set of lectures on the Westminster Confession during the 1670s and 1680s (published in 1726 as a *Compleat Body of Divinity*). But theology in action rather than just theology by the book was the key to what made American Puritanism work.

Encounter with Native Americans

Almost all ventures in European colonization proclaimed an intention to evangelize Native Americans. None succeeded, at least with anything like the success so easily anticipated. Sharp differences in world-view, the largely unintended destruction of native populations by European diseases, the assumption accepted almost universally that Christianity entailed European forms of civilization, and an inability to segregate altruistic missionary efforts from the acquisitive pursuit of land doomed efforts at Christianizing the native peoples.

In Acadia, the earliest Jesuit missionaries established a North American precedent when in 1611 they began serious study of the Micmac language. Later mission work in Acadia would be taken up by the Capuchins, another renewed Franciscan order, but this effort was crushed at mid-century during armed conflict with New Englanders. Along the St Lawrence, Jesuits took the lead with Algonquian-speaking tribes by establishing a settlement for converted Indians at Sillery near Quebec. Similar efforts would later include an important settlement organized by the Sulpicians on Mount Royal in the present Montreal. The most significant early mission effort throughout all of North America, however, was the Jesuit work among the Iroquoian-speaking Huron far to the west on Georgian Bay.

The Jesuit Jean Le Brébeuf had first travelled to Huronia in 1626 where he remained for three years to study the language and culture. After a hiatus caused by conflict with England, Brébeuf reopened the mission in 1634. By 1647, there were nineteen Jesuits at work, and converts numbered in the thousands. The relative success of the Jesuits was in part a product of hard-won lessons drawn from the order's missionary experience in China (especially Matteo Ricci) and India (especially Robert de Nobili) that had accepted the possibility that non-western religions might contain a positive base on which Christianity could build. Thus, the Canadian Jesuits found at least some common ground in Huron commitment to personal relationships, Huron trust in visions, and Huron familiarity with migration (as an analogy to pilgrimage). For his part, Brébeuf translated biblical and liturgical material into Huron and probably composed at least one Christmas carol, which, however, has been translated with the name of an Algonquian deity: 'Twas the moon of wintertime when all the birds had fled, That mighty Gitchi Manitou sent angel choirs instead'.[7]

The relative cultural flexibility of the Jesuits notwithstanding, external factors were probably more important in the conversion of the Huron. Contact with the French had led to devastating epidemics of measles and influenza. Simultaneously the Huron were being pressed hard by the Iroquoian Five Nations Confederacy to the south. The Jesuits' arrival, in other words, coincided with personal and community trauma. Brébeuf and his colleagues struggled zealously to strengthen this Christian outpost in the American wilderness, but a final push by the Five Nations in 1648 and 1649 led not only to the destruction of the Huron mission, but of Huronia itself. In this debacle, many Jesuits were faithful unto death, including Brébeuf (who fell in 1649). In keeping with well-established Indian practice, Brébeuf as the honoured leader of a foe was subjected to exquisite torture, which he bore so stoically that when he died his captors respectfully ate his heart and drank his blood.

Converted Indians included the Huron Joseph Chihwatenha who joined the Jesuits in observing the *Spiritual Exercises* of Ignatius Loyola. Later in the century, Kateri Tekakwitha, of mixed Algonquian-Iroquoian parentage, went to such lengths of pious self-mortification that even before her early death in 1680 she was an object of admiration for many. It was, however, a sign indicating the relatively superficial results of missionary activity that, although the Sulpicians eventually accepted a few native nuns, no native priests were ordained in the seventeenth century.

In the English colonies, missionary efforts came later and were even less effective. A very occasional convert might provide reason for self-congratulation, like Pocahontas, daughter of the Algonquian chief Powhatan, who espoused Christianity at Jamestown in 1614. But her life as a Christian was short, since she died three years later in England where she had been taken by her English husband, John Rolfe. More commonly in Virginia as also in New England, early English–Indian relations were marked by suspicion, conflict, and even massacre. Exceptions included Roger Williams, who interacted sympathetically with the Narragansett Indians, and the Jesuit Andrew White, whose work in Maryland with the Piscataway was cut short when English authorities exiled him from the colony in 1645.

The most extensive Puritan efforts were undertaken by two Massachusetts pastors, John Eliot (1604–90) of Roxborough, and Thomas Mayhew, Jr. (1621– 57) of Martha's Vineyard. Eliot succeeded in gathering a number of Indian converts into 'praying towns' organized after Old Testament models, and his Algonquian translation was the first full Bible of any sort printed in the English colonies. But Eliot's work was all but destroyed during King Philip's War (1675– 76) when fearful Puritans quarantined the converted Indians in unhealthy conditions on Deer Island in Boston Harbour. Mayhew, his father, and other members of the family enjoyed longer-lasting success in their work because the relatively isolated character of Martha's Vineyard protected converted Indians from the depredations of warfare and the acquisitiveness of land-hungry Europeans.

The most effective Protestant mission to Native Americans did not begin until well into the eighteenth century. It was undertaken by Moravians, who were also the Protestant pioneers in effective outreach to enslaved Africans. In 1732, only a few years after the modern rejuvenation of the Moravian church, their leader, Count Ludwig Nicholas von Zinzendorf, dispatched Leonhard Dober and David Nitschman from Herrnhut in Saxony to St Thomas in the Virgin Islands. Moravians, who enjoyed no stake in land or authority and who practised a Pietistic religion of the heart, enjoyed considerable success in this venture, which led then to fruitful ministry with the black populations of Jamaica (1754), Antigua (1756), and Barbados (1765).

As part of the same missionary spirit, in 1742 two Moravians, Christian Rauch and Gottlob Büttner, began work with the Mahicans at Shekomeko near the Massachusetts–New York border. Among their converts were several women whose expressions of faith testified to a substantial indigenizing of Moravian piety. One of these converts, Rachel (who had been Wampanosch), left a record in December 1743 of what it meant for her to participate in a Moravian communion. As recorded by Büttner, her experience mingled the Moravian theology of Christ's blood and wounds with her understanding of native practices of ritual torture: 'She saw nothing with her eyes, but her heart believed so in the Saviour as if she had seen him and she had then such a feeling of it, that she thought that if any one should pull the flesh from her bones she would nevertheless abide with him, and she said, "I believe I should not have felt it neither, for my whole body and heart felt a power from his wounds and blood".'[8]

In just a few more years Moravians succeeded in establishing a second mission, this one conducted by David Zeisberger, among the Delaware of Pennsylvania. But then the French and Indian War greatly damaged the Shekomeko and Delaware missions, since Indians were suspect for being Indian, and Moravians were regularly charged with being papists. Zeisberger eventually found a temporary refuge for his converts at Friedenshütten (meaning 'sheltered by peace') on the Susquehanna River. But hostility from white Pennsylvanians soon drove the Moravians and their converts into the western wilderness, where after much further trauma they eventually established a secure settlement in modern Ontario.

Native American cultures operated on principles greatly at odds with European culture, for relations with divinity as well as for relations with the land, for reconciliation with enemies as well as for reconciliation with God. Perhaps the wonder is not that Europeans found it so difficult to evangelize Native Americans but that even a few of the Indians adopted the Christian message for themselves.

Revival and war

During the early decades of the eighteenth century the European powers treated their colonies with benign neglect. The result for the churches was not drift, but an evolutionary adaptation of immigrant faith to new-world conditions.

In New France, the work of the Jesuits was interrupted when they were ensnared in political manoeuvrings at home. But along with Récollets, Capuchins, and Sulpicians, the Jesuits persevered in a significant, but diminishing work among the Indians even as their religious centre of gravity swung increasingly to the European settlements. Although interminable quarrels among bishops and leaders of the orders marked a clear spiritual descent from the heroism of the previous century, the structures of an organic Catholic society were nonetheless strengthened. Catholics in Acadia, where political control passed to the British with the Treaty of Utrecht in 1713, carried on uneasily until the outbreak of imperial warfare in 1754. In the intervening decades, notable mission work by the Jesuit Sébastien Rale and Pierre Maillard of the Seminary of the Holy Spirit (Paris) had complicated relations with Britain, especially since these fathers recruited natives as warriors to harass New England settlements as they also tended to more narrowly religious concerns. At the start of the French and Indian War, Britain took the draconian step of expelling the French-descended Acadians to Louisiana and elsewhere.

Only from this tumultuous period in the mid-1750s did a continuous Protestant history begin in Canada, as British authorities recruited New Englanders and various European Protestants to fill up the Acadian land they had evacuated.

In Quebec, similar traumas faced the church with the triumph of British arms at Quebec (1759) and at Montreal (1760). Overlords in London looked for a speedy extirpation of the French and Catholic presence along the St Lawrence, but leaders on site were more realistic. Gov. James Murray disregarded instructions to exclude Roman jurisdiction from Quebec (though the Treaty of Paris of 1763 did allow for the practice of Catholicism). His tact was matched by the skilful diplomacy of Jean-Olivier Briand who, after reassuring Murray and the British of Quebecois loyalty, was in 1764 consecrated as the new bishop. Through delicate negotiations between Murray and Briand, Britain eventually provided funds and other support for the Catholic Church in British North America, more than sixty years before it conceded full civil rights to Catholics on its own soil. In 1760, about 180 priests and 190 nuns were at work among Quebec's roughly 70,000 inhabitants.

The ratio of people to ministers was considerably higher in the thirteen colonies to the south, but the construction of churches, the calling of pastors, and the encouragement of Christian practices was for the most part keeping up with a rapid rise in population. At mid-century, with white colonists in the thirteen colonies totalling roughly one million, there was about one church for every 600 New Englanders (living mostly in well-defined towns and adjacent farms), one for about every 470 middle colonists (mostly rural, though with Philadelphia and New York as rising urban centres), and one for about every 1,050 whites in the southern colonies (with the population mostly dispersed along waterways).[9] As an indication of how influential old-world patterns of state establishments for religion remained, in 1740 over half of all the churches were 'established', either Congregational (423) or Anglican (246). In Virginia at this date there were no non-Anglican churches, and the colony's leaders intended to keep it that way. New England had come to tolerate a few non-Congregationalists, but only grudgingly. In both the south and New England, governments still controlled religion more tightly than was the case in England. By contrast, in the middle colonies denominational pluralism had become a fact of life. This was the region where in 1740 most of the thirteen colonies' non-established churches were found: Presbyterian (160), German and Dutch Reformed (129), Baptist (96), Lutheran (95), Quaker (c. 50), Mennonite and Moravian and Brethren (c. 30), and Catholic (27).

Well before tumults at mid-century drastically altered the shape of religion, incremental developments brought evolutionary change. The Bloodless

Revolution of 1688 and the European entanglements of the new monarchs, William and Mary, pulled New Englanders out of their Puritan shell and made all colonial Protestants more self-conscious about the controversy with Rome that was so inextricably a part of the conflict with France. This heightened sensibility was expressed clearly when, for example, in 1698 a Congregational minister preached a sermon entitled *New-England's Duty and Interest* in which that interest was described as lying with 'the Protestant People, and [God's] Witnesses in Germany, Bohemia, Hungarra, France, the Valleys of the Piedmont; and many other places in Europe: where for his Name and Gospel sake they have been Killed all the day long'.[10]

The careers of notable Protestant leaders further illustrate the temper of the times. Cotton Mather (1663–1728), long-time colleague minister with his father, Increase, at Boston's Second Church, was famously hyper-active, but also learned, conscientious, and touchingly pious. His *Magnalia Christi Americana* (1702) represented a filiopietistic paean to the unique virtues of New England's founders, but Mather also corresponded with the Halle Pietist August Hermann Francke, he nudged norms of religious experience towards the new affectional philosophy of the eighteenth century, he eventually welcomed non-Congregational churches to Boston (though not Anglicans), and he manifested the Enlightenment's fascination with nature by urging inoculation against smallpox and writing a considerable work of natural theology, *The Christian Philosopher* (1721). Mather regarded Benjamin Colman as a theological trimmer when in 1699 Colman was named the pastor of Boston's new Brattle Street Church, where new expressions of English architecture, English liturgy, and English sensibility seemed to be replacing New England's historic Puritan distinctiveness. Yet Colman, who had lived in London before taking this charge, was not so much a liberal as an internationally attuned evangelical who valued closer ties with an array of European Protestants. In the 1730s Colman would connect Jonathan Edwards with leading British Dissenters and also provide Boston's official welcome for George Whitefield. Together, Mather and Colman were reflecting an altered landscape. They participated in the era's explosion of print, they shared a heightened sense of world-wide Catholic menace, and their congregations were financially supported by an ever-expanding trans-Atlantic trade.

Such tectonic movement prepared the way for revivalistic eruption. New England had long witnessed recurring episodes of local revival, for example, several 'harvests' at the Northampton, Massachusetts, church of Solomon Stoddard (1643–1729), the dominant religious figure in the Connecticut River Valley for more than half a century. By the mid-1720s similar local episodes were occurring among the Dutch in New Jersey where Theodore Frelinghuysen promoted the standard emphases of European Pietism: personal repentance, Christ-centred faith, and suspicion of inherited church authority. Presbyterians who had come to America from Ulster were also drawn to these emphases more readily than their fellows from Scotland. In the early 1740s a Scots–Irish party led by Gilbert Tennent, who had been pointed towards Pietistic concerns by Frelinghuysen, joined forces with transplanted New Englanders led by Jonathan Dickinson to create a dynamic movement of New Side Presbyterian revival. It eventually produced a corps of eager young preachers, among whom the most effective was Samuel Davies (1723–61). Davies, who settled permanently in Virginia in 1748, laboured patiently to win recognition for Presbyterian churches there – first by appealing to the British Toleration Act of 1689 and then by preaching intensely patriotic sermons during the war with France. By the time of Davies' departure from Virginia to serve as president of the College of New Jersey at Princeton, a Presbyterianism that combined respect for the Scottish confessional legacy with a Pietistic urgency was spreading fast in several middle and southern colonies.

The most visible expression of the new religious forces, however, came from a local revival in Massachusetts and the exertions of an Anglican itinerant. In late 1734, Jonathan Edwards (1703–58), the grandson and successor of Solomon Stoddard, preached a short series of sermons to his Northampton congregation on justification by faith. Response in the town was electric, as described in Edwards' initial report: 'Those that were most disposed to contemn vital and experimental religion, and those that had the greatest conceit of their own reason, the highest families in the town, and the oldest persons in the town, and many little children were affected remarkably; no one family that I know of, and scarcely a person, has been exempt'.[11]

The particular history of Northampton and Edwards' persistent preaching against what he viewed as Arminian tendencies help explain this revival, just as the suicide of Edwards' uncle, Joseph Hawley, in May 1735 helps explain why the revival cooled. But what local circumstances cannot explain is the clamour that greeted Edwards' account – *A Faithful Narrative of the Surprizing Work of God in the Conversion of Many Hundred Souls in Northampton, and the Neighboring Towns and Villages* – when in 1737 it was published in London under the auspices of Isaac Watts. Edwards' stark depiction of the damning dreadfulness of human sin and his equally powerful depiction of the palpable joy of salvation struck chords of sympathy in Boston and elsewhere in the colonies, in Scotland, England, and Wales, and even on the continent. Edwards would go on to a chequered career with his Northampton congregation, which in 1750 expelled him when he tried to alter sacramental practices inherited from Stoddard. But the reception that greeted his rendering of the 1735 revival showed that the day of a more affectional, more conversionistic, less traditional, and less hierarchical Protestantism had arrived.

Even more broadly indicative of a new religious era was the labour of George Whitefield, who first came to America in 1738. Whitefield was a young man who preached traditional Calvinism, an ordained Anglican who flouted church conventions by preaching out-of-doors or wherever he could gather a crowd, an advocate of the older Puritan spirituality who exploited the most up-to-date strategies of marketing and communications, and a person of genuinely self-effacing piety who became one of the great celebrities of the age. Whitefield came to America ostensibly to manage an orphanage in Georgia modelled after the Pietist institution in Halle. But his real business was to preach. Especially memorable tours in and around Philadelphia from 3 April to 5 June 1740 (during which he mesmerized the secular Benjamin Franklin) and in New England from 14 September to 13 October of the same year (during which he and Jonathan Edwards explored their considerable spiritual affinity) marked Whitefield as the first person widely known in all of the colonies that would later constitute the United States. More importantly, his preaching – direct, personal, improvisational, dramatic, popular, and affecting – pointed away from religion conceived as an inherited frame of life to religion conceived as a function of personal choice. That Whitefield inspired many imitators and drew the fire of many enemies was less important for the long term than that he had inaugurated a new approach to religion that would flourish in North America as nowhere else in the world. The key was a faith that embraced much of traditional Christianity but was appropriated personally in a more modern individualistic form.

The revival was both a sign and precipitate of fundamental change. It left New England Puritanism shattered into competing parties – liberals like Charles Chauncy and Jonathan Mayhew, who were pushed by revival enthusiasms to stronger advocacy of rational moralism; conservative Old Lights like Isaac Stiles of North Haven, Connecticut, who struggled to maintain Calvinism in its traditional establishmentarian form; New Lights who followed Edwards in seeking to rejuvenate the comprehensive Puritan churches with the new wine of revival; and Separates who held that the experimental Calvinism preached by Edwards and Whitefield required congregations of true believers to come out of the stultifying established churches. In New England as throughout the rest of the colonies, the revivals spurred the labours of energetic Baptists like the theologically and politically astute Isaac Backus, who stood with Edwards in promoting heart-felt Calvinism but against all forms of religious establishment as violating the rights of conscience. Anglicans also benefited because they seemed to offer a calm refuge from revival enthusiasms.

The mid-century awakenings operated as a great stimulus to theology. Clerics like Ebenezer Gay of Hingham, Massachusetts, who opposed the revivals, took the first steps towards Unitarianism by subjecting inherited belief to the eighteenth century's new standards of rationality and common sense. But the great theological monument of the awakenings came in the work of Jonathan Edwards, who strove to baptize the era's new moral philosophy for the revival of Calvinistic piety. In a series of works of ever more painstaking discrimination, culminating in the *Treatise Concerning Religious Affections* (1746), he laboured to spell out what were and what were not reliable signs of God's true working. In *The Freedom of the Will* (1754) he deployed up-to-date casuistry to argue against rapidly rising notions of human freedom understood as self-determination. In the posthumously published *Two treatises: Concerning the End for which God Created the World (and) The Nature of True Virtue* (1765) he argued that biblical reasoning and contemporary affectional psychology both defined genuine goodness as love of God for God's own perfectly holy sake. Edwards's own attitude towards the church (as made up essentially of the redeemed) and salvation (as dependent wholly upon the grace of God) had the ironic effect of weakening the commitment of his theological heirs to careful thought. His own labours, by contrast, are increasingly recognized as the intellectual, as well as theological, highpoint of the age.

The awakenings also gave an unusual voice to women. Susanna Anthony of Newport, Rhode Island, for example, joined her local congregation in 1742 after a sermon on Hebrews 7:25 ('Wherefore, he is able to save them to the uttermost, that come unto God by him') led her to experience 'the Spirit of God . . . powerfully . . . Thus, thus, infinitely lovely did Christ appear to me'.[12] Anthony went on, as did many women touched by the revival, to lead a women's 'society' that met weekly for many decades. Less typically, she also played a significant role in the call of Samuel Hopkins, a student of Edwards, to the pulpit of her Newport church. Esther Edwards Burr (1732–58), daughter of the distinguished theologian and husband of Princeton College president Aaron Burr, gained a considerable measure of self-confidence by undergoing the same gracious experiences that the awakeners preached so forcefully. When a college tutor once spoke disparagingly in her presence of female capacities for friendship and rational personal development, she responded with a full flight of argument and 'talked him quite silent'.[13] Among

Baptists and Separates (that is, Congregationalists who broke away from the establishment to form their own churches), awakened women in the first years of revival were allowed unprecedented opportunities of exhorting and participating fully in deliberations of the congregation.

Even more significant for the world history of Christianity were efforts inspired by the revival to communicate the gospel to African Americans. Protests against slavery appeared sporadically during the colonial period, from Mennonites and Quakers in Pennsylvania late in the seventeenth century, from the Puritan judge Samuel Sewall in 1700, and from the Quaker John Woolman (1720–72) throughout his adult life. But evangelism of slaves and freed blacks had almost never succeeded. In the 1740s revival preaching and practices, which paid less attention to church order than to experiential religion, began to break through. Whitefield and Davies, who, as it happens, both owned slaves, were the most effective preachers to African Americans, but they were joined by many others. Phillis Wheatley, an African-born slave who had been manumitted by her Boston owners, memorialized this evangelistic activity in a tribute published at Whitefield's death in 1770. Wheatley, who had herself heard Whitefield preach, recorded especially his address to the slaves:

> Take him, ye *Africans*, he longs for you,
> *Impartial Saviour* is his title due:
> If you will chuse to walk in grace's road,
> You shall be sons, and kings, and Priests to God.[14]

Such a message, applied with a minimum of manipulation, represented one of the most unexpected, and yet most important, innovations occasioned by the expansion of Europe. In outreach to African Americans, Christianity took root in a group with no social standing, no inherited tradition of Christian faith, no stock in church establishments, and no history of European Christendom. In a way that none could foresee in that century, it was a prescription for the future.

What people could see clearly in the wake of revival was a renewal of imperial warfare and the beginning of cataclysmic change for the colonies. Britain's victory over France, which was finalized by the Treaty of Paris in 1763, seemed at first to simplify colonial life. In many sermons of thanksgiving it was proclaimed that Protestant British liberty had been vindicated in a struggle against French Catholic despotism. But when Britain tried to regularize its newly expanded empire with taxes, soldiers, and tighter administration, it was not long before colonials were blasting George III and his parliament as the despots. In that unexpected development the churches would be fully engaged, and in it would be found yet more unexpected fruit from seed planted in North American colonial Christian experience.

Notes

1. What colonists called the French and Indian War began in 1754, two years before the fighting in Europe's Seven Years' War.

2. Samuel Davies, 'God the sovereign of all nations', in S. Davies, *Sermons on important subjects*, 4th edn, 3 vols. (New York: J. and J. Harper, 1828), vol. 3, p. 173.

3. J. Butler, 'Protestant pluralism', *Encyclopedia of the North American colonies*, ed. Jacob Ernest Cooke, 3 vols. (New York: Charles Scribner's Sons, 1993), vol. 3, p. 609.

4. R. Williams, *The complete writings of Roger Williams*, 7 vols. (New York: Russell & Russell, 1963), vol. 3, pp. 3–4.

5. William Bradford, *Of Plymouth Plantation*, ed. S. E. Morison (New York: Knopf, 1959), pp. 61, 62–3.

6. Edmund S. Morgan (ed.), *Puritan political ideas* (Indianapolis: Bobbs-Merrill, 1965), pp. 90, 93.

7. On the translation, John Webster Grant, *Moon of wintertime: Missionaries and the Indians of Canada in encounter since 1534* (Toronto: University of Toronto Press, 1984), p. vii.

8. In Rachel Wheeler, 'Women and Christian practice in a Mahican Village', *Religion and American culture*, 13 (Winter 2003), p. 36.

9. Patricia U. Bonomi and Peter R. Eisenstadt, 'Church adherence in the eighteenth-century British American colonies', *William and Mary quarterly*, 39 (1982), p. 273. The number of churches is from Edwin S. Gaustad and Philip L. Barlow, *New historical atlas of religion in America* (New York: Oxford University Press, 2000).

10. Thomas S. Kidd, '"Let hell and Rome do their worst": world news and anti-Catholicism, and international Protestantism in early-eighteenth-century Boston', *New England quarterly*, 86 (2003), p. 270.

11. J. Edwards, 'Letter of May 30, 1735', in *The works of Jonathan Edwards*, vol. 4: *The Great Awakening*, ed. C. C. Goen (New Haven: Yale University Press, 1972), p. 101.

12. Samuel Hopkins, *The life and character of Miss Susanna Anthony* (Hartford, CT: Hudson and Goodwin, 1799), pp. 30–1.

13. E. E. Burr, *The journal of Esther Edwards Burr, 1754–1757*, ed. Carol F. Karlsen and Laurie Crumpacker (New Haven: Yale University Press, 1984), p. 257.

14. P. Wheatley, *The poems of Phillis Wheatley*, ed. Julian D. Mason, Jr. (Chapel Hill: University of North Carolina Press, 1966), p. 68.

21

Christianity in Africa

LAMIN SANNEH

Led by Catholic Spain and Portugal, and later joined by Protestant England and the Netherlands, the explosion of maritime exploration from the late fifteenth century made for a shift from land-based power to sea-based power. In the era before Vasco da Gama rounded the Cape in 1498, the dominant world powers had been land-based. After 1500, the dominant powers were those with unchallenged suzerainty over the sea lanes, from Lisbon and Genoa, or Plymouth and Rotterdam, to Goa and Canton. Sea-based power brought into play a new mercantile class whose entrepreneurial spirit sent them looking for wealth and profit in hitherto unknown or unexplored lands. As one such adventurer expressed it, they crossed the seas 'to serve God and His majesty, to give light to those who were in darkness', but also most emphatically 'to grow rich, as all men desire to do'.[1] Or, as Columbus expressed it, 'Gold, what an excellent product! It is from gold that riches come. He who has gold can do whatever he pleases in this world. With gold one can even bring souls into Paradise.'[2] For these entrepreneurs, mission was not just necessary, it was profitable.

The Catholic missions in West and East Africa

The first European sea-based power to colonize extensively in Africa was Portugal, a small monarchy that had arisen amid the twelfth-century Christian crusade against the Moors in the Iberian peninsula. Seeking gold and slaves, and perhaps the fabled Christian kingdom of Prester John, fifteenth-century Portuguese kings sent expedition after expedition to sail ever further southwards along the western African coast. These Portuguese maritime expeditions brought with them priests and some viewed the explorations as part of the Christian crusade. In the early 1480s, Portuguese expeditions reached the kingdom of the Kongo, a sophisticated African state along the River Zaire. Missionaries arrived in 1491, receiving a warm welcome and baptizing the king and hundreds of his subjects. Afonso, the 'apostle of the Kongo', came to the Kongolese throne as a Christian convert in 1506, and reigned until 1543, establishing a Christian monarchy, learning Portuguese, building churches, promoting missions, and indeed sending his son, Henry, to Portugal to be educated and ordained for missionary service in the Kongo. The Jesuits arrived in the mid-sixteenth century and formed Christian villages. In 1596, the papacy established the diocese of São Salvador for the Kongolese Kingdom and the neighbouring territory of Angola. The Jesuits established a college at São Salvador in 1624; the first rector, Fr Cardosa, translated the standard Portuguese catechism into the local Kikongo language, and distributed hundreds of copies. These Kikongo catechisms were used by lay catechists, the *maestri*, who handed on the teachings in the villages from generation to generation, much of the time without clerical presence.

In 1645 the Capuchins, including Italian and Spanish friars, began a mission in the Kongolese Kingdom, as part of a larger initiative of *Propaganda Fide* to promote mission activity directed from Rome in West Africa. In what marked the beginning of nearly two centuries of Capuchin involvement in the Kongo, the Capuchins established schools in São Salvador and Soyo, learned Kikongo, and began systematic evangelization in the rural districts. They established confraternities among the Africans, among them the Confraternity of Our Lady of the Rosary, which was formed in Luanda in 1658 and which became a forum for promoting African rights. Between 1672 and 1700, thirty-seven Capuchin fathers recorded a total of 341,000 baptisms. Other Capuchin missions were established on the Guinea Coast and Sierra Leone in 1644, in Benin in 1647, and in the small state of Warri in the 1650s. Queen Nzinga of Matamba, in eastern Angola, embraced Christianity through the influence of a captured Capuchin father in 1656, and sought to create a Christian state, personally carrying stones for the building of the church of Our Lady of Matamba, which was completed in 1665, the year of her death.

After the Portuguese rounded the Cape, they set up colonies in East Africa, including fortified trading cities along the coasts. The island-city of Mozambique became the main administrative centre of Portuguese East Africa, and the city had an estimated 2,000 Christians by 1586. The Mutapa Empire in Zimbabwe came under Dominican influence in the seventeenth century, and its kings accepted baptism. In the Zambezi valley, the Portuguese crown made large grants of land (*prazos*) to settlers. Jesuits and Dominicans from Portugal accompanied the colonists, and in some cases the fathers held *prazos*. According to a Portuguese Jesuit in 1667, there were sixteen places of worship pursuing missionary work in the lower Zambezi valley – six conducted by

Figure 7 Crucifix from the Christian Kongolese Kingdom, south-western Africa, seventeenth century. It provides an early example of an Africanized vision of the suffering Christ. (Photograph in the Butler Collection, Centre for the Study of Christianity in the Non-Western World, University of Edinburgh.)

the Jesuits, nine by the Dominicans and one by a secular priest. In 1697, the Jesuits established a college at Sena, for the children of both the Portuguese and African elite. For a time in the early to mid-seventeenth century, there was a real prospect of the large-scale spread of Catholic Christianity in Africa, supported by a network of African kings and their ruling elite, and pushed forward by a number of remarkable priests and friars. While many Africans may have embraced Christianity in order to placate the Portuguese overlords, there is also evidence of real belief and commitment. When, for example, the city of Mombassa temporarily fell to a Muslim force in 1631, seventy-two African men and women – the 'Martyrs of Mombassa' – accepted death with their fellow European Christians rather than deny their Christian faith.

By the early eighteenth century, however, the prospects for African Christianity had become greatly reduced. The Christian Kongolese Kingdom was shattered by civil warfare and the power and authority of the Kongolese king considerably restricted. The capital of São Salvador was sacked by a warring faction in 1678 and was then deserted for a quarter century. Reoccupied in the early eighteenth century, its twelve churches were in ruins, and only a single priest, Estavo Botelho, remained in the capital – and he was a slave-trader who lived with concubines. Of the several provinces of the kingdom, only the coastal province of Soyo retained a significant Christian population. The Capuchin mission in the Kongo was reduced to two or three friars. By 1750, this fell to one Capuchin missionary, the remarkable Fr Cherubina da Savona, who bravely carried on traversing the country until 1777 and baptizing some 700,000 during his lonely mission of twenty-seven years. Although later Capuchins attempted to carry on the mission, the last regular Capuchin priest withdrew in 1795. In some rural villages, the *maestri* continued to convey Christian teachings, and the people observed Christian rituals and chanted canticles. French missionaries discovered one such village north of the River Zaire in 1773, its identity proclaimed by a great cross. However, without a regular priesthood empowered to baptize, such communities in time lapsed from their Christian faith. Despite periodic but short-lived missions in Warri and other countries in West Africa, Christianity struggled to survive. In East Africa, the religious orders and secular priests increasingly restricted their ministry to the Portuguese ruling class, and by 1712, missions to Africans continued only in Zambesia. Soon these also died out. Everywhere, Christianity was becoming a mere appendage of the colonial settlements, with the clergy becoming largely chaplains to the colonizers and supporters of the colonial governments.

There were a number of reasons for this decline of the Catholic missions. The waning power of Portugal reduced its ability to recruit and maintain missionaries, while at the same time increasing its suspicion of missionaries of other nationalities. Rome, moreover, experienced a declining interest in the world mission movement during the eighteenth century, and the supply of missionaries gradually diminished. There were never enough priests for the African mission field, and while many of the missionary priests were exemplary in their piety and commitment, others proved disappointing. Often isolated and lacking regular episcopal supervision or encouragement, some grew discouraged, took concubines or became slavers, bringing scandal and disrepute to their church and their calling. Many missionaries succumbed to the African climate and fever. Of 438 known Capuchin fathers active in the mission to the Kongo between 1645 and 1835, 229 died after a few years in the mission field, while others returned home in poor health. Portugal's decision in 1759 to expel the Jesuits from its colonial territories further reduced the numbers of missionaries, especially in Zambesia. While efforts were made to recruit and educate an African priesthood, these proved insufficient and there were never enough African priests. Capuchin fathers, moreover, were suspicious of the lay *maestri* and often declined to give them the necessary support.

Catholic missions in other parts of the world, however, confronted similar difficulties, without the collapse that was experienced in sub-Saharan Africa. What was distinctive about Africa was the social devastation caused by the slave trade. While slavery and the slave trade co-existed with Christianity in the past, in Africa the sheer scale of this trade was unprecedented. From the mid-seventeenth century, tens of thousands of Africans were shipped off each year to plantations in the Americas. Portugal's African empire became primarily a source of slaves. In order to feed the burgeoning demand for human labour, the slavers began seizing whole villages and devastating and depopulating whole districts. This in turn contributed to civil warfare and social breakdown. It is estimated that 40 per cent of the total number of slaves crossing the Atlantic came from the Kongo-Angola area – a figure out of all proportion to the population of the region, and one of the main reasons for the disintegration of the Christian Kongolese Kingdom. Some of the clergy in Africa, it must be noted, owned slaves or engaged in the slave trade. For example, Fr Pedro de S. S. Trinidade, who lived at Zumbo on the Zambezi between 1710 and 1754, owned 1,600 slaves and worked a gold mine. Nearly all the clergy received financial support through the slave trade. Nonetheless, many of the clergy were prepared to speak out against slavery and the slave trade. In 1686, in response to appeals from the Capuchins and petitions orchestrated by a former Afro-Brazilian slave, Lourenço da Silva (who claimed to be of royal Kongolese blood), the Holy Office in Rome had condemned the Atlantic slave trade. Despite this condemnation, the trade continued, with ruinous effects for the Catholic missions until well into the early nineteenth century. When the famed Scottish missionary David Livingstone reached Angola in 1854 on his trek across the continent, he found only the ruins of Jesuit and Capuchin churches and Christianity reduced to a folk memory. The recovery of the Catholic missions would come, but only after the close of our period.

A new beginning: The Protestant missions in West Africa

In time, the antislavery note that had been sounded for so long, and with so little effect, in Rome became a dominant theme in the renewal of the worldwide missionary movement in a Protestant Christianity that for the most part rejected mission as a Roman Catholic preserve. The first such Protestant organization, the Society for the Propagation of Christian Knowledge (SPCK), was founded in London in 1698. Its stated purpose was 'to promote religion and learning in the Plantations abroad and to propagate Christian knowledge at home', and it decided to allow, as a spin-off activity, the formation of a missionary arm called the Society for the Propagation of the Gospel in Foreign Parts (SPG) with the goal of sending out and maintaining missionaries. A Royal Charter in 1701 established the SPG on that basis. But even such early signs of commitment to mission among Protestants remained largely ad hoc and contingent, and often derivative from the work of others. The SPCK's educational and publishing work, however, had a significant impact at home and on the work that others were doing in the mission field. In particular, by 1720 there was an extensive programme of Bible translation. The SPCK had by that date produced 10,000 Arabic New Testaments, 6,000 Psalters, and 5,000 Catechetical Instructions. The targets were communities in the Ottoman dominions, and in Russia, Persia and India. The SPCK began a mission to the Scilly Isles in 1765 that lasted until 1841.

Direct SPG involvement in Africa was prompted by the needs of British trading concerns. Accordingly, between 1752 and 1824 the SPG sent out at the request of the Royal African Company (RAC) English clergymen who were commissioned as chaplains at Cape Coast in the then Gold Coast. One of these clergymen, Thomas Thompson, served for five years and recorded his impressions in a journal entitled, *An Account of Two Missionary Voyages*, which he published in 1758. Reflecting the prevailing opinions of the RAC, Thompson took the view that slavery was not an evil, and he wrote approvingly of the slave trade. But in the attention he paid to the value of African languages in the work of missions, Thompson unwittingly signalled a crucial shift to African cultural materials as the appropriate framework for the transmission of Christianity. He stressed the importance of developing Fanti-language education, and, appropriately, arranged for three Fanti boys to accompany him to England for education. Two of them died, but the third, Philip Quaque, was ordained in the Anglican Church and in 1765 returned to Cape Coast where he served as schoolmaster, catechist, and missionary. He died in 1816 in those positions.

The Danes had also been involved at the fort of Christiansborg, Accra, a garrison fortress held by Denmark from which they regulated trade in the adjacent area. The chaplains who arrived in the Gold Coast were not strictly speaking missionaries, but, significantly enough, some took a close interest in African life and religion. For example, Wilhelm Johann Mueller, a chaplain between 1662 and 1670 at Fort Frederiksborg near Cape Coast, argued for missionary effort among the local population and asked for the Bible to be translated into the local languages. He followed his own advice when he collected some 800 practical words and phrases. He also demonstrated knowledge of local religious practices, the first such attempt at understanding by an outsider.

Two other chaplains based at Christiansborg found the restricted boundaries of fortress life too confining, and ventured further afield. One was Johann Rask, who served between 1709 and 1712, and the other was H. S. Monrad, who served between 1805 and 1809. Both condemned slavery and the trade that fostered it, and both expressed the classic doubt about the viability of establishing the church in Africa under the compromising shadow of European commercial enclaves. Without a missionary organization behind them, they did the next best thing and encouraged African pupils to enrol in the school at the castle.

Among the bright talents drawn to the school were William Amo of Axim who later obtained a doctorate degree at Wittenberg University, Jacob Capitein who graduated from the University of Leiden in the Netherlands (producing for his dissertation an ironic defence of the slave trade as not being inconsistent with Christian teaching), Frederck Svane who graduated from the University of Copenhagen, and Jacob Protten. Such early missionary work was the first bloom of the evangelical awakening that eventually spread to Africa. Svane belonged to the Ga tribe and returned with a Danish wife to serve briefly at Christiansborg as a catechist and teacher before returning to Denmark in 1746.

Jacob Protten also returned to the Gold Coast but disappeared into neighbouring Togoland, later to re-emerge for a brief spell in faraway Germany. He was then at Christiansborg between 1756 and 1761, and again from 1765 until his death in 1769. The haphazard nature of such careers was a fitting testament to the centuries of dogged effort to take Christianity into Bilád al-Súdán, 'land of the blacks', as Arab geographers called sub-Saharan Africa. By 1776, the year of the American Revolution, the missions across Africa had become marginal, weakened under the global strain of the slave trade. Saving souls had yielded to selling them.

Christian antislavery movements and the return of former slaves to Africa

Nevertheless, change was afoot, thanks in large part to the unforeseen and far-reaching consequences of the American Revolution. It is relevant to the story of Christianity in modern Africa to point out that what became the United States contained the largest population of Africans anywhere outside Africa. The vast majority of these Africans were slaves, some 700,000 by 1790, with an additional 59,000 free Africans. Antislavery sentiments acquired a new urgency in the context of the anti-colonial politics of the Thirteen Colonies on the Atlantic seaboard. Many of the leading voices for independence from Britain expressed similar objections to the continuation of slavery on American soil. The first antislavery society was founded in 1775 in Philadelphia, and in 1785 Benjamin Franklin became its president. Franklin joined the emancipation of slaves to the national cause of political independence, vowing, for example, to boycott sugar because it was dyed with the blood of slave labour. A related motive in such ideas of boycott was undoubtedly the attack on the economic interests of the plantation system on which Britain's colonial power was based. The political and economic basis of antislavery agitation connected with the Second Great Awakening that from the 1790s swept the American colonies and drew in throngs of African converts. It was an eventful connection with long-range ramifications for the course of the history of Christianity in Africa. The evangelical awakening brought about an African mass movement in Christianity that was the first of any such movement among non-European populations, and in scale and effectiveness it went beyond anything that had impacted Africa, before or since.

Long before the American Revolution there had been a movement among New England puritans to suppress the slave trade. In 1640 in the Puritan colony of Massachusetts a slave captain had been arrested and his slave cargo confiscated and ordered to return to Africa at the colony's expense. When later the slave trade gained enough support that it could defy Puritan strictures, it was justified on grounds of economic expedience, not on religion.[3] In 1773,

Samuel Hopkins of Rhode Island and a disciple of the leader of the First Great Awakening, Jonathan Edwards (1703–58), approached a fellow clergyman and a future president of Yale University, Ezra Stiles, about organizing a batch of black converts for repatriation to Africa as the bridgehead of a Christianization errand into the continent. Hopkins in 1775 appealed to John Adams (1735–1826), the future president of the United States, for a contribution to the cause of Christian colonization. By the outbreak of the war in 1776 over $500 had been raised through private donations, but the war interrupted the plans. Hopkins returned to the idea even before the war was formally concluded in 1783, and later in 1794 under the aegis of the African Society of Providence James McKenzie was sent to the West African coast to prospect for a colony.

The wave of conversion spurred by the First Great Awakening had affected large numbers of American blacks who were subsequently caught up in the American Revolution, and afterwards these blacks, reformed and tempered, crossed the ocean back to Africa as new emissaries of the gospel. At the conclusion of the war, black loyalist troops were demobilized under British command and transported to Canada in 1783. Later, in January, 1792, a freedom Armada of just under 1,200 of these blacks, disillusioned with life in Canada, set sail from Nova Scotia. They arrived in Freetown, Sierra Leone, in March of the same year, to commence a new phase in Africa's experiment with Christianity and with freedom from slavery. The original colony of free London blacks, settled in 1787 in this 'Province of Freedom', had from numerous causes disintegrated beyond being retrievable, and the cause of the new Christian experiment in Africa appeared to have all but foundered. At this point came the new impetus from the New World, with a gallant British parliament backing the enterprise by paying the full cost of repatriation to the tune of £9,600. Perhaps this was simply Britain's ironic way of repaying the Americans for their disloyalty, as George Washington had reason to suspect.

At any rate, here they were, these blacks originally uprooted from their homes, bound in chains, crammed in slave ships and hauled across the ocean, returning from the horrors of enslavement and racial castigation to the source of their misfortune. They came with a new and different message: liberation for captives, release for prisoners, time of favour for outcasts, and good news for the poor.

Old World missions had targeted kings, chiefs, princes and the other eminences of the land as the principal candidates for conversion, but the kings and chiefs and their circle of officials had sooner or later repudiated Christianity, if they had adopted it, reverting instead to the exploitative ways of the old politics that sanctioned slavery and the slave trade. Now, New World ideas of freedom combined with the revival message of redemption and personal promise to declare reprieve for outcasts, the downtrodden, and the bound and gagged. Former slaves, ex-captives, victim populations and marginal social groups stood in the first line of appeal, a situation that represented a stunning public repudiation of the old venerable principle of political pedigree and social privilege and of public custom as immutable law. This message ignited the dormant forces of indigenous discontent and disaffection.

Eighteenth-century African Christian leaders

A brief exposé of the careers of some of these eighteenth-century figures will carry our story forward. There is the biography of Olaudah Equiano, an indefatigable antislavery campaigner who worked on both sides of the Atlantic to mobilize progressive opinion to abolish the slave trade and advance Africa's economic development. There is, to be sure, a question about Equiano's African credentials, with some indication that he was in fact born in the American South and not in Nigeria, as he himself claimed. Be that as it may, Equiano's importance for our subject is independent of any questions about his birth. Tradition claims an Igbo origin for him as 'Ekwuno'. He himself claimed that he arrived as a slave on a Virginia plantation in 1757. He went through a series of remarkable adventures, and in one place he recounted his conversion experience on a ship in Cadiz. Campaigning in Britain in 1789 in the year of the French Revolution, Equiano described slavery as a human rights issue, and insisted that its perpetuation was an obstacle both to human progress and to Africa's economic advancement. Motives of self-interest, he contended, should be joined to those of justice and humanity to give no quarter to the slave trade and slavery.

Equiano made an early bid for a leadership role in the antislavery movement. His autobiographical work, *The Life of Olaudah Equiano*, was an acute study of the social effects of slavery on the African continent and on Europeans' relations with Africans. He recounts how in 1779 his request to be ordained for missionary service in Africa was turned down by the Bishop of London. In 1783 he was in London calling on Granville Sharp, the antislavery humanitarian, to bring to Sharp's attention the fate of 130 Africans who were thrown into the sea from a slave ship to allow the owners fraudulently to claim insurance compensation, a revelation that had a profound and immediate effect on Sharp and on parliament. Equiano joined forces with another ex-slave, the Fanti, Ottobah Cugoano, who in 1787 had written a book, *Thoughts and Sentiments on the Evils of the Slavery*, possibly with the collaboration of Equiano. Cugoano's work was a scathing indictment of the slave trade and of the Europeans who promoted it in the name of Christianity. The book appeared in a French translation in 1788. In it, Cugoano called slavery an injury and a robbery, saying there was not a trace in it of reason, justice, charity, or civilization. The Scots and the Dutch, he said, claimed to follow the Protestant religion and yet are among the worst specimens of 'floggers and Negro-drivers'.

After Equiano's bid to lead the antislavery mission to Africa was rebuffed in London, it fell to the black veterans of the American Revolutionary War to pursue beyond the New World that dual vocation of antislavery and Christianity. Thomas Peters was one of these. Peters had been born around 1740 in Nigeria of Yoruba Egba parents. Kidnapped in 1760, he was sold to the French slave ship, the *Henri Quatre*. He eventually arrived in French Louisiana where his French master sold him to an Englishman. By 1770 he had been sold yet again, this time to William Campbell, a Scotsman in Wilmington, North Carolina, where Peters learned his trade as a millwright. When the war broke out in 1776, the town was evacuated, whereupon Peters joined the British side in the hope of gaining his freedom. After the British lost control of Philadelphia at the end of 1777, Peters, who had gone there, left with a contingent of demobilized troops bound for Nova Scotia. Twice wounded in battle, he survived the war and went with his wife to settle in Nova Scotia.

Peters organized a petition among the blacks in Nova Scotia, describing the harsh living conditions there in spite of assurances to the contrary by officials. In 1791, he took the petition to London and presented it to William Granville of the Foreign Office. The petition had immediate effect, with the directors of the newly formed Sierra Leone Company saying they 'concurred in applying to His Majesty's Ministers for a passage for [the blacks] at the expense of government, and having obtained a favourable answer to their application, they immediately availed themselves of the services of Lieut. [John] Clarkson, who very handsomely offered to go to Nova Scotia in order to make the necessary proposals, and to superintend the collecting and bringing over such free blacks to Sierra Leone, as might be willing to emigrate.'

Peters then returned to Nova Scotia to assist in organizing a disembarkation party amidst much misapprehension among the blacks as well as opposition among whites who worried about the drain on black labour. But in spite of the odds, the repatriation drive got underway, with Peters duly signing up for it, and succeeded in laying a trans-Atlantic trail that numerous others, and not only blacks, would follow.

The story of David George is a fitting testament to that repatriation effort. Born in slavery in the state of Virginia in about 1742, George was later converted in the evangelical movement that swept through the ranks of New World blacks. He undertook missionary drives in the south where he succeeded in setting up Baptist churches in the state of Georgia. At the outbreak of the Revolution, George was already an accomplished religious pioneer, as became evident when he was evacuated to Nova Scotia, where he arrived in 1782. There he resumed his preaching activity, putting up what he called 'a meeting house' and holding revival sessions. John Clarkson, brother of Thomas Clarkson and who arrived in Nova Scotia after Thomas Peters' intervention in London, went to one of George's revival meetings and testified about George's talent for the vocation. 'I never remember', said Clarkson, 'to have heard the Psalms sung so charmingly in my life before'. No business, obstacle, or thought of favour was capable of deterring George 'from offering up his praises to his Creator'. When in 1792 Clarkson as an 'unlikely Pied Piper' led the Nova Scotian blacks 'across the sea to the coasts of Africa', George, not surprisingly, was among their number. New World antislavery sentiments crossed the Atlantic to the African continent to decisive effect, for good and ill.

In Freetown, George expanded the scope of his work. He continued with his preaching duties, naturally, but he assumed an increasing role as community leader and unpaid ombudsman for the settlers. He defended what he called 'the religious rights' of the Nova Scotians against attempts by the authorities to impose an official Christianity as safeguard against seditiously inclined black preachers. Britain was a recovering protagonist of the American Revolution, still allergic to republican ideas in religion and politics, and still wary of the contagion in the colony of 'open house' religion, that is, with homes serving also as places of worship. But the settlers would not budge, with George making the argument on their behalf that the status of blacks before God as carrying no stigma or prejudice should be reflected in their freedom and equality in state and society, however objectionably republican that might sound.

Officials decried such views as antinomian and they instituted the Colony Chaplaincy as a deterrent, refusing to recognize, or perhaps fearing, that the settlers were not preaching anarchy or subjective retreat, but a social activism of their own vintage. The charge of antinomianism was based on a theological misunderstanding, namely, the erroneous view that the settlers were appealing to the doctrine which says that 'to the pure all things are pure', so that those who are saved consider themselves exempt from moral and political accountability. That was, however, far from the case with the settlers. On a visit to London in 1793, for example, George urged commitment to the cause of abolition and mission in Africa, pleading with his English friends to bestir themselves to a similar end in England. On that visit George met John Newton, co-author of the popular hymn, 'Amazing Grace', and a one-time slave trader on the west coast who had since converted to evangelical religion. In 1793, we may recall, the idea of overseas missionary service was far from the mind of churches in Britain, though the Wesleyan revival had awakened society to a larger responsibility at home, with William Carey taking such homebred impulses abroad when he set out for India in 1792. George's appeal was, in the circumstances, a significant gesture that placed Africa right at the centre of the antislavery movement and of the missionary awakening allied to it. It was a matter of time before the growing sentiment for abolition would prevail in parliament where William Wilberforce led the drive to abolish the slave trade in 1807.

The charge of antinomian heresy met with a convincing refutation in the person of Paul Cuffee, an African American from New England, and one of the wealthiest and most influential blacks of the eighteenth and nineteenth centuries. Born in 1759 in Dartmouth, Massachusetts, Cuffee grew up in the slave household of the Slocum Quaker family, and later converted to that faith. The name Cuffee or Cuffe ('Kofi') was adopted in 1778, hinting at his paternal Ghanaian Ashanti origins. He was freed by his conscience-stricken Quaker master, and at age of sixteen, Cuffee entered the whaling trade in which he rose eventually to great wealth. He achieved the unusual distinction of being a black ship-owner, commissioning in 1800 the 162-ton vessel, the *Hero*, a ship that on one of its voyages rounded the Cape of Good Hope. In 1806, he fitted out two more and larger ships, one a 268-ton vessel, the *Alpha*, which travelled from Wilmington and Savannah to Gottenburg, Sweden, eventually returning to Philadelphia.

In the other ship, the *Traveller*, in which he owned three-quarters interest, Cuffee made a fateful voyage to West Africa. He left Philadelphia in December 1810, travelling via England where early in 1811 he arrived at Liverpool, then a significant slave port. There he obtained the release of a slave named Aaron Richards, having sent a petition on the matter to the Board of Admiralty set up under the terms of the 1807 act abolishing the slave trade. Cuffee consulted widely with leading figures of the antislavery and evangelical movements, including William Wilberforce – born, coincidentally, in the same year as Cuffee – and Zachary Macaulay, since retired as governor of Sierra Leone, and father of the celebrated historian, Thomas Babington Macaulay. Cuffee also met the Duke of Gloucester, president of the African Institution, an influential and active antislavery and humanitarian organization whose directors included Wilberforce and William Allen, the prominent Quaker leader with known sympathies for the Mennonite cause in southern Russia. In September 1811, Cuffee resumed his journey to West Africa, arriving in Freetown in November of that year. He gave free passage to a British Methodist missionary and three schoolteachers, proof here, too, that the missionary impetus even in Europe was enabled by black initiative. That was even more so in field practice abroad, though missiologists conveniently often ignored that fact.

The immediate impetus for Cuffee's West African odyssey was the act of 1807 abolishing the British slave trade, an act that itself was inspired in large measure by the successful establishment of the American blacks from Nova Scotia in West Africa. His purpose was to establish a base for legitimate trade at the source of the slave trade in an attempt to discredit the human traffic there. He also wished to create a different triangular trade connecting Africa, the New World, and Europe – a trading pattern in which African Americans would form an indispensable link. Tropical produce grown by means of scientific agriculture would be carried to America in ships owned by blacks, and profits from that would be used to purchase machinery and goods, which would in turn create the economic infrastructure required for settling more free and productive American blacks in West Africa. Their example, Cuffee argued, would prove contagious among Africans. Legitimate trade and profit, as William Thornton, the Quaker philanthropist, had also argued in 1785, would forge a moral chain to strangle the vicious slave trade to the direct benefit of the long-suffering Africans themselves.

Yet formidable obstacles stood in the way, not least of which was the grip of European traders who reduced their African partners to crippling indebtedness. It was difficult, Cuffee calculated, to raise an African entrepreneurial class against such odds. So he confessed that it appeared to him clearly that a new economic foundation had to be laid among the Africans in the colony. 'I had to encourage them to exert themselves on their own behalf and become their own shippers and importers that they may be able to employ their own citizens for at present their colony is stript of their young men for as soon as they are discharged from school they have no business to go into and they enter on board foreigners so the Colony is Continually stript of her [population].'[4]

Chiefs also stood in the path of such progress, for whatever their promises of co-operation, Cuffee reckoned, their heart was not in abolition, or in legitimate trade, for that matter, with its free enterprise culture. 'I May also add further that in conversing with the African chiefs that it was with great reluctance they gave up the slave trade saying that it made them poor and they Could not git things as they used to git when they traded in slaves.'[5] In the old order of the slave trade, local rulers and princes shared an identity of interest with the captains of slave ships, and slave profits helped to strengthen indigenous political institutions. But enslaving your neighbours risked a similar fate for yourself. Pre-emptive raids as a strategy and a deterrent increased the certainty of retaliation. Slave raids benefited no one in the long run, though in the short run no one could afford to do without them. It was that short-run reality that stumped the ameliorative plans of Cuffee and others, and particularly those of the British parliament.

To push forward his economic ideas, Cuffee founded the Quaker-inspired Friendly Society of Sierra Leone, and later wrote to its secretary, the African American, James Wise: 'I instruct thee to endeavor that she, the Friendly Society, may not give up her commercial pursuits, for that is the greatest outlet to her national advancement. – I foresee this to be the means of improving both your country and nation.'[6] Cuffee returned to the United States, departing Freetown on 4 April 1813 and arriving after a fifty-four-day voyage.

Thomas Clarkson, the Cambridge anti-slavery campaigner, in a notice of 24 January 1814, drew the public's attention to Cuffee's Friendly Society, saying it existed 'to devise means of disposing of [the settlers'] produce on the most advantageous terms, and of promoting habits of industry among each other. This association continues but', he cautioned, 'it cannot carry its useful plans into execution, without assistance from England'.[7] Clarkson's apprehensions about the Friendly Society were echoed by William Allen who rallied to Cuffee's cause, which was then under attack from white trading interests in the Sierra Leone colony.

Later in 1814, a petition was presented to the Congress of the United States on Cuffee's behalf. The Speaker of the House remitted it to the Committee on Commerce and Manufacture. The Senate then tabled a resolution authorizing the President to allow Cuffee to leave for West Africa with a cargo of goods, but, as Britain and the United States were then at war, the measure was defeated on the grounds that it would let British goods elude the blockade imposed by Congress. A similar request to the British parliament on Cuffee's behalf was turned down as too risky given the current state of navigation laws, which were deemed to need special support as a result of the damaging effects of the Anglo–American War of 1812 as well as the continuing Napoleonic Wars.

Far from being discouraged by such setbacks, an undaunted Cuffee persisted with his efforts. With the help of fellow Quakers in Westport, he fitted out the *Traveller* again and set sail in November 1815. The *Traveller* was laden with a cargo of tobacco, soap, candles, naval stores, flour, iron to build a sawmill, a wagon, grindstones, nails, glass, and a plough. There were thirty-eight passengers, eighteen heads of family and twenty children, and common labourers who would till the soil.

On board the *Traveller* was Perry Locke, a licensed Methodist preacher, 'with a hard voice for a preacher', Cuffee commented delicately. (Cuffee reminded Locke in Freetown that Locke had complained in America about being denied his liberties and was again murmuring because he was called upon to serve as a juror. 'Go and fill thy seat and do as well as thou canst', Cuffee told him.[8]) Another passenger, Anthony Survance, was a native of Senegal. He had been sold to the French in Saint Domingue and escaped to Philadelphia during the Revolution. He learned to read and write and studied navigation, though, in spite of professional interest, life at sea ill suited him because of his susceptibility to seasickness. Cuffee mused privately that Survance would not make a good mariner. Survance joined the voyage at his own expense, intending eventually to make it to his home in Senegal.

The party dropped anchor in Freetown on 3 February 1816. Unbeknownst to Cuffee, the attitude of the Freetown establishment towards him had meanwhile hardened, and he was beset with landing difficulties. He was subjected to heavy customs duties for his goods, diminishing any hope he entertained of making a profitable going of his venture. For consolation, the governor and chief justice granted Cuffee an audience. The Freetown traders and commercial interests who conspired to shut out Cuffee were determined to prevent any American penetration of the West African market. Thwarted in Sierra Leone, Cuffee returned to America to continue his antislavery and missionary campaign. He died there in July 1817.

Sierra Leone as a 'Christian experiment' was substantially changed for good with the introduction of African 'recaptives' following the abolition of the slave trade in 1807. The British Naval Squadron patrolled the extended West African coastline, impounding slaves bound for the New World and landing them in Freetown. They were resettled into parish communities organized around church, school, and farm. These recaptives hailed from all parts of the African continent and in time formed the backbone of the settlement. They swamped the original Nova Scotian settlers, and took over much of the work of education, community government, and evangelization. From their ranks emerged a new mobile middle class with an influence far beyond its size. That middle class would later become the ironic nemesis of colonialism, and of much else besides.

Paul Cuffee's legacy in America was an enduring one, and it led directly to the establishment of Liberia as a settlement for freed slaves from the southern United States. Robert S. Finley, a Presbyterian minister from New Jersey and later president of the University of Georgia, had been campaigning for the creation of a settlement in Africa for freed slaves. He made contact with

Cuffee and wrote to him saying, 'The great desire of those whose minds are impressed with the subject is to give opportunity to the free people of color to rise to their proper level and at the same time to provide a powerful means of putting an end to the slave trade, and sending civilization and Christianity to Africa'.[9] Finley became an architect of the Liberian colonization scheme.

When eventually the American Colonization Society (ACS) was formed in December 1816 in a hall in the United States House of Representatives, Cuffee's proposals and example were the inspiration, and Sierra Leone the model that people had in mind. The board of managers of the ACS paid fulsome tribute to Cuffee in a memorial note, praising him for his clear and unwavering judgement, his informed opinion, his unyielding commitment and unstinting devotion, and, above all, for his hands-on experience of life in West Africa, experience that counteracted the effects of unfounded prejudice. The tribute to him ended with the point that any future engagement with Africa would have to be based on partnership of an uncommon order, one in which fact and knowledge would replace prejudice and aspersion, an order that must be evaluated in terms of its 'usefulness to the native Africans and their descendants in this country'.[10] With the antislavery cause in West Africa, the African theme in Christianity acquired a trans-Atlantic range.

Protestant missions and African rights in South Africa

The eighteenth-century Protestant evangelical movement, as we have seen, served to revive missionary interest in general. Thus was founded in 1795 the London Missionary Society (LMS), and other related bodies such as the Netherlands Missionary Society of Rotterdam (1797), the mission school in Berlin founded in 1800 by Pastor Johann Jänicke of the Brethren Church, and in 1815 the Basel school that supplied recruits for British missions. The Netherlands Missionary Society picked up the African connection established by the Moravians in the 1740s when John Theodore Vanderkemp went out as a missionary to South Africa. The Cape had been colonized by the Protestant Dutch from 1652, with the Dutch settlers, or Boers, pressing inland in search of land, viewing themselves as a people in covenant with God, and encroaching upon the local African populations. In 1795, the Cape had been occupied by Britain, then at war with the Netherlands; the occupation became permanent after 1806. Vanderkemp arrived at the Cape in 1799, establishing a mission to the hard-pressed Khoi at Bethelsdorp on Algoa Bay, 400 miles east of Cape Town. He made a dramatic entrance into the politics of the slave trade when he purchased from slavery a girl of seventeen whom he then married. The young girl's African mother was from Madagascar. Vanderkemp's personal example of a radical and politically uncompromising evangelical faith that openly endorsed the principle of social and political equality influenced many who followed him in missionary service.

Upon his arrival in South Africa, Vanderkemp was immediately stumped by the language question. Unlike the Zulus, the Khoi in Cape Colony had some knowledge of Dutch and so could act as intermediaries with the missionaries. In that role, the Khoi could also function as teachers and catechists and thus as second-tier missionaries to their own people, a role that would help accelerate the process of naturalizing Christianity in Africa. The more astute of the European missionaries saw such African agency as implying inescapably a sharp role reversal, with Christian Africans becoming the chief agents of Christianization and setting the agenda for mission. Furthermore, the achievements of African agency had the prospects of permanency in a way that foreign agency manifestly did not.

Much in that idea and in its implications of cost-effectiveness resonates well with the logic of the local reception and adaptation of Christianity rather than with missionary notions of transmission and wholesale indigenous uprooting. Those setbacks of transmission were precisely what occurred in other parts of the mission field, prompting the missionary statesman, Henry Venn (d. 1872), for example, to propound his theory about 'the euthanasia of a mission'. Vanderkemp's insights were promptly adopted as sound policy by other missionaries, though the fact that Vanderkemp was working with South African Khoi with some knowledge of Dutch gave an advantage to his ideas.

Yet the rigours of frontier life among Africans on the fringes of a colonial white society which was on the path of unrelenting expansion into native lands took a terrible toll on him, and he died relatively young in 1811. The leading agent of the London Missionary Society and chief architect of its work in South Africa was John Philip of Aberdeen, Scotland, who was appointed to that position in 1820. He was an eloquent and passionate defender of the rights of Africans against whites in South Africa, carrying the antislavery banner into opposition strongholds.

Appointed to a commission of enquiry into the state of the mission following Vanderkemp's death, Philip found that the colonial government appeared unhappy with the work of missionaries, and that puzzled him at first. However, upon further enquiry, and given what he came to know of the nature of that unhappiness, sadly, he saw little chance of reconciliation. To the bitter dismay of the colonial authorities, the missions had championed the interests of the Africans against the whites. In the course of his investigations Philip found that the mission station at Bethelsdorp had been converted into what he called a virtual 'slave lodge', with the Africans there drafted as labourers at a work camp. For their back-breaking work, they were paid pittance or no wages at all, and the women and children were abandoned. A more bewildered and forlorn people he had not met. Everything the missionaries had laboured so valiantly to establish and to promote was torn down by a ruthless colonial government. The defining issue for the missions became African advancement, precisely the ground the government had chosen for throwing down the gauntlet. Without choosing it, missions had the race problem tied round their necks like an albatross, and it is a credit to Vanderkemp and to Philip, his worthy successor, that they refused to flinch from the challenge. Predictably, the race problem went on to dominate the religious and political landscape in South Africa throughout the nineteenth and twentieth centuries. Philip's book, *Researches in South Africa*, contains a robust defence of his evangelical and humanitarian views.

The Sierra Leone experiment to 1815

In West Africa the evangelical cause was represented by the Church Missionary Society (CMS) of the Church of England, founded in 1799, although, instructively, the first CMS recruits were German evangelicals, Melchio Renner and Peter Hartwig, who arrived in Sierra Leone in 1804. With its hints of unruly enthusiasm, evangelical religion was suspect among probably most Anglicans, and churchmen found the idea of missionary service unfamiliar and unacceptable. Consequently, the CMS became by force of circumstance an ecumenical and trans-national missionary organization. Even then, it was a rocky beginning for the CMS. Hartwig abandoned the missionary life, disappeared promptly into Susu country, not to convert Africans but to become a slave trader. Undaunted, the CMS dispatched a second batch of missionaries, all Germans, who arrived in 1806: Leopold Butscher, Johann Prasse and Gustavus Nÿlander. Nÿlander was to become the pioneer agent of the CMS in Sierra Leone, and he stayed in Freetown as agent of the Sierra Leone Company. (Sierra Leone became a British crown possession after 1807.) He was a man who wore many hats: as chaplain he ministered to a flock of European churchgoers, and at home he played husband to a Nova Scotian. The tropics stripped whatever surviving religious habits his European parishioners retained, and they deserted the chapel, leaving Nÿlander with no flock to tend. The chapel fell into disrepair and was abandoned, its functions absorbed into Nÿlander's other household responsibilities.

Nÿlander began to make headway with the mission only when he directed his attention to the country beyond the Freetown peninsula. On the Bulom Shore he commenced in 1818 the language work that was to distinguish Christianity's mission and encounter with modern Africa. He compiled a *Bulom grammar and vocabulary*, and translated Saint Matthew's Gospel into Bulom. It was the first Bible translation in Sierra Leone, although in 1801 the missionary Henry Brunton, then back in Scotland after a period of service in the African mission field, had published a Susu grammar and some catechisms.

With respect to the other two missionary companions of Nÿlander, a similar pattern can be discerned in their work. Johann Prasse went with Butscher and Melchio Renner to the Rio Pongas for work among the Susu, following the new CMS doctrine that metropolitan Freetown was an inauspicious environment for mission, and accordingly shifting the focus to indigenous hinterland populations. It was a policy change representing a quiet but momentous repudiation of Christianity and civilization as identical twins, and it ran counter to prevailing settler opinion about the irredeemability of uncivilized 'tribes' so-called. Butscher eventually returned in 1814 to Freetown to head a settlement of new re-captives in Leicester.

Butscher's experiences from living among the Susus led him to formulate some sharp ideas about the deep impact of the slave trade on societies beyond the coast, and the facilitating but limited role of colonial guardianship. What he said on the subject had echoes, for example, of ideas in ancient Roman north Africa, and yet it was also in a significant measure in advance of his time. It was not till 1837, when Thomas Fowell Buxton (1786–1845) published his much acclaimed *The slave trade and its remedy*, that belated attention was drawn to what Butscher had described as far back as 1812. From his experience, Butscher said the slave trade was the most important source of income for inland societies and that the recent abolition had threatened the very foundation of their economic survival. Seizing slaves on the high seas, as was the policy of the British government, did not strike at the root cause of enslavement; what was needed, Butscher said, was an export commodity that could profitably and effectively replace slaves as a commodity. It should therefore be the single most urgent objective of missions and governments alike to develop an alternative source of wealth for African societies. Butscher, accordingly, set about seeking to secure the support and co-operation of government authorities, thus suggesting a strong partnership between mission and government, with the flag following the Bible rather than the Bible following the flag, as would happen later.

It was under Butscher's plan that Governor Maxwell (1811–15) organized an administrative scheme for the resettling of re-captives who were arriving in the colony in increasing numbers. In 1807 Freetown's population was 1,871, including ninety-five military personnel. In the census of April 1811, it had increased to around 3,500, thanks to an influx of re-captives. In July 1814 there was a further big jump to 5,520 re-captives. In a report drawn on 31 December 1818, the number of re-captives was put at 6,406. The total population, including settlers, was about 17,300 in 1816. The rapid rise in these figures is not due exclusively, if at all, to the British Naval Squadron becoming more effective at seizing slave ships, but, more ominously, to the uncomfortable fact that the pace of the slave trade had quickened since, and in spite of, the legal abolition of the trade, so that there were more slave ships to be seized. It is, for example, estimated that during 1810 alone some 80,000 slaves were illegally shipped across the Atlantic, mostly to markets in Brazil, Cuba, and the southern United States. It was this demographic pressure felt in the Freetown peninsula that Governor Maxwell was asked to address, though the task fell to his successor, Sir Charles MacCarthy, who for that purpose devised an effective network of supervised village settlements, called the Parish Scheme – though it is questionable if such a scheme was appropriate for the sea-borne indigenous influx it sought to channel.

With energy and imagination, MacCarthy, a Roman Catholic by background, took up the task that fell to him, and responded to Butscher's call for a genuine partnership between mission and government in the cause of African rehabilitation. The re-captives were farmed out to newly created villages on the peninsula, each village directed by a clergyman. There was a chapel, with required attendance, which during the week would also serve as a school. Before 1815 there were three such villages: Leicester, founded in 1809; Wilberforce (formerly Cabenda), established in 1810; and Regent (formerly Hogbrook), founded in 1812. Between 1815 and 1820, ten more villages were created to absorb the newcomers, among them Kissy and Gloucester in 1816; Charlotte and Leopold (the latter renamed Bathurst) in 1817, and Wellington, Hastings, and Waterloo in 1819. After the disbanding of the Royal African Corps in 1819, the demobilized troops were resettled appropriately in Gibraltar Town in recognition of the servicemen who had served in Gibraltar.

These parish-style villages transformed Freetown into a black diaspora, and Freetown became a Caribbean-style cultural settlement on African soil, an auspicious crossroad of indigenous and western ideas. African re-captives who originated from many different parts of the continent, some from as far away as the Congo and Mozambique, intermingled with those from Nigeria to share in common a sense of native dispossession and in Freetown the availability of faith-based Christian communities. The shrines and altars of indigenous communities arrived in the settlement with the re-captives and co-existed quite amicably with Christian rituals. Re-captive Yoruba diviners, for example, welcomed the challenge of missionaries, saying they were happy to add the Christian divinity to the Yoruba pantheon because a place already existed for that. It showed how in the conditions of dislocation, mobility, and resettlement precipitated by the slave trade Christianity was welcomed as African restoration. The transmission of Christianity engaged the terms of indigenous discovery to commence a long-term intercultural process of conversion and readjustment in Sierra Leone and beyond.

Notes

1. J. H. Parry, *The age of reconnaissance* (New York: Mentor Books, 1964), p. 33.
2. Cited in Jean Comby, *How to understand the history of Christian mission* (London: SCM Press, 1996), p. 60.
3. W. E. B. DuBois, *The suppression of the African slave trade to the United States of America: 1638–1870* (1898, repr. New York: Russell & Russell, 1965), pp. 30–1.
4. *Captain Paul Cuffe's logs and letters, 1808–1817: A black Quaker's 'Voice from within the veil'*, ed. Rosalind Cobb Wiggins (Washington, DC: Howard University Press, 1996), p. 341.
5. *Ibid.*, p. 342.
6. Henry Noble Sherwood, 'Paul Cuffe', *Journal of Negro history*, 8 (April 1923), p. 204.
7. Thomas Clarkson, 'Society for the Purpose of Encouraging the Black Settlers at Sierra Leone, and the Natives of Africa Generally, in the Cultivation of their soil, and by the sale of their produce', 28 January 1814, Public Record Office, London, CO 267/41.
8. *Cuffe's logs and letters*, ed. Wiggins, p. 434.
9. Sherwood, 'Paul Cuffe', p. 213.
10. *First Annual Report of the American Colonization Society*, p. 5, cited in Sherwood, 'Paul Cuffe', p. 220.

22

Christianity in south and south-east Asia

CHARLES J. BORGES

This chapter will explore the spread of Christianity from the sixteenth to the early nineteenth centuries within the various parts of undivided India and, more briefly, in some other areas of south and south-east Asia. We will begin with India. The history of India goes back some 5,000 years to the Indus Valley civilization with its sophisticated urban culture found in the cities of Harappa and Mohenjo-Daro. The Indo-Aryan civilization probably came to India from central Asia around 1500 BC and formed much of India's living tradition and impressive religious system. Indian culture was always a rich mosaic of new elements and foreign influences merged into its ancient roots.

The oldest of its religious traditions was Hinduism. Under the broad rubric of Hinduism, there existed an enormous fluidity of beliefs and practices which in turn evolved by interacting with the other religions of India. Hinduism was a way of life. It had no single book or god or prophet and every village could have its own deity. It was a religion of deep philosophy and metaphysics, existing side by side with rituals and ceremonies that marked the days, seasons and events in life. Gods were either distant or near, and were part of every household and clan. One worshipped them through silent meditation, communal singing, or joyful festivity. Closely linked to this religious system was a social system. Society came to be divided into four castes, the Brahmans (priestly class in charge of the rituals and chants), the Kshatriyas (warriors), the Vaishyas (merchants), and the Shudras (menial workers).

Besides Hinduism, three other great religions were born in India over the centuries: Jainism and Buddhism, founded in the sixth century BCE, respectively by Mahavir (the Great Hero) and Gautama Buddha (the Enlightened One); and Sikhism, founded by Guru Nanak in the sixteenth century. But other major religions arrived from the outside. Christianity, as we will see below, may have appeared as early as the first or second centuries; and Zoroastrianism arrived in the ninth century, taking refuge in India after fleeing persecution in Persia. Islam first came to India in the tenth century through a series of

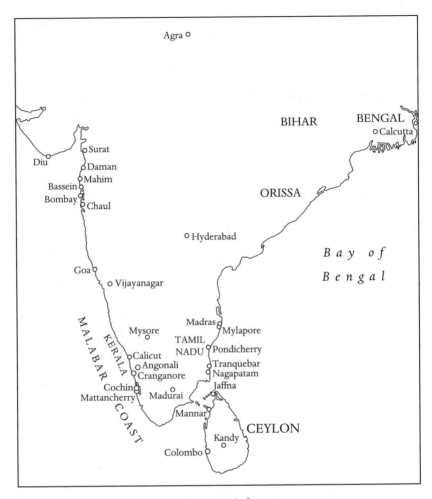

Map 3 Missions in India *c.* 1800

raids on the subcontinent, but it established a permanent dynasty only in 1206. The great Mughal dynasty, established by Babur in 1526, ruled India for over 300 years. Mughal patronage of the arts brought a blending of the best of the Islamic, Hindu and Christian traditions, thanks in large measure to the presence of Sufi preachers and Jesuit priests within its kingdom. By the end of the seventeenth century, however, the Mughals had been gradually weakened through a combination of religious wars and invasions from the north-west. Their political weakness allowed various European powers to establish their commercial and territorial sway in the subcontinent.

The first Europeans to come to India were the Portuguese, arriving in the persons of Vasco da Gama and his crew on 27 May 1498 at Calicut on the west coast. The Portuguese made substantial territorial gains in the following years, taking Goa in 1510. Though a strong power in the sixteenth century, they lost most of their territories, except for Goa, Daman and Diu, to the Dutch and the English in the following century, a period during which French and Danish traders also arrived on the coasts of the subcontinent. By the eighteenth century, the Dutch had been largely pushed out by the English.

The English, later the British, East India Company was created by royal charter in December 1600 and granted a monopoly of English trade with the whole of Asia and the Pacific basin. The Company established trading settlements, or factories, on the coasts of India, beginning with Surat on the western coast in 1608. The Company was trading in Bengal from the 1650s, and in 1702 they completed Fort William on the Hugli to protect their trading interests there. The city of Calcutta grew around Fort William, which by the later eighteenth century became the centre of British power in India. The French, meanwhile, had set up the French East India Company (*Compagnie des Indies*) in 1674 and by the early eighteenth century had made Pondicherry on the east coast the base of French power. The eighteenth century saw a major confrontation between the English and the French, who fought three wars in India between 1740 and 1763. After the Battle of Plassey (1757) the British Company established its Raj (rule) over Bengal, Bihar and Orissa in eastern India. From 1773, the British parliament started to exercise complete control over the Company's affairs, appointing Warren Hastings as the first Governor in 1772 and then as the first Governor General two years later. The Doctrine of Lapse ensured that lands belonging to any Indian ruler dying without a direct heir to the throne went into British hands, and this meant a steady expansion of British-held territory. In 1793, the Lord Cornwallis Code laid the firm foundations for British rule in nineteenth-century India, setting standards for service, law courts, and revenue collection.

The Thomas Christians

According to tradition, Christianity first came to India in the person of Saint Thomas, who is said to have arrived on the western coast of Kerala about the year 52, and whose apostolate was preserved in the memory which his converts conveyed to later generations in India. This Christian community was in communion with the Syrian Church of the east whose metropolitan lived first in Seleucia-Ktesiphon and in the eighth century moved to Baghdad.

The Thomas Christians were largely upper class, maintaining their Hindu culture while they practised the Christian faith with strong Syrian influences in their liturgy and worship. They continued to flourish in south India long after the disappearance of Christians from many other parts of Asia.

Following their first encounter with the Thomas Christians at Cranganore on the coast of Kerala, the Portuguese worked at bringing these communities more in line with the Roman Church and the Latin tradition. The Thomas Christians were initially willing to accept the primacy of the see of Rome, which they did formally at the Synod of Diamper in 1599, but great tension soon developed over the continuing attempts to alter their liturgy and remove other eastern traditions from their church life. According to the Portuguese, there could be only one law, that of Christ, and not two laws, one of St Thomas and the other of St Peter. Driven to distraction by these pressures, the majority of the Thomas priests (*kattanars*) met on 3 January 1653 at the ancient Coonan Cross of Mattancherry and there swore an oath never to accept the authority of the Archbishop of Cranganore, who was primate of the Roman Catholic Church in Kerala. These events led to the birth of a new Christian communion, the Malankara Syrian Orthodox Church, sometimes referred to as 'Jacobites', a nomenclature they reject.

Rome acted promptly in response to this crisis. The Congregation for the Propaganda of the Faith sent out Carmelite fathers to India to attempt to deal with the situation. This initiative was forced on the Propaganda since the Thomas Christians refused to have anything more to do with the Jesuits, with whom they had been dealing. Though often high-handed, the Carmelites were able to reconcile many of the Thomas Christians so that a majority returned to communion with Rome in 1662. This move had been greatly helped by Propaganda appointing in 1661 a vicar apostolic for Kerala, which gave the Thomas Christians in communion with Rome, known as the Syro-Malabar Catholic Christians, their own *de facto* bishop.

At that time the separatist Malankara Church attempted to re-establish its links with the East Syrian Patriarchate (sometimes referred to as the Chaldean Church) but these attempts failed. Eventually the West Syrian Patriarch, based in Damascus, made contact with them and they became an autonomous church within the Syrian Patriarchate, after having made some nominal changes in their customs to conform to the West Syrian as opposed to East Syrian traditions.

Meanwhile, the Syro-Malabar Catholics continued to complain to Rome about the Carmelites and bombarded the Holy See with requests for an Indian bishop to replace the missionary vicar apostolic. In 1780, they sent a delegation led by Fr Joseph Kariattil to Rome to petition personally for the appointment of an Indian bishop for their church, though in Rome this delegation was apparently not taken seriously. There was, however, a dramatic change in their fortunes when the delegates arrived in Lisbon to begin their journey home. Under the powers of the *Padroado*, the Queen of Portugal appointed Fr Kariattil as Archbishop of Cranganore. When he landed at Goa, the excitement of the Thomas Christians was at fever pitch but then, to their despair, he fell ill and died in 1783 before leaving Goa. Some have speculated that had he lived, the two communities of Thomas Christians, those in communion with the Syrian Church and those in communion with the Roman Church, might have come together again.

At this critical juncture, the Archbishop of Goa made Kariattil's companion, Fr Thomas Parreamakal, administrator of the vicariate apostolic, but this did not satisfy the people, who widely believed that Kariattil had been poisoned. There was widespread agitation and at a meeting in 1787 at Ankamali the Thomas Christian leaders in communion with Rome vowed to recognize Parreamakal as their bishop and no other. The archdiocesan authorities refused to accept this, and after some time the agitation did subside. The result was that the Thomas Christians had to wait until 1887 to have bishops from their own communities.

Catholic missions in India

The Portuguese governor, Afonso de Albuquerque, had taken over the western coastal city of Goa in 1510 and it soon became the capital of the Portuguese possessions in the entire east, the *Estado da India* (as these possessions were called) spreading from Hormuz at the mouth of the Persian Gulf to Malacca and to the Indonesian Spice islands. Within Goa, the Portuguese made vigorous efforts to convert the people to the Christian faith. Along with the Portuguese government officials, merchants and soldiers, groups of religious priests and brothers and secular priests came to Goa each year from Portugal. Goa also became an important educational centre, with priests and catechists receiving training there and then moving to missions in other parts of India and beyond. Goa was raised to the status of a diocese in 1534 and to that of an archdiocese in 1557. The Franciscans arrived there as early as 1510, the Jesuits in 1542, the Dominicans in 1548, the Augustinians in 1572, and the Carmelites in 1607. Among the well-known educational institutions located in Goa were the Colleges of St Aquinas (Dominicans), St Bonaventure (Franciscans), Populo (Augustinians), and St Paul's and St Roque (Jesuits). The many Goan churches

Figure 8 'Virgin and Child', fashioned in Goa, India, *c.* 1700. Ivory statuette, about 23 centimetres in height, with hair and robe edges coloured and gilt. A common Baroque image, but here with features and dress clearly adopted to India. (Photograph in the Butler Collection, Centre for the Study of Christianity in the Non-Western World, University of Edinburgh.)

(for example, Bom Jesus, Se Cathedral, St Francis of Assisi, Holy Spirit of Margao) remain rich expressions of the architecture, sculpture, painting, and wood-carving styles of the time.

During the sixteenth century, Christianity made remarkable progress in the numbers of converts made both inside the Portuguese-held territories and in the various Portuguese trading centres. There were, however, no close contacts with the higher classes of the Hindus. Saint Francis Xavier contributed much to evangelizing the people of India. Arriving in Goa on 6 May 1542, he was active in charitable works while he preached to the Portuguese settlers and catechized among the local people. Within five months he had left Goa for the east coast of India, and by August 1549, he was in Japan. The Italian Jesuit, Fr Alessandro Valignano (1539–1606), built on the foundations laid by Xavier and came to be known as the foremost organizer of the Indian missions of his day. He stressed the need to learn local languages and he set up schools for this purpose. He laboured long on the problem of the church in Malabar and pondered the best ways to bring them fully back to the Catholic Church.

It was in 1581, during Valignano's tenure as Provincial of Goa, that the Enlightened Mughal emperor, Jalal-ud-din Muhammad Akbar, invited the Jesuits to his royal court in north India. Akbar hoped to gather religious men from different faiths to help him found a new religion, the Din-i-Ilahi. Jesuits like Fr Rudolf Acquaviva and others participated in three successive Jesuit missions to the Mughal court over the next hundred years. Although these Jesuit missions failed to convert the various Mughal emperors, they did help bring about a better understanding between Islam and Christianity. They built up a fruitful connection with the imperial courts, a connection which enabled them to open mission stations in various parts of the Muslim Empire and even in Nepal and Tibet. Akbar was succeeded by Jahangir (who aided British attempts to trade in India), then by Shah Jahan (builder of the Taj Mahal), and finally by the ruthless Aurangzeb whose death in 1707 marked the effective end of the Mughal Empire, although it continued in a reduced form until the end of the rule of emperor Bahadur Shah in 1858.

Besides the Mughal court, Jesuits had an important presence at different times in the royal courts of the southern kingdoms of Vijayanagara, Gunji, Madurai, and Thanjavur. Jesuit superiors and subjects wrote regularly to Rome detailing their mission work, successes, failures, and needs. This system of regular correspondence within the Society of Jesus had been designed by Saint Ignatius, the founder of the order, as a way to strengthen the bonds of union among its members and facilitate good government. The *Litterae Indicae*, or

Indian letters, soon became an effective instrument of propaganda in Europe for overseas missions.

The correspondence is revealing of the innovations and originality of the great Italian Jesuit missionary in south India, Fr Roberto de Nobili. He began his missionary work in 1606 at Madurai, one of the ancient centres of Tamil culture. In order to gain broad acceptance, he declared himself to be a member of the Italian nobility and of the raja (kingly) class, and a twice-born Roman Brahman. He dressed in the Brahman *sanyasi* mode, wore the sacred thread, the *kudumi*, and put on wooden sandals. He learnt Tamil, Telugu and Sanskrit and began reformulating Christianity in the terms and thought patterns of Indian religious civilization. He eventually made over 30,000 converts and a century after his death, the mission he established could boast of over 200,000 Christians. His religious motto was, appropriately, '*Aperire portam*' (to open the door).

De Nobili's intellectual gifts, his capacity to absorb and communicate the learning that he found in the land of his adoption, were outstanding. Though accused of being fixated on high caste, his perspectives went beyond caste and custom. He possessed an impressive spirit of penance and was called '*Tattuva Podagar*' (the Brahman mendicant) by all. However, he encountered opposition from the Hindus, and even more from some of his fellow missionaries and church leaders. Although the Jesuits in Rome and even Pope Gregory XV initially supported his innovations, eventually many of the practices he proposed for his new converts were banned by Rome. He had continually sought to understand Hinduism from within; his aim had been not merely to convert the high-caste Brahmans, but through them to bring the whole of India to Christ.

The de Nobili method of mission remained a contentious issue through the seventeenth and eighteenth centuries. In 1703, Charles Maillard de Tournon was sent as papal delegate to China and then to India to settle matters of the 'Chinese Rites' and 'Malabar Rites'. He ruled that there should be no compromise in the matter and that the two rites must be rejected. In 1739, Pope Clement XII required all missionaries to sign an oath to this effect. Pope Benedict XIV, by his instruction *Omnium Sollicitudinum* of 12 September 1744, ruled that all Catholics, whatever their caste, should hear Mass and receive communion in the same church and at the same time. The Jesuits adhered to the ruling, but they built separate entrances for believers from the low castes to enter the common churches and installed small divisions within the churches to separate the low from the high castes.

Not as intellectually gifted as de Nobili, yet equally sympathetic to Hinduism, was the Portuguese Jesuit, St João de Brito. He dressed in the garb of a Hindu *sanyasi* (mendicant) and worked exclusively with the low castes of south India. For his forthrightness he was tortured and then beheaded in February 1693 at Oriyur in Tamilnadu. According to his biographer, 'he was a man of the rank and file. He may have had the zeal and enthusiasm of a Francis Xavier but he was never called upon to exercise them on the whole east, his labour being practically confined to Tamil Nadu. Nor was it his lot to inaugurate new missionary methods like Robert de Nobili. He came to a field ripe for the harvest and without casting about for new tools or new methods he seized the old sickle and joined the reapers.'[1]

The founder of the Madurai, Kanara and Mysore Jesuit missions was Fr Leonardo Cinnami. He came to recognize that his initial four years in the missions had not borne fruit, mainly because he had been viewed as a Portuguese priest. By 1649 he began dressing as a *sanyasi*, had his ears pierced and his head and neck smeared with ashes. Besides his great mission work, he left several devotional works in the local Kanada language, the most notable being *Istoria del Canara* (1648).

What is striking about the growth of the church in seventeenth- and eighteenth-century India is the number of priests and laymen who produced important literary and religious works. One recalls such sixteenth-century works as *Homem das Trinta e duas perfeições* (Archbishop Francisco Garcia Mendes), *Discursos sobre a vida do apóstolo Sam Pedro* (Estevão da Cruz), *Colóquios dos simples e drogas medicinais* (Garcia da Orta); and such seventeenth-century works as *História do Malavar* (Diogo Gonçalves), and the treatises on Hinduism by Jean Venance Bouchet and a Konkani grammar by Karel Prikryl. The Italian Jesuit Constanzo Guiseppe Beschi (1680–1747) wrote classical epics, philosophical treatises, commentaries, dictionaries, grammars, translations, and tracts for both Hindus and Christians. His epic poem *Tembavani* ('Unfading Garland') and his public disputations with Hindu scholars won him great renown, ensuring him a lasting legacy as a scholar of Sanskrit and Tamil literature.

Others who were equally well known as writers included Heinrich Roth (1620–68) who composed a Sanskrit grammar in Latin, and John Ernest Hanxleden (1681–1732), author of *Mishiada Pana* (1728) and of a Sanskrit Malayalam Portuguese dictionary and a Malayalam grammar in Portuguese. Gaston Coeurdoux (1691–1777) had served in Pondicherry, Kanara, and Tranquebar. He was well versed in the Sanskrit and Telugu languages and wrote a Telugu–Sanskrit–French dictionary and was the first to show the linguistic connections of Sanskrit with Latin, Greek, German, and Russian. Jean Calmette (1693–1739) served in the Tamil mission in Kanara and was the first European to get a copy of all the four Hindu Vedas while Francis Pons (1698–1752) was an astronomer, geographer, canonist, and a Sanskrit scholar who composed a Sanskrit grammar.

Non-Jesuit religious orders and congregations also did commendable work but on a much smaller scale, given their limited numbers and paucity of funds. The activities of the Franciscans during the seventeenth and eighteenth centuries were directed more towards consolidation than expansion. By 1629 they had two provinces in India, with about 600 friars. They had houses in Goa and also in Bassein, and their houses suffered under Maratha attacks in the eighteenth century. In 1766 they had to withdraw from the parishes they had held in the Bardez area of Goa, handing them over to local Goan secular priests who had become very numerous by that time and who were eager to run the parishes.

After their arrival in Goa in 1548 the Dominicans also set up houses at Bassein, Mahim, Tarapur, Chaul, Daman, Diu, Cochin, Nagapatanam, and Mylapore, all coastal towns on the west and east coasts of India. They were subsequently able to expand their missions to Mozambique and to Malacca, and to the islands of Timor and Solor in Indonesia. The Augustinians were the last to arrive in Goa, establishing the college of Our Lady of Grace after September 1572. From 1599 they expanded into Bengal, the region which they viewed as their most successful missionary field. They also worked in Persia and on the east coast of Africa.

Other religious orders, including the Carmelites, the Capuchins, and the Theatines, arrived in the course of the seventeenth century. They worked under the direct supervision of the Propaganda and had jurisdictional difficulties with the Portuguese. The Carmelites had charge of the vicariates of Malabar and the Great Mughal. The Capuchins worked in Surat, Madras and Pondicherry, and the Theatines served in Golconda. Under the Padroado regime of Goa, there were both Portuguese and Goan priests. Under the Roman Propaganda system, there were vicars apostolic in Bombay, Kerala, Pondicherry, and Tibet. Italian Carmelites served in Bombay and Kerala; French Capuchins and secular priests of the *Société des Missions Estrangéres* in Tamilnadu; French Capuchins in Madras and Italian Capuchins in north India. The Theatines (Clerics Regular of Divine Providence of St Cajetan) were also present in Goa, although they lacked funds and personnel in comparison with other orders. However, the Oratory of the Holy Cross of Miracles, founded in Goa in 1682 and patterned on the Oratory of Saint Philip Neri, grew to be an influential body, especially as it was the first religious congregation made up of clerics of local origin. Though all of these orders and congregations were engaged in the same general purpose of Christianization, a considerable amount of jealousy and exclusiveness existed among them.

In 1703, the Propaganda erected the Prefecture of Tibet-Hindustan, entrusting it to the Capuchins. They were able to maintain a presence in Lhasa from 1707 to 1745, when religious persecution forced them to move back to Kathmandu in Nepal, where the order had been established since 1715. But ultimately, in 1769, political unrest forced them to leave this kingdom as well and to relocate in India. In the meantime, many Nepalese Christians and catechumens relocated to Bettiah, Bihar in 1745. The Prefecture of Tibet-Hindustan was elevated into a vicariate in 1812.

The Jesuits moved into Tibet even earlier, with a mission at Tsaparang which ended in 1641. In 1713, a fresh start was made by two Jesuits, Ippolito Desideri and Manoel Freyre, even though the Capuchins considered Tibet part of their mission field and out of bounds to all other orders. Desideri was soon left alone in Tibet, and in the face of severe Capuchin opposition to his presence, he was ordered out of Lhasa in 1719. He was a great geographer, and his account of the mission was very reliable, revealing a deep understanding of Tibetan society and literature.

The first convent for women in the east, the convent of Santa Monica, was established in Goa in 1606, largely through the efforts of Archbishop Dom Aleixio de Menezes. It was intended mainly for the widows of Portuguese soldiers. Although tensions prevailed for some years between two factions within the cloister, the nuns continued to perform their regular religious duties, excelled in literary and musical works, and were also known for their skill in the fine arts and in culinary innovations.

The year 1759 marked the beginning of a difficult period for the Jesuits in both Portugal and in India. In that year, the Marquis of Pombal, virtual ruler of Portugal, managed to have the Society suppressed. The order's extensive landed properties and their houses in Goa were confiscated. In 1760, 127 Jesuits, working in various parts of India, were arrested and shipped back to Europe from Goa. Following the suppression, Pombal pursued a number of popular reforms in the colony. He disbanded the Inquisition in 1774 (it had conducted over seventy *autos-da-fé*, or sessions of examination, since its beginnings in Goa). He revamped the educational system and worked to improve conditions for the local clergy. Priests came to be selected for parish posts on the basis of their learning and virtue rather than on their race.

Disturbances continued in Goa. The Portuguese presence there did not remain unchallenged and there were many popular revolts. In 1654, for example, Dom Mathias de Castro, unhappy over being bypassed for an episcopal post in Goa, joined with Adil Shah, ruler of Bijapur, in a failed attempt to overthrow the Portuguese. In 1787, the conspiracy of the Pintos of Candolim brought to the fore Caetano Francisco de Couto, José António Gonçalves, and Caetano Victorino de Faria – all Goan priests – who had developed an abortive plan to overthrow Portuguese rule in Goa, after they had failed to persuade the Holy See to fill vacant episcopal posts of the *Padroado* in Goa with Indian appointees.

Protestant missions in India

The Dutch, British, and Danish merchants who set up trading stations, or factories, along the coasts of India in the seventeenth century brought along with them their own chaplains. With the founding of the Lutheran mission at Tranquebar on the east coast of south India in the early years of the eighteenth century, the monopoly which the Roman Catholic Church had till then held in the mission field was challenged. From 1706 till the beginning of the nineteenth century, the Lutheran Mission supported a total of fifty-six missionaries in India.

The mission owed its success to the efforts of two pioneering individuals from Denmark, Bartholomaus Ziegenbalg and Heinrich Plutschau. The Danes had been in Tranquebar since 1620, when the rajah of Thanjavur had allowed them to lease the area. Two churches existed there in the later seventeenth century, one, the Zion church, and the other, a Roman Catholic church. But the situation was transformed with the arrival of Ziegenbalg and Plutschau, both in their twenties, on 6 July 1706.

From the start the two Danish missionaries concentrated on education. Together, they established a school called the Charity School. In 1708, we learn of Ziegenbalg being imprisoned for a brief period on the orders of the Danish commandant. In 1709, we come across him expressing admiration for Indians as a civilized people, and for the depth of their moral insights. By 1711 he had translated the Bible into the local Tamil language, and in 1713, he published a genealogy of the Malabarian gods.

Ziegenbalg prided himself on being a High Church Lutheran and he had a strong sense of his calling to the mission. Anxious to make it a success, he developed a variety of original approaches. He used the Tamil language and Indian music in church services, and in general he sought to have the mission directed from India itself rather than from Europe. Confronted with the caste system, he believed that it had to be weakened within the church, even though it could never be totally abolished. His converts were mainly the

Shudras or Dalits, and the larger part of his church was reserved for them. Only a smaller transept was kept separate for the believers of all other castes. In 1714, Ziegenbalg visited Europe to sort out certain problems concerning the mission, and he returned to India two years later as a married man. He was not, however, to enjoy his new condition for long and he died on 23 February 1719, his health weakened as a result of the many difficulties he experienced with his colleagues in running the mission.

Another well-known missionary at Tranquebar was Benjamin Schultze who served in the mission on and off from 1720 through to 1740, and who received support from the Society for the Propagation of Christian Knowledge. His efforts on behalf of the local church resulted in three Indian catechists being ordained pastors. John Philip Fabricius, who arrived in India in 1740, also spent two years at Tranquebar. Thereafter, he moved to Madras, joining the English mission there, though he always remained linked to the Danish mission. By 1750 he had translated the New Testament into Tamil and had composed a short Tamil grammar in English. When he died in 1791, he had served for over fifty years in India.

The greatest of all the Tranquebar missionaries was Christian Friedrich Schwartz, who arrived in Tranquebar, aged twenty-four, on 30 July 1750. He came to know and speak Tamil, Telugu, Marathi, Persian, and Sanskrit, as well as a number of European languages, modern and classical. Noted for his holiness and purity, he was a preacher, teacher, diplomat, and statesman. He was highly regarded by soldiers, and the men of the English regiments delighted in his company. Schwartz eventually moved from Madras to Thanjavur, where he came to be treated as the royal priest of the city – able to exercise immense influence over the rajah and his political affairs. He also managed to be on good terms with the Muslim ruler, Hyder Ali of Mysore (1722–82). After the exit of the Jesuits from India in 1759, he looked after the areas in south India where the Jesuits had worked. He helped to form large congregations of Christians in Madras, Tranquebar, Tiruchirapalli, Thanjavur, and Palayamkottai. At his death in 1798, he had spent forty-eight years in India.

What was remarkable about such missionaries as Ziegenbalg, Schultze, and Schwartz was that they conducted much of their mission work through the local languages, promoted extensive lay participation, and placed the practical management of their missions largely in Indian hands. From its inception, the Tranquebar mission benefited from the services of European missionaries who were trained at the college founded by August Hermann Francke at the end of the seventeenth century in the German city of Halle. Francke had been a pioneer in education and had defined true theology as living religion.

His educational system stressed active, experiential learning, including the actual handling of objects in the natural sciences and practical training in technology.

Turning to the English contribution to missions, the policy of the East India Company had been largely hostile to Christian missions within Company territories, viewing the missions as a disruptive presence that would create tensions between the Company and local inhabitants. However, from 1792 pressures from evangelical public opinion upon the British parliament forced the Company to allow missionary chaplains to enter the East India Company's service in India. The father of the modern missionary movement among the British Protestants was William Carey, an evangelical who greatly admired the work of the German Evangelicals in India. He arrived in India in 1792 but he encountered many difficulties at the hands of the British East India Company and he was initially banned from Calcutta. With the Baptists Joshua Marshman and William Ward, Carey established a mission at Serampore, a Danish colonial enclave near Calcutta. Along with the Christian mission, Carey and his associates promoted the study of languages in order to translate the Scriptures and they created both western-style schools and a printing press. He was later able to enter Calcutta, but only by virtue of his ability to teach Indian languages at Fort William College. Carey's presence in Bengal not only advanced the Christian mission, but also contributed to enhanced cultural interactions between India and the west. In 1813, by the act renewing the East India Company Charter, the British parliament granted Christian missionaries the right to enter into British territories in India. At the same time, parliament created an Anglican establishment in India, endowed by Company revenues, with a Bishop of Calcutta exercising diocesan authority over the British territories, assisted by archdeacons in Calcutta, Madras, and Bombay. The first Bishop of Calcutta, the moderate High Churchman, Thomas F. Middleton, was consecrated in London in May 1814, and arrived in Calcutta in November 1814. This Anglican establishment and the growing number of missionaries of all denominations led to a steady increase in the numbers of missionary schools, colleges, and hospitals. Nevertheless, the tension between British officials looking primarily for stability and British missionaries working for social reform and conversions would continue to trouble the Raj throughout the nineteenth century.

The impact of English education also proved a mixed blessing for the British Empire in India. William Jones, an undogmatic Christian with an abiding respect for the religions of India, founded the Asiatic Society of Bengal in Calcutta in 1784, to promote the study of Indian culture and religion. Following the Charter Act of 1813, the work of the missionaries, the influence of trade and the introduction of western education served to stimulate a cultural revival among Bengal's growing intelligentsia. After 1814, the learned Brahman, Ram Mohan Roy (1772–1833) began making his mark in Calcutta as the father of this Hindu Renaissance. Well versed in English and the western classics, as well as his native Hindu culture, he inspired a movement among Indians for a fresh appreciation of the *Upanishads* and other Hindu texts.

As a whole, the Protestant impact on missions in India began to be felt only from the beginning of the eighteenth century. The pioneering Protestant missions in India before 1815 had been those of the Tranquebar mission and the Serampore mission of William Carey and his associates. Both missionary movements gave pride of place to the Bible and worked to translate it into several local languages, while the Serampore mission, in particular, stressed education and journalism.

South and south-east Asia outside India

There is not room here to explore the course of Christian missions across the whole of south and south-east Asia. Instead, we will focus on three mission fields: Sri Lanka, Timor and some of the neighbouring islands, and Vietnam.

In 1505, the Portuguese had reached Galle and Colombo in present-day Sri Lanka; they called the country Taprobane or Ceylon. At that time, the Jaffna peninsula of Ceylon had Hindu rulers and Hindu subjects, but the rest of the island was Buddhist. The Catholic mission began with the arrival of a group of Franciscans in 1543. Vikrama Bahu, the Buddhist King of Kandy, converted to Christianity in the 1540s in return for Portuguese help. Many others converted for material advantages from the Portuguese, and by 1560 there was a flourishing Christian community in Mannar on the eastern side of the island. Various Catholic orders under Portuguese patronage, including the Jesuits from 1602 and later the Augustinians and Dominicans, conducted missions on Ceylon. However, they failed to encourage local inhabitants to enter the priesthood. When the Dutch overran the island in 1658, they forced the withdrawal of the Portuguese priests, decreeing the death penalty for anyone harbouring a Roman Catholic priest. Many Catholic churches were now used for Protestant worship and the Catholics of Ceylon found themselves deprived of their pastors. In 1686, the Goan Oratorian priest, Blessed José Vaz (1651–1711), arrived in Ceylon and worked there amid poverty and danger for twenty-four years until his death. He developed ingenious ways of keeping the Catholic faith alive on the island, including reliance on native missionaries and catechists. As a result of his efforts, by the end of the eighteenth century, after 140 years of official Dutch efforts to suppress Catholicism, there were still an estimated 67,000 Roman Catholics on the island.

The Dutch East India Company by its renewed charter of 1623 had made provision for the promotion of the Protestant faith, and the company set up a seminary in Leyden, which trained missionaries for service in the Dutch possessions in the east. After their occupation of Ceylon, they set up a Protestant ecclesiastical structure, and restricted all official employment to Protestants, and in some cases confiscated the property of those refusing Protestant baptism. In 1722, there were said to be nearly 425,000 Protestant Christians in Ceylon, though most of these were nominal; indeed, they could hardly be other than nominal, as in 1747 there were only five Protestant ministers on the whole island. The British seized the coastline of Ceylon from the Netherlands in 1796, and formally annexed the island in 1815. The British occupation was followed by the arrival of representatives of the main British missionary societies – the London Missionary Society in 1804, the Baptist Missionary Society in 1812, the Wesleyan Methodists in 1814, and the Church Missionary Society in 1817.

The Christian mission on the island of Timor in the East Indies began in the mid-sixteenth century. The Timorese had been always animists, with a vague monotheism. The Franciscan, António Taveira, arrived in 1556 and began a preaching mission. The Dominicans came in 1562, and took the lead in evangelizing the island, concentrating on converting local rulers, who then became vassals of Portugal. By 1577, there were an estimated 50,000 converts. The Dominicans effectively ruled the island for over a century, without interference from civil or military authorities.

The Dominicans built their first church in 1590 at Mena and later they set up churches on the neighbouring islands of Sawu, Adunara, and Flores. As the faith advanced in Timor, it became linked in matters of jurisdiction both to the vicar-general of the Dominicans at Goa and to the Bishop of Malacca. In the first quarter of the eighteenth century, the Dominicans encountered the first serious challenge to their predominance on the islands of Timor and Solor. A Portuguese royal order of 25 March 1722 declared that Jesuits attached to the provinces of Goa, China and Macau would also be allowed to work in Timor. Another order of 10 March 1723 recommended that the Oratorians of the Miraculous Cross in Goa should be permitted in Timor. On 8 October 1738 a seminary was established under the Oratorians' care in Timor for the training of local aspirants to the priesthood. Not until 1812, however, did the Dominicans' temporal power in Timor begin to wane. In 1834 the suppression of all religious orders in Portugal and in its overseas provinces finally brought an end to the Dominican mission in Timor.

In the Moluccas and in East Flores, the Christian faith initially spread during the sixteenth century through the efforts of Portuguese missionaries. They had arrived along with Portuguese merchants, who were searching for spices and sandalwood. After nearly a century under Portuguese dominance, Amboina fell into the hands of the Dutch East India Company in 1605, Batavia in 1619, Malacca in 1641, Solor in 1646, Makassar in 1667, and Ternate in 1683. The Dutch East India Company promoted the spread of the Reformed Protestant faith and forbade the Catholic Church to operate within its territories, with the exception of East Flores, Solor and Timor. Until 1644 the Jesuit provinces of Malabar and Japan attended to the Roman Catholic ecclesiastical needs of the islands. However, for over a century, Catholicism in Indonesia was largely cut off from the rest of Catholic Christendom. The Dutch East India Company, meanwhile, supported Protestant missionaries and insisted that all its employees be members of the officially recognized Reformed Church. Growth in the numbers of Protestant converts, however, was slow. In 1799, the Dutch East India Company was dissolved and the Reformed dominance over the region brought to an end, opening Indonesia once again to a variety of missionary activities.

In Vietnam, the first record of Christian activity was in 1533 when a royal edict was issued by King Le Trang Tong forbidding the preaching of the doctrines of 'Gia-To' (Jesus), which were being spread by a man described by a Vietnamese word that usually means European. Later in the sixteenth century, a number of Dominicans entered the country, but widespread evangelization began only in the seventeenth century, with the arrival in 1615 of the Jesuit missionaries. The most famous of these Jesuit missionaries, Alexandre de Rhodes, came in 1625. He was eventually expelled, but not before he made two massive contributions to the creation of a Vietnamese Christianity. First, he led a team of missionaries who produced the Quoc-Ngu system of transliterating the Vietnamese language using the Latin alphabet, with an additional five signs to indicate the five tones of Vietnamese. This has been used by the Vietnamese people ever since. Second, de Rhodes produced a Vietnamese Catechism which had a long-lasting influence on Vietnamese Catholicism.

As a result of the lobbying of the Holy See by de Rhodes, Pope Alexander VII, in 1660, appointed two missionaries as the vicars apostolic of the two new dioceses of north and south Vietnam, then called Tonkin and Cochin China respectively. At that time, the missionaries who took over the work in Vietnam were those of the *Société des Missions Etrangères*. This latter society worked very hard in the subsequent decades at the creation of a native priesthood while the church was undergoing intermittent, but at times severe, persecution both in Tonkin and Cochin China.

In the eighteenth century, there was a breakdown of central authority in the north and south, and the people suffered through a series of civil wars which developed into a rivalry between the princes of the Nguyen and Trin clans. A decisive moment came both for the nation and for the church when Fr Pierre-Joseph Pigneaux negotiated a treaty between the French court and the Nguyen party, which brought the latter French military help in return for commercial concessions. French troops from Pondicherry arrived in 1788 and helped to achieve a Nguyen victory. The leading Nguyen prince became the Emperor Gian Long. Although he was and remained a Buddhist, the emperor showed favour to the Christian community. In 1802 the community was divided into three dioceses, each headed by a missionary Vicar Apostolic. There were 121 Vietnamese priests, fifty-five missionary priests, and 320,000 communicants. This development was also the beginning of a dangerous connection between the Christian church and French colonialism, which contributed to continuing, intermittent periods of severe persecution of the church in Vietnam.

The period between 1660 and 1815 in India and parts of south Asia and south-east Asia marked a tempestuous time politically, culturally, economically, and religiously. During these years, India witnessed within its confines the consolidation of control by western powers, the steady growth of the Christian faith, the spread of Islamic art and culture, and the flowering of various strands of Hindu philosophical thought and devotion. India also became the starting point and the funding agency for further missionary movements to various parts of Asia.

Note

1. A. Sauliere, *Red sand: A life of St. John de Brito, S. J. Martyr of the Madurai Mission* (Mathura: De Nobili Press, 1947), p. 487.

23

Christianity in East Asia

R. G. TIEDEMANN

The mid-seventeenth century was, generally speaking, not a good time for Christianity in East Asia. China was taking a long time to recover from the upheavals of internal rebellion and conquest by the alien Manchus. In Tokugawa Japan, Christianity had been all but eliminated and in Korea it was still virtually unknown. Only in the Philippines had the Catholic Church established a relatively stable presence.

The Philippines: A Catholic enclave in East Asia

The conversion of the Philippines constitutes a remarkable chapter in the history of Christianity in East Asia. By the mid-seventeenth century, only two or three generations after the Spanish conquest, most of the principal islands in the archipelago, except for the Muslim-controlled regions of Mindanao and the uplands of northern Luzon, had become permanently Christian. The Philippines thus formed an early Catholic enclave within the larger non-Christian world of Asia.

Crucial to the spiritual conquest of the Philippines were the friar missionaries who had arrived with the early Spanish colonizers. In addition to the friars, the Jesuits also played a part in the rapid conversion of the Philippines. It should be noted that the religious institutes in the Philippines received their personnel almost entirely from Spain and to a lesser extent Mexico. In time each of the orders established a Philippine province under a provincial superior based in Manila. The Philippine provinces of the friars comprised not only the territories under their care in the archipelago but also their respective missions on the Asian mainland.

Besides the provinces of the religious orders, the secular clergy was also established in the decades after the conquest. In 1595 Pope Clement VIII had raised the diocese of Manila to the status of an archdiocese and created three new dioceses: Nueva Cáceres (now the city of Naga), Nueva Segovia (transferred to Vigan in the mid-eighteenth century), and Cebu. This structure remained in place throughout the period 1660 to 1815. However, due to an acute shortage of secular priests in the Philippines during the early Spanish colonial period, regular clergy, trained in Spain by their respective orders for missionary service, often found themselves assigned as parish priests. Periodically this situation led to serious tensions over jurisdiction between the religious orders and the ecclesiastical hierarchy.

During the last decades of the seventeenth century, the Habsburg kings of Spain continued to take seriously their role as promoters of the Catholic faith in their colonial possessions, and they looked to the Spanish clergy, especially the friars, to play their part. 'As missionaries, the friars worked within the context of the Spanish colonial policies. They were agents of the State as well as servants of the Church.'[1] From the start, the mendicant orders had been intimately involved in the *encomienda* programme of pacification and colonization. The *encomienda* system consisted of feudal holdings entrusted by the King of Spain to the colonizers as reward for their services. It was a means for extracting produce and labour services from the conquered indigenous populations in return for their protection. The early friars worked through this system to pursue mass evangelization among pacified and settled native groups.[2] The regulars remained a potent force in the Philippine church throughout the Spanish era.

Through the ardour and thoroughness of the early missionaries, Christian communities were established in the lowland Philippines within two or three generations after the Spanish arrival. Both the friars and the Jesuits insisted that neophytes memorize the entire *Doctrina Cristiana* – a compendium of common Catholic prayers and religious practices – together with the fundamental doctrinal principles. Thus new practices (the sacraments, confessions, penance) and new concepts (the idea of original sin and the idea of salvation) entered the Philippine world. At the same time, converts had to conform to the new Catholic morality, which included the renunciation of polygamy, ritual drinking, chattel-slavery, and usury.

While the regular clergy played an important part in shaping the beliefs of the neophytes, other factors also contributed to the successful evangelization of the Philippine lowlands. Charles Macdonald has alerted us to the 'transformative continuity between old religious rituals and present-day Catholicism', which was achieved 'by using the same belief structure within a new framework or by simply transposing a pre-existing structure into a new idiom'. Macdonald argues that some of the later Spanish friars were 'probably simple peasants', who brought with them 'their own brand of folk Christianity, including the veneration of the saints, and a host of "superstitions" (belief in ghosts, evil spirits, and the like). The folk beliefs of missionaries probably matched some native beliefs, bringing the two religious worlds closer together.' Thus, many folk beliefs 'could prosper with the blessing of the clergy, while retaining their polytheistic structure and fulfilling pre-Christian religious needs'.[3]

Religious communities for women

Although women had played important roles as priestesses in pre-Hispanic Filipino society, their transition into Christian institutional life proved difficult. On the one hand, Catholic monastic values such as personal sanctification and perfection, removal from one's own family, obedience, poverty, and celibacy were alien concepts to indigenous women. On the other hand, the Spanish church and civil authorities resisted the acceptance of native women into religious orders. Thus the Royal Monastery of the Immaculate Conception of the Poor Clares (*Real Monasterio de Sta. Clara*), a community of the Second Order of St Francis established in Manila in 1621, was exclusively for women of pure Spanish heritage, whether born in Spain or in the colony. This remained the only community for nuns in the Philippines until the twentieth century.

It was only towards the end of the seventeenth century that the first quasi-religious communities came into being for indigenous women and women of mixed ethnicity (*mestiza*) who sought lives of spiritual perfection. These pious women, many of whom had been accepted as tertiaries by one of the mendicant orders, had hitherto lived in solitude or with their families. Opting for lives of rigorous penitence and contemplation, these women, known as *beatas* ('blessed women'), also assisted with the poor and sick, with the instruction of girls and with various menial tasks for the church. Eventually, the *beatas* were permitted to wear a habit and profess what in effect were private vows of chastity, poverty, and obedience. These communities, known as *beaterios*, were never recognized as religious congregations under canon law but were simply considered as 'pious unions', that is, 'associations of the faithful founded to further some work of piety or charity'.[4]

The tentative beginnings of a permanent *beaterio* in the Philippines can be traced to the early 1680s when two childless young widows, the sisters-in-law Antonia Esguerra, widow of Captain Simón de Fuentes, and Francisca de Fuentes, having received the tertiary habit of St Dominic, began to meet with other women – Spanish, creole, and native – in the Esguerra home in Manila. As *beatas*, they involved themselves in works of charity and invited other pious women to join them in their spiritual endeavours, including Sebastiana

Salcedo, a mystic and member of the old native nobility. In 1686 the group asked the prior of the Dominican convent to be allowed to live in community with the permission of the Provincial Chapter. Although this date can be regarded as the beginning of their religious community, it was not until 1696 that the Beaterio of St Catherine of Siena was formally inaugurated, with Mother Francisca del Espiritu Santo as the first prioress. Native women were accepted only as 'sisters of obedience' (*hermanas de la obediencia*), without voting rights.

A second such institution, the *Beaterio de la Compañía de Jesús*, was founded by the Chinese *mestiza* Mother Ignacia de Espiritu Santo, with the help of the Jesuit priest Paul Klein. From the 1730s, it received girls who, after undergoing a two-year novitiate, were initially allowed to make simple, temporary vows, for a seven-year period, at the end of which they could make perpetual vows of chastity and obedience as members of the *beaterio*. In addition to engaging in education, it organized retreats for native, *mestiza*, and Spanish lay women. 'All these women of diverse races gathered as one, lived in community during the eight days of each retreat, and together performed the spiritual exercises within the *beaterio*, "to the great benefit not only of themselves but of the communities they came from"'.[5] In 1719, two indigenous blood sisters, Dionisia Mitas Talangpaz and Cecilia Rosa Talangpaz of Calumpit, Bulacan, founded the third major Philippine religious community. In 1725 they received the habit of the Third Order of Augustinian Recollects as well as a small house in Manila. This was in effect the beginning of the *Beaterio de San Sebastián de Calumpang*.

Given the ambiguity of their status, the *beatas* could not avoid being drawn into jurisdictional struggles. As Luciano Santiago has aptly put it:

> The beatas had to contend with three entities, united nominally yet fiercely independent of each other, and often with conflicting views on the nature of the beaterios: the governor-general as the king's representative who had the prerogative of whether or not to implement royal decrees; the bishop of the diocese; and the provincial of the religious order which supervised the beata's community.[6]

Despite much official hostility, the three major sister communities managed to survive into the twentieth century, when they were finally given the status of regular religious congregations.

Controversies in the colonial church

By the middle of the seventeenth century the combined force of the friars, the church and the state had created a relatively stable, Christianized society in the settled areas of the lowland Philippines. During the following decades, however, the colonial partnership began to break down. Tensions developed into what became a complex three-cornered contest between royal administrators, the secular hierarchy, and the mendicant orders.

A number of the quarrels between bishops and colonial functionaries concerned abuses connected with the *encomienda* system. As the Dominican Bishop Andrés Gonzáles of Nueva Cáceres remarked in 1687, exactions under this system had become oppressive and unjust, as neither the feudal holders (or *encomenderos*) nor the royal officials had acted fairly towards the natives. Though the *encomienda* system was formally abolished at the beginning of the eighteenth century, colonial officials continued to enforce the institutional structures that had sustained it for their own private gain. The Franciscan Manuel Matos, since 1754 Bishop of Nueva Cáceres, became a particularly outspoken critic of exploitation of native labour by abusive *encomenderos* and colonial administrators, unfair commerce (for example, the compulsory exaction of produce from the subject people, often without payment), arbitrary taxation, and the suppression of basic rights.

Since the colonial government in the Philippines showed little interest in remedying the abuses, the only recourse for the indigenous people was to turn to the 'paternal protection of the ecclesiastics, particularly their bishops'. But as Danilo Gerona has pointed out, few bishops paid serious attention to the colonial abuses, and those who did were not opposed to the colonial institutions as such. Their interventions were simply intended to mitigate the oppression. Nor was the church itself as a colonial institution free from corruption. Some friars were accused of leading a 'princely life' at the expense of the indigenous Filipinos, something the increasingly hostile colonial officials were quick to point out. The bishops, for their part, 'apparently saw the need to consolidate their powers in view of the relentless abuses perpetrated by colonial authorities and the constant challenge they posed to the hierarchy'.[7]

One of the controversies in the early Spanish regime that profoundly affected the course of Philippine history involved a dispute between the bishops and the friars over the issue of canonical visitation. Since few Spanish secular priests were attracted to the Philippines, the regular clergy, who had arrived prior to the creation of the dioceses, had been drafted to serve as parish priests. Their dual status created an unusual situation: as *friars*, they were subject to the authority of their respective provincials, but as *parish priests*, they were under the authority of the bishop. The friars claimed that they should be exempted from episcopal visitation because they had come to the Philippines to evangelize amongst the heathen, not to administer parishes. But the bishops insisted on visiting the parishes administered by friar-curates.[8]

The jurisdictional conflicts became particularly intense in 1697–1705 under Archbishop Camacho, who was determined to subject the mendicant orders to his visitation. The friars' representatives in Madrid protested against Camacho's actions, in a memorandum to the Spanish king dated 13 February 1699. They intimated that if visitations were forced upon the friars the latter would withdraw from the parishes or even leave the Philippines altogether. However, the king supported Camacho's stand and directed royal officials in Manila to assist the archbishop in enforcing the right of visitation. Further support for Camacho's stand came from Pope Clement XI's brief of 30 January 1705, which stated that 'the right of visiting the parochial regulars belonged to the said archbishop and other bishops'. Undeterred by the royal and papal injunctions, the regulars continued to oppose the archbishop, and the dispute remained unresolved when Camacho was transferred to the see of Guadalajara in Mexico. In 1707 Camacho's successor, Francisco de la Cuesta, revived the fight against the regulars and attempted to enforce both the papal brief and the royal decree. The regulars, in turn, requested that the implementation of the papal brief be delayed, pending a decision on their appeal in Spain. Alarmed by the continuing dispute in the Philippines, the king ordered the archbishop to halt his attempts at implementing visitations until further notice.[9] However, Pope Benedict XIV later issued bulls on 6 November 1744 and 24 February 1745, both of them supported by King Ferdinand IV, ordering the friar-curates to submit to episcopal visitation.

Decline of the Philippine church

The period after 1770 was one of decline for the Catholic Church in the Philippines. As John Schumacher has argued, this decline was precipitated by events in Europe. In the later eighteenth century, the Bourbon kings, as 'Enlightened despots', increasingly 'saw the Church primarily as an instrument of the Crown to preserve its subjects in their loyalty and direct their activities in accord with royal purposes'. Charles III, in particular, introduced measures that were designed 'to reduce the Church to the role of State servant which were to have especially disastrous consequences in the Philippines'. Particularly significant, according to Schumacher, were: (1) the expulsion of the Jesuits from the Spanish dominions, decreed in Madrid in 1767 but not executed in the Philippines until 1768–69; (2) the subjection of the friars to royal and episcopal control; and (3) the decision by the Archbishop of Manila to appoint large numbers of Filipino secular priests.[10]

The British occupation of Manila in 1762–64 during the Seven Years' War was an additional factor behind the church's decline. It was the Spanish religious orders who organized the resistance against the British, with the militant Augustinians particularly successful in mobilizing Filipinos against the 'heretics'. However, these efforts at resistance did not occur everywhere, for the British occupation coincided with and indeed stimulated the outbreak of uprisings against abuses by the colonial administration in the provinces of Pangasinan, Cagayan, and Ilocos. Diego Silang's insurrection in Ilocos, in particular, challenged both Spanish civil and ecclesiastical authority, and the Bishop of Vigan and the Augustinians felt compelled to raise a large army against him.

In the late 1760s, another attempt was made to settle the visitation problem in accordance with Pope Benedict XIV's bulls of 1744 and 1745. When Basilio Sancho, a court prelate, arrived in 1767 as the new Archbishop of Manila, he immediately directed the friars in the parishes to submit to visitation. The tensions increased when Simón de Anda, the hero of Spanish resistance to the British occupation of Manila, returned to the Philippines as governor-general in July 1770. Known for his antagonism towards the mendicants, he also demanded that they submit to the requirements of the royal patronage (*patronato real*) system. The first Council of Manila was convened in 1771 to implement reforms, including the subordination of the friar-curates to episcopal jurisdiction. In October 1771, after the Augustinians in the province of Pampanga failed to comply with orders from the archbishop and the governor-general, Anda sent troops to apprehend the recalcitrant friars who 'were herded to Manila and then shipped to Spain'.[11]

The vexed jurisdictional dispute between bishops and friars was closely related to the controversy between the regular and the secular clergy for possession of the parishes. As has been indicated, the secular clergy were never very numerous. In any case, since the ecclesiastical territory had largely been divided amongst the religious orders, there was little scope for the seculars. Moreover, most of the latter preferred the prebendaries and benefices of the Manila cathedral rather than parish work in the isolated hinterlands. Two decrees of King Ferdinand IV in 1752 and 1757 required a gradual takeover of parishes by the secular clergy upon the death of the incumbent friars. However, as a result of the expulsion of the Jesuits as well as of some Augustinians, a considerable number of parishes suddenly became vacant in the early 1770s.

Archbishop Sancho, determined to cripple the religious orders, hurriedly ordained a large number of Filipino seculars, after rudimentary training in the seminary, and assigned them to the vacant parishes. The poorly trained Filipino priests, however, were not ready for the sudden imposition of full responsibility in the local churches. Consequently, on 11 December 1776 the Spanish king, having received numerous complaints against the Filipino seculars, including one from Governor-General Anda himself, suspended the transfer of parishes to the Filipino clergy. According to the king's decree the friars in charge of parishes would subject themselves to canonical visitation, but only by their own superiors, while the archbishop would retain the right only to visit parishes held by secular clergy. The Spanish friars thus consolidated their power and influence in Philippine society, while the Filipino secular priests were denied the rights and privileges granted to the Spanish mendicants. The antagonism between the two groups deepened in the course of the nineteenth century into national and racial enmity.

The events of the 1760s and early 1770s contributed significantly to the decline of the Philippine church. To make matters worse, the mendicant orders found it harder to attract new recruits from Spain, as a consequence of the disruptions during the Revolutionary and Napoleonic warfare in Europe. Thus, while the Catholic faith remained strong in the Philippine lowlands, the upland regions were neglected because of a lack of properly trained priests, and a consequent decline of missionary ardour. This regional dichotomy in religious identity would persist to the present day.

China: Toleration, suppression and survival

Although the Manchu armies had taken Beijing and installed the Shunzhi Emperor of the Qing dynasty in the Forbidden City in 1644, it would be the early 1680s before peace was restored throughout the Chinese Empire. Especially in the south the political situation remained fluid, due to the incomplete military control of the Manchus and the existence of Ming loyalist resistance movements. The Chinese Christian communities, particularly in the provinces of Fujian and Sichuan, were seriously affected by these internal conflicts.

The Catholic missionary enterprise in late seventeenth-century China

The precarious condition of Christianity during these years was not improved by the increasing rivalries among the missionaries. During the early decades of the seventeenth century, the Society of Jesus had enjoyed the exclusive right to propagate the gospel in Japan and China. From this position of independence the Jesuits had devised a policy of accommodation or adaptation to Chinese culture and to the life-style and etiquette of the Confucian scholar-elites. By addressing themselves to the literate elite, they engaged in evangelization 'from the top down'. Moreover, they used European science and technology in order to attract the attention of the educated Chinese, sending well-trained scientists, astronomers and artists to the court to work for the emperor. Their monopoly of the directorship of the important Astronomical Bureau from 1644 gave these Court Jesuits influence with the emperor or at least with some court officials. Of more general significance is the fact that they adopted a tolerant attitude towards certain Chinese rites, like ancestral worship and the veneration of Confucius, which they declared to be 'civil rites'.

However, the exclusive position of the Society of Jesus was challenged in the 1630s by the arrival of Spanish mendicants (Dominicans in Fujian and Discalced Franciscans in Shandong) from the Philippines. In the 1680s the Spanish Augustinians also became active in a somewhat more modest capacity. Of greater significance was the introduction of the vicariate system to the eastern missions which permitted direct papal action in China. The appointment of the first vicars apostolic under the direct authority of the Sacred Congregation for the Propagation of the Faith (or *Propaganda Fide*) was closely connected to the foundation of the Foreign Mission Society of Paris (*Société des Missions Etrangères de Paris*) in 1659. This new society of secular priests sent to China missionaries who were less willing to practise accommodation. *Propaganda Fide* sent the first Reformed Franciscans from Italy to China in the 1680s.

The new situation demanded the establishment of a clear ecclesiastical structure in the Middle Kingdom. The Portuguese *padroado* had been in charge of one diocese in the Portuguese settlement of Macao since 1576; however, the extent of this diocese had never been clearly defined. Thus, the appointment of the first vicars apostolic was not surprisingly accompanied by protracted intra-church conflicts between the *padroado* and *Propaganda Fide*. The ensuing jurisdictional issues were finally settled by Pope Innocent XII in 1696. China was divided into three *padroado* dioceses with limited territory: the diocese of Beijing included the provinces of Zhili and Shandong as well as the territory of Liaodung in Manchuria; the diocese of Nanjing consisted of Anhui, Jiangsu, and Henan; and the diocese of Macao included Guangdong, Guangxi, and the island of Hainan. Each of the remaining provinces became vicariates apostolic: Fujian, Jiangxi, Huguang (later divided into Hunan and Hubei), Sichuan, Guizhou, Shanxi, Shaanxi, Yunnan, and Zhejiang.[12]

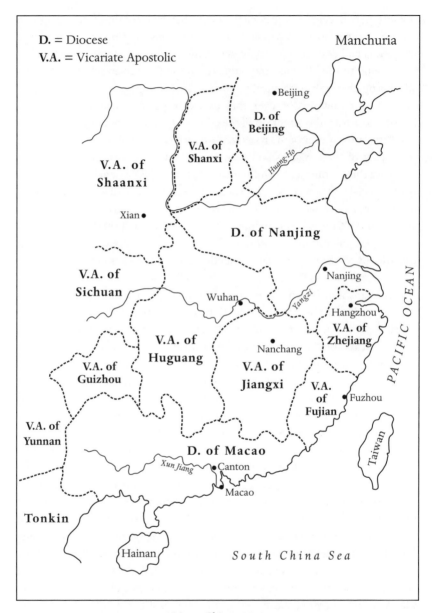

Map 4 China c. 1696

As for the Jesuits of China, they were by no means homogeneous as a group. A distinction had long existed between the court Jesuits and those based in the provinces. The situation was further complicated by the arrival of the first French Jesuits in Beijing. In an attempt to extend his influence to East Asia, King Louis XIV sent six French Jesuits to China in 1687, all of them well trained in science and with the title of 'Mathématiciens du Roy'. They successfully demonstrated their skills to the Kangxi emperor and as a result were given a piece of land within the imperial precinct, where later the famous Northern Church (*Beitang*) was erected.[13] However, a conflict soon developed between the French Jesuits and the Portuguese-sponsored Jesuits working at the Astronomical Bureau. It was both a clash of national interests and a competition for scientific influence.[14] As a result of this conflict, the French Jesuit mission was separated from the Portuguese Jesuit vice-province in November 1700.

A time of persecution and recovery

The appointment of the Jesuit Adam Schall von Bell as director of the Astronomical Bureau by the Shunzhi Emperor in 1645 suggested that the missionaries and Christianity had been accepted by the new regime. For a while the prestige attached to the court Jesuits' position afforded a degree of protection to priests and converts. However, this relatively trouble-free period came to an end as a result of the so-called 'Calendar Case' instigated by Yang Guangxian. Having made several attempts to have the foreigners in charge of the Astronomical Bureau removed, Yang attacked both Christianity and western learning. His report of September 1664 convinced the regents of the young Kangxi emperor that Schall had not only made several astronomical errors but that the Jesuit missionaries were plotting rebellion and indoctrinating the people with false ideas. After lengthy investigation, Schall and seven officials in the Astronomical Bureau, including five Christians, were sentenced to death. Although Schall was pardoned, the Christian officials were executed in 1665, most of the missionaries were imprisoned in Guangzhou (Canton), and the churches in the provinces were closed.

The Calendar Case resulted from several factors, some of which had been smouldering before Yang launched his attack – such as personal rivalry among the Jesuits, tensions between pro- and anti-Christian factions at court, and bitterness among the Muslim astronomers whom Schall had displaced. This episode marked the first comprehensive attack on western learning, and the judgement was followed in 1669 with the first prohibition of the propagation of Christianity among Han subjects. In 1671, the suppression of the Catholic mission was partially lifted, but with the qualification that the missionaries could not make new converts or build new churches. The Kangxi emperor again bestowed personal favours on the court missionaries, including a tablet with the text *Jingtian* (Revere Heaven) to be distributed to all churches. This apparent imperial protection, on the one hand, and the prohibition of further propagation, on the other, led to an ambiguous situation between 1671 and 1691 which Ad Dudink has called 'tacit toleration'.[15]

The same ambiguity characterized the so-called Edict of Toleration of 1692, which the missionaries obtained as a reward for their casting of cannon and their help in the negotiations with Russia (Treaty of Nerchinsk, 1689). The edict confirmed that the Christian religion had not proven to be seditious and therefore did not need to be proscribed. Christians were placed on the same level as Buddhists and Daoists who were allowed to have temples and offer incense. As long as Christians remained subordinated to Confucian state orthodoxy and did not create trouble, they were to be allowed to practise their rituals in their places of worship. However the edict did not mention further Christian religious propaganda or the building of new churches. In light of subsequent events, the Edict of Toleration was 'a fleeting moment . . . , an ideal that was immediately surrounded with controversy and constant disappointment, claims and counter-claims'.[16]

The Rites Controversy intensified

The uncertainties arising from the Edict of Toleration coincided with the culmination of the fateful Rites Controversy amongst the European missionaries, a controversy which had started with Matteo Ricci's policy of accommodation. Essentially but by no means exclusively a contest between the Jesuits and the mendicants, it involved three distinct problems. The first was the so-called 'Term question', that is, how to express the name God and other important concepts in Chinese. The second was the question of whether or not Christians should be forbidden to take part in ceremonies honouring Confucius and the cult of ancestors. Finally, there was the question of whether Christians should be permitted to participate in community activities that involved honouring non-Christian divinities.

The conflict between the two camps intensified when the French secular priest Charles Maigrot, Vicar Apostolic of Fujian, attacked the Jesuit position on the Chinese rites in his *Mandate* of 1693. It condemned Jesuit practices and rejected the use of the Chinese terms *shangdi* ('lord on high') and *tian* ('heaven') for God. After lengthy deliberations in Rome, the pope issued the anti-rites decree *Cum Deus optimus* of 20 November 1704. It forbade the use of *tian* and *shangdi*, while approving *tianzhu* ('Lord of Heaven'). At the same time, Christians were forbidden to take part in sacrifices to Confucius or to ancestors. Rome's decisions were taken to China by the papal legate Charles Thomas Maillard de Tournon. However, his audience with the Kangxi emperor in July 1706 went rather badly, and in response, the irritated Kangxi emperor issued an order that all missionaries, in order to obtain an imperial permit (*piao*) to stay in China, would have to declare that they would follow 'the rules of Matteo Ricci'. De Tournon, for his part, countered with a set of rules on precisely how the missionaries were to answer the emperor's questions, threatening the disobedient with excommunication and leaving no room for interpretation. Finally, the apostolic constitution *Ex illa die* (1715) reiterated the papal pronouncements of the 1704 bull.

The conflict became more complicated when in 1721 the papal legate Carlo Ambrogio Mezzabarba approved eight 'concessions' proposed by those opposed to the papal decrees. These concessions were, however, later annulled by Rome. The apostolic constitution *Ex quo Singulari* (1742) reinforced the papal decrees with sanctions and included an obligatory oath of observance to be taken by all priests leaving for the China mission. This constitution ruled conclusively against the Chinese Rites and effectively closed the controversy. Because it fundamentally challenged Chinese beliefs and was perceived as a threat to the Chinese social order, this decision has often been considered as one of the main causes for the 'failure' of Christianity in China. The dissolution of the Society of Jesus by Pope Clement XIV in 1773, promulgated in China in 1775, can be seen as an epilogue to this long affair.

As David Mungello has remarked, 'interpretations of the Rites Controversy can be placed on a spectrum between two extremes. One extreme regards the Rites Controversy as a watershed in the early modern history of Sino-western cultural relations while the other extreme views the Controversy as a purely European affair which can be easily omitted when attempting to understand the history of Christianity in China from a Chinese perspective.'[17] Whereas from a missionary perspective the focus is on the sharp demarcation between the so-called 'Jesuit' and 'Dominican' positions, the role of the Chinese converts has been largely ignored. 'Their involvement in the controversy through books, pamphlets, letters of protest etc. shows that they were truly imbedded in a Chinese society in which rites occupied an important place.'[18]

Suppression and survival of Christianity 1724–1815

From the early eighteenth century the toleration of Christianity in China was being increasingly questioned. Indeed, in January 1721 the Kangxi emperor indicated that he wished to proscribe this troublesome creed. It was, however, not until January 1724, shortly after the accession of the Yongzheng emperor, that an edict proscribing Christianity was actually issued. The foreign missionaries were deported to Canton and, later, to Macao (except those who worked at the court and those who had managed to hide in the provinces). Urban churches were gradually closed and converted into temples, granaries, schools, or other public facilities. Initially, there was no large-scale persecution of Chinese Christians or of missionaries working clandestinely in the provinces. From time to time new missionaries even managed to enter China. The first local persecution seems to have occurred in Fujian in late 1733. For the remainder of the eighteenth century, there were periodic local persecutions, but these were 'usually followed by a period of comparative quiet, with opportunity for recuperation'.[19] Only the persecutions in the late 1740s and the mid-1780s can be described as anti-Christian agitation on a large scale. Nevertheless, in the long run the climate of hostility forced a gradual retreat of Catholicism into the remoter parts of rural China.

While much has been written about the work of foreign missionaries in the Manchu Empire, the contribution made by indigenous Christians is alluded to only in passing. Yet a careful examination of the history of the China missions reveals that from the beginning, Chinese Christians were vital to the introduction, preservation and subsequent expansion of Christianity in the country. Given the extreme paucity of European missionaries, the vast size of China and the many social and linguistic problems that foreign priests had to face, Rome soon came to recognize the importance of training a native clergy. Indeed, as early as 1659 the newly appointed vicars apostolic were instructed by *Propaganda Fide* to train indigenous priests who could read Latin, even if they did not understand it. In 1666 the *Missions Etrangères de Paris* opened a central seminary in Ayutthaya, the capital of Siam, to prepare Chinese, Vietnamese and other East Asians for the priesthood. When the Burmese invaded the Siamese capital in 1767, the seminary was first moved to Hon-dat near Ha-tiên, Vietnam, and soon afterwards to Virampatnam near Pondicherry in French India – where it remained until its closure in 1781. In 1807 a new *Missions Etrangères de Paris* seminary was established in Penang in the Strait of Malacca, a British possession since 1786.

After 1724, in view of the growing insecurity of the Catholic Church in China, training for the priesthood continued primarily outside the empire, and many Chinese were sent to Europe. The 'Propaganda' missionary Matteo Ripa founded the College of the Holy Family of Jesus Christ in Naples in 1732 for the purpose of training Chinese secular priests. The Jesuits likewise sent some Chinese to study in Europe, at their college in Rome or at Louis-le-Grand College in Paris. There some joined the Society of Jesus, before returning to China as priests. In addition, a small number of Chinese clerics were trained by the Dominicans in Manila at the expense of the Spanish crown.

But deracinization during their prolonged formation in Europe (and even in Siam and Macao) made it difficult for the new priests to reintegrate into Chinese society. They gradually lost the ability to speak and write Chinese and were alienated from their own culture. Towards the end of the eighteenth century tentative beginnings were made, in spite of the precarious situation, to train the native clergy in China. Nevertheless, because of the high cost of such training as well as a certain reticence amongst the foreign missionaries to educate Chinese clerics, the number of indigenous priests remained relatively small. Thus, in the late 1740s the remarkable Li Ande (Andreas Ly) was the only priest ministering to many Christian communities in the large province of Sichuan. It was, in fact, he who founded the first seminary for native priests in that province (and indeed in all of inland China) in 1764.

Given the paucity of both foreign and indigenous clergy, the mission enterprise came to rely on various kinds of Chinese lay personnel to manage local church affairs as well as to preserve and extend the faith. It is useful to distinguish among three types of lay leadership: male itinerant catechists, local congregational leaders (huizhang), and – of particular importance – certain single laywomen known as the 'institute of virgins'.

The 'institute of virgins' warrants particular attention. In consequence of the custom of strictly segregating the sexes in traditional Chinese society, the evangelization of women presented a particular challenge for Catholic missionaries. Although women often played a pivotal role in the conversion of families, Chinese mores made it all but impossible for priests – foreign or Chinese – to establish direct contact with them. Since it was also impractical to establish proper Catholic convents prior to the Sino-foreign treaties of the mid-nineteenth century, the indigenous laywomen known as 'virgins' became a vital element in the propagation and preservation of the Catholic faith amongst Chinese females. The earliest evidence of their activities comes from seventeenth-century Fujian province, where Spanish Dominican friars introduced the beata system which had developed in the Philippines. To some extent influenced by the Fujian experience, the *Missions Etrangères de Paris* priests established the institute of virgins in their mission in the 1740s. Under this system, single women consecrated their lives to the service of God and the mission. Usually bound by a private vow of chastity, they continued to live with their families, where they instructed the women and children. In Sichuan they were also involved in external evangelization and the care of abandoned girls. The rules for such women concerning the formation of character and the cultivation of a religious life and Christian virtues, especially chastity, were approved by *Propaganda Fide* in 1784 and further elaborated by the Sichuan Synod of 1803. These rules remained in force well into the twentieth century. Thus the essential value of the virgins to the apostolate was recognized. Indeed, in times of persecution they became pillars of the faith within extended kinship networks and local Christian communities.

Non-Catholic Christians in China

Although the Christianizing of China was primarily undertaken by Roman Catholics, brief mention must be made of the rather marginal Russian Orthodox and Protestant efforts during the period 1660–1815. The Russian Ecclesiastical Mission in Beijing was founded in 1727 to provide pastoral care for the Russian prisoners from Albazin and their descendants. The Russian Orthodox Church placed more emphasis on political-diplomatic, commercial, and later scientific activities, than on evangelization. Moreover, Russian clerics, unlike Catholic priests, did not stay for the rest of their lives in China, but returned to Russia after a decade. Theirs remained a small church with only a few Russian members.

Protestant missionary activities are hardly noteworthy during this period. The first Protestant attempt to propagate the gospel in the Middle Kingdom ended in the 1660s when the Dutch East India Company was expelled from Taiwan by the Ming loyalist Zheng Chenggong (Koxinga). It was not until 1807 that more lasting Protestant missionary work was initiated with the arrival in Guangzhou of Robert Morrison of the London Missionary Society.

At the beginning of the nineteenth century, after nearly a century of sporadic persecutions, Christianity had been reduced to a marginal religion in China. Nevertheless, after 1800 the Chinese state renewed its efforts to eradicate what it still perceived to be a dangerous creed. The persecutions of 1805 and 1811 targeted not only some foreign priests but also the Christian community at Beijing (including Manchus), a community that had thus far enjoyed a degree of freedom on account of their being served by the westerners who worked at the court. Further afield, the vicar apostolic of Sichuan, Gabriel-Taurin Dufresse, was beheaded in 1815.

But developments in China were not the only factors contributing to the precarious state of the Christian enterprise around 1800. External factors such as the declining power of Spain and Portugal, the dissolution of the Society of Jesus in 1773 and the impact of the French Revolution all contributed to a waning of the missionary spirit in Catholic Europe, bringing about declining financial support which considerably weakened the missionary endeavour in China. Although the Congregation of the Mission (Lazarists or Vincentians) – designated to continue the work of the suppressed Jesuit order – sent its first missionaries to China in 1784, by 1820 only twenty-eight Lazarist priests had arrived in China. The *Missions Etrangères de Paris* also experienced a decline in personnel for the China mission field, and there is no reason to believe that the situation was different for the vicariates apostolic of the Italian Friars Minor or the Spanish Dominicans. The Christian endeavour in China had reached a low point in 1815.

Japan: survival of the 'secret' Christians

The establishment of the Tokugawa *bakufu* government following the Battle of Sekigehara (1600) soon brought to a close the 'Christian Century' in Japan. The third *shōgun* (military ruler), Tokugawa Iemitsu, strengthened the *bakufu* regime by thoroughly prohibiting the Christian religion and promoting a policy of national isolation (*sakoku*). The closure of the country to the outside world was intended as a means of extirpating Christianity, by preventing the smuggling of missionaries into the country and keeping any Christian influences from filtering in from abroad. Japanese Christianity received its severest blow in the wake of the Shimabara Rebellion (1637–38) on the island of Kyushu, a place where Christianity had become well established. In the aftermath of the rebellion, an Office of Inquisition for Christian Affairs was established at Edo (modern Tokyo) in 1640. It was put under the direction of a special commissioner who was entrusted with the task of exterminating all surviving Christians and eliminating the last remnants of the alien creed from the country. It maintained a prison (*Kirishitan yashiki*), where captured missionaries and influential Christians were examined, tortured, or imprisoned until their death. The Office of Inquisition remained in operation uninterruptedly until 1792.

Some 150,000 Japanese converts had gone underground to escape the severe persecutions, and the government employed various means to destroy these 'secret Christians' (*senpuku Kirishitan*). They included the practice of rewarding those who denounced Christians, in conjunction with the *gonin-gumi* system, that is, the five-family neighbourhood groups who were mutually responsible for the behaviour of their members. The ceremony of *efumi* or 'picture treading' (stepping on images representing Christ or the Virgin Mary), held annually at the beginning of the year, was likewise introduced by the Inquisition as a method for eradicating the foreign religion. Finally, the supervision of religious matters and the investigation of subversive sects were entrusted to Buddhist monks. Every family had to register at a Buddhist temple and obtain a temple certificate. The combination of these measures proved effective, resulting in several wholesale arrests and punishment, called *kuzure* ('crumblings'), in the mid-seventeenth century. These institutions to eradicate Christianity remained in place until the end of the *bakufu* government in the second half of the nineteenth century.

In spite of intense government investigations, underground Christians managed to survive in a few places, principally in the Nagasaki area and some nearby smaller islands. In the absence of priests, the various religious sodalities and confraternities that foreign priests had created amongst local converts before *sakoku* now 'constituted the religious core of the community'.[20] Since the Christian communities could not openly employ images of their faith, they adopted Buddhist images like that of a Goddess of Mercy holding a child in her arms (*Koyasu Kannon*) or of a Goddess of Motherly Love (*Jibo Kannon*) instead of an image of Mary (*Mariya Kannon*). Thus, gradually the faith of the underground Christians tended to move away from a God who was a strict father and judge, and focus on Mary as the forgiving mother of infinite tenderness.

This trend can also be observed in the only surviving doctrinal text compiled by the underground Christians themselves, namely the *Tenchi Hajimari no Koto* ('Concerning the Creation of Heaven and Earth'), whose topics are the creation of heaven and earth, the angels and the fall of humankind, Mary, the life of Christ, and the end of the world. The text is 'a blend of Christian catechetical materials and prayers with a rich mixture of native tradition and belief, and appears as a classic example of acculturation, whereby the Christian message has taken Japanese roots, and flowered as an exotic bloom'.[21]

A few foreign missionaries did attempt to enter Japan after 1640, but they were unsuccessful. When the Italian priest Giovanni Battista Sidotti was dropped by a ship on an island off Kyushu in 1708, he was almost immediately captured and transferred to Edo, where he was imprisoned in the *Kirishitan yashiki* and interrogated by the famous Confucian scholar Arai Hakuseki. In his report of 8 January 1710, Arai noted: 'When the people of those [Christian]

Figure 9 'Mary as patroness of the Japanese martyrs'. This silk painting by the early twentieth-century Japanese artist, Lukas Hasegawa, reflects the emphasis on the Virgin in the underground church in Japan. Her features and dress have here been adapted to Japan, while the martyred Japanese Christians are visible on the background landscape. (Photograph in the Butler Collection, Centre for the Study of Christianity in the Non-Western World, University of Edinburgh.)

countries spread their doctrine to other lands, that is not a plot of aggression; this fact is clear. However, once that doctrine begins to flourish, rebellious subjects *ipso facto* arise in the land; that also is the inevitable natural consequence.'[22] Yet the unexpected arrival of this last missionary during the period of seclusion rekindled Japanese interest in western civilization. While the Christian religion and civilization were still condemned as evil and subversive, Arai Hakuseki became aware of the practical value of western sciences. Indeed, he became an ardent advocate of western learning, although he rejected Christianity. His report on Sidotti helped bring about a change of policy by the *bakufu* concerning the importation of Chinese books on western sciences written by the Jesuit missionaries.

Although the intensity of the anti-Christian persecution gradually abated after 1700, Japanese Christians were nevertheless discovered from time to time. Thus as late as the 1790s a *kuzure* occurred at Urakami in Nagasaki and another in the Amakusa area (in Higo Domain, now a part of Kumamoto Prefecture) in 1805, when over 5,000 underground *Kirishitan* were apprehended. It is indeed remarkable that in spite of complete isolation and persecution, the faith was kept and transmitted from generation to generation in the remote villages and fishing hamlets of Kyushu. It was here that the *Kakure Kirishitan* (Hidden Christians) re-emerged at the end of the Tokugawa shogunate.

Korea: The formation of a self-evangelized church

The early history of Catholicism in Korea is a unique example of church planting without missionary intervention. Although a few foreign missionaries had attempted to enter Korea in the late sixteenth and seventeenth centuries, including the Spanish priest Gregorio de Cespedes, who had accompanied the Japanese army as chaplain in 1593–95, these encounters do not seem to have had any consequence.

Of greater significance was the introduction of Catholic ideas through Korean Confucian scholars in the late seventeenth and eighteenth centuries. It was customary for the King of Korea to send annual tribute missions to Beijing to present compliments and gifts to the Emperor of China. Some members of these tribute missions came into contact with the Jesuit missionaries who had produced Chinese works explaining both western science and the Catholic religion. Over the years members of the tribute mission returned to Korea with many of these works, including Matteo Ricci's *Tianzhu shiyi* ('The True Lord of Heaven') and Diego de Pantoja's *Qike* ('The Seven Victories'). By the early eighteenth century, members of the *Sirhak-p'a* (School of Practical Learning), which had developed among Korean neo-Confucian literati, were studying these works. The prominent scholar Yi Ik (1682–1763), in particular, recognized in the Jesuit publications a system of wisdom and ethics that was compatible with Confucianism. But he was sceptical of the overtly religious elements in the missionary writings, and some of his disciples subsequently called for action against the foreign religion.

In spite of a generally negative reception of Catholicism, a few followers of the philosophy of Yi Ik, from the *Namin* (southerner) elite, were nevertheless moved to take the faith more seriously. Well versed in Confucian thought and deeply committed to Confucianism, they sought in Catholicism a way to correct the growing political and social corruption of the stagnating Chosun Dynasty. The group consisted of Kwŏn Ch'ŏl-sin, the three brothers Chŏng Yag-yong, Chŏng Yak-chŏn, Chŏng Yak-chong, as well as Kwŏn Il-sin and Yi Pyŏk (Lee Pyuk). Deeply impressed with what he had read, Yi Pyŏk subsequently asked his brother-in-law Yi Sŭng-hun, a member of the Korean tribute mission sent to the Chinese imperial court in 1783, to obtain more information on Christianity. While visiting the foreign priests in Beijing, Yi Sŭng-hun received instruction in Catholicism and was baptized. Returning to Korea with books and religious objects in the spring of 1784, he and other ardent 'evangelists' began to preach the gospel to their friends and relatives, many of whom they converted. In the same year Yi Pyŏk wrote the Korean Christian book, *Sung-gyo Yo-ji* ('Essentials of the Holy Teaching').

These early converts established the first Korean Catholic Church in 1784, based upon what they knew of the church in China. Organized around a system of 'lay priests', it respected the traditional patriarchal family system and ancestor worship, helping to shape the early Korean Christian church as a family-based movement. Donald Baker has recently argued that the first converts 'used their common philosophical concerns and their political and marriage ties with fellow *Namin* to propagate their religion'. Most converts 'were persuaded of the superiority of Catholic doctrine and ethical practices by some relative or friend whom they trusted'.[23] For early Korean Catholics, Confucian values and thought patterns played a vital role in interpreting some Christian doctrines. For example, such Christian doctrines as the resurrection of believers and eternal life resonated with Confucian beliefs and practices regarding the ancestors. Indeed, for the early Korean Catholics, the Christian memorial service for one's deceased parents was similar to ritual practices relating to ancestor worship.

While the circle of friends and relatives around Yi Pyŏk was able to reconcile Confucian and Catholic beliefs and practices, the vast majority of the Korean literati remained firmly opposed to Catholicism. The situation deteriorated further when instructions coming from Bishop Alexandre de Gouvea (1751–1808) in Beijing forbade both the appointment of 'lay priests' in the Korean churches and Catholic participation in ancestral rituals. This had tragic consequences. When Paulus Yun Chi-ch'ung burnt his mother's ancestral tablets, in accordance with de Gouvea's instructions, he was executed on 8 December 1791 for his offence against Confucian tradition. Some prominent converts now withdrew from the church; however, the overall number of adherents continued to grow, aided by the general policy of toleration maintained by the Korean King Chŏngjo. By the end of the eighteenth century, the number of Korean converts had increased to over 10,000.

King Chŏngjo's policy of toleration, however, came to an end with his sudden death in 1800. The *Shinyu* Persecution of 1801 began as soon as the formal mourning period for the king was over. In the course of the persecution, perhaps as many as 300 Catholics died as a result of either formal execution or from wounds suffered under torture. The Chinese priest, Jacobus Zhou Wenmo, who had secretly entered Korea in 1794 and assumed leadership of the Korean Christians, was executed in 1801. Yi Sŭng-hun was beheaded, even though he had publicly renounced his faith years earlier. Among other prominent Christians who perished was Hwang Sa-yŏng. At the start of the persecution, Hwang had gone into hiding in the countryside where he wrote a letter to Bishop de Gouvea in Beijing. In this famous 'silk letter', he described the persecution in detail and asked for western military assistance to rescue the beleaguered Catholics and compel the Korean government to grant religious freedom. The interception of Hwang's letter led to a change in official Korean government policy towards Catholics. Until now, the Korean authorities had sought to suppress the Catholics primarily as an intellectual and moral threat. After 1801, however, they began to view Catholicism as a more serious threat to Korea's political independence. Yet the self-evangelizing Korean church not only survived but continued to grow in the face of the ferocious anti-Christian campaigns during the early decades of the nineteenth century.

Notes

1. Arthur Leonard Tuggy, *The Philippine Church: Growth in a changing society* (Grand Rapids, MI: Eerdmans, 1971), p. 48.
2. *Ibid.*, pp. 50–1.

3. Charles J.-H. Macdonald, 'Folk Catholicism and pre-Spanish religions in the Philippines', *Philippine studies*, 52 (2004), pp. 83, 88, 89.
4. Reginald D. Cruz, '"Devotion and defiance": Religious communities for women established in colonial Philippines prior to 1750', in Anne C. Kwantes (ed.), *Chapters in Philippine church history* (Manila: OMF Literature, 2001), p. 36, note 3.
5. Nick Joaquin, 'The Beatas of 17th-century Manila', in Joaquin, *Culture and history: Occasional notes on the process of Philippine becoming* (Manila: Solar, 1988), p. 121.
6. Luciano P. R. Santiago, 'The development of the religious congregations for women in the Philippines during the Spanish period (1565–1898)', *Journal of Sophia Asia studies*, 12 (1994), p. 53.
7. See D. Gerona, 'In defence of the natives: The church in the midst of colonial abuses (1600–1790)', Ateneo de Naga University, 16 August 2003, http://www.adnu.edu.ph/MainWeb/research/art02.html.
8. On the visitation controversy, see Horacio de la Costa, 'Episcopal jurisdiction in the Philippines during the Spanish regime', in Gerald H. Anderson (ed.), *Studies in Philippine church history* (Ithaca: Cornell University Press, 1969), pp. 44–64.
9. Pablo Fernandez, *History of the church in the Philippines (1521–1898)* (Manila: National Book Store, 1979), pp. 112–13.
10. John N. Schumacher, 'Syncretism in Philippine Catholicism: Its historical causes', *Philippine studies*, 32 (1984), p. 257.
11. Salvador P. Escoto, 'The ecclesiastical controversy of 1767–1776: A catalyst of Philippine nationalism', *Journal of Asian history*, 10 (1976), p. 105.
12. See the relevant maps in Joseph de Moidrey, *La hiérarchie catholique en Chine, en Corée et au Japon (1307–1914)* (Shanghai: T'ou-sè-wè, 1914).
13. Claudia von Collani, *P. Joachim Bouvet S. J. Sein Leben und sein Werk* (Nettetal: Steyler Verlag, 1985), pp, 11–17.
14. Catherine Jami, 'For whose greater glory? Jesuit strategies and science during the Kangxi Reign (1662–1722)', in Wu Xiaoxin (ed.), *Encounters and dialogues: Changing perspectives on Chinese–Western exchanges from the sixteenth to eighteenth centuries* (Nettetal: Steyler Verlag, 2005).
15. Ad Dudink, in Nicolas Standaert (ed.), *Handbook of Christianity in China*, vol. 1: *635–1800* (Leiden: Brill, 2001), p. 515.
16. Jonathan D. Spence, 'Claims and counter-claims: The Kangxi emperor and the Europeans (1661–1722)', in D. E. Mungello (ed.), *The Chinese Rites Controversy: Its history and meaning* (Nettetal: Steyler Verlag, 1994), p. 15.
17. D. E. Mungello, 'An introduction to the Chinese Rites Controversy', in Mungello (ed.), *Rites Controversy*, pp. 4–5.
18. Nicolas Standaert, 'Rites Controversy', in Standaert (ed.), *Handbook of Christianity in China*, p. 685.
19. Kenneth Scott Latourette, *A history of Christian missions in China* (London: SPCK, 1929), p. 156.
20. Christal Whelan, 'Introduction', in Whelan (trans.), *The beginning of heaven and earth: The sacred book of Japan's hidden Christians* (Honolulu: University of Hawaii Press, 1996), pp. 9–10.

21. Stephen Turnbull, 'Acculturation among the *Kakure Kirishitan*: Some conclusions from the *Tenchi Hajimari no Koto*', in John Breen and Mark Williams (eds.), *Japan and Christianity: Impact and responses* (Basingstoke: Macmillan, 1996), pp. 63–74.

22. Cited in George Elison, *Deus destroyed: The image of Christianity in early modern Japan* (Cambridge, MA: Council on East Asian Studies, Harvard University, 1988), pp. 237–8.

23. Don Baker, 'A Confucian confronts Catholicism: Truth collides with morality in eighteenth century Korea', *Korean studies forum*, 6 (1979–80), p. 6.

24

Christian encounters with other
world religions

ANDREW C. ROSS

The massive Christian missionary effort that had begun with the opening of the Spanish and Portuguese overseas empires was, by 1660, in full flood. This effort was undertaken by the religious orders, particularly the Dominicans and Franciscans in the early days. Because of this intimate association of missionary activity with Iberian imperial expansion and because of the 'Reconquista' tradition of these two empires, the Christian encounter with other religions was perceived in terms of conquest. This was soon seen by some of the missionaries involved as a problem, and a minority struggled, with only limited success, to disentangle Christianity from its role as the spiritual wing of Christendom's expansion. A dynamic new element broke into this situation with the creation of the Society of Jesus in 1542. The Jesuits became, with astonishing rapidity, the leading missionary society, with half of their 1,000 members working outside Europe by 1600.

The Jesuit effort to disengage religious outreach from Spanish or Portuguese expansion was reinforced in 1622 by the papal institution of the Sacred Congregation for the Propagation of the Faith (colloquially 'the Propaganda'). The purpose of the new congregation was to oversee the missionary activities of the Roman Catholic Church free from the restrictions of the *Padroado Real* and *Patronato Real*, the concordats with the Holy See which gave so much control over the church outside Europe to the Portuguese and Spanish crowns, respectively. This conflict between royal and papal authority over the worldwide mission of the church was an inhibiting and ever-present factor in this period of Catholic outreach. Despite these problems, there was a massive expansion of Catholic Christianity outside Europe between 1500 and 1740.

This expansion involved conflict with other religions, but it also opened areas of fruitful interaction between Christianity and two other religious traditions, Hinduism and Confucianism. The fruitful relationship with Confucianism has led some historians to suggest that the high point of this missionary effort was reached in March 1692 when the greatest of all the Qin emperors of

China, Kangxi, issued his edict on Christianity at Beijing. In effect this edict granted Christianity, as practised in the pro-Confucian tradition of the Jesuit pioneer, Matteo Ricci, the same imperial recognition as had been granted to Buddhism centuries before. In this same period in south India a parallel fruitful interaction between Christianity and Hinduism was taking place under Jesuit leadership.

We will return to these areas and their significance later. In 1660, encounters with Confucianism, Hinduism, and Buddhism were comparatively new experiences for western Christians. This was not so, however, in the case of Islam. Islam is the religious tradition, other than Judaism, with which Christianity has had the longest interaction and it thus deserves to be considered first.

Christianity and Islam

In 1660, western Europe, free from a Muslim political presence since the fall of Granada, saw Islam primarily in terms of the threat to its security posed by the powerful Ottoman Empire. The reality of this threat was confirmed when, in 1683, Ottoman armies reached the gates of Vienna. Soon after this dramatic event, however, Ottoman power entered a period of decline and both Catholic Austria and Orthodox Russia began to make significant military advances against the Turks. It was these conflicts which characterized Christian–Muslim relations in the eighteenth century, with the result that the relations should be perceived as those between two hostile powers rather than those between one religion and another. In the popular mind of the Catholic and Protestant communities of Europe, the Muslim was seen in the guise of the Barbary corsair or the Ottoman janissary.

Some genuine, if limited, religious encounter between Latin Christianity and Islam had taken place, however, in the sixteenth and early seventeenth centuries. The Society of Jesus, as part of its worldwide missionary effort, had placed missions at the court of the Shah in Persia and at the court of the great Moghul in Delhi. As a result of such encounters, a number of western Christians became experts in Arabic and Persian and attempted to engage in a dialogue of sorts with Muslim intellectuals and to produce books aimed at a Muslim readership. By 1660, however, that kind of dialogical encounter was over. The last piece of serious writing in Arabic or Persian which attempted to explain the Christian faith to the Muslim was written by Fr Aimé Chésaud in 1656. This missionary effort did, nevertheless, leave one important legacy – that is, there was now agreement that the days of crusade and forced conversion were over.

The outcome of this fruitless missionary encounter with Islam exposed two major flaws in the new Christian approaches to the Muslim. (Christians, it should be noted, initiated the approaches throughout this period of profound indifference on the part of Islamic thinkers towards Christianity.) The first was the failure to recognize Islam as a religion in its own right. Islam as a Christian heresy or as a confused misunderstanding of Judaism and Christianity was the perception that persisted throughout this period among Catholic writers and missionaries, even those expert in Arabic and Persian. This understanding of Islam also dominated Protestant thinking, as we shall see. What was good in Islam, according to this understanding, consisted of Christian residues, what was bad was always the work of 'the impostor Muhammad' as the Prophet was usually designated.

The second flaw was that the dialogue, when initiated, was always one of intellectual controversy. Muslims were to be encouraged to state their objections to Christianity and then these were answered, the falsity of Islam proved and the sinfulness of Muhammad shown from Muslim writings. This was an approach that had been shaped by Catholic–Protestant encounters in Europe in the sixteenth century, an inappropriate model that also ignored the earlier vigorous rejection by St Thomas Aquinas of the controversialist approach to Islam.[1]

When, by the 1650s, it appeared that the missionary efforts in Isfahan and Delhi were failures, the Catholic Church entered a period of theological indifference towards Islam as a religion. This Catholic indifference coincided with a period of intellectual stagnation within Islam itself, which Muslim scholars refer to as *gumud*.[2] Thus, during the eighteenth century there was no significant interchange between the two religious traditions – with this lack of real interaction taking place despite a significant number of Latin Catholic priests living in Muslim lands throughout the century. Their tasks were limited to caring for the Christian slaves within those lands, running medical dispensaries and, if asked, dispelling in quiet conversation only the wrong notions of the faith that the Muslim enquirer might have. This situation did not begin to change until the revival of Catholic missionary concern and activity in the second quarter of the nineteenth century.

Within the frontiers of the Ottoman Empire there were many non-western Christian churches: Greek Orthodox, Armenian, Assyrian, Coptic, and Monophysite. Their presence, however, produced no fruitful encounter between Christianity and Islam in this period. Under the rule of the Ottoman Empire, whose internal policy was to keep everything as it was, each Christian community or *melet*, under its patriarch or archbishop who acted as its secular as well as its religious head, concentrated on its own affairs. The leader of each *melet* was, understandably, primarily concerned with the survival of his community and with achieving the best relations possible with the Ottoman authorities. Those authorities were extraordinarily tolerant of the ancient Christian communities so long as nobody attempted to change the status quo. This toleration was remarked upon by western Christian writers, both Catholic and Protestant, who visited the Ottoman Empire. It was also commented on favourably by various sceptical and deist writers, like Voltaire, who sought to draw attention to the intolerance of Christianity. In the case of these latter writers, their complimentary remarks about Islam have sometimes been seen as part of a positive response to Islam, which, in the case of Voltaire and most others, it was not.[3]

As Protestant missionary concerns grew from small beginnings early in the eighteenth century to a significant movement in its last decades and the first decades of the nineteenth century, they did not produce any significant or creative encounters with Islam. Protestant Christianity had had little direct contact with Islam. What encounters there were involved travellers or diplomats rather than anyone with theological training. The one important Protestant theological writer of the period who dealt with Islam was the Dutch theologian and man of letters, Hugo Grotius, in his *De veritate religionis Christianae*, the first Latin edition of which appeared in 1627. This book was, however, of great importance because of the prestige of the author and its wide distribution. The book was translated into English and French and reprinted a number of times in the eighteenth century in both languages. Grotius, who had no knowledge of Arabic nor had had any direct contact with Islam, created for the Protestant public a profoundly distorted image of that faith. He asserted that the Muslim 'laity' were not allowed to read their holy books and that Islam was a religion of violence which only expanded by war. Further, like the Catholic writers of the time, he denigrated the private and public life of the Prophet.

The other widely influential book written by a Protestant and dealing with Islam, was James Porter's *Observations on the religion, law, government and manners of the Turks* of 1768. Porter had been the British Ambassador at Constantinople and was a distinguished linguist whose work on Islamic civil law was both accurate and groundbreaking in terms of western understanding of that aspect of Islam. Yet Porter's writing did not contribute anything meaningful to a religious encounter between Christianity and Islam. He dismissed the Quran as religiously unhelpful, a meaningless jumble of Jewish and Christian ideas, and he treated the Prophet as a licentious charlatan. In the writings of Porter and the few other Protestant writers of the time who had actually encountered Islam – none of whom were missionaries or clergymen – there were approving references to some of the practices of Islam. When these favourable references to Islam are looked at carefully, however, one sees that they were simply conceptual devices for criticizing aspects of Roman Catholic piety and practice which Protestants considered superstitious or idolatrous.[4]

Christianity and Hinduism

The first encounter of western Christianity with what has come to be called Hinduism came with the creation of a number of Portuguese bases on the coast of India in the first decade of the sixteenth century. Christianity and Hinduism had already met in the early centuries of Christian history as the presence of the Christians of St Thomas, or Syrian Christians, in southern India attested; however, that encounter had had little or no impact on western Christianity. The Syrian Christian community had, by the time of the arrival of the Portuguese, come to be an acceptable part of Indian society and made no attempt to reach out to people beyond the bounds of their own community. They were to all intents and purposes a caste, following caste rules like endogenous marriage, ritual cleansing when in touch with members of lower castes and so on. Indeed in Kerala where the majority of the community lived, this Christian community was treated as one of the highest castes, only Brahmans being superior.[5]

The initial reaction of the clergy who came with the Portuguese conquerors was to see Indians either as 'Musulmans' (their ancient enemies) or as 'pagans'. There was no attempt to study or understand what form this 'paganism' took. Inside the various small Portuguese enclaves, many non-Muslim Indians became Christians in a way that meant they also became Portuguese. The noted Catholic historian, Henri Bernard-Maître, referred to this process as 'Portugalization'.[6]

It was the missionaries of the Society of Jesus who initiated a genuine encounter between western Christianity and the complex system of philosophies, and religious, economic, and social practices that the west came to call Hinduism. This was slow to develop. For example, Francis Xavier, founder of the Jesuit mission in the east, did not encounter Hinduism directly during his stay in India. Goa was simply Portugal in the east, and later, while working among the Paravas in the south, Xavier still did not encounter Hinduism directly, because there he was attempting to raise the quality of Christian life in what was already a Christianized community.

When Jesuit fathers and other missionaries did encounter Hinduism, they were deeply confused, because they had no previous intellectual experience to draw on that helped them to comprehend it. They attempted, on the whole unsuccessfully, to use their knowledge of Greek and Roman religion as a way into understanding Hinduism. The integral role played by caste in the religious, social and economic system, for example, was one which took some time for them to begin to recognize let alone understand. Hinduism, a word that only came into general use in the 1830s, was and is a social system, an economic system, a complex, many-faceted religious system, including in its embrace a range of practices and theologies stretching from monotheism to belief in a pantheon of almost innumerable deities, as well as a number of markedly different philosophic schools.

In the eighteenth century, 'Hinduism' varied markedly in details of thought and practice from one part of the Indian sub-continent to another. It was the aristocratic Italian Jesuit, Roberto de Nobili, who initiated a fruitful encounter with the Hinduism of Tamil-speaking southern India.[7] At the time of his arrival in India in 1606, Nobili saw that an Indian Christian was seen as a *parangi*, that is, as a Portuguese or a European, and that outside the areas of Portuguese control, becoming a Christian was to cut oneself off from all that constituted normal life. Converts ceased in a deeply serious sense to be Indian. The exceptions to this were the members of the two outcaste communities of the *Paravas* and the *Makuas*, who had become Christian by way of group conversion. By this means the individual *Parava* or *Makua* was not an isolated individual but continued to live an acceptable life in the bosom of his or her family and community, although to other Indians the two groups had become *parangi*.

Nobili went to live in Madurai, the great southern centre of Hindu pilgrimage and of Tamil Hindu literary and philosophic activity. There he cut himself off not only from the Portuguese but also from *Makua* and *Parava* Christians and began to live the life of a *sannyassi*, that is a high-caste penitent who has given up the world. He emphasized that he was not Portuguese and that he was of noble birth, 'a Roman *rajah*'. As such a *sannyassi* he became accepted gradually as someone with whom Brahmans and other high-caste Indians could have social intercourse. He became fluent in Tamil and he also learned Sanskrit, the classic language of the fundamental texts of Hinduism. The Brahman who taught him Sanskrit became his friend and through long conversations with him Nobili came to realize that there were books, vital to an understanding of Hinduism, of which he knew nothing. He persuaded his friend to give him access to these sacred texts. This was a dangerous thing for the Brahman to do. These books were not only forbidden to outsiders but also to all men not of the twice-born castes and to all women. Punishment for revealing them could be severe. We do not now know what specific texts were made available to Nobili, but he was the first European to have access to some of the Sanskrit texts at the heart of Hinduism. He was then fully equipped to enter into genuine discussions, both philosophic and religious, with Brahmans and others of high caste. He did slowly gain some converts from the higher castes. With the agreement of the Bishop of Cranganore, he allowed them to continue to wear the signs of their caste, to conform to its customs and to continue to take part in many, though not all, of their family and caste festivals. These Christians were deemed by other Indians not to have lost caste and thus remained part of Indian society.

Nobili then turned to the rest of southern Hindu society. He reached out to them, the majority of caste Indians, through the means of a new religious order of *pandaraswami*. These were Jesuits who accepted the life of a penitent seeking holiness, while conforming to the rules of a class of holy man who could relate to the rest of Hindu society, including, under certain severe restrictions, relating to outcastes. Again the converts they made were allowed to retain enough of the customs of their caste so as not to be seen as *parangi*.

The Portuguese authorities were unhappy about the specific rejection of Portugal by this movement, while missionaries from other orders saw the whole movement as one which betrayed the faith. Despite the fierce condemnation that the Jesuit policy produced, the matter was settled in favour of the Jesuits when Pope Gregory XV ruled in his Apostolic Constitution, the *Romanae sedis antistes* of 1623, that Nobili's procedures were acceptable. With this support, a genuine, if geographically limited, encounter of Christianity and Hinduism continued. By the time that Fr John Britto, the outstanding Jesuit *pandaraswami* of the period, was martyred in 1693, the Hinduized Christian or Christianized Hindu community in the south Indian kingdoms of Mathurai, Thanjavur, Gingi, and Vellore amounted to between 1 and 2 per cent of the total population of the area.[8] All, however, was about to change.

In the original defence of his position, Nobili had referred, not only to the support he believed he had in the theology of the Church Fathers, but also to the work going on in his own time in China, inspired by his fellow Jesuit, Matteo Ricci. By 1700, Ricci's policy of the enculturation of Christianity within the world of Confucianism had been under bitter attack in Rome for some time.[9] Into that situation there arrived in Rome a formal letter of complaint from the French Capuchins of Pondicherry, the French post on the Coramandel coast of India, which raised thirty-six points against the practices of the churches following the Nobili tradition. It had already been decided in Rome to send a Legate with exceptional powers to China, Thomas de Tournon, to settle the dispute over the Jesuit policy towards Confucianism. His instructions were, in fact, to settle the dispute by condemning the practices usually referred to as the 'Mandarin Rites' and bring their practice to an end. With the arrival in Rome of the complaints from the Capuchins, de Tournon was instructed to go to Pondicherry and there settle this Indian dispute also.

De Tournon stayed in Pondicherry for eight months, before leaving for China in July 1704. He interviewed a large number of witnesses but how far he understood the issues has to be queried, as he knew no Indian language and was ill most of the time. He issued his judgement on 23 June 1704. It condemned the structure of accommodation begun by Roberto de Nobili, a structure which at that very moment appeared to receive sanctification in the eyes of many within the Catholic Church by the initiation of the process of beatification of the martyred Jesuit *pandaraswami*, John Britto. Despite an intellectually rigorous defence of the Nobili position by Francisco Laynes, Procurator of the Madurai mission, which briefly gave some hope of reprieve, none came. The Holy Office endorsed de Tournon's decisions. The Malabar Rites, as the system was named, not entirely appropriately, were again formally condemned and any disobedience threatened with severe punishment in papal briefs *Compertum* of August 1734 and *Concredita nobis* of May 1739. The papacy, in effect, relegated Hinduism officially to the position it would hold in the eyes of most European observers, Catholic or Protestant, throughout the eighteenth century – that is, it was portrayed as a mixture of idolatry and depraved superstition.

It was just as this crisis was developing that the first Protestant missionaries to India arrived at the Danish factory at Tranquebar on the Coramandel coast of south India. Heinrich Plutschau and Bartholomaus Ziegenbalg had been sent there by the pious King of Denmark, Frederick IV. Ziegenbalg plunged into the study of Tamil but showed no knowledge of the existence of the many Catholic books in the language until, during an effort to collect Tamil palm-leaf books, he discovered that a number of them were Christian books. His study progressed rapidly and this devout orthodox Lutheran became an authority on south Indian Hinduism. In 1713 he produced a well-researched book, *The Genealogy of the Malabarian Gods*. He sent it to Halle, the mission-training centre in Germany where he had studied, intending it to be published in Europe as an aid to Christians in their understanding of Hinduism. However, the response of the director at Halle, A. H. Franke, was to put it on a shelf in the library, where it lay until discovered in the 1860s. Franke remarked that missionaries were sent to extirpate heathenism and not to spread what he called 'heathenish nonsense' in Europe.[10]

Despite the attitude of Franke in Halle, the Lutheran Church in south India remained remarkably sympathetic to Hindu culture and grew, albeit slowly. Through the influence of the Danish and British royal families, the mission gained significant financial help from the Society for Promoting Christian Knowledge. The new Lutheran community as it developed made significant concessions to the Christian converts on the issue of caste. Arrangements were made at services and meetings so that the *Sudra* Christians, who were in the majority, could preserve their caste status despite a large minority of outcastes among the church members. There was also a widespread absorption of Tamil culture into the church's life, one example being the singing of hymns which were based upon different forms of Tamil poetry and music. Indeed in 1809, the Indian poet Vedenayaka Sastri was widely feted for a substantial body of poetry on Christian themes in the classical Tamil form called *kuravanci* – poetry to be recited in public with musical accompaniment. Historians of Tamil literature have recognized it as a notable contribution to the *kuravanci* form. Equally significant, a large section of the Christians were from the *Saiva* Hindu tradition dominant in the area. Each *Saiva* sect has its own special master narrative poem for public recitation and singing, a *purana*, and Sastri's work fulfilled that role in the new Indian Christian community.[11] Whatever this new community was, it had clear characteristics which could be called Hindu, and its members were certainly not *parangi*. Again, as with the Jesuit mission, we have here a form of Christian and Hindu encounter that was fruitful and creative rather than simply negative and hostile.

This Lutheran development in south India is in marked contrast with the main Protestant Christian encounter with Hinduism. This was to take place primarily in the nineteenth century but the foundations and style of that encounter were set by 1815. However, before the encounter between organized Protestantism and Hinduism took place on a large scale, there developed a body of writing about Hinduism by scholars writing in English. All were formally Protestant Christians and most were servants of the British East India Company. There was one notable exception, the outstanding academic and leader in the Church of Scotland, Principal William Robertson of the University of Edinburgh. These writers presented an attractive face of Hinduism to a western and Christian audience. Nathaniel Halhed's *A code of Gentoo laws* of 1776 was the first of these English-language books based on genuine Hindu texts. Then ten years later came Charles Wilkin's English translation of the *Bhagavadgita*, the first classical Sanskrit text to be published in a European language. This development of interest in Indian culture led a group of scholarly East India Company civil servants to set up a society for the study of Indian culture in 1784, the Asiatic Society of Bengal. In the first two volumes, those for 1789 and 1790, of that society's journal, *Asiatik Researches*, Sir James Jones published three seminal articles sympathetic to Hinduism, which reached a wide audience not only in Britain but also in western Europe. Principal Robertson's *An historical disquisition of the knowledge the ancients had of India* (1791), which had gone through four editions by 1804, completed the leading echelon of sympathetic writings on India. Robertson, like Jones and the others, admired much in Indian society and culture, particularly its long continuity with the past that neither Muslim nor European conqueror had been able to break. Robertson, who never visited India, defended caste in terms that made it sound like a kind of welfare state, or at least an arrangement that led to social stability and relative prosperity for all. In his discussion of caste he insisted that,

> The arrangements of civil government are made, not for what is extraordinary, but for what is common; not for the few, but for the many. The object of the first Indian legislators was to employ the most effectual means of providing for the subsistence, the security, and happiness of all the members of the community over which they presided.[12]

Jones, Robertson and the others who presented a sympathetic picture of Hindu society to the west were, however, all agreed on their aversion to much of Hindu 'religion' or 'popular Hinduism' as some termed it. Most of them insisted that some of the practices were so awful that they could not be recounted. In making this distinction they were doing what some twenty-first century scholars do: write as if it were possible to divide neatly and clearly Hindu 'religion' from Hindu social relations and Hindu philosophy. Most modern scholars of Hinduism, whether Indian or European, do not consider such a tidy separation possible to sustain.[13]

Just as fifty years earlier, Deists and anti-Christian intellectuals had used the Jesuit enthusiasm for Confucianism to challenge the authority of the Bible and the uniqueness of Christianity, so, in the last quarter of the eighteenth century, similar intellectuals used the writings of these admirers of Hindu philosophy and society to the same end. These writings, needless to say, did not encourage the new wave of evangelical Protestant activists, whether they were formally missionaries or not, to adopt a sympathetic attitude towards Hinduism.

It was William Ward of the Baptist mission at Serampore in Bengal (founded in 1793) who set the tone of the new Protestant Christian approach to Hinduism. It should be noted that, like all the other members of that mission,

Ward encouraged converts to retain their Indian dress, diet, and even their Hindu names. On the issue of caste, however, the Serampore missionaries were adamant that all those who sought baptism had to renounce caste utterly. Thus, they rejected the south Indian Lutheran compromise. This Serampore approach to caste became the standard approach to caste for the later Protestant missions in India, in contrast with the same movement's rejection, on the whole, of the Serampore enthusiasm for Indian dress, diet and the retention of Indian names by converts.

The most important impact of the Serampore mission on the encounter of Protestant Christianity with Hinduism was made by Ward's two books, *An Account of the writings, religion, and manners of the Hindoos* published in 1811 and *Farewell letters to a few friends in Britain and America on returning to Bengal*, published in 1823. These books were to be reprinted many times and set the overall tone for the Protestant encounter with Hinduism. Ward's descriptions of Hindu practices and beliefs in the Bengal of his day were not inaccurate, but he had no knowledge of Hinduism elsewhere in India, where Hinduism varied considerably from what he described in Bengal. Further, he had little or no knowledge of Hindu philosophy. What was of fundamental importance was that Ward found nothing at all of any value in any aspect of Hinduism. This was in stark contrast with his Christian predecessors, Catholic and Lutheran, who had been able to find at least a 'trail of grains of gold in the sand of the riverbed' as one put it. Responding to those who perceived some good in Hinduism, Ward asked,

> how should a people be moral, whose gods are monsters of vice; whose priests are their ringleaders in crimes, whose scriptures encourage pride, impurity, falsehood, revenge, and murder; whose worship is connected with indescribable abominations, and whose heaven is a brothel?[14]

It is important, however, to note that a powerful reaction against the largely favourable attitude of Jones and Robertson towards Indians, India and Hinduism appeared also at this time among what might be termed secular writers. The two most important of these writers, Charles Grant and James Mill, wrote specifically to refute the positive perceptions of Hindus and Hinduism displayed in the writing of Jones and Robertson. It has often been pointed out that Grant was a fervent evangelical Christian, but what is important about his writing on India is that it is part of reaction against Hinduism that stems as much from Enlightenment ideas about 'progress' as from evangelical Protestantism. Mill's and Grant's attitudes towards Hinduism were representative of a new approach towards cultures and religions outside Europe, which assessed these phenomena on a scale of how far they contributed to or hindered the 'progress' of the people. Grant's attitude was that if Hinduism were eliminated, the people would have restored to them the use of their reason and would rise in what he called 'the scale of human beings'. James Mill, a tireless advocate of the utilitarian gospel, was as concerned about freeing the British people from the corruption that tarnished British society as he was in freeing the Indian people from what he perceived as their ignorance perpetuated by the authority and power of the Brahmans. The evangelical Protestantism of the period, which supported missions and the abolition of slavery, owed a deep intellectual debt to the Enlightenment even as it attempted to repudiate some aspects of that development in European thought. The impact of the Enlightenment was such that most Protestants, evangelical or not, came to share the perspective on history and culture summed up by Hegel when he argued that the Europe of his day represented the end of history. In such a view, history had its beginning and childhood in Asia, but it reached its maturity in the west, whose culture was destined to be the culture of the world.[15] By 1815, the approach of Protestant Christianity towards Hinduism, shaped as much by Enlightenment thought as by evangelical individualism, was set on a collision course leading to mutual antipathy and distrust.[16]

Christianity and Buddhism

In a textbook on Buddhism widely used at the end of the twentieth century, the author asserts that 'Buddhism was "discovered" in the west during the first half of the nineteenth century.'[17] The author goes on to say that of course there had been encounters in the past between westerners and what came to be called Buddhism in the west. However, these 'disparate accounts of the encounter of the West with indistinct aspects of the Orient' were only recognized retrospectively as relating to Buddhism, after 'Buddhism' had been 'constructed'. This may very well be true of the intellectual world of the west in general, but a real encounter between Christianity and Buddhism happened during the sixteenth, seventeenth, and eighteenth centuries in Japan, China and Indo-China primarily, though latterly also in Thailand, Ceylon, and Burma. The longest period of Christian–Buddhist contact was that between the Catholic missions and Buddhism in Japan, China, and Indo-China. This began with Francis Xavier's arrival in Japan and the creation of the Catholic mission there. The Jesuits gradually developed a picture of a religious tradition coming from India that had taken root in China, Japan, and Indo-China. They did not map out the full extent of its diffusion in Asia nor did they have any detailed knowledge of its history. They were aware, however, that it was a major religious tradition of importance over a vast area of Asia and that it originated in India.

Although from the mid-seventeenth century Jesuit correspondence from the east was widely read in western Europe, by Protestants as well as Catholics, these reports did little to bring any understanding of Buddhism to the west. This is partially explained in China by the concentration of the Jesuits upon Confucianism and in Japan on the ferocious repression and its heroic martyr-doms.

However, despite the length of time it took for the western intellectual world to recognize Buddhism for what it was, Catholic missionaries certainly recognized it in Japan, China, Indo-China, and Siam not as 'indistinct aspects of the Orient', but as a powerful, coherent religious tradition. On his first encounter with this religious tradition in Japan, Xavier described accurately the many Buddhist sects in Japan and clearly understood that, despite their contradictory teachings and conflicting practices and theologies, they were sects of the same religion, whose common origins lay elsewhere.[18] Thirty years later, Alessandro Valignano (1539–1606), Visitor of the Society of Jesus in the east, organized the Society and its auxiliaries in Japan according to a system of ranks, rules of diet and patterns of courtesy based upon those of the Zen monastic order.[19] He was so deeply impressed by the prestige of Buddhist monks in Japan that he encouraged Fathers Ruggieri and Ricci to dress in a manner close to that of Buddhist monks as they began their work in China. This was so they might communicate that they were teachers of religion while attempting in their dress, diet, and manners to reject European and conform to Chinese norms. It was in China that missionaries became aware that what they came to call the 'religion of the idolaters' had its origins in India. This they recognized despite the fact that after more than a hundred years of western Christian activity in India Catholic missionaries had not encountered Buddhism there, except briefly in Ceylon.

Because there were so many outward similarities between Catholic Chris-tianity and Japanese Buddhism, there were in Xavier's time a number of sym-pathetic encounters between followers of the two faiths. This initial sympathy and apparent agreement, however, led to all the more bitter disillusion on both sides when the real differences became clear. When one also takes into account the hatred that the early patron of the Christian mission, the dictator Oda Nobunaga (1533–82), had for the Buddhist monastic communities, it is not surprising that the relationship between the two faiths in Japan developed into one of constant argument and conflict. In China, relations also rapidly became entirely negative. Once Ricci understood the nature of Chinese society and became first an admirer, then a scholar of the Confucian classics, he saw the Christian future in China as one of interaction with Confucianism. From 1595, Jesuits in China discarded Buddhist-type robes and dressed in the manner of the literati or scholar/administrators of the empire. The majority of this powerful group scorned Buddhism as idolatrous superstition and this had a powerful effect on the attitude to Buddhism adopted by Ricci and the Jesuit mission. Further, on this subject at least, all the other Catholic orders that arrived in China subsequently agreed with the Jesuits.

This antagonism between Christianity and Buddhism was repeated in Indo-China where again the Christian church was much more sympathetic to Confucianism, which, as in China, was the faith or philosophy of the intellectual and political elite. Despite the existence of some creative elements in the encounter with Buddhism in Japan, then, Christian relations with Buddhism were entirely negative throughout the eighteenth century. The coming into being of Protestant outreach did not change this situation before 1815.

The one positive note that the Catholic missionaries struck was their admiration for the devotion and piety of so many of the Buddhist laity. This links directly with what might be seen as incongruous by some – that is, the number of missionaries in Indo-China and Japan who reported that many of the most devoted new Christians had been devout Buddhists. The reason might lie in the fact that the various Chinese, Japanese and northern Indo-Chinese Buddhist sects were derived from the *Mahayana* tradition, and had become varieties of a religion of personal salvation, most unambiguously the very popular schools of *Chan* (in Japan, *Zen*) and *Jing-tu* (Pure Land). Thus the Christian encounter was with a form of Buddhism that was much closer to Christianity in its understanding of the human predicament than was *Theravada* Buddhism, the older and original Buddhist tradition which Catholic missionaries encountered only briefly in Ceylon and later in eighteenth-century Burma and Siam.

Christianity and Confucianism

As already noticed, the Jesuit mission in China – which began with the arrival of Fathers Michele Ruggieri and Francesco Pasio in 1582 and was soon to be dominated by Matteo Ricci (1552–1610) – began a fruitful encounter with Confucianism. Despite the presence in ninth- and tenth-century China of the Nestorian Mission and the presence in China of Franciscans and of Marco Polo in the medieval period, the Christian west appeared to have no knowledge of what is called in Chinese *ru-jia* or *ru-jiao*, 'the School of the Literati', until

Ruggieri and Ricci began to write about it with great enthusiasm. It was Ricci who gave Confucius to the west by translating what in China are called the Classics and by romanizing the name of the central teacher of the tradition, *Kongfuzi* (551–479 BCE), as Confucius.

What then was 'the School of the Literati'? It has been defined as an intellectual tradition drawing upon the ongoing interpretation of those Chinese writings that have been generally accepted as the 'Classics'. There has been much discussion over the centuries as to whether it was a religion or a philosophy, but it is best perhaps to point out it was defined centuries before words for 'religion' or 'philosophy' existed in Chinese. Ricci believed what he called 'original Confucianism' had a clear monotheistic core but agreed that what he called 'neo-Confucianism', the Confucianism as defined by the commentators of the Sung dynasty which had become official state Confucianism, was fundamentally atheistic. He was not alone then or now in believing this. What was important was that for Ricci, Confucian morality in both its ancient and contemporary forms was compatible with the moral concerns of the Christian faith. Indeed he insisted it was more readily compatible than the classical culture of the west of which Christianity had absorbed so much. This compatibility was such that he was able to use Confucian Classical texts to help explain and justify Christian thought in his book, *Tianzhu shiyi* ('The true meaning of the Lord of Heaven'). This important book played a role in the foundations of Christianity in Korea as well as in China.

As a result of Ricci's study of the Classics, which initially had been at the insistence of Alessandro Valignano, both men agreed that all European Jesuit recruits would learn Mandarin (i.e., Classical Chinese, the language of literature and government) by studying the Chinese Classics. They would thus not only learn a language but also enter the mental world of the literati, the intellectual meritocracy who effectively ran China for a thousand years up until 1900. They would thus be able to continue the development of the Confucian–Christian dialogue, which by 1660 had produced a Catholic Christianity in China that conformed to many Confucian norms.

This development in China was significantly different from the accommodation to Japanese culture which the Jesuits had also spearheaded. In Japan the missionaries had conformed to Japanese norms in terms of dress, diet, and forms of politeness and behaviour, as well as in the architecture of their buildings. The relationship of Christianity and Confucianism in China that was initiated and fundamentally shaped by Ricci reached a much more profound level. Christianity in its intellectual articulation and in its practices absorbed elements of Confucianism much as the early church had interacted with

Greek thought, an interaction that many late twentieth-century scholars would prefer to term enculturation rather than accommodation.

When they first arrived in China, the Franciscan and Dominican fathers had been shocked at this development and had protested to Rome. So in 1645 the pope issued an instruction that appeared to condemn the Riccian position. The Jesuits in China, however, sent a delegation to Rome to appeal against Rome's 1645 instructions. In response to this delegation, Pope Alexander VII issued a decree in 1656 permitting the Chinese experiment to continue. It is important to note that the majority of the missionaries of the other orders who served in China for a significant period of time had come by the 1680s to agree broadly with the Riccian position.

What was it that had so shocked the Franciscan and Dominican pioneers? What they found shocking is perhaps encapsulated in the way in which many Chinese, including the imperial household, regarded Matteo Ricci as both a Christian priest and a Confucian intellectual. He thus personified for the church in China that it was possible to be both Confucian and Christian. This position enabled leading Mandarins like Xu Guangqi, Professor in the Hanlin Academy in Beijing and subsequently Grand Secretary of the Empire, to become Christians and leaders in the church. It was a position summed up by another leading Christian Mandarin, Li Yingshi, when he asserted of the Christian message 'it does away with idols and completes the law of the literati'.[20]

According to Ricci, not only did the Chinese Classics contain a morality that was acceptable to Christianity, but also what he called 'original' Confucianism contained cosmological and religious ideas consistent with Christian teachings. What were the practical results of this position for the life of Chinese Christians? It meant they were allowed to continue participating in the ancestral rites of the family and clan. If they were graduates, moreover, they were allowed to participate in the rites that honoured Confucius, matters that were fundamental to Chinese culture. Christians were able to do so because these rites, despite the superstitious and religious connotations attached to them by the uneducated, were essentially social and civic activities, and not religious. Ricci insisted that it should be left to a future indigenous hierarchy, as it developed, to deal with the problem of popular superstition.

An associated issue was what Chinese words could be used to translate God? Here there had been considerable difficulty in coming to a decision. Among Ricci's successors, some argued that although terms like *shangdi* ('lord on high') and *tian* ('heaven') had had a transcendent meaning when the Classics were written, since Sung times neo-Confucianism had robbed them of that meaning.

Even the term from the Classics settled upon, *tianzhu* ('lord of heaven') was considered doubtful by some, but in the end missionaries of all the orders accepted it.

The general acceptance by the missionaries in China of the Riccian tradition enabled the *Kangxi* emperor, seen by some as the greatest of the emperors of the *Qing* dynasty, to issue his edict on Christianity on 22 March 1692. This edict, in effect, recognized Christianity, as understood and practised according to the Confucianist pattern established by Ricci, as a licit religion in the empire. Indeed the emperor specifically compared the new status of Christianity with that of Buddhism, also a religion of foreign origin but now accepted as licit by the imperial authorities.

At the same time, attacks were again being mounted in Europe against the 'Mandarin Rites'. What some saw as a creative encounter between Christianity and Confucianism was decried by many others as a betrayal of Christianity at worst or the laying of a superficial veneer of Christianity upon Confucianism at best. Unlike the conflicts of the mid-seventeenth century, the beginning of the eighteenth century saw clergy other than Jesuits now emerging as leading apologists for what might be termed 'Confucian Christianity'. These were the Dominican, Lo Wenzao, the first Chinese to be consecrated a bishop of the Roman Catholic Church, and the Augustinian, Alvaro Benevente, Vicar Apostolic of Guangxi. The Jesuits in China attempted to end the problem once and for all by having their interpretation of the nature of the familial rites, the rites in honour of Confucius, and their general understanding of *ru-jiao* confirmed as accurate by the source of correctness in these matters, the emperor. They appealed to the *Kangxi* emperor, who issued an imperial rescript on 30 November 1700. This unambiguously endorsed Ricci's understanding of this tradition. The result, however, was the opposite of what the missionaries in China had hoped for. Not only in Rome, but also across Christian Europe, Catholic and Protestant, the missionaries' action was interpreted as appealing to a pagan ruler to settle a church dispute. This was, in truth, a total misrepresentation of what the missionaries had done: they had asked for a ruling about a non-Christian tradition from the official source of that tradition in order to help the church make a decision about the appropriate relationship of Christianity to it. In the climate of the time, the misrepresentation of their action is understandable. What is bewildering is the number of twentieth-century historians who have misrepresented it in the same way.

As we already noted in our discussion of Hinduism, Pope Clement XI appointed Charles de Tournon as a papal legate to go to both India and China to deal with the problems presented by the controversies over the Malabar

Rites and the Mandarin Rites. Arriving in China in April 1705, de Tournon took as his advisor Charles Maigrot of the *Société des Missions Estrangères de Paris*. It was Maigrot who had reopened the matter of Confucian Christianity by banning Christians under his authority from participating in familial rites in 1693. When this was condemned in China by all save his colleagues in the Paris Society, Maigrot reopened the controversy in Europe by appealing to the Theology Faculty of the Sorbonne for support. The *Kangxi* emperor, meanwhile, treated the papal legate with courtesy and patience. His patience gave out, however, when he realized that the legate had come not for discussions but to bring to an end the 'ways of *Li Madou*'. He was infuriated when he discovered that the legate's advisor, Maigrot, could not easily read Mandarin and had read neither the Classics nor even Ricci's *Tianzhu Shiyi*. He expelled Maigrot and had the Portuguese imprison de Tournon at Macao.[21] The emperor then decreed in 1706 that only missionaries who promised to follow the ways of *Li Madou* could obtain an Imperial *biao* without which they could not stay in China. Clement XI's bull, *Ex illa die* of 1715, then rendered the position of all priests, missionary and indigenous, impossible. The bull condemned the Mandarin Rites in careful detail and added a strongly worded oath that all Catholic clergy in China had to swear rejecting the traditions of Ricci under penalty of excommunication for refusal. Although appeals against this went on until the promulgation of Benedict XIV's bull, *Ex quo singulari* of 1742, ended the matter; the development of Confucian Christianity was over. Some twentieth-century scholars have questioned whether Ricci understood Confucianism; eighteenth-century Confucian scholars certainly believed he had. When members of the Confucian establishment on the orders of the emperor were putting together the massive official bibliographical compilation, the *Ssuku Chuanshu* ('The Complete Library of the Four Branches of Knowledge'), they included Ricci's *Tianshu Shiyi*!

Two Protestant missionaries, Robert Morrison (1782–1834) and Dr William Milne (1785–1822), began work in China before 1815. Serious and devoted men though they were, they contributed nothing positive towards a Christian–Confucian encounter. Their entirely negative attitude appears to have been well described by Milne: 'It is therefore absolutely necessary, before this nation can be truly virtuous and happy, that its veneration of ancient names be destroyed, or at least greatly weakened.'[22]

In reviewing the Christian encounter with other world religions during the period 1660 to 1815, the encounter with Islam can be summed up most readily: there was no religious encounter. Rather, it was a political encounter of two power blocks, the Christian and the Islamic worlds, regarding each other somewhat as the Soviet Union and the United States viewed one another during the twentieth-century Cold War. The Christian encounter with Buddhism, which took place principally in China and Japan, was more of a genuine religious encounter. However, despite some initial episodes of sympathetic discussion, relations soon took a negative turn, principally because the missionaries' most powerful converts and their leading local sympathizers were themselves already anti-Buddhist. With Confucianism and with Hinduism, the situation was dramatically different, at least for a time. The Jesuit missions initiated and maintained a creative dialogue with both traditions until this development was finally ended by the papal bull *Ex quo singulari* of 1742. After that, the encounter was overwhelmingly negative. Despite a brief but creative Lutheran/Hindu encounter in south India, the impact of the new, rapidly expanding Protestant missionary endeavour was equally negative. As a result, by 1815 Protestant and Roman Catholic Christianity, so hostile to each other otherwise, were united in their condemnation of the other great religious traditions in the world, dismissing them as wrong at best, and as demonic at worst.

Notes

1. Jean-Marie Gaudel, *Encounters and clashes: Islam and Christianity in history* (Rome: Pontificio Instituto di Studi Arabi e Islamici, 1990), vol. 1, pp. 232–5.
2. *Ibid.*, p. 186.
3. Ahmad Gunny, *Images of Islam in eighteenth-century writings* (London, Grey Seal, 1996).
4. Gunny, *Images of Islam*, p. 194.
5. Duncan Forrester, *Caste and Christianity: Attitudes and policy on caste of Anglo-Saxon Missions in India* (London: Curzon Press, 1980), chap. 5.
6. S. Delacroix (ed.), *Histoire universelle des missions Catholiques*, 4 vols. (Paris: Grund, 1956), vol. 2, p. 43.
7. Although referred to in many books as 'de Nobili', Fr Wicki has shown that he always wrote his name 'Nobili' when writing in Italian or Portuguese. J. W. Wicki, *Neue Zeitschrift fur Missionwissenschaft*, 33 (1977), p. 136.
8. S. Neill, *A history of Christianity in India: From the beginning to 1707* (Cambridge: Cambridge University Press, 1984), p. 309.
9. What 'accommodation' is in contrast with 'inculturation' and which is the more appropriate designation for the Jesuit policy in Madurai and in China we will turn to later.
10. Quoted in S. Neill, *A history of Christianity in India*, vol. 1, p. 33.
11. Indira Viswanathan, 'The Bethlehem Kuravanci of Vedanayaka Sastri', in Brown and Frykenberg (eds.), *Christians, cultural interactions, and India's religious tradition* (Grand Rapids, MI: Eerdmans, 2002).
12. Quoted in Geoffrey Carnall, 'Robertson and contemporary images of India', in S. J. Brown (ed.), *William Robertson and the expansion of empire* (Cambridge: Cambridge University Press, 1997), p. 215.
13. Forrester, *Caste and Christianity*, chap. I.

14. William Ward, *Farewell letters to a few friends in Britain and America*, 2nd edn (London, 1821), p. 57.

15. David Bosch, *Transforming Mission* (New York: Orbis Books, 1991), chap. 6.

16. Brian Stanley (ed.), *Christian Missions and the Enlightenment* (Grand Rapids, MI: Eerdmans, 2001). In particular Ian D. Maxwell, 'Civilisation or Christianity: The Scottish debate on Mission methods, 1750–1835'.

17. Philip C. Almond, *The British discovery of Buddhism* (Cambridge: Cambridge University Press, 1988), p. 7.

18. Georg Schurhammer, *Francis Xavier: His life, his times*, 4 vols. (Rome: Jesuit Historical Institute, 1982), vol. 4, pp. 442–5.

19. J. F. Schutte, *Valignano's Mission principles for Japan*, 1 vol., 2 parts (St Louis: Institute for Jesuit Sources, 1985), part 2, pp. 126–89.

20. Louis J. Gallagher, *China in the sixteenth century: The journals of Matteo Ricci* (New York: Random House, 1953), p. 448.

21. Andrew C. Ross, *A vision betrayed: The Jesuits in Japan and China, 1542–1742* (Maryknoll, NY: Orbis Books, 1994), pp. 190–9.

22. Quoted in Robert Philip, *The life and opinions of the Reverend Dr. William Milne* (London: John Snow, 1840), p. 256.

PART V

★

REVOLUTION AND THE CHRISTIAN WORLD

25

The American Revolution and religion, 1765–1815

MARTIN E. MARTY

The War of Independence (1776–83), fought by the British colonies in North America against the British government, was the dominant but by no means the only defining event in American religion between 1765 and 1815. The period also saw colonists living off the spiritual capital they had created in the First Great Awakening, which had climaxed in the 1740s, and then citizens realizing what many historians have called a Second Great Awakening beginning around the turn of the nineteenth century.

Further, in the aftermath of the war, the colonists came together to form a new nation. The central act of that formation was the writing and acceptance of the United States Constitution (1787) with its Bill of Rights (1789) that dealt with religious issues.[1] The new charter of religious liberties in that Bill of Rights was one of the many stimuli for developing denominational patterns and practices which American citizens adopted so rapidly and with such enthusiasm that these would provide a framework for much religious life in the United States ever after.

Through the period, the overwhelmingly predominant religion was Christianity; among Christians, Protestantism possessed a near monopoly and among Protestants, English-speaking Protestants made up a majority. They played the most visible role in the Revolution and in the shaping of national life. As for the others: in a population estimated at 2.5–3 million people at the time of the nation's founding in 1787, African American slaves counted for little in public life, deprived as they were of rights. Demographers estimate that approximately 30,000 citizens of colonies were Roman Catholics, most of them living in Maryland and Pennsylvania. While Catholics and the very few Jews played their parts in the Revolution, any strong national influence on their part would await the immigration of their fellow-adherents decades after 1815.

Church-based orthodox Protestantism was not the only form available. In the middle of this period many elite Americans came to favour the beliefs and ideas associated with the European Enlightenment, while giving these beliefs and ideas a cast favourable to Protestantism. Leaders of the Revolution and drafters of the Constitution – people of influence such as George Washington, John Adams, Thomas Jefferson, James Madison, and many more–while remaining responsible members of the Congregational churches in the north and the Anglican, later Episcopal, church in the south, breathed the spirit of this version of the Enlightenment.[2]

So strong was their attachment to its broad principles and so articulate were they in expressing these principles that one historian, Crane Brinton, noted that there arose what he called 'clearly a new religion', which he named 'simply Enlightenment, with a capital E'.[3] It is oversimplifying, but not grossly so, to see the division in the religious ranks as featuring on the one hand, the religion of the heart – the Awakenings accented the emotive and experiential features of Christianity – and on the other, the religion of the head – the American Enlightenment leaders saw themselves being devoted to reason above all. There were many reasons for believers and other citizens to expect a clash between the two. Yet, curiously, many of the themes and approaches of both came to be blended in the public expression of religion in the life of the new nation.[4]

Those who reckon with American religion also pay attention to the powerful but narrowly focused faith embodied in formal religious institutions that came to be called denominations – Congregational, Episcopal, Presbyterian, and the like – and to the more generalized civic and public forms of faith. The sociologist Peter Berger has called such genera a 'sacred canopy' over the conventional religious forms, covering as it did aspects of church religion, public prayer, and the invocation of the divine in military and state-making affairs.[5]

To speak in these two sets of terms is to assume certain definitions or descriptions of religion as such. Religion, first, is focused on that which concerns people ultimately. This was evident at that time in fierce debates over personal conversion and morality in the churches, but also in religious devotion to state and nation. Secondly, people form communities in the name of religion. It was in this context that the modern denomination was born, denomination being a neutral term applied to all faiths, which now occupied a level playing-field as the once-established churches lost their legal privileges. Further, religious people gravitate towards the use of myths and symbols, rites, and ceremonies. These were evident throughout the period in the services of Christian worship, which included preaching, prayer, and sacramental life. But the Revolution also impelled and inspired leaders to make use of mythic and symbolic images in the waging of the war.[6] They spoke of devoting their 'sacred honour' to the fight for independence and convoked God-in-general when recruiting troops, sending them into battle, or presiding over funeral rites.

The religion of the American Revolution, like other religions, implied what we might call a metaphysical background, a sense or claim that behind the ordinary appearances of national life there existed a larger narrative and set of meanings and expectations. Thus Thomas Jefferson and his colleagues in the Declaration of Independence made the religious claim that their rights were 'endowed by their Creator'. George Washington and other military and constitutional leaders joined Jefferson in speaking of 'Nature's God' unconfined by a particular set of scriptures. They invoked 'Providence' and 'Heaven' to guide them in battle and in drafting documents for the new nation.[7]

Finally, religious groups expect certain behavioural consequences as a result of the commitments just mentioned. Thus the colonials determined and proclaimed that the British were enslaving them by depriving them of representation in policies that affected them all, and that it was their sacred duty to rebel against such slavery. Just as they expected citizens to lay their lives on the line in the war, so they also stressed the need for virtue and morality, ordinarily based on or related to religion. Washington said as much in his major speeches and as the Congress proclaimed in the Northwest Ordinance, which in 1787 envisioned terms of citizen life in the north-west territories far beyond the eastern coasts.[8]

The Great Awakening

The religious beginning of the emergent story of the Revolution, in the minds of an ever-increasing number of historians, lay in the Great Awakening. The Awakening is seen as the first true inter-colonial intellectual and spiritual event and complex. The heart of the revivalists' or awakeners' message was, of course, the need for individuals to turn from their wicked ways and to let God the Father of Jesus Christ draw them to God's self. But not only individual salvation was at issue. The evangelists began to use millennial language, which spoke of the need for citizens to be converted and to become moral together, in order to make the world attractive for Jesus Christ's return.

That call included the demand that the colonies as colonies and then the new nation as nation had to manifest awareness of their shortcomings and their readiness for God to work for their common purposes and common good. Historians who study the phrases about the colonies in the newspapers of the day can chronicle the rise of talk not about this or that colony, or about His Majesty's colonies, but, for the first time broadly 'the American colonies' or the nation, where a returning Jesus would be expected and welcomed to guide and fulfil the destiny of citizens believing and working together.[9]

If, as many then believed, the fires of revival had been banked or slowed as the Awakening was gradually spent, this did not mean that people deserted the churches. It is true that a new passion came along to redirect some of the energies that had previously gone into church, now into nation. Some of the talent of the sons of colonials were turned from ministerial vocations in religion to politics and statecraft. Language once used to draw people to the Kingdom of God now got translated to the language that demanded loyalty and urged liberty. The churches did not empty because of the challenges of war-making and the attractiveness of nation-building, but many scholars believe that church life was at its lowest ebb to date at the time of the war. The Second Great Awakening and the revivals that followed it then attracted ever-growing numbers of converts and adherents through the nineteenth century. Majorities during the war had something else on their mind than being attentive to sermons and private prayer.

In a letter to Thomas Jefferson in 1815, John Adams, the second president of the United States, spelled out the terms of Revolution as he remembered it. The war, he contended, was not part of the Revolution; it was an effect and consequence of the Revolution. 'The Revolution was in the minds of the people, and this was effected, from 1760 to 1775, in the course of fifteen years before a drop of blood was shed at Lexington.'[10] New religious forces were coming to the scene, and they had a bearing on the Revolution and its aftermath.

Establishment and dissent

Nine of the thirteen colonies inherited some version or other of church establishment. This meant that citizens subsidized the privileged church in each case through taxation, revenues exacted whether they shared the faith or were members of the particular body these supported. Such an official church provided the minister to pray or preach at public occasions such as Fast Days or Election Days. Dissenters were handicapped in various ways. They often had to acquire licenses to preach and gather at particular places. By 1765, many of the establishments had become quite relaxed and political leaders found it expedient not to impose penalties on dissenters too lightly. Yet young James Madison in 1774 could write to a friend that he was enraged over the 'diabolical, hell-conceived principle of persecution' which left some ministers of the gospel in prison for failing to get licenses and thus preaching in unlawful situations.[11]

In the northern colonies the Congregational Church was established except in Rhode Island, a colony founded by dissenters, especially Baptists, and which also provided a welcoming home to Quakers. The Congregationalists, descendants of the New England Puritans and in many cases enlivened by the Great Awakening revivalists and preachers, began to use religious language against the British. Some of these, among them Jonathan Mayhew, were theological liberals who were moving from rigid Calvinism towards Arminianism. This was a form of Protestantism that stressed the benevolence of God and the duties of humans – one of these duties now being, Mayhew said as early as 1750, to throw off the yoke of British-imposed slavery, meaning its taxation policies.[12]

While Mayhew and other Arminians, ancestors of what became the Unitarian denomination in the nineteenth century, occupied fashionable pulpits and gave learned discourses on liberty, in the shadow of their steeples or in the backwoods, less-prestigious, often less-educated, and almost always more fervent ministers took up the cause of liberty. Among practices that caused many to chafe were the efforts by the Anglican church establishment in England to gain footholds in New England. Some prominent citizens in Massachusetts and Connecticut had set the pace by converting to Anglicanism. But more ominous in the eyes of Congregationalists were endeavours by Anglicans through the Society for the Propagation of the Gospel (SPG) not only to fulfil stated intentions to convert Native Americans but also to promote religious rule by bishops. And bishops, symbols of repression in their eyes, were abhorrent to members of the 749 Congregational churches that existed at the time of the Revolution.[13] The Baptist Isaac Backus, in a book of history in 1784, was typical in citing the episcopal encroachment as the greatest single cause of the Revolution. Fighting against the intrusion of the SPG and the threat of bishops led many of these independent-minded Congregationalists to oppose anything British and to call, increasingly, for independence.

In the southern colonies the Anglican or Episcopal Church was everywhere established. At the time of the Revolution there were 406 such parish churches in these colonies. While George Whitefield, the most effective revivalist in the Great Awakening, had been an Episcopalian, few Anglicans were caught up in the revivals and they often disdained emotional religious expressions. Most scholars agree that Anglicans of the established churches in the colonies were a comparatively weak presence.

Anglicans faced a notoriously difficult problem as the War of Independence loomed: their clergy, though lacking a resident bishop in America, were all ordained in England and as part of their ordination they had taken an oath of loyalty to the British crown. If they were conscientious about it, they had to be loyalists opposed to the Revolution. When war came in 1775, many of them fled to Canada, some returned to England, and of those who remained most had to be at best quiet about their commitments. Meanwhile, many of their prominent members turned their back on the clergy's preachments and became leading patriots. This is the company in which General, and later President, George Washington was prime.

Between the nine colonies represented by the northern and southern religious establishments were the middle colonies, notably Pennsylvania, New York, and New Jersey. While Congregationalists and Episcopalians were represented lightly in these colonies, there was a different population mix that included non-English speaking immigrants: Lutherans and Reformed as well as members of more radical and often pacifist churches such as the Mennonites, Dunkers ('Church of the Brethren'), and other heirs of Anabaptist and similar radical movements dating back to Protestantism's beginnings in the sixteenth century. In Pennsylvania they built upon the foundations of liberty that had been first laid by the Quakers under the colony's proprietor and founder, William Penn. Quakers gradually yielded power among the Pennsylvania elites to Anglicans, some of whom had been converted from Quakerism. They also came to be outnumbered by the common folk of the newer immigrant churches. Quakers and the adherents of these immigrant 'peace churches' were pacifist. That is, they refused to bear arms when the war began and many of them would not even engage in the 'alternate service' that was congenial to many of patriotic sentiment who aided in relief work and cared for the wounded in battle.

Another force in these middle colonies were the Presbyterians, some of whom had New England Congregational roots. The Presbyterians governed themselves through a well-defined hierarchy of church courts, presbyteries and synods, which set them apart from the Congregationalists, with their independent congregations. The Presbyterians' organization gave them coherence and disproportionate influence, along with the ability to spread the signals and effects both of revivalist movements and of support for political independence. Not only did some of the Presbyterians descend from Congregational stock. Their cohorts were also enlarged and enriched by migrants of Scots–Irish background. Some of these were stalwart Calvinists who came to believe that a provident God had called them to the cause of independence and liberty. So passionate did some of them become that British and some loyalist colonials occasionally sneered that the Revolution was simply a Presbyterian war.

Others of the Scots–Irish were influenced by a particular movement called the Scottish Enlightenment, which fed teachers and tutors to the colonies. Among them were those who taught founding fathers such as James Madison. They also prepared potential leaders among them to attend and excel at the College of New Jersey, which became Princeton University. The most influential of these leaders was John Witherspoon, who successfully blended a staunch Calvinist faith with a new-found faith in reason and science that came with that Scottish Enlightenment background. He and his colleagues helped provide rationales for opposing the crown, figuratively deposing the king, and composing a constitutional republic. Witherspoon himself became a signer of the Declaration of Independence in 1776.

As a result of the Awakening and the growth of dissent in New England under Baptist leaders like the influential Isaac Backus, critics of the established churches divided congregation after congregation. Backus asked how Congregationalists could complain of 'taxation without representation' by the British parliament without noticing that they were guilty of establishing such a policy over against tax-resistant Baptists and other dissenters. Many of these, to put the seal of dissent on their practices, refused to pay taxes – Backus once went to jail for this – and also would not baptize infants. Rather, they delayed baptism until children became sufficiently adult to make their own profession of faith. This practice both made them unwelcome in settled Congregational New England and convinced many to move to Virginia and elsewhere in the south. There they converted many of their neighbours to the Baptist cause and, along with this cause, they spread dissent against church establishments. Thus the orthodox Baptist elder John Leland both converted souls and campaigned at the side of Thomas Jefferson for new laws that later led to disestablishment of Anglicanism and the assurance of religious freedom in Virginia.

The Methodists, another new force on the scene between 1765 and 1815, were not unambiguous in support of Revolution. They had represented a revitalized group within Anglicanism in England under the leadership of John Wesley and his colleagues, but had then gone their separate way. With their highly evangelical faith, they felt called to convert the colonials to Methodism, but had found only a toe-hold when the war broke out. Many, being devoted to the crown, shared the discomfort of mainstream Anglicans. Some returned to England or remained hardly visible as a church movement until after the war. However, after they organized as a body in Baltimore in 1784 and with leadership personified by the energetic missionary and administrator Francis

Asbury, they spread their word and became agents of both the gospel and the republic. They experienced growth which matched that of the Baptists and often were explicit rivals. By 1815, the Baptists and Methodists had displaced the colonial 'big three' of Congregationalism, Episcopalianism, and Presbyterianism, in numbers and, in some places and respects – particularly in the south and, after the west opened early in the new century – everywhere west.

The loyalists and the churches

The loyalist story is most difficult to reconstruct. Estimates of the number in their camp vary, but many scholars believe that at least one-third of the population would have preferred to remain citizens of Great Britain. Many of these loyalists had religious reasons for doing so. Thus Henry Melchior Muhlenberg, the most prominent colonial Lutheran cleric and the father of John Peter Gabriel Muhlenberg, one of George Washington's notable generals, remained loyal to King George III until at least 1776 on both rather simplistic and dedicated biblical grounds. Lutherans had learned and often in the colonies still taught that the prime biblical text on this subject was Romans 13. There Paul the apostle had written that the 'powers that be', in this case, the king, were ordained of God. Every Christian soul was to be subject to such powers, and those who resisted them would receive damnation. That was a pretty heavy penalty for joining the patriot cause. However, Muhlenberg and most hitherto reluctant Lutherans segued and even turned to the patriot cause after the Declaration of Independence and the establishment of new colonial authority. Now he and they could sign up with Washington and the other founders, who were the new 'powers that be', ordained of God, worthy of obedience.

The Anglicans and the few Methodists could not move so deftly. Their oaths and their instincts were not revocable or to be changed because some American militants wielding muskets and drums and flags came along to agitate against and then set out to dethrone the king. For them, an oath was an oath, binding and permanent. Habits led them to be sincerely devoted to long traditions of Britain and to English liberties. They tried to make the case that English laws by and large were among the most protective and lenient of the day. If parliament and the crown were momentarily insensitive and obtuse enough to impose taxes on colonists, often and especially to pay for their own policing and the expenses that their colonial status imposed on all of England, these loyalists were sympathetic to those parliamentary figures across the Atlantic who were counselling patience and working for change.

Certainly, in their eyes, the grievances that led colonists, including religious leaders, to see the Stamp Act of 1765, a revenue-producing inconvenience and burden, as the devil's work, could be addressed through means other than bullets and torches. The Boston Massacre, an event of 1770 in which British soldiers fired on and killed a few insurgent colonists, was not enough to lead them to call for war and independence.

The imposition by England of taxes on tea imports to the colonies, burdens that led some partisans of revolution to engage in a famed Tea Party, in which they dumped shiploads of tea into Boston harbour, they saw again as an irritation to be addressed through politics, not incendiary acts. When the British parliament passed the Quebec Act in 1774, a policy designed to keep Canada within the British Empire, anti-Catholic American patriots found new reason to be agitated and wary. British opinion thought the Act was reasonable, providing as it did a means of keeping the 100,000 mainly Catholic citizens in the fold. For the Americans, on the other hand, granting the Canadian Catholics religious liberty was one thing. Granting Canada, with its Catholics, rights to much of the old north-west of what was to become the United States was another, and it understandably evoked fierce negative reaction. Still, war did not come.

Religion and American identity

While many loyalists left the colonies and others, reading the handwriting on colonial walls, turned recessive and sullen, the more intense energies of colonists went to support the cause of independence and colonial liberty. The Stamp Act and the Tea Party had been justified in colonial, especially New England pulpits, and British policy came to be described as tyranny. The more staid preachers in prominent pulpits showed how the philosopher John Locke, the prophets in the Hebrew Scriptures, and Paul the apostle as preacher of liberty and not blind obedience, would have backed the colonists' rebellions. Meanwhile, some evangelizers on horseback found biblical grounds for similar messages in villages on the frontier and in the forests. They amassed a spiritual capital from which the colonists could draw. Among their favoured biblical texts was one in the Old Testament, in which the city of Meroz was cursed because it did not come to the defence of the Lord. Similarly cursed would be those villages, churches, and individuals who did not now do battle for the Lord, who did not see the Americans' righteous cause as divinely inspired.[14]

One can easily overstress the role of religion in triggering and sustaining the Revolution – just as, decades ago, historians tended to overlook it. The passion that leads to war always draws on a mixture of motives, some of them having to do with markets, budgets, simple economic self-interest, the creation of an image of a demonic foe to be used to rally the indifferent, and the contagious spirit that the sound of battle sets afire. All these were present. But it did not hurt and in the end it helped immensely that so many believers made 'the sacred cause of liberty' their own by claiming that a Provident God would bless their efforts, ennoble their sacrifices, and bless their beginnings as a new nation. In 1776, a national seal included the Latin slogan 'Annuit Cœptis' – the divine has 'blessed our beginnings'. That sentiment came naturally.

The religion of the Enlightenment

Speaking of what came naturally leads to concern for the other religious force that Crane Brinton denominated the religion of the Enlightenment with a Big 'E'. While members of the various churches could fight at each other's side and demonize the king and the British, they did not share enough premises to enable them to devise the sets of common purposes that would be needed for nation-building. Here, fortuitously or providentially, this new Enlightened philosophy held sufficient sway among leaders who articulated visions and formulated laws. They were able to transcend sectarian boundaries.

The first traces of the new language that spoke of the God of Nature or the God of Reason were heard among some educated British troops during the colonial wars, around 1758. Never did the advocates who spoke that language attract congregations or large followings. Their ranks were peopled by attorneys and merchants, many of whom had graduated from Harvard and Yale in the north, Princeton in the middle colonies, and William and Mary in the south. Others received some of their education in England, and there picked up the nuances and claims of this religion. They began to apply these in the American colonies.

In the Anglican Church some of these liberalizing viewpoints were called Arminian, accenting, as we have noted, the benevolence of a God who dealt genially and generously with humans who were devoted to virtue. Beyond the church, in most cases, in the circle of religiously minded philosophers, some called themselves deists. Thomas Jefferson would be classified a deist, while Philadelphia patriot and founder Benjamin Franklin, a printer and scientist, though nominally a Presbyterian, paid little attention to the Calvinist creed and, when he did do so he was critical. Let it be noted, however, that as a promoter of virtue Franklin could support the work but not the message of revivalists like George Whitefield. Though the 'sects' disagreed with each other over creeds that Franklin found irrelevant, he celebrated their contribution to moral seriousness.[15]

Franklin outlined his creed, one that matched that of the deists. He was not non-religious, and was anything but secular. Without needing the Bible or any other book of revealed religion, he would promote morality. For him, there was a God of Reason and Law, who held humans responsible. They could do good or evil, and would be rewarded or punished in this life or in a life to come. The churches, he thought, had a right to exist and could be allies of people of good will who did not adhere to their dogmas. But these dogmas were irrelevant, except insofar as they inspired and motivated people to good works. Some followers of Jesus, in his eyes, were good and some were bad. Some non-believers in the divinity of Jesus were also good or bad. So, he reasoned, it could not be the belief in the divinity of Jesus or any other Christian doctrine that was the mark of good citizenship.[16]

People like Franklin worked at the side of Whitefield and other clerics, and took pains not to antagonize them. Patriot Tom Paine, visiting for some years from England, was a more militant deist. In the model of more radical continental proponents of Enlightenment, he saw church religion as a distraction from the cause of liberty and maybe a barrier to it. Paine did inspire some of the church people to support liberty, without, of course, accepting his attack on the churches. But he was too radical for most domestic consumption.

Somewhere between Franklin and Paine was Thomas Jefferson, also a critic of Calvinism, 'priestcraft', dogma, and many church practices that struck him as incongruent with rational religion. With Paine he could say that his own mind was his church. Yet he could ally with professedly religious figures, especially dissenters against establishments, to fire up revolutionaries during the war and fighters for religious liberty thereafter.[17]

Religion and revolution

War time was not the moment for these two sets of religious forces to oppose each other overtly and flagrantly. It was after the forming of the new nation that the revivalists, who began to surge in the early 1790s, could score and scorn people like Jefferson, especially when he ran for president in 1800. Then, repelled by the anti-religion of French revolutionaries, these revivalists and other clerics, especially those who were also Federalists, spoke of Jefferson as an arch-infidel. Those in New England who kept trying to retain religious establishments until past 1815 in Connecticut and, finally, Massachusetts, abhorred the efforts of Jefferson and his supporters to erect a 'wall of separation between church and state'.[18]

Serious grievances against revenue policies or belief in a provident or benevolent God were necessary but not sufficient bases for the Revolution. The revolutionaries also came to claim that monarchy itself, at least in the British style, was against the will of God. Baptists spoke of soul liberty, a theme that might have irritated conservatives in the staid establishments, but Baptists could link with Enlightenment-minded statesmen in calling for an enlargement of human liberty on any of a number of grounds. Humans, such church people claimed, were made in the divine image, and they could realize the effects of this only if arbitrary authority – and King George III and all he stood for, were such – were removed. Still, Baptists and other Calvinists often came to the patriot side more or less by instinct, not by ideology.

With rebellious doctrines came what already shows up as a positive affirmation: that is, individuals were capable of making decisions about their politics on the basis of informed conscience. Indeed, their separate faiths now demanded that they do so. They came to claim that their version of Christianity was supportive of this revolutionary individualism and expressive of freedom. The political philosopher Hannah Arendt noted how they all came to aver this, but she asked, with good credence, why it had taken so long for the biblical support of republican (and democratic) liberties to appear. Where were Christian advocates like those of 1776 from the beginnings until then? She did not want to take away from their impulses and claims, and she did not disagree that the sacred cause of liberty had been latent in biblical and other religious texts. But she said that before developing the claim they at least ought to acknowledge – I would say they ought figuratively to send a card of thanks to modernity, also known as the Enlightenment – for having provided a rationale and a motivator.[19]

One of the more radical steps eventually taken was an explicit call for independence. Throwing off the yoke of a colonizing power was unprecedented. Benjamin Franklin, who always kept a soft spot in his heart and a hard argument in his head in respect to England, where he lived during much of this period, was reluctant to make the call for a break early on. Curiously, one of the first to foresee independence was not a Protestant. The wealthy Catholic, Charles Carroll of Carrollton in Maryland, was a member of a landed clan of Catholics. While studying in England in 1763, he came to see the logic of independence and to envision that America 'will and must be independent'. He became the only Catholic signer of the Declaration of Independence. Moreover, his distant cousin, John Carroll, America's first Catholic bishop, was a member of a small party sent by Congress to try to attract Canada into an alliance against England.[20]

Other non-Protestants also took part. Thus Haym Salomon, a Jewish immigrant from Poland who gravitated to the militant Sons of Liberty, came to be known as 'freedom's financier'. Jews at the time lacked rabbinical presence in the colonies, and were on their own in the few synagogues. Salomon helped found one in Philadelphia in 1783. So far as can be known, Jews drew on the prophetic Jewish tradition to call for liberty and independence.

Not prominent, at least as articulators, on the revolutionary stage and not reasonably liberated in the constitution-making period were three sets of people. First were members of that half of the population who were women. They were not enfranchised, and did not have a clerical voice in the male-dominated established or in most dissenting churches. There were some prominent individuals among them. We might take special note of Abigail Adams, wife of the lawyer and later the second President, John Adams. She revealed a consistent support of the cause of independence and nation-building. Some diaries and observations by others show that many of them participated by supporting and tending to the wounds of fighting men, providing food for revolutionary forces, and helping sustain them in prayer. A century and a half would pass before they could express their liberation by access to the voting booth.

A second set of people were the Native Americans, the Indians, many of whom had sided with the French in the recently prosecuted colonial wars. They had been displaced for more than a century by the east coast immigrants, decimated in wars with whites, devastated by diseases that came with the immigrants, and displaced to the frontiers to which whites were moving in this period. When the founders drafted the Constitution, the original population was classified as a set of foreign powers. This was not their war, their victory, or their nation with the benefits it could have provided. In the Northwest Ordinance of 1787 the authors stipulated that 'the utmost good faith shall always be observed toward the Indians; their lands and property shall never be taken from them without their consent; and in their property, rights and liberty, they shall never be invaded or disturbed, unless in just and lawful wars authorized by Congress'. The nation kept no part of this 'utmost good faith'.[21]

Similarly, a third set of people, the African blacks in America, received no liberties as a result of the Revolution and fabrication of a Constitution. In order to win power, southern colonists wanted to boast large populations for the sake of representation, so they counted Africans in those numberings. But blacks were each valued as only three-fifths of a human in the count and, frankly, were usually treated as far less than three-fifths of a human in their bondage. They were not to be emancipated for almost 100 years. Those who bought their freedom or escaped to it were segregated. Richard Allen and Absalom Jones remember that it was in 1787, the year of the drafting of the Constitution, that they were displaced from pews to galleries in a Philadelphia church, an act that helped inspire them to found their own denominations. Blacks could form their own churches, and most of them were Baptist and Methodist, but they could not preach freedom or enjoy liberty.

Religion in the new nation

That left white men to determine what life in the independent colonies should look like. The common religious ethos developed in the Great Awakening and the much more passionate sense of commonality that grew while people from thirteen colonies had to be united as they risked death and gave lives during the war meant that it was possible to conceive of their thirteen separate colonies virtually as ready for a new, more interactive polity. They did this first through the frail and ineffective Articles of Confederation, which had to give place to a federal union signalled by the Constitution drafted in 1787 and ratified by 1789. Much of the rhetoric for the federal union came from clergy from across most of the colonies, though they did oppose each other in respect to major details of life in the republic as Federalist and Republican parties formed. Again, clergy became ideologues and spokespersons for these parties, often setting out as they did to find biblical warrants for their separate approaches to the new nation.

While the fifty-five drafters who gathered in Independence Hall in Philadelphia between May and September, 1787, kept religion at a distance when writing a Constitution, it is clear that many of them recognized the need to deal with the religious situation. They could not establish the religion of the Enlightenment. Such a religion was not well institutionalized – where were its sanctuaries, who were its clerics? – and any attempt to establish it would have been bitterly opposed by the churches. Yet it was inconceivable that the churches would come to sudden agreement, overcome their historic differences, graciously yield to each other, and cease competition. What should the drafters do?

It has been said that the constitutionalists solved the problem of religion by not solving the problem of religion.[22] That is, they were silent, keeping it at a distance. One clause in the Constitution, Article IV, dramatically insisted that 'No religious Test shall ever be required as a Qualification to any Office or public Trust under the United States'. Otherwise, the Constitution was godless, unless one wants to count the phrase 'in the year of Our Lord 1787' in the final line. Ratification also presented its own problems. How sell the Constitution in places like Connecticut and Massachusetts, which still had established Congregationalism? How assure the rights of minorities across the nation, a place where, as some founders contended, Jews, Turks and Infidels should have the same rights as the most intense and established believers?[23]

The church historian Philip Schaff classically described the course the new Congress of the assembled and confederated colonies had to take in respect to the religious resolution of the Revolution. Since, he maintained, the sects could not have come together to provide a grounding for the republic – they were in too many ways in competition, jealous of their rights and lacking a single philosophy of government – Congress was 'shut up' to its course.[24] This meant being wary of the various states' addresses to religion, while assuring liberty at least on the federal level. The Constitution-writers had not done justice to this theme. Congress, asked to help assure liberties, produced a Bill of Rights, which formed the first Ten Amendments to the Constitution. James Madison, a major drafter, was not alone in calling religious liberty 'the first liberty'. Assure this liberty and most of the others, such as free speech, freedom of the press, and the like, would be protected.

Leading up to the debates that produced the First Amendment, which represented a truly revolutionary proposal and assurance, was a series of struggles in the thirteen colonies. Rhode Island, Pennsylvania, and similar states had no difficulty; in these states, disestablishment and religious freedom had long been effected. Connecticut and Massachusetts were still struggling. Among the southern states, Virginia stood out as the most decisive. This was the state of Washington, Jefferson, Madison, another patriot Patrick Henry (the orator whose speech that climaxed with 'Give me liberty or give me death' inspired colonists during the war) and many others. Most of them were members of Anglican parish councils and vestries, though few of them were as devoted to the particulars of their faith as Henry, a Presbyterian, was to his.

Virginians pondered what to do about religious freedom there. In 1779, Thomas Jefferson had drafted a 'Bill for Establishing Religious Freedom in Virginia', an act that made him so proud that he wanted the fact engraved on his tombstone. He had then argued that 'Truth is great and will prevail if left to herself'. But after making bold proposals for the Virginia state constitution, he had left in 1784 to become ambassador to France. James Madison carried on. Washington and Henry were among those who favoured what came to be called 'multiple establishment': let the state subsidize religious institutions, but do so for all, apportioning funds according to their size.

Madison's view was clearly expressed in his *Memorial and remonstrance against religious assessments*. Religion, he maintained, was a matter of opinion, and the government dared not try to coerce assent, as, he claimed, Virginia was doing. Henry was the main opponent of Madison's proposal to disestablish all churches. Madison, an adept politician, helped see to Henry's election to the governorship, thus depriving the state legislature of his voice. Madison and his colleagues then gathered support around the state and in 1786 Jefferson's bill passed by a vote of 76:20.[25]

A couple of years later, Madison busied himself in selling the Constitution to the states, whose legislatures had to ratify it. Contributing to the *Federalist Papers*, he argued that 'security for civil rights must be the same as for religious rights; it consists in the one case in a multiplicity of interests and in the other in a multiplicity of sects'.[26]

In 1789, with the Constitution ratified and in force, arguments like those in Virginia now reached representatives of all the states. After agonizing argument, the formulators came up with two clauses, totalling sixteen words: 'Congress shall make no law respecting an establishment of religion nor prohibiting the free exercise thereof'. They had to settle for that first word, 'Congress'. They dared not interfere directly with cherished state policies, but they had set in motion a force of understanding that eventually came to prevail in federal courts. The two clauses, meanwhile, were seen from the beginning sometimes to be in conflict: undercutting establishment could mean that some forums, which religious groups had hitherto considered places for free access, were now beyond their reach. That did not look like 'free exercise'.

What, one might ask, was so revolutionary about this amendment? Taking a long historical view the answer is a great deal, a revolutionarily great deal. For 1,400 years, since the age of Constantine in the Roman Empire, wherever Christians were a strong presence they favoured and often held a monopoly or at least a privileged status at the hands of a complicit government. Christians then could do to others what had been done to them by the Romans: try to force compliance and then to deprive non-Christians of rights or citizenship or even survival. That period and approach ended with the First Amendment.

Those like Henry in Virginia and any number of New Englanders who feared that disestablishment would mean a decline in morals and virtue, to say nothing of church growth – who would finance religion, and how would they do so? – protested or turned sullen and uncooperative. Yet experience after the passing of the First Amendment was astonishing. As revivalists invaded the south and the west, church membership grew impressively, with little legal help from the state.

With new revivals being reported all the way from Yale College to the mountain ridges and hollows of pioneer Kentucky, the effects were often paradoxical. On one level they were democratic, levelling. Gone were the heavy layers of hierarchy, hands of bureaucracies, and ties of many precedents. People had equal access to God for conversion and at least in theory equal status before God after it. Uneducated citizens could feel the Spirit and get up and preach, beginning steps that led them from place to place to start new communities, new churches. They brought order and stability, once the emotional highs of revivals had passed.

On the other side of the paradox, it became clear that revivals were also instruments of social control. Before long the new institutions in frontier towns, now rivals of the outposts of Congregationalism, Presbyterianism, and Episcopalianism, competed for a market share and acquired means for doing so. The Methodists developed intricate networks for chartering and supervising 'circuit riders' and missionaries, in patterns that allowed for little deviation from norms set by higher-ups. The Baptists were more unrestrained: any Christian among them could set up shop as a missionary or pastor, and many did, to spread their churches especially across the south.

The post-Revolutionary churches developed a style that has been called voluntaryistic (as opposed to 'voluntaristic'), which meant that they were seen as agencies dependent upon the will and decision of the individuals who made them up. They depended less on an ontology of the church, on a sense of its 'givenness', with its existence independent of the will of people, and more on a sense of what seemed manifest: that the people, to be sure, 'under God', were the creators and determiners of the church. They were free to compete, and they did.

Chaos could have ensued, but did not always do so. The most prominent example of the voluntary church in action was the development of what the historian Charles Foster called 'An Errand of Mercy'.[27] This was a network, one that replicated and was connected in many cases with counterparts in Great Britain, of agencies designed to effect legislation, assure educations, develop charities, and promote morals. These were often lay-run efforts by leaders who came from across denominational lines. They crusaded against alcohol, duelling, sometimes against slavery and for patriotic support of the nation and its symbols, Christian education as in Sunday Schools, and various efforts to effect justice.

One final function of the churches that were heirs of the Revolution and the constitutional drawing of a line of distinction between religion and the civil authorities (James Madison's term for 'the separation of church and state') was the supplying of morale, common language, and national spirit. This had diminished since the colonies had momentarily united during the Revolutionary War, now decades before. Yet many in the clergy who had once used scriptural passages to justify independence now found other scriptural passages that helped them to see the nation as a whole as God's vineyard, a new Zion, an arena in which God-pleasing activity went on. Often they were propelled by millennial enthusiasm, still drawing on visions of an ever-improving world made attractive for Christ's return.

Far from being a Utopia, the new nation was often a scene of lawlessness and violence – just as it had been, especially on the frontiers, before the War of Independence. And the ideology of common nationhood began to be tested early as the North and South went separate ways in dealing with slavery. There had been many slaveholders in the North, but slavery was not as economically necessary or feasible as it seemed to be in the agricultural plantation world in the southern states. By the second decade of the new century some northerners in particular started dreaming of ways to resolve the moral dilemmas that came with slavery. Some advocated the purchase of freedom for slaves followed by their emigration back to Africa. A very few worked for the abolition of slavery without worrying about economic consequences.

In the South, slavery was taken for granted, its economic necessity implied and defended. And when challenge to the institution came, no group was more forceful and effective among the ideological and practical defenders of slavery than the clergy. Like their forebears and counterparts, they put abundant biblical texts to work justifying the enslaving of other humans. The Revolution was thus at best half-finished, if Revolution meant the striving for and effecting of basic human liberties.

Many have seen the War of Independence and its aftermath as a conservative revolution by American lawyers, landowners, and merchants who assured for themselves the kind of economic liberties their counterparts in England knew. However, the legal assurance of religious freedom and the rise of voluntary churches made up a more radical revolution. The degree that that was so, the one-time British colonials had to their satisfaction effected the beginning of what another Latin phrase on their national motto so triumphantly affirmed: this meant a *novus ordo seclorum*, a new order of ages.

Notes

1. B. Preiss and D. Osterlund, *The Constitution of the United States* (New York: Bantam, 1987), pp. 19–47, 51–83.
2. H. F. May, *The Enlightenment in America* (New York: Oxford University Press, 1976).
3. C. Brinton, 'Many mansions', *American historical review*, 49 (1964), p. 315.
4. M. Noll, *America's God: From Jonathan Edwards to Abraham Lincoln* (New York: Oxford University Press, 2002) pp. 53–157.
5. P. Berger, *The Sacred canopy: Elements of a sociological theory of religion* (Garden City, NY: Doubleday, 1967).
6. C. Albanese, *Sons of the fathers: The civil religion of the American Revolution* (Philadelphia: Temple University Press, 1976).
7. P. F. Boller Jr., *George Washington and religion* (Dallas: Southern Methodist University Press, 1963).
8. E. S. Gaustad, *Faith of our fathers: Religion and the new nation* (San Francisco: Harper and Row, 1987), pp. 151–6.
9. R. L. Merritt, *Symbols of American community 1735–1775* (New Haven: Yale University Press, 1966), pp. 130–3.
10. B. Bailyn, *The ideological origins of the American Revolution* (Cambridge, MA: Harvard University Press, 1967), p. 1.
11. W. R. Hutchison and W. M. E. Rachel (eds.), *The papers of James Madison*, 6 vols. (Chicago: University of Chicago Press, 1962), vol. 1, p. 106.
12. C. W. Akers, *Called unto liberty: A life of Jonathan Mayhew, 1720–1766* (Cambridge, MA: Harvard University Press, 1964).
13. C. Bridenbaugh, *Mitre and sceptre: Transatlantic faiths, ideas, personalities and politics, 1689–1775* (New York: Oxford University Press, 1962).
14. A. Heimert, *Religion and the American mind: From the Great Awakening to the Revolution* (Cambridge, MA: Harvard University Press, 1966).
15. D. F. Hawke, *Franklin* (New York: Harper and Row, 1976), pp. 56–7, 86, 93.
16. S. E. Mead, *The lively experiment: The shaping of Christianity in America* (New York: Harper and Row, 1963), pp. 39–45.
17. *Ibid.*, pp. 45–8, 57–9.
18. P. Hamburger, *Separation of church and state* (Cambridge, MA: Harvard University Press, 2002), pp. 1–9.
19. H. Arendt, *On revolution* (New York: Viking, 1963), pp. 18–19.
20. T. O. Hanley, *The American Revolution and religion* (Washington, DC: Catholic University Press, 1971).
21. P. B. Kurland and R. Lerner (eds.), *The Founders' Constitution*, 5 vols. (Chicago: University of Chicago Press, 1987), vol. 1, pp. 27–9.
22. W. Berns, *The First Amendment and the future of American democracy* (New York: Basic, 1976).
23. M. Borden, *Jews, Turks, and infidels* (Chapel Hill, NC: University of North Carolina Press, 1984).
24. P. Schaff, *Church and state in the United States or the American idea of religious liberty and its practical effects* (New York: G. P. Putnam's Sons, 1888), p. 23.

25. D. Peterson and R. C. Vaughan (eds.), *The Virginia Statute for Religious Freedom: Its evolution and consequences in American history* (New York: Cambridge University Press, 1988).

26. A. Hamilton, J. Jay, and J. Madison, *The Federalist* (Washington: Robert B. Luce, 1976), pp. 53–62 and 335–41.

27. C. Foster, *An errand of mercy: The Evangelical United Front, 1790–1837* (Chapel Hill, NC: University of North Carolina Press, 1960).

Christianity and the campaign against slavery and the slave trade

CHRISTOPHER LESLIE BROWN

The British abolitionist Thomas Clarkson, author of the first history of the Anglo-American antislavery movements, attributed the public campaigns against the slave trade to the influence of religious progress. The 1807 abolition of the American and British slave trades represented, he thought, the fulfilment of Christian teachings and a vindication of the faith. In other cultures and at other times, Clarkson acknowledged, religious leaders had encouraged and facilitated beneficence to the weak and the needy. Only Christianity, however, had made possible the more ambitious commitment to rid entire societies of long-accepted customs and practices that degraded the human race. The Christian faith, and Protestantism in particular, had invested the impulse to benevolence with a new vitality and had extended its reach across the widest possible domain. 'To Christianity alone', Clarkson insisted, 'we are indebted for the new and sublime spectacle of seeing men and women go beyond the bands of individual usefulness to each other; of seeing them associate for the extirpation of private and public misery; and of seeing them carry their charity, as a united brotherhood, into distant lands'.[1]

Over the proceeding four centuries, however, as Thomas Clarkson knew, it was Christian Europe that had devised and operated a vast transatlantic traffic which had conveyed, as of 1808, more than 8 million African men, women, and children to the Americas and led to the death and enslavement in Africa and the Americas of many millions more. Professed Christians sold, purchased, and worked African slaves everywhere in the new American settlements, from Quebec to Quito. Indeed, the institution of slavery helped make possible the expansion of Christendom to and through the Americas. For, without the labour of African slaves, Europeans would have found it exceptionally difficult to forge colonial societies and develop productive transatlantic economies. The most pious, like the most profane, had acquired a stake in human bondage. The religious leaders of every Protestant denomination and every Catholic order regarded slaveholding among their brethren as unexceptional and unobjectionable. With more than 17,000 enslaved men and women on their estates in Brazil, Paraguay, Chile, Peru, Quito, and New Granada, the Jesuits as of 1760 were the largest slaveholders in South America, to cite only the most egregious example of church investment in unfree labour.[2]

The clergy, moreover, had provided the institution of slavery with crucial ideological support. The proslavery ideas mobilized by the defenders of slavery during the eighteenth century drew upon traditions that dated back to the founding of the faith. Christian slaveholders cited Paul and his instructions to both slaves and masters to honour their respective duties to one another. Further, Saint Augustine had taught that slavery represented just one of many consequences of the sinful condition of humanity; it was original sin that had made subjection to established authority a necessity. The morally and spiritually weak, Aquinas had added, stood to benefit from the supervision and authority of the strong. This cultural tradition provided a useful resource for Europeans looking to justify African slavery in the Americas. It helped cast slavery as part of the sacred order, even though slavery had been declining in western Europe during the late medieval and early modern eras. The confrontation with Islam over the preceding centuries had encouraged a tendency to consider adherence to the Christian faith a distinctive marker of identity that conveyed privileges as well as duties. If Christians could hold heathens in captivity, it was wrong to enslave other Christians. This emphasis on differences between those within and outside the faith helped theologians decide that Africans suffered from the Curse of Ham, which decreed that the progeny of his son Canaan would be consigned to slavery in perpetuity – a point of view to which defenders of slavery in the Americas would return with some frequency. For these benighted children of Africa, some slaveholders argued, the Atlantic slave trade might be regarded as providing a rescue from heathen lands. These arguments were made by churchmen as well as by their parishioners. The defenders of slavery included the most prominent and influential of theologians in Europe and the Americas, from New England to New Spain.[3]

Christianity, then, was as important to the expansion of slavery in the Americas, as it was to its demise. In crucial ways, the antislavery movements of the late eighteenth century had 'secular' origins. The campaigns represented one consequence of the emergence and expansion of print culture, the ethos of politeness and sensibility, new theories of economic behaviour and new definitions of economic interests, a growing scepticism towards prescriptive authority, and, perhaps most importantly, a consequential series of conflicts between colonial and imperial powers from 1775 to 1815, during the 'Age of Revolution'. These contexts and trends, however, would have had very different consequences for the history of antislavery if they had not been accompanied by much broader movements for spiritual revival within certain Protestant communities during the last half of the eighteenth century. The evangelical revival instilled within particular individuals and groups a commitment to seek religious purity in this world, to campaign vigorously against earthly sins. To long-standing inert antislavery impulses, the revival brought an inclination to act. In the context of a history of Christianity, Anglo-American abolitionism may be understood as one part of the much broader effort during the evangelical revivals to give religion greater sway over both public and private life. At the same time, in that attempt to extend the influence of Christianity, abolitionists would invite, inadvertently in many instances, the radical reinterpretation of Scripture by Africans and their descendants, who would find in the Christian tradition a message of liberation that their erstwhile guides had feared or had failed to see.

Moral objections to human bondage in the Americas surfaced not long after the establishment of colonial slavery and the opening of the Atlantic slave trade. In most instances, denunciations came from Catholic priests who had spent several years in the colonies ministering to exiled Africans. Typically, the target was the Atlantic slave trade, and not slaveholding itself. The ideal of Christian servitude, sanctioned by both custom and Scripture, could insulate the institution of slavery from attack. It proved far more difficult to justify the kidnapping of Africans (man-stealing in biblical terms) that clergy knew produced captives for the middle passage. As early as 1555, the Portuguese Dominican Fernando Oliveira described the Atlantic slave trade as piracy and a sin. This was also the view of Tomas Mercado, a Spanish Dominican who fourteen years later published a meditation on the ways the morals of European traders had been corrupted by New World riches: the slave trade, by encouraging in Africa wars and raids for innocent captives, represented only the most egregious example. Miguel Garcia, a Spanish Jesuit serving in Brazil, lost his teaching post in 1583 for refusing communion to Portuguese slaveholders. These slaveholders all lived in sin, Garcia insisted, since they had partaken in the injustice of the slave trade. The Jesuit Alonso de Sandoval of Cartagena stopped short of condemning the Atlantic slave system as a whole. But after having spent a half-century tending to the involuntary migrants disembarked in the South American port, he made clear his contempt for the slave trade in 1647 by graphically describing in print the horrors of the Atlantic crossing.[4]

These protests against illicit enslavement would be repeated in the late seventeenth and early eighteenth centuries. A particularly dramatic confrontation took place in Havana, where the deputy to the Bishop of Cuba in 1681 excommunicated two Capuchin missionaries who had begun urging slaveholders to liberate their slaves and had denied absolution to those who refused. In 1686, their views on slavery came to the attention of the papacy, which just then was contemplating a very rare instance of antislavery mobilization in colonial Brazil. Lourenco Da Silva de Mendouca, the mixed-race procurator of the black and mulatto Christian brotherhoods in Iberia and Brazil, had travelled to Rome at the behest of other free Christians of colour hoping to bring an end to the enslavement of Africans baptized in the faith. These Capuchin and Christian African appeals together produced a sustained enquiry by the cardinals assembled in the *Propaganda Fide* which led in turn to what the historian Richard Gray has described as 'the most significant debate ever held within the curia concerning the injustices of the Atlantic slave trade'. The outcome was a formal declaration by the Holy Office in 1686 that endorsed each of the antislavery propositions put forward by the excommunicated Capuchin missionaries. But that judgement could bring no major adjustment to how the slave trade or slavery operated while the crowns of Spain and Portugal exercised final authority over their American colonies. It would be the last antislavery statement to emerge from Rome for a century and a half.[5]

Antislavery opinion circulated rather more extensively in the British settlements in North America and the Caribbean founded in the seventeenth century – within communities that allowed more room for the articulation of dissent and the exploration of heterodox opinion. In England, the occasional criticism of colonial slavery before and during the early eighteenth century took shape most commonly in the imaginative literature preoccupied with tensions between primitive innocence and European luxury. In the Americas, by contrast, antislavery sentiment emerged out of more specific social conflicts between the pursuit of religious purity and the more pervasive commitment to the acquisition of wealth. The faultlines developed most consistently and consequentially within the Religious Society of Friends, where a belief in continuing revelation, an impulse to challenge an accommodation with worldly aims and institutions, and the comparatively limited influence of spiritual elders combined to encourage dissenters within the Society to confront publicly the Quaker majority that profited from slave labour. A similar concern with how the owning of slaves might cause spiritual and moral harm to the owners of slaves would move several Anglican philanthropists in the 1730s and 1740s to fight on behalf of the short-lived ban on slaveholding in the new colony of Georgia, a ban designed to prevent the formation of a planter class preoccupied with the acquisition of outsized wealth. The antislavery impulse in the British colonies often originated in a concern for the spiritual health of the slaveholder.[6]

Those preoccupied with the welfare of captive Africans typically advocated the conversion of slaves to Christianity. Before 1760, the humanitarian impulse was channelled into missionary work. This was as true in the new British and French American settlements as in the established Spanish and the Portuguese colonies. The Christianization of slavery was the aim of religious leaders as diverse as the Jesuit Anthony Vieira in Brazil, the Quaker George Fox in Barbados, and the Puritan Cotton Mather in Massachusetts. Dependence on lay patronage meant that the clergy had little room for independent action on the question of slavery, even if inclined. The slaveholding elite developed a habit of harassing or running off those ministers excessively critical of the established order. It seemed more practical and most useful to find ways to civilize slavery, to make slaveholding conform with the ideal of Christian servitude, and to render the institution more humane and more just, so that 'servants' and masters recognized and honoured their duties and obligations to each other. An attack on slavery, all understood, entailed also an attack on private property and the social order. The promotion of Christianity, by contrast, seemed to offer the most promising way to sanctify human bondage and restrain its worst abuses without fomenting revolutionary change.

These impulses received official support in the European capitals with overseas colonies, particularly in the late seventeenth and early eighteenth centuries. In 1701, the Portuguese Monarch Peter II directed sugar-mill owners to allow slaves to cultivate their provision plots on Saturdays so that they would be free to attend religious services on Sundays. In the same year, the Church of England responded to the rapid growth of the British slave trade by establishing a missionary organization, the Society for the Propagation of the Gospel in Foreign Parts, which was charged to promote conversion to the Anglican faith in the British colonies. Such endorsements of missionary work aimed to remind masters that they too owed obedience to higher authorities, both temporal and sacred. This orientation was most apparent in the *Code Noir* promulgated in 1685 to provide a legal framework for slavery in the French Caribbean colonies. The *Code Noir* addressed almost every aspect of plantation life, the mode of justice, forms of punishment, the work regime, and the respective rights of masters and slaves. The first fourteen articles of the Code prescribed the various ways the Catholic Church was to shape the moral character of Caribbean slavery by requiring baptism, by encouraging slaves to marry, and by insisting on the keeping of the Sabbath.[7]

State support for missions to the slaves would be supplemented by activities organized by the several religious orders and societies competing for influence in the Americas during the eighteenth century. The Dominicans, Jesuits, and Capuchins had been active in South America, the Caribbean, and New Spain before 1660. Several Protestant missions would develop in the century that followed. Both Puritans and Quakers showed some interest in converting enslaved men and women to Christianity during the initial phases of settlement in both the West Indies and New England. An English philanthropic society, 'The Associates of Dr Bray', was instituted in 1723 with the primary mission of instructing slaves in Christianity. Both the Associates of Dr Bray and the Society for the Propagation of the Gospel would find particularly energetic workers among recent Huguenot settlers in North America, who had experienced their own exile and persecution. The impact of these initial attempts sponsored by the Church of England, however, would pale in comparison to the influence of the evangelical revivals that began in the 1740s and returned in sporadic bursts into the nineteenth century. Methodists, Moravians, Baptists, and New Light Presbyterians proselytized among enslaved Africans across North America, and in the Chesapeake and the Carolinas in particular, during the third quarter of the eighteenth century. Missions to the slaves would revive with even greater intensity in the two decades after American independence, as tens of thousands of men and women of African descent came to embrace Christianity. The evangelical movement had only the most limited impact on the British West Indies before the American Revolution. It would have a profound influence thereafter, however, as Methodist and Baptist preachers, both black and white, laboured assiduously and successfully to win new converts in the British sugar colonies.[8]

These missions to the slaves aimed to improve slavery, not overthrow it. In key respects, they sought to place colonial slavery on a more secure moral footing. The clergy told the enslaved that salvation lay in Christ, not in liberation on earth. And they explained that obedience to established authorities in the household and on the plantations was God's will. A yearning for liberty, in this way of thinking, could be cast as a vice. Across the Americas, political elites enacted laws or rendered judgements during the late seventeenth and early eighteenth centuries that ruptured the customary tie between Christianity and liberty. The French government, for example, directed Catholic priests in the Caribbean to discourage wrongdoing among the slaves by threatening eternal punishment for those who committed crimes. If before, Christians could not enslave other Christians, that rule would no longer apply to those Christians who were of African descent. These rulings helped the clergy at work on the plantations to argue that Christian conversion would advance the interests of slaveholders, not subvert them. That had been the message that several Jesuit priests communicated in the late seventeenth century to recalcitrant plantation owners in Brazil. It would be the primary theme of every sermon and pamphlet published or distributed by the Society for the Propagation of the Gospel during the eighteenth century.[9]

The missionary impulse, nonetheless, met with mixed results. Catholic priests, generally, enjoyed more success than Protestant ministers, in part because of greater support from the state and in part because of a greater willingness to tolerate syncretic, if not heretic, forms of the faith. The clergy won more converts, proportionally, in colonial cities and towns than on the plantations. And the work proved slightly less difficult in settlements where slave labour did not predominate, in societies with slaves rather than slave societies. Even so, the clergy faced some degree of resistance to slave missions in most of the American colonies; only the Spanish colonies seem to have constituted an exception. That opposition arose from several concerns. Some masters worried that admitting slaves to the Christian fellowship would blur the social boundaries essential to the preservation of slavery. Some thought that too much attention to religion would distract workers and compromise profits. Most disliked the prospect of ministers meddling in plantation life. And some feared that Christianity would encourage enslaved Africans, typically of diverse ethnic backgrounds, to view themselves as a community of believers, perhaps equal to those who held them in bondage. Masters, as a consequence, typically harassed those zealous for Christian conversion, especially in those colonies where slave labour produced great wealth. Some slaveholders might tolerate the baptism of slaves. Most plantation owners thought rather less of allowing enslaved men and women regular access to Christian counsellors.[10]

The minister who worked regularly among the enslaved often developed sympathies with their needs, interests, and outlook, as slaveholders feared. Missionaries could become advocates for those to whom they preached on Sundays. Such relationships seem to have become particularly common in the French Caribbean during the eighteenth century, where some Jesuits, as the Capuchins had done before, forged close ties with the enslaved community. Jean Mogin, an especially conscientious Saint-Christophe priest, acted as an attorney for enslaved Africans victimized by sadistic slaveholders in the late seventeenth century. He represented in court a woman who had been raped by her overseer and filed charges against a slaveholder who had murdered her slaves. Such patronage, from the perspective of slaveholders, represented just one instance of the more general threat posed by missions to the slaves. By treating enslaved men and women as members of the faith, by training black catechists, holding separate worship services, and allowing for the development of a black religious leadership, the Jesuits seemed to undermine the perpetuation of social distance and racial difference upon which slavery depended.[11] Similar anxieties arose among landholders in the Chesapeake region during the evangelical revivals that commenced in the mid-eighteenth century, as black men and women attended open-air meetings with whites, sharing with them the love feasts and prayers that bound together the community of believers seeking salvation.[12]

This nascent sympathy for the enslaved and the persistent obstruction by the planters drove some missionaries to open criticism of the slaveholding elite. True Christians, these sceptics decided, would not force their workers to labour on the Sabbath. Nor would they block efforts to bring plantation life more closely in line with the ideal of Christian servitude. The slaveholders, according to these critics, had assumed a place that rightfully belonged to God. Rather than obedience to the Lord, they demanded submission to the lord of the estate. In practice, moreover, slavery too frequently left captives unable to choose virtue over vice, to live free from sin. Too often, they had neither the guidance nor the freedom to live and die as Christians. In many colonial societies, slaves were not permitted to marry. Left in spiritual darkness because of slaveholder neglect, they were allowed or even encouraged to violate the Sabbath. In this way, the institution of slavery, if not sinful in itself, had become a source of vice. It also seemed to corrupt the slave owners themselves, encouraging arrogance, pride, and cruelty, and setting the conditions that allowed for the sexual exploitation of enslaved women. More than a few missionaries in every plantation colony in the Americas decided that the slaveholders were worse heathens than their slaves. Too often these masters of women and men held religion in contempt and treated enslaved Africans like beasts of burden. This 'rustic theology', the Portuguese critic Manoel Ribeiro Rocha wrote in 1758, was 'the reverse of Christian theology'.[13] The obsession with profits had displaced the true Christian's obligation to practise charity, humility, justice, and piety. In this way, a critique of human bondage emerged from a concern with the fate of Christianity in plantation societies.

The solution, a small few concluded, lay in reforms that would improve colonial slavery. In crucial respects, these amelioration proposals, which surfaced as early as the late seventeenth century and became more common by the third quarter of the eighteenth century, represented the first attempts at humanitarian intervention. Conversion to Christianity constituted just one element of the programme. Reformers hoped to encourage marriage among slaves. And they wanted to eliminate or reduce the cruelties that made slavery distinctively inhumane. To this end, they argued for the enforcement of existing laws and called for the enactment of new legislation that would protect slaves from the worst abuses. At the same time, they hoped to interest colonial and imperial administrators in establishing more sustained oversight of the master–slave relationship in the Americas. The reform ethos seems to have had some influence on individual slaveholders in the British and Portuguese colonies in particular, as those who regarded themselves as devout or Enlightened looked for ways to practise a 'gentle' form of slavery. The political and institutional obstacles to comprehensive reform, however, could suggest the need for more radical remedies. The Reverend James Ramsay, an influential figure in the early antislavery campaigns in Britain during the 1780s, came to espouse slave trade abolition only after two decades of failing to persuade plantation owners in his St Kitts parish to endorse the conversion of slaves to Christianity.[14]

The prospects for reform owed much to the opportunities for dissent. Spanish and Portuguese officials would not permit critics of slavery to do more than call for humane treatment and Christian instruction. In the eighteenth century, this was as far as the Catholic Church was prepared to go.[15] The Church of England proved no more amenable to innovation on the question of slavery. Protestant Dissenters who lived under the far more tolerant British state, however, had the freedom to reach their own decisions regarding the customary religious justifications for human bondage. For this reason, slaveholders in the British plantation colonies, in particular, left themselves unusually vulnerable when they blocked attempts to bring slavery in line with the ideal of Christian servitude. Their resistance to Christian conversions helped certain uncompromising seekers of moral purity decide that slavery was not only unpleasant (and perhaps, therefore, justifiable on pragmatic grounds) but also a sin, and therefore a violation of divine law. This meant that slaveholding could be listed among the many other wicked habits that true Christians could and should renounce, such as gambling, cursing, intemperance, and profanation of the Sabbath. The institution of slavery could be seen not as the inevitable consequence of the sinful condition of humanity but, instead, as a voluntary and unfortunate choice of the sinner.

A willingness to renounce slavery became a test of moral purity for certain religious communities in North America during the last half of the eighteenth century. Several eccentric Quakers had already reached this decision early in the eighteenth century. They urged Quaker elders to liberate the Religious Society of Friends from the sin of holding slaves. These urgings would have little effect, though, until the traumas of the Seven Years' War, which crystallized for the Quaker elite of Pennsylvania the stark choice between worldly compromise and religious duty. The spiritual reformers within the Religious Society persuaded the influential Philadelphia Yearly Meeting in 1761 to ban Friends from purchasing slaves and later, in 1774, disown Friends who possessed slaves. This moral renewal within the Society of Friends, itself affected by George Whitfield and the Great Awakening, in turn would affect how some Baptists and Methodists thought about the institution of slavery in the era of the American Revolution. The second born, those who had passed through the experience of contrition, redemption, regeneration, and sanctification, looked for ways to demonstrate transcendence of the self. Some chose to manumit their slaves as a sign of their rebirth. To be sure, manumission as an act of piety frequently occurred elsewhere, outside of North America and without the influence of evangelicalism. Only the Protestant revivalists in the new United States, however, followed the Quaker example, albeit briefly, by advising followers to free themselves from slaveholding and promote the abolition of slavery. And only in the new American republic did acts of manumission conclude, as they did in the middle and northern United States, in the gradual but comprehensive abolition of slavery.[16]

These more aggressive stands against slavery by specific Protestant denominations during the 1780s owed much to the influence of the American Revolution. Quaker and evangelical discomfort with slavery otherwise might have concluded with attempts at reform within their own religious communities. They might have ended with individual and sectarian movements for purity, rather than attempts at societal change through government action. The politics of the American Revolution, however, made colonial slavery and the Atlantic slave trade the subject of sustained and persistent controversy for the first time anywhere in the Atlantic world. Antagonists in both Britain and North America politicized involvement in the slave system by treating it as evidence of moral corruption. The antislavery impulses long dormant in Anglo-American culture burst forth in a spasm of accusation, recrimination, and apologetics, as each side insisted, when attempting to ennoble their cause, that the other bore primary responsibility for the inhumane exploitation of Africans. This new definition of the problem as collective and public, rather than individual and private, meant that the locus of change might lie with the nation itself. The sense of crisis contributed to self-scrutiny, as well as fault-finding, as men and women on both sides of the Atlantic looked for reasons that might explain how a civil war had emerged within the British Empire.

Religious enthusiasts seized on the opportunity. For those inclined to interpret collective misfortunes as providential, it seemed that God was punishing the British Empire for its sins. More than a few commentators pointed to the enslavement of Africans, a view particularly common in New England among the Calvinist theologians of the New Divinity who declared that patriots could only expect to escape God's judgement and achieve independence if they prohibited the slave trade to America and set the enslaved free. These views acquired importance in England too, where the deeply pious antislavery pioneer Granville Sharp explained the civil war within the empire as proof of God's displeasure with both the British nation and the American colonies. Some in Britain came to agree with Sharp during the 1780s and suggested that the loss of thirteen colonies represented divine punishment for the buying and selling of African men, women and children. Only 'Acts of Benevolence and Righteousness', Reverend Gilbert Wakefield declared in 1784, could save Britain from 'the pit of Destruction, into which we have been gradually sinking'.[17]

If dependence on slavery was becoming a sign of collective vice during the 1770s, an organized attack on slavery now could be interpreted as proof of collective virtue. Some American patriots described their emergent antislavery agenda as one way to sanctify the pursuit of colonial independence. The only way to restore the affections of those patriots now in rebellion and to restore the moral authority of the British Empire, Granville Sharp argued in response, was to align imperial practice with the laws of God, a project that might begin by abolishing the Atlantic slave trade. The British abolition movement, which commenced in 1787, would acquire much of its urgency from the desire for national redemption. And this aim to rectify a shameful record held within it the hope, among British evangelicals in particular, that through abolitionism activists might restore the image of the nation, improve the reputation of Christianity, and clear a path for its advance. British abolitionists, in particular, waxed rhapsodic when contemplating the ways in which the abolition of the slave trade would enable Christian missionaries to settle on the West African coast and teach the gospel of love, fellowship and forbearance, in the place of war and avarice. The antislavery campaigns of the late eighteenth and early nineteenth centuries inspired the first sustained attempts to establish on the Upper Guinea Coast, in the new British province of Sierra Leone, a beachhead for the propagation of the faith.[18]

Through the campaign against the Atlantic slave trade, some British abolitionists hoped to make the British people better Christians. That was the possibility first anticipated by Anglican evangelicals gathered at Barham Court in Teston, Kent during the 1780s and subsequently at Clapham Common south of London. These evangelicals within the Church of England – Hannah More, William Wilberforce, James Ramsay, Charles and Margaret Middleton – had grown uncomfortable with the distaste for earnest Christianity among certain elements of polite and fashionable society. Like many of their contemporaries, they had been profoundly affected by the humiliating outcome of the American War. Unlike their peers, however, they responded by looking for ways to enhance the role of religion in private and public life. For these purposes, abolitionism looked like an ideal cause. It would not alarm those usually suspicious of moral reform movements, since the crusade against the slave trade could be understood also as a campaign for liberty, a triumph of the humanitarian sensibility, and a blow against outworn tradition. These pious and well-placed men and women did think of the slave trade as a sin, and hoped for the gradual abolition of slavery. Yet what gave the antislavery movement unusual importance to them was the opportunity to bring Christianity into politics. Slave trade abolition, accomplished with overwhelming public support in 1807 but orchestrated by Clapham Sect leadership, offered concrete proof that the British people had come to embrace in form and substance a devotion to practical Christianity. The evangelicals' crusade for the reform of British manners and morals in the early nineteenth century would be indebted to the moral capital the Clapham Sect first accrued during the campaign against the slave trade.

Antislavery commitments often took shape in the context of religious fellowship. The Society of Friends provides the best and most important example. Quakers not only set a model for Christian witness by renouncing their involvement in slavery during the third quarter of the eighteenth century. They also devised the tactics that would force the imperial and colonial governments to take up the question of slavery as a matter of government policy. The rise in antislavery pamphleteering during the last quarter of the eighteenth century depended considerably on Quaker efforts. Several opponents of slavery, the Methodist leader John Wesley most famously, took their cue from the writings of Anthony Benezet and other Friends who devised in the 1760s and 1770s a detailed case against the Atlantic slave trade. The Quakers helped guide antislavery tracts into print, subsidizing, in many instances, their publication and distribution. Perhaps most importantly, Friends organized the first antislavery societies, not only in Britain but also across the new United States from

North Carolina to Rhode Island. Quaker networks facilitated the sharing of information, ideas, and personnel and helped create the impression that the sometimes discrete initiatives constituted a movement. Friends in England represented the first petitioners and fundraisers for the cause of abolition in the 1780s. Their example would lead other denominations in Britain, particularly the Methodists and Separate Baptists, to make support for antislavery one measure of a commitment to the faith. Within the Society of Friends, this marriage was so complete that, by the last two decades of the eighteenth century, to be a Quaker was to be an abolitionist. The Methodists and Baptists, by contrast, with their desire to convert the slave-holding south and later the British West Indian colonies, found it far more difficult to require that members embrace abolitionist principles. In those regions, antislavery threatened to split the church.

Churches also provided a context in which the enslaved themselves could seek their liberty. As slaveholders feared, the conversion of enslaved men and women to Christianity had the unintended effect of producing new avenues for the pursuit of freedom. Converts sometimes made use of their admission to the Christian fellowship to assert a claim to the liberty enjoyed by other members of the faith, even though, in every instance, the clergy and the slaveholding elite denied that conversion bestowed such benefits. These expectations for social advancement could lead to unrest, as when black communicants in Virginia revolted in 1730 as a response to rumours that British instructions to free enslaved black Christians had been suppressed. Enslaved African Catholics born in the Kingdom of the Kongo, under Portuguese control, fled to Spanish territory from British and Dutch settlements in the Americas in search of religious liberty, as well as freedom itself. In part, Methodist and Baptist preachers in North America attracted more black converts than their Anglican predecessors during the last half of the eighteenth century because the promise of freedom from sin also seemed ultimately to offer the prospect of freedom from slavery. The evangelicals offered blacks new tools with which to resist their bondage. They fostered literacy among the enslaved. Some learned to write as well as to read. So it became possible to disseminate antislavery protests in a way that could circulate beyond one's immediate environs, and in the cultural idiom of the dominant society.

The first black abolitionists – Phillis Wheatley, Lemuel Haynes, Ottobah Cugoano, Olaudah Equiano, among others – were steeped in Calvinist theology. It was conventional for these writers to cast their personal salvation in terms that recommended the potential for repentance and purification for society as a whole. Their position within the faith allowed them to question whether Christians who owned slaves were Christians at all. These new students of Scripture did not find in the Bible a justification of slavery or the enslavement of Africans in particular. The mixed-race clergyman Lemuel Haynes and the African-born Ottobah Cugoano in London denied that blacks bore the Mark of Cain or suffered from the Curse of Ham. (Cugoano, indeed, thought that the Canaanites perhaps had come to settle in the Americas as West Indian slaveholders.) These writers instead called for a shift in emphasis in the definition of Christian ethics. They found in the Bible the principle of justice and charity, not a sacred basis for servitude and oppression. They found an avenging God who humbled the great and raised the meek. 'How hateful slavery is in the sight of God', wrote the black Methodist preachers Richard Allen and Absalom Jones in 1794, 'who hath destroyed King and Princes for the oppression of slaves'. Following the lead of both Quakers and the Calvinist theologians of the New Divinity, this first generation of black abolitionists insisted that religious purity and the laws of God must take precedence over the laws of man.[19]

The abolition of slavery in the northern and middle United States in the years after the American Revolution made possible the establishment of the first independent black churches. Absalom Jones and Richard Allen would be responsible in 1816 for the founding of the African Methodist Episcopal Church in Philadelphia, the first independent black church in the Americas. Their work occurred simultaneously with an extraordinary growth of black Baptist congregations across the English-speaking world, in Nova Scotia, the Chesapeake, Georgia and the Carolinas, and in Jamaica. These new congregations were led by black preachers who brought the evangelical revival to tens of thousands of black men and women, free and slave alike. They promoted communal and cultural autonomy. In the middle and northern United States they also emerged as institutional bases for the promotion of abolitionism. Religious leaders in these churches came forward as an incipient leadership class, positioned to speak for and speak to the great many black men and women who lacked a public voice. It was in the black churches, historian Richard Newman has argued, that the case for immediate emancipation was sustained in the United States between 1790 and 1830, as the enthusiasm for abolitionism subsided after the revolutionary era, and after the abolition of the US slave trade in 1807, a decision that owed more to a collective assessment of social and economic interests than to a commitment to revolutionary principles or religious ideals.[20]

As centres of community life, the churches also helped foster a sense of nationhood among newly freed slaves. They helped black men and women see their personal and collective history in the context of sacred history. Evangelicalism, with its emphasis on spiritual death, purification, and rebirth seemed to describe particularly well the torturous journey of Africans in the Americas from enslavement, violent passage, captivity, and, perhaps, liberation. This legacy suggested that God had a special purpose for black people in the Americas. Black preachers across the United States characterized Americans of African descent as God's chosen people, now suffering under the bondage of 'Our Modern Egyptians', as Phillis Wheatley famously suggested, but destined for redemption, salvation, and freedom through God's saving grace. Unlike the Puritan settlers, blacks could not think of themselves as entering a new Eden. Instead, they were arising like Lazarus, from deprivation and despair to reclaim their rightful heritage. In this interpretive framework, what lay ahead for men and women of African descent was a new Exodus, an escape from bondage, the day of jubilee when all wrongs would be redressed and blacks, as latter day Hebrews, would enjoy divine protection. This was the radical potential invoked by black ministers from the pulpit in the last years of the British and American slave trades. It was not unusual for these same preachers to see the new Zion in West Africa, where black Americans, the descendants of African heathens, would return to bring civilization and the gospel.[21]

The Africanization of Catholicism also figured in the Haitian Revolution, the most radical of the antislavery movements of the late eighteenth and early nineteenth centuries. In Saint Domingue, as elsewhere in the French Caribbean, Jesuit missionaries had experienced some success in converting enslaved Africans to Christianity, though always under the watchful eye of the planter class. In this respect, the history of Christianity in Saint Domingue differed little from the history of Christianity in other plantation colonies in the West Indies or South America. It would seem, however, that the expulsion of the Jesuits from San Domingue in 1763 expedited the development of a highly unorthodox version of Catholicism, deeply inflected by African rituals, beliefs, and cosmologies, that helped provide enslaved men and women with a common framework in which to understand their condition and themselves. This absorption of Catholic iconography into Vodun rites may explain why leaders of the uprising appropriated and manipulated Christian symbolism to impress and inspire their followers. The rebel leader Romaine Rivière, to give just one example, declared himself a prophet in the summer of 1791 and established a camp in an abandoned church where he claimed to enjoy 'direct communication with the Virgin Mary'. In this way, black political leaders invoked and appropriated the spiritual and moral authority of Catholic saints to enhance the legitimacy of rebellion and revolution. Across Saint Domingue, the insurgents presented themselves as defending church and king in the first years of the uprising. Their subsequent alliance with the Jacobin government of revolutionary France, which authorized a comprehensive emancipation of slaves in the French colonies in 1794, had little impact on the popular Catholicism that remained an animating force in the revolution. The founders of Haiti at independence in 1804 and after made a point to contrast the embrace of Catholicism in this the second free republic in the Americas with the godlessness of Napoleonic France which restored slavery and the Atlantic slave trade in 1802.[22]

Such contrasts between a pious attack on slavery and its impious defence mark a profound transformation in Christian attitudes towards human bondage. In the age of revolution, several of the most dynamic religious movements in Christendom were beginning to regard the venerable proslavery tradition in Christian thought as an embarrassment, an affront to true faith. The exponents of this new perspective denounced those who would invoke Scripture to justify inhumanity. Anglo-American Protestantism during the late eighteenth century tended to square itself with the Enlightenment faith in moral progress, but to reinterpret beneficial change as the workings of divine providence. The decision of Napoleonic France to restore slavery in 1802 seemed to show one consequence of valuing too highly the dictates of utility and reason. 'For Britons, at least', as the historian David Brion Davis has written, 'the long struggle with "infidel France" reinforced the conviction that Christianity, if unadulterated and wedded to free institutions, would inevitably promote the moral and material progress of every human race'.[23] Revealed religion could achieve for humanity what the new science of man, with its preoccupation with human difference, would not: the individual and collective commitment to the salvation and dignity of mankind.

In most respects, the British critique of the Catholic powers was correct. Antislavery movements failed to develop in the Spanish and Portuguese empires during the long eighteenth century. The more pervasive antislavery sentiment in France produced only a short-lived antislavery movement, and then only among those bourgeois reformers conspicuously sympathetic to the British campaigns and sceptical of the religious authority of the Catholic Church. Abbé Henri Grégoire, a consistent opponent of slavery and racial prejudice, was the exception who proved the rule. Grégoire hoped that Haitian independence would contribute to the spiritual regeneration of the church and invest it with a new sense of purpose. He looked forward to the formation of an indigenous clergy who would promote Christianity in Haiti and beyond. Grégoire was, however, a singular figure, and his comfortable position within the regime allowed him to escape, for a time, the official suppression of anti-slavery publications in Napoleonic France after 1802. Then, before, and after, abolitionism would not flourish in societies ruled by absolutist states.

In crucial ways, however, the achievements of Anglo-American Protestantism were the product of its failures. No set of colonial settlements proved more impervious to the Christian conversion of enslaved Africans than the plantation societies of the British Empire. The attention elsewhere to what the historian Frank Tannenbaum once called the 'moral personality' of the slave, however imperfect and incomplete, had helped sustain the view that human bondage could be reconciled to the ideal of Christian servitude.[24] British colonists neglected the 'moral personality' of the enslaved almost completely until the very end of the eighteenth century. They made little effort to cast slavery as consistent with Christian practice. That choice left them highly vulnerable to evangelicals who called for a return to earnest Christianity and the promotion of moral purity.

Notes

1. Thomas Clarkson, *The history of the rise, progress and accomplishment of abolition of the African slave trade by the British Parliament*, 2 vols. (London: Longmans, 1808), vol. 2, pp. 8, 11.

2. Dauril Alden, *The making of an enterprise: The Society of Jesus in Portugal, its empire, and beyond, 1540–1770* (Palo Alto, CA: Standford University Press, 1996), p. 525.

3. David Brion Davis, *The problem of slavery in western culture* (New York: Oxford University Press, 1988), pp. 62–121; Robin Blackburn, *The making of New World slavery: From the Baroque to the modern, 1492–1800* (London: Verso, 1997), pp. 42–4, 64–76; Larry E. Tise, *Proslavery: A history of the defense of slavery in America* (Athens, GA: University of Georgia Press, 1987).

4. Davis, *Problem of slavery in western culture*, pp. 187–92; Boxer, *The church militant and Iberian expansion, 1440–1770* (Baltimore: The Johns Hopkins University Press, 1978), pp. 32–4; Blackburn, *The making of New World slavery*, pp. 120–1, 150–6.

5. Richard Gray, 'The papacy and the Atlantic slave trade: Lourenco da Silva, the Capuchins and the decisions of the Holy Office', *Past and present*, 115 (1987), p. 58.

6. Davis, *Problem of slavery in western culture*, pp. 144–50, 291–348, 472–82; Wylie Sypher, *Guinea's captive kings: British anti-slavery literature of the XVIIIth century* (Chapel Hill: University of North Carolina Press, 1942); Thomas E. Drake, *Quakers and slavery in America* (New Haven: Yale University Press, 1950).

7. Robert Edgar Conrad, *Children of God's fire: A documentary history of black slavery in Brazil* (Princeton: Princeton University Press, 1983), p. 60; Sylvia Frey and Betty Wood, *Come shouting to Zion: African American Protestantism in the American south and British Caribbean to 1830* (Chapel Hill: University of North Carolina Press, 1998), pp. 63–79; Sue Peabody, '"A dangerous zeal": Catholic missions to slaves in the French Antilles, 1635–1800', *French historical studies*, 25 (2002), pp. 69–70.

8. Frey and Wood, *Come shouting to Zion*, pp. 80–148.

9. Carolyn Fick, *The making of Haiti: The Saint Domingue revolution from below* (Knoxville: University of Tennessee Press, 1990), p. 65; Davis, *Problem of slavery in western culture*, pp. 203–11; Conrad, *Children of God's fire*, pp. 163–74.

10. James H. Sweet, *Recreating Africa: Culture, kinship, and religion in the African-Portuguese world, 1441–1770* (Chapel Hill: University of North Carolina Press, 2003), pp. 200–01; Laennec Hurbon, 'The church and slavery in eighteenth-century Saint Domingue', in Marcel Dorigny (ed.), *The abolitions of slavery from L. F. Sonthonax to Victor Schoelcher, 1793, 1794, 1848* (New York: Berghahn Books, 2003), pp. 58–61; Thomas Ingersoll, *Mammon and Manon in early New Orleans: The first slave society in the Deep South, 1718–1819* (Knoxville: University of Tennessee Press, 1999), pp. 111–12; Marcus Jernegan, 'Slavery and conversion in the American colonies', *American historical review*, 21 (1916), pp. 504–27.

11. Peabody, 'A dangerous zeal', pp. 67, 81–2.

12. Frey and Wood, *Come shouting to Zion*, pp. 80–117.

13. Conrad, *Children of God's fire*, p. 294.

14. Christopher L. Brown, 'Empire without slaves: British concepts of emancipation in the age of the American Revolution', *William and Mary quarterly*, 3rd ser., 56 (1999), pp. 298–303.

15. J. M. Lenhart, 'Capuchin champions of Negro emancipation in Cuba, 1681–1685', *Franciscan studies*, 6 (1946), pp. 209–10; Eugene Genovese, *Roll Jordan roll: The world the slaves made* (New York: Vintage, 1976), pp. 177–9; Colin M. Maclachlan, 'Slavery, ideology, and institutional change: The impact of the Enlightenment on slavery in late eighteenth-century Maranhao', *Journal of Latin American studies*, 11 (1979), pp. 14–15.

16. Sydney V. James, *A people among peoples: Quaker benevolence in eighteenth-century America* (Cambridge, MA: Harvard University Press, 1963); James D. Essig, *The bonds of wickedness: American Evangelicals against slavery, 1770–1808* (Philadelphia: Temple University Press, 1982).

17. David Brion Davis, *The problem of slavery in the age of revolution, 1770–1823* (Ithaca: Cornell University Press, 1975), pp. 285–99, 392–8; Gilbert Wakefield, *A sermon preached at Richmond in Surry on July 29th, 1784, the day appointed for a general thanksgiving on account of the peace* (London, 1784), p. 16.

18. Linda Colley, *Britons: Forging the nation, 1707–1837* (London: Pimlico, 1992), pp. 350–60; Stiv Jakobbson, *Am I not a man and a brother? British missions and the abolition of the slave trade and slavery in West Africa and the West Indies, 1786–1838* (Lund: Gleerup, 1972).

19. Davis, *Problem of slavery in the age of revolution*, pp. 196–8, 213–32; Judith Jennings, *The business of abolishing the slave trade, 1783–1807* (London: Frank Cass, 1997).

20. Anthony Parent, *Foul means: The formation of a slave society in Virginia, 1660–1740* (Chapel Hill: University of North Carolina Press, 2003), pp. 259–60; John K. Thornton, 'African dimensions of the Stono rebellion', *American historical review*, 96 (1991), pp. 1103, 1107–1108; Armando Lampe, 'Christianity and slavery in the Dutch Caribbean', in Lampe (ed.), *Christianity in the Caribbean: Essays on church history* (Barbardos: University of the West Indies Press, 2001), p. 142.

21. Adam Potkay and Sandra Burr (eds.), *Black Atlantic writers of the 18th century* (Basingstoke: Macmillan, 1995), pp. 3–16; John Saillant, 'Slavery and Divine Providence in New England Calvinism: The New Divinity and black protest', *New England quarterly*, 8 (1995),

pp. 584–608; Keith A. Sandiford, *Measuring the moment: Strategies of protest in eighteenth-century Afro-English writing* (Selinsgrove: Susquehanna University Press, 1988), pp. 100–01; Absalom Jones and Richard Allen cited in Richard S. Newman, *The transformation of American abolitionism: Fighting slavery in the early republic* (Chapel Hill: University of North Carolina Press, 2002), p. 95.

22. Peabody, 'A dangerous zeal', pp. 85–7; John K. Thornton, '"I serve the King of Congo": African political ideology and the Haitian revolution', *Journal of world history*, 4 (1993), pp. 187–99; Hein Vanhee, 'Central African popular Christianity and the making of the Haitian Vodou religion', and Terry Rey, 'Kongolese Catholic influences on Haitian popular Catholicism: A sociohistorical explanation', both in Linda Heywood (ed.), *Central Africans and cultural transformations in the African diaspora* (Cambridge: Cambridge University Press, 2002), pp. 243–64, 265–85.

23. David Brion Davis, *Slavery and human progress* (New York: Oxford University Press, 1984), p. 133.

24. Frank Tannenbaum, *Slave and citizen: The Negro in the Americas* (New York: Vintage Books, 1946) p. 98.

27

The French Revolution and religion
to 1794

TIMOTHY TACKETT

In its impact on France and on Europe, the French Revolution stands as one
of the pivotal moments in the recent history of Christianity. It led not only to
a decade-long schism within the Catholic Church, but also, for a time, to a
state-sponsored assault on Christianity itself unlike anything in the European
experience since the early Roman Empire. In its later stages it produced the
first full separation of church and state in modern times. Although some of
these conflicts were attenuated under the Napoleonic regime, the memory of
the Revolution continued to exercise a powerful influence on anticlerical and
antireligious movements and on the church itself well into the nineteenth and
twentieth centuries.

Religion in France on the eve of the Revolution

The strength of religion and the church in France on the eve of the Revolution
has been much debated by specialists in the field. For Michel Vovelle and a
number of French historians, the Catholic Church was already in full decline
at the end of the *ancien régime* and the term 'de-Christianization' might well
be used for describing certain trends among the laity. In the view of John
McManners, by contrast, the period constituted a 'golden age of the French
Church'. 'Never', he argues, 'had there been . . . so many laymen living lives
of well-informed belief and pious practice'.[1] In fact, as we shall argue here,
there are elements of truth in both interpretations, depending on the period,
the region, and the social group under consideration.

The overwhelming majority of the French population in 1789 – some 28
million souls – had been baptized in the Roman Catholic Church. Though it
had been seriously challenged during the Wars of Religion, Catholicism had
made a remarkable recovery in the seventeenth century, and by the end of the
ancien régime it totally dominated the French religious landscape, with tens of
thousands of churches, chapels, monasteries, convents, schools, and hospitals

in every corner of the kingdom. Only three religious minorities maintained a significant presence in certain provinces. Some half a million Calvinists or 'Huguenots' were concentrated primarily in a crescent of territory around the southern rim of the Massif-Central, where they had struggled to maintain their faith and their identity since the Revocation of the Edict of Nantes in 1685. Though the royal government had ceased active repression of the Calvinists and though the edict of 1787 had given formal recognition to their births and marriages, they were still legally forbidden to practise their religion or to hold most positions of political or social importance. By contrast, the 200,000 French Lutherans, almost all of them living in Alsace, were protected from most discrimination by the Treaty of Westphalia. They maintained an influential presence in the provinces, notably in the city of Strasbourg. In addition to the Protestants, France held a small Jewish population of perhaps 50,000 people. The majority were Ashkenazim, dwelling predominantly in the rural areas of Alsace and Lorraine, tenaciously clinging to their traditional customs and clothing in a regime that excluded them even from landholding. The remainder were Sephardim, descendants of refugees from Spain and Portugal, living in largely assimilated urban communities in Bordeaux, Bayonne, and Avignon.

Compared to the marginal existence of Calvinist pastors and Jewish rabbis, the French Catholic clergy was among the most powerful corporate bodies in the kingdom. In 1789 it included some 170,000 individuals – regular and secular, masculine and feminine – just over one half of one per cent of the total population. Yet the numerical and economic strength of that body varied significantly from one region to another. In general, the clergy was substantially more numerous in the cities than in the countryside, but it also maintained a significant rural presence in large portions of northern, north-eastern, and western France, where the parish priest or 'curé' might live in company with an assistant priest (*vicaire*) and in proximity to various communities of regulars or seculars. By contrast, in many areas of the Parisian Basin and central and southern France, a solitary *curé* was commonly the only priest encountered by the inhabitants in their day-to-day lives. Ecclesiastical wealth – from land-holdings, tithing rights, and seigniorial dues – also differed substantially from region to region. In much of northern France, especially between Paris and the Austrian Lowlands, clerical lands might constitute 20 to 40 per cent of the territory. Though most of this wealth was controlled by regulars, bishops, and canons, a significant amount was shared with the parish clergy, so that many *curés* lived like local squires with impressive rectories and glebe lands. In much of southern and especially south-eastern France, however, the far more meagre ecclesiastical possessions were monopolized by the upper and regular clergies, leaving the majority of parish priests with only a fixed salary – the so-called *portion congrue* – that was badly eroded by inflation in the second half of the century.

In addition to its economic and social influence, the French clergy still wielded significant political power. Even at the end of the *ancien régime* and at the beginning of the Revolution, individual bishops continued to hold major ministerial positions in the royal government. Moreover, since the sixteenth century the Gallican church had developed one of the most powerful bureaucracies in the country. A General Assembly of the Clergy met at regular intervals to vote 'free gifts' of money to the crown, while two 'agents-general' and a permanent staff of assistants jealously guarded the clergy's tax privileges and other prerogatives. By threatening to lower or withdraw its contributions, the clergy might substantially influence specific decisions of the crown.

Among both the clergy and the laity, Catholicism remained vital and active in France to the very eve of the Revolution. Indeed, it might be argued that the Catholic Reformation, long hampered by wars and problems of finance, reached a pinnacle of success in the kingdom only in the mid-eighteenth century. By the early decades of that century every French diocese had a designated seminary – usually within the diocese itself – for the training of its parish clergy. The priests formed by such institutions were arguably better educated and prepared for pastoral care than ever before. Intellectual and moral standards were reinforced by regular conferences and retreats for clergymen, and by periodic pastoral visits by the bishops or their representatives. The bishops themselves were for the most part responsible administrators, leading morally acceptable lives. However, in 1789 all, without exception, were aristocrats, and many held themselves at a substantial social and pastoral distance from the commoner parish clergy – especially by comparison with their episcopal predecessors of the seventeenth century. Their greatest failing was perhaps their non-residence, with many dwelling in Paris or on family estates for substantial periods of time and administering their dioceses through their vicars-general.

As for the lay population, the overwhelming majority of the popular classes closely identified with a Catholic religion which continued to frame the central moments of their lives and their work. In rural areas, where over 80 per cent of the population lived, there was near universal participation in catechism and the 'Easter duties' of confession and communion during Lent. Equally impressive was the huge output of religious books of all kinds, published to the very end of the *ancien régime*, especially by presses outside Paris. Whatever the importance of secular books in the French capital, the great bestsellers of the age for France as a whole were undoubtedly the cheap lives of saints, books of hours, devotional works, and simple spiritual guides produced in publishing centres like Nancy, Rouen, Caen, and Toulouse. At least to 1750, the number of families sending sons and daughters into the clergy also remained high, with overall recruitment at that time probably unequalled since the sixteenth century. In certain regions of the kingdom – notably in the western provinces of Brittany and Poitou – Catholic revival missions seem to have been met with particular enthusiasm. And in Alsace and Lorraine, Marian and other devotional confraternities are known to have been vital and active to the very eve of the Revolution.

Yet whatever the continuities of faith and practice among the rural masses, the religious culture of many elements of the urban elites seems to have experienced a clear transformation after mid-century. Beginning in the 1750s or 1760s, a sharp decline in clerical recruitment of both seculars and regulars seems primarily to have affected families of town notables. A remarkably similar chronology was registered in the 'secularization' of wills in certain regions of France, as men, in particular, reduced or eliminated the religious invocations to such wills and donated far less money for requiem Masses and church charities. At almost the same period the library holdings of many elite families revealed a significant shift in reading interests from religious and theological books to works on a wide range of secular subjects, some of them authored by the better-known anticlerical writers of the age. Finally, we should not overlook the veritable explosion of new freemason lodges in the second half of the century. Although most masons were probably not overtly anticlerical or deist, and though the majority claimed an attachment to Christianity and even engaged chaplains for their lodges, the masonic experience nevertheless helped reinforce a more secular culture and style of ethical thinking.

The meaning and origins of this apparent shift in religious sensibilities have been much debated by historians. Some writers argue, for example, that transformations in the language of wills reflect changes in the quality but not the intensity of faith, a trend towards an internalization or privatization of religious belief.[2] Yet the concurrence of so many independent indicators strongly suggests a more fundamental cultural evolution, particularly among the urban professional classes. Though the term 'de-Christianization' is perhaps too strong to describe such trends, it seems likely that anticlericalism and laxity in religious practice were on the increase among the elites and may even have effected certain elements of the Parisian working class.

Indeed, in the period after mid-century there were at least four major sources of intensifying attacks against the Catholic clergy, two originating primarily outside the church and two primarily from within. The most visible of such attacks, at least in the eyes of later generations, emerged from the writings of the French *philosophes*. It would seem more than a coincidence that many of the most important and influential publications of the French Enlightenment appeared precisely during the same critical period of the 1750s and 1760s when clerical recruitment and religious references in wills were undergoing sharp declines. Such writings were complex and often contradictory in their positions on a whole range of questions, yet attacks on the clergy and on revealed religion – far more intense in France than in any other region of Europe – were arguably among the single most important common denominators. But historians have given much less attention to the broad attacks against the rights and privileges of the clergy pursued by the magistrates of the various French *parlements* or sovereign courts during much the same period. Strongly imbued with an ideology of 'parliamentary Gallicanism' that claimed sweeping powers for the courts over church affairs, the royal magistrates readily intervened in issues as diverse as ecclesiastical benefices, church lands, tithing rights, clerical salaries, and even the dispensing of sacraments. Thus, the courts strongly encouraged a veritable 'revolt against the tithes' on the part of rural inhabitants in many parts of the kingdom and played a central role in the expulsion of the Jesuits from France. The magistrates' anticlerical positions in many of their decisions were all the more influential in that they were given wide publicity through published judicial briefs known as *mémoires judiciaires*.

Two other sources of late eighteenth-century attacks against elements of the clergy arose essentially from within the church itself. First, the period was marked by a particularly intense stage in the long-standing Jansenist–Jesuit struggle, a struggle that generated at least as much anti-papal and anticlerical rhetoric from the pens of writers as did the Enlightenment. The defeat and ultimate suppression of the Society of Jesus in the mid-1760s – part of an international assault on the order – was led in France by groups of Jansenists, strongly supported by the Gallican *parlements*. The destruction of the Jesuits set the precedent for a major investigation and reordering of all religious clergy in France – by a royal Commission on Regulars beginning in 1768. It led also to a significant restructuring of French secondary education, previously dominated by the Jesuits, and perhaps to a decline in the importance of religious instruction in the curriculum. Second, there was a growing antagonism between many French *curés* and the upper and regular clergy over the unjust division of the church's wealth. Some *curé* activists drew on a French version of the 'Christian Enlightenment', emphasizing the 'utility' of the *curés* in promoting the 'happiness' and economic improvement of their parishioners – as well as their salvation – and castigating the 'useless' non-resident tithe-owning clergy, the canons, monks, and other clergymen, who were parasites on the resources of the parish. On the eve of the Revolution, numerous pamphlets were published by *curés* who identified their own struggle for justice against an aristocratic upper clergy with the struggle of French commoners in general.

Yet not all French elites were won over by these anticlerical attacks. It is important not to underestimate the importance of the vigorous French Catholic 'counter-Enlightenment' in the last decades of the *ancien régime* that was explicitly pro-clerical in its conception.[3] In numerous books, reviews, pamphlets, and essays, authors such as Stanislaus Fréron and abbé Barruel, a former Jesuit, argued the dangers for religion, morality, and monarchy of the 'godless philosophy' of the age. Many were convinced of the existence of an invidious conspiracy between the Enlightenment and the Protestants to destroy the Catholic Church. They were thus particularly outraged by the 'Edict of Toleration' of 1787. These 'counter-revolutionaries' before the Revolution promoted a church and a society structured on the basis of hierarchy, authority, and tradition rather than on reason and utility.

Religious transformations in the early Revolution, 1789–1791

It is impossible here to explore the complex question of the origins of the French Revolution. Dale Van Kley has made a compelling case that religious debates themselves, and above all the writings of Jansenists, were of central importance in 'desacralizing' the monarchy and thus delegitimizing the *ancien régime*. Other historians have argued that any such desacralization was far less profound in its impact than Van Kley contends; and that insofar as it did exist, it was a much longer-term phenomenon, by no means specific to the late eighteenth century.[4] In any case, the grave fiscal crisis of the 1780s that placed the French state on the brink of bankruptcy (engendered in large measure by France's involvement in the American Revolution) and the failure of leadership by King Louis XVI were probably far more important in initiating the events of 1789 than the impact of religion or ideology.

When the deputies to the Estates General arrived in Versailles in May of that year, summoned by the king to advise him on the crisis, few of them anticipated the sweeping transformations of the French clergy which would soon be instituted. To be sure, on the basis of their pre-revolutionary writings and personal correspondence, a number of the commoner deputies of the 'Third Estate' appear to have held strongly anticlerical sentiments and personal beliefs close to deism. Yet, as many of the eighteenth-century philosophical writers, such deputies clearly held to a double standard on religion: whatever their personal views towards the Christian faith, they were convinced it was 'useful' for social cohesion and stability among the masses. Moreover, the *cahiers de doléances* or 'statements of grievances' which they brought with them to Versailles and which had been largely drafted by urban elites like themselves, generally demanded only moderate reforms of ecclesiastical abuses, and gave no indication of a desire for massive transformations and suppressions within the clergy. While the deputies' views on religion were invariably influenced by Jansenism, Gallicanism, and the Enlightenment, the actual policies they developed arose primarily out of the unanticipated contingencies of the revolutionary process itself, evolving in stages over a period of months and years.

In the earliest stages of the Revolution, the 200-odd deputies from the parish clergy played a key role in events. The decision by the majority of *curés* in mid-June to break with their bishops and to sit and vote jointly with the commoner deputies was of fundamental importance in the transformation of the Estates into a National Assembly. But the critical turning point for the future of the clergy, as for most of the institutions of the *ancien régime*, was the extraordinary series of decrees passed on the night of 4 August 1789. Through a curious mixture of fear, altruism, and group psychology, the plan of a small minority to move the suppression of some seigniorial rights produced a wave of wholesale denunciations of much of the political and social complex of pre-revolutionary France. More than any other single event, the achievements of 4 August led to the assumption that almost anything was possible, initiating a process by which virtually all previously accepted institutions and values were put into question.

The night of 4 August was particularly important for the clergy in that it brought the total suppression both of the tithes and of the seigniorial rights controlled by the church. Two days later a deputy proposed that the state also take control of the church's landholdings, the third major source of ecclesiastical revenues. But the majority was initially opposed to such a measure, and it was only in early November, as the Revolution found itself facing the same impending bankruptcy that had destroyed the *ancien régime*, that a majority of moderates could be convinced to put church property 'at the disposal of the nation'. And it was yet another five months before the Assembly agreed that virtually all clerical landholdings would be confiscated and sold for the benefit of the nation. Without a doubt it was the impending fiscal disaster and not hostility towards religion that convinced a majority of the Assembly to nationalize church lands.

The suppression of the regular clergy likewise took place in stages, over much the same period. The monastic orders had long suffered from a poor image in public opinion, but their suppression at this point in time was partly conceived to facilitate the rapid seizure of monastic property. Religious vows were suspended in late October 1789 and most regular orders – with the exception of congregations directly involved in teaching or in various social services – were dissolved the following February. Though provisions were made for individuals who wished to live out their lives in a conventual setting, a large number of male religious – though far fewer women – now left their convents, some returning to their families, others moving into the secular clergy.

The most contentious issue concerning the church during the first year of the Assembly's existence may well have been the status of Protestants and Jews. The proposal that freedom of religion be included in the 'rights of man and the citizen' aroused a great storm of protest among conservatives in late August 1789. The compromise wording, that 'No one should be troubled because of their opinions, even religious, provided that the expression of those opinions does not disturb public order', pleased no one and seemed to leave open the possibility of administrative or judicial restrictions on religious freedom. Only on Christmas Eve 1789, after several weeks of careful preparation and persuasion by the liberal 'left' side of the Assembly, were full political and civil rights granted to Protestants. Similar rights were given to Sephardic Jews one month later and to the generally less assimilated Ashkenazim in September 1791, shortly before the Assembly was dissolved. Although the Catholic Church remained established in theory to 1795, the sole denomination supported by the revolutionary state, all careers and political participation were now opened to Protestants and Jews alike. The decrees thus marked a signal moment in the history of toleration in France and in Europe.

But such provisions left the conservatives in the Assembly more fearful than ever of the status of the Catholic Church in the new revolutionary regime. On three successive occasions motions to declare Catholicism the official 'state religion' went down to defeat. The third of these motions, by the Carthusian monk Dom Gerle on 12 April 1790, led to what was perhaps the single most impassioned and divisive debate since the beginning of the Revolution. When the motion was finally rejected, on a very close vote, a whole segment of the deputies convinced themselves that the left was attempting to 'destroy religion'. The nationwide campaign which the 'right' now launched in opposition to the Assembly's religious polices was one of the earliest steps in the development of an organized counter-revolution.

In any case, the proclamations of toleration and civil rights for Protestants and Jews did not necessarily mean the acceptance of such principles by the general population. Alsace and Lorraine would experience waves of popular anti-Semitism throughout the revolutionary period, encouraged on occasion by elements of the elites. And in the wake of the Dom Gerle affair, the southern towns of Montauban and Nîmes were torn by episodes of sectarian violence leading to the deaths of several hundred people – both incidents intensified by social tensions between Catholic workers and wealthy Calvinist merchants and manufacturers. Throughout large areas of southern France, Catholic populations now came to view the Revolution as a 'Protestant attack' against their faith.

In the meantime, a combination of circumstances was pushing the majority of the National Assembly towards a reorganization of the Catholic clergy far more sweeping than most of its members would ever have imagined just one year earlier. With the church's loss of the three pillars of its independent endowment – landed property, tithes, and seigniorial dues – and with the state's commitment to assume the financial support of the clergy, ecclesiastics were converted into a corps of 'civil servants', whose status was to be governed in part by the logic of efficient budgetary management. Yet the views of the majority in the Assembly were also coloured by political hostility towards an alignment of bishops and conservative Catholics who were increasingly associated with opposition to the whole Revolution. It was in a mood of anger and frustration with such opposition, combined with a desire for fiscal restraint, that the majority adopted the 'Civil Constitution of the Clergy' on 12 July 1790.

The package of legislation reforms, assembled in the Ecclesiastical Committee by a small group of Gallican lawyers and Jansenist sympathizers, was by almost any standard extraordinarily radical. In an effort to impose a more rational administration, the 135 dioceses of *ancien régime* France were reduced to 83, designed to coincide with the new civil administrative 'departments'. The posts of cathedral and collegiate canons, of chaplains, and of virtually all those holding positions without cure of souls were eliminated, and the thousands of clergymen who held such positions were retired with modest pensions – joining the ranks of the regular clergy and the bishops who had lost their dioceses. Episcopal revenues were also vastly diminished, while the revenues of the parish priests were standardized, bringing higher incomes for some and lower for others, depending on the amount they had received under the *ancien régime*. In the future, moreover, all new bishops and parish priests would be chosen by the same lay electoral assemblies which selected local administrators – assemblies which might even include Protestants or free thinkers, as long as such individuals were willing to attend a preliminary Mass. No confirmation of new bishops would be asked of the pope. Rome would simply be notified of the election in the name of 'the unity of the faith'.

In November 1790, the vast majority of the *ancien régime* bishops accepted an *Exposition of principles*, penned by the Archbishop of Aix, objecting to many elements of the Civil Constitution, but agreeing to cooperate temporarily while they awaited a decision from the pope. Yet some individual bishops were far less accommodating, issuing statements opposing the sale of church property or the suppression of their dioceses. On 27 November, in an atmosphere of growing impatience, the National Assembly took the fateful step of imposing a clerical oath of allegiance to the new Constitution. In the minds of the deputies, the oath was directed primarily against the bishops, viewed as the principal source of opposition. Almost as an afterthought, it was also required of parish clergymen and ecclesiastics who were serving as teachers. Anyone who refused to swear the oath would be stripped of his position.

At the end of December, after much soul-searching, the king formally sanctioned the oath legislation. During the next three months, tens of thousands of priests in cathedrals and parish churches in every corner of the kingdom were required to stand before their congregations following Sunday Mass and affirm their solemn, religious acquiescence to the Constitution in the precise words specified by the Assembly. To no one's surprise, virtually all of the bishops refused to comply. Only four diocesan prelates – along with two coadjutors – out of the eighty-three formally held to the oath ultimately accepted it. Far more unexpected and disconcerting were the results registered among the parish clergy. The vast majority were probably eager to show their acceptance of the Revolution in general, and almost all were willing to take some form of oath. But some 48 per cent of a total of 51,000 *curés* and *vicaires* insisted on amending various kinds of restrictions, typically specifying that their allegiance to the state could not extend to spiritual matters. According to the amended oath legislation, such restrictions were judged unacceptable and the priests in question would be forced to leave their posts.

The proportion of oath-takers varied enormously from region to region, with individual districts ranging from 100 per cent compliance to total rejection. The reasons for this regional diversity were complex. In some of the strongly 'constitutional' areas (Dauphiné, Provence, portions of the Pyrenees) the parish clergy had been particularly disinherited from the wealth of the *ancien régime* church. Long-standing patterns of organized opposition to the episcopacy over economic and ecclesiological issues made a break in 1791 relatively easy. Most of the strongest oath-taking zones (including the expanded Parisian Basin and much of central France, as well as the previously mentioned regions) were also areas in which the clergy was relatively sparse and where solitary *curés*, with only limited links to an ecclesiastical society, tended to identify much more fully with the lay society in which they lived. Most of the predominantly 'refractory' regions had much denser concentrations of ecclesiastics – a reality that may also explain the high rejection rate in most of the large towns. Several of the refractory regions (like Franche-Comté, Roussillon, and the provinces touching the Austrian Netherlands) were in frontier zones that had entered relatively late into the French realm and had retained a stronger ultramontane tradition from their long years under the Spanish Habsburgs. In Languedoc, as we have seen, the substantial Protestant presence pushed many people to identify the Civil Constitution itself with Protestantism and an attack on their Catholic faith. Many non-juring regions in western France (such as Brittany, Anjou, and parts of Poitou) had been the terrain of particularly vigorous and successful missionary activity in the eighteenth century, activities which may have oriented both clergy and laity towards a more traditional clerical and ultramontane view of Catholicism. Indeed, almost everywhere laypeople exerted pressure on the clergy to accept or reject the oath, with the oath ceremony providing the occasion for a *de facto* referendum on the general religious and secular policies of the Revolution.

Yet it is also evident from oath speeches preserved for individual priests that the jurors and non-jurors tended to favour two very different images of the priesthood itself. Many constitutionals placed an emphasis on the 'citizen priest', the servant of local society, with particular responsibilities as a cultural intermediary and a tutor for the economic and political life of the community. The reforms, they argued, had in no way touched the fundamental theological and spiritual aspects of religion, but were only concerned with reforming abuses in ecclesiastical organization and returning to the traditions of the early church. Refractories, on the contrary, viewed the National Assembly's decrees instituting the lay election of bishops and reorganizing the dioceses without the consent of the church as a transgression into spiritual matters over which the state had no authority. They tended rather to embrace a more traditional Tridentine conception of the priest as primarily a man of God, tightly linked to the lines of hierarchy and authority within the Roman Church.

Only in April and May 1791, after the clergy had already been compelled to take a stance, was the opinion of Pope Pius VI finally made public in France. Influenced in part by the French ambassador to Rome, a holdover from the *ancien régime* who had never been replaced, the pope issued two briefs which condemned virtually all aspects of the revolutionary transformation of the church as 'heretical and schismatic' and comparable to the policies of Wycliffe and Luther. At the same time he attacked many of the founding principles of the Revolution itself, notably the concepts of liberty, equality, and the rights of man. Such principles, he argued, were 'sacrilegious' and sought only to overthrow the Catholic religion.[5]

Even some members of the French episcopacy were surprised by the intransigence of the pope's condemnation, and a few took pains to justify their previous acceptance of the achievements of 1789 in the secular domain. But the bishops were now left with no room for retreat or compromise, and within a few months nearly all of them went into exile.

In the end, Pius VI's pronouncements had relatively little immediate effect on the situation in France. Nearly all parish clergymen had already made their decisions, for or against the Civil Constitution, and only a small proportion of jurors now retracted their oaths. The two briefs contributed above all in further polarizing the situation in the kingdom. Opponents of the Revolution found additional justification for condemning the Constitution as being not only antithetical to the rights and privileges of the *ancien régime*, but 'godless' as well. Patriots in Paris, on the contrary, enthusiastically mocked the briefs and burned the pope in effigy in the Palais Royal. In the face of the Roman father's position the revolutionary government felt it had no choice but to break off all diplomatic relations. The decade-long schism that resulted would engender intense religious bitterness, as both sides castigated their opponents and proclaimed the non-efficacy of their rivals' sacraments. It would also render the political task of ending the Revolution and stabilizing the country enormously more difficult.

Religious divisions in France, 1791–1793

With the crisis of the Civil Constitution and the ecclesiastical oath, a three-way confrontation emerged in France. The clergy and most of the laity soon took sides for either the 'Constitutional' Church or the 'Roman' or 'Refractory' Church. But over the next three years a smaller contingent of anticlerical deists and a handful of self-proclaimed atheists, impatient with Catholicism and Christianity altogether, grew increasingly influential.

For over a year after the schism began the orthodox Roman Catholic Church maintained a legal existence in France, at least in the eyes of the Parisian legislators. Following the logic of religious toleration – and despite the bitter opposition of the Gallican-Jansenist faction that had devised the Civil Constitution – the deputies in Paris passed a 'toleration decree' in May 1791. This decree permitted non-jurors to continue celebrating Mass and even to share the parish church with the jurors, as long as they did not cause disturbances or attack the Revolution and its policies. The law also specified that no refractories could be dismissed until replacements had been found. In zones where the oath had been massively rejected, it was often impossible to find sufficient substitutes, and local authorities were forced to leave refractories at their posts, sometimes well into 1792.

The strength of the Roman Church in a given diocese depended not only on the number of non-jurors and the support of the laity, but also on the vigour and organization of the *ancien régime* bishop. By the summer of 1792, all but a handful of the bishops had moved safely beyond the French frontiers. They had to rely on vicars-general or on other appointed delegates who had remained behind to provide local leadership. In most cases, the leadership in question was directed above all at denouncing the revolutionary church and circulating the relevant papal pronouncements. Since, as chance would have it, the initial crisis almost coincided with the Lenten season, many displaced *curés* made full use of the Easter confessional to attack the 'intruders' who had been sent to replace them.

In strongly juring regions a priest who had rejected the oath might be the target of considerable popular animosity and even violence. A clergyman's refusal to embrace the Constitution was viewed as evidence that he was an enemy and potential conspirator against the Revolution. Yet some measure of lay support for refractories was to be found almost everywhere. In most regions women played a particularly active role in defending the traditional church – even though other women fervently supported the Revolution. Women's religious orders – which widely sympathized with the non-jurors – frequently provided chapels for the celebration of refractory Masses. Contingents of laywomen, sometimes organized through *ancien régime* confraternities, were commonly at the forefront of those opposing and even physically abusing or rioting against the jurors.

Faced with such opposition, many local revolutionary officials became disillusioned with the policy of toleration imposed from above. Especially in the wake of Louis XVI's abortive attempt to flee the country and his arrest in Varennes on 21 June 1791, officials in several departments began organizing illegal repression against the non-jurors, compelling them to leave their former parishes, and sometimes imprisoning them or deporting them from their dioceses.

In any case, the Refractory Church lost all semblance of official protection after the 'Second French Revolution' and the overthrow of the monarchy in the summer of 1792. The law of 26 August 1792 ordered all non-jurors under 60 years of age to leave the country immediately, while placing elderly and disabled refractories in detention. Thereafter, and for the next several years, the dissident church existed in France only through the action of a small number of clandestine priests, and through the independent organization of the laity. If such clergymen were captured by the revolutionaries, they were not treated gently. As many as 3,000 priests were killed during the Revolution through judicial procedures or summary execution, the overwhelming majority of them refractories.

In the meantime, the Constitutional Church set about organizing itself with considerable energy and determination. The first task was the election and consecration of a corps of bishops to head the newly redrawn dioceses, in only three of which the *ancien régime* prelates had agreed to serve. The line of canonical authority was maintained when Bishop Talleyrand – who had, in fact, already resigned his See of Autun – agreed to consecrate the first bishops elected by the laity. Most of the new diocesan leaders (55 of 80), were chosen from among the *curés*, many of them former participants in pre-revolutionary movements for church reform. With rare exceptions, they were qualified and dedicated men, and they quickly began organizing seminaries and episcopal councils and publishing formal missives for the guidance of the laity. Much of the constitutional parish clergy, both holdovers from the *ancien régime* and newly elected *curés*, were also committed to their pastoral functions, though they readily assumed the role of 'citizen priests' and closely cooperated with revolutionary administrators and national guardsmen. There can be no doubt, however, that many of the former regulars, who won election in the parishes as they sought out new careers, were poorly prepared for their pastoral duties. In dioceses where numerous replacements had to be found, the arrival of large numbers of such clerics from other dioceses, many with opportunist motives and uncertain vocations, undoubtedly tarnished the reputation of the Constitutional Church.

During the first years of the Revolution, a significant segment of both the clergy and the laity were persuaded that the Revolution was the handiwork of God Himself, and that the Civil Constitution had laid the groundwork for a profound spiritual renewal. Many were inspired by the primitive church, arguing that 'citizen Jesus', as some now preferred to call him, would certainly have embraced the Revolution. They were convinced – and elaborated their beliefs in numerous books and pamphlets – that Christ would have approved the sale of church property and the pruning of those abuses and 'useless' elements of the church imposed by men over the centuries.

In towns and rural areas where the overwhelming majority had taken the oath, the transition to the Revolutionary Church might take place with relatively little ado. There is some evidence that attendance at Mass even increased as religious participation came to be associated with patriotism. Most of the major political events and revolutionary celebrations, like the Festival of the Federation marking the anniversary of the fall of the Bastille, continued to be framed with religious ceremonial. Traditional Catholic feast days and processions were also widely celebrated in both Paris and the provinces, at least through the summer of 1793. Indeed, before that date, efforts by certain radicals to halt processions in Paris were roundly opposed by the population itself.

But the period also saw the rise of a movement of belligerent anticlericalism and even anti-religion, ultimately directed against both churches. There was a clear change in tone at the governmental level following the completion of the Constitution and the appearance of the new 'Legislative Assembly' in October 1791. All members of the first National Assembly had been excluded from re-election and the new deputies numbered only about twenty clergymen, compared to almost 300 who sat previously. Moreover, a large majority of the representatives had been local revolutionary administrators, with direct experience in the long and frustrating struggle to implement laws concerning the clergy. Indeed, one of the first major questions taken up by the legislators was the repression of refractory priests. The radical 'Girondin' faction proved particularly aggressive in rhetoric directed against all non-jurors, regardless of whether they had actually disobeyed the law. In the course of debates a few deputies even proposed that the new regime entirely separate itself from the church – a proposal passionately opposed by the constitutional bishops. In the end, the assembly voted a decree defining all refractories as enemies of the nation and requiring their immediate exile. Even though Louis XVI vetoed the measure, some local administrators unilaterally implemented elements of the decree, continuing a strategy of illegal repression begun at the time of the king's flight to Varennes.

Hostility towards refractories was raised to a new level after April 1792 when France became involved in a war with Austria and Prussia. Many revolutionaries were convinced that priests who had refused the oath might well be in league with the foreign enemies. With the overthrow of the monarchy that summer, the provisional government revived the deportation law previously vetoed by Louis XVI, and an estimated 35,000 clergymen – regulars and seculars, men and women – departed for exile in Spain, England, Switzerland, or various of the German and Italian states. But the radicals in power also took measures to limit the influence of priests who had long supported the Revolution. Decrees were pushed through stripping the *curés* of responsibility for registering births, marriages, and deaths in the parishes; restricting their right to wear clerical garb in public; and disbanding the regulars still serving in schools and hospitals. Another law imposed a new pledge of allegiance to the government, the so-called 'oath of liberty and equality', required now of all clergy – both regular and secular – not just those with cure of souls. In early September, in a climate of fear and anarchy and with an invading army approaching the capital, rumours spread wildly that counter-revolutionary inmates were plotting to break out and attack the unprotected Parisians. Crowds of local citizens broke into prisons and murdered hundreds of people, including three bishops and some 220 other refractory clergymen who happened to be incarcerated there. Similar killings took place in several provincial towns.

Thereafter, relations between the government and the clergy continued to deteriorate. Large popular uprisings broke out in western France (Brittany, Maine, Normandy, and the 'Vendée') and in portions of the Protestant south, all motivated in part by the Revolution's religious polices, and led – or thought to be led – by elements of the refractory clergy. The 'Federalist' revolts of the summer of 1793 – protesting the domination of the Revolution by radical factions in Paris – saw the participation of several leaders of the Constitutional Church. Many anticlerical radicals had committed themselves to supporting that church precisely because they believed it could help promote social stability. But when a minority of constitutionals seemed to follow the refractories in lending support to rebellions, many revolutionaries lost all patience with both the clergy and religion.

De-Christianization

For close to two centuries historians have debated the origins and significance of the movement of 'de-Christianization', generally dated between the autumn of 1793 and the summer of 1794. To what extent was the attack on Christianity coerced from above by a small group of revolutionary fanatics? To what extent did it represent a dramatic shift in values among larger segments of the population? Research pursued over the last thirty years has substantially illuminated the question, but the various currents of de-Christianization were complex and at times contradictory, and much uncertainty still remains.[6]

Clearly the movement must be placed in the political context of the 'Reign of Terror' with which it closely coincided. It was a period in which France was beset not only by foreign invasions and bitter civil wars, but also by deep internal struggles for the control of the government between different factions of radicals. In the midst of such pressures, the obsession with conspiracy was intensified as never before, leading to widespread suspicion against the privileged classes of the *ancien régime*, both nobles and clergymen. But war and internal disruption alone cannot explain the transformation from anticlericalism to anti-religion; nor why some French regions seemed more susceptible to the movement than others. In fact, the period also corresponded to the most radical phase of the Revolution, in which a whole array of political, social, and cultural values were questioned or overturned. It was in a quasi-millenarian context that certain aggressively anti-religious or atheistic positions, positions advocated by a marginal fringe of eighteenth-century philosophers and by a tiny minority of Parisian intellectuals early in the Revolution, acquired for a time a substantially larger following. For some elements of the urban elite, whose commitment to the Christian church had already been weakened in the last decades of the *ancien régime*, de-Christianization now became an appealing option. But that option was also taken up by portions of the urban working class, notably in the milieu of the 'sans-culottes' – that group of intensely politicized Parisian artisans, shopkeepers, and petty officials. A variety of pamphlets, speeches, and administrative directives promoted the idea that Christianity was an illusion, foisted on the people by clergymen in order to maintain themselves in power; a positive evil obstructing the spread of revolutionary ideas. The Revolution had produced a new phase in western culture, it was argued, in which people should either set aside the 'superstition' of religion altogether, or develop a new, patriotic cult closely akin to the 'civil religion' recommended by Jean-Jacques Rousseau in his *Social Contract*. But it is clear that coercion and fear also played a major role in the instigation of de-Christianization. In most parts of the country it was directly incited by outside forces arriving from Paris, either by representatives on mission from the Convention or by bands of the popular 'revolutionary armies', circulating in the countryside to promote the Terror.

The first systematic efforts in this regard seem to have occurred in September and October 1793 through the actions of representatives in Picardy and in central France. Similar campaigns were launched in Paris itself in November, and then spread to most of the country over the following months. There can be no doubt that the majority of the population was hostile to such campaigns, and that a great many people readily returned to traditional Christian practice after the end of the Terror. Yet such actions could not have been initiated and enforced without some cooperation on the part of local leaders and militant national guardsmen. There is also evidence that some towns and regions were substantially more receptive than others to the goals of de-Christianization. It may have been least successful in precisely those zones, like western and north-eastern France, where Catholicism seems to have been exceptionally vital on the eve of Revolution.

As many historians have noted, de-Christianization entailed both destructive attacks against existing religious symbols and practices and a variety of efforts to evolve a new 'revolutionary religion'. It was in October 1793 that a revolutionary calendar – commissioned by the Convention ten months earlier – was first formally adopted, instituting a ten-day week without reference to the Christian Sabbath and marking the beginning of a new era in time with the creation of the French Republic, rather than with the birth of Christ. At almost the same period, thousands of names of towns and streets and businesses were changed to remove all allusions to saints or the Virgin – or to kings, queens, and aristocrats. But there were also more direct attacks on physical objects integral to Christianity. Hundreds of church bells were removed and melted down, ostensibly for cannons to defend the nation. Religious statuary was battered and defaced. On occasion the de-Christianizers held veritable autos-da-fé of ecclesiastical vestments and sacred ornaments or texts. And almost everywhere there were efforts to close down churches altogether, sometimes converting them to factories or stables or anti-Christian temples for revolutionary ceremonies. Though the principal targets were the buildings devoted to the Catholic religion, virtually all Protestant churches and Jewish synagogues were closed as well.

But the central symbolic event in this process was the attack on the clerical leadership, the constitutional clergy and the Protestant pastors. Throughout France, priests and pastors were forced to resign their posts and cease celebrating the sacred Offices. And in large areas of the nation, revolutionary leaders went even further, pushing Catholic clergymen to repudiate the priesthood altogether and, if at all possible, to marry. Those who failed to follow such directives were sometimes imprisoned. Whether through fear or conviction, a certain number of priests enthusiastically denounced their previous sacerdotal functions. But by far the greater number quietly retired, profoundly disillusioned with a revolutionary process which most of them had long supported and which had now turned against them.

During the same period many officials made vigorous attempts to establish new revolutionary cults to replace the Christian religion. A first wave of 'cults of reason' was self-consciously atheistic in inspiration and involved various rituals in honour of Reason or Nature, usually depicted by sculptured or human representations of the appropriate 'goddess'. But a competing, deistically inclined cult of the Supreme Being became progressively more popular, particularly after Maximilien Robespierre and his closest associates mobilized their influence in its favour. Through the end of the Terror in the summer of 1794 hundreds of such cults were celebrated in communities large and small in virtually every department of France. Though the details of such ceremonies differed substantially from town to town, they usually involved close adaptations of elements of Catholic practice, including sermons, hymns, altars, processions, and references to revolutionary 'martyrs' or 'saints'. Most de-Christianizers were dismissive of or positively hostile to Christian theology. Yet they commonly favoured an ethics adapted from the teachings of Christ, invariably portrayed as an early revolutionary. The extreme left de-Christianizer, Jacques Hébert, was not alone in his enthusiastic praise for 'the sans-culotte from Nazareth'.

Most of the attacks on Christianity were abandoned after the fall of Robespierre and the end of the Terror in July 1794, although there would be periodic waves of renewed state anticlericalism over the next five years. For the most part, the revolutionary cults had aroused little or no support outside the larger towns. But by the end of the century substantial segments of both the Catholic and Protestant clergies had been dispersed, imprisoned, or exiled, and their churches disaffected or destroyed. For months and in some cases years, open religious practice would cease to exist. In the meantime, revolutionary armies were carrying similar attacks on the clergy and the church to many other parts of Europe.

In the following years, as the next chapter will explore, the French clergy and laity would successfully manage to reinstate both the Catholic and Protestant churches. Indeed, the early nineteenth century would witness significant movements of religious revival, in large measure in reaction to the events of the Revolution. Yet the traumatic experience of the revolutionary decade had shaken the church to its very foundations. It would leave a legacy of division and hostility between the Catholic Church and progressive politics, between clericalism and anticlericalism that would persist in France and in Europe into the twentieth century.

Notes

1. John McManners, *Church and society in eighteenth-century France*. Vol. 1: *The clerical establishment and its social ramifications* (Oxford: Oxford University Press, 1998), p. 3. Cf. Michel Vovelle, *Piété baroque et déchristianisation en Provence au XVIIIe siècle* (Paris: Editions du Seuil, 1978).

2. Philippe Ariès, *L'homme devant la mort* (Paris, Editions du Seuil, 1977), pp. 317–22; John McManners, *Death and the Enlightenment: Changing attitudes to death among Christians and unbelievers in eighteenth century France* (Oxford: Oxford University Press, 1981). Cf. Vovelle, *Piété baroque*, pp. 265–300.

3. Darrin M. McMahon, *Enemies of the Enlightenment: The French counter-Enlightenment and the making of modernity* (Oxford: Oxford University Press, 2001), esp. chap. 1.

4. See, especially, Dale Van Kley, *The religious origins of the French Revolution: From Calvin to the Civil Constitution: 1560–1791* (New Haven: Yale University Press, 1996), esp. chap. 4. Compare Roger Chartier, *The cultural origins of the French Revolution* (Durham, NC: Duke University Press, 1991), chap. 6; and Timothy Tackett, *Becoming a revolutionary: The deputies of the French National Assembly and the emergence of a revolutionary culture (1789–1790)* (Princeton: Princeton University Press, 1996), pp. 102 and 304.

5. See Albert Mathiez, *Rome et le clergé français sous la Constituante* (Paris: Armand Colin, 1911), pp. 490–3 and 510.

6. E.g., cf. Michel Vovelle, *Religion et révolution: La déchristianisation de l'An II* (Paris: Hachette, 1976), esp. pp. 285–300; with Nigel Aston, *Religion and revolution in France, 1780–1804* (Washington, DC: Catholic University of America Press, 2000), pp. 260–1; and Dale Van Kley, 'Christianity as casualty and chrysallis of modernity: The problem of dechristianization in the French Revolution', *American historical review*, 108 (2003), pp. 1081–1104.

28

The French Revolution and religion, 1795–1815

SUZANNE DESAN

Between 1795 and 1815, France underwent astonishing political changes as Revolution gave way to empire-building, followed by military collapse and the Restoration of the monarchy. The political experimentation of the revolutionary and Napoleonic eras precipitated momentous religious transformations. By 1794, the radical revolutionaries had literally attempted to 'de-Christianize' France by closing down churches, forcing priests to resign or emigrate, and inventing new republican cults to replace Christianity. Over the next twenty years, as Catholics struggled to restore religious practice, France's leaders worked to define a new relationship between nation and religion. In the later years of the Revolution, the Directory (1795–99) experimented with separating church and state yet continued to view Christianity as potentially subversive and to pursue anticlerical or de-Christianizing policies. When Napoleon came to power, he negotiated a new settlement that re-established Catholicism as the 'religion of the majority of the French' and sought to make it dependent upon the state. This era also demanded flexibility from the nation's some 650,000 Protestants and 50,000 Jews. They welcomed the legal recognition of rights brought by the Revolution, but also strove to adapt to fluctuating politics, as the revolutionary assault on religious practice gave way to intermittent toleration and then new oversight by the state. Ever ambitious, when he built his empire, Napoleon also exported a controversial set of religious policies, such as appropriating church lands, streamlining worship, increasing state surveillance of religion, and instituting religious toleration. Focusing primarily on France and then on the empire, this chapter explores the creative adaptations of laity and clergy to this era of political turmoil.

The struggle to revive religion: France during the later years of Revolution, 1795–1799

The fall of Robespierre in July 1794 brought widespread hopes among believers for a return to public religious practice. As chapter 27 explored, the early years of the Revolution had been deeply disruptive. Over the early 1790s, the Revolution's initial attempts to create a national church had given way to escalating anticlericalism and attacks on religious worship and institutions. In 1790–91 the National Assembly began the sale of church lands, abolished religious orders, and demanded that priests take an oath of allegiance to the new nation and to a reorganized version of the church (the Civil Constitution of the Clergy). By dividing oath-taking 'constitutional' clergy from 'refractory' or 'non-juror' priests who refused to take the oath, the Civil Constitution created a deep schism among the clergy and their parishioners. In addition, the de-Christianization campaign of 1793–94 closed down the public practice of Catholicism.

In 1794–95, then, Catholics faced a confusing and uncertain situation. Local revolutionaries in many areas continued to celebrate republican festivals. Clergy were scarce; refractory and constitutional priests remained deeply divided. Their legal status was often shifting or unclear and they confronted renewed government demands for oaths over the later 1790s. Furthermore, in the years between Thermidor and Napoleon's 1801 Concordat with the pope, national leaders did not manage to create coherent and consistent religious policies. Most republican leaders continued to regard Catholicism with suspicion: at worst, as an ally of royalism or counter-revolution; at best, as degrading fanaticism. National politics were marked by political changeability, as the Thermidoreans and the Directory tried to balance the demands of the Left and the Right. According to these twists and turns of national politics, the government vacillated between tolerating limited forms of public practice and then pursuing greater police surveillance or outright repression of worship. But broadly speaking, religious policy had two distinct phases: first, a gradual return to *partial* freedom of worship from February 1795 to autumn 1797; second, a two-year return to the de-Christianization campaign between the left-wing *coup d'état* of September 1797 and Napoleon's coup in December 1799.

In February 1795, the Thermidorean Convention initiated a striking new policy. Hoping to pacify religious resistance in the counter-revolutionary Vendée and elsewhere, the legislature literally separated church and state: the state would no longer recognize nor fund any religion but it would allow religious assemblies in private spaces. Further laws in 1795 permitted citizens to reopen churches under strict regulations, and clergy who swore a new oath of loyalty to the nation could practise again. But the Directory continued to advocate republican festivals and calendar and to curtail and police Catholic practice. Notably, refractory priests, religious processions, habits, inscriptions, bell-ringing, and religious foundations were still outlawed.

Moreover, when the revolutionary leadership took a marked swing to the left in the autumn of 1797, the Directory advanced a 'second de-Christianization campaign' that vigorously renewed many of the goals of 1793–94. The Directors worked to replace Sunday worship with a cycle of republican festivals, the *culte décadaire*, to be celebrated every tenth day of the revolutionary calendar. These national festivals aimed at instilling moral values and patriotism: their subjects ranged from youth, marriage, or agriculture to more explicitly political festivals, such as the Founding of the Republic or the 9th of Thermidor. At the suggestion of Director La Revellière-Lépeaux, the government also promoted a new cult known as Theophilanthropy. Originating from an essay contest at the Institut National, Theophilanthropy was essentially an attempt to transform deism into a practising religion. Its followers professed belief in one God and the immortality of the soul. Its ceremonies attempted to replace the elaborate rituals of Catholicism with a simple grandeur and an eclectic synthesis of moral teachings from sources as varied as Confucius and Calvin. With few exceptions, neither the *fêtes décadaires* nor Theophilanthropy met with sustained success. Their following was especially weak in rural areas. But the official attempt to enforce the republican calendar and its festivals nonetheless created difficulties for Catholics.

Paradoxically, the obstacles and challenges of the late 1790s paved the way for religious creativity among both laity and clergy as they strove to reinvent modes of religious practice. Within the complex legal and political context, the late 1790s witnessed a veritable religious revival. Parishioners and their *curés* used a wide variety of means – both political and religious – to reclaim their right to practise or to invent new forms of religious expression.

Given the shortage of clergy and the limitations on public practice for the laity, clandestine or domestic rituals and prayers necessarily played a crucial role in cultivating the religious renaissance. Nineteenth-century memoirs abound with images of familial devotion from the late 1790s: fathers recounting or reading aloud the lives of the saints, children learning catechism at a mother's knee, believers reciting the rosary by the hearth or at a spinning bee. As Olwen Hufton has suggested, the rosary may have held special salience for women, as they drew reassurance from a Marianized faith and from communal recitation of the rosary in all-female *veillées*. Whenever possible, parishioners gathered in households, barns, or forest clearings to hear a Mass said in secret by a priest. These covert rituals could attract large and determined crowds. In one village in the Haut-Rhin, when the police tried to arrest a non-juror saying an illicit Mass for 200 people in a hayloft, the gendarmes got no help from the municipal officer, while his wife admonished them, 'Yes, we want the Mass and we'll have it . . . Watch yourself for everybody detests you.'[1]

As this example reminds us, Catholicism had always drawn its strength and character from the public and collective expression of faith. The religious revival of the mid- to late 1790s was above all an attempt to restore public practice: to recover the village church, ring bells freely once again, take part in pilgrimages or outdoor saints' festivals, or make it possible for a local *curé* to say Mass publicly. In 1795, many French villagers echoed the sentiments of one pastor in the Vendée: 'Their promises for religion are worthless, because there will be no solemn and public cult, no bells, no processions, not even religious vestments outside of church'.[2]

Catholics used a variety of means to regain their churches and religious symbols and to reinstate public ritual. Parishioners peppered local authorities and the distant legislature with petitions imploring them to return their churches or bells or to free priests from prison. Particularly in areas that generally supported the Revolution, some Catholics proclaimed loyalty to religion and republic and appropriated revolutionary ideology to demand religious freedom as a natural 'right', newly won by the Revolution. Petition after petition clamoured for the use of a local parish church and reminded the authorities that support for religion was 'the general will' of the sovereign people and that 'the Constitution of the Republic guarantees the freedom of religion'. These Catholics often sought to align a legal re-establishment of religion with a return to peaceful republicanism: for example, fifty-six petitioners from Laroquebron in Cantal assured the Directors, 'We are resolved to shed the last drop of our blood to uphold Religion and Republic, one and indivisible: this is our wish. *Vive la république! Vive la liberté!*'[3]

Although some Catholics supported the republic, more frequently Catholicism was allied with counter-revolutionary sentiment, and many parishioners turned to violence to reclaim their faith. Notably, the counter-revolutionary rebels who engaged in guerrilla activity over large areas of the Vendée, Brittany, Anjou, and Normandy had many interlocking reasons for hating the Republic and fighting for a return to communal autonomy. Catholic resentment of de-Christianizing policies acted as one important element fuelling these persistent resistance movements. On a much smaller scale, other parishioners in all areas of France engaged in more localized acts of religious rioting: they simply broke into their churches, stole back sacred objects, and began to celebrate public rituals without formal permission. The attitudes of local officials towards illicit assemblies varied immensely, but everywhere they felt the pressure of parishioners who did not hesitate to appropriate civil and religious authority. The women of Dollon in the Sarthe compelled their mayor to reinstall their statue of Christ and then forced the mayor's son to kiss the ground before the crucifix. Next, they coerced one citizen Volet to give back the altar he had bought earlier in the Revolution. With each passing day, the local administrators granted more concessions to the women. All across France, just as they had led opposition to jurors in the early 1790s, women played an especially central role in reclaiming sacred spaces, maintaining both public and private worship, and harbouring priests from arrest. This female activism both grew out of and promoted a gradual feminization of religion in France.

Clerical leadership was crucial to these varied attempts to resurrect public rituals. Although they remained leery of offending republican authorities too directly, both constitutional and refractory bishops and priests struggled to reinstate pastoral care and rebuild institutional structures for the church. As these two groups of clergy emerged from hiding or slipped back into France to rejoin their communities, they faced complex conditions and difficult decisions. Each new clerical oath demanded by the national government forced individual *curés* to wrestle with their consciences: many agonized over the decision of whether to swear loyalty to the republic in order to gain legal access to the use of the village church. The attitudes of local officials were crucial for these re-emerging priests, for their legal status remained perilous. Moreover, in some regions, refractory and constitutional priests competed for the allegiance of lay parishioners. But the scarcity of priests was a more frequent problem, for their ranks had been decimated.

If higher numbers of non-jurors had emigrated or experienced imprisonment, the ranks of the constitutional clergy had been especially hard hit by abdications. Out of 28,000 jurors, some 22,000 had either resigned or abdicated; many others had married, died, or retracted their oaths and decamped to the refractory side. Only twenty-five of eighty-three bishops from 1792 were still serving the Constitutional Church by 1795. Despite its earlier official position, that Church received no support from the Directors, although local authorities in peaceful regions often preferred jurors to non-jurors in the hope that they would be less likely to stir up political opposition. Although the church had lost the support of the regime, its leaders nonetheless worked to regroup as a national church. Tirelessly devoted to the cause of making Catholicism compatible with republicanism, Bishop Henri Grégoire organized his fellow Gallican bishops into a group known as the 'United Bishops', and founded a national journal entitled *Les Annales de la religion*, dedicated to reconciling refractories to the Constitutional Church. The bishops held two National Councils in 1797 and 1801 to coordinate decisions about liturgy and politics, rid their church of married priests, and work towards filling vacant parishes and bishoprics.

On the local level, constitutional clergy improvised, made the best of shifting circumstances, and hoped not to lose too many constitutional colleagues to the refractories' appeals for retractions of the original oath. Hostilities between the two churches usually ran deep. In Toulouse, the constitutional bishop Sermet worried that the growing strength of refractories had enticed many jurors to shift their allegiances: 'I anticipate that this epidemic sickness is going to grow and win over the region', he commented in a dramatic letter to Grégoire in 1797.[4] Yet, lay parishioners could be fiercely loyal to a juror who had stood by them over the dark years of the radical revolution: the women of Fretin (Nord) defended the right of the local constitutional priest to say Mass by driving away his non-juring missionary rival with screams and threats. Constitutional clergy succeeded in rebuilding their congregations especially in areas where oath-taking had been high in 1790–91 and where royalist leanings were weak among the populace at large.

No sooner had Robespierre been overthrown than the first non-jurors began to steal back into France from the Rhineland, Switzerland, Spain, and England. If the frontier areas were the first to benefit, refractories moved swiftly to develop networks in multiple regions across France. In certain regions, such as the north, Lyonnais, Upper Normandy, Maine, Morvan, and parts of Auvergne and the Alps, émigré bishops sent vicars-general into France to develop clandestine missions of clergy. Intrepid leaders, such as abbé Linsolas in Lyon and abbé Dubourg in Toulouse, organized their fellow non-jurors to purify desecrated churches and say Mass. They also cultivated networks of lay *chefs de paroisse* and pious women to spread the word about imminent arrivals of non-jurors, hide them from authorities when necessary, and lead private prayer sessions when no priests could be present. Anxious to restore the sacramental life of their followers, non-jurors also conducted clandestine baptisms, marriages, funeral ceremonies, and even first communion ceremonies (when local officials looked the other way). These rituals often also staked out the legitimacy of the Roman Church over the Constitutional Church or republican culture: for example, in 1796 the refractory priest Durançon of the diocese of

Avignon rebaptized the three-month-old 'Jean-Baptiste Mucius-Scaevola' with the simple saint's name 'Pierre'.

Some non-juror leaders, notably abbé Emery, the former director of the Sulpicians in Paris, advised the priests to make peace with the regime, take the promise of submission of 1795, and regain public access to churches and public worship. Many other refractories, allied with royalism, argued against any cooperation whatsoever with the republic. This issue reached a head after the left-wing coup in the autumn of 1797, when the Directory demanded that all priests swear an oath of 'hatred of royalty'. Only about one-fifth of the refractories of 1791 acceded to this oath. The rest faced the risk of deportation or exile. Enforcement of this anticlerical policy was particularly harsh in the areas newly occupied by French armies: 8,000 of the 10,000 priests condemned to deportation were Belgians. Local opposition to the policy in both France and Belgium meant that most sentences were never carried out. Several thousand priests were nonetheless imprisoned and 256 were deported to French Guiana.

In situations where clergy were unavailable, lay believers remained intent on collective, public ritual. While parishioners led each other in hymns and prayer all over France, in certain areas lay leaders, often schoolteachers, went so far as to perform 'white Masses' without any priest present. Rare was the lay minister who dared to consecrate the communion host, though they replicated the rest of the Mass, complete with vestments, clerical gestures, and Latin chants. Some distributed 'blessed bread', performed funerals and benedictions, or sang vespers or morning prayer. While these lay cults existed in parts of the Vendée, Poitou, Brittany, Lyonnais, and Franche-Comté, they seem to have been especially prevalent and persistent (often even continuing beyond the Concordat) in areas later known for weak devotion and post-Concordat shortages of clergy, such as the Paris Basin and other parts of north-central France.

Without clerical oversight, many laity resurrected and transformed popular cultural practices from the *ancien régime*. In some cases, they fused religious and political expression. For example, in the west local people unofficially canonized quite a few victims of the civil war, whether 'bleu' (prorevolution-ary) or 'blanc' (royalist/counter-revolutionary). In the spring of 1796 a band of counter-revolutionary *chouans* murdered Perrine Dugué, a nineteen-year-old daughter of a republican family. Neighbouring pro-revolutionary Catholics in the Mayenne declared her a martyr and a saint and flocked to her grave, which became a site of miracle cures and pilgrimages drawing hundreds of faithful. Other similar local cults sprang up and persisted, despite the attempts of both republican and clerical authorities to suppress them. These novel saints' cults emerged spontaneously and almost always took place at newly sacred outdoor locations. Displaying a remarkable syncretism between religious and political martyrdom, they bore testimony to the creativity and resilience of believers, as well as to the richness of popular cultural expression.

In fact, the Revolution in certain ways reinforced the centrality of popular cultural practices for Catholics. During the Directory, parishioners partook in an upsurge in outdoor pilgrimages, devotional rituals at shrines or outdoor crosses, and above all, celebrations of age-old saints' festivals, complete with illegal processions, ceremonies, and dancing. In the process, believers not only flagrantly defied the republican calendar, but also resurrected practices that the Catholic Reformation clergy had so often attempted to repress and replace during the *ancien régime*. As the *curé* of Tronchoy (Yonne) commented in his own defence to the administrators of Epineuil, 'Haven't I been forced to concede to the wishes of the inhabitants and *celebrate festivals suppressed many years ago*, but to which they are still attached?'[5]

This grassroots struggle to rebuild Catholicism found certain parallels in the Protestant attempts to renew rituals and clerical networks as well. Interestingly, the decree in 1795 separating church and state placed Catholicism and Protestantism into the same legal category for the first time: neither religion received state recognition nor aid, and both were subject to the same laws regulating and curtailing public worship. If France's 470,000 Calvinists and 200,000 Lutherans shared this legal status (or non-status) with Catholics, they also faced some of the same difficulties. But these hardships were multiplied for a faith whose numbers were smaller and whose official position had barely begun to be regularized before the Revolution. Despite the marginal status of Protestantism, its clergy had been very hard hit by de-Christianization and widespread abdications. In all of France excluding Alsace, only about 120 pastors returned to lead worship in the mid-1790s, compared to perhaps 210 active ministers in 1793. Moreover, their organizational networks had been devastated by the Revolution: according to surviving records, only one Protestant synod met during the Directory, a small gathering in Haut-Languedoc in 1796.

The Protestant revival after the Terror took place on the congregational level and was markedly uneven in the different Protestant strongholds. In the countryside in Alsace and in many pockets of traditional strength in the Midi, parishioners and their pastors managed to return to collective practice between 1795 and 1798. They either made declarations to share churches or resumed outdoor worship modelled on the *ancien régime* 'Church of the Desert'. Daniel Robert has suggested that the rural return to religious practice outpaced the urban one because middle-class, urban Protestant notables seemed slower to embrace their former faith and had often experienced the political divisiveness of the Revolution more deeply. These divisions hindered the renewal of worship in Marseille, Montauban, Caen, and Bordeaux and its surrounding area. Regular practice did not begin again in Marseille until 1801 and until as late as 1805 in Toulouse.

When Napoleon overthrew the Directory with the coup of 18 Brumaire (9 November 1799), the religious situation in France remained deeply problematic. Although Catholics and Protestants, laity and clergy, had displayed persistence and imagination in reviving their faith, most believers longed for a return to normalcy – in terms of both public practice and a clarified legal stature for their religions.

The Napoleonic Era: The Concordat and its impact

As Napoleon sought to consolidate his power in the early years of the Consulate, he recognized the urgent need to achieve a new religious settlement. Dissident clergy continued to re-enter the country; armed resistance persisted in the ever troublesome Vendée. The First Consul hoped to defuse the potent link between Catholicism and royalism and, more generally, he wanted to garner popular support by regularizing the religious situation. While not spiritually inclined, Napoleon believed that religion was useful to instil moral behaviour and social stability. Ever the pragmatist, Napoleon later claimed that he aimed 'to govern as the majority desires to be governed. That, I believe, is the best way to recognize popular sovereignty. By turning Catholic I ended the war in the Vendée, by becoming a Moslem I established myself in Egypt... If I governed a people of Jews, I would rebuild the temple of Solomon.'[6] Bonaparte knew that an accord with Rome would make it easier for him to assimilate newly conquered Catholic areas, such as Belgium or northern Italy. Finally, he also sought to put the church under state control. If Napoleon had good reasons for resolving France's religious dilemmas, the new pope, Pius VII, was also anxious to end the religious schism within the French church and to restore public worship. Agreement between representatives of pope and Consul did not come easily however. Only after twenty-one drafts and eight months of discussion in 1800–1801 did a hard-won compromise emerge.

This agreement, promulgated in churches across France on Easter Sunday 1802, was known as the Concordat. It granted Catholics the full freedom to public worship and put an end to the Directory's experiment with separating church and state. But the Concordat did not re-create the confessional state of the *ancien régime*. In this post-revolutionary France that accorded legal status to Protestants and Jews, Catholicism was acknowledged as 'the religion of the majority of the French'. To resolve yet another legacy from the Revolution, Napoleon convinced the pope to recognize as permanent the sale and transfer of church lands (*biens nationaux*) during the 1790s. In creating a new form of Gallicanism, the Concordat – and the Organic Articles that Napoleon added to the original agreement – followed certain practices set up by the Civil Constitution of the Clergy, but tempered others. As in 1790, the secular clergy and the bishops would become salaried employees of the state and there would be no attempt to resurrect the vast system of regular clergy from the *ancien régime*. Avoiding the debacle of the oath of 1790–91, Napoleon specified that the clergy must declare loyalty to the government but did not demand an oath to the specifics of the Concordat. Nor would there be elections of *curés* or bishops.

Rather, bishops would appoint *curés*. Napoleon himself would nominate all bishops and the pope would invest them with holy office. The number of dioceses would once again be reduced: only fifty bishops would be appointed within France's pre-1792 borders (sixty including the Belgian and Rhineland areas). Despite Pius VII's hesitations and regrets, the final agreement also stipulated that all current bishops – whether juror or non-juror – had to resign. In essence, this provision gave Napoleon the opportunity to weed out the most oppositional Gallican and Roman prelates and to designate a new clerical leadership that should be loyal and dependent upon him. The Concordat created deep divisions among the episcopate. Thirty-eight of ninety-three bishops surviving from the *ancien régime* refused to accept it, and some would play an integral role in setting up local resistance known as the Petite Eglise. Moreover, Bonaparte and the pope soon became involved in struggles over the choice of bishops. In the short term, Napoleon managed to override the pope's rejection of twelve constitutional prelates, but years later, when imprisoned by the emperor, the pope simply refused to invest bishops nominated by his captor.

Just before the promulgation of the Concordat, Napoleon added his own set of Organic Articles to the Concordat without the knowledge or agreement of the papal envoy. These seventy-three Articles clarified state supervision of the church hierarchy. Specific regulations curtailed clerical independence. No papal bull could be promulgated without state sanction. Bishops required government permission to leave their dioceses or establish chapters or seminaries. The state retained the right to remove most *curés* from their posts. Moreover, the Organic Articles created a new Ministry of Religion (*Cultes*) to oversee and negotiate with the church. The first Minister of Religion, Jean-Etienne-Marie Portalis, shared Napoleon's pragmatic desire to allay the old divisions among the clergy. Overall, he favoured the return to worship and proved to be an adept overseer of the new alignment between church and state. He urged local authorities as well as the other government ministries to reduce their interference in parish affairs and he allowed working clergy a certain, limited independence from the state. For example, they were permitted to deny the sacraments as they judged necessary and to refuse remarriage to divorced individuals. The Ministry also managed the growing budget that paid clerical salaries and aided Catholics by providing scholarships for seminarians and stipends for novices of the growing female congregations.

In a nutshell, the Concordat facilitated the recovery from the religious conflicts of the 1790s and ushered in a new era in the relations between church and state. In the secular state that emerged from the Revolution, the clergy became salaried civil servants. They no longer held their privileged, corporate status and their own endowed lands as under the *ancien régime*. Napoleon sought to garner ceremonial as well as social support from Catholicism: in 1804, he successfully pressured Pope Pius VII into participating in his elaborate coronation ceremony at Notre Dame in Paris. Yet, although Bonaparte worked to forge a new kind of Gallicanism and an imperial alliance between throne and altar, in the long term the Concordat and Napoleon's religious manoeuvres helped to foster the ultramontanism of the French Catholic Church.

The Organic Articles also regularized the position of Protestants and offered an unprecedented degree of official recognition to the two dominant groups of Protestants, the Lutherans and Calvinists (Reformed Church). Smaller Protestant sects, like the Mennonites or Methodists, were not recognized but were unofficially tolerated. The state paid and supervised Lutheran and Reformed ministers. Lutheran communities were concentrated for the most part in eastern France and the Rhineland. The Ministry of Religion worked out a hierarchical structure for their religious governance: a central 'general consistory' in Strasbourg presided over local parishes and included several appointees by the First Consul. Calvinists were geographically more widespread, living mainly in a crescent that ran south from the Charente across the Midi up to the Drôme. The Articles deprived the Reformed Church of its pyramidal system of synods and local self-governance. Mistrusting Calvinist traditions of communal autonomy, Napoleon sought to create rationalized ecclesiastical boundaries and institutions that paralleled department structures and reinforced social hierarchy. Synods required the Ministry's permission in order to assemble. In the name of social stability, the Articles stipulated that six to eight notables of a certain stature would join pastors in forming consistories. Each consistory would govern a group of 6,000 or more souls and oversee the appointment of pastors for individual parishes, rather than allowing congregations to recruit their own ministers.

As French Calvinists worked to adapt to the new organizational structures, they continued to face shortages of pastors and solicited help from migratory foreign clergymen, often from Switzerland. Napoleon allowed the Calvinists to open a seminary in Montauban in 1809 and enabled them to claim some seventy-five buildings across France, mainly churches that had formerly belonged to the Catholic Church. Out of tradition and necessity, outdoor worship also continued in some regions. Despite the efforts of the French state to normalize Protestants' status, on the local level old animosities between Protestants and Catholics persisted. Notably, in the Gard in 1815, royalist bands wreaked vengeance on Protestants and even murdered some who were vilified as former revolutionaries or who served as government officials during the Hundred Days.

Although Jews were legally tolerated, they were not included within the 1802 settlement. But between 1806 and 1809, Napoleon set up several institutions to incorporate Jews under state supervision and facilitate negotiations between the Ministry of Religion and Jewish leaders. Staffed by Jewish notables, these institutions, such as the governing Central Consistory and departmental consistories, tied Judaism more closely to the state and often created tensions among Jewish communities accustomed to local decision-making. But Jews did not surrender authority over their communal practices. Rabbis and notables strove to cultivate good relations with Napoleon while simultaneously forging a unique Jewish identity. As Frederic Cople Jaher notes, 'Consistories faced both ways, policing Jews at the behest of the government while defending the community against official and unofficial persecution and encouraging cohesion'.[7]

The majority of Catholics welcomed the Concordat, although members of the breakaway 'Petite Eglise' fused royalist opposition to Napoleon with resentment of the Concordat. The mainstream church gradually whittled away at these tenacious pockets of clandestine practice and resistance in the west, Normandy, and Lyonnais. Across France as a whole, Catholics faced two more pressing and widespread problems. The church had to overcome great losses of property and personnel from the revolutionary decade. Beyond the massive sale of church lands, individual parishes struggled to repair damaged churches and to replace lost sacred objects, statues, bells, or crosses. In 1808, of the 60,000 secular and religious clergy remaining from the 1790s, only 55 per cent still exercised the priesthood. Twenty-five per cent had married or definitively abdicated, while another 20 per cent lived as clergymen but did not embrace pastoral duties. Moreover, ordinations of new priests remained far below *ancien régime* levels. A distinct shift occurred: nineteenth-century clerical recruits came disproportionately from the countryside, and clerical shortages became an ongoing problem in certain areas, most notably the Paris Basin.

The disparities in clerical recruitment suggest a second profound problem for the post-Concordat church. Side-by-side with renewed religious fervour, the early 1800s witnessed decline in religious practice. For some, revolutionary anticlericalism held lasting resonance. For others, the Revolution exacerbated a drift away from weekly worship, already begun in the *ancien régime*. A division emerged within Catholicism between those who practised their faith regularly and those who remained Catholic but rarely entered a church building. 'Faith is being lost . . . France is decatholicizing itself', lamented one vicar-general in the diocese of Soissons in 1813.[8] It is inordinately difficult to measure religiosity, but it is clear that regional and gender-based variations in practice emerged and grew over the early 1800s. As Timothy Tackett has argued, the divisive experience of the oath of 1791 was one crucial factor influencing regional religious culture: the areas that rejected the oath correlate surprisingly well with regions of strong allegiance to Catholicism into the modern era. Much of the Massif-Central, Alsace-Lorraine, and the west, especially Brittany, became known for religious fervour, while Limousin, parts of southeastern France, the Loire valley, and the Paris Basin experienced a decline in observance.

Likewise, a movement towards the feminization of religion had begun in the *ancien régime*, and circumstances during the Revolution and empire heightened this trend. Napoleon provided secular secondary education only for boys, and the army exposed massive numbers of young men to anticlericalism. In contrast, most girls received all their schooling from the female congregations that were founded or revived during the empire. As Claude Langlois has shown, the Napoleonic era set a pattern that escalated over the course of the nineteenth century: female religious orders grew at spectacular rates, with 12,300 members in 1808, 15,000 in 1815, and 104,000 by 1861. The Revolution had sparked the fervour and the audacity of many Catholic women, both lay and religious. For example, when priests were scarce in the 1790s, Anne Marie Rivier virtually took on the role of *curé* in her village, leading worship and opening schools. She later founded the Présentation de Marie, which became the largest teaching congregation in the south-east by the end of the empire. For countless less well-known women, the church became a central arena of sociability and social activism that fit well with the developing codes of domesticity.

If various patterns of detachment became increasingly apparent during the empire, the Concordat had nonetheless paved the way for a vibrant resurgence of public and organized religiosity. As Nigel Aston has put it succinctly, 'It was clear that, in the early 1800s, lay Catholics, for the most part, wanted a return to traditional, localised religiosity'.[9] Pilgrimages flourished as the laity flocked to shrines dedicated to Mary or to healing local saints, such as Saints Barbe, Blaise, and Brigitte in the Moselle. Confraternities that had gone underground during the 1790s reappeared as crucial groups that spurred revival, especially in the south-east. Napoleon grew so wary of their collective power that he outlawed them in the late years of the empire. Hoping both to tap into the new religious energy and reinspire non-practising Catholics, teams of priests orchestrated interior missions, which drew crowds of several thousand to attend Masses or participate in outdoor stations of the cross. In short, by the 1810s, while some French remained either apathetic in their practice or politically opposed to the church, Catholicism had once again become a prominent public force in French life.

Religious policies and practices in the empire

As Napoleon expanded the borders of France, he also sought to export his religious policies into annexed territories, satellite republics, and eventually the empire. The revolutionaries before him had attempted to promote republican cults in place of Christianity and to give rights to religious minorities in the newly acquired French departments. Napoleon assimilated and altered these goals to fit his views on state-building and the social utility of religion. As within France, he sought to establish state authority over religions, institute religious toleration on behalf of social stability, and create rational and uniform mechanisms of governance by religious elites. He applied the Concordat of 1801–02 to the Belgian, Rhineland, and Piedmont departments. With difficulty, over the course of 1803–04, he negotiated a concordat for the Italian Republic, albeit one less favourable to him than the French version. Eventually, even in other parts of the empire not governed by these concordats, he also initiated a host of controversial religious reforms, such as the nationalization of church lands, the abolition of monasteries, and the partial implementation of religious toleration.

Napoleon's concordats and religious course of action had entirely different effects in France and the conquered territories. In France, his settlement in many ways reversed the de-Christianizing manoeuvres of the radical Revolution and managed to defuse and weaken counter-revolutionary sentiment. In contrast, the other areas of Europe, with the exception of Belgium, had not experienced the full force of the zealous de-Christianization campaign of the Revolution. Across Europe, Napoleon's religious policies wreaked havoc with local practices and provoked substantial resistance across classes and across both urban and rural populations. Some Protestant and Catholic elites, who had grown disillusioned with revolution, war, and the unmet promises of the Enlightenment, rejected Napoleon and embraced a new Christian romanticism, kindled by popular writers, such as Novalis or Chateaubriand. Even more widespread was the grassroots resistance of peasants from Spain to Italy to Tyrol who felt their very way of life threatened by Napoleonic cultural reforms. By unleashing widespread resentment, the emperor's religious policies played a crucial role in arousing opposition and contributed to his eventual downfall.

In the early 1800s, Napoleon anticipated that his aim of strengthening state control over churches and simplifying religious practice would win the support of secular princes and reform-minded administrators. In the Holy Roman Empire, the politics of religious reform became entangled with the complex issue of how to redraw territorial boundaries as the old empire was dismantled bit by bit. By the Treaty of Lunéville in 1801, the prince-bishoprics were divided up between Napoleon and the German princes. Some territorial rulers welcomed the opportunity to appropriate monastic lands and to expand their state boundaries. Elector Max-Joseph of Bavaria had already undertaken a reformist agenda inspired by Joseph II of Austria; the Bavarian ruler and Maximilian von Montgelas, his Enlightenment-inspired minister, happily gobbled up smaller states, including Bamberg, Nuremberg, Augsburg, Freising, and Passau, as well as the Tyrol. Montgelas of Bavaria and Melzi d'Eril of Milan became prime examples of ministers bent on expediting secularization and restructuring church life, but many administrators from Württemberg to Naples pursued a similar set of goals.

For ordinary citizens, the Napoleonic religious reforms struck deep into popular customs and local social organization. The texture of religious life changed in many ways. Catholicism was now meant to be streamlined and centred on the parish church and the local clergyman. Authorities frequently reduced the number of parishes and closed down chapters, confraternity chapels, monasteries, and convents. In Italy, for example, the number of parishes declined from fifty-three to eighteen in Bologna and eighteen to six in Rimini. Disbanding abbeys, priories, and convents enabled state administrators to confiscate art and lands, move entire libraries to secular sites, and sell off valuable properties. With their lives disrupted, monks and nuns were expected to return to their families of origin. With few economic options, nuns in particular tended to remain together and even to re-establish clandestine convents. The laity felt the loss of convents that had provided charitable and medical aid. Italian confraternities had frequently been allied with religious orders and now could become focal points for resistance against French integration. In Turin, for example, the aristocratic confraternity of Saint Paul and the more populist Saint Francis confraternity became strongholds of opposition to the new prefect, while the Association of Christian Friendship circulated anonymous tracts against the Concordat.

At the same time, some secular authorities cracked down on all sorts of popular religious practices that were considered either superstitious or disorderly. When Napoleon called a national church council in 1811, its formal document, 'Views on the organization of Catholic worship', summarized official attitudes: it was the duty of the church 'to lend a hand in the eradication of superstitious practices, those shameful leftovers of medieval barbarism'. Napoleon's own attitude was pragmatic; he was scornful of popular religion, but had more interest in maintaining social and religious order than in repressing specific beliefs. Many of his administrators nonetheless worked hard to eradicate local festivals, suppress pilgrimages, reduce the number of saints' days, and close down confraternities. Authorities who remembered the divisive 1790s in France moved with caution. French administrators in the Rhineland, for example, chose local religious feast days to celebrate new revolutionary festivals. But some tactics were blatantly insensitive: one French official worried that the adjutant-general in Rome had created unnecessary offence by galloping 'with twenty-four dragoons through a canonization ceremony of some new saints'.[10] Napoleonic policies fostered a defiant defence of outdoor processions, healing rituals, clandestine confraternities, Marian devotional practices, and saints' cults.

The Napoleonic attempt to institute religious toleration also proved deeply controversial. Certain groups, such as Dutch Catholics, Protestant minorities in former German bishoprics, and Jews in many locations, stood to benefit from this innovation. Two factors, however, made the process especially difficult to implement. First, local animosities between sects ran deep. If subgroups of Protestants and Catholics often viewed each other with profound suspicion, the emancipation of the Jews was particularly resented and resisted across the empire. Only Westphalia attempted to bring about full emancipation. Second, the Napoleonic agenda combined legal toleration with a drive towards rationalizing religious organizations and creating legal uniformity. As Stuart Woolf has argued, this process ran roughshod over complex social relationships between and within denominations. In Holland for example, Napoleon wanted to replace the 'anarchy of practical toleration' with a stream-lined system merging the smaller sects into three official religions. Charles Lebrun, his representative, sought to temper Napoleon's regimen, acknowl-edging the divisions and differences, for example, between Anabaptists and Calvinists, old and new Lutherans, Sephardic and Ashkenazic Jews.[11]

Priests had a mixed reaction to Napoleonic religious policies. Administrators enlisted them as civil servants and, if possible, as agents of order in the countryside. Although some reformist clergy seconded the suppression of 'superstitions' or used their influence to support the empire, it was not always so easy to convert them to the total Napoleonic vision. Some priests in Italian, Spanish, and German lands were potential allies who had been inspired by Jansenist or democratizing ideas. But for them – as for Grégoire and many constitutional clergy in France – the concordats and policies of the early 1800s marked a moment of disillusionment, a missed opportunity for clerical democratization and inner reform of the church. Many other priests, especially those with ultramontane sympathies in locations like Belgium or Naples, only paid lip-service to ecclesiastical reforms. Michael Broers has found countless incidences in Italy of priests who used the liturgy as a political weapon and blatantly refused to celebrate the required Te Deums or public prayers for the emperor and his victories. Most famously, the clergy of Rome deserted the stalls of St Peter's when it came time to 'celebrate the birth of the King of Rome "in his own city" in 1811'.[12] Nowhere did the clergy play a greater role in fomenting opposition to Napoleon than in Spain. Especially once Napoleon had appointed his brother Joseph to replace the Spanish Bour-bons in 1808, clergymen from Galicia to Andalusia championed a veritable cru-sade of guerrilla warfare against the 'Antichrist' Napoleon and his anticlerical armies.

Napoleon did not improve matters by undermining his diplomatic relations with Pope Pius VII. Although the two men never saw eye to eye, at least in the early 1800s they had negotiated two concordats and the pope had participated, albeit reluctantly, in Napoleon's coronation as emperor. However, as Napoleon continued to expand his empire, the pope strove to maintain his political independence and quietly declined to accede to Napoleon's growing list of demands, despite the emperor's repeated threats. In 1806, Pius VII denied recognition to Napoleon's brother Joseph Bonaparte as the newly installed King of Naples. Although he agreed to begin negotiations with Napoleon for a new concordat to govern the German states, the pope balked in 1807 at joining the alliance against Britain and granting the French use of his ports. Napoleon fulminated in a letter to his Italian viceroy Eugène de Beauharnais, 'What does Pius VII want to do . . . put my thrones under interdiction, excommunicate me? . . . Does he believe that our century has returned to the ignorance and brutishness of the ninth century? Why doesn't the pope want to render unto Caesar what is Caesar's?'[13]

Within months imperial troops had occupied Rome and made Pius VII a prisoner within the Vatican. (They later moved him to Liguria and eventually to Fontainebleau in 1812.) In 1809, Napoleon annexed the Papal State as two new French departments. Calmly recalcitrant, the pope withheld investiture from new bishops and refused to bless Napoleon's new marriage with Marie-Louise of Austria. As a result, their son, defiantly named the King of Rome, was illegitimate in the eyes of the church. Napoleon's original Concordat with the church had essentially crumbled, while Pius's stature rose dramatically and his ill treatment fostered ever-greater resentment towards Napoleon in Catholic Europe. Bonaparte pressured the pope into signing a new even more Gallican agreement, the Concordat of Fontainebleau, but the empire collapsed before its implementation and Napoleon finally sent Pius back to Italy in 1814.

The disastrous breakdown of Napoleon's relations with the papacy and the Catholic Church in some ways paralleled the broader trajectory of Napoleon's rule. Just as his geopolitical reach had far exceeded his grasp by 1813, so too his religious policy had suffered because he overestimated his own power and his ability to effect far-reaching change. In moving too far beyond the successful religious pacification of France in 1802, Napoleon had proved only too well his own insight that political peace demanded a secure religious settlement within Europe. While Europeans rejoiced at Napoleon's downfall, many Catholics in France welcomed back the Bourbon monarchy, deeply allied with the church.

For all that the Bourbons might dream of returning to the *ancien régime*, the revolutionary and Napoleonic eras had fundamentally transformed Catholicism. Until the 1905 separation of church and state, the Concordat of 1801–02 framed the complex relationship between the newly secular state and the Catholic Church, debunked from its *ancien régime* dominance yet solidly acknowledged as the 'religion of the majority of the French'. Moreover, the divisive religious politics of the 1790s lived on in French memory: Catholicism, most often allied with the Right, remained deeply embroiled in the political struggles between Left and Right. Last but not least, in France and the empire, the revolutionary and Napoleonic eras had fostered both secularization and religious zeal: over the course of the nineteenth century, the decline in religious practice would co-exist with currents of deep devotion.

Notes

1. Quoted in Nigel Aston, *Religion and revolution in France, 1780–1804* (Washington, DC: Catholic University of America Press, 2000), p. 288.

2. Quoted in Claude Langlois and Timothy Tackett, 'A l'épreuve de la Révolution (1770–1830)', in François Lebrun (ed.), *Histoire des Catholiques en France du XVe siècle à nos jours* (Toulouse: Privat, 1980), p. 265.

3. Citations from Suzanne Desan, *Reclaiming the sacred: Lay religion and popular politics in revolutionary France* (Ithaca: Cornell University Press, 1990), chap. 4; and André Latreille, *L'Eglise catholique et la Révolution française*, 2 vols. (Paris: Hachette, 1946–50), vol. 1, p. 224.

4. Cited in Jean-Claude Meyer 'Les réactions populaires à la lutte antireligieuse menée en Haute-Garonne', in Bernard Plongeron (ed.), *Pratiques religieuses dans l'Europe révolutionnaire (1770–1820). Actes du colloque à Chantilly, 27–29 novembre 1986* (Paris: Brepols, 1988), p. 341.

5. My emphasis. Archives nationales, F⁷ 7424, letter from *curé* Tronchoy to the cantonal administration in Epineuil, 20 Ventôse An VI (10 March 1798).

6. Cited in Ralph Gibson, *A social history of French Catholicism, 1789–1914* (London: Routledge, 1989), p. 47, and Martin Lyons, *Napoleon Bonaparte and the legacy of the French Revolution* (New York: St Martin's Press, 1994), p. 83.

7. Frederic Cople Jaher, *The Jews and the nation: Revolution, emancipation, state formation, and the liberal paradigm in America and France* (Princeton: Princeton University Press, 2002), p. 121. See also Ronald Schechter, *Obstinate Hebrews: Representations of Jews in France, 1715–1815* (Berkeley: University of California Press, 2003), chap. 6.

8. Cited in Jacques-Olivier Boudon, *Napoléon et les cultes. Les religions en Europe à l'aube du XIXe siècle, 1800–1815* (Paris: Fayard, 2002), p. 100.

9. Aston, *Religion and revolution*, p. 345.

10. Citations from Nigel Aston, *Christianity and revolutionary Europe, c. 1750–1830* (Cambridge: Cambridge University Press, 2002), pp. 282–3; Stuart Woolf, *Napoleon's integration of Europe* (London: Routledge, 1991), pp. 206–7.

11. Woolf, *Napoleon's integration of Europe*, pp. 210–11.

12. Michael Broers, *The politics of religion in Napoleonic Italy: The war against God, 1801–1814* (London: Routledge, 2002), p. 80.

13. Quoted in Boudon, *Napoléon et les cultes*, pp. 241–2.

29

Movements of Christian awakening in revolutionary Europe, 1790–1815

STEWART J. BROWN

On 10 September 1815, Tsar Alexander I of Russia held a review of his army to celebrate the final allied victory over Napoleonic France. Over 150,000 soldiers assembled on the Plain of Vertus, a vast natural amphitheatre located some eighty miles east of Paris. Amid glorious late summer weather, the troops conducted elaborate manoeuvres, punctuated by the sound of 540 cannon, in the presence of the Tsar and his brother sovereigns, the Emperor of Austria and the King of Prussia. Seated in a court barouche near the Tsar, dressed in a blue serge dress and straw hat, was Julie, Baroness de Krüdener. Informal spiritual advisor to the Tsar and self-proclaimed prophetess, the Baroness was, in the words of the French Protestant author, Madame de Stäel, 'the forerunner of a great religious epoch which is dawning for the human race'.[1] On the following day, the feast day of St Alexander Nevsky, 150,000 soldiers celebrated Mass on the plain, organized into seven squares before seven altars. In describing the event, Baroness de Krüdener was ecstatic. 'I saw at the head of the army', she observed of the Tsar, 'the man of great destinies, the man prepared before the ages and for the ages. The Eternal had summoned Alexander and, obediently, Alexander had answered the call of the Eternal.'[2] Fifteen days later, the sovereigns of Russia, Austria, and Prussia signed a document, largely drafted by Alexander, which would become known as the 'Holy Alliance'. By this, they solemnly pledged to govern their lands and conduct their mutual relations in accordance with 'the sublime truths which the Holy Religion of our Saviour teaches'. In the following months, most of the states of Europe subscribed. The triumph over Napoleonic France, it seemed, was destined to usher in the revival of Christendom in Europe.

The great event staged on the Plain of Vertus reflected the belief shared by much of Europe that the victory over Napoleon had been the fulfilment of God's plan and the fruit of a Christian reawakening. The quarter century dominated by the French Revolution and Napoleonic empire had been a time of devastating warfare, economic distress and social dislocation. It had also been a time of profound challenge to the churches of Europe, perhaps the greatest challenge to Christianity since the Reformation. The attacks upon Christian beliefs and practices, the pillaging of churches across continental Europe, the seizures of church lands, and the assault upon the traditional social order had raised questions about the survival of organized Christianity. But those twenty-five years of war and upheaval had also witnessed Christian revival movements across Europe. Amid the storm and stress, many came to reject the rationalism of the later Enlightenment and the revolutionary promises of a new order, and returned to Christian interpretations of human nature and human destiny. Men and women turned to Christianity to seek meaning behind the forces that were violently transforming European civilization, to gain consolation over the losses experienced through warfare, and to find emotional stability amid the dislocations of the times. They looked to Christianity for the regeneration of individuals and nations. In 1815, many believed, their faithfulness was rewarded.

Revolution and awakening

At its beginning in 1789, the French Revolution had not been widely perceived outside France as a challenge to Christianity. While some conservatives, most famously the Irish politician and philosopher, Edmund Burke, did predict that the Revolution would desecrate all things holy, many European Christians had looked favourably upon the early phase of the French Revolution. The Revolution, they had believed, would free the church in France from its enthralment with royal absolutism and aristocratic patronage. That church would no longer be a wealthy and privileged corporation, drawing excessive tithes, rents, and dues from society, and placing heavy burdens on the poor. Its clergy would learn to live more modestly as true pastors to the people. In the Rhineland of Germany, probably the majority of the Catholic laity looked with favour upon the reforms imposed in 1789–91 by the French National Assembly on the Catholic Church in France – especially the reduction of the church's tithes, properties and feudal privileges. In Britain, Protestant Dissenters pointed to the new rights of citizenship granted by the French National Assembly to French Protestants and they argued that the Revolution would in time promote religious freedom and Christian morality. In his 'Discourse on the love of our country', delivered in November 1789, the Unitarian preacher, Richard Price, portrayed the Revolution as destined to unite all the nations in 'ardour for liberty'. 'The dominion of priests', he proclaimed, 'was giving way to the dominion of reason and conscience'.[3] This new dispensation was destined to spread beyond France, undermining the old alliance of church and state across

Europe, and bringing religious liberty. In Prussia, the young Reformed clergy-man, Friedrich Schleiermacher, confided to his father as late as February 1793 that 'upon the whole I heartily sympathize with the French Revolution'.[4] This early support for the Revolution, however, faded as the Revolution grew more violent, and as members of the clergy began fleeing France in large numbers, bringing with them harrowing tales of atrocities. As reports of the Terror and de-Christianization campaign in France spread, it grew clear that the Revolution was becoming an unparalleled challenge to European Christianity.

The fear and unrest stirred by the Revolution in France also contributed to religious yearnings, as many Europeans responded to the political tensions by embracing a gospel that promised both salvation in the next world and a sense of individual dignity and worth in the present. In the United Kingdom, the 1790s witnessed a new religious zeal among Protestant Dissenters, and especially Wesleyan Methodists, and a resurgence of the Evangelical movement that had first emerged in the 1730s. This revival movement, to be sure, was not solely a response to the Revolution. Along with the political ferment, much of Britain was now experiencing the social dislocations of early industrialization, with the spread of mechanized production bringing large-scale movements of population, threatening livelihoods and ways of life, and driving many into dire poverty. Amid this social unrest, there emerged a growing number of itinerant evangelists, many of them labouring people, barely literate and without ordination in any church. Some of them were supported by Dissenting congregations or voluntary religious societies; some supported themselves through labour or relied on the goodwill of local people. The itinerants moved through the countryside, preaching in barns, in cottages, on roadsides, or in fields. They entered the new industrial villages that were mushrooming in the north and midlands of England, and the central lowlands of Scotland. These were often rough and violent places, growing up largely outside the pastoral care of the established churches. The evangelists brought to the inhabitants a simple gospel of human sin and depravity, of salvation through the atoning sacrifice of Christ, and of sanctification under the influence of the Holy Spirit. They preached in a direct, homespun language, aimed at the understandings of labouring people. Their meetings were often loud and unruly, punctuated by spontaneous prayer, singing, shouts and the violent convulsions of sinners in agony. These meetings also provided a sense of communal belonging, and when the itinerating evangelists moved on to the next village, the converts they left behind would often form themselves into congregations, which might meet in a cottage, barn, or rented room. These congregations, in turn, frequently began sending out lay evangelists to neighbouring villages. As well as labouring men, the itinerants included forceful women preachers, such as Ann ('Praying Nanny') Cutler, Mary Barritt or Elizabeth Tomlinson.

The growth of evangelical Dissent between 1790 and 1815 in Britain was unprecedented, as tens of thousands experienced conversion. By law, Dissenting congregations were required to register with the local magistrates. Between 1781 and 1790, 1,405 new Dissenting congregations were registered in England. This number rose to 4,245 new congregations between 1791 and 1800, and to 5,434 new Dissenting congregations between 1801 and 1810. The numbers of Methodists in England increased from about 47,000 in 1786 to 190,000 by 1816.[5] In Ireland, Methodist numbers rose from about 14,000 to 29,000 between 1791 and 1815, with most of this growth occurring among the linen weavers in Ulster.[6] In Scotland, the Society for Propagating the Gospel at Home, formed in 1798, conducted a vigorous evangelical mission, resulting in the formation of scores of Independent and later Baptist congregations by 1815. Connections were formed with the revival movement, known as the Second Great Awakening, now emerging across the Atlantic in the new American republic. From 1805, American itinerant preachers, such as Lorenzo 'Crazy' Dow – with his long patriarchal beard and wild eyes – began arriving in Britain and Ireland, bringing with them the revival methods of the American frontier, including the 'camp meetings', large outdoor gatherings which continued for several days. The first English camp meeting was held by Methodists in May 1807 at Mow Cop in Staffordshire.

The evangelistic activity was accompanied by efforts to instil basic literacy among the lower social orders through the Sunday school movement. Sunday schools, largely non-denominational in nature, provided instruction in reading as well as Christian doctrine, and they were largely organized and taught by lay Christians from the labouring orders. In 1788, there were about 60,000 Sunday school enrolments in England. This number increased to over 94,000 in 1795, 206,000 in 1801, and 415,000 in 1811.[7]

Within the established churches in Britain and Ireland, a growing number were also drawn into this movement of Christian revival. A circle of wealthy and committed evangelicals, mainly members of the established Church of England and based in the London neighbourhood of Clapham, began in the 1790s to cultivate a strict personal and family piety and to organize home and overseas mission work. This circle included William Wilberforce, the opponent of slavery, whose *Practical view of the prevailing religious system of professed Christians* was published in 1797 and had an immense effect in spreading an evangelical Christianity among the upper social orders. It also included Hannah More, the patron of Sunday schools, whose 'Cheap repository tracts', published in the 1790s with the aim of instilling Christian virtues among the labouring orders, had a massive distribution. In Scotland and Ireland, evangelical parties grew in influence within the established churches from the 1790s. The conversion of Thomas Chalmers in 1811 produced an impassioned and highly influential evangelical preacher within the Church of Scotland. The 1790s also witnessed the beginning of the modern British overseas mission movement, with the formation of the Baptist Missionary Society in 1792, the London Missionary Society in 1795, and the Church Missionary Society in 1799. The Baptist shoemaker and preacher, William Carey, proclaimed in 1792 that Christians were under an obligation to bring the gospel immediately to all the world, including distant lands sunk 'in the most deplorable state of heathen darkness'[8]; within a year, he sailed to India as a missionary.

There was heightened Protestant evangelical activity elsewhere in Europe, much of it, as in Britain, driven by the laity and occurring outside the established churches. In Protestant Germany, Pietist communities viewed the French Revolution as the fruit of the false philosophies of the Enlightenment, as a judgement of God upon a corrupt social and religious order, and as a divine call for social regeneration. Pietism, which for much of the eighteenth century had been restricted to conservative, inward-looking groups of the nobility and upper bourgeoisie – the 'quiet voices in the land' – became more assertive in the 1790s, more ready to challenge the existing order in church and state, and to evangelize among artisans and peasants. In Württemberg, the ascetic Pietist lay evangelist of peasant background, Johann Michael Hahn, gathered a large, mainly peasant following in the 1790s and began organizing his converts on a congregational pattern outside the established church. The preaching of Christian Gottlob Pregizer led in the same decade to the formation of conventicles of fervent hymn-singing converts, known as the 'Hurrah Christians', located mainly in the Black Forest. By 1800, more than fifty voluntary Christian societies had been established in Württemberg. Pietist evangelical outreach was also promoted by the Christianity Society (*Christentumgesellschaft*) which had been founded in 1780 in Basel for the purpose of providing charity and supporting evangelism. During the 1790s it established branch societies in Swiss and German towns and cities, and became active in circulating Christian tracts. In Berlin, the saintly Moravian preacher, Johannes Jänicke, gathered a considerable following, especially among pious aristocrats, with his simple, humble, and emotional preaching; in 1800, he founded a school in Berlin for the training of missionaries. The revival movement was stimulated by the warm, emotional writings of the Pietist layman, Johann Heinrich Jung-Stilling, Christian mystic, physician, professor of economics, and councillor to the Grand

Duke of Baden. Jung-Stilling's novel, *Heimweh*, published in 1794, exercised a profound influence with its view of life as pilgrimage. The revival also found support from the writings of the Swiss Christian educationalist, Johann Heinrich Pestalozzi, with his passionate belief that all children, regardless of social background, had an equal claim on educational opportunity.

The evangelical activity spread among the Lutherans in Scandinavia. In eastern Denmark and western Norway, the 1790s saw the beginnings of a rural lay evangelical movement, with a Pietist character. Hans Nielson Hauge, a farmer's son, experienced conversion in 1796 and embarked on a career as an itinerant lay preacher. He travelled some 10,000 miles over the next six years, preaching almost daily and criticizing what he viewed as the dead orthodoxy of the established church. From 1804 to 1814, the civil authorities intermittently imprisoned him for breaking the laws against lay preaching. Nonetheless, he organized a large popular movement in the rural areas, training followers as lay preachers and establishing mills and workshops to provide employment. A Danish Evangelical Society was formed in 1801. In Sweden, a revival movement emerged about 1800, associated with 'New Readers', lay people who read and interpreted Scripture to households in the scattered farmsteads. An Evangelical Society was organized under Moravian influence in Stockholm in 1808 and awakenings occurred in the south-west of Sweden from about 1810, associated with the impassioned preaching of Jacob Otto Hoof. Revivals, rooted in Pietism, occurred in Finland from about 1800; a leading figure was the farmer and lay preacher, Paavo Ruotsalainen, who was converted in 1796. There were further revivals after 1800 in the Baltic regions of Estonia and Latvia, inspired largely by the work of Moravians.

In Catholic regions, new movements of popular devotion emerged in the 1790s. Antipathy to both the anti-Catholic campaigns of the French revolutionaries and to reforms imposed by the Habsburg state on the Catholic Church contributed to a popular devotional movement among Catholics in the mountainous Tyrol region in the early 1790s. Despite initial opposition from the imperial government, the movement, which drew inspiration from the cult of the Sacred Heart, gained a large following – with processions, feasts and passion plays, and visions of saints and the Virgin. There were further revivals of popular devotion to the Virgin in northern and central Italy. During one six-month period in 1796, the Papal States had 114 reported incidents of statues of the Madonna moving her eyes, of which twenty-four were judged by the authorities as miraculous.[9] In 1801–02, Fr Luigi Mozzi, a former Jesuit, led a series of popular missions in the diocese of Treviso, spreading popular devotion to both the Virgin and the Stations of the Cross.

The popular revival movements emerging across Europe during the 1790s shared certain common characteristics. They opposed the scepticism and materialism prevalent in the later Enlightenment, and the rationalism and moderatism pervading the established churches. They viewed the French Revolution as a divine visitation, and they looked to a revival of Christianity as a means of averting or alleviating the judgement of God. But the revival movements were not simply reactions against the Revolution. They also shared some of the ideals of the Revolution, including an emphasis on elevating the condition of the common people. The evangelical work was directed largely to the middle and lower social orders, and emphasized the belief that every individual was of equal value before God. In a time of turbulence, it spread the message that God was on the side of the common people. It included efforts to expand popular education. The revival movements were also largely driven by lay activists from the middle and lower social orders. These leaders were characterized more by passion and commitment, than by social status, education, ordination, and clerical career patterns. The movements were largely outside the established churches and indeed were frequently opposed by the authorities in church and state. They were, to an extent, about the empowerment of the common people. For those touched by these movements, God redeemed individuals, regardless of their social status, and God's spirit entered into the redeemed, enabling them to do His will in the world.

Millenarianism and Romanticism

In the 1790s, as the armies of the French Republic moved beyond the borders of France into the Rhineland, the Low Countries, and Italy, they brought with them the anti-Christian attitudes and policies of the revolutionary regime. In Belgium, French republicans purged the Catholic Church in the later 1790s, suppressing monasteries, selling off monastic lands, listing nearly 8,000 priests for deportation and actually deporting nearly 2,000 priests.[10] In the Rhineland, French forces and their local republican supporters abolished tithes, banned the ringing of church bells, religious ceremonies, processions and symbols outside church buildings, made civil marriage compulsory and imposed a system of election of parish priests. French soldiers could be coarse in their blasphemy, mutilating statues, building fires on altars, defecating into tabernacles, and parodying Christian worship.[11] In Italy, the invading French armies looted churches and broke up monasteries, friaries, and convents. In February 1798, French troops occupied Rome and established a Roman Republic. The frail Pope Pius VI was removed from Rome, and died in Valence in the south of France in August 1799. After some months of confusion, a conclave of cardinals met in the Venetian lagoon and elected in 1800 a new pope, Luigi Chiaramonti, Bishop of Imola, who was widely believed to sympathize with the Revolution. The Catholic Austrian empire opposed the election and it was by no means clear that Chiaramonti, who took the name Pius VII, would be accepted as pope by the church at large. For some critics, the papacy seemed to be tottering.

In 1799, Napoleon Bonaparte's seizure of power in France opened a new phase of violent upheaval in Europe. Napoleon restored the Catholic Church in France with the Concordat of 1801, which he extended to Belgium and the Rhineland; he negotiated a further Concordat for the Catholic Church in Italy in 1803–04. The concordats, however, gave his regime considerable control over the Catholic Church. In 1804, Napoleon raised himself, with the pope's sanction, to the imperial throne. Napoleon's victories in Germany, meanwhile, led to fundamental territorial revisions, including the abolition of ecclesiastical states and the redrawing of political boundaries without reference to the confessional identities of populations. The old formula of 'cuius regio eius religio' ceased to have meaning; the political-religious order that had prevailed since the Peace of Westphalia of 1648 came to an end. In 1806, the abolition of the Holy Roman Empire closed a millennium of European history.

Amid the unprecedented assault on Christianity and unparalleled social and political upheavals, many in Europe turned to Scripture, and especially scriptural prophecy, in the search for meaning behind the events. Some saw the victories of the French armies, the weakening of the papacy, and the elevation of a Corsican adventurer to an imperial throne as signs and wonders that according to Scripture would presage the Second Coming of Christ in glory and the beginning of the millennium of rule by the saints. New prophetic voices were heard. In France, there had been millenarian currents before the Revolution, associated with cells of Convulsionaries, charismatic elements of the Jansenist movement that met quietly for prayer, devotion, and the study of unfulfilled biblical prophecy. Their influence extended beyond France. In the 1780s and early 1790s, one such group, the Avignon Society, attracted enthusiasts from throughout Europe for the study of biblical prophecy.

There were prophetic and millenarian movements in England, and especially London, from the later 1780s. Some visionaries, including two London artisans who had lived for several months with the Avignon Society, embraced the mystical writings of Emmanuel Swedenborg, the Swedish natural philosopher who had died in London in 1772. The Church of the New Jerusalem, inspired by Swedenborg's teachings, was established in London in 1787, and spread to other English cities in the early 1790s. The poet and illustrator, William Blake, was drawn to the Swedenborgian belief in the coming of the New Jerusalem. Some visionaries revived the teachings of the Muggletonians, an obscure seventeenth-century sect; for them, the age of the Holy Spirit had begun and the reign of the saints was imminent. Others were drawn to the belief, rooted in the eschatological claims of the biblical books of Daniel and Revelation, that the Second Coming of Christ would be immediately preceded by the restoration of the Jews to the holy land. The rational Dissenter, Joseph Priestley, came to believe that the restoration of the Jews was imminent. In 1793, he declared in a sermon that the three great prophecies of Scripture – the fall of the papal Antichrist, the collapse of the Ottoman Empire, and the restoration of the Jews to the holy land – were now being fulfilled. He was convinced that he would personally witness Christ's return in glory.

In the mid-1790s, Richard Brothers, a retired naval officer, proclaimed himself to be the nephew of God and king of the Hebrews, and prophesied the destruction of London by earthquake. He promised to gather all the Jews, including the 'hidden Jews' who had assimilated into gentile society and lost their identity, and lead them back to the holy land in anticipation of the millennium. His prophetic claims attracted a following. 'All the madmen and enthusiasts in England', observed the poet Robert Southey in 1807, 'made a common cause with this King of the Hebrews'. 'One madman', Southey continued,

> printed his dreams, another his day-visions; one had seen an angel come out of the sun with a sword drawn in his hand, another had seen fiery dragons in the air, and hosts of angels in battle array; these signs and tokens were represented in rude engravings and the lower classes of people . . . began to believe that the seven seals were about to be opened, and the wonders of the Apocalypse would be displayed.[12]

Brothers was declared insane in 1795 and placed in a private asylum, where he remained until 1806. By then, his influence was eclipsed by that of a new prophetess, Joanna Southcott, a labouring woman from Devon, who had begun conveying divine messages in 1792 and who came to London in 1802. Claiming to be the 'woman clothed in the sun' as described in Revelation 12, she also insisted that she had been called by the Holy Spirit to 'seal' believers in advance of the Last Judgement, which was fast approaching. For her, the French Revolution was a visitation from God, a final summons to the world to turn from sin. By 1814, some 20,000 people, mainly from the London artisan classes, had received her seal. Southcott promised to give birth to Shiloh, a shadowy messianic figure, but she died in 1814 after a false pregnancy. Her followers convinced themselves that the birth of Shiloh had occurred in a spiritual sense and they continued to adhere to her teachings.

The passion for prophecy spread through British society. Samuel Horsley, Church of England Bishop of Rochester, interpreted the French Revolution in apocalyptic terms. In 1800, he discerned in 'the raging sea of Anarchy and Irre-ligion . . . the dreadful Apocalyptic Beast . . . in its ancient form'. By 1806, he had become convinced that Napoleon would return most of the Jews to Palestine and proclaim himself the Messiah, before being revealed as the Antichrist.[13] Spencer Perceval, prime minister from 1809 until his assassination in 1812, poured over biblical prophecy in an effort to understand the unfolding world events. Millenarian beliefs infused the work of Samuel Frey, a German-born Jewish convert who studied at Jänicke's Berlin mission school, immigrated to London in 1801 and established the London Society for Promoting Christian-ity amongst the Jews in 1809. In Ireland, 'prophecy men' spread millenarian visions through Ulster and Connaught in the mid 1790s, while in the same decade Trinity College, Dublin, emerged as a centre for prophetic speculation based on analysis of biblical chronology.

In Germany, Pietist communities embraced prophetic teachings amid the upheavals of revolution and invasion. Many believed that the Enlightenment had represented the false teachings of the Antichrist, and that the triumphs of the revolutionary and Napoleonic armies marked the raging of Satan on earth, which was the prelude to the return of Christ and the advent of the millennium. According to the historian Hartmut Lehmann, a quarter of Protestants in Württemberg at the end of the eighteenth century adhered to some form of millenarianism.[14] In 1800, a Protestant clergyman in Württemberg, Johann Jakob Friederich, published a work of prophecy, in which he claimed that God had called the poor and oppressed of the world to make their way to the holy land. There they were to build on Mount Zion a temple, which would be more beautiful than could be imagined. From this temple, a fountain would flow, the waters of which would cure all diseases and irrigate the land, transforming Palestine into a garden. Those living in the holy land would be safe from the final raging of the Antichrist, and would welcome Christ on his return in glory. In calling the faithful to make their way to Mount Zion, God also promised to the pilgrims, including the blind, the lame, the elderly and women about to give birth, His divine protection.[15]

Among those who heeded this call was Marie Kummer, a daughter of a Pietist lay preacher, who in 1801 joined a group of thirty pilgrims on the journey to Mount Zion. The pilgrims got as far as Vienna before they were turned back by the Austrian authorities. On her return Kummer continued her career as prophetess of the millennium. Influenced by such apocalyptic visions, others made different kinds of pilgrimages. The Württemberg Pietist weaver, Johann George Rapp, who believed he would live to see Christ's Second Coming, emigrated during 1803–04 with some 1,600 of his followers to North America. There they formed a community, which they named New Harmony, where they hoped for refuge during the time of the devil's raging before the coming of the millennium. Still other millenarian Pietists withdrew into their conventicles in Germany to await the world's last days.

Perhaps the most celebrated figure of the prophetic movement was the Baroness Julie de Krüdener (1764–1824), a German aristocrat from the Baltic region. The estranged wife of a diplomat, Julie de Krüdener was wealthy, affected, attractive, and flirtatious, and had spent much of her life travelling about Europe in search of pleasure. Her sentimental novel, *Valérie*, had received acclaim in fashionable circles at its publication in 1803. Then amid the warfare of 1805–07, and the crushing defeats of Austria, Prussia, and Russia, Julie was drawn into millenarian circles. She met the Pietist mystic, Jung-Stilling, who was now predicting that the millennium would begin in 1818 or 1819. In 1807, she became the confidante of Queen Louise of Prussia, a renowned beauty who had embraced an ascetic Christian piety amid her country's devastating defeat. By 1808, Julie had become part of an extravagant mystical Pietist coterie in Baden, led by Frederick Fontaines and including Marie Kummer. Preaching and prophesying to the common people, the coterie was harried from place to place by nervous authorities – until it was broken up. Julie, however, continued her mission as a self-proclaimed prophetess of the Second Coming. By 1814, she was an emaciated, prematurely aged figure, her thinning hair severely parted in the middle, her clothing plain and her manners stern. She had come to view Tsar Alexander I of Russia as God's chosen one, who would come from the north and lead the nations of Europe into a new Christian era.

Julie de Krüdener was not alone among the intellectuals of Europe in finding her way to a personal Christian faith or seeking in Christianity a new world-order of peace and unity. Disillusioned by the directions taken by the Revolution, a number of poets, authors and artists of the Romantic movement, with its celebration of subjective feeling, intuitive insight and freedom from convention, moved towards Christianity from about 1800. Friedrich Schleiermacher, a Protestant pastor with roots in Pietism, was part of the Jena circle of young Romantics surrounding the author Friedrich Schlegel; his friends convinced him to write an apology for Christianity, directed to intellectuals who rejected religion. Schleiermacher's *On religion: Speeches to its cultured despisers* appeared in 1799 and received immediate acclaim. Defining religion as 'a sense and a taste for the infinite', he portrayed religious motivation as rooted in a primal feeling, an intuitive sense of 'absolute dependence' on something totally other. A few years later, in 1802, François-René de Chateaubriand published his *Genius of Christianity*, with its praise of the creative, aesthetic spirit of Christianity. Influenced by such celebrations of religious feeling, kindred spirits began looking to religion as well as art for individual self-discovery. Friedrich Schlegel and his gifted wife, Dorothea Mendelssohn, converted to Catholicism in 1808. The idealist philosopher, Friedrich Schelling, moved towards Catholic Christianity from about 1806. A young Hamburg Jew, David Mendel, was converted to Christianity in part by Schleiermacher's *On Religion*. Taking the name 'Neander' at his baptism in 1806, he taught church history with a poetic passion at the University of Berlin from 1813. In England, the Romantic poet, Robert Southey, embraced a High Anglican faith in 1810.

Some Romantics were drawn to Christianity, and especially medieval Christianity, out of a longing for familial and communal order amid the political upheavals of the times. Friedrich von Hardenberg, a Romantic poet who wrote under the name of Novalis, had found consolation in Christianity following the death of his young fiancée. His essay, 'Christendom or Europe', written in 1799, employed an ecstatic, mystical language to extol the harmonies of a Christian world-order and to call upon the nations to return to this unity. Since the Reformation, sectarian and national divisions had brought only warfare; there must be a return to the common Christian faith of the Middle Ages. 'Blood will flow across Europe', he prophesied,

> Until the nations become aware of the terrible madness which drives them around in circles and until, affected and soothed by holy music, all in a varied group they approach their former altars to undertake the work of peace . . . Only religion can awaken Europe again and make the peoples secure.[16]

The essay circulated widely in manuscript – it was considered too controversial for publication in the *Athenäum*, the organ of the Jena circle – and it contributed significantly to a revived interest in medieval Catholicism. Also drawn to medieval institutions and the religious basis of community was the conservative political philosopher, Adam Müller, who converted to Roman Catholicism in 1805. His *Elements of Statecraft* (1808) promoted the notion of an organic national unity rooted in Christian teaching. Several German painters, including Johann Friedrich Overbeck, Franz Pforr, and Peter von Cornelius, embraced this veneration of medieval faith. Known as the Nazarines, they established a community in Rome in 1811, and sought to recover the styles and techniques of medieval Christendom.

Elements of both the millenarian enthusiasm for Christ's return and the Romantic longings for the unity of Christendom can be discerned in the Bible Society movement which swept across Europe in the early decades of the nineteenth century. The British and Foreign Bible Society was founded in London in 1804. Its aim was breathtaking in its simplicity and ambition: it would unite Christians of all denominations in the quest to provide every inhabitant of the world with access to a Bible, without note or comment, and printed in his or her native language. As the influence of the Bible reached into every home and heart, it would convert the world's population to a pure, scriptural Christianity, uniting all peoples in a common faith and bringing an end to war, oppression and injustice. The world would be made ready for the Second Coming. The London parent society promoted the organization of a network of auxiliary societies across Britain and Europe. The first continental auxiliary, the German Bible Society, was established at Nuremberg in May 1804. It moved its headquarters in 1806 to Basel, which became the principal centre for the printing and distribution of Bibles in central Europe. With the patronage of Frederick William III of Prussia, a Prussian Bible Society was established in 1805 in Berlin. It survived the defeat and occupation of Prussia in 1806–07, and was active in distributing Bibles in Poland and Bohemia. Largely through the efforts of a Scottish agent, the Congregationalist John Paterson, the Bible Society movement was carried across Scandinavia from 1807. In the summer of 1812, amid the momentous events of the invasion by Napoleon's grand army, Paterson arrived in Russia, visiting Moscow only days before the city fell to the French. Gaining the support of Prince Alexander Golitzin, minister for public worship and a mystical Pietist, Paterson convinced Tsar Alexander to approve the formation of a Russian Bible Society in January 1813. It soon established auxiliaries in Russia and Poland, becoming one of the most influential forces for publishing and popular education in Russia during the coming decade.

Religion, resistance, and national identity

The advance of the revolutionary armies beyond the borders of France in the 1790s had initially been welcomed by many in the occupied districts. They had looked on the French as liberators from oppressive regimes and antiquated social structures, and as representatives of Enlightenment thought and revolutionary ideals. Many others, however, hated the French invaders. They resented

French disdain for their traditions, feared conscription into the French armies, felt crushed by the financial exactions demanded by the French occupiers, and loathed their arrogance. Prominent among opponents of the French invaders were members of the clergy. The churches, as we have seen, suffered under French occupation. For the clergy, French occupation meant not only reduced incomes, but also their marginalization in the new social and political order. In response, clerics frequently denounced from the pulpit the Revolution and its works. They refused to take oaths of loyalty to the governments imposed by the French, and did not obey laws which they deemed anti-Christian. Some clerics went further and joined resistance movements, giving these movements the character of religious crusades, of struggles for God.

The late 1790s saw a number of popular counter-revolutionary resistance movements which received clerical support and employed Christian imagery. Catholic priests and the imagery of the Sacred Heart played a significant role in the popular resistance to French invasion in the Tyrol in 1796–97 (this was also the case in the popular resistance to the Revolution in the French Vendée, a struggle that was still raging in 1796–97). Catholic priests were prominent in the peasant risings against the French in Switzerland and Belgium in 1798; in consequence French vengeance fell heavily on the church. There were risings in northern Italy in 1799, with peasant bands fighting the French under banners emblazoned with images of the Virgin. In the south of Italy, religion was a vital element in the popular rising against the Parthenopean Republic that had been established with French support in January 1799 in Naples. Cardinal Fabrizio Ruffo gathered and led a peasant army, the 'Santafede', or 'Most Christian Armada of the Holy Faith'. Soon numbering 17,000, the Santafede overthrew the Parthenopean Republic with British naval support in June 1799, in the first successful counter-revolutionary rising in Europe. The warfare, with its religious sanctions, was brutal, and the Santafedist victory was followed by massacres of republicans, portrayed as enemies of God. In Italy, popular counter-revolutionary violence was also directed against Jews, who were seen as benefiting from the secularized order imposed by the French. During the 'revolt of the Roman Vespers' in February 1798, drunken crowds in Rome murdered any Jew, as well as Frenchmen, they encountered. The taking of Siena by counter-revolutionary peasant forces in 1799 was followed by a pogrom, including the burning alive of thirteen Jews on the 'liberty tree'.[17]

With the establishment of the French Empire in 1804 and the expansion of Napoleonic imperial domination in Europe, popular resistance movements became increasingly national in character. They used the language of national liberation and national destiny, with the nation defined as the people as a whole, its history, culture, and religion. In these movements, Christianity became linked to emerging nationalist fervour. The popular revolt against French dominance that began in Madrid in May 1808 and quickly spread across Spain employed the imagery of the crusade – with supporters comparing it to the medieval struggle for the liberation of Christian Spain from the Moors. Members of the clergy, and especially friars and monks, were active in the fighting; indeed some battalions were made up entirely of monks or friars. Franciscans defended heroically a key fort during the siege of Gerona, and Franciscans commanded guerrilla units in the hills. Bishops of the church in Spain presided over many of the local juntas set up to co-ordinate resistance. Priests portrayed Napoleon in Old Testament terms as a 'lash of punishment' from God, meant to summon the Spanish nation to righteousness, so that a repentant Spain could fulfil its destiny as God's chosen people of the Christian era. Preaching at a memorial service in 1809 in Cervera for the victims of the rising, a priest assured his congregation that in the midst of the present 'terrible convulsions, a golden century of prosperity and grandeur will be born'. 'May God', he added, 'finish this great work'.[18] In December 1808, Napoleon described the Spanish rising as 'an insurrection of monks' and French troops took murderous reprisals upon the Spanish clergy. This created martyrs and strengthened popular loyalty to the church. Catholicism was also a vital element in the peasant rising against French control in the Tyrol in the summer of 1809. Andreas Hofer, the leader of the rising, proclaimed that it was a struggle for 'God, Emperor and Fatherland', while a Capuchin friar, Joachim Haspringer, commanded part of Hofer's peasant army. In 1809, the pope resisted with a bull of excommunication the incorporation of the Papal States into the French Empire. In consequence he was arrested and eventually removed to France. His courageous refusal to submit to Napoleon's demands enhanced the popular image of the papacy across Catholic Europe.

When Napoleon's grand army invaded Russia in June 1812, the Tsar proclaimed the struggle 'a national Holy War for the Fatherland' while popular rage over the devastation wreaked by the invaders on churches and icons contributed to the resistance.[19] On the day before the battle of Borodino, when the Russian army confronted the Napoleonic forces outside Moscow, a solemn procession of priests and chanters moved along the Russian line, carrying on white linen bands the centuries-old icon of the Mother of God, rescued from the destruction of Smolensk. Soldiers, including the Russian commander, Marshall Kutusov, fell to their knees as the procession passed. During these bitter months, Tsar Alexander, who had been raised in the scepticism and anticlericalism prevalent in the later Enlightenment, experienced something akin to a religious conversion. The great fire that consumed Moscow, he later claimed, 'shed light in his soul'.[20] The destruction of the grand army on the retreat from Moscow was for many Europeans the work of God. As an English clergyman observed of Napoleon's Russian nemesis in a sermon in 1814:

> The valour and perseverance of the Russians did much, but the elements did more. God sent forth his own armies against him, the snow, the frost, the piercing cold, accompanied with disease and famine; and by these irresistible foes, his proud legions were in a few days almost annihilated.[21]

The destruction of Napoleon's army in Russia provided the occasion early in 1813 for a national rising in Prussia – a rising which also had the character of a Christian awakening. Many Prussians believed that the defeat and dismemberment of Prussia in the war of 1806–07 had been the bitter fruit of national sin and that national regeneration would come only through the Christian faith. After 1807, a number of Prussian clergymen, including Friedrich Schleiermacher, Gottfried Hanstein, H. T. Ribbeck and Ludwig Borowski, used sermons to prepare the population for national renewal and a war of liberation. As Schleiermacher assured a friend in 1808, Prussia was 'a chosen instrument and people of God' and was destined to rise again 'in full glory'.[22] When in 1813 Prussia declared war on Napoleonic France, its king called on all Germany 'to join us in our mission of liberation', while from their pulpits Protestant pastors portrayed the war as a holy crusade, and aroused patriotic fervour with the language of martyrdom, redemption and resurrection. For some clerics, the war was an opportunity to strengthen the traditional alliance of throne and altar in Prussia, and make the church again the principal bulwark of royal absolutism. For others, and especially Schleiermacher, the war promised to align the clergy with popular and liberal causes. In taking their part in the national struggle, the clergy would lay claim to the role of tribunes of the people. Many Germans viewed the 'Battle of the Nations' at Leipzig in October 1813 and the subsequent fall of Napoleonic France in providential terms. This was the view of the Pietist Ludwig Nicolovius, director of ecclesiastical affairs in Prussia. 'We are now witnessing God's miracles', he wrote to Countess Luise Stolberg in the spring of 1814, 'This is the beginning . . . of a new Jerusalem in which God Himself will be the center and source of everything'.[23]

This belief that Providence was guiding the nations took hold of Tsar Alexander. He was a tortured soul, ravaged by guilt over his complicity in the murder of his father that had brought him to the throne in 1801. Amid the devastation of his country in 1812, the Tsar had begun pouring over the Scriptures, under the influence of Prince Golitzin and other mystical masons in his court.

In July 1814, he met the Pietist mystic, Jung-Stilling, who urged him to take up the cause of Europe's salvation. Then on 4 June 1815, two weeks before the allies' final victory over Napoleonic France at Waterloo, the Tsar met the Baroness de Krüdener in curious circumstances at Heilbronn. He had been alone reading Scripture when he recalled hearing reports of the prophetess. As he did so, he was suddenly informed that she had arrived at the house seeking an audience. Believing her arrival to be a message from God, the Tsar closeted with her for three hours, listening intently to her assurances that he was chosen by God to lead the nations of Europe to a new Christian dispensation. The Baroness followed him in his subsequent movements to Heidelberg and Paris, and the two met regularly, usually clandestinely at night, for prayer and the study of prophecy. Under her influence, Alexander revived an idea for a European league of nations that he had first outlined in 1804. He now combined this league with a vision of revived Christendom to form the idea of the Holy Alliance. After September 1815, most of the European states – led by Russia, Austria, and Prussia – subscribed 'in the name of the Most Holy and Indivisible Trinity' to the treaty of three articles, pledging to govern according to the 'Principles of the Christian Religion', to pursue their relations with one another in a spirit of Christian love, and to promote Christian teachings among their peoples.

Christianity and the Restoration

With the end of the Napoleonic Wars came moves to strengthen the alliance of church and state, of throne and altar, throughout Europe. The fall of Napoleon was accompanied by efforts to place 'legitimate' rulers back on their thrones and to restore social hierarchies. Political leaders working to restore the old order looked to the churches to denounce the 'principles of 1789', to instruct the common people in patient acceptance of their place within the social hierarchy and to alleviate social tensions by providing charity and caring for war widows and orphans. The churches were to teach that authority in this world came, not from the people, but from God, and that it was communicated from above through divinely ordained rulers. Their message for Restoration Europe became less one of popular empowerment and liberation, and more one of human sinfulness and the need for order. For some politicians, to be sure, these appeals to Christian sentiment were a calculated means of restoring hierarchies of wealth and power. But there was also much genuine belief among such rulers as Tsar Alexander, Frederick William III of Prussia and Francis I of Austria. The churches for their part looked to the restored European rulers to support the reawakened Christianity. They called upon rulers to assist in rebuilding parish churches, cathedrals, abbeys, friaries, and convents, and in restoring, where possible, ecclesiastical lands and revenues. They expected the social elites to set examples of public and private devotion. Some looked to the Holy Alliance to unite the states of Europe in shared Christian values and preserve Europe from what they viewed as the twin evils of atheism and revolution.

The Roman Catholic Church, which in the later 1790s had been so severely weakened, now entered a new era of power and influence. Pope Pius VII returned to Rome from his French captivity amid popular adulation in 1814, and the representatives of the great powers meeting at Vienna agreed to restore most of the former papal territories to his temporal authority. Pius re-established the Jesuit order in 1814, and worked with new confidence to rebuild the structures of the church in war-torn Europe. Significantly, he did not subscribe to the Holy Alliance, on the grounds that the pope could not join with Protestant and Orthodox schismatics in rebuilding Christendom; that was the responsibility of the one true church. In France, the Restoration of the Bourbons to the throne brought increased influence for the Catholic Church. Conservative French thinkers, including Vicomte de Bonald, Joseph de Maistre, and the young Felicité de Lamennais, convinced many that only a strong Catholic Church could impose authority over the rebellious hearts and minds of fallen humanity and thus protect the social order from a renewal of revolution. In Spain, the hierarchy restored the Inquisition and silenced liberal reformers among the clergy who supported a constitutional monarchy. In the Habsburg territories, a triumphalist Catholic Church received political support from Prince Metternich and intellectual support from such Catholic romantics as Adam Müller and Friedrich Schlegel, who both glorified medieval Christendom.

European Protestantism also entered a new era of confidence and missionary outreach. In the United Kingdom, the state had in 1809 begun a programme of reforms of the established Protestant churches in England, Ireland, and Scotland, combined with large-scale investment of public money in strengthening pastoral care and religious instruction for the masses. A major parliamentary grant in 1818 contributed to the erection of hundreds of new churches in the urban districts of England. These so-called 'Waterloo churches' were intended as a national monument to the victory over Napoleonic France, and as a defence against the contagion of revolution among urban and industrial workers. There was also an increase of missionary activity, as the British State in 1813 officially opened its possessions in India to missionary activity and formed an Anglican Church establishment for India, with a bishopric at Calcutta. British missionaries and Bible Society agents were also active on the continent. High Church Anglicans raised money for post-war relief work in Germany; the Scottish evangelist, Robert Haldane, played a leading role in the revival that swept through French-speaking Protestant communities in Switzerland and France after 1816; and British evangelicals formed a Continental Society in 1818 to co-ordinate missionary activity. In Prussia, the Protestant awakenings continued after 1815. In rural districts, revival activity was promoted by aristocratic families, for whom evangelical Protestantism was a means of enhancing their local influence. In the towns and cities, the awakening was promoted by philanthropic and educational societies, which combined evangelism with practical charity, much of it initially inspired by the needs of war widows and orphans. Revival activity also continued in Scandinavia into the 1840s, while in Russia the Bible Society remained influential into the 1820s.

Christianity was again a powerful force in the Europe of 1815. For those with property, Christianity provided the antidote to the social resentments that led to revolutionary violence; for many artists and writers, it provided an affirming faith in opposition to the dry materialism and scepticism of the later Enlightenment. Among the lower social orders, church adherence offered mutual support and a sense of community, which became increasingly important as western Europe experienced the new upheavals of industrialization and rapid urbanization. For the clergy, the years after 1815 brought an enhanced sense of vocation and improved status in society; they were, for many, the guardians of the faith and the true defenders of the social order.

In the post-war years, the alliance of throne and altar would grow reactionary, and the Holy Alliance would change from the harbinger of a new Christian and moral European order into a symbol of oppression. Baroness de Krüdener died in the Crimea in December 1824, and Tsar Alexander died in the Crimea a year later; by then, their millenarian hopes had faded, along with their vision of a Christian concert of nations. The profound challenges to Christianity that we have explored in this volume were, moreover, re-emerging amid growing disillusionment with the Restoration. The nineteenth century would indeed witness further political revolutions, with revolutionaries denouncing Christianity as an obstacle to human progress and reform. The challenge to Christianity of the later Enlightenment would also resurface, with scientific materialism increasingly calling into question belief in God and providence. The Christian religion, however, would nonetheless remain a vital presence in Europe, a body of beliefs that had broad popular support and that proved capable of adapting to the changing social and political circumstances. Despite the powerful, unprecedented anti-Christian forces that had emerged in the later eighteenth century, the nineteenth century would be the 'great century' of Christian expansion and diversification in the world and of the campaign for the end of the moral stain of slavery. The Christian awakenings between 1790 and 1815, with their belief in divine intervention in human affairs, their emphasis on personal faith and devotion, and their calls for social activism, did much not only to preserve European Christianity against the unprecedented onslaught of the French Revolution, but also to strengthen it for the challenges and opportunities of the nineteenth century.

Notes

1. J. C. Herold, *Mistress to an age: A life of Madame de Staël* (London, 1959), p. 451.
2. H. Troyat, *Alexander of Russia: Napoleon's conqueror*, trans. J. Pinkham (New York: E. P. Dutton, 1982), p. 232.
3. R. Price, *A discourse on the love of our country* (London, 1790), pp. 40–1.
4. F. Schleiermacher, *The life of Schleiermacher, as unfolded in his autobiography and letters*, trans. F. Rowan, 2 vols. (London: Smith, Elder & Co., 1860), vol. 1, p. 109.
5. A. D. Gilbert, *Religion and society in industrial England: Church, chapel and social change 1740–1914* (London: Longman, 1976), pp. 34, 31.
6. G. M. Ditchfield, *The evangelical revival* (London: UCL Press, 1998), p. 92.
7. T. W. Laquer, *Religion and respectability: Sunday schools and working class culture 1780–1850* (New Haven: Yale University Press, 1976), p. 44.
8. W. Carey, *An enquiry into the obligations of Christians to use means for the conversion of heathens* (Leicester: Ann Ireland, 1792), p. 62.
9. M. Broers, *The politics of religion in Napoleonic Italy: The war against God, 1801–1814* (New York: Routledge, 2002), p. 55.
10. D. Beales, *Prosperity and plunder: European Catholic monasteries in the age of revolution* (Cambridge: Cambridge University Press, 2003), pp. 272–4.
11. T. C. W. Blanning, *The French Revolution in Germany: Occupation and resistance in the Rhineland, 1792–1802* (Oxford: Oxford University Press, 1983), pp. 220–5; Beales, *Prosperity and plunder*, pp. 282–6.
12. R. Southey, *Letters from England* (1807), ed. J. Simmons (London: Cresset, 1951), p. 431.
13. R. A. Soloway, *Prelates and people: Ecclesiastical social thought in England 1783–1852* (London: Routledge & Kegan Paul, 1969), pp. 39–40.
14. H. Lehmann, 'Pietistic millenarianism in late eighteenth-century Germany', in E. Hellmuth (ed.), *The transformation of political culture: England and Germany in the late eighteenth century* (Oxford: Oxford University Press, 1990), p. 333.
15. *Ibid.*, pp. 327–30.
16. [F. von Hardenberg], *Novalis: Philosophical writings*, trans. and ed. M. Mahony Stoljar (Albany, NY: State University of New York Press, 1997), p. 150.
17. N. Aston, *Christianity and revolutionary Europe c.1750–1830* (Cambridge: Cambridge University Press, 2002), pp. 230–1.

18. W. J. Callahan, *Church, politics, and society in Spain, 1750–1874* (Cambridge, MA: Harvard University Press, 1984), p. 91.

19. A. Palmer, *Alexander I: Tsar of war and peace* (London: Weidenfeld and Nicolson, 1974), p. 236.

20. Troyat, *Alexander of Russia*, p. 241.

21. G. Young, *The downfall of Napoleon and the deliverance of Europe* (Whitby: R. Rodgers, 1814), pp. 18–19.

22. K. S. Pinson, *Pietism as a factor in the rise of German nationalism* (New York: Columbia University Press, 1934), p. 195.

23. R. M. Bigler, *The politics of German Protestantism* (Berkeley: University of California Press, 1972), p. 30.

Chronology

Date	Continental Europe	Great Britain and Ireland	The Americas	Asia and Africa	Date
1640	Augustinus by Cornelieus Jansen	English Civil War begins		Inquisition against Christians in Japan	1640
				Qing Dynasty to power in Beijing; Jesuit Schall in Chinese Astron. Bureau	1645
1645	Peace of Westphalia	Westminster Confession of Faith drafted			
1650	Bull *Cum occasione* against Jansenists	Execution of Charles I	Toleration Act in Maryland	Cape Colony founded in South Africa	1650
1655	Mission étrangère founded in Paris	Death of Oliver Cromwell	Arrival of first resident bishop in Quebec	Roberto de Nobili dies in India	1655
1660	Personal reign of Louis XIV begins	Restoration of Stuart Monarchy Corporation Act, England Act of Uniformity, England	Half-way Covenant, Massachusetts	Death of Alexander of Rhodes	1660
	French establish Compagnie des Indes		Colony of Carolina established	Thomas Christians link to Roman Church	

	Asia / Missions	America	Europe
1665	Christian persecution begins in China; Ayutthaya seminary for Asian priests		Covenanters' Pentland Rising, Scotland
1670			Independence of Portugal; Spinoza's *Tractus theologico-politicus*; Penn's *Great Case of Liberty of Conscious*; Test Act in England
1675	First apostolic vicar in China		Spener's *Pia Desideria* published; Hardouin-Mansart begins Invalides in Paris; Wren begins Saint Paul's Cathedral
1680		William Penn founds Philadelphia	Francke opens Bible Society in Leipzig; Four Gallican Articles in France; Siege of Vienna by the Turks; Exclusion Crisis 1679–81
1685	French *Code noir* for slaves; First *beateria* for women in the Philippines	First Presbytery in America	Anti-Convenanter 'Killing Times', Scotland; Revocation of Edict of Nantes
1690	Calcutta founded; Edict recognizing Christianity in China	Salem witch trials	Newton's *Principia*; Glorious Revolution in England; English Toleration Act; Presbyterianism re-established in Scotland; Saint Paul's Cathedral in London; Quesnel's *Réflexions morales*

(cont.)

Date	Continental Europe	Great Britain and Ireland	The Americas	Asia and Africa	Date
1695		Locke's *Reasonableness of Christianity* Toland's *Christianity Not Mysterious*		China divided into dioceses and vacariates Jesuits found College at Sena, Zambesia	1695
1700	Boubons to throne in Spain War of Spanish Succession (1701–14)	Society for Propogating Christian Knowledge Society for the Propagation of the Gospel Irish Test Act		First Protestant missionaries in India Prefecture of Tibet-Hindustan erected Malabar Rites condemned	1700
1705	Peace of Altranstädt Destruction of Port-Royal near Paris	Parliamentary Union of England & Scotland	Philadelphia Association of Regular Baptists established	Chinese Rites condemned	1705
1710	Leibniz's *Essai de théodicée* Bull *Unigenitus* against Jansenists	Sacheverell affair, Church of England Occasional Conformity Act, England Scottish Toleration Act and Patronage Act Accession of George I; Schism Act			1710

1715	Jacobite rising Suspension of Anglican Convocation		Oath required against Mandarin Rites
	Peace of Passarowitz		
1720	Irish Toleration Act; repeal of Schism Act		
	Zinzendorf's Moravian Brothers, Herrnhut Jews recognized in Bordeaux		
1725	Non-subscribing Presbytery of Antrim, Ireland		Chinese imperial edict against Christians
1730	Protestants expelled from Salzburg		
	Protestant Dissenting Deputies formed Erskines' Secession from Church of Scotland	Colony of Georgia founded	
	Voltaire's *English Letters*	Revival in Northampton, Mass (1734–35) John Wesley in Georgia 1735–37	Malabar Rites in India condemned by Rome
1735	Zinzendorf banished from Saxony	George Whitefield's first visit to America	
	Warburton's *Alliance . . . Church & State* John Wesley begins itinerant preaching		

(cont.)

Date	Continental Europe	Great Britain and Ireland	The Americas	Asia and Africa	Date
1740	War of Austrian Succession (1740–48)		First Great Awakening		1740
	Concordat with Sardinia	Cambuslang Revival, Scotland (1741–42)	Break-up of Philadelphia Synod	Pope orders one Mass for all Indian castes	
1745	Concordat with Kingdom of Naples	Jacobite rising			1745
			Regulars ousted from Spanish American Parishes		
1750	First volume of the *Encyclopédie*		Jonathan Edwards dismissed, Northampton	C. F. Schwartz arrives in Tranquebar	1750
	Concordat with Spain				
	Jesuits expelled from Portugal				
1755	Seven Years' War (1756–63)		Death of Jonathan Edwards		1755
	Helvetius' *De l'esprit*				
1760	Rousseau's *Vicaire savoyard*	Accession of Geoge III		Pombal forbids missionaries to Congo	1760
	Febronius' *De statu ecclesiae*	Relief Church formed in Scotland			
	Jesuits expelled from France				
1765	Jesuits expelled from Spain and Naples		Stamp Act Congress in American Colonies		1765
	Committee on regulars in France				

1770	Swedenborg's *True Christianity* First Partition of Poland Jesuits dissolved by the papacy	Death of George Whitefield Feathers Tavern Petition in England		
1775	War of American Revolution (1775–83)		Quebec Act Declaration of Independence in America	Pombal disbands Inquisition in Goa
1780	Reduction of regulars in Austria Edict of Toleration in Austria State-run seminaries in Austria *Lettres patentes* for Jewish rights in Alsace	Catholic Relief Acts in England & Ireland Anti-Catholic Gordon Riots in London	Slavery illegal in Massachusetts	Asiatic Society of Bengal established
1785	Pistoia Synod in Tuscany Edict of Toleration in France French Revolution: Rights of Man & Citizen	William Paley, 'Of Religious Establishments'	Virgina statutes on religious freedom Drafting of US Constitution	C. Wilkins' English translation of *Bhagavagita*
1790	Civil Constitution of the Clergy in France Religious schism begins in France French Revolutionary Wars begin (1792–99) De-Christianization in France (1793–94) Jung–Stilling's *Heimweh*	Death of John Wesley British Baptist Missionary Society established	Bill of Rights ratified in US	W. Robertson's *India* Baptist William Carey arrives in India Lord Cornwallis Code in India

(cont.)

Date	Continental Europe	Great Britain and Ireland	The Americas	Asia and Africa	Date
1795	First church–state Separation in France	London Missionary Society established			1795
	French troops occupy Rome	Wilberforce's *Practical View*			
	Napoleon to power in France	United Irishmen rising			
		Church Missionary Society established			
1800	Napoleonic Wars (1800–1815)	Parliamentary Union of Britain and Ireland			1800
	Danish Evangelical Society			Anti-Christian persecution begins in Korea	
	French Concordat with pope implemented	William Paley's *Natural Theology*			
		British and Foreign Bible Society established	Consolidación of church assets in Spanish America		1805
1805	End of Holy Roman Empire	Parliament abolishes British slave trade			
	Napoleon's decree on the Jews				1810
1810	Napoleon's invasion of Russia			British India opened to missionaries	
	Russian Bible Society			First Anglican Bishop of Calcutta	
	Jesuits re-established by papacy	Death of Joanna Southcott			
1815	Holy Alliance proposed			European powers abolish slave trade	1815

Bibliography

GENERAL

Aston, Nigel, *Christianity and revolutionary Europe, 1750–1830*, Cambridge: Cambridge University Press, 2002.

Boxer, Charles R., *The Church militant and Iberian expansion, 1440–1770*, Baltimore: The Johns Hopkins University Press, 1978.

Bradley, James E. and Dale K. Van Kley (eds.), *Religion and politics in Enlightenment Europe*, Notre Dame, IN: University of Notre Dame Press, 2001.

Callahan, William J., *Church, politics and society in Spain, 1750–1874*, Cambridge, MA: Harvard University Press, 1984.

Callahan, William J. and David Higgs (eds.), *Church and society in Catholic Europe of the eighteenth century*, Cambridge: Cambridge University Press, 1979.

Chadwick, Owen, *The popes and European revolution*, Oxford: Clarendon Press, 1990.

Châtellier, Louis, *The Europe of the devout: The Catholic reformation and the formation of a new society*, Cambridge: Cambridge University Press, 1990.

Clark, J. C. D., *English society 1660–1832: Religion, ideology and politics during the ancien régime*, Cambridge: Cambridge University Press, 2000.

Farriss, Nancy, *Crown and clergy in colonial Mexico, 1759–1821*, London: Athlone Press, 1968.

Fulbrook, Mary, *Piety and politics: Religion and the rise of absolutism in England, Württemberg and Prussia*, Cambridge: Cambridge University Press, 1983.

Gernet, Jacques, *China and the Christian impact: A conflict of cultures*, Cambridge: Cambridge University Press, 1985.

Hastings, Adrian, *The church in Africa, 1450–1950*, Oxford: Clarendon Press, 1994.

Hope, Nicholas, *German and Scandinavian Protestantism: 1700 to 1918*, Oxford: Oxford University Press, 1999.

Hsia, Ronnie Po-Chia, *The world of Catholic renewal, 1540–1770*, Cambridge: Cambridge University Press, 1998.

Marty, Martin, *Religion, awakening and revolution*, New York: Consortium, 1977.

McMahon, Darrin, *Enemies of the Enlightenment*, Oxford: Oxford University Press, 2001.

McManners, John, *Church and society in eighteenth-century France*, 2 vols., Oxford: Oxford University Press, 1998.

Neill, Stephen, *A history of Christianity in India 1707–1858*, Cambridge: Cambridge University Press, 1985.

Noll, Mark A., *A history of Christianity in the United States and Canada*, Grand Rapids, MI: Eerdmans, 1992.

Palmer, Robert R., *Catholics and unbelievers in eighteenth-century France*, New York: Cooper Square, 1961.

Van Kley, Dale K., *The religious origins of the French Revolution: From Calvin to the civil constitution, 1560–1791*, New Haven: Yale University Press, 1996.

Walsh, John, Colin Haydon, and Stephen Taylor (eds.), *The Church of England c. 1689 – c. 1833: From toleration to tractarianism*, Cambridge: Cambridge University Press, 1993.

Ward, W. R., *Christianity under the ancien régime, 1648–1789*, Cambridge: Cambridge University Press, 1999.

   The Protestant evangelical awakening, Cambridge: Cambridge University Press, 1992.

Wiesner-Hanks, Merry E., *Christianity and sexuality in the early modern world: Regulating desire, reforming practice*, London: Routledge, 2000.

I CONTINENTAL CATHOLIC EUROPE

Beales, Derek, *Joseph II*, vol. 1: *In the shadow of Maria Theresa*, Cambridge: Cambridge University Press, 1987.

Bergin, Joseph, *The French episcopate in the reign of Louis XIV 1661–1715*, New Haven: Yale University Press, 2004.

Blanning, T. C. W., *Reform and revolution in Mainz 1743–1803*, Cambridge: Cambridge University Press, 1974.

Chittolini, Giorgio, and Giovanni Miccoli (eds.), *La chiesa e il potere politico dal medioevo all'eta contemporanea*, Turin: G. Einaudi, 1986.

Collins, Jeffrey, *Papacy and politics in eighteenth-century Rome: Pius VI and the arts*, Cambridge: Cambridge University Press, 2004.

Dickson, P. G. M., 'Joseph II's reshaping of the Austrian church', *Historical journal*, 36 (1993), pp. 89–114.

Duffy, Eamon, *Saints and sinners: A history of the popes*, New Haven: Yale University Press, 1987.

Eyck, Frank, *Religion and politics in German history: From the beginnings to the French Revolution*, Basingstoke: Macmillan, 1997.

Garcia Villoslada, Ricardo (ed.), *Historia de la iglesia en España*, vols. 4 and 5, Madrid: Ed. catolica, 1978–80.

Gross, Hanns, *Rome in the age of the Enlightenment: The post-Tridentine syndrome and the ancien régime*, Cambridge: Cambridge University Press, 1990.

Guimera, Agustin (ed.), *El reformismo borbonico*, Madrid: CSIC Alianza ed., 1996.

   Carlos III y la Illustracion, 2 vols., Madrid: Ministerio de cultura, 1988–90.

Hermann, Christian, *L'Eglise d'Espagne sous le patronage royal, 1476–1834*, Madrid: Casa de Valazquez, 1988.

Jacob, Margaret C., *Living the Enlightenment: Freemasonry and politics in eighteenth-century Europe*, Oxford: Oxford University Press, 1991.

Johns, Christopher M. S., *Papal art and cultural politics in the age of Clement XI*, Cambridge: Cambridge University Press, 1993.

Jonard, Norbert, *L'Italie des Lumières: Histoire, société et culture du XVIIIe siècle italien*, Paris: Champion, 1996.

Milan au siècle des Lumières, Dijon: University of Dijon, 1974.

Joutard, Philippe (ed.), *Histoire de la France religieuse*, vol. 3: *Du roi Très Chrétien à la laïcité républicaine, XVIIIe–XIXe siècle*, Paris: Seuil, 1991.

Kovacs, Elisabeth (ed.), *Katholische Aufklärung und Josephinismus*, Munich: R. Oldenbourg, 1979.

Ultramontanismus und Staatskirchentum im Theresianisch-Josephischen Staat, Vienna: Wiener Dom-Verlag, 1975.

Lebrun, François (ed.), *Histoire des Catholiques en France*, 2nd edn Paris: Hachette, 1985.

Levillain, Philippe (ed.), *Dictionnaire historique de la papauté*, Paris: Fayard, 1994.

Maxwell, Kenneth, *Pombal: Paradox of the Enlightenment*, Cambridge: Cambridge University Press 1995.

O'Brien, C. H., 'Ideas of religious toleration at the time of Joseph II: A study of the Enlightenment among Catholics in Austria', *Transactions of the American Philosophical Society*, 59 (part 7), Philadelphia: American Philosophical Society, 1969.

Olaechea, Rafael, *Las Relaciones hispano-romans en la Segunda mitad del XVIII: La agencia de preces*, 2 vols., Zaragoza: Universidad de Zaragosa, 1965.

Porter, Roy, and O. Grell (eds.), *The rise of toleration*, Cambridge: Cambridge University Press, 2000.

Reb, Sylvaine, *L'Aufklärung catholique à Salzburg: L'œuvre réformatrice (1772–1803) de Hieronymas von Colloredo*, Berne: P. Lang, 1995.

Rosa, Mario, *Settecento religioso: Politica della ragione e religione del cuore*, Venice: Marsilio, 1999.

Schnurer, Gustav, *Katholische Kirche und Kultur im 18. Jahrhundert*, Paderborn: Ferdinand Schöningh, 1941.

Valensise, M., 'Le sacre du roi: stratégie symbolique et doctrine politique de la monarchie française', *Annales Economies, Sociétés, Civilisations*, 41 (1986), pp. 543–77.

Van Kley, Dale K., *The Damiens affair*, New Haven: Yale University Press, 1984.

The Jansenists and the expulsion of the Jesuits from France, 1757–65, New Haven: Yale University Press, 1975.

Venturi, Franco, 'Church reform in Enlightenment Italy: The sixties of the eighteenth century', *Journal of modern history*, 48 (1976), pp. 215–32.

Vanysacker, Dries, *Cardinal Giuseppe Garampi (1725–92), an Enlightened Ultramontane*, Brussels: Brepols, 1995.

Wagner, H., 'Die Idee der Toleranz in Österreich', in *Religion und Kirche in Österreich*, Vienna: Hirt, 1972, pp. 11–128.

Wright, Anthony David, *The early modern papacy: From the Council of Trent to the French Revolution, 1564–1789*, Harlow: Longman, 2000.

2 CONTINENTAL PROTESTANT EUROPE

Albrecht-Birkner, Veronika, *Reformation des Lebens: Die Reformen Herzog Ernst des Frommen von Sachsen-Gotha und ihre Auswirkungen auf Frömmigkeit, Schule und Alltag im ländlichen Raum (1640–1675)*, Leipzig: Evangelische Verlags-Anstalt, 2002.

Aner, Karl, *Die Theologie der Lessingzeit, Nachdruck der Ausgabe*, Halle: Niemeyer, 1929; repr. Hildesheim: Olms, 1964.

Barnett, S. J., *The Enlightenment and religion: The myths of modernity*, Manchester: Manchester University Press, 2003.

Brecht, Martin (ed.), *Geschichte des Pietismus, Band I: Der Pietismus vom siebzehnten bis zum frühen achtzehnten Jahrhundert*, Göttingen: Vandenhoeck & Ruprecht, 1993.

Brecht, Martin and Klaus Deppermann (eds.), *Geschichte des Pietismus, Band II: Der Pietismus im achtzehnten Jahrhundert*, Göttingen: Vandenhoeck & Ruprecht, 1995.

Dantine, Johannes (ed.), *Protestantische Mentalitäten*, Vienna: Passagen-Verlag, 1999.

Deppermann, Andreas, *Johann Jakob Schütz und die Anfänge des Pietismus*, Tübingen: Mohr, 2002.

Deppermann, Klaus, *Der hallesche Pietismus und der preußische Staat unter Friedrich III*, Göttingen: Vandenhoeck & Ruprecht, 1961.

Dissertori, Alois, *Auswanderung der Defregger Protestanten 1666–1725*, Innsbruck: Wagner, 2001.

Feiereis, Konrad, *Die Umprägung der natürlichen Theologie in Religionsphilosophie: ein Beitrag zur deutschen Geistesgeschichte des 18. Jahrhunderts*, Leipzig: St Benno-Verlag, 1965.

Fischbeck, Hans-Jürgen (ed.), *Der Protestantismus und die (Erneuerung der) Aufklärung*, Mülheim/R.: Evangelische Akademie, 2001.

Gestrich, Andreas and Rainer Lächele (eds.), *Johann Jacob Moser. Politiker, Pietist, Publizist*, Karlsruhe: Braun, 2002.

Geyer-Kordesch, Johanna, *Pietismus, Medizin und Aufklärung in Preußen im 18. Jahrhundert. Das Leben und Werk Georg Ernst Stahls*, Tübingen: Niemeyer, 2000.

Greyerz, Kaspar von, *Religion und Kultur in Europa 1500–1800*, Göttingen: Vandenhoeck & Ruprecht, 2000.

Gründer, Karlfried and Karl Heinrich Rengstorf, *Religionskritik und Religiosität in der deutschen Aufklärung*, Heidelberg: Schneider, 1989.

Haakonssen, Knud (ed.), *Enlightenment and religion: Rational dissent in eighteenth-century Britain*, Cambridge: Cambridge University Press, 1996.

Hammann, Konrad, *Universitätsgottesdienst und Aufklärungspredigt. Die Göttinger Universitätskirche im 18. Jahrhundert und ihr Ort in der Geschichte des Universitätsgottesdienstes im deutschen Protestantismus*, Tübingen: Mohr, 2000.

Harrison, Peter, *'Religion' and the religions in the English Enlightenment*, Cambridge: Cambridge University Press, 1990.

Hinrichs, Carl, *Preußen und Pietismus. Der Pietismus in Brandenburg-Preußen als religiös- soziale Reformbewegung*, Göttingen: Vandenhoeck & Ruprecht, 1971.

Ingen, Ferdinand van (ed.), *Gebetsliteratur der Frühen Neuzeit als Hausfrömmigkeit. Funktionen und Formen in Deutschland und den Niederlanden*, Wiesbaden: Harrassowitz, 2001.

Jung, Martin H. (ed.), *'Mein Herz brannte richtig in der Liebe Jesu'. Autobiographien frommer Frauen aus Pietismus und Erweckungsbewegung. Eine Quellensammlung*, Aachen: Shaker, 1999.

Kang, Chi-Won, *Frömmigkeit und Gelehrsamkeit. Die Reform des Theologiestudiums im lutherischen Pietismus des 17. und des frühen 18. Jahrhunderts*, Gießen: Brunnen-Verlag, 2001.

Kemper, Hans-Georg and Hans Schneider-Halle (eds.), *Goethe und der Pietismus*, Tübingen: Niemeyer, 2001.

Bibliography

Kraft, Thomas, *Pietismus und Methodismus. Sozialethik und Reformprogramme von August Hermann Francke (1663–1727) und Wesley (1703–1791) im Vergleich*, Stuttgart: Medienwerk der Evangelisch-Methodistischen Kirche, 2001.

Lächele, Rainer (ed.), *Das Echo Halles. Kulturelle Wirkungen des Pietismus*, Tübingen: Bibliotheca Academica Verlag, 2001.

Landes, Wallace B. (ed.), *Radical Pietism in contemporary perspective*, Richmond, IN: Bethany Theological Seminary, 1998.

Lehmann, Hartmut, Heinz Schilling and Hans-Jürgen Schrader (eds.), *Jansenismus, Quietismus, Pietismus*, Göttingen: Vandenhoeck & Ruprecht, 2002.

Lehmann, Hartmut, *Pietismus und weltliche Ordnung in Württemberg. Vom 17. bis zum 20. Jahrhundert*, Stuttgart: Kohlhammer, 1969.

Löffler, Ulrich, *Lissabons Fall – Europas Schrecken. Die Deutung des Erdbebens von Lissabon im deutschsprachigen Protestantismus des 18. Jahrhunderts*, Berlin: de Gruyter, 1999.

Meyer, Dietrich, *Zinzendorf und die Herrnhuter Brüdergemeine. 1700–2000*, Göttingen: Vandenhoeck & Ruprecht, 2000.

Miersemann, Wolfgang (ed.), *Pietismus und Liedkultur*, Tübingen: Niemeyer, 2002.

Mondot, Jean (ed.), *Les Lumières et les leur combat. La critique de la religion et des Eglises a l'époque des Lumières*, Berlin: Berliner Wissenschafts-Verlag, 2004.

Müller-Bahlke, Thomas (ed.), *Gott zur Ehr und zu des Landes Besten. Die Franckeschen Stiftungen in Preußen. Aspekte einer alten Allianz*, Halle: Verlag der Franckeschen Stiftungen zu Halle, 2001.

Neumann, Josef N. (ed.), *Das Kind in Pietismus und Aufklärung*, Tübingen: Niemeyer, 2000.

Obst, Helmut, *August Hermann Francke und die Franckeschen Stiftungen in Halle*, Göttingen: Vandenhoeck & Ruprecht, 2002.

Peters, Christian and Martin Brecht (eds.), *Zwischen Spener und Volkening. Pietismus in Minden-Ravensberg im 18. und frühen 19. Jahrhundert*, Bielefeld: Luther-Verlag, 2002.

Ruppel, Karl August, *Theologie und Wirtschaft. Konzepte protestantischer Wirtschaftsethik zwischen Aufklärung und Industrialisierung*, Hildesheim: Georg Olms, 1999.

Schicketanz, Peter, *Der Pietismus von 1675 bis 1800*, Leipzig: Evangelische Verlags-Anstalt, 2001.

Schilling, Heinz, *Die neue Zeit. Vom Christenheitseuropa zum Europa der Staaten, 1250–1750*, Berlin: Siedler, 1999.

Seidel, Johannes Jürgen, *Die Anfänge des Pietismus in Graubünden*, Zurich: Chronos Verlag, 2001.

Sparn, Walter, *Vernünftiges Christentum. Über die geschichtliche Aufgabe der theologischen Aufklärung im 18. Jahrhundert in Deutschland*, in: *Rudolf Vierhaus, Wissenschaften im Zeitalter der Aufklarung*, Göttingen: Vandenhoeck & Ruprecht, 1985, S. 18–57.

Sträter, Udo (ed.), *Waisenhäuser in der Frühen Neuzeit*, Tübingen: Niemeyer, 2003.

Temme, Willi, *Krise der Leiblichkeit. Die Sozietät der Mutter Eva (Buttlarsche Rotte) und der radikale Pietismus um 1700*, Göttingen: Vandenhoeck & Ruprecht, 1998.

Walker, Mack, *The Salzburg transaction: Expulsion and redemption in eighteenth-century Germany*, Ithaca: Cornell University Press, 1992.

Wallmann, Johannes (ed.), *Halle und Osteuropa. Zur europäischen Ausstrahlung des hallischen Pietismus*, Tübingen: Niemeyer, 1998.

Philipp Jakob Spener und die Anfänge des Pietismus, Tübingen: Mohr, 1986.

Walter, Peter (ed.), *Theologen des 17. und 18. Jahrhunderts. Konfessionelles Zeitalter, Pietismus, Aufklärung*, Darmstadt: Wissenschaftliche Buchgesellschaft, 2003.

3 GREAT BRITAIN AND IRELAND

Best, G. F. A., *Temporal pillars: Queen Anne's bounty, the ecclesiastical commissioners, and the Church of England*, Cambridge: Cambridge University Press, 1964.

Bolton, F. R., *The Caroline tradition of the Church of Ireland*, London: SPCK, 1958.

Brooke, Peter, *Ulster Presbyterianism: The historical perspective 1610–1970*, 2nd edn, Belfast: Athol Books, 1994.

Buckroyd, Julia, *Church and state in Scotland*, Edinburgh: John Donald, 1980.

Chart, D. A., 'The close alliance of church and state', in Walter Allison Phillips (ed.), *History of the Church of Ireland from the earliest times to the present day*, Oxford: Oxford University Press, 1933, vol. 2, pp. 175–241.

Clark, J. C. D., *The language of liberty 1660–1832: Political discourse and social dynamics in the Anglo-American world*, Cambridge: Cambridge University Press, 1994.

Connolly, S. J., *Religion, law and power: The making of Protestant Ireland, 1660–1760*, Oxford: Clarendon Press, 1992.

Cornwall, Robert D., *Visible and apostolic: The constitution of the church in High Church Anglican and non-juror thought*, Newark: University of Delaware Press, 1993.

Drummond, Andrew L., and James Bulloch, *The Scottish church 1688–1843: The age of the moderates*, Edinburgh: The Saint Andrew Press, 1973.

Dunlop, A. Ian, *William Carstares and the kirk by law established*, Edinburgh: Saint Andrew Press, 1967.

Eccleshall, Robert, 'Richard Hooker and the peculiarities of the English: The reception of the *ecclesiastical polity* in the seventeenth and eighteenth centuries', *History of political thought*, 2 (1981), pp. 63–117.

Ford, Alan, James McGuire and Kenneth Milne (eds.), *As by law established: The Church of Ireland since the Reformation*, Dublin: Lilliput Press, 1995.

Foster, Walter Rowland, *Bishop and presbytery: The Church of Scotland, 1661–1688*, London: SPCK, 1958.

Gascoigne, John, 'The unity of church and state challenged: Responses to Hooker from the Restoration to the nineteenth-century age of reform', *Journal of religious history*, 21 (1997), pp. 60–79.

Gibson, William, *Enlightenment prelate: Benjamin Hoadly, 1676–1761*, Cambridge: James Clarke, 2004.

Goldie, Mark, 'The theory of religious intolerance in Restoration England', in Ole Peter Grell, Jonathan I. Israel and Nicholas Tyacke (eds.), *From persecution to toleration*, Oxford, 1991, pp. 331–68.

Greaves, R. W., 'The working of the alliance: A comment on Warburton', in G. V. Bennett and J. D. Walsh (eds.), *Essays in modern English church history: In memory of Norman Sykes*, London: Adam and Charles Black, 1966, pp. 163–80.

Green, I. M., *The re-establishment of the Church of England, 1660–1663*, Oxford: Oxford University Press, 1978.

Herron, Andrew, *Kirk by divine right: Church and state: A peaceful co-existence*, Edinburgh: Saint Andrew Press, 1985.

Lathbury, Thomas, *A history of the convocation of the Church of England*, 2nd edn, London: J. Leslie, 1853.

Mant, Richard, *History of the Church of Ireland, from the revolution to the union of the churches of England and Ireland, January 1, 1801*, London: Parker, 1840.

Marshall, J., 'The ecclesiology of the latitude-men 1660–1689: Stillingfleet, Tillotson and "Hobbism"', *Journal of ecclesiastical history*, 36 (1985), pp. 407–27.

Mather, F. C., *High Church prophet: Bishop Samuel Horsley (1733–1806) and the Caroline tradition in the later Georgian church*, Oxford: Clarendon Press, 1992.

Nockles, Peter, *The Oxford movement in context: Anglican High Churchmanship 1760–1857*, Cambridge: Cambridge University Press, 1994.

   'Church or Protestant sect? The Church of Ireland, High Churchmanship and the Oxford Movement, 1822–1869', *Historical journal*, 41 (1998), pp. 457–93.

Schochet, Gordon, 'Between Lambeth and Leviathan: Samuel Parker on the Church of England and political order', in Nicholas Phillipson and Quentin Skinner (eds.), *Political discourse in early modern Britain*, Cambridge: Cambridge University Press, 1993, pp. 189–208.

Spellman, W. M., *The Latitudinarians and the Church of England, 1660–1700*, Athens, GA: University of Georgia Press, 1993.

Spurr, John, *The Restoration Church of England, 1646–1689*, New Haven: Yale University Press, 1991.

Sykes, Norman, *Church and state in England in the XVIIIth century*, Cambridge: Cambridge University Press, 1934.

   From Sheldon to Secker: Aspects of English church history, 1660–1768, Cambridge: Cambridge University Press, 1959.

Taylor, Stephen, 'William Warburton and the alliance of church and state', *Journal of ecclesiastical history*, 43 (1992), pp. 271–86.

   '"Dr. Codex" and the Whig "Pope": Edmund Gibson, Bishop of Lincoln and London, 1716–1748', in R. W. Davis (ed.), *Lords of Parliament: Studies, 1714–1914*, Stanford: Stanford University Press, 1995, pp. 9–28.

Wall, Maureen, *The penal laws, 1691–1760: Church and state from the treaty of Limerick to the accession of George III*, 2nd edn, Dundalk: Dundalgan Press, 1967.

Waterman, A. M. C., 'The nexus between theology and political doctrine in church and dissent', in Knud Haakonssen (ed.), *Enlightenment and religion: Rational dissent in eighteenth-century Britain*, Cambridge: Cambridge University Press, 1996, pp. 193–218.

4 THE CHURCH IN ECONOMY AND SOCIETY

Anstey, Roger, *The Atlantic slave trade and British abolition, 1760–1810*, London: Macmillan, 1975.

Aretin, Karl Otmar Freiherr von, *Vom Deutschen Reich zum Deutschen Bund, Deutsche Geschichte*, ed. Joachim Leuschner, Göttingen: Vandenhoeck & Ruprecht, 1980.

Beales, Derek, *Prosperity and plunder: European Catholic monasteries in the age of revolution, 1650–1815*, Cambridge: Cambridge University Press, 2003.

Bercé, Yves-Marie, *Fête et révolte: Des mentalités populaires du XVIe au XVIIIe siècle*, Paris: Hachette, 1976.

Benedict, Philip, 'Faith, fortune and social structure in seventeenth-century Montpellier', *Past and present*, 152 (1996), pp. 46–78.

The faith and fortunes of France's Huguenots, 1600–85, Aldershot: Ashgate, 2001.

Bergin, Joseph, *Cardinal Richelieu: Power and the pursuit of wealth*, New Haven: Yale University Press, 1985.

The making of the French episcopate, 1589–1661, New Haven and London: Yale University Press, 1996.

Bodinier, Bernard, 'La dimension foncière de la question agraire: La vente des biens nationaux: Essai de synthèse', *Annales historiques de la Révolution française*, 71 (1999), pp. 7–19.

Bossy, John, *Christianity in the west: 1400–1700*, Oxford: Oxford University Press, 1985.

Brown, Richard, *Church and state in modern Britain, 1700–1850*, London: Routledge, 1991.

Chamberlain, Jeffrey S., *Accommodating High Churchmen: The clergy of Sussex, 1700–45*, Urbana: University of Illinois Press, 1997.

Clark, Gregory and Ysbrand Van Der Werf, 'Work in progress? The industrious revolution', *Journal of economic history*, 58 (1998), pp. 840–43.

De Vries, Jan, 'Between purchasing power and the world of goods: Understanding the household economy in early modern Europe', in Roy Porter and John Brewer (eds.), *Consumption and the world of goods*, London: Routledge, 1993, pp. 85–132.

'The industrial revolution and the industrious revolution', *Journal of economic history*, 54 (1994), pp. 249–70.

Dinet, Dominique, 'Les grands domaines des réguliers en France (1560–1790): Une stabilité apparente?' in *Proceedings of the twelfth international economic history congress*, Rimini: Guaraldi, 1988, pp. 233–52.

Guiso, Luigi, Paola Sapienza, and Luigi Zingales, 'People's opium? Religion and economic attitudes', *Journal of monetary economics*, 50 (2003), pp. 225–82.

Gutton, Jean-Pierre, *La société et les pauvres; l'exemple de la généralité de Lyon, 1534–1789*, Paris: Les Belles Lettres, 1971.

Hoffman, Philip T., *Growth in a traditional society: The French countryside, 1450–1815*, Princeton: Princeton University Press, 1996.

Church and community in the diocese of Lyon, 1500–1789, New Haven: Yale University Press, 1984.

Hickey, Daniel, *Local hospitals in ancien régime France: Rationalization, resistance, renewal, 1530–1789*, Montreal: McGill–Queen's University Press, 1997.

Jacob, Margaret C., *Scientific culture and the making of the industrial west*, Oxford: Oxford University Press, 1997.

Jacob, Margaret C. and Matthew Kadane, 'Missing, now found in the eighteenth century: Weber's Protestant capitalist', *American historical review*, 108 (2003), pp. 20–49.

Kellenbenz, Hermann and Paolo Prodi (eds.), *Fiskus, Kirche und Staat im konfessionellen Zeitalter*, Berlin: Duncker und Humblot, 1994.

Landes, David S., *The wealth and poverty of nations: Why some are so rich and some so poor*, New York: Norton, 1998.

Landi, Fiorenzo (ed.), 'Accumulation and dissolution of large estates of the regular clergy in early modern Europe', in *Proceedings of the twelfth international economic history congress*, Rimini: Guaraldi, 1988.

Bibliography

'Introduction', in *Accumulation and dissolution of large estates of the regular clergy in early modern europe*, in *Proceedings of the twelfth international economic history congress*, Rimini: Guaraldi, 1988, pp. 5–14.

La Vopa, Anthony J., *Grace, talent, and merit: Poor students, clerical careers, and professional ideology in eighteenth-century Germany*, Cambridge: Cambridge University Press, 1988.

Lebrun, François *et al.*, *Histoire des catholiques en France*, Paris: Privat, 1980.

Lindert, Peter H., *Growing public: Social spending and economic growth since the eighteenth century*, 2 vols., Cambridge: Cambridge University Press, 2004.

Maurer, Michael, *Kirche, Staat und Gesellschaft im 17. und 18. Jahrhundert*, Munich: R. Olderbourg, 1999.

McManners, John, *French ecclesiastical society under the ancien régime: A study of Angers in the eighteenth century*, Manchester: Manchester University Press, 1960.

Michaud, Claude, *L'Eglise et l'argent sous l'ancien régime: les receveurs généraux du clergé de France aux XVIe et XVIIe siècles*, Paris: Fayard, 1991.

Mitzman, Arthur, *The iron cage: An historical interpretation of Max Weber*, New York: Knopf, 1970.

Mokyr, Joel, *The lever of riches: Technological creativity and economic progress*, Oxford: Oxford University Press, 1990.

The gifts of Athena: Historical origins of the knowledge economy, Princeton: Princeton University Press, 2002.

Norberg, Kathryn, *Rich and poor in Grenoble, 1600–1814*, Berkeley: University of California Press, 1985.

Raab, Heribert, *Reich und Kirche in der frühen Neuzeit*, Freiburg: Freiburg University Press, 1988.

Reinhardt, Rudolf, 'Die hochadeligen Dynastien in der Reichskirche des 17 und 18 Jahrhunderts', *Römische Quartalschrift*, 83 (1988), pp. 213–55.

Reinhard, Wolfgang, 'Papstfinanz, Benefizienwesen und Staatsfinanz im konfessionellen Zeitalter', in Hermann Kellenbenz and Paolo Prodi (eds.), *Fiskus, Kirche und Staat im konfessionellen Zeitalter*, Berlin: Duncker und Humblot, 1994, pp. 337–72.

Stroup, John, *The struggle for identity in the clerical estate: Northwest German Protestant opposition to absolutist policy in the eighteenth century*, Leiden: E. J. Brill, 1984.

Sutherland, D. M. G., *The French Revolution and empire: The quest for a civic order*, Malden: Blackwell, 2003.

Tackett, Timothy, *Priest and parish in eighteenth-century France: A social and political study of the curés in a diocese in Dauphiné, 1750–1791*, Princeton: Princeton University Press, 1977.

Toscani, Xenio, *Il clero lombardo dall'ancien régime alla restaurazione*, Bologna: Il Mulino, 1979.

Vierhaus, Rudolf, *Deutschland im Zeitalter des Absolutismus*, in Joachim Leuschner (ed.), *Deutsche Geschichte*, Göttingen: Vandenhoeck & Ruprecht, 1984.

Wangermann, Ernst, *The Austrian achievement: 1700–1800*, London: Thames and Hudson, 1973.

Weber, Christoph, *Familienkanonikate und Patronatsbistümer: Ein Beitrag zur Geschichte von Adel und Klerus im neuzeitlichen Italien*, Berlin: Duncker & Humblot, 1988.

Weber, Max, *Die Wirtschaftsethik der Weltreligionen*, ed. Helwig Schmidt-Glintzer and Petra Kolonko, in Horst Baier *et al.* (eds.), *Gesamtausgabe*, Series 1, vol. 19, Tübingen: J. C. B. Mohr, 1989.

The Protestant ethic and the spirit of capitalism, ed. Talcott Parsons, New York: Charles Scribner's Sons, 1930.

5 THE CATHOLIC CLERGY IN EUROPE

Châtellier, Louis, *Le catholicisme en France*, vol. 2: *Le XVIIe siècle, 1600–1650*, Paris: SEDES, 1995.

Chittolini, Giorgio and Giovanni Miccoli (eds.), *Storia d'Italia, Annali 9, La Chiesa e il potere politico dal Medioevo all'età contemporanea*, Turini Einaudi, 1986. (In particular, the essay by Claudio Donati, 'La Chiesa di Roma tra antico regime e riforme settecentesche (1675–1760)', pp. 721–66.)

Citterio, Ferdinando and Luciano Vaccaro, *Storia religiosa dell'Austria*, Milan: Centro ambrosiano, 1997.

Greco, Gaetano, *La Chiesa in Italia nell'età moderna*, Rome and Bari: Laterza, 1999.

História religiosa de Portugal, vol. 2: *Humanismos e reformas*, Lisbon: Círculo de Leitores, 2000.

Kloczowski, Jerzy, *A history of Polish Christianity*, Cambridge: Cambridge University Press, 2000.

Ortiz, Antonio Domínguez, *Las clases privilegiadas en la España del Antiguo Regímen*, 3rd edn, Madrid: Ediciones ISTMO, 1973.

Plongeron, Bernard, *La vie quotidienne du clergé français au XVIIIe siècle*, Paris: Hachette, 1974.

Rosa, Mario (ed.), *Clero e società nell'Italia moderna*, Rome and Bari: Laterza, 1992.

Tackett, Timothy, *Priest and parish in eighteenth-century France*, Princeton: Princeton University Press, 1977.

Taveneaux, René, *La vie quotidienne des jansénistes aux XVIIe et XVIIIe siècles*, Paris: Hachett, 1973.

Le catholicisme dans la France classique, 1610–1715, 2 vols., Paris: SEDES, 1980.

6 THE PROTESTANT CLERGIES IN THE EUROPEAN WORLD

Akenson, D. H., *The Church of Ireland: Ecclesiastical reform and revolution, 1800–1885*, New Haven: Yale University Press, 1971.

Aston, Nigel and Nigel Cragoe (eds.), *Anticlericalism in Britain c. 1500–1914*, Stroud: Sutton Publishing, 2000.

Baker, Frank, 'The people called Methodists 3. Polity', in Rupert Davies, A. R. George and Gordon Rupp (eds.), *A history of the Methodist Church in Great Britain*, 4 vols., London: Epworth Press, 1965–88, vol. 1, pp. 211–55.

Barkley, J. M., 'The Presbyterian minister in eighteenth-century Ireland', in J. L. M. Haire, et al., *Challenge and conflict: Essays in Irish Presbyterian history and doctrine*, Belfast: W&G Baird, 1981, pp. 46–71.

Barnard, Toby, *A new anatomy of Ireland: The Irish protestants, 1649–1770*, New Haven: Yale University Press, 2003.

'Improving clergymen, 1660–1760', in *Irish Protestant ascents and descents, 1641–1770*, Dublin: Four Courts Press, 2004, pp. 306–29.

Beckett, J. C., *Protestant dissent in Ireland, 1687–1780*, London: Faber & Faber, 1948.

Benedict, Philip, *Christ's churches purely reformed: A social history of Calvinism*, New Haven: Yale University Press, 2002.

Dixon, C. Scott and Luise Schorn-Schütte (eds.), *The Protestant clergy of early modern Europe*, Basingstoke: Palgrave Macmillan, 2003.

Drummond, A. L., *German Protestantism since Luther*, London: Epworth Press, 1951.

Greaves, R. L., *God's other children: Protestant Nonconformists and the emergence of denominational churches in Ireland, 1660–1700*, Stanford: Stanford University Press, 1997.

Green, Ian, '"Reformed pastors" and *bons curés*: The changing role of the parish clergy in early modern Europe', in W. J. Sheils and Diana Wood (eds.), *The ministry: Clerical and lay*, Studies in Church History, 26, Oxford, 1989, pp. 249–86.

Gregory, Jeremy, *Restoration, reformation and reform, 1660–1828: Archbishops of Canterbury and their diocese*, Oxford: Oxford University Press, 2000.

Gugerli, David, 'Protestant pastors in late eighteenth-century Zürich: Their families and society', *Journal of interdisciplinary history*, 22 (1992), pp. 369–85.

Harding, Alan, *The Countess of Huntingdon's connexion: A sect in action in eighteenth-century England*, Oxford: Oxford University Press, 2003.

Hempton, David, 'A tale of preachers and beggars: Methodism and money in the great age of transatlantic expansion, 1780–1830', in M. A. Noll (ed.), *God and mammon: Protestants, money, and the market*, New York: Oxford University Press, 2002, pp. 123–46.

Hsia, R. Po-Chia, *Social discipline in the Reformation: Central Europe 1550–1750*, London and New York: Routledge, 1989.

Israel, Jonathan, *The Dutch republic: Its rise, greatness, and fall, 1477–1806*, Oxford: Clarendon Press, 1995.

Jacob, W. M., *Lay people and religion in the early eighteenth century*, Cambridge: Cambridge University Press, 1996.

Mechie, Stewart, 'Education for the ministry in Scotland since the Reformation', *Records of the Scottish Church History Society*, 14 (1961–2), pp. 115–33, 161–78; 15 (1963), pp. 1–20.

O'Day, Rosemary, *The professions in early modern England, 1450–1800*, Harlow: Longmans, 2000.

Révész, Imre, *History of the Hungarian Reformed Church*, trans. G. A. F. Knight, Washington: Hungarian Reformed Federation of America, 1956.

Révész, Emeric, J. S. Kováts, and Ladislaus Ravasz, *Hungarian Protestantism: Its past, present and future*, Budapest: n.p., 1927.

Schorn-Schütte, Luise, 'Priest, preacher, pastor: Research on clerical office in early modern Europe', *Central European history*, 33 (2000), pp. 1–39.

Selles, O. H. 'A case of hidden identity: Antoine Court, Bénédict Picet, and Geneva's aid to France's Desert Churches', in J. B. Roney and M. I. Klauber (eds.), *The identity of Geneva: The Christian commonwealth 1564–1864*, Westport, CT: Greenwood Press, 1998, pp. 93–109.

Sher, Richard and Alexander Murdoch, 'Patronage and party in the Church of Scotland', in Norman MacDougall (ed.), *Church, politics and society: Scotland 1408–1929*, Edinburgh: John Donald, 1983, pp. 197–220.

Smiles, Samuel, *The Huguenots in France after the revocations of the Edict of Nantes*, London: George Routledge and Sons, 1893.

Virgin, Peter, *The church in an age of negligence: Ecclesiastical structure and problems of church reform, 1700–1840*, Cambridge: James Clarke & Co., 1989.

Watts, M. R., *The dissenters: From the Reformation to the French Revolution*, Oxford: Oxford University Press, 1985.

Wykes, D. L., 'The contribution of the Dissenting academies to the emergence of rational Dissent', in Knud Haakonssen (ed.), *Enlightenment and religion: Rational dissent in eighteenth-century Britain*, Cambridge: Cambridge University Press, 1996, pp. 99–139.

7 REACHING AUDIENCES: SERMONS AND ORATORY IN EUROPE

Beutel, Albrecht, 'Evangelische Predigt vom 16. bis 18. Jahrhundert', *Theologische Realenzyklopädie*, 27 (1997), pp. 296–311.

Bitter, Gottfried, 'Katholische Predigt der Neuzeit', *Theologische Realenzyklopädie*, 27 (1997), pp. 262–96.

Boge, Birgit and Ralf Georg Bogner (eds.), *Oratio Funebris. Die katholische Leichenpredigt der frühen Neuzeit. Zwölf Studien*, Amsterdam: Rodopi, 1999.

Bosch, Gerrit Vanden, *Hemel, hel en vagevuur. Preken over het hiernamaals in de Zuidelijke Nederlanden tijdens de 17de en 18de eeuw*, Leuven: Davidfonds, 1991.

Bosma, Jelle, *Woorden van een gezond verstand. De invloed van de Verlichting op de in het Nederlands uitgegeven preken van 1750 tot 1800. Monografie & bibliografie*, Nieuwkoop: De Graaf, 1997.

Boucher, Edouard, *L'Eloquence de la chaire. Histoire littéraire de la prédication*, Lille: 1894.

Bowman, Frank Paul, *Le discours sur l'éloquence sacrée à l'époque romantique. Rhétorique, apologétique, herméneutique (1777–1851)*, Geneva: Librairie Droz, 1980.

Dargan, Edwin Charles, *A history of preaching*, 2 vols. (1905–1912), repr. Grand Rapids, MI: Baker Book House, 1954.

Downey, James, *The eighteenth-century pulpit: A study of the sermons of Butler, Berkeley, Secker, Sterne, Whitefield and Wesley*, Oxford: Oxford University Press, 1969.

Dreesman, Ulrich, 'Erbauliche Aufklärung. Zur Predigttheorie Johann Lorenz von Mosheims', in Christian Albrecht and Martin Weeber (eds.), *Klassiker der protestantischen Predigtlehre. Ein führungen in homiletische Theorieentwürfe von Luther bis Lange*, Tübingen: Mohr Siebeck, 2002, pp. 74–92.

Edwards, O. C., *A history of preaching*, Nashville, TN: Abingdon Press, 2004.

Eybl, Franz M., *Abraham a Sancta Clara. Vom Prediger zum Schrifsteller*, Tübingen: Niemeyer, 1992.

Feugère, Anatole, *Bourdaloue. Sa prédication et son temps*, 5th edn, Paris: Poitiers, 1889.

Goyet, Thérèse and Jean-Pierre Collinet, *Journées Bossuet. La prédication au XVIIe siècle*, Paris: Librairie A.-G. Nizet, 1980.

Herzog, Urs, *Geistliche Wohlredenheit. Die katholische Barockpredigt*, Munich: Verlag C. H. Beck, 1991.

Holtz, Sabine, *Theologie und Alltag. Lehre und Leben in den Predigten der Tübinger Theologen 1550–1750*, Tübingen: J. C. B. Mohr (P. Siebeck), 1993.

Ihalainen, Pasi, *Protestant nations redefined: changing perceptions of national identity in the rhetoric of the English, Dutch and Swedish public churches, 1685–1772*, Leiden: Brill, 2005.

Kastl, Maria, *Das Schriftwort in Leopoldspredigten des 17. und 18. Jahrhunderts. Untersuchungen zur Heiligenpredigt als lobender und beratschlagender Rede*, Vienna: Braumüller, 1988.

Krause, Reinhard, *Die Predigt der späten deutschen Aufklärung (1770–1805)*, Stuttgart: Calwer Verlag, 1965.

Lambert, Frank, *George Whitefield and the transatlantic revivals, 1737–1770*, Princeton: Princeton University Press, 1994.

Lebrun, François, 'La prédication au XVIIIe siècle', in Jean Delumeau (ed.), *Histoire vécue du peuple chrétien*, 2 vols., Toulouse: Privat, 1979, vol. 2, pp. 43–66.

Lenz, Rudolf, *De mortuis nil nisi bene? Leichenpredigten als multidisziplinäre Quelle unter besonderer Berücksichtigung der Historischen Familienforschung, der Bildungsgeschichte und der Literaturgeschichte*, Sigmaringen: Thorbecke, 1990.

Lessenich, Rolf P., *Elements of pulpit oratory in eighteenth-century England (1660–1800)*, Cologne and Vienna: Böhlau, 1972.

Lyons, [Abbé], *Les trois génies de la chaire: Bossuet, Bourdaloue, Massillon ou leurs œuvres oratoires en tebleaux synoptiques*, Nice, 1896.

Matheson, Ann, *Theories of rhetoric in the eighteenth-century Scottish sermon*, Lewiston, NY: Edwin Mellen, 1995.

Mitchell, W. F., *English pulpit oratory from Andrewes to Tillotson*, 2nd edn, New York: Russell & Russell, 1962.

Nye, Robert (ed.), *The English sermon. Volume III: 1750–1850*, Cheadle: Carcanet Press, 1976.

Saugnieux, Joël, *Les jansénistes et le renouveau de la prédication dans l'Espagne de la seconde moitié du XVIIIe siècle*, Lyon: Presses Universitaires de Lyon, [1976].

Saul, Nicholas, *'Prediger aus der neuen romantischen Clique': Zur Interaktion von Romantik und Homiletik um 1800*, Würzburg: Königshausen & Neumann, 1999.

Schneyer, Johann Baptist, *Geschichte der katholischen Predigt*, Freiburg: Seelsorge Verlag, 1968.

Schütz, Werner, *Geschichte der christlichen Predigt*, Berlin: de Gruyter, 1972.

Sisson, C. H. (ed.), *The English sermon. Volume II: 1650–1750*. Cheadle: Carcanet Press, 1976.

Storme, H. 'Gedrukte preekboeken: een verwaarloosde bron voor de geschiedenis van godsdienst, mentaliteit en dagelijks leven', in M. Cloet and F. Daelemans (eds.), *Religion, mentalité et vie quotidienne. Histoire religieuse en Belgique depuis 1970*, Brussels: Archief- en Bibliotheekwezen in België, 1988, pp. 89–109.

Taylor, Larissa (ed.), *Preachers and people in the Reformation and early modern period*, Leiden: Brill, 2001.

Truchet, Jacques, *La prédication de Bossuet: Etude des thèmes*, 2 vols., Paris: Editions du Cerf, 1960.

Welzig, Werner (ed.), *Predigt und soziale Wirklichkeit. Beiträge zur Erforschung der Predigtliteratur*, Amsterdam: Rodopi, 1981.

Predigten der Barockzeit. Texte und Kommentar. In zusammenarbeit mit Heinrich Kabas und Roswitha Woytek herausgegeben und durch Zeugnisse zur Predigt in der deutschen Literatur vom 18. zum 20. Jahrhundert ergänzt, Vienna: Verlag der Österreichischen Akademie der Wissenschaften, 1995.

8 CHRISTIAN EDUCATION

Brizzi, Gian Paolo, *La formazione della classe dirigente nel Sei-Settecento*, Bologna: Il Mulino, 1976.

Caspard, Pierre, 'Pourquoi on a envie d'apprendre. L'autodidaxie ordinaire à Neuchâtel (XVIIIe siècle)', *Histoire de l'éducation*, 70 (May 1996), pp. 65–110.

'Examen de soi-même, examen public, examen Etat de l'admission à la Sainte-Cène aux certificats de fin d'études, XVIe–XIXe siècle', *Histoire de l'éducation*, 94 (May 2002), pp. 17–74.

Chisick, Harvey, *The limits of reform in the Enlightenment: Attitudes towards the education of the lower classes in eighteenth-century France*, Princeton: Princeton University Press, 1981.

Delgado Criado, Buenaventura (ed.), *Historia de la educación en España y América*, vol. 2: *La educación en la España moderna (Siglos XVI–XVIII)*, Madrid: Fundación Santa Maria, 1993.

Engelbrecht, Helmut, *Geschichte des östereichischen Bildungswesens. Erziehung und Unterricht auf dem Boden Österreichs*, vol. 2: *Das 16. und 17. Jahrhundert*; vol. 3: *Von der frühen Aufklärung bis zum Vormärz*, Vienna: Osterreichischer Bundesverlag, 1983–84.

Eygun, Jean, *Au risque de Babel. Le texte religieux occitan de 1600 à 1850*, Bordeaux: Association d'étude du texte occitan, 2002.

Frijhoff, Wilhelmus Theodorus Maria, *La société néerlandaise et ses gradués 1575–1814*, Amsterdam: Holland University Press, 1981.

Graff, Harvey J. (ed.), *Literacy and social development in the West: A reader*, Cambridge: Cambrige University Press, 1981.

The legacies of literacy: Continuities and contradictions in western culture and society, Bloomington: Indiana University Press, 1991.

François, Etienne, 'Die Volksbildung im ausgehenden 18 Jahrhundert. Eine Untersuchung über dem vermeintlichen "Bildungsrückstand" der katholischen Bevölkerung Deutschlands im Ancien Régime', *Jahrbuch für westdeutsche Landesgeschiechte*, 3 (1977), pp. 277–304.

Hammerstein, Notker (ed.), *Handbuch der deutschen Bildungsgeschichte*, vol. 1: *15. bis 17. Jahrhundert. Von der Renaissance und der Reformation bis zum Ende der Glaubenskämpfe*, Munich: C. H. Beck, 1996.

Universitäten und Aufklärung, Göttingen: Wallstein, 1995.

Hans, Nicholas, *New trends in education in the eighteenth century*, London: Routledge and Kegan Paul, 1951.

Houston, R. A., *Literacy in early modern Europe: Culture and education, 1500–1800*, London and New York: Longman, 1988.

Kistenich, Johannes, *Bettelmönche im öffentlichen Schulwesen. Ein Handbuch für die Erzdiözese Köln, 1600 bis 1850*, 2 vols., Cologne: Böhlau Verl, 2001.

Konrads, Nobert, *Ritterakademien der frühen Neuzeit. Bildung als Standesprivilag im 16 und 17 Jahrhundert*, Göttingen: Vandenhoeck and Ruprecht, 1982.

Lawson, John and H. Silver, *A social history of education in England*, London: Methuen, 1973.

Motley, Mark, *Becoming a French aristocrat: The education of the court nobility 1580–1715*, Princeton: Princeton University Press, 1990.

Neugebauer, Wolfgang, *Absolutischer Staat und Schulwirklichkeit in Brandeburg-Preussen*, Berlin: W. de Gruyter, 1985.

Norden, N., 'Die Alphabetisierung der oldenburgischen Küstenmarsch im 17 und 18 Jahrhundert', in Ernst Hinrichs and Wilhelm Norden (eds.), *Regionalgeschichte. Probleme und Beispiele*, Hildesheim: Lax, 1980.

Paulsen, Friedrich, *Geschichte des gelehrten Unterrichts in den deutschen Schulen und Universitäten vom Ausgang des Mittelalters bis zur Gegenwart*, 2nd edn, 2 vols., Leipzig: Veit, 1896.

Roggero, Marina, *Scuola e riforme nello stato sabaudo*, Turin: Diputazione subalpina di storia patria, 1981.

Il sapere e la virtù. Stato, Università e professioni nel Piemonte tra Settecento e Ottocento, Turin: Diputazione subalpina di storia patria, 1987.

Rüegg, Walter, *A history of the university in Europe*, vol. 2: *Universities in early modern Europe (1500–1800)*, ed. H. De Ridder-Symoens, Cambridge: Cambridge University Press, 1996.

Schindling, Anton, 'Die protestantischen Universitäten im Heiligen Römischen Reich deutscher Nation im Zeitalter der Aufklärung', in Notker Hammerstein (ed.), *Universitäten und Aufklärung*, Göttingen: Wallstein, 1995.

Schmale, Wolfgang and Nan L. Dodde, *Revolution des Wissens Europa und seine Schulen (1750–1825): Ein Handbuch zur europäischen Schulgeschichte*, Bochum: Verlag Dieter Winkler, 1991.

Stone, Lawrence (ed.), *The university in society*, vol. 1: *Oxford and Cambridge from the fourteenth to the early nineteenth century*; vol. 2: *Europe, Scotland, and the United States from the sixteenth in the twentieth century*, Princeton: Princeton University Press, 1974.

Schooling and society: Studies in the history of education, Baltimore: The Johns Hopkins University Press, 1976.

Viñao Frago, Antonio, 'Aprender a leer en el Antiguo Regimen: cartillas, silabarios y catones', in Agustín Escolaño Benito (ed.), *Historia ilustrada del libro escolar en España. Del Antiguo Regimen a la Segunda Republica*, Madrid: Ed. Pirámide, 1997, pp. 148–91.

9 CHRISTIANITY AND GENDER

Primary sources

Arenal, Electa and Stacey Schlau (eds.), *Untold sisters: Hispanic nuns in their own works*, Albuquerque: University of New Mexico Press, 1989.

Arnold, Gottfried, *Unpartheiische Kirchen und Ketzerhistorie vom Anfang des Neuen Testaments bis auf das Jahr Christi 1688*, Frankfurt: Thomas Fritschens sel. Erben, 1729.

Humez, Jean M. (ed.), *Mother's first-born daughters: Early Shaker writings on women and religion*, Bloomington: Indiana University Press, 1993.

Lierheimer, Linda, *Spiritual autobiography and the construction of self: The mémoires of Antoinette Micolon*, Milwaukee: Marquette University Press, 2004.

Pascal, Jacqueline, *A rule for children and other writings*, ed. and trans. John Conley, S. J., Chicago: University of Chicago Press, 2003.

Petersen von Merlau, Eleonora, *Pietism and women's autobiography*, ed. and trans. Barbara Becker-Cantarino, Chicago: University of Chicago Press, 2005.

San José, María de, *Word from New Spain: The spiritual autobiography of Madre María de San José (1656–1719)*, ed. and trans. Kathleen Ann Myers, Liverpool: Liverpool University Press, 1993.

Secondary sources

Andaya, Barbara Watson, 'The changing religious role of women in pre-modern Southeast Asia', *Southeast Asian research*, 2 (1994), pp. 99–116.

Atwood, Craig D., 'Sleeping in the arms of Christ: Sanctifying sexuality in the eighteenth-century Moravian church', *Journal of the history of sexuality*, 8 (1997), pp. 25–47.

'The mother of God's people: The adoration of the Holy Spirit in the eighteenth-century Brüdergemeinde', *Church history*, 68 (1999), pp. 886–909.

Bilinkoff, Jodi, *Related lives: confessors and their female penitents, 1450–1750*, Ithaca: Cornell University Press, 2005.

Blussé, Leonard, *Strange company: Chinese settlers, mestizo women and the Dutch in VOC Batavia*, Dordrecht: Foris, 1986.

Boxer, C. R., *Mary and misogyny: Women in Iberian expansion overseas 1415–1815*, New York: Oxford University Press, 1975.

Boyer, Richard E., *Lives of the bigamists: Marriage, family, and community in colonial Mexico*, Albuquerque: University of New Mexico Press, 1995.

Brewer, Carolyn, *Shamanism, Catholicism, and gender relations in Colonial Philippines, 1521–1695*, London: Ashgate, 2004.

Carr, Thomas M. Jr., 'Les Abbesses et la Parole au dix-septième siècle: les discours monastiques à la lumière des interdictions pauliniennes', *Rhétorica*, 21, 1 (Winter 2003), pp. 1–23.

Chilcote, Paul Wesley, *John Wesley and the women preachers of early Methodism*, Metuchen, NJ: Scarecrow Press, 1991.

She offered them Christ: The legacy of women preachers in early Methodism, Nashville: Abingdon Press, 1993.

Choquette, Leslie, '"Ces amazons du Grand Dieu": Women and missions in seventeenth-century Canada', *French historical studies*, 17 (1992), pp. 626–55.

Conley, John J., *The suspicion of virtue: Women philosophers in neoclassical France*, Ithaca: Cornell University Press, 2002.

Conrad, Anne, *Zwischen Closter und Welt: Ursulinen und Jesuitinnen in der Katholischen Reformbewegung des 16./17. Jahrhunderts*, Mainz: Zabern, 1991.

Cope, Esther S., *Handmaid of the Holy Spirit: Dame Eleanor Davies, never so mad a ladie*, Ann Arbor: University of Michigan Press, 1993.

Crawford, Patricia, *Women and religion in England, 1500–1750*, London: Routledge, 1993.

Dailey, Barbara Ritter, 'The visitation of Sarah Wight: Holy Carnival and the revolution of the saints in civil war London', *Church history*, 55 (1986), pp. 438–55.

Davis, Natalie Zemon, *Women on the margins: Three seventeenth-century lives*, Cambridge, MA: Harvard University Press, 1995.

Diefendorf, Barbara, *From penitence to charity: Pious women and the Catholic Reformation in Paris*, Oxford: Oxford University Press, 2004.

Dinan, Susan E. and Debra Meters (eds.), *Women and religion in old and new worlds*, London: Routledge, 2001.

Gutiérrez, Ramón A., *When Jesus came, the corn mothers went away: Marriage, sexuality, and power in New Mexico 1500–1846*, Stanford: Stanford University Press, 1988.

Hambrick-Stowe, Charles, 'The spiritual pilgrimage of Sarah Osborne (1714–1796)', *Church history*, 61 (1992), pp. 408–21.

Hernández, María Leticia Sánchez, *Patronato, regio y órdenes religiosas femeninas en el Madrid de los Austrias*, Madrid: Fundación Universitaria Española, 1997.

Hoffman, Barbara, *Radikalpietismus um 1700: Der Streit um das Recht auf eine neue Gesellschaft*, Frankfurt: Campus, 1996.

'"Daß es süße Träume und Versuchungen seyen": Geschriebene und gelebte Utopien im Radikalen Pietismus', in Hartmut Lehmann and Anne-Charlott Trepp (eds.), *Im Zeichen der Krise: Religiosität im Europa des 17. Jahrhunderts*, Göttingen: Vandenhoek & Ruprecht, 1999, pp. 101–28.

Irwin, Joyce, 'Anna Maria von Schurman and Antoinette Bourignon: Contrasting examples of seventeenth-century Pietism', *Church history*, 60 (1991), pp. 301–35.

Juster, Susan, *Disorderly women: Sexual politics and evangelicalism in revolutionary New England*, Ithaca: Cornell University Press, 1994.

Kostroun, Daniella, 'A formula for disobedience: Jansenism, gender, and the feminist paradox', *Journal of modern history*, 75 (2003), pp. 483–522.

Kunze, Bonnelyn Young, *Margaret Fell and the rise of Quakerism*, Stanford: Stanford University Press, 1994.

Mack, Phyllis, *Visionary women: Ecstatic prophecy in seventeenth-century England*, Berkeley: University of California Press, 1992.

'Die Prophetin als Mutter: Antoinette Bourignon', in Hartmut Lehmann and Anne-Charlott Trepp (eds.), *Im Zeichen der Krise: Religiosität im Europa des 17. Jahrhunderts*, Göttingen: Vandenhoek & Ruprecht, 1999, pp. 79–101.

Medioli, Francesca, 'The dimensions of the cloister: Enclosure, constraint, and protection in seventeenth-century Italy', in Anne Jacobson Schutte, Thomas Kuehn, and Silvana Seidel Menchi (eds.), *Time, space and women's lives in early modern Europe*, Kirksville, Miss.: Sixteenth Century Journal Publishers, 2001, pp. 165–80.

Procter-Smith, Marjorie, *Women in Shaker community and worship: A feminist analysis of the uses of religious symbolism*, Lewiston, NY: E. Mellen, 1985.

Rapley, Elizabeth, *The Dévotes: Women and church in seventeenth-century France*, Montreal: McGill-Queens University Press, 1990.

The social history of the cloister: Daily life in the teaching monasteries of the old regime, Montreal: McGill-Queens University Press, 2002.

Schutte, Anne Jacobson, *Aspiring saints: Pretense of holiness, Inquisition, and gender in the Republic of Venice, 1618–1750*, Baltimore: The Johns Hopkins University Press, 2001.

Shell, Robert C.-H., *Children of bondage: A social history of the slave society at the Cape of Good Hope, 1652–1838*, Hanover: Wesleyan University Press, 1994.

Smith, Hilda, *Reason's disciples: Seventeenth-century English feminists*, Urbana: University of Illinois Press, 1982.

Smith, Merril D. (ed.), *Sex and sexuality in early America*, New York: New York University Press, 1998.

Ullbrich, Claudia, *Shulamith and Margarete: power, gender, and religion in a rural society in eighteenth-century Europe*, trans. Thomas Dunlap, Leiden: Brill, 2005.

Van Deusen, Nancy, 'Defining the sacred and the worldly: *Beatas* and *recogidas* in late seventeenth-century Lima', *Colonial Latin American historical review*, 6 (1997), pp. 456–83.

Walker, Claire, *Gender and politics in early modern Europe: English convents in France and the Low Countries*, London: Palgrave-Macmillan, 2003.

Wallace, Jr., Charles, '"Some stated employment of your mind": Reading, writing, and religion in the life of Susanna Wesley', *Church history*, 58 (1989), pp. 354–66.

Ward, Patricia A., 'Madam Guyon and experiential theology in America', *Church history*, 67 (1998), pp. 484–98.

Watt, Diane, *Sectaries of God: Women prophets in late medieval and early modern England*, Rochester, NY: Boydell & Brewer, 1997.

Weaver, F. Ellen, *La contre-réforme et les constitutions de Port-Royal*, Paris: Cerf, 2002.

'Erudition, spirituality, and women: The Jansenist contribution', in Sherrin Marshall (ed.), *Women in Reformation and Counter-reformation Europe: Public and private worlds*, Bloomington: Indiana University Press, 1989, pp. 189–206.

Weaver, Elissa B., *Convent theatre in early modern Italy: Spiritual fun and learning for women*, Cambridge: Cambridge University Press, 2002.

Wilcox, Catherine M., *Theology and women's ministry in seventeenth-century English Quakerism: Handmaids of the Lord*, London: E. Mellen, 1995.

Willen, Diane, 'Godly women in early modern England: Puritanism and gender', *Journal of ecclesiastical history*, 43 (1992), pp. 561–80.

Witt, Ulrike, *Bekehrung, Bildung und Biographie: Frauen im Umkries des Halleschen Pietismus*, Halle: M. Niemeyer, 1996.

Zarri, Gabriella, *Recinti: Donne, clausura, e matrimonio nella prima età moderna*, Bologna: Il mulino, 2000.

10 POPULAR RELIGION

Behringer, Wolfgang, *Witches and witch-hunts: A global history*, Cambridge: Polity Press, 2004.

Bell, Catherine, *Ritual theory, ritual practice*, Oxford and New York: Oxford University Press, 1992.

Bercé, Yves-Marie, *Fête et révolte. Des mentalités populaires du XVIe au XVIIIe siècle. Essai*, Paris: Hachette, 1976.

Beyer, Jürgen, Albrecht Burkardt, Fred van Lieburg, and Marc Wingens (eds.), *Confessional sanctity (c. 1500–c. 1800)*, Mayence: Verlag Philipp von Zabern, 2003.

Bloch, Marc, *The royal touch: Sacred monarchy and scrofula in England and France*, trans. J. E. Anderson, London: Routeledge and K. Paul, 1973.

Boutry, Philippe, Pierre-Antoine Fabre, and Dominique Julia (eds.), *Rendre ses vœux: Les identités pèlerines dans l'Europe moderne (XVIe–XVIIIe siècle)*, Paris: Ecole des hautes études en sciences sociales, 2000.

Boutry, Philippe, and Dominique Julia (eds.), *Pèlerins et pèlerinages dans l'Europe moderne*, Rome: Ecole française de Rome, 2000.

Briggs, Robin, *Witches and neighbors: The social and cultural context of European witchcraft*, Harmondsworth: Viking, 1996.

Brückner, Wolfgang, Gottfried Korff, and Martin Scharfe, *Volksfrömmigkeitsforschung*, Würzburg and Munich: Bayerisches Nationalmuseum, 1986.

Burkardt, Albrecht, *Les clients des saints. Maladie et quête du miracle à travers les procès de canonisation de la première moitié du XVIIe siècle en France*, Rome: Ecole française de Rome, 2004.

Burke, Peter, *Popular culture in early modern Europe*, London: Temple Smith, 1978.

Certeau, Michel de, *La possession de Loudun*, Paris: Gallimard, 1970.

Châtellier, Louis, *La religion des pauvres: Les missions rurales en Europe et la formation du catholicisme moderne, XVIe–XIXe siècle*, Paris: Aubier, 1993.

The Europe of the devout: The Catholic Reformation and the formation of a new society, Cambridge: Cambridge University Press, 1989.

Christian Jr., William A., *Local religion in sixteenth-century Spain*, Princeton: Princeton University Press, 1981.

Clark, Stuart, *Thinking with demons: The idea of witchcraft in early modern Europe*, Oxford: Clarendon Press, 1997.

Cunningham, Andrew, and Ole Peter Grell, *The four horsemen of the Apocalypse: Religion, war, famine and death in Reformation Europe*, Cambridge: Cambridge University Press, 2000.

Daston, Lorraine J., and Katherine Park, *Wonders and the order of nature, 1150–1750*, New York: Zone Books, 1998.

Davis, Natalie Zemon, 'From "popular religion" to "religious culture"', in Steven Ozment (ed.), *Reformation Europe: A guide to research*, St Louis: Center for Reformation Research, 1982, pp. 321–41.

Delumeau, Jean, *Catholicism between Luther and Voltaire: A new view of the Counter-Reformation*, trans. Jeremy Moiser, London: Burns & Oates, 1977.

Sin and fear: The emergence of a western guilt culture, 13th–18th centuries, New York: St Martin's Press, 1990.

Devlin, Judith, *The superstitious mind: French peasants and the supernatural in the nineteenth century*, New Haven: Yale University Press, 1987.

Ferber, Sarah, *Demonic possession and exorcism in early modern France*, London and New York: Routledge, 2004.

Frijhoff, Willem, *Embodied belief: Ten essays on religious culture in Dutch history*, Hilversum: Verloren, 2002.

Garrett, Clark, *Spirit possession and popular religion: From the Camisards to the Shakers*, Baltimore: The Johns Hopkins University Press, 1987.

Ginzburg, Carlo, *Ecstasies: Deciphering the witches' sabbath*, trans. Raymond Rosenthal, ed. Gregory Elliott, London: Hutchinson Radius, 1991.

The night battles: Witchcraft and agrarian cults in the sixteenth and seventeenth centuries, London: Routledge & Kegan Paul, 1983.

Israel, Jonathan I., *Radical Enlightenment: Philosophy and the making of modernity*, Oxford: Oxford University Press, 2001.

Karant-Nunn, Susan C., *The reformation of ritual: An interpretation of early modern Germany*, London & New York: Routledge, 1997.

Klaniczay, Gábor, *The uses of supernatural power: The transformation of popular religion in medieval and early modern Europe*, Cambridge: Polity Press, 1991.

McManners, John, *Church and society in eighteenth-century France*, vol. 2: *The religion of the people and the politics of religion*, Oxford: Clarendon Press, 1998.

Monter, William E., *Ritual, myth and magic in early modern Europe*, Athens, OH: Ohio University Press, 1984.

Muchembled, Robert, *Popular culture and elite culture in France, 1400 to 1750*, trans. Lydia Cochrane, Baton Rouge: Louisiana State University Press, 1985.

A history of the devil from the Middle Ages to the present, trans. Jean Birrell, Cambridge: Polity Press, 2003.

Parish, Helen, and William G. Naphy (eds.), *Religion and superstition in Reformation Europe*, Manchester and New York: Manchester University Press, 2002.

Po-chia Hsia, Ronnie, and Robert W. Scribner (eds.), *Problems in the historical anthropology of early modern Europe*, Wiesbaden: Harrassowitz, 1997.

Po-chia Hsia, Ronnie, *Social discipline in the Reformation: Central Europe, 1550–1750*, London and New York: Routledge, 1989.

The world of Catholic renewal, 1540–1770, Cambridge: Cambridge University Press, 1998.

Reinhard, Wolfgang, and Heinz Schilling (eds.), *Die katholische Konfessionaliserung*, Gütersloh: Gütersloher Verlagshaus, 1993.

Roper, Lyndal, *Oedipus and the devil: Witchcraft, sexuality and religion in early modern Europe*, London and New York: Routledge, 1994.

Sabean, David Warren, *Power in the blood: Popular culture and village discourse in early modern Germany*, Cambridge: Cambridge University Press, 1984.

Schilling, Heinz, 'Confessional Europe', in Thomas A. Brady Jr., Heiko A. Oberman, and James D. Tracy (eds.), *Handbook of European history, 1400–1600: Late Middle Ages, Renaissance and Reformation*, vol. 2: *Visions, programs and outcomes*, Leiden: Brill, 1995, pp. 641–82.

Scribner, Bob, and Trevor Johnson (eds.), *Popular religion in Germany and Central Europe, 1400–1800*, Basingstoke: Macmillan, 1996.

Scribner, R. W., *For the sake of the simple folk: Popular propaganda for the German Reformation*, Cambridge: Cambridge University Press, 1981.

Popular culture and popular movements in Reformation Germany, London and Ronceverte: The Hambledon Press, 1987.

Religion and culture in Germany (1400–1800), ed. Lyndal Roper, Leiden: Brill, 2001.

Thomas, Keith, *Religion and the decline of magic: Studies in popular beliefs in sixteenth-and seventeenth-century England*, London: Weidenfeld and Nicolson, 1971.

Tracy, James D., and Marguerite Ragnow (eds.), *Religion and the early modern state: Views from China, Russia, and the West*, Cambridge: Cambridge University Press, 2005.

Vrijhof, Pieter H., and Jacques Waardenburg (eds.), *Official and popular religion: Analysis of a theme for religious studies*, The Hague: Mouton, 1979.

Walsham, Alexandra, *Providence in early modern England*, Oxford: Oxford University Press, 1999.

II JEWISH–CHRISTIAN RELATIONS

Primary sources

Autobiography of a seventeenth-century Venetian Rabbi, ed. and trans. Mark R. Cohen, Princeton: Princeton University Press, 1988.

Memoirs of Glückel of Hameln, trans. Marvin Lowenthal, New York: Schocken Books, 1977.

Mendelssohn, Moses, *Schreiben an den Herrn Diaconus Lavatter zu Zürich*, Berlin & Stettin, 1770.

Mendes-Flohr, Paul, and Jehuda Reinharz (eds.), *The Jew in the modern world*, Oxford: Oxford University Press, 1995.

Secondary sources

Cohen, Mark R., 'Leone da Modena's Riti: A seventeenth-century plea for social toleration of Jews', *Jewish social studies*, 24 (1972), pp. 297–319.

Endelman, Todd, *The Jews of Georgian England, 1714–1830*, Ann Arbor: University of Michigan Press, 1991.

Hertzberg, Arthur, *The French Enlightenment and the Jews*, New York: Columbia University Press, 1968.

Israel, Jonathan, *European Jewry in the age of mercantilism, 1550–1750*, 3rd edn, London: Littman Library, 1998.

Kahn, Léon, *Les Juifs de Paris*, Paris, 1895.

Katz, Jacob, *Tradition and crisis: Jewish society at the end of the Middle Ages*, trans. Bernard Dov Cooperman, New York: New York University Press, 1993.

Malino, Frances, *The Sephardic Jews of Bordeaux*, University, AL: University of Alabama Press, 1978.

A Jew in the French Revolution: The life of Zalkind Hourwitz, Oxford: Basil Blackwell, 1996.

Meyer, Michael, *The origins of the modern Jew*, Detroit: Wayne State University Press, 1967.

Mortier, Roland, 'Les "philosophes" français du 18e siècle devant le judaïsme et la judéité', in Bernhard Blumenkranz (ed.), *Juifs en France au XVIIIe siècle*, Paris: Commission française des archives juives, 1994.

Ruderman, David, *Jewish Enlightenment in an English key*, Princeton: Princeton University Press, 2000.

Schechter, Ronald, *Obstinate Hebrews: representations of Jews in France, 1715–1815*, Berkeley, CA: University of California Press, 2003.

Schwarzfuchs, Simon, *Napoleon, the Jews and the Sanhedrin*, London: Routledge and Kegan Paul, 1979.

Shohat, Azriel, *Im Hilufei Tekufot: Reshit ha-Haskalah be-Yahadut Germanya*, Jerusalem: Mosad Bialiik, 1960.

Sorkin, David, *The Berlin Haskalah and German religious thought*, London: Valentine Mitchell, 2000.

Stern, Selma, *The court Jew*, trans. Ralph Weiman, New Brunswick: Transaction Books, 1985.

12 ARCHITECTURE AND CHRISTIANITY

Arminjon, Catherine and Denis Lavalle (eds.), *20 siècles en cathédrales*, Paris: Editions du patrimoine, 2001.

Bazin, Germain, *L'Architecture religieuse baroque au Brésil*, Sao Paulo: Museu de Arte, 1956–58.

Bouchon, Chantal, Catherine Brisac, Nadine-Josette Chaline, and Jean-Michel Leniaud, *Ces églises du dix-neuvième siècle*, Amiens: Encrage, 1993.

Du Colombier, Pierre, *L'Architecture française en Allemagne au XVIIIe siècle*, Paris: PUF, 1956.

Hitchcock, Henry Russell, *Rococo architecture in southern Germany*, London: Phaidon, 1968.

Leniaud, Jean-Michel, *Les cathédrales au XIXe siècle*, Paris: Economica, 1993.

Lours, Mathieu, 'L'éclaircissement des églises parisiennes au XVIIIe siècle. Gestion et spiritualité', *Mémoires publiés par la fédération des sociétés historiques et archéologiques de Paris et de l'Île-de-France* (2001), pp. 139–98.

Middleton, Robin, and David Watkin, *Neoclassical and nineteenth-century architecture*, New York: Electa-Rizzoli, 1987.

Norberg-Schultz, Christian, *Architecture baroque*, Paris: Gallimard/Electa, 1992.

Architecture baroque tardive et rococo, Paris, Gallimard/Electa, 1989.

Pérouse de Montclos, Jean-Marie, *Histoire de l'architecture français. De la Renaissance à la Révolution*, Paris: Mengès, 1989.

Selbach, Vanessa, 'Représentation et interprétations des antiquités hébraïques dans les bibles du XVIe au XVIIIe siècle', in Jean-Michel Leniaud and Béatrice Bouvier (eds.), *Le livre d'architecture. XVe–XXe siècle, édition, représentations et bibliothèques*, Paris: Ecole des chartes, 2002, pp. 125–38.

Summerson, John Newenham, *Georgian London*, 2nd edn, London: Pimlico, 1988.

13 CHRISTIANITY AND THE RISE OF SCIENCE, 1660–1815

Blunt, W., *The complete naturalist: A life of Linnaeus*, London: G. Rainbird, 1971.

Châtellier, Louis, *Les espaces infinis et le silence de Dieu. Science et religion, XVIe–XIXe siècle*, Paris: Aubier-Flammarion, 2003.

Cohen, I. Bernard, *Introduction to Newton's 'Principia'*, Cambridge, MA: Harvard University Press, 1971.

Cohn, J., *Histoire de l'infini. Le problème de l'infini dans la pensée occidentale jusqu'à Kant*, trans. J. Seidengart, Paris: Editions du Cerf, 1994.

Coleman, William R., *Georges Cuvier zoologist: A study in the history of evolution theory*, Cambridge, MA: Harvard University Press, 1964.

Davillé, L., *Leibniz historien*, Paris, 1909.

Frängsmyr, Tore (ed.), *Linnaeus: The man and his work*, Berkeley: University of California Press, 1984.

Gillispie, Charles Coulston, *Genesis and geology: A study in the relations of scientific thought, natural theology and social opinion in Great Britain*, Cambridge, MA: Harvard University Press, 1996.

Gillispie, Charles Coulston, Robert Fox, and Ivor Grattan-Guinness, *Pierre-Simon Laplace (1749–1827): A life in exact science*, Princeton: Princeton University Press, 1997.

Gohau, G., *Les Sciences de la Terre aux XVIIe et XVIIIe siècles: naissance de la géologie*, Paris: Albin Michel, 1990.

Golinski, Jan, *Science as public culture: Chemistry and Enlightenment in Britain, 1760–1820*, Cambridge: Cambridge University Press, 1992.

Gusdorf, Georges, *La révolution galiléenne*, vol. 1, Paris: Payot, 1969.

Hahn, Roger, *The anatomy of a scientific institution: The Paris Academy of Science, 1666–1803*, Berkeley: University of California Press, 1971.

Hall, A. Rupert, *Philosophers at war*, Cambridge: Cambridge University Press, 1980.

Isaac Newton, adventurer in thought, new edn, Cambridge: Cambridge University Press, 1996.

Hofmann, James R., *André-Marie Ampère: Enlightenment and electrodynamics*, Cambridge: Cambridge University Press, 1995.

Larson, James L., *Reason and experience: The representation of natural order in the work of Carl von Linné*, Berkeley: University of California Press, 1971.

Laudan, R., *From Mineralogy to geology: The foundation of a science, 1650–1830*, Chicago: Chicago University Press, 1987.

Laurent, G. (dir.), *Jean-Baptiste Lamarck, 1744–1829*, Paris: Editions du CTHS, 1997.

Mancosu, P., *Philosophy of mathematics and mathematical practice in the seventeenth century*, Oxford: Oxford University Press, 1996.

Manuel, Frank E., *Isaac Newton, historian*, Cambridge: Cambridge University Press, 1963.

The religion of Isaac Newton, Oxford: Oxford University Press, 1974.

Metzger, Hélène, *Newton, Stahl, Boerhaave et la doctrine chimique*, Paris: Alcan, 1930.

Monnoyeur, F. (ed), *Infini des mathématiciens, infini des philosophes*, Paris: Belin, 1992.

Neveu, Bernard, *Erudition et religion aux XVIIe et XVIIIe siècles*, Paris: Albin Michel, 1994.

Pomeau, René, *La religion de Voltaire*, new edn, Paris: Nizet, 1969.

Proust, Jacques, *Diderot et l'Encyclopédie*, Paris: Armand Colin, 1962.

Redondi, Pietro, *Galileo eretico*, Turin: Einaudi, 1988.

Rodis-Lewis, Geneviève, *Descartes: Biographie*, Paris: Calmann-Lévy, 1995.

Roger, Jacques, *Les sciences de la vie dans la pensée française du XVIIIe siècle*, Paris: Armand Colin, 1964.

Romano, Antonella, *La Contre-Réforme mathématique. Constitution et diffusion d'une culture mathématique jésuite à la Rénaissance*, Rome: Ecole française de Rome, 1999.

Stafleu, Frans Antonie, *Linnaeus and the Linnaeans: The spreading of their ideas in systematic botany: 1735–1789*, Utrecht: A. Oosthoek's Uitgeversmaatschappij, 1971.

Taton, René and Curtis Wilson (eds.), *Planetary astronomy from the renaissance to the rise of astrophysics. Part. B: The eighteenth and nineteenth centuries*, Cambridge: Cambridge University Press, 1995.

Westfall, Richard S., *Never at rest: A biography of Isaac Newton*, Cambridge: Cambridge University Press, 1980.

14 THE ENLIGHTENMENT CRITIQUE OF CHRISTIANITY

Berti, Sylvia,'The religious sources of unbelief', *Journal of the history of ideas*, 56 (1995), pp. 555–75.

Champion, Justin, *Republican learning*, Manchester: Manchester University Press, 2003.

Goldgar, Anne, *Impolite learning: Conduct and community in the republic of letters, 1680–1750*, New Haven: Yale University Press, 1995.

Jacob, Margaret C., *The Newtonians and the English revolution, 1689–1720*, Ithaca: Cornell University Press, 1976.

The Enlightenment: a brief history with documents, Boston, MA: Bedford, 2001.

The radical Enlightenment: Pantheists, freemasons and republicans, 2nd edn, Morristown, NJ: Temple Publishers, 2003.

Jacob, Margaret C. and James R. Jacob (eds.), *The origins of Anglo-American radicalism*, Amherst: Humanity Books, 1991.

Klein, Lawrence E., *Shaftesbury and the culture of politeness: Moral discourse and cultural politics in early eighteenth-century England*, Cambridge: Cambridge University Press, 1994.

Lund, Roger (ed.), *The margins of orthodoxy: Heterodox writing and cultural response, 1660–1750*, Cambridge: Cambridge University Press, 1995.

Miller, Peter N., '"Freethinking" and "freedom of thought" in eighteenth-century Britain', *The historical journal*, 36 (1993), pp. 599–671.

O'Higgins, J., S. J., *Anthony Collins*, The Hague: Nijhoff, 1970.

Page, Anthony, *John Jebb and the Enlightenment: Origins of British radicalism*, Westport, CT Praeger, 2003.

Porter, Roy, 'Mixed feelings: The Enlightenment and sexuality in eighteenth-century Britain', in Paul-Gabriel Broucé (ed.), *Sensuality in eighteenth-century Britain*, Manchester: Manchester University Press, 1982.

Robinson, Eric, 'The Derby philosophical society', *Annals of science*, 9 (1953), pp. 359–67.

Roche, Daniel, *France in the Enlightenment*, trans. Arthur Goldhammer, Cambridge, MA: Harvard University Press, 1998.

Rousseau, G. S., 'In the House of Madam Van der Tasse, on the long bridge: A homosexual university club in early modern Europe', in Kent Gerard and Gert Hekma (eds.), *The pursuit of sodomy: Male homosexuality in Renaissance and Enlightenment Europe*, New York: Harrington Park Press, 1989, pp. 311–48.

Rousseau, G. S. and Roy Porter (eds.), *Sexual underworlds of the Enlightenment*, Chapel Hill: University of North Carolina Press, 1988.

15 THE CHRISTIAN ENLIGHTENMENT

Benin, Stephen, *The footprints of God: Divine accommodation in Jewish and Christian thought*, Albany, NY: State University of New York Press, 1993.

Bernard, A., *Le sermon au XVIIIe siècle. Etude historique et critique sur la prédication en France, de 1715 à 1789*, Paris: Thrin et fils, 1901.

Blanning, T. C. W., 'The Enlightenment in Catholic Germany', in Roy Porter and Mikulas Teich (eds.), *The Enlightenment in national context*, Cambridge: Cambridge University Press, 1981.

Brown, Stewart J., 'William Robertson (1721–1793) and the Scottish Enlightenment', in Stewart J. Brown (ed.), *William Robertson and the expansion of empire*, Cambridge: Cambridge University Press, 1997.

Cottret, Bernard, *Le Christ des Lumières. Jésus de Newton à Voltaire (1680–1760)*, Paris: Les Editions du Cerf, 1990.

Cottret, Monique, *Jansénismes et Lumières. Pour un autre XVIIIe siècle*, Paris: Albin Michel, 1998.

Dickey, Laurence, *Hegel: Religion, economics and the politics of spirit, 1770–1807*, Cambridge: Cambridge University Press, 1986.

Elwell, Clarence, *The influence of the Enlightenment on the Catholic theory of religious education in France*, New York: Russell & Russell, 1942.

Everdell, William, *Christian apologetics in France, 1730–1790: The roots of romantic religion*, Lewiston, NY: Edwin Mellen, 1987.

Gargett, Graham, *Jacob Vernet, Geneva, and the philosophes*, Oxford: The Voltaire Foundation, 1994.

Gascoigne, John, *Cambridge in the age of Enlightenment*, Cambridge: Cambridge University Press, 1989.

Heyd, Michael, *'Be sober and reasonable': The critique of enthusiasm in the seventeenth and early eighteenth centuries*, Leiden: E. J. Brill, 1995.

Hunter, Ian, *Rival Enlightenments: Civil and metaphysical philosophy in early modern Germany*, New York: Cambridge University Press, 2001.

Israel, Jonathan, *The radical Enlightenment: Philosophy and the making of modernity*, Oxford: Oxford University Press, 2001.

Masseau, Didier, *Les ennemis des philosophes. L'antiphilosophie au temps des Lumieres*, Paris: Albin Michel, 2000.

Maza, Sarah, *Private lives and public affairs: The causes célèbres of prerevolutionary France*, Berkeley: University of California Press, 1993.

Menozzi, Daniele, *Les interprétations politiques de Jésus de l'ancien régime à la Révolution*, Paris: Les Editions du Cerf, 1983.

Mossner, Ernest Campbell, *Bishop Butler and the age of reason*, New York: The Macmillan Company, 1936.

Northeast, Catherine, *The Parisian Jesuits and the Enlightenment 1700–1762*, Oxford: The Voltaire Foundation, 1991.

Phillipson, Nicholas, 'The Scottish Enlightenment', in Roy Porter and Mikulas Teich (eds.), *The Enlightenment in national context*, Cambridge: Cambridge University Press, 1981, pp. 19–40.

'Providence and progress: An introduction to the historical thought of William Robertson', in Stewart J. Brown (ed.), *William Robertson and the expansion of empire*, Cambridge: Cambridge University Press, 1997.

Pitassi, Maria-Cristina, *De l'orthodoxie aux Lumières: Genève 1670–1737*, Geneva: Labor et Fides, 1992.

Le Christ entre orthodoxie et Lumières. Actes du colloque tenu à Genève en aout 1993, Geneva: Droz, 1994.

Edifier ou Instruire? Les avatars de la liturgie réformée du XVIe au XVIIIe siècle, Paris, Champion, 2000.

Apologétique 1680–1740: sauvetage ou naufrage de la théologie? Geneva: Labor et Fides, 1991.

Plongeron, Bernard, 'Recherches sur l' "Aufklärung" catholique en Europe occidental, 1770–1830', *Revue d'histoire moderne et contemporaine*, 16 (1969), pp. 555–605.

Théologie et politique au siècle des Lumières, 1770–1820, Geneva: Droz, 1973.

Pocock, J. G. A., *Barbarism and religion*, 2 vols., Cambridge: Cambridge University Press, 1999.

'Clergy and commerce: The conservative Enlightenment in England', in *L'Eta dei Lumi: Studi Storici sul Settecento Europeo in Onore di Franco Venturi*, 2 vols., Naples, 1985, vol. 1, pp. 523–61.

'Post-Puritan England and the problem of the Enlightenment', in P. Zagorin (ed.), *Culture and politics from puritanism to the Enlightenment*, Berkeley, 1980, pp. 91–111.

'Enthusiasm: The antiself of Enlightenment', in Lawrence E. Klein and Anthony J. La Vopa (eds.), *Enthusiasm and Enlightenment in Europe, 1650–1850*, San Marino, CA: Huntington Library, 1998, pp. 7–28.

Porter, Roy, *The creation of the modern world: The untold story of the British Enlightenment*, New York: W. W. Norton, 2000.

Porter, Roy and Mikulas Teich, (eds.), *The Enlightenment in national context*, Cambridge: Cambridge University Press, 1981.

Reddy, William, *The navigation of feeling: A framework for the history of emotions*, Cambridge: Cambridge University Press, 2001.

Reill, Peter, *The German Enlightenment and the rise of historicism*, Berkeley: University of California Press, 1975.

Rivers, Isabel, *Reason, grace and sentiment: A study of the language of religion and ethics in England, 1660–1780*, 2 vols., Cambridge: Cambridge University Press, 2000.

Rosa, Susan, '"Il était possible aussi que cette conversion fut sincère": Turenne's conversion in context', *French historical studies*, 18 (Spring 1994), pp. 632–66.

'Seventeenth-century Catholic polemic and the rise of cultural rationalism: An example from the empire', *Journal of the history of ideas*, (1996), pp. 87–107.

Sell, Alan, *John Locke and the eighteenth-century divines*, Cardiff: University of Wales Press, 1997.

Sher, Richard, *Church and university in the Scottish Enlightenment: The moderate literati of Edinburgh*, Princeton: Princeton University Press, 1985.

Sorkin, David, '"A wise, enlightened and reliable piety": The religious Enlightenment in central and western Europe, 1689–1789', Parkes Institute Pamphlet 1, University of Southampton, 2002.

'Reclaiming theology for the Enlightenment: The case of Siegmund Jacob Baumgarten (1706–1757)', *Central European history*, 36 (2003), pp. 503–30.

'William Warburton: The middle way of "heroic moderation"', *Dutch review of Church history*, 82, 2 (July 2002), pp. 1–39.

Tackett, Timothy, *Priest and parish in eighteenth-century France: A social and political study of the curés in a diocese of Dauphiné, 1750–1791*, Princeton: Princeton University Press, 1977.

Whelan, Ruth, 'Between two worlds: The political theory of Jacques Abbadie', *Lias*, 14 (1987), pp. 101–117, 143–57.

'From Christian apologetics to Enlightened deism: The case of Jacques Abbadie (1656–1727)', *Modern language review*, 87 (1992), pp. 32–40.

Yolton, John, *John Locke and the way of ideas*, London: Oxford University Press, 1956.

Young, B. W., *Religion and Enlightenment in eighteenth-century England: Theological debate from Locke to Burke*, Oxford: Clarendon Press, 1998.

16 JANSENISM AND THE INTERNATIONAL SUPPRESSION OF THE JESUITS

Appolis, Emile, *Les jansénistes espagnols*, Bordeaux: Société bordelaise de diffusion de travaux des lettres et sciences humaines, 1966.

Caeiro, José, *Historia da Expulsas de Companhia de Jesus de Provincia de Portugal*, Lisbon: Ed. Varbo, 1991.

Cottret, Monique, *Jansénismes et lumières: pour un autre XVIIIe siècle*, Paris: Albin Michel, 1998.

Crétineau-Joly, Jacques, *Histoire religieuse, politique et littéraire de la Compagnie de Jésus composée sur les documents inédits et authentiques*, 6 vols., Paris: Mellier Frères, 1846.

Delattre, Pierre, *Les établissements des jésuites en France depuis quatre siècles: Répertoire topobibliographique*, 5 vols., Enghien, Belgium: Institut supérieu de théologie, 1949–57.

Egido López, Teófanes and Isidoro Pinedo, *Las causas 'gravísimas' y secretas de la expulsión de los jesuitas por Carlos III*, Madrid: Fundación Universitaria Española, 1994.

Egret, Jean, 'Le procès des jésuites devant les parlements de France, 1760–1774', *Revue historique*, 204, (July-Dec. 1950), pp. 1–27.

Bibliography

Ferrer Benimelli, José A., 'Carlos III y la extinción de los jesuitas', in *Actas del Congreso Internacional sobre 'Carlos III y la Ilustración'*, 2 vols., Madrid: Ministerio de cultura, 1989, vol. 1, pp. 239–59.

'El motín de Esquilache y sus consecuencias según la correspondencia diplomática francesca. Primera fase de la expulsión y de la extinción de los jesuitas', *Archivum historicum Societatis Jesu*, 53, 105 (1984), pp. 193–219.

Giménez López, Enrique (ed.), *Expulsión y exilio de los jesuitas españoles*, Alicante: Universidad de Alicante, 1997.

Lafage, Franck, *L'Espagne de la Contre-révolution: développement et déclin, XVIIIème XXème siècles*, Paris: Edinons Harmattan, 1993.

Lynch, John, *Bourbon Spain, 1700–1808*, Oxford and London: Basil Blackwell, 1989.

Michel, Marie-Jose, *Jansénisme et Paris, 1640–1730*, Paris: Klincksieck, 2000.

Miller, Samuel J., *Portugal and Rome, c.1748–1830: An aspect of the Catholic Enlightenment*, Rome: Università Gregorianna Editrice, 1978.

Mischaud, Claude, 'Un anti-jésuite au service de Pombal: l'abbé Platel', in Maria Helena Carvalho dos Santos (ed.), *Pombal revisitado: communicações ao colóquio internacional organizado pela Commissão do 2.° centenario da morte do marquês de Pombal*, 2 vols., Lisbon: Imprensa Universitaria no. 34, Edital Estampa, 1984, vol. 1, pp. 389–401.

Northeast, Catherine, *The Parisian Jesuits and the Enlightenment, 1700–62*, Geneva: Voltaire Foundation, 1991.

Pastor, Ludwid Freiherr von, *The history of the popes from the close of the Middle Ages*, 40 vols., London: Routledge and Kegan Paul, 1938–68.

Plongeron, Bernard, et al., *Histoire du christianisme des origines à nos jours*, vol. 10: *Les défis de la modernité, 1750–1840*, ed. Jean-Marie Mayer, Charles and Luce Pietri, André Vauchez, Marc Venard, Paris: Desclée, 1997.

Ravignan, Gustave-Xavier de La Croix de, *Clément XIII et Clément XIV*, 2 vols., Paris: Julien, Lanier et Cie, 1854.

Rodríguez, Laura, 'The Spanish riots of 1766', *Past and present*, 59 (May 1973), pp. 117–46.

'The riots of 1766 in Madrid', *European studies review*, 3 (1973), pp. 223–42.

Rodríguez Casado, Vicente, *La política y los politícos en el reinado de Carlos III*, Madrid: Ediciones Riap, 1962.

Saugnieux, Joël, *Le jansénisme espagnol du XVIIIe siècle: Ses composants et ses sources*, Oveido: Universidad Cátedra Feijoo, 1975.

Scott, H. M., 'Religion and real politik: The doc de Choiseul, the Bourbon family compact and the Society of Jesus, 1758–1773', *International history review*, 25 (2003), pp. 37–62.

Stein, Stanley J. and Barbara H. Stein, *Apogee of empire: Spain and New Spain in the age of Charles III, 1759–1789*, Baltimore: The Johns Hopkins University Press, 2003.

Tallon, Alain, *Le concile de Trente*, Paris: Editions du Cerf, 2000.

Thompson, Dorothy Gillian, 'French Jesuit leaders and the destruction of the Jesuit Order, 1756–1762', *French history*, 2 (1988), pp. 237–63.

'General Ricci and the suppression of the Jesuit order in France, 1760–1764', *Journal of ecclesiastical history*, 37 (July 1986), pp. 426–41.

'The persecution of the Jesuits by the parlement of Paris, 1761–1771', *Studies in church history*, 21 (1984), pp. 289–301.

Tietz, Manfred (ed.), *Los jesuitas españoles expulsos. Su imagen y su contribición al saber sobre el mundo hispánico en la Europa del siglo XVIII. Actas del coloquio internacional de Berlin*

(7–10 de abril de 1999), Madrid and Frankfurt am Main: Iberoamericana and Vervuert, 2001.

Van Kley, Dale K., *The Jansenists and the expulsion of the Jesuits from France, 1757–1765*, New Haven: Yale University Press, 1975.

Vogel, Christine, 'Der Untergang des Gesellschaft Jesu als europäisches Edienereignis' Inaugural-Dissertation zur Erlangung des Doktorgrades des Philosophie des Fach-bereiches 04 der Justus-Liebig-Universität Giessen, 2003.

17 EVANGELICAL AWAKENINGS IN THE NORTH
ATLANTIC WORLD

Beyreuther, Erich, *Der junge Zinzendorf*, 2nd edn, Marburg an der Land: Verlag der Francke Buchhandlung, 1957.

   Zinzendorf und die Christenheit, Marburg an der Land: Verlag der Francke Buchhandlung, 1961.

   Zinzendorf und die sich allhier beisammen finden, Marburg an der Land: Verlag der Francke Buchhandlung, 1959.

Brecht, M. et al., *Geschichte des Pietismus*, 4 vols., Göttingen: Vandenhoeck & Ruprecht, 1993–2004.

Dellsperger, Rudolph, *Die Anfänge des Pietismus in Bern*, Göttingen: Vandenhoeck & Ruprecht, 1984.

Deppermann, Andreas, *Johann Jakob Schütz und die Anfänge des Pietismus*, Tübingen: J. C. B. Mohr (Paul Siebeck), 2002.

Fawcett, Arthur, *The Cambuslang revival of the eighteenth century*, London: Banner of Truth, 1971.

Hempton, David, *Methodism: Empire of the spirit*, New Haven: Yale University Press, 2005.

Hinrichs, Carl, *Preussentum und Pietismus*, Göttingen: Vanderhoeck & Reprecht, 1971.

MacInnes, J., *The evangelical revival in the highlands of Scotland*, Aberdeen: Aberdeen University Press, 1951.

Noll, Mark, *The rise of evangelicalism: The age of Edwards, Whitefield and the Wesleys*, Leicester: Apollos, 2004.

Podmore, C. J., *The Moravian church in England, 1728–1760*, Oxford: Oxford University Press, 1998.

Rack, Henry D., *Reasonable enthusiast: John Wesley and the rise of Methodism*, 3rd edn, Peterborough: Epworth Press, 2002.

Richey, Russell E., *Early American Methodism*, Bloomington: Indiana University Press, 1991.

Schlenther, Boyd S., *Queen of the Methodists: The Countess of Huntingdon and the eighteenth-century crisis of faith*, Bishop Auckland: Durham Academic Press, 1997.

Stead, G. and M. Stead, *The exotic plant: A history of the Moravian Church in Great Britain 1742–2000*, Peterborough: Epworth Press, 2003.

Stoeffler, F. E., *German Pietism during the eighteenth century*, Lieden: E. J. Brill, 1973.

   The Rise of evangelical Pietism, Leiden: E. J. Brill, 1971.

Strieff, Patrick, *Reluctant saint? A theological biography of Fletcher of Madeley*, Peterborough: Epworth Press, 2001.

Tudur, Geraint, *Howell Harris: From conversion to separation, 1735–1750*, Cardiff: University of Wales Press, 2000.

Wallmann, Johannes, *Phillip Jakob Spener und die Anfänge des Pietismus*, Tübingen: J. C. B. Mohr (Paul Siebeck), 1970.

Wernle, Paul, *Der Schweizerische Protestantismus im 18. Jahrhundert*, vols. 1–3, Tübingen: J. C. B. Mohr (Paul Siebeck), 1923–25.

Westerkamp, Marilyn J., *Triumph of the laity: Scots-Irish piety and the Great Awakening, 1625–1760*, New York: Oxford University Press, 1988.

Uttendörfer, Otto, *Zinzendorf und die Mystik*, Berlin: Christlicher Zeitschrifts Verlag, 1950.

18 TOLERATION AND MOVEMENTS OF CHRISTIAN
REUNION, 1660–1789

Primary sources

Abernethy, John, *Religious obedience founded on personal persuasion*, Belfast, 1720.

Blackburne, Francis, *The confessional*, London, 1766.

Calamy, Edmund, *A defence of moderate Non-Conformity*, 3 vols., London, 1703–05.

Hoadly, Benjamin, *The nature of the kingdom, or church of Christ*, London, 1717.

Kippis, Andrew, *A vindication of the Protestant Dissenting ministers, with regard to their late application to Parliament*, 2nd edn, London, 1773.

Locke, John, *A letter concerning toleration* (1689), ed. James H. Tully, Indianapolis: Hackett Publishing, 1983.

Montesquieu, *The spirit of the laws*, trans. and ed. Anne M. Cohler, Basia Carolyn Miller and Harold Samuel Stone, Cambridge: Cambridge University Press, 1989.

Nevin, Thomas, *The trial of Thomas Nevin. M. A. pastor of a church, of the Presbyterian denomination*, Belfast, 1725.

Palmer, Samuel, *The Protestant-Dissenter's catechism*, 3rd edn, London, 1774.

Priestley, Joseph, *An essay on the first principles of government*, London, 1768.

Voltaire, *Treatise on tolerance and other writings*, ed. Samuel Harvey, Cambridge: Cambridge University Press, 2000.

Secondary sources

Barlow, Richard Burgess, *Citizenship and conscience: A study in the theory and practice of religious toleration in England during the eighteenth century*, Philadelphia: University of Pennsylvania Press, 1962.

Berkvens-Stevelinck, C., J. Israel, and G. H. M. Posthumus Meyjes (eds.), *The emergence of tolerance in the Dutch Republic*, Leiden: Brill, 1997.

Coffey, John, *Persecution and toleration in Protestant England, 1558–1689*, Harlow: Longman, 2000

Ditchfield, G. M., 'The parliamentary struggle over the repeal of the Test and Corporation Acts, 1787–1790', *English historical review*, 89 (1974), pp. 551–77.

Flaningam, John, 'The occasional conformity controversy: Ideology and party politics, 1697–1711', *Journal of British studies*, 17 (1977), pp. 38–62.

Gibson, William, *Enlightenment prelate: Benjamin Hoadly, 1676–1761*, Cambridge: James Clarke & Co., 2003.

Grell, Ole Peter, and Roy Porter (eds.), *Toleration in Enlightenment Europe*, Cambridge: Cambridge University Press, 2000.

Grell, Ole Peter, Jonathan I. Israel, and Nicholas Tyacke (eds.), *From persecution to toleration: The Glorious Revolution and religion in England*, Oxford: Clarendon Press, 1991.

Haakonssen, Knud (ed.), *Enlightenment and religion: Rational Dissent in eighteenth-century Britain*, Cambridge: Cambridge University Press, 1996.

Haydon, Colin, *Anti-Catholicism in eighteenth-century England: A political and social study*, Manchester: Manchester University Press, 1993.

Hoak, Dale, and Mordechai Feingold (eds.), *The world of William and Mary: Anglo-Dutch perspectives on the revolution of 1688–89*, Stanford: Stanford University Press, 1996.

Hsia, R. Po-Chia, and H. F. K. van Nierop (eds.), *Calvinism and religious toleration in the Dutch Golden Age*, Cambridge: Cambridge University Press, 2003.

Hunt, N. C., *Two early political associations: The Quakers and the Dissenting deputies in the age of Sir Robert Walpole*, Oxford: Clarendon Press, 1961.

Israel, Jonathan I. (ed.), *The Anglo-Dutch moment: Essays on the Glorious Revolution and its world impact*, Cambridge: Cambridge University Press, 1991.

Lacey, Douglas R., *Dissent and parliamentary politics in England, 1661–1689*, New Brunswick: Rutgers University Press, 1969.

Laursen, John Christian, and Cary J. Nederman, (eds.), *Beyond the persecuting society: Religious toleration before the Enlightenment*, Philadelphia: University of Pennsylvania Press, 1998.

Murphy, Andrew R., *Conscience and community: Revisiting toleration and religious Dissent in early modern England and America*, University Park: Pennsylvania State University Press, 2001.

Nuttall, Geoffrey F., and Owen Chadwick (eds.), *From uniformity to unity, 1662–1962*, London: SPCK, 1962.

Poland, Burdette C., *French Protestantism and the French Revolution: A study in church and state, thought and religion, 1685–1815*, Princeton: Princeton University Press, 1957.

Rouse, Ruth, and Stephen C. Neill (eds.), *A history of the ecumenical movement 1517–1948*, Philadelphia: Westminster, 1954.

Sheils, W. J. (ed.), *Persecution and toleration*, vol. 21 of Studies in Church History, Oxford: Basil Blackwell, 1984.

Sher, Richard B., *Church and university in the Scottish Enlightenment: The moderate literati of Edinburgh*, Princeton: Princeton University Press, 1985.

Sykes, Norman, *William Wake, Archbishop of Canterbury 1657–1737*, 2 vols., Cambridge: Cambridge University Press, 1957.

Taylor, Stephen, 'Sir Robert Walpole, the Church of England and the Quakers Tithe Bill of 1736', *Historical journal*, 28 (1985), pp. 51–77.

Van Eijnatten, Joris, *Mutua Christianorum tolerantia: Irenicism and toleration in the Netherlands: The Stinstra Affair 1740–1745*, Florence: Leo S. Olschki, 1998.

Watts, Michael R., *The Dissenters from the Reformation to the French Revolution*, Oxford: Clarendon Press, 1978.

Wykes, David L., 'Quaker schoolmasters, toleration and the law, 1689–1714', *Journal of religious history*, 21 (1997), pp. 186–7.

Young, B. W., *Religion and Enlightenment in eighteenth-century England: Theological debate from Locke to Burke*, Oxford: Clarendon Press, 1998.

Zagorin, Perez, *How the idea of religious toleration came to the West*, Princeton: Princeton University Press, 2003.

19 CHRISTIANITY IN IBERIAN AMERICA

Alden, Dauril, *The making of an enterprise: The Society of Jesus in Portugal, its empire, and beyond, 1540–1750*, Stanford: Stanford University Press, 1996.

Block, David, *Mission culture on the upper Amazon: Native tradition, Jesuit enterprise and secular policy in Moxos, 1600–1880*, Lincoln, NB: University of Nebraska Press, 1994.

Brading, D. A., *Church and state in Michoacán, 1749–1810*, Cambridge: Cambridge University Press, 1994.

Mexican Phoenix: Our Lady of Guadalupe: Image and tradition across five centuries, Cambridge: Cambridge University Press, 2001.

Burns, Kathryn, *Colonial habits: Convents and the spiritual economy of Cuzco, Peru*, Durham, NC: Duke University Press, 1999.

Cahill, David, 'Popular religion and appropriation: The example of Corpus Christi in eighteenth-century Cuzco', *Latin American research review*, 31 (1996), pp. 67–110.

Celestino, Olinda and Albert Meyers (eds.), *Las cofradías en el Peru: region central*, Frankfurt: K. D. Vervuert, 1981.

Cervantes, Fernando, *The devil in the new world: The impact of diabolism in New Spain*, New Haven: Yale University Press, 1994.

Cervantes, Fernando and Nicolas Griffiths (eds.), *Spiritual encounters: Interactions between Christianity and native religions in colonial America*, Lincoln, NB: University of Nebraska Press, 1999.

Chowning, Margaret, 'The *consolidación de vales reales* in the bishopric of Michoacán', *Hispanic American historical review*, 69 (1989), pp. 451–78.

Crosby, Harry W., *Antigua California: Mission and colony on the peninsular frontier, 1697–1768*, Albuquerque: University of New Mexico Press, 1994.

Curcio-Nagy, Linda A., 'Native icon to city protectress to royal patroness: Ritual political symbolism and the Virgin of Remedies', *The Americas*, 52 (1996), pp. 367–93.

'Giants and gypsies: Corpus Christi in colonial Mexico City', in William H. Beezley, Cheryl English Martin and William E. French (eds.), *Rituals of rule, rituals of resistance: Public celebrations and popular culture in Mexico*, Wilmington: Scholarly Resources Books, 1994, pp. 1–26.

'Rosa de Escalante's private party: Popular female religiosity in colonial Mexico City', in Mary E. Giles (ed.), *Women in the Inquisition: Spain and the New World*, Baltimore: The Johns Hopkins University Press, 1999, pp. 254–69.

Dean, Carolyn, *Inka bodies and the Body of Christ: Corpus Christi in colonial Cuzco, Peru*, Durham, NC: Duke University Press, 1999.

Egaña, Antonio de, S. J., *Historia de la iglesia en la América Española*, vol. 2: *Hemispherio sur*, Madrid: Editorial catolica, 1966.

Farriss, Nancy, *Maya society under colonial rule: The collective enterprise of survival*, Princeton: Princeton University Press, 1984.

Foz y Foz, Pilar, *La revolución pedagógica en Nueva España, 1754–1820*, Madrid: Instituto de estudios americanos, 1981.

Gallagher, Ann M., 'The Indian nuns of Mexico City: Monasterio of Corpus Christi, 1724–1821', in Asunción Lavrin (ed.), *Latin American women: Historical perspectives*, Westport, CT: Greenwood Press, 1978, pp. 150–72.

García Añoveros, Jesús María, *La monarquía y la Iglesia en America*, Valencia: Asociación Francisco López de Gómara, 1991.

Griffiths, Nicolas, *The cross and the serpent: Religious repression and resurgence in colonial Peru*, Norman, OK: University of Oklahoma Press, 1996.

Harrington, Raymond P., 'The secular clergy in the diocese of Mérida de Yucatán, 1780–1850: Their origins, careers, wealth and activities', Ph.D. thesis, The Catholic University of America (1982).

Iwasaki Cauti, Fernando, 'Mujeres al borde de la perfección: Rosa de Santa Maria y las alumbradas de Lima', *Hispanic American historical review*, 73 (1993), pp. 581–613.

Karasch, Mary, *Slave life in Rio de Janeiro, 1808–1850*, Princeton: Princeton University Press, 1987.

Klaiber, Jeffrey, 'Religion y justicia en Túpac Amaru', *Alpachis* (Cuzco, Peru), 16 (1982), pp. 173–86.

Langer, Erick and Robert H. Jackson (eds.), *The new Latin American mission history*, Lincoln, NB: University of Nebraska Press, 1995.

Lavalle, Bernard, 'Las doctrinas de indigenas como núcleos de explotación colonial, siglos XVI–XVII', *Alpachis* (Cuzco, Peru), 16 (1982), pp. 151–71.

Lavrin, Asunción, 'El capital eclesiástico y las elites sociales en Nueva España a fines del siglo XVIII', *Estudios Mexicanos/Mexican Studies*, 1 (1985), pp. 1–28.

Lea, Henry Charles, *The Inquisition in the Spanish dependencies*, New York, 1908.

Levaggi, Abelardo (ed.), *La Inquisicion en Hispanoamerica*, Buenos Aires: Universidad del Museo social argentino, 1997.

Lipsett-Rivera, Sonya, '"Mira lo que hace el diablo": The devil in Mexican popular culture, 1750–1856', *The Americas*, 59 (2002), pp. 201–20.

Lockhart, James, *The Nahuas after the conquest: A social and cultural history of the Indians of central Mexico, sixteenth through eighteenth centuries*, Stanford: Stanford University Press, 1992.

Lópetegui, Leon and Félix Zubillaga, *Historia de la iglesia en la América Española*, vol. 1: *México y las Antillas*, Madrid: Editorial catolica, 1966.

López, Celia, *Con la cruz y con el dinero: Los Jesuitas del San Juan colonial*, San Juan, Argentina: Editorial Fundación Universidad Nacional de San Juan, 2001.

López, Rosalva Loreto, 'The devil, women and the body in seventeenth-century Puebla convents', *The Americas*, 59 (2002), pp. 181–200.

López Sarrelangue, Delfina, 'Mestizaje y Catolicismo en la Nueva España', *Historia Mexicana*, 23 (1973), pp. 1–42.

Los Dominicos y el Nuevo Mundo. Siglos XVIII y XIX. Actas del IV Congreso Internacional, 1993, Salamanca: Ed. San Estaban, 1995.

Marsilli, Maria, 'God and evil in the gardens of the Andean south: Mid-colonial rural religion in the diocese of Arequipa', Ph.D. thesis, Emory University, 2002.

Mazin Gómez, Oscar, *Entre dos majestades: el obispo y la iglesia del gran michoacán ante las reformas borbónicas, 1758–1772*, Zamora, Mexico: El Colegio de Michoacán, 1987.

Meyers, Albert and D. E. Hopkins (eds.), *Manipulating the saints*, Hamburg: Wayasbah, 1988.

Mills, Kenneth, *Idolatry and its enemies: Colonial Andean religion and extirpation, 1640–1750*, Princeton: Princeton University Press, 1997.

Morgan, Ronald J., *Spanish American saints and the rhetoric of identity, 1600–1810*, Tucson: University of Arizona Press, 2002.

Myers, Kathleen, 'Testimony for canonization or proof of blasphemy? The new Spanish Inquisition and the hagiographic biography of Catarina de San Juan', in Mary E. Giles (ed.), *Women in the Inquisition: Spain and the New World*, Baltimore: The Johns Hopkins University Press, 1999, pp. 270–95.

Poole, Deborah, 'Los santuarios religiosos en la economía regional andina (Cuzco)', *Alpachis* (Cuzco, Peru), 16 (1982), pp. 79–116.

Poole, Stafford, C. M., *Our Lady of Guadalupe: The origins and sources of a Mexican national symbol, 1531–1797*, Tucson: University of Arizona Press, 1996.

Saeger, James Schofield, *The Chaco mission frontier: The Guaycuruan experience*, Tucson: University of Arizona Press, 2000.

Taylor, William B., *Magistrates of the sacred: Priests and parishioners in eighteenth-century Mexico*, Stanford: Stanford University Press, 1996.

Thornton, John, *Africa and Africans in the making of the Atlantic world, 1400–1680*, Cambridge: Cambridge University Press, 1992.

Van Deusen, Nancy E., *Between the sacred and the worldly: The institutional and cultural practice of recogimiento in colonial Lima*, Stanford: Stanford University Press, 2001.

Van Oss, Adriaan C., *Catholic colonialism: A parish history of Guatemala, 1524–1821*, Cambridge Latin American Studies 57, Cambridge: Cambridge University Press, 1986.

Vargas Ugarte, Ruben, S. J., *Concilios limenses, 1551–1772*, vol. 3: *Historia*, Lima, 1954.

Voekel, Pamela, *Alone before God: The religious origins of modernity in Mexico*, Durham, NC: Duke University Press, 2002.

Wobeser, Gisela von, 'La inquisición como institución creditícia en el siglo XVIII', *Historia Mexicana*, 39 (1990), pp. 849–79.

 Vida eternal y preocupaciones terrenales: las capellanías de Misas en la Nueva España, 1700–1821, Serie historia novohispana 64, Mexico City: Universidad Autónoma de México, 1999.

20 BRITISH AND FRENCH NORTH AMERICA TO 1765

Primary sources

Bradford, William, *Of Plymouth Plantation*, ed. S. E. Morison, New York: Knopf, 1959.

Burr, Esther Edwards, *The journal of Esther Edwards Burr, 1754–1757*, ed. Carol F. Karlsen and Laurie Crumpacker, New Haven: Yale University Press, 1984.

Edwards, Jonathan, *The works of Jonathan Edwards*, vol. 4: *The Great Awakening*, ed. C. C. Goen, New Haven: Yale University Press, 1972.

Hopkins, Samuel. *The life and character of Miss Susanna Anthony*, Hartford, CT: Hudson and Goodwin, 1799.

Wheatley, Phillis, *The poems of Phillis Wheatley*, ed. Julian D. Mason, Jr., Chapel Hill: University of North Carolina Press, 1966.

Bibliography

Secondary sources: general

Butler, Jon, *Awash in a sea of faith: Christianizing the American people*, Cambridge, MA: Harvard University Press, 1990.
  'Protestant pluralism', in *Encyclopedia of the North American colonies*, ed. Jacob Ernest Cooke, 3 vols., New York: Charles Scribner's Sons, 1993, vol. 3: pp. 609–31.
Gaustad, Edwin S., and Philip L. Barlow, *New historical atlas of religion in America*, New York: Oxford University Press, 2000.
Hamm, Thomas, *Quakers in America*, New York: Columbia University Press, 2003.
Miller, Perry, *Errand into the wilderness*, Cambridge, MA: Harvard University Press, 1956.
Stout, Harry S., *The New England soul: Preaching and religious culture in colonial New England*, New York: Oxford University Press, 1986.
Taylor, Alan, *American colonies: The settling of North America*, New York: Penguin, 2001.
Westerkamp, Marilyn J., *Women and religion in early America, 1600–1850*, New York: Routledge, 1999.

Secondary sources: seventeenth-century British

Bremer, Francis J., *John Winthrop: America's forgotten founding father*, New York: Oxford University Press, 2003.
Cohen, Charles I., *God's caress: The psychology of Puritan religious experience*, New York: Oxford University Press, 1986.
Foster, Stephen, *The long argument: English Puritanism and the shaping of New England culture, 1570–1700*, Chapel Hill: University of North Carolina Press, 1991.
Gaustad, E. S., *Liberty of conscience: Roger Williams in America*, Grand Rapids, MI: Eerdmans, 1991.
Hall, David D., *Worlds of wonder, days of judgment: Popular religious belief in early New England*, New York: Knopf, 1989.
Hambrick-Stowe, Charles, *The practice of piety: Puritan devotional disciplines in seventeenth-century New England*, Chapel Hill: University of North Carolina Press, 1982.
Heimert, Alan, and Andrew Delbanco (eds.), *The Puritans in America: A narrative anthology*, Cambridge, MA: Harvard University Press, 1985.
Middlekauf, Robert, *The Mathers: Three generations of Puritan intellectuals, 1596–1728*, New York: Oxford University Press, 1971.
Morgan, E. S. (ed.), *Puritan political ideas*, Indianapolis: Bobbs-Merrill, 1965.
  The Puritan dilemma: The story of John Winthrop, Boston: Little, Brown, 1958.
  Visible saints: The history of a Puritan idea, New York: New York University Press, 1963.
Pope, Robert G., *The Half-Way Covenant: Church membership in Puritan New England*, Princeton: Princeton University Press, 1969.
Winship, Michael P., *Making heretics: Militant Protestantism and free grace in Massachusetts, 1636–1641*, Princeton: Princeton University Press, 2002.

Secondary sources: eighteenth-century British

Anderson, Fred, *Crucible of war: The Seven Years' War and the fate of empire in British North America, 1754–1766*, New York: Knopf, 2000.

Bibliography

Bonomi, Patricia U., and Peter R. Eisenstadt, 'Church Adherence in the eighteenth-century British American colonies', *William and Mary Quarterly*, 39 (1982), pp. 245–86.

Cogley, Richard W., *John Eliot's mission to the Indians before King Philip's War*, Cambridge, MA: Harvard University Press, 1999.

Fiering, Norman, *Jonathan Edwards's moral thought and its British context*, Chapel Hill: University of North Carolina Press, 1981.

Frey, Sylvia R., and Betty Wood, *Come shouting to Zion: African American Protestantism in the American South and British Caribbean to 1830*, Chapel Hill: University of North Carolina Press, 1998.

Guelzo, Allen C., 'God's designs: The literature of the colonial revivals of religion, 1725–1760', in Harry S. Stout and D. G. Hart (eds.), *New directions in American intellectual history*, New York: Oxford University Press, 1997.

Heimert, A., and Perry Miller (eds.), *The Great Awakening*, Indianapolis: Bobbs-Merrill, 1967.

Juster, Susan, *Disorderly women: Sexual politics and evangelicalism in revolutionary New England*, Ithaca: Cornell University Press, 1994.

Kidd, Thomas S., ' "Let hell and Rome do their worst": World news and anti-Catholicism, and international Protestantism in early-eighteenth-century Boston', *New England quarterly*, 86 (2003), pp. 265–90.

McLoughlin, William G., *New England dissent: The Baptists and the separation of church and state*, 2 vols., Cambridge, MA: Harvard University Press, 1971.

Marsden, George, *Jonathan Edwards: A life*, New Haven: Yale University Press, 2003.

Murrin, John M., 'Religion and politics in America from the first settlements to the Civil War', in Mark A. Noll (ed.), *Religion and American politics*, New York: Oxford University Press, 1990.

Noll, Mark A., *The rise of Evangelicalism*, Leicester: Apollos, 2004.

Pointer, Richard W., *Protestant pluralism and the New York experience: A study of eighteenth-century religious diversity*, Bloomington: Indiana University Press, 1988.

Roeber, A. G., *Palatines, liberty, and property: German Lutherans in colonial British America*, Baltimore: The Johns Hopkins University Press, 1993.

Stout, Harry S. *The divine dramatist: George Whitefield and the rise of modern evangelicalism*, Grand Rapids, MI: Eerdmans, 1991.

Wheeler, Rachel, 'Women and Christian practice in a Mahican village', *Religion and American culture*, 13 (Winter 2003), pp. 27–68.

Secondary sources: French Canada

Blackburn, Carole, *Harvest of souls: The Jesuit missions and colonialism in North America, 1632–1650*, Montreal: McGill-Queen's University Press, 2000.

Choquette, Robert, 'French Catholicism comes to the Americas', in C. H. Lippy, R. Choquette, and S. Poole (eds.), *Christianity comes to the Americas*, New York: Paragon, 1992.

Grant, John Webster, *Moon of wintertime: Missionaries and the Indians of Canada in encounter since 1534*, Toronto: University of Toronto Press, 1984.

Greer, Allan, *Mohawk Saint: Catherine Tekakwitha and the Jesuits*, New York: Oxford University Press, 2004.

Murphy, Terrence, and Roberto Perin (eds.), *A concise history of Christianity in Canada*, Toronto: Oxford University Press, 1996.

Thwaites, R. G. (ed.), *Jesuit relations and allied documents*, Cleveland: Burrows Brothers, 1896–1901.

21 CHRISTIANITY IN AFRICA

Anstey, Roger, *The Atlantic slave trade and British abolition: 1760–1810*, London: Macmillan, 1975.

Baur, John, *2000 years of Christianity in Africa: An African history 62–1992*, Nairobi: Paulines, 1994.

Cuffee, Paul, *Paul Cuffe's logs and letters: 1808–1817: A Black Quaker's 'Voice from Within the Veil'*, ed. Rosalind Cobb Wiggins, Washington, DC: Howard University Press, 1996.

DuBois, W. E. B., *The suppression of the African slave trade to the United States of America: 1638–1870* (1898), repr. New York: Russell & Russell, 1965.

Du Plessis, J., *A History of Christian missions in South Africa*, London: Longmans, Green and Co., 1911, repr. Cape Town: C. Struik, 1965.

Fiddles, Edward, 'Lord Mansfield and the Sommersett Case', *Law quarterly review*, 200 (October 1934).

Flint, John E. (ed.), *Cambridge history of Africa*, vol. 5: *c.1790–c.1870*, Cambridge: Cambridge University Press, 1976.

Fyfe, Christopher, *A history of Sierra Leone*, London: Oxford University Press, 1962.

George, David, 'An account of the life of Mr. David George, from Sierra Leone in Africa, given by himself in a conversation with Brother Rippon of London, and Brother Pearce of Birmingham', *The annual Baptist register* (1790, 1791, 1792 and 1793).

Goodell, William, *Slavery and anti-slavery: A history of the great struggle in both hemispheres, with a view of the slavery question in the United States*, New York: William Harned, 1852.

Hancock, David Leslie, *Citizens of the world: London merchants and the integration of the British Atlantic community: 1735–1785*, Cambridge: Cambridge University Press, 1995.

Latourette, Kenneth Scott, *The history of the expansion of Christianity*, vol. 5: *The Great century in the Americas, Australasia, and Africa, 1800–1914*, and vol. 6: *The great century in northern Africa and Asia, 1800–1914*, Grand Rapids, MI: Zondervan Publishing House, 1970.

Sanneh, Lamin, *Abolitionists abroad: American Blacks and the making of modern West Africa*, Cambridge, MA: Harvard University Press, 1999.

Sherwood, Henry Noble, 'Paul Cuffe', *Journal of Negro history*, 8 (April 1923).

Sundkler, Bengt, and Christopher Steed, *A history of the church in Africa*, Cambridge: Cambridge University Press, 2000.

Wadström, Carl B., *Essay on colonization, particularly applied to the Western Coast of Africa, with some free thoughts on cultivation and commerce; also brief descriptions of the colonies already formed, or attempted, in Africa, including those of Sierra Leone and Bulama*, 2 vols., London: Darton & Harvey, 1794.

22 CHRISTIANITY IN SOUTH AND SOUTH-EAST ASIA

Ballhatchet, Kenneth, *Caste, class and Catholicism in India, 1789–1914*, Surrey: Curzon Press, 1998.

Borges, Charles, *The economics of the Goa Jesuits, 1542–1759: An explanation of their rise and fall*, New Delhi: Concept, 1994.

Borges, Charles, Hannes Stubbe, and Oscar Pereira (eds.), *Goa and Portugal: History and development*, New Delhi: Concept, 2000.

Boxer, Charles R., *The Portuguese seaborne empire 1415–1825*, Harmondsworth: Penguin Books, 1973.

Portuguese India in the mid-seventeenth century, New Delhi: Oxford University Press, 1980.

Coelho, Victor, 'Music in Portuguese India and Renaissance music histories', in Teotónio R. de Souza and José Manuel Garcia (eds.), *Vasco da Gama e a l'India*, 3 vols., Lisbon: Fundação Calouste Gulbenkian, 1999, vol. 1, pp. 185–94.

Correia-Afonso, John, *The Jesuits in India, 1542–1773*, Anand: Gujarat Sahitya Prakash, 1997.

Cronin, V., *A Pearl to India: The life of Roberto de Nobili*, London: Rupert Hart-Davis, 1959.

Daniélou, Alain, *A brief history of India*, Vermont: Inner Traditions India, 2003.

D'Costa, Anthony, *The Christianization of the Goa Islands*, Bombay: Heras Institute, 1965.

Fenning, Hugh, 'Records of the Dominicans of Goa, 1700–1835', in *Archivum Fratrum Praedicatorum*, vol. 1, Rome, 1980.

'Dominican mission reports in Goa 1686–1832', in *Archivum Fratrum Praedicatorum*, vol. 52, Rome, 1982.

Ferroli, Domenico, *The Jesuits in Malabar*, vol. 1, Bangalore: Bangalore Press, 1939.

The Jesuits in Malabar, vol. 2, Bangalore: King and Co., 1951.

The Jesuits in Mysore, Kozhikode: Xavier Press, 1955.

Frykenberg, Robert E. (ed.), *Christians and missionaries in India: Cross-cultural communication since 1500*, London: Routledge and Curzon, 2003.

Hartmann, Arnaulf (ed.), 'The Augustinians in golden Goa: A manuscript of Felix of Jesus, O.S.A.', *Analecta Augustiniana*, 30, Rome, 1967.

Houtart, F., *Religion and ideology in Sri Lanka*, Bangalore: TPI, 1974.

Hull, Ernest R., *Bombay mission history with a special study of the Padroado question*, vol. 1, Bombay: Examiner Press, 1927.

Jackson, Kenneth D., *A hidden presence: 500 years of Portuguese culture in India and Sri Lanka*, Macau: Fundação Macau, 1995.

Maclagan, Edward, *The Jesuits and the Great Moghul*, London: Burns Oates & Washbourne, 1932.

Meersman, Achilles, *The Friars Minor or Franciscans in India, 1291–1942*, Karachi: Rotti Press, 1943.

Melo, Carlos M. de, *The recruitment and formation of the native clergy in India, 16th–19th century: A historico-canonical study*, Lisbon: Agencia Geral do Ultramar, 1955.

Mundadan, Mathias A., *History of Christianity in India*, vol. 1: *From the beginning up to the middle of the sixteenth century*, Bangalore: Theological Publications in India, 1984.

Nevett, Albert M., *John de Britto and his times*, Anand: Gujarat Sahitya Prakash, 1980.

Perniola, V., *The Catholic Church in Sri Lanka (the Dutch period 1658–1795)*, Dehiwala, Sri Lanka: Tisara Prakasakayo, 1983–85.

The Catholic Church in Sri Lanka (the Portuguese period 1505–1658), 3 vols. Dehiwala, Sri Lanka: Tisara Prakasakayo, 1989–2003.

Perumalil, H. C., and E. R. Hambye (eds.), *Christianity in India: A history in ecumenical perspective*, Alleppey: Prakasam Publications, 1972.

Phan, Peter C., *Mission and catechesis: Alexandre de Rhodes and inculturation in seventeenth-century Vietnam*, New York: Orbis Books, 1998.

Sauliere, A, *Red sand: A life of St. John de Brito, S. J., martyr of the Madura mission*, Mathura: De Nobili Press, 1947.

Souza, George Bryan, *The Survival of Empire: Portuguese trade and society in China and the South China Seas, 1630–1754*, Cambridge: Cambridge University Press, 1986.

Souza, Francisco de, *Oriente Conquistado a Jesus Cristo pelos padres da Companhia de Jesus da Provincia de Goa*, repr., Porto: Lello & Irmão, 1979.

Souza, Teotónio R. de, *Medieval Goa: A socio-economic history*, New Delhi: Concept, 1979.

Souza, Teotónio R. de, and Charles J. Borges (eds.), *Jesuits in India: In historical perspective*, Macau: ICM, 1992.

Thekedathu, Joseph, *History of Christianity in India: From the middle of the sixteenth century to the end of the seventeenth century*, vol. 2, Bangalore: Theological Publications of India, 1982.

Trindade, Paulo da, *Conquista Espiritual do Oriente*, 3 vols., Lisbon: Centro de Estudos Históricos Ultramarinos, 1962.

Wolpert, Stanley, *A new history of India*, New York: Oxford University Press, 2004.

Wessels, Cornelius, *Early Jesuit travellers in Central Asia, 1603–1721*, The Hague: Martinus Nijhoff, 1924.

Wicki, J. (ed.), *História do Malavar 1615 by Fr. Diogo Gonçalves, S. J.*, Munster: Aschendorffsche Verlagsbuchhandlung, 1955.

23 CHRISTIANITY IN EAST ASIA

Philippines

De la Costa, Horacio, 'The development of the native clergy in the Philippines', in Horacio de la Costa and John N. Schumacher (eds.), *The Filipino clergy: Historical studies and future perspectives*, Manila: Loyola Papers Board of Editors, Loyola School of Theology, Ateneo de Manila University, 1980, pp. 58–9.

The Jesuits in the Philippines, Cambridge, MA: Harvard University Press, 1961.

Escoto, Salvador P., 'The ecclesiastical controversy of 1767–1776: A catalyst of Philippine nationalism', *Journal of Asian history*, 10 (1976), pp. 97–133.

Fernandez, Pablo, *Dominicos donde nace el sol. Historia de la Provincia del Santísimo Rosario de Filipinas de la Orden de Predicadores*, 2nd edn, Barcelona: Yuste, 1958.

History of the church in the Philippines (1521–1898), Manila: National Book Store, 1979.

Kwantes, Anne C. (ed.), *Chapters in Philippine church history*, Manila: OMF Literature, 2001.

Macdonald, Charles J.-H., 'Folk Catholicism and pre-Spanish religions in the Philippines', *Philippine studies*, 52 (2004), pp. 78–93.

Palanco, Fernando, 'Diego Silang's revolt: A new approach', *Philippine studies*, 50 (2002), pp. 512–37.

Santiago, Luciano P. R., 'The development of the religious congregations for women in the Philippines during the Spanish period (1565–1898)', *Journal of Sophia Asia*, 12 (1994), pp. 49–71.

Schumacher, John N., 'The early Filipino clergy: 1698–1762', *Philippine studies*, 51 (2003), pp. 7–62.

'Syncretism in Philippine Catholicism: Its historical causes', *Philippine studies*, 32 (1984), pp. 251–72.

Tuggy, Arthur Leonard, *The Philippine church: Growth in a changing society*, Grand Rapids, MI: Eerdmans, 1971.

China

Collani, Claudia von, *P. Joachim Bouvet S. J. Sein Leben und sein Werk*, Nettetal: Steyler Verlag, 1985.

Duteil, Jean-Pierre, *Le mandat du ciel: Le rôle des jésuites en Chine*, Paris: Arguments, 1994.

Entenmann, Robert E., 'Christian virgins in eighteenth-century Sichuan', in Daniel H. Bays (ed.), *Christianity in China: From the eighteenth century to the present*, Stanford: Stanford University Press, 1996, pp. 180–93.

Latourette, Kenneth Scott, *A history of Christian missions in China*, London: Society for Promoting Christian Knowledge, 1929.

Malek, Roman (ed.), *Western learning and Christianity in China: The contribution and impact of Johann Adam Schall von Bell, S. J. (1592–1666)*, Nettetal: Steyler Verlag, 1998.

Menegon, Eugenio, 'Ancestors, virgins, and friars: The localization of Christianity in late imperial Mindong (Fujian, China), 1632–1863', unpublished Ph.D. thesis, University of California, Berkeley, 2002.

Mungello, D. E. (ed.), *The Chinese Rites Controversy: Its history and meaning*, Nettetal: Steyler Verlag, 1994.

Ronan, Charles E., and Bonnie B. C. Oh (eds.), *East meets West: The Jesuits in China, 1582–1773*, Chicago: Loyola University Press, 1988.

Rosso, Antonio Sixto, *Apostolic legations to China of the eighteenth century*, Pasadena: Perkins, 1948.

Serruys, Henri, 'Andrew Li, Chinese priest 1692 (1693?)–1774', *Neue Zeitschrift für Missionswissenschaft*, 32 (1976), pp. 39–55, 130–44.

Standaert, Nicolas (ed.), *Handbook of Christianity in China*, vol. 1: 635–1800, Leiden: Brill, 2001.

Uhalley, Stephen, Jr., and Xiaoxin Wu (eds.), *China and Christianity: Burdened past, hopeful future*, Armonk, NY: M. E. Sharpe, 2001.

Widmer, Eric, *The Russian ecclesiastical mission in Peking during the eighteenth century*, Cambridge, MA: Harvard University Press, 1976.

Willeke, Bernward H., *Imperial government and Catholic missions in China during the years 1784–1785*, New York: Bonaventura, 1948.

Witek, John W. (ed.), *Ferdinand Verbiest (1623–1688): Jesuit missionary, scientist, engineer and diplomat*, Nettetal: Steyler Verlag, 1994.

Japan

Breen, John, and Mark Williams (eds.), *Japan and Christianity: Impact and responses*, Basingstoke: Macmillan, 1996.

Elison, George, *Deus destroyed: The image of Christianity in early modern Japan*, Cambridge, MA: Council on East Asian Studies, Harvard University, 1988.

Jennes, Joseph, *A history of the Catholic Church in Japan: From its beginnings to the early Meiji era (1549–1873)*, rev. edn, Tokyo: Oriens Institute for Religious Research, 1973.

Mullins, Mark R. (ed.), *Handbook of Christianity in Japan*, Leiden: Brill, 2003.

Voss, Gustav, and Hubert Cieslik (trans.), *Kirishito-ki und Sayo-yoroku: japanische Dokumente zur Missionsgeschichte des 17. Jahrhunderts*, Tokyo: Sophia University, 1940.

Whelan, Christal (trans.), *The beginning of heaven and earth: The sacred book of Japan's hidden Christians*, Honolulu: University of Hawaii Press, 1996.

Korea

Baker, Don, 'A Confucian confronts Catholicism: Truth collides with morality in eighteenth-century Korea', *Korean studies forum*, 6 (1979–80), pp. 1–44.

Choi, André, *L'érection du premier Vicariat Apostolique et les origines du catholicisme en Corée, 1592–1837*, Immensee: Neue Zeitschrift für Missionswissenschaft, 1961.

Chung, Chai-sik, 'Christianity as a heterodoxy: An aspect of general cultural orientation in traditional Korea', in Yung-hwan Jo (ed.), *Korea's response to the West*, Kalamazoo, MI: Korea Research and Publications, 1971, pp. 57–86.

Dallet, Charles, *Histoire de l'Eglise de Corée*, vol. 1, Paris: Victor Palmé, 1874.

Diaz, Hector, *A Korean theology: Chu-Gyo Yo-Ji: Essentials of the Lord's teaching by Chŏng Yak-jong Augustine (1760–1801)*, Immensee: Neue Zeitschrift für Missionswissenschaft, 1986.

Ruiz de Medina, Juan, *The Catholic Church in Korea: Its origins, 1566–1784*, Seoul: Royal Asiatic Society, 1991.

24 CHRISTIAN ENCOUNTERS WITH OTHER WORLD RELIGIONS

Almond, Philip E., *The British discovery of Buddhism*, Cambridge: Cambridge University Press, 1988.

Arkiasamy, Soosai, *Dharma, Hindu and Christian according to Roberto de Nobili*, Rome: Pontificia Universita Gregoriana, 1986.

Arthur, Mildred, *Early views of India*, London: Thames and Hudson, 1980.

Bosch, David, *Transforming mission: Paradigm shifts in the theology of missions*, New York: Orbis Books, 1991.

Carnall, Geoffrey, 'Robertson and contemporary images of India', in S. J. Brown (ed.), *William Robertson and the expansion of empire*, Cambridge: Cambridge University Press, 1997.

Da Trinadade, Paulo, *Chapters on the introduction of Christianity to Ceylon*, Chilaw: Edmund Peiris, 1972.

Delacroix, S. (ed.), *Histoire universelle des missions Catholiques*, 4 vols., Paris: Grund, 1956.

Du Bois, J. A., *Description of the character and manners etc. of the peoples of India*, London: Longman, Hurst, Bees, Orme and Brown, 1817.

Du Jarric, Pierre, *Akbar and the Jesuits*, London: George Routledge and Sons, 1926.

Forrester, Duncan, *Caste and Christianity in India: Attitudes and policy on caste of Anglo-Saxon missions in India*, London: Curzon Press, 1980.

Gaudel, Jean-Marie, *Encounters and clashes: Islam and Christianity in history*, Rome: Pontificia Instituto di Studi Arabici e Islamici, 1990.

Goddard, Hugh, *History of Christian–Muslim relations*, Edinburgh: Edinburgh University Press, 2000.

Gunny, Ahmad, *Images of Islam in eighteenth-century writings*, London: Grey Seal, 1996.

Hudson, D. D., *Protestant origins in India*, Richmond: Curzon, 2000.

Koilpillai, Victor, *SPCK in India*, Delhi: SPCK, 1985.

Launay, Adrien, *Histoire de la mission de Cochinchine (1658–1823)*. *Documents historique*, Paris: P. Téqui, 1920.

Marshall, P. J., *The British discovery of Hinduism in the eighteenth century*, Cambridge: Cambridge University Press, 1970.

Mungello, D. E. (ed.), *The Chinese Rites Controversy: Its history and meaning*, Chicago: Loyola Press, 1995.

    Curious land: Jesuit accommodation and the origins of Sinology, Stuttgart: F. Steyner Verlag, 1985.

    The Forgotten Christians of Hangzhou, Honolulu: University of Hawaii Press, 1984.

    The spirit and the flesh in Shangdong 1650–1785, Oxford: Rowman and Littlefield, 1999.

Neill, Stephen, *A history of Christianity in India: From the beginning to 1707*, Cambridge: Cambridge University Press, 1984.

Ross, Andrew C., *A vision betrayed: The Jesuits in Japan and China, 1542–1742*, New York: Orbis Books, 1994.

Stanley, Brian (ed.), *Christian missions and the Enlightenment*, Grand Rapids, MI: Eerdmans, 2001.

Teltscher, Kate, *India inscribed: European and British writing on India*, Oxford: Oxford University Press, 1995.

Wellesz, Emmy, *Akbar's religious thought*, London: Allen and Unwin, 1952.

Witek, J. W. (ed.), *Ferdinand Verbeist (1623–1688): Jesuit missionary, scientist, engineer and diplomat*, Nettetal: Steyler Verlag, 1994.

Wright, A. D., *The Counter-Reformation: Catholic Europe and the non-Christian world*, London: Weidenfeld and Nicolson, 1982.

Zupanov, Ines G., *Disputed mission: Jesuit experiments and Brahmanical knowledge*, Oxford: Oxford University Press, 2001.

25 THE AMERICAN REVOLUTION AND RELIGION, 1765–1815

Akers, C. W., *Called unto liberty: A life of Jonathan Mayhew, 1720–1766*, Cambridge, MA: Harvard University Press, 1964.

Albanese, C., *Sons of the fathers: The civil religion of the American Revolution*, Philadelphia: Temple University Press, 1976.

Andrews, D. E., *The Methodists and revolutionary America, 1760–1800: The shaping of an evangelical culture*, Princeton: Princeton University Press, 2000.

Bailyn, B., *The ideological origins of the American Revolution*, Cambridge, MA: Harvard University Press, 1967.

Berger, P., *The Sacred canopy: Elements of a sociological theory of religion*, Garden City, NY: Doubleday, 1967.

Berns, W., *The First Amendment and the future of American democracy*, New York: Basic, 1976.

Boller, P. F. Jr., *George Washington and religion*, Dallas: Southern Methodist University Press, 1963.

Borden, M., *Jews, Turks, and infidels*, Chapel Hill: University of North Carolina Press, 1984.

Bridenbaugh, C., *Mitre and sceptre: Transatlantic faiths, ideas, personalities and politics, 1689–1776*, New York: Oxford University Press, 1962.

Brinton, C., 'Many mansions', *American historical review*, 49 (1964).

Davis, H. D., *Religion and the continental congress 1774–1789: Contributions to original intent*, New York: Oxford University Press, 2000.

Foster, C., *An errand of mercy: The evangelical United Front, 1790–1827*, Chapel Hill: University of North Carolina Press, 1960.

Gaustad, E. S., *Faith of our fathers: Religion and the new nation*, San Francisco: Harper and Row, 1987.

Hamburger, P., *Separation of church and state*, Cambridge, MA: Harvard University Press, 2002.

Hamilton, A., J. Jay, and J. Madison, *The Federalist*, Washington: Robert B. Luce, 1976.

Hanley, T. O., *The American Revolution and religion*, Washington, DC: Catholic University Press, 1971.

Hawke, D. F., *Franklin*, New York: Harper and Row, 1976.

Heimert, A., *Religion and the American mind: From the Great Awakening to the Revolution*, Cambridge, MA: Harvard University Press, 1966.

Kurland, P. B., and Lerner, R. (eds.), *The founders' constitution*, 5 vols., Chicago: University of Chicago Press, 1987.

McGarvie, M. D., *One nation under law: America's early national struggles to separate church and state*, DeKalb: Northern Illinois University Press, 2004.

May, H. F., *The Enlightenment in America*, New York: Oxford University Press, 1976.

Mead, S. E., *The lively experiment: The shaping of Christianity in America*, New York: Harper and Row, 1963.

Merritt, R. L., *Symbols of American community in America*, New Haven: Yale University Press, 1966.

Meyer, D. H., *Democratic Enlightenment*, New York: Putnam's, 1976.

Noll, M., *America's God: From Jonathan Edwards to Abraham Lincoln*, New York: Oxford University Press, 2002.

Peterson, D. and Vaughan, R. C. (eds.), *The Virginia statute for religious freedom: Its evolution and consequences in American history*, New York: Cambridge University Press, 1988.

Preiss, B., and Osterlund, D., *The constitution of the United States*, New York: Bantam, 1987.

Schaff, P., *Church and state in the United States, or the American idea of religious liberty and its practical effects*, New York: G. P. Putnam's Sons, 1888.

Shaw, P., *American patriots and the rituals of revolution*, Cambridge, MA: Harvard University Press, 1981.

26 CHRISTIANITY AND THE CAMPAIGN AGAINST SLAVERY AND THE SLAVE TRADE

Alden, Dauril, *The making of an enterprise: The Society of Jesus in Portugal, its empire, and beyond, 1540–1750*, Palo Alto, CA: Stanford University Press, 1996.

Anstey, Roger, *The Atlantic slave trade and British abolition, 1760–1810*, London: Macmillan, 1975.

Basker, James (ed.), *Amazing Grace: An anthology of poems about slavery, 1660–1830*, New Haven: Yale University Press, 2002.

Bennett, J. H., *Bondsmen and bishops: Slavery and apprenticeship on the Codrington plantations of Barbados, 1710–1838*, Berkeley: University of California Press, 1958.

Blackburn, Robin, *The making of New World slavery: From the Baroque to the modern, 1492–1800*, London: Verso, 1997.

Brooks, Joanna, *American Lazarus: Religion and the rise of African-American and Native American literatures*, Oxford: Oxford University Press, 2003.

Brooks, Joanna, and John Saillant, John (eds.), *'Face Zion forward': First writers of the black Atlantic*, Boston: Northeastern University Press, 2002.

Brown, Christopher L., 'Empire without slaves: British concepts of emancipation in the age of the American Revolution', *William and Mary quarterly*, 3rd Ser., 56 (1999), pp. 273–306.

Clarkson, Thomas, *The history of the rise, progress and accomplishment of the abolition of the African slave trade by the British parliament*, 2 vols., London: Longman, 1808.

Colley, Linda, *Britons: Forging the nation, 1707–1837*, London: Pimlico, 1992.

Conrad, Robert Edgar, *Children of God's fire: A documentary history of black slavery in Brazil*, Princeton: Princeton University Press, 1983.

Davis, David Brion, *The problem of slavery in western culture*, New York: Oxford University Press, 1988.

The problem of slavery in the age of revolution, 1770–1823, Ithaca: Cornell University Press, 1975.

Slavery and human progress, New York: Oxford University Press, 1984.

Dayan, Joan, *Haiti, history, and the gods*, Berkeley: University of California Press, 1995.

Dayfoot, Arthur Charles, *The shaping of the West Indian church, 1492–1962*, Gainesville: University Press of Florida, 1998.

Drake, Thomas, *Quakers and slavery in America*, New Haven: Yale University Press, 1950.

Essig, James D., *The bonds of wickedness: American evangelicals against slavery, 1770–1808*, Philadelphia: Temple University Press, 1982.

Ferguson, Moira, *British women writers and colonial slavery, 1670–1834*, London: Routledge, 1992.

Fick, Carolyn, *The making of Haiti: The Saint Domingue revolution from below*, Knoxville: University of Tennessee Press, 1990.

Frey, Sylvia and Betty Wood, *Come shouting to Zion: African American Protestantism in the American South and British Caribbean to 1830*, Chapel Hill: University of North Carolina Press, 1998.

Genovese, Eugene, *Roll Jordan roll: The world the slaves made*, New York: Vintage Books, 1976.

Gray, Richard, 'The papacy and the Atlantic slave trade: Lourenco da Silva, the Capuchins and the decisions of the Holy Office', *Past and present*, 115 (1987), pp. 52–68.

Heywood, Linda (ed.), *Central Africans and cultural transformations in the African diaspora*, Cambridge: Cambridge University Press, 2002.

Hurbon, Laennec, 'The church and slavery in eighteenth-century Saint Domingue', in Marcel Dorigny (ed.), *The abolitions of slavery from L. F. Sonthonax to Victor Schoelcher, 1793, 1794, 1848*, New York: Berghahn Books, 2003.

Ingersoll, Thomas, *Mammon and Manon in early New Orleans: The first slave society in the deep South, 1718–1819*, Knoxville: University of Tennessee Press, 1999.

Jakobbson, Stiv, *Am I not a man and a brother? British missions and the abolition of the slave trade and slavery in West Africa and the West Indies, 1786–1838*, Lund: Gleerup, 1972.

James, Sydney V., *A People among peoples: Quaker benevolence in eighteenth-century America*, Cambridge, MA: Harvard University Press, 1963.

Jenergan, Marcus, 'Slavery and conversion in the American colonies', *American historical review*, 21 (1916), pp. 504–27.

Lampe, Armando, *Christianity in the Caribbean: Essays on church history*, Barbardos: University of the West Indies Press, 2001.

Lenhart, J. M., 'Capuchin champions of Negro emancipation in Cuba, 1681–1685', *Franciscan studies*, 6 (1946), pp. 195–217.

Maclachlan, Colin M., 'Slavery, ideology, and institutional change: The impact of the Enlightenment on slavery in late eighteenth-century Marahnao', *Journal of Latin American studies*, 11 (1979), pp. 1–17.

Mathews, Donald G., *Slavery and Methodism: A chapter in American morality*, Princeton: Princeton University Press, 1965.

Maxwell, John F., *Slavery and the Catholic Church: The history of Catholic teaching concerning the moral legitimacy of the institution of slavery*, Chichester: Anti-Slavery Society for the Protection of Human Rights, 1975.

Newman, Richard S., *The transformation of American abolitionism: Fighting slavery in the early republic*, Chapel Hill: University of North Carolina Press, 2002.

Parent, Anthony, *Foul means: The formation of a slave society in Virginia, 1660–1740*, Chapel Hill: University of North Carolina Press, 2003.

Peabody, Sue, '"A dangerous zeal": Catholic missions to slaves in the French Antilles, 1635–1800', *French historical studies*, 25 (2002).

Potkay, Adam and Sandra Burr (eds.), *Black Atlantic writers of the eighteenth century*, Basingstoke: Macmillan, 1995.

Raboteau, Albert J., *Slave religion: The 'invisible institution' in the Antebellum South*, New York, Oxford University Press, 1978.

Russell-Wood, A. J. R., 'Iberian expansion and the issue of Black slavery: Changing Portuguese attitudes, 1440–1770', *American historical review*, 83 (1978), pp. 16–42.

Saillant, John, 'Slavery and divine providence in New England Calvinism: the new divinity and black protest', *New England quarterly*, 8 (1995), pp. 584–608.

Sandiford, Keith A., *Measuring the moment: Strategies of protest in eighteenth-century Afro-English writing*, Selinsgrove: Susquehanna University Press, 1988.

Schwartz, Stuart, 'The plantations of St. Benedict: The Benedictine sugar mills of colonial Brazil', *The Americas*, 39 (1982), pp. 1–22.

Soderlund, Jean R., *Quakers and slavery: A divided spirit*, Princeton: Princeton University Press, 1985.

Sweet, David G., '"Black robes and Black destiny": Jesuit views of African slavery in seventeenth-century Latin America', *Revista de historia de America*, 86 (1978), pp. 87–133.

Sweet, James H., *Recreating Africa: Culture, kinship, and religion in the African-Portuguese world, 1441–1770*, Chapel Hill: University of North Carolina Press, 2003.

Sypher, Wylie, *Guinea's captive kings: British anti-slavery literature in the XVIIIth century*, Chapel Hill: University of North Carolina Press, 1942.

Tannenbaum, Frank, *Slave and citizen: The Negro in the Americas*, New York: Vintage Books, 1946.

Thornton, John K., 'African dimensions of the Stono rebellion', *American historical review*, 96 (1991).

'"I serve the King of Congo": African political ideology and the Haitian revolution', *Journal of world history*, 4 (1993), pp. 187–99.

Tise, Larry E., *Proslavery: A history of the defense of slavery in America, 1701–1840*, Athens, GA: University of Georgia Press, 1987.

27 AND 28 THE FRENCH REVOLUTION AND RELIGION

Primary sources

Tackett, Timothy (ed.), *The French Revolution research collection. Section 8. Religion*, Oxford: Pergamon Press, 1990.

Secondary sources

Ariès, Philippe, *L'homme devant la mort*, Paris: Editions du Seuil, 1977

Aston, Nigel, *The end of an 'élite': The French bishops and the coming of the Revolution, 1786–1790*, Oxford: Clarendon Press, 1992.

Religion and revolution in France, 1780–1804, Washington, DC: The Catholic University of America Press, 2000.

Aulard, François-Alphonse, *Le culte de la raison et le culte de l'être suprême (1793–1794)*, Paris: Alcan, 1892.

Le christianisme et la Révolution française, Paris: Rieder, 1925.

Boudon, Jacques-Olivier, Jean-Claude Caron, and Jean-Claude Yon, *Religion et culture en Europe au 19e siècle*, Paris: Armand-Colin, 2001.

Boudon, Jacques-Olivier, *Napoléon et les cultes. Les religions en Europe à l'aube du XIXe siècle, 1800–1815*, Paris: Fayard, 2002.

Broers, Michael, *Europe under Napoleon, 1799–1815*, London: Arnold Press, 1996.

The politics of religion in Napoleonic Italy: The war against God, 1801–1814, London: Routledge, 2002.

Chartier, Roger, *The cultural origins of the French Revolution*, Durham, NC: Duke University Press, 1991.

Cholvy, Gérard, *Histoire religieuse de la France contemporaine. 1800/1880*, Toulouse: Privat, 1985.

Cousin, Bernard, Monique Cubells, and René Moulinas, *La pique et la croix. Histoire religieuse de la Révolution française*, Paris: Centurion, 1989.

Desan, Suzanne, *Reclaiming the sacred: Lay religion and popular politics in revolutionary France*, Ithaca: Cornell University Press, 1990.

Encrevé, André, *Les Protestants en France. De 1800 à nos jours*, Paris: Stock, 1985.

Gibson, Ralph, *A social history of French Catholicism, 1789–1914*, London: Routledge, 1989.

Godechot, Jacques, 'La Révolution française et les Juifs', in Bernhard Blumenkranz and Albert Soboul (eds.), *Les Juifs et la Révolution française*, Paris: Commission française des archives juives, 1976, pp. 47–70.

Godel, Jean, *La réconstruction concordataire dans le diocèse de Grenoble après la Révolution (1802–1809)*, Grenoble: La Tronche, 1968.

Histoire des Protestants en France, Toulouse: Privat, 1977.

Hufton, Olwen, 'The reconstruction of a church, 1796–1801', in Gwynne Lewis and Colin Lucas (eds.), *Beyond the Terror: Essays in French regional history, 1794–1815*, Cambridge: Cambridge University Press, 1983, pp. 21–52.

Women and the limits of citizenship in the French Revolution, Toronto: University of Toronto Press, 1992.

Jacob, Margaret C., *Living the Enlightenment: Freemasonry and politics in eighteenth-century Europe*, Oxford: Oxford University Press, 1991.

Jaher, Frederic Cople, *The Jews and the nation: Revolution, emancipation, state formation, and the liberal paradigm in America and France*, Princeton: Princeton University Press, 2002.

Joutard, Philippe (ed.), *Histoire de la France religieuse*, vol. 3. *Du roi Très Chrétien à la laicité républicaine*, Paris: Editions du Seuil, 1991.

Lagrée, Michel, 'Piété populaire et Révolution en Bretagne: l'exemple de canonisations spontanées (1793–1815)', in *Voies nouvelles pour l'histoire de la Révolution française. Colloque Albert Mathiez/Georges Lefebvre, 30 novembre-16 décembre, 1974*, Paris: Bibliothèque nationale, 1978, pp. 265–79.

Langlois, Claude, *Un diocèse breton au début du dix-neuvième siècle*, Paris: Klincksieck, 1974.

Le catholicisme au féminin: Les congrégations françaises à supérieure générale au XIXe siècle, Paris: Les éditions du Cerf, 1984.

'La rupture entre l'église catholique et la Révolution', in François Furet and Mona Ozouf (eds.), *The French Revolution and the creation of modern political culture*, vol. 3: *The transformation of political culture, 1789–1848*, Oxford: Pergamon Press, 1989, pp. 375–90.

Langlois, Claude, and T. J. A. Le Goff, 'Pour une sociologie des prêtres mariés', in *Voies nouvelles pour l'histoire de la Révolution française. Colloque Albert Mathiez/Georges Lefebvre, 30 novembre-16 décembre, 1974*, Paris: Bibliothèque nationale, 1978, pp. 281–312.

Langlois, Claude, and Timothy Tackett, 'A l'épreuve de la Révolution (1770–1830)', in François Lebrun (ed.), *Histoire des Catholiques en France du XVe siècle à nos jours*, Toulouse: Privat, 1980, pp. 215–89.

'Ecclesiastical structures and clerical geography on the eve of the French Revolution', *French historical studies*, 11 (1980), pp, 352–70.

Langlois, Claude, Timothy Tackett and Michel Vovelle, *Atlas de la Révolution française*, vol. 9: *Religion*, Paris: Editions de l'EHESS, 1996.

Latreille, André, *L'Eglise catholique et la Révolution française*, 2 vols., Paris: Hachette, 1946–50.

Leflon, Jean, *La crise révolutionnaire, 1789–1846*, Paris: Bloud et Gay, 1949.

Lewis, Gwynne, *The second Vendée: The continuity of counter-revolution in the department of the Gard, 1789–1815*, Oxford: Clarendon Press, 1978.

Lyons, Martin, *France under the Directory*, Cambridge: Cambridge University Press, 1975.

Napoleon Bonaparte and the legacy of the French Revolution, New York: Saint Martin's Press, 1994.

Martin, Jean-Clément (ed.), *Religion et Révolution. Colloque de Saint-Florent-le-Vieil 13-14-15 mai 1993*, Paris: Anthropos, 1994.

Mathiez, Albert, *Les origines des cultes révolutionnaires, 1789–1792*, Paris: Bellais, 1904.

Contributions à l'histoire religieuse de la Révolution française, Paris: Alcan, 1907.

La Révolution et l'église, Paris: A. Colin, 1910.

Rome et le clergé français sous la Constituante. La Constitution civile du clergé. L'affaire d'Avignon, Paris: Armand Collin, 1911.

Mazoyer, Louis, 'La question protestante dans les cahiers des Etats généraux', *Bulletin de la société de l'histoire du Protestantisme français*, 80 (1931), pp. 41–73.

McManners, John, *The French Revolution and the church*, London: SPCK, 1969.

Menozzi, Daniele, *Les interprétations politiques de Jésus de l'Ancien régime à la Révolution*, Paris: Editions du Cerf, 1983.

Pisani, Paul, *Répertoire biographique de l'épiscopat constitutionnel (1791–1802)*, Paris: Picard, 1907.

Plongeron, Bernard, *Conscience religieuse en Révolution*, Paris: Picard, 1969.

'Recherches sur l'Aufklärung catholique en Europe occidentale (1770–1830)', *Revue d'histoire moderne et contemporaine*, 16 (1969), pp. 555–605.

Plongeron, Bernard (ed.), *Pratiques religieuses dans l'Europe révolutionnaire (1770–1820). Actes du colloque à Chantilly 27–29 novembre 1986*, Paris: Brepols, 1988.

Poland, Burdette C., *French Protestantism and the French Revolution: A study in church and state, thought and religion, 1685–1815*, Princeton: Princeton University Press, 1957.

Ravitch, Norman, *Sword and mitre: Government and episcopate in France and England in the age of aristocracy*, Paris: Mouton, 1966.

Reinhard, Marcel, *et al.*, 'Les prêtres abdicataires pendant la Révolution', in *Actes du 89e congrès national des sociétés savantes, Lyon, 1964*, Paris: Imprimerie nationale, 1965, pp. 27–228.

Reuss, Rudolphe, *Les églises protestantes en Alsace pendant la Révolution (1789–1802)*, Paris: Fishbacher, 1906.

Robert, Daniel, *Les eglises réformées en France, 1800–1830*, Paris: Presses universitaires de France, 1961.

Roche, Daniel, *Le siècle des Lumières en province: académies et académiciens provinciaux, 1680–1789*, 2 vols., Paris: Mouton, 1978.

Schechter, Ronald, *Obstinate Hebrews: Representations of Jews in France, 1715–1815*, Berkeley: University of California Press, 2003.

Scheidhauer, Marcel, *Les églises luthériennes en France, 1800–1815*, Strasbourg: Oberlin, 1975.

Sepinwall, Alyssa Goldstein, *Regenerating the world: The Abbé Grégoire, the French Revolution, and the making of modern universalism*, Berkeley: University of California Press, 2005.

Sicard, Augustin, *Le clergé de France pendant la Révolution*, 2 vols., Paris: Picard, 1912–27.

Soboul, Albert, 'Sentiment religieux et cultes populaires pendant la Révolution: saintes patriotes et martyrs de la liberté', *Archives de sociologie des religions*, 2 (1956), pp. 73–87.

Sottocasa, Valérie, *Mémoires affrontées. Protestants et Catholiques face à la Révolution dans les montagnes du Languedoc*, Rennes: Presses universitaires de Rennes, 2004.

Sutherland, D. M. G., *France 1789–1815: Revolution and counterrevolution*, New York: Oxford University Press, 1986.

Tackett, Timothy, *Priest and parish in eighteenth-century France: A social and political study of the curés in a diocese of Dauphiné*, Princeton: Princeton University Press, 1977.

'The west in France in 1789: The religious factor in the origins of the counterrevolution', *The journal of modern history*, 54 (1982), pp. 715–45.

'The social history of the diocesan clergy in eighteenth-century France', in Richard Golden (ed.), *Church and society in early-modern France*, Lawrence: Kansas University Press, 1982, pp. 327–79.

Religion, revolution, and regional culture in eighteenth-century France, Princeton: Princeton University Press, 1986.

Becoming a revolutionary: The deputies of the French National Assembly and the emergence of a revolutionary culture (1789–1790), Princeton: Princeton University Press, 1996.

Van Kley, Dale, 'The Jansenist constitutional legacy in the French Revolution', in *The French Revolution and the creation of modern political culture*, vol. 1. *The political culture of the Old Regime*, ed. Keith Michael Baker, Oxford: Pergamon Press, 1987, pp. 169–202.

'Christianity as casualty and chrysallis of modernity: The problem of dechristianization in the French Revolution', *American historical review*, 108 (2003), pp. 1081–1104.

Vovelle, Michel, *Piété baroque et déchristianisation en Provence au XVIIIe siècle*, Paris: Plon, 1973.

Religion et révolution: La déchristianisation de l'an II, Paris: Hachette, 1976.

The revolution against the church: From reason to the Supreme Being, trans. Alan José, Cambridge: Polity Press, 1991.

Woolf, Stuart, *Napoleon's integration of Europe*, London: Routledge, 1991.

29 CHRISTIAN AWAKENINGS IN REVOLUTIONARY EUROPE, 1790–1815

Batalden, Stephen K., 'Printing the Bible in the reign of Alexander I', in G. A. Hosking (ed.), *Church, nation and state in Russia and the Ukraine*, London: Macmillan, 1991, pp. 65–78.

Bigler, Robert M., *The politics of German Protestantism: The rise of the Protestant Church elite in Prussia, 1815–1848*, Berkeley: University of California Press, 1972.

Blanning, T. C. W., *The French Revolution in Germany: Occupation and resistance in the Rhineland, 1792–1802*, Oxford: Oxford University Press, 1983.

'The role of religion in European counter-revolution, 1789–1815', in D. Beales and G. Best (eds.), *History, society and the churches*, Cambridge: Cambridge University Press, 1985, pp. 195–214.

Broers, Michael, *The politics of religion in Napoleonic Italy: The war against God, 1801–1814*, London: Routledge, 2002.

Brown, Stewart J., *The national churches of England, Ireland and Scotland 1801–46*, Oxford: Oxford University Press, 2001.

Canton, William, *A history of the British and foreign Bible society*, 5 vols., London: John Murray, 1904.

Clark, Christopher M, 'The politics of revival: Pietists, aristocrats, and the state church in early nineteenth-century Prussia', in Larry E. Jones and James Retallack (eds.), *Between reform, reaction and resistance: Studies in the history of German conservatism from 1789 to 1945*, Providence, Rhode Island: Berg, 1993, pp. 31–60.

Cole, Lawrence, 'Nation, anti-enlightenment, and religious revival in Austria: Tyrol in the 1790s', *Historical journal*, 43 (2000), pp. 475–97.

Davis, John A., 'The "Santafede" and the crisis of the "ancien régime" in southern Italy', in John A. Davis and Paul Ginsborg (eds.), *Society and politics in the age of the Risorgimento*, Cambridge: Cambridge University Press, 1991, pp. 1–25.

Forstman, Jack, *A Romantic triangle: Schleiermacher and early German Romanticism*, Missoula, MT: Scholar's Press, 1977.

Garrett, Clarke, *Respectable folly: Millenarians and the French Revolution in France and England*, Baltimore: The Johns Hopkins University Press, 1975.

Geiger, Max, 'Politik und Religion nach dem Programm der Heiligen Allianz', *Theologische Zeitschrift*, 15 (1959), pp. 107–25.

Harrison, J. F. C., *The Second Coming: Popular millenarianism, 1780–1850*, London: Routledge & Kegan Paul, 1979.

Knapton, John Ernest, *The lady of the holy alliance: The life of Julie de Krüdener*, New York: Columbia University Press, 1939.

Latourette, Kenneth Scott, *Christianity in a revolutionary age*, 5 vols., London: Eyre and Spottiswoode, 1959–63.

Lehmann, Hartmut, *Pietismus und weltliche Ordnung in Württemberg*, Stuttgart: W. Kohlhammer, 1969.

  'Pietistic millenarianism in late eighteenth-century Germany', in Eckhart Hellmuth (ed.), *The transformation of political culture: England and Germany in the late eighteenth century*, Oxford: Oxford University Press, 1990, pp. 327–38.

Lovegrove, Deryck W., *Established church, sectarian people: Itinerancy and the transformation of English dissent, 1780–1830*, Cambridge: Cambridge University Press, 1988.

McCalman, Iain, 'New Jerusalems: Prophecy, dissent and radical culture in England, 1785–1830', in Knud Haakonssen (ed.), *Enlightenment and religion: Rational dissent in eighteenth-century Britain*, Cambridge: Cambridge University Press, pp. 312–35.

Nichols, Robert L., 'Orthodoxy and Russia's Enlightenment, 1762–1825', in R. L. Nichols and T. G. Stavrou (eds.), *Russian Orthodoxy under the old regime*, Minneapolis: University of Minnesota Press, 1978, pp. 65–89.

Palmer, Alan, *Alexander I: Tsar of war and peace*, London: Weidenfeld and Nicolson, 1974.

Pinson, Koppel S., *Pietism as a factor in the rise of German nationalism*, New York: Columbia University Press, 1934.

Raack, R. C., 'Schleiermacher's political thought and activity, 1806–1813', *Church history*, 28 (1959), pp. 374–90.

Thompson, E. P., *Witness against the beast: William Blake and the moral law*, Cambridge: Cambridge University Press, 1993.

Troyat, Henri, *Alexander of Russia*, trans. Joan Pinkham, New York: E. P. Dutton, 1982.

Valence, Deborah M., *Prophetic sons and daughters: Female preaching and popular religion in industrial England*, Princeton: Princeton University Press, 1985.

Index

Note: Page references in *italics* indicate illustrations, while those in **bold type** indicate maps.

in North America 395, 403–4
in Philippines 453–4
in Portugal 97
and slavery 522
in Spain 25, 100–2
for women 175–6
  in France 104, 548, 568
  in India 443
  in Italy 105
  in Latin America 383, 384
  in Philippines 453–4
  in Poland 108
  in Spain 101–2
see also individual orders
organs, church 240
Orientalism 5
orthodoxy, Protestant 41–3, 110
Othman II 20
Ottoman Empire 3, 16, 20, 94, 476, 477–8
Our Lady of Copacabana 381
Overbeck, Johann Friedrich 586

pacifism 354, 395, 502
Padroado Real 315, 437, 444, 459, 475
Paine, Thomas 507
Palestine, and the Jews 40, 583, 584
Paley, William 55, 62–3, 67
Palmer, Robert R. 290
pamphlets, by women 168, 169, 170
pandaraswami, Jesuit 481, 482
pantheism 269, 271, 275, 279
papacy: and administration 21
  and church property 74
  and church and state 15, 18, 19–21, 31, 308, 475
  and elections to papacy 21
  and French Revolution 546–7, 582, 589
  and Italian church 92–3
  and Jansenism 308, 309, 312, 318, 324, 333
  and Jesuits 302–4, 307, 312, 314, 316, 317–18, 320, 592
    suppression 4, 19, 31, 90, 164, 302, 322–5
  and nunciature 21, 28
  and Ottoman Turks 20
  and Uniate Churches 20–1
Papal State 20, 26, 93, 104, 573, 589
Paracelsus/Paracelsianism 331, 334
Paris: church buildings
  La Madeleine 238
  Les Invalides 232, *234*, 235, 241, 244
  Notre-Dame 239, 244
  Saint-Sulpice 238, 245
  Val-de-Grâce 232, *233*, 235, 240, 243

parlement 310, 311–14, 317, 322
University 156
Paris, Treaty (1763) 404, 409
parish missions 385–6
parish system 110, 341, 431
Parker, Samuel 57–8
parlements, French 310, 311–14, 317, 322, 540
Parliament, English, and Convocation 59, 61
Parma: and Jesuits 302, 304, 321–2
  and papacy 26, 93
Pascal, Blaise 8, 255, 306, 309, 311, 314
Passionei, Cardinal 311, 317, 318
Passowitz, Peace of (1718) 20
Paterson, John 587
Patrick, Simon 57
patronage: of the arts 94
  in Catholic Europe 18, 20, 23, 24, 29, 73, 76, 98, 100
  in England 118
  in Finland 118
  in Germany 118
  in Ireland 64
  in Netherlands 118
  in Scotland 68–9, 344, 345, 360, 365–6
  in Sweden 117–19
patronato real 457, 475
Paul IV, Pope 306
Paul V, Pope 306
Paul, St Vincent de 91, 97, 103, 176
pedagogy, modern 153–4
Pelagius/Pelagianism 305, 306, 307
Penn, William 355, 395, 397, 502
Pennsylvania: and Protestantism 35, 41, 43, 502
  and Quakers 395, 502, 526
  and revivalism 339–40
  and toleration 355, 367–8, 397, 497, 511
Péréfix, Archbishop 178
periodicals 143, 324, 364
Perrault, Claude 235, 238
persecution: in China 461–2, 464, 466
  in England 270, 354–5
  in France 9, 110, 123, 266–8, 270, 349
  in Japan 4, 467–8, 470
  in Korea 472
  of Pietists 37
  of Quakers 170, 355
  of Shakers 173
  in South-east Asia 4, 450
Peru: and *beaterios* 383–4
  and religious orders 378, 385
Pestalozzi, Johann Heinrich 580
Peter II of Portugal 521

Peter Leopold, Duke of Tuscany 27, 93, 99,
    105, 324
Peters, Thomas 421
Petersen, Johanna Eleanora 171, 172, 173
Petite Eglise (France) 565, 567
Pforr, Franz 586
Philadelphian Society 171
Philip III of Spain 101
Philip IV of Spain 24, 101
Philip V of Spain, and papacy 20
Philip, John 428–9
Philippines: and church and state 454–6
    decline of the church 456–8
    and female convents 181, 453–4
    and Roman Catholicism 4, 451–3
philosophes 24, 75, 276, 289, 292, 350, 540
physico-theology 273, 285, 290
Piarists 96, 100, 106, 154
Pietism 33–41, 42, 47, 110–11, 329–31
    and clergy 116, 117, 126
    conventicles 7, 33–5, 36–7, 42, 128
    decline 40–1
    and education 153, 154, 163
    and Enlightenment thought 49
    expulsion from Salzburg 5, 17
    and mission 4, 7, 37, 39, 181
    and revivalism 579–80
    and role of women 128, 167, 171–3, 181
    and science and learning 8
    and sermons 128, 142
    in Silesia 335–6
    see also enthusiasm; renewal
Pietism (movement) 329, 335, 367, 396
pilgrimage 95, 188, 196, 200, 563, 569, 571
Pius V, Pope 104
Pius VI, Pope 19, 21
    and Austria 30
    and France 325, 546–7, 581
    and Jansenism 324
    and Naples 27
    and Portugal 26
Pius VII, Pope: and Jesuits 323, 592
    and Napoleon 326, 564–6, 572–3, 582
    return to Rome 592
Pluche, Abbé Noel-Antoine 273, 290
pluralism 64, 122, 347, 364, 396, 404
Plutschau, Heinrich 444, 482
pogroms, in Poland 331
Poiret, Pierre 333, 338
Poland: architecture 236
    bishops 95–6
    clergy 100, 107–8
    and church and state 18

and Jews 331
partitions 20, 96, 107
politics: and antislavery movement 528
    and Christian Enlightenment 284, 287,
        297–9
    and French Revolution 557
    and Jansenism 310
    and popular religion 382
    and preaching 138–41
    and role of women 169–71
    see also church and state; republicanism
Pombal, Sebastiao de Carvalho e Melo de 97,
        102, 373
    and church in Brazil 378–9
    and expulsion of the Jesuits 18, 26, 90,
        315–17, 323, 443
Poor Clares 384, 453
Popular Party (Scotland) 366
pornography, and materialism 274–5
Port-Royal convent 177, 308, 309
Porter, James 478–9
Porter, Roy 276
Portugal: African colonies 411–16
    and architecture 236
    bishops 90
    and China 459
    and church and state 17, 18, 20, 26, 315,
        373
    clergy 97, 102
    and India 435, 436, 437, 443–4, 479–80
    and Jesuits 18, 26, 90, 164, 307, 378–9, 415,
        443
    and mission 3–4, 475
    and slavery 521, 525
    and South and South-east Asia 447–9
    see also Brazil
Potter, John 58–9
poverty, and education 152–4
Prasse, Johann 429–30
prayer, and women 168, 169, 171
praying towns 402
preaching 110, 128–44
    aims 132–8
    appearance 128–32
    changing content 141–4
    in colonies 183, 399
    confessional and polite 138–41
    court sermons 129, 141
    discriminating 338, 341
    funeral 122, 131, 132, 137
    itinerant 577–8, 580
    length 130, 143
    listeners 129, 135